The Blue G

Ireland

Brian Lalor

BLUE GUIDE

A&C Black • London
WW Norton • New York

Eighth edition 1998 © Brian Lalor

Published by A&C Black (Publishers) Limited
35 Bedford Row, London WC1R 4JH

1st edition Findlay Muirhead
2nd–3rd editions L. Russell Muirhead
4th–6th editions © Ian Robertson
7th edition © Brian Lalor and Ian Robertson

All rights reserved. No part of this publication may be reproduced or used in any form or by any means—photographic, electronic or mechanical, including photocopying, recording, taping or information storage and retrieval systems without permission of the publishers.

The rights of Brian Lalor to be identified as author of this work have been asserted by him in accordance with the Copyright, Designs and Patents Act, 1988.

ISBN 0 7136 4550–4

'Blue Guides' is a registered trademark.

Illustrations © Brian Lalor
Cover photograph: Back to back pre-Christian stone idols in Caldragh graveyard, Boa Island, Lower Lough Erne © Christopher Hill Photographic
Maps and plans © A&C Black. Town plans updated for this edition by Map Creation Ltd. Colour map and map of regions by Robert Smith. Regional maps and key by Peter McClure

A CIP catalogue record of this book is available from the British Library.

Published in the United States of America by
WW Norton & Company, Inc
500 Fifth Avenue, New York NY 10110

Published simultaneously in Canada by
Penguin Books Canada Limited
10 Alcorn Avenue, Toronto, Ontario M4V 3B2

ISBN 0-393-31801-X

The author and the publisher have done their best to ensure the accuracy of all the information in Blue Guide Ireland; however, they can accept no responsibility for any loss, injury or inconvenience sustained by any traveller as a result of information or advice contained in this guide.

Brian Lalor has pursued a multi-disciplinary career in art, archaeology and architecture, and is the author of numerous books (including four on Dublin), which he has also illustrated. When not drawing, writing or travelling in Ireland and more distant parts, he has in recent years been involved in excavating at Yodefat, a classical site in Galilee. His most enduring contribution to archaeology was in solving the century-long mystery of 'Robinson's Arch' at the Temple Mount in Jerusalem. In 1993 he took over authorship of Blue Guide Ireland; he lives in Dublin.

The publishers and the author welcome comments, suggestions and corrections for the next edition of Blue Guide Ireland. Writers of the most informative letters will be awarded a free Blue Guide of their choice.

Printed and bound in Great Britain by Butler & Tanner, Frome and London.

Contents

The Regions

Maps and Plans

Ireland, colour map *inside front and back covers*
Ireland Regional map showing corresponding chapters   52

Introduction

Despite its small size (84.459 sq km), slightly smaller than New York State, about the size of Maine, Ireland presents to the visitor some of the finest unspoilt landscape, dramatic coastline and wilderness areas in Europe, with the attractive prospect of travelling almost anywhere on uncrowded roads in an environment of rain-washed translucent skies while breathing the fresh air of Atlantic breezes. It provides a perfect recreational destination for sailing and fishing, hill and long-distance walking, cycling, camping and relaxed touring. The abundance of antiquities and historic architecture in the countryside provide continuity in every region, and the combination of sites from the Neolithic to the 19C set in extraordinarily beautiful landscape is one of the characteristic features of rural Ireland.

The cities form a total contrast; there has been a wide growth of facilities for the visual and performing arts, mainly concentrated in urban areas. In Dublin a remarkable number of museums and libraries display the greatest artworks of Celtic, early Christian, medieval and Georgian Ireland. The Dublin cultural institutions of theatre, music and the spoken arts present works from the wide repertoire of Irish literature and the cities of Belfast, Cork, Derry, Galway and Limerick all possess a lively cultural and social life. However, virtually any town or population centre of any size is likely to have an arts centre, theatre, gallery or group of craftsworkers situated in its vicinity, or to be the base for a festival. In specific areas these developments are particularly evident and the coastal rim appears to have attracted a rich variety of creative talent from Donegal to Waterford. The musical life of the city and country is one of the most vital to be experienced anywhere, and the particular ambience of Irish Traditional Music and Irish pubs can be found in any part of the country.

Contemporary Irish writing, novels, poetry and drama, as well as recent Irish films can give the intending visitor an idea of what to expect of daily life. Ireland is both a small European island-nation, and conversely, a place unto itself, with a singularly individual character and people. The informality of Irish life, friendliness of people towards visitors and accessibility of the attractions of the country contribute towards easy appreciation of the best of what Ireland has to offer.

Acknowledgements
I would like to take this opportunity of thanking all those who assisted me in any way during my work on this edition; in particular Dr. Maurice Craig for his careful reading of the previous edition; Colin Rynne; Rosemary McQuillan and FAS; Bernard Loughlin and the Tyrone Guthrie Centre, Annaghmakerrig; Noelle Campbell-Sharp and the Cill Rialaig Project, Ballinskelligs; the Northern Ireland Tourist Board; the directors and staff of the following institutions; Arts Council of Northern Ireland; Bord Failte; Cork County Council; Crawford Municipal Art Gallery; Dublin Corporation; Derry City Council; Dublin County Council; Foyle Valley Trust; Government Publications Office; Hugh Lane Municipal Gallery of Modern Art; Hunt Museum Limerick; Inner City Trust, Derry; Irish Architectural Archive; Laganside Corporation; Limerick Civic Trust; National Library of Ireland; National Gallery of Ireland; National Museum of Ireland; Northern

Ireland Tourist Board; Office of Public Works; Royal Gunpowder Mill, Ballincollig; Royal Irish Academy; Shannon Development; Ulster Folk and Transport Museum, Cultra; Ulster Architectural Heritage Society; Ulster Museum; Waterford Town Hall.

The Guide

The 8th edition of the Blue Guide to Ireland is organised on a regional basis, with 20 independent areas, each accompanied by a sketch map of its principal features. The regions are arranged, beginning in Dublin, and following an anti-clockwise direction around the coast, with inland digressions where the region does not have a coastline. Where the geography of the region allows it, round routes are indicated—region 8: Killarney and the Ring of Kerry, for example—otherwise the road-system is presented without presupposing that the traveller will wish to go in a specific direction. Distances within regions are short, making everything extremely accessible. Depending on the character of each locality, the size of individual regions varies from those in which everything might be seen in a good day's touring, to more extensive regions requiring many days. Although Ireland is administratively divided on a county basis, and local loyalties in sport and politics are strong, county boundaries are of no great significance to the visitor and only relate to the regions in a general sense.

Points of arrival by sea and air are located in 11 of the 20 regions, ensuring that visitors with little time at their disposal the possibility of swift access from Europe or the US to most areas, without necessitating cross-country travel by road or train.

Restaurants and places to stay are mentioned on a basis of a combination of good quality accommodation with attractive food, in buildings of historic interest with diversity of facilities; some areas of the country are richly served, others poorly provided for.

Events in Northern Ireland are notoriously difficult to predict, but with the reopening of long-closed border roads and a widespread desire for peace within the province, media reports should not be interpreted as a deterrent to visiting the North. The island of Ireland is here presented as a single unit, the border should have no real significance for visitors, as it can create an imaginary barrier to visiting some of the loveliest countryside on the island. The greatest inconvenience a visitor is likely to experience, travelling north-south or vice versa is having to exchange miles and sterling north of the border for kilometres and punts in the south.

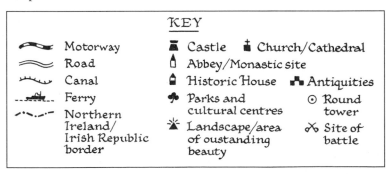

KEY

Motorway	Castle	Church/Cathedral	
Road	Abbey/Monastic site		
Canal	Historic House	Antiquities	
Ferry	Parks and cultural centres	Round tower	
Northern Ireland/Irish Republic border	Landscape/area of oustanding beauty	Site of battle	

Practical Information

Planning your Trip

When to go

The climate of Ireland is temperate; the winters mild. Only on the east coastal strip are there fewer than 200 rainy days a year. Snow remains on the ground rarely except in upland locations. May and June are the sunniest months, but an 'Irish Summer' tends to be a moveable feast. Waterproofs, or at least a light rain-coat, may be required at any season, but it should be remembered that a period of continuous rain is the exception; what appears to be a persistent downpour may well be followed by a day of brilliant sunshine; more predictably, all four seasons can be encountered in a single day. It is worth noting that getting to the islands off the west and northwest coasts may be affected by weather conditions.

The more well known or picturesque attractions (**Killarney, the Ring of Kerry, Achill, Connemara**), are likely to be crowded during July and August, and accommodation should be booked well in advance (see p. 25 for major festival dates). The latter half of May and June are more comfortable, but September and October are probably the months in which the country is to be seen at its best; the weather is at its most settled, the banks of fuchsia are in flower, and the colour of both valley and mountain is particularly striking, the only drawback being the comparative shortness of the evenings.

National Tourist Organisations

The **Irish Tourist Board** (*Bord Fáilte*; pronounced 'Board Falcha'), with their main offices at Baggot St Bridge, Dublin 2, will provide general information gratis, and book accommodation. Postal enquiries should be addressed to *Bord Fáilte*, PO Box 273, Dublin 8. Otherwise the Irish Tourist Board can be contacted at the following addresses:

UK. 150 New Bond Street, London W1Y 0AQ (☎ 0171-4933201).

Northern Ireland. 53 Castle Street, Belfast BT1 1GH, and Foyle St, Derry BT48 6AR.

Europe. Amsterdam, Leidsestraat 32, 1017 PB Amsterdam (☎ 02-6223101). Brussels, Avenue de Beaulieu 25, 1160 Brussels (☎ 02-6739940); Copenhagen, Box 104, 1004 Kobenhavn k (☎ 033-158045); Frankfurt, Irishe Fremdenverkehrszentrale, Untermainanlage 7, W 6000 Frankfurt Main 1 (☎ 069-236492); Milan, Via S. Mario Segreta 6, 20123 Milano (☎ 02-8690541); Paris, 33 Rue Miromesnil, 75008 Paris (☎ 331-47420336); Stockholm; Box 5292, 102 46 Stockholm (☎ 08-6628510).

USA. New York, 5th Floor, Suite 500, 276 Fifth Ave, New York, NY 1001 (☎ 212-4180800; fax 212-3719052).

Canada. 160 Bloor St East, Suite 934, Toronto, Ontario, M43 1B99; 38 Level, MLC Centre, Martin Pl. (☎ 416-9292777; fax 416-9296783).

Australia. 5th level, 36 Carrington St, Sydney, NSW 2000 (☎ 02-2996177; fax 02-2296323).

New Zealand. 87 Queen St, Auckland.

Japan. 3rd Floor, Azabu-dai, Minato-ku, Tokyo.

The **Northern Ireland Tourist Board** is at St. Anne's Court, 59 North St, Belfast BT1 1ND (☎ 0232-231-221; fax 0232-240-960).
In the Republic: 16 Nassau Street, Dublin 2 (☎ 679-1977; fax 679-863).
UK. 11 Berkeley St, London W1X 5AD (☎ 0171-493-0601), and 38 High St, Sutton Coldfield, West Midlands B72 1UP.
Europe. Taunusstrasse 52–60, W6000 Frankfurt am Main (☎ 069-234-504).
USA. 276 5th Ave, 5th Floor, Suite 500, New York, NY 10001 (☎ 212-686-6250; fax 212-686-8061).

Elsewhere, information may be obtained from branches of the British Tourist Authority. Very useful leaflets giving a full list of these tourist facilities are available from Bord Fáilte and the Northern Ireland Tourist Board. The **British Travel Centre** at 12 Regent St, London SW1Y 4PQ, now provides information on the island as a whole, without distinction.

Tour Operators

Any accredited member of the Association of British Travel Agents (ABTA) will advise on the latest schedule for ferry, rail and bus services from London and elsewhere in the UK to the ferry ports (and in Ireland) also flights from airports in the UK, car-hire facilities, etc. They will also book tickets, and accommodation. **Specialist tour operators**: Colclough Tours, 71 Waterloo Rd, Dublin 4 (☎ 01-668-6463), organises the most interesting and individual range of tours available in the country.

Getting to Ireland

By Air

Regular air services between Great Britain and Ireland are maintained by **Aer Lingus**, 223 Regent St, London W1 (☎ 0181-569-5555); **British Airways**, 75 Regent St, London W1 (☎ 0171-897-4000; for N Ireland only); **British Midland** 2–5 Warwick Court, London WC1R 5 (☎ 0171-5489-5599) and **Ryanair** 235 Finchley Rd, London NW3 6LS (☎ 0171-436-7101; for the Republic only). Less frequent services are provided by other companies. Full information is also available from travel agents.

Regular flights are scheduled from mainland Europe (Aer Lingus, British Airways), from North America (**Aer Lingus, Delta**), and elsewhere, together with an increasing number of internal flights in Ireland itself.

There are regular bus services from airports to town terminals, while taxis will also meet planes. Car-hire firms have offices at airports, all of which have the usual restaurants, shopping, exchange, hotel-booking facilities, and information bureaux.

Holiday Packages. Aer Lingus can also advise on different types of fare, and also on interesting combinations in the way of tours, etc. which can be arranged, which are worth considering to reduce costs. Among these are Dublin Weekends; Country Weekends; 'Castles in the air' (weekends in Irish castles); Golf Weekends; Fly-Drive holidays, with or without accommodation booked in advance; fishing holidays; holidays in horse-drawn caravans, or Shannon cruisers; reductions for students, children, or spouse, etc.; and other facilities which may be available and which may assist in the planning of holidays, business congresses and conventions.

By Sea

Car ferries provide a number of sailings daily, throughout the year; at peak periods Christmas, Easter and certain Bank Holidays, a sailing ticket is required as well as the general open ticket, to ensure a place on the ferry. Telephone numbers given are the Irish offices of the shipping companies.

Irish Republic

Fishguard & Pembroke–Rosslare, **B & I Line** (☎ 053-33158).

Holyhead–Dun Laoghaire, **Stena Line** (☎ 01-204-7777).

Holyhead–Dublin Port, **B & I Line** (☎ 01-661-0511; 24-hr information: ☎ 01-661-0715).

Douglas–Dublin Port, **Isle of Man Steam Packet Co.** (☎ 01-874-1231).

Swansea–Cork, **Swansea Cork Ferries** (☎ 021-271-166).

Roscoff–Cork, **Brittany Ferries** (☎ 021-277-801).

Le Havre/Roscoff–Cork (☎ 021-277-801), Cherbourg–Rosslare (☎ 053-33311), Cherbourg–Rosslare, **Irish Ferries** (☎ 01-661-0551).

Northern Ireland

Stranraer–Belfast, **Stena Line** (☎ 0990-204-204).

Stranraer–Belfast, **Seacat Scotland** (☎ 0345-523-523).

Cairnryan–Larne, **P & O European Ferries** (☎ 01574-274321).

Liverpool–Belfast, **Norse Irish Ferries** (☎ 080232-779090).

Douglas–Belfast, **Isle of Man Steam Packet Company** (☎ 01232-351009).

For full information contact: **B&I Line**, 150 New Bond St, London W1Y 0AQ (☎ 0171-734-4681); **Stena Line**, Charter House, Park St, Ashford, Kent TN24 8EX (☎ 0233-647047); **P&O European Ferries**, Cairnryan, near Stranraer, Wigtownshire, Scotland (☎ 05812-276); **Isle of Man Steam Packet Co. Ltd.**, PO Box No 5, Douglas, Isle of Man (☎ 0624-661661); **Sealink Scotland**, Sea Terminal, Stranraer, Dumfries & Galloway DG9 8EL (☎ 0776-2262).

Travelling formalities

Passports

Passports and identity cards are not required for British travellers entering the Republic of Ireland from British ports and airports, or from Northern Ireland. Travellers arriving direct from the Continent or America, and elsewhere, must be in the possession of passports. Citizens of non-EU and US countries may require a visa.

Customs

For security reasons, scrutiny of air travellers to and from Ireland is fairly comprehensive. Passengers are given the option to declare dutiable goods, but spot-checks are to be expected. Travellers between Great Britain and Northern Ireland are not normally subject to customs examination, but their luggage is also liable to be opened for reasons of security, and likewise when entering from the Republic from Northern Ireland or vice-versa.

Currency

There is no restriction on the importation of currency into the Republic of Ireland. Irish notes may be exported to a total value not exceeding IR£150 (in denominations not exceeding IR£20) and any foreign currency to a total value not exceeding IR£1200. If visitors enter the Republic with more than IR£1200 in foreign currency notes, this should be declared to Customs on entry, since proof of importation may be asked for on departure from the country.

The Dublin and Shannon Airport bureaux de change remain open 364 days a year.

The Irish pound (*punt*) no longer has parity with Sterling (since mid-1979), although the differential is slight, usually favouring Sterling by a few pence. Irish coins, issued since 1928 are now identical in shape and size to the British coinage; e.g. 2p, 5p, 10p, 20p, 50p and £1. Irish currency notes are issued in denominations of £5, £10, £20, £50 and £100. Irish coins and notes are not accepted in Great Britain, but are increasingly more acceptable in Northern Ireland, particularly in the Border regions.

Banks in the Republic are open from Monday to Friday from 10.00–12.30, and 13.30–15.00, and in Dublin remain open until 17.00 on Thursdays. On busy shopping streets they now remain open during lunch-hour; the late-opening day varies elsewhere. Some agencies in the larger centres provide foreign exchange facilities, while travellers' cheques and credit cards are widely accepted. Travelling Banks may occasionally be found in remote country districts.

In Northern Ireland banks are open from Monday to Friday from 10.00–12.30 and 13.30–15.30. There are exchange facilities on the main Dublin/Belfast road near Newry, and at 68 Strand Rd, Londonderry, at Thomas Cook, 11 Donegall Pl., Belfast, and Belfast International Airport.

Arriving in Ireland

Regional Tourist Information

Tourist offices in the airports and ferryports provide a full service, and will provide information on booking accommodation, car hire and other internal transport facilities, as well as a wide range of general tourist information. They are normally open throughout the year from 09.00–18.00 Monday to Friday, and 09.00–13.00 on Saturday.

Dublin Tourism (1 Clarinda Park North, Dun Laoghaire, Co. Dublin) runs the tourist offices in the Dublin area, for which there is a central telephone number (☎ 284-4768). In Dublin itself, the **Tourist Information Centre** in the city centre (Suffolk St, Dublin 2, ☎ 603-7700), is the principal tourist information facility.

Regional tourist offices have the same opening hours in all the principal cities, towns and villages of scenic, historic or cultural interest. Offices open in many other places on a seasonal basis, and tourist information points which carry literature are also widespread.

Regional tourism in the Republic is divided into six areas:

Shannon (Clare, Limerick, North Kerry, North Tipperary). Shannon Development, Tourism Division, Shannon Town Centre, Shannon, Co. Clare (☎ 061-361555; fax 061-361903).

South East (Carlow, Kilkenny, South Tipperary, Waterford, Wexford). South East Tourism, 41 The Quay, Waterford (☎ 051-75823; fax 051-77388).

South West (Cork, South Kerry). Cork/Kerry Tourism, Grand Parade, Cork (☎ 021-273251; fax 021-273505).

West (Galway, Mayo, Roscommon). Ireland West Tourism, *Aras Fáilte*, Eyre Square, Galway (☎ 091-63081; fax 091-63201).

North West (Cavan, Donegal, Leitrim, Monaghan, Sligo). North West Tourism, Aras Reddan, Temple St, Sligo (☎ 071-61201; fax 071-60360).

Midlands East (Kildare, Laois, Longford, Louth, Meath, North Offaly, Westmeath, Wicklow). Midlands East Tourism, Dublin Road, Mullingar, Co. Westmeath (☎ 044-48761; fax 044-40413).

In **Northern Ireland**, Networked Tourist Information Centres are organised on a county basis, with offices in most large towns.

Co. Armagh. Old Bank Building, 40 English St, Armagh (☎ 0861-527808).

Co. Antrim. Council Offices, 14 Charles St, Ballymoney (☎ 02656-62280); The Castle, Carrickfergus (☎ 09603-51604); Giants Causeway Visitor Centre, Bushmills (☎ 02657-31853).

Co. Down. Tower House, 34 Quay St, Bangor (☎ 027-270069); Market St, Downpatrick (☎ 0396-613426).

Co. Fermanagh. Lakeland Visitor Centre, Shore Rd, Enniskillen (☎ 0365-323110).

Co. Tyrone. Sperrin Heritage Centre, 27 Glenelly Rd, Cranagh (☎ 066-26 48124); Abercorn Sq, Strabane (☎ 0504-883733).

Accommodation

Hotels and Country Houses

The art of hospitality is a gift natural to the Irish, and visitors will as a rule find a warm welcome at an Irish hotel, often more informal than in other countries, and in general a high standard of service and cleanliness. Most hotels provide a full meal service. The majority have bars, and a surprising number offer a baby-sitting service. There is an increasing number of country houses and castles which have been adapted to accommodate guests, to obtain the latest editions of *The Hidden Ireland* (private country house accommodation), contact Kensington Hall, Grove Park, Dublin 6 (☎ 01-668-463; fax 01-668 6578). *The Blue Book* lists exceptional country-houses and restaurants; contact Ardbraccan Glebe, Navan, Co. Meath (☎ 046-23416; fax 046-23292). *Friendly Homes of Ireland* lists family homes and small hotels; contact 71 Waterloo Rd, Dublin 4 (☎ 01-686-463; fax 01-686-578).

Other brochures are *Irish Country Houses and Restaurants* (ICHRA) and *Manor House Hotels* and *Country Havens of Northern Ireland*.

They are annually classified by the Irish Tourist Board, and are included in their *Official List of Hotels* and *Guesthouses*, a copy of which may be requested. They are graded as either A*, A, B*, B and C (most bedrooms in the scale A hotels have private bathrooms *en suite)*.

Bed and Breakfast/Guesthouses

Bed and breakfast/guesthouses, or 'B&B's, are smaller in scale than hotels, and not open to non-residents. They may give a more personal service, but generally only provide breakfasts and evening meals. They are similarly graded from A to C, and should certainly not be overlooked; by staying in this type of accommodation the visitor comes in contact with a wider cross-section of the population than the hotels are likely to provide, and the proprietors will have an intimate knowledge of their area.

The Board produces an annual a list of approved *Town and Country Homes and Guesthouses*, in which a more traditional and homely way of life will be experienced. Evening meals will be provided if reasonable notice is given. A circular 'shamrock' sign, on which the current year and the words 'Approved Bord Fáilte' are printed, should be displayed on each house so listed. An illustrated guide to *Farmhouse Accommodation* is also available from the Tourist Board on request.

Hostels

A list of hostels in Ireland may be obtained from **An Óige** (Irish Youth Hostel Association, IYHA), 39 Mountjoy Sq., Dublin 1, and from **YHANI** (Youth Hostel Association of Northern Ireland), 56 Bradbury Pl., Belfast BT7 1RU. The Tourist Board publishes an information sheet listing Youth Hostels and their location throughout the Republic. The **Independent Hostels Organisation** (IHO), an ever-growing group of attractive individually-owned hostels, operate on a more informal basis, and generally in smaller, more casual premises; contact Vary Finlay, Bantry Hostel, Bishop Lucy Place, Bantry, Co. Cork, (☎ and fax 027-51672) for information map of hostel distribution.

The Irish Tourist Board have a **Central Reservation Service** at Suffolk St, (PO Box 273, Dublin; ☎ 01-284-4768), which will make reservations, not only in hotels and guesthouses, but also on river-cruisers, and for horse-drawn caravans. It will also give information about car hire. A small fee is payable for these services.

Publications of the Northern Ireland Tourist Board, NITB (59 North St, Belfast BT1 1NB, ☎ 0232-240960), *Where to Stay in Northern Ireland,* and *Where to Eat in Northern Ireland,* cover a wide cross-section of recommended locations.

Visitors to Dublin or Belfast are recommended to book accommodation as far in advance as possible. With the increase in tourism, conferences, rugby matches etc, not only the larger hotels get booked up, but also many of the smaller central ones, and if you try at short notice you risk being accommodated some considerable distance from town.

Where a service charge is included, no tipping is expected except in the case of exceptional service. VAT is, by law, included in all Irish hotel prices and restaurants.

The Tourist Board, which encourages the use of approved accommodation only, can also supply lists of self-catering accommodation in rented cottages, chalets and villas, and likewise camping parks, with details of their amenities and equipment for hire. Unapproved accommodation, while not corresponding to the boards precise guidelines, can provide excellent service also.

Eating and Drinking

Wholemeal breads, widely available, are among the best items of staple food to be found throughout Ireland; soda bread, soda farls, potato bread, tea-brack, baps, are among some of the variants. When eaten with Irish creamery butter, you have a very satisfying combination. Farmhouse cheeses are a rewarding end to any meal, generally produced in small quantities on family farms (**Gubeen**, **Derrynaflan**, **Cashel Blue**, **Desmond**, **Millens**), the variety reflects the European cheesemaking tradition in microcosm.

The oysters of the Galway region go superlatively with a pint of Guinness; for meat eaters, the *Ulster Fry* is a mammoth encounter with puddings and bacon, capable of nourishing a traveller for days. Colcannon and champ are northern specialities; in Cork drisheen, tripe and Clonakilty black puddings are local specialities; most regions have local dishes, but these may have to be sought out.

Drinking is both a national preoccupation and failing, and pubs, *the* point of social contact in any part of the island. Guinness is the national drink, a thick black stout with creamy white head, and Murphys a regional alternative. Irish Whiskey (*uisce beatha*, 'the water of life') was originally distilled in many parts of the country, its manufacture is now concentrated at Bushmills, Co. Antrim, and Middleton, Co. Cork. It is frequently drunk as a 'chaser' to a pint of stout, 'a pint and a drop', in local parlance. Irish whiskey, spelt with an 'e' to distinguish it from mere whisky, is bottled only after it has been matured in wooden casks for at least seven years. It has a distinctive flavour unlike Scotch, Bourbon or rye. 'Irish coffee' and 'Irish Cream Liqueurs' are modern inventions, combining native spirits with fresh cream.

The percentage of pubs to population, even in the smallest of villages, is remarkably high, and only in recent years have they ceased to be fortresses of male company; many still contain 'snugs', screened cubicles for discreet conversations, or to accommodate women patrons. The rural phenomenon of the 'pub-grocery' deserves special mention. In such premises the bar counter may be bolstered by wheelbarrows at one end, packages of detergent at the other. Morrisseys in Abbeyleix is a museum quality example, even to the glass-fronted tins for 'loose biscuits'. All over Ireland, pubs are becoming more conscious of the need to provide bar-food, and the results can be excellent.

Restaurants

This is an area in which a veritable revolution has occurred in Ireland during the past 25 years. The era when quantity (mountains of fluffy potatoes, and bacon with the life boiled out of it) was believed to equate with quality, has been replaced by one in which a generation of chefs and restaurant-owners who display great flair and originality are creating menus capable of attracting even the most critical of diners. An asset which any chef in Ireland has at their disposal is the best locally-produced pollution-free vegetables, sea food and meat. On every level of price and style of food, choice is available, although some areas tend to represent a black hole in the generally widespread improvements. Ethnic restaurants, previously uncommon in Ireland, which lacks long-established foreign communities, are now more widespread, and restaurants specialising in French, Italian, Greek, Mexican, Japanese and Chinese food are becoming common. Fish restaurants should be more commonplace than they are in an island location, however when found they are generally worth visiting; Irish wild salmon and trout are exceptional. Gourmet establishments can be found in the unlikeliest of places, and the west and southwest coastal regions have some of the best restaurants in the country **Clifden, Co. Galway; Kinsale** and **West Cork** generally). Places serving traditional Irish food are rare in any part of Ireland (Gallagher's Boxty House, Fleet St, Temple Bar, Dublin). Vegetarian restaurants are becoming more common, and many places have vegetarian dishes on their menus. Among a growing literature on where to eat in Ireland, the *Bridgestone Guides* by John and Sally McKenna (Estragon Press) are an invaluable source of perceptive advice on mouth-watering and interesting places to eat.

Opening Hours
The hours during which alcohol is legally on sale in the Republic are now only slightly more liberal than those applying in Great Britain (and Northern Ireland; see below). On weekdays its sale is officially permitted between 10.30–23.30. On Sundays the opening hours are from 12.30–14.00, and from 16.00–23.00. Hotel residents can usually obtain a drink at any time, while non-residents may order refreshments with their meals. Pubs in Northern Ireland are open between 11.30–23.00 from Monday to Saturday (those with late licences to 01.00), and on Sundays from 12.30–14.30, and from 19.00–22.00.

Travelling around Ireland
Nowhere in Ireland is further than an extended day's car journey from the point of arrival, but when public transport is being used, connections may not always allow a long journey to be completed within a single day. With the exception of the principal routes, Irish roads can be narrow and tortuous, making longer journeys of what on a map may appear as a short distance. Possession of an adequate map is recommended; here are some suggestions: Ireland 1:250.000 in four sheets; the Discovery series 1:50.000, 89 sheets with archaeological sites highlighted (highly recommended); Ordnance Survey Road Atlas 1:250.000 in book format.

By Rail
In addition to the fast DART coastal commuter services in the Dublin area, Dublin is connected by main line to Rosslare (ferry port), Waterford (airport), Cork (airport and ferry port), Tralee (airport), Limerick (airport), Galway (airport), Westport, Sligo (airport) and Belfast (airport and ferry port), while Belfast is connected to Larne (ferry port), Portrush and Derry (airport). Full details of all services throughout the network are available from tourist offices and railway stations. An extensive area (see map), of south Ulster is unserviced by the network. The train service is swifter but both more limited and more expensive than travelling by bus.

By Bus
The **Expressway** network provides a wide range of coach services linking the main towns throughout the island. There is also an extensive network of local services, together with **Ulsterbus** services in the North. Latest schedules can be obtained from tourist offices, bus and railway stations, which can advise on the variety of tourist and excursion tickets available. **Bus Éireann** (desk at Tourist Office, Suffolk St., Dublin2) offers a wide range of bus and rail tickets including the 8 or 15-day Rambler ticket which gives unlimited travel by bus or rail or a

combination of the two. The Overlander ticket allows you unlimited travel into Northern Ireland. In the capital, Dublin Bus, has an 'Explorer' ticket, valid for four days on Dublin buses and suburban trains after 09.45. Private bus companies provide services in some outlying regions. Tickets are sold in bus stations, but are generally also available from the bus driver. Fridays, Saturday, Sundays are very busy times for the bus service, when the entire student and young working population of the country decides to go home from the cities to the provinces for the weekend.

It should be noted that in the Republic, the destinations of some buses are still indicated on the vehicle in Irish only, which may well confuse the visitor, who should always check with the conductor or driver.

By Car

Motorists visiting Ireland are advised to join one of the driving associations (such as the AA or RAC) which will provide any necessary documents, as well as information about rules of the road in Ireland, restrictions regarding caravans and trailers, arrangements for spare parts, insurance, etc. The speed limit is 55 mph (90kph) and 30 mph (65 kph) in built-up areas.

Restrictions. Although there are certain restrictions on the use of their vehicle while in Ireland, visitors may import and re-export their cars without any formality, but unless they are registered in Northern Ireland they must carry a nationality plate while in the Republic. Motorists not the owners of their vehicle should possess the owner's permit for its use abroad. It should also be noted that in the towns of Northern Ireland there are areas to which vehicle entry is restricted, or in which unattended vehicles may not be parked.

Some **petrol stations** are closed on Sundays; motorists should not let their tanks become low too late in the evenings.

Car hire. All important towns, ports and airports provide car-hire facilities. Avis (☎ 01-677-6971); Budget (☎ 01-837-9802); Hertz (☎ 01-844-5466); Murray Europcar (☎ 01-668-1777). **Casey Auto Rentals**, based in Shannon, Castlebar and Knock Co. Mayo (☎ 094-21411, offers a 5% discount to Blue Guide readers.

The roads in Ireland, comparatively few of which are subject to heavy traffic, are particularly suitable for tourists, although in some of the narrower and winding roads in remoter districts there are occasional steep gradients or sharp bends. In some areas cows, sheep, horses and other livestock are liable to wander onto the highway, pursuing a time-honoured tradition of *grazing the long acre*. Most but by no means all places are sign-posted, some in both miles and kilometres. In Northern Ireland, signs are in English, distances in miles. Road sign tend to be scarce in out-of-the-way places, often misleading, sometimes non-existent. The ends of a remarkable number of signs have been broken or knocked off, or the signs twisted in another direction so travellers should refer to a detailed map as well.

In the Republic, the roads are divided into three categories: the main network of National roads, e.g. N2; and those with the prefix R (R123, etc.), although some are still marked as Trunk roads (T2) or Link roads (L93), together with an extensive range of minor roads and tracks. In Northern Ireland the equivalent roads are marked A2, or B6 as in Great Britain, apart from the two main motorways driving southwest and northwest from Belfast, indicated as M1 and M2 respectively.

By Air
Internal flights are available from the major international airports, Belfast, Cork, Dublin and Shannon, as well as the regional ones, but are quite expensive relative to any other means of transport; there are regional airports at Carrick Finn (north Donegal), Derry; Galway; Knock, (Co, Mayo); Sligo, Tralee and Waterford.

By Bicycle
All parts of Ireland are particularly suitable for exploration by bicycle, and visitors' bicycles are treated as personal effects and may enter the country free of duty. Bicycles may also be hired from **Rent-a-bike** dealers, among others, and further information may be obtained at any tourist office. **Irish Cycling Safaris**, 7 Dartry Park, Dublin 6 (☎ 260-0749), organise cycling holidays along the more romantic areas of the western seaboard, which provide an ideal way for the visitor to experience little known and spectacularly beautiful areas of the country.

Walking
The longest established and most extensive waymarked walking trail in Ireland is the 560 ml/929 km, **Ulster Way,** which makes a grand circuit of Northern Ireland, passing through the finest scenery of the region. It is sub-divided into 14 walks. In the Republic there are now twenty waymarked routes, distributed in the most interesting regions of the country. From Dublin, the **Wicklow Way** links southwest to the **South Leinster Way**, running as far as Carrick-on-Suir, and the Grand and Royal Canal Ways link Dublin to the Shannon region. In West Cork/South Kerry are three of the finest **walks** in the country, and north of Galway is the **Western Way**, from Connemara to Mayo.

Walking is without doubt the most exhilarating manner in which to see the best countryside in Ireland; good regional publications on walking routes are available, but these should always be used in conjunction with the appropriate Ordnance maps.

By Horse
Tourist offices can likewise advise on holiday transport by horse-drawn caravan, now less popular than twenty years ago, due to increased road traffic. Riding holidays in trackless regions remain an attractive alternative

Inland Waterways
It is possible to traverse the country from Dublin on the east coast to Limerick on the west, and from Waterford in the extreme southeast to Lough Erne in the northwest, on the quite extensive and little used inland waterways (a combination of 18C navigational canals and natural river courses) entirely avoiding cars, roads, or any suggestion of speed or urgency.

The Shannon and its lake system is the busiest and most developed region of the waterways, with all the necessary apparatus of boats and cruisers for hire, harbours and lakeside pubs and restaurants, but the long neglected canal network is also slowly being brought back into operation. The recently restored Shannon–Erne Waterway, closed for a hundred years (only eight boats ever travelled on it between its inception in the 1860s and its prompt closure), unites Limerick through 16 locks with Belleek. The *Shell Guide to the River Shannon* is an excellent source book.

General Information

Embassies and Consulates abroad
UK. 17 Grosvenor Pl., London SW1X 7HR; **USA**. 2234 Massachusetts Av., Washington (with Consulates at 515 Madison Av., New York 10022; 655 Montgomery 54335, San Francisco 9411; and 400 N Michigan Av., Chicago, Illinois 60611); **Canada**. 170 Metcalfe St, Ottawa K2P IP3; **Australia**. 20 Arkana St, Yarrulumla, Canberra 2600.

Embassies and Consulates in Dublin
British Embassy, 31 Merrion Rd. 4 (☎ 269-5211); **USA** Embassy and Consulate, 42 Elgin Rd, 4 (☎ 668-8777); **Canadian** Embassy, 65 St. Stephen's Green, 2 (☎ 478-1988); **Australian** Embassy, Fitzwilliam House, Wilton Terrace, 2 (☎ 676-1517).

A full list of other Consulates and Trade Delegations may be obtained from the Department of Foreign Affairs, Iveagh House, 80 St. Stephen's Green, 2, Dublin.

Cultural organizations
The Irish Arts Council (*An Chomhairle Ealaíon*), 70 Merrion Sq., 2
The National Trust for Ireland (*An Taisce*; pronounced An Tash-ke), The Tailors' Hall, Back Lane, 8
The Military Historical Society for Ireland, 86 St. Stephen's Green, 2
The Old Dublin Society, 58 S William St. 2
Royal Inst. of the Architects of Ireland, 8 Merrion Sq.
Royal Irish Academy, 19 Dawson St, 2
Royal Society of Antiquaries of Ireland 3 Merrion Sq.
The Irish Architectural Archive, 73 Merrion Sq.
The Irish Georgian Society, 74 Merrion Square, Dublin 2
National Archives, Bishop St, Dublin 8
Office of Public Works, 51 St. Stephen's Green
National Monuments Advisory Council, Ely Place Upper, 2
Royal Dublin Society, Ballsbridge, 4
Royal Society for Industrial Archaeology, c/o The RDS; Royal Horticultural Society, 16 St. Stephen's Green, 2.
For information on the Gaeltacht; *Gaeltarra Eireann, Na Forbacha, Gaillimh.*

Health
Visitors from EC countries are entitled to medical treatment in Ireland under an EC reciprocal medical treatment arrangement. The Pharmacy at 55 O'Connell St, Dublin is open daily until 22.00.

Personal Security
In the Republic the police or Civic Guard are known as the **Garda Síochána** (or

more simply, the Garda; plural Gardaí, pronounced 'Gardee'). They are unarmed unless undertaking special duties. The crime rate in rural Ireland is exceptionally low, particularly regarding crimes against tourists. In the cities however, precautions which are advisable in any urban area should be observed; in Dublin it is unwise to leave anything of value visible in an unattended car, walking around the city very late at night can be hazardous, and certainly should not be done when alone.

In Northern Ireland, the armed **Royal Ulster Constabulary** (RUC) is supported by a reserve force, and by regiments of the British Army. As in the south, the countryside is very safe. Because of the high security presence in urban areas, crimes against the individual are less common, yet in Belfast, precautions should also be taken.

In **emergencies**, dial 999 to call the Fire Brigade, Ambulance, or Police.

Disabled Travellers

Facilities for the disabled are improving in Ireland, but nothing should be taken for granted. Most public museums and galleries now have wheelchair access ramps and adequate lifts, but the smaller regional institutions are less likely to have convenient access. Historic sites by their very nature are mostly inaccessible, except in the case of prominent locations with high visitor numbers. Disabled toilets are likewise to be found in public institutions, but should not be expected anywhere.

For advice contact: Disabled Driver's Association, Carmichael House, North Brunswick St, Dublin 7 (☎ 721-233); National Rehabilitation Board, 25 Clyde Road, Ballsbridge, Dublin 4 (☎ 684-181).

Postal and Telephone Services

Most **post offices** are open between 08.00 or 09.00–17.30 or 18.00 on weekdays, but may close between 13.00–14.15 (some may close at 13.00 one day a week). In Northern Ireland they all close at 13.00 on Saturday. The GPO in O'Connell St, Dublin, is open with a Bureau de Change, 08.00–20.00 Monday to Saturday, and 10.30–18.30 on Sunday and Bank Holidays.

Irish postage stamps must be used on letters posted from the Republic; letter boxes are painted green. British stamps are used in Northern Ireland, where letter boxes are painted red, but the narrowed slit of the latter (for security reasons) will not accept anything but the thinnest envelopes and larger packets must be posted at post offices.

Telephones

Public call-boxes may be found at most post offices, railway stations, at hotels, pubs, and in kiosks; most now accept phone cards although a small number still take coins. Telephone numbers given in this book are supplied with local (ie Irish) codes except Dublin. If you are calling Ireland from Britain the code is 00 353. The prefix for Dublin is '1'. For NI codes are as given.

Opening Hours

Shops and businesses are open 09.00–18.00, and sometimes later depending on the location and type of trade. In Dublin city centre late opening is on Thursday, to 21.00. Late opening days and half-days vary in different regions.

Newspapers

The *Irish Times* is the leading Dublin-published liberal newspaper; the *Irish Independent* and *Sunday Independent* are more populist broadsheets. The *Sunday Tribune* is a 'quality' Sunday paper, while *The Sunday Business Post* is its principal rival.

As well as the Irish newspapers, standard British broadsheet and tabloid papers are available on the date of issue in all cities and most towns, the range of titles may be more limited the further one is from an airport. American papers are available in cities and international hotels on the date of issue. Continental papers are only available in the cities.

Public Toilets

Not a national strong-point, the standards vary from the excellent to the unspeakable. Quaint rural pubs of delightfully undisturbed character are liable not to have disturbed their toilet facilities since Oliver Cromwell last used them. However, standards are improving. In public toilets, *Fír* denotes men, *Mna*, women; the first words of Irish which every visitor must learn.

Taxis

Service or *dolmus* taxis only exist in the cities of Northern Ireland, where 'Black Taxis' serve particular suburban regions. In general, bargaining should not be necessary in any part of the country if the driver turns on the meter (which he may have to be reminded to do). Other than for long and obscure trips the taxi service is not expensive; with permanent grid-lock threatening Dublin's rush hour traffic, its mobility and cheapness is to be recommended.

Area and Population

Island of Ireland (1991 census)
84.459 sq km
pop. 5.101.401

Republic of Ireland
70.282 sq km
pop. 3.523.401
pop density 130 ppsm
pop Dublin 1.024.429

Northern Ireland
14.177 sq km
pop. 1.578.000
pop density 280 ppsm
pop Belfast 524.700

Measurements

The measurements of buildings are given in metres (m), as are the altitudes of hills, cliffs and mountains.

Local Customs

Irish tribalism manifests itself in both militant and benign forms. Among the most tribal and well known are the celebration of the 'Marching Season' in Northern Ireland, the highlight of which is Orange Day, the 'Glorious Twelfth' (12 July), when the Orangemen of Ulster commemorate the Battle of the Boyne (1690), with drum-beating parades, the sash-wearing participants clad in dark suits and bowler hats. Irish clan rallies, more convivial and less parochial, bring together people from the Irish Diaspora (now scattered across the globe), in search of their family roots. All Irish family names are associated with a particular territory, and this provides the location for clan rallies. For further information consult the Genealogical Office, Kildare St, Dublin 2.

In rural areas on December 26, St. Stephen's Day, the 'Wran Boys' celebrate by dressing in fancy dress and touring the locality, at least nominally in pursuit of the inoffensive wren. Many similar folk customs survive in different parts of the country.

Emblems

The national flag of the **Irish Republic** is a tricolour of green, white, and orange, green being displayed next to the staff. It is said to have been introduced in 1848 as an emblem of the Young Ireland movement by Thomas Francis Meagher, and at Easter 1916 flew above the General Post Office, Dublin. The colours represent the Gaelic and Anglo-Norman stock, and the supporters of William of Orange, the Protestant planters; Meagher suggested that the white signified the lasting truce between the Orange and Green, beneath whose folds 'the hands of the Irish Protestant and the Irish Catholic may be clasped in heroic brotherhood'.

The standard of the President is a golden harp on an azure field; the harp, the official Government emblem, replaced the earlier three crowns on Irish coinage in the early 16C.

The shamrock is said to have been used by St. Patrick to explain the idea of the 'Trinity' to the pagan Gaels, although this legend first appeared in the 18C, and it is still frequently displayed as an emblem of Ireland in general, but is not used in any official context.

The National Anthem was written in 1907 by Peadar Kearney (1883–1942), who with Patrick Heeney, also composed the music. First published in the newspaper *Irish Freedom* (1912), it is known as *The Soldier's Song* (*Amhrán na bhFiann*), and its chorus, displacing the earlier Fenian anthem *God Save Ireland*—which might have been disparagingly misinterpreted—was adopted in 1926; it is always sung in Irish. The replacement of the current anthem is frequently discussed.

The Union Jack is the national flag of **Northern Ireland** and more specifically an emblem of the Union. Flying of the tricolour by Nationalists in Northern Ireland is widespread but illegal. The origin of the arms of the province of Ulster—shorn of legendary trappings—is that it was derived from those borne by De Burgo, Earl of Ulster at the period of the Norman invasion, with the addition of the O'Neill escutcheon, the 'Red Hand of O'Neill'—argent a dexter hand gules (red right hand on white background). The right hand is severed at the wrist, from which no blood should flow. Some confusion has arisen in the past by the indiscriminate use of both dexter and sinister hands by the Order of Baronets of Ulster, instituted by James I, when 'a hand gules', otherwise unspecified, was adopted as their device.

The Troubles

Readers may be somewhat dismayed on crossing the political frontier between the Republic of Ireland and Northern Ireland. It is always disturbing to cross borders under the scrutiny of armed guards and to pass military patrols. The sight of police stations incongruously surrounded by chicken-wire barricades tends to make the country look more beleaguered than it is. A decrease in such manifestations of security can be expected in the future, should peace in Northern Ireland become permanent.

However, it must be stated that Northern Ireland is as replete with the charms and beauties of the island as any other region, and the traveller should not be put off by the negative impression generally purveyed by the media. Away from the well-known trouble-spots, life and conditions are tranquil, and the people unfailingly hospitable.

Urban Ireland

Recent historical research and extensive archaeological excavations in urban Ireland have led to a considerable re-assessment of the role of the Vikings in Irish history. The greater body of information on the Viking Age had been, in the past, the Irish manuscript sources, and inevitably these documents present the Norse invaders in the poorest possible light, as ruthless plunderers of monastic treasures. Archaeology attempts to present a more objective view, and it is in their role as the creators of urban Ireland that Viking significance really lies. Also at the latter end of over a millennium of urban growth which began in the 9C, the conclusion of the 20C demands a more detailed evaluation of contemporary architectural developments which have received greater attention.

The transition from a predominantly rurally based population to the emergence of a substantial urban one which has taken place in the second half of the 20C is the most fundamental change to occur in population movements in Ireland since the catastrophic years of the mid 19C. The long-term significance of such radical demographic changes which are still taking place are difficult to predict except to observe that Ireland, the least densely populated country in the EU, is likely if present trends continue, to display in its western regions and hinterland a dangerously low density which may undermine the viability of life in some areas of the countryside.

Sporting and Leisure activities

Sport in Ireland can be divided into two categories, 'Gaelic Games', and games also played elsewhere, ie. rugby, soccer, cricket, basketball, golf etc. Of the traditional Irish sports (Gaelic football, hurling, road bowls, camogie (women's hurling), handball), hurling is the most unusual, and an excellent spectator sport. Played by two 15-member teams with ash sticks curved at the end, the 25cm leather ball is hit at extraordinary speeds of up to 80mph; hurling is called 'the fastest game on earth', and whatever the accuracy of the claim, it is indeed a game requiring prodigious skill, strength and mobility. The All Ireland hurling and football finals, played in Croke Park, Dublin, excite great interest. The country has an abundance of fine golf facilities, both of the links and course variety, many sited on beautiful stretches of the coastline. Horse racing takes place on tracks in many parts of the country, the principal fixtures are held at the Curragh in Co. Kildare, but regional events are widespread. Greyhound racing tracks are located in the cities.

Information sheets and brochures on all sports may be obtained from the Irish Tourist Board (see above) and in Northern Ireland from the Sports Council, Upper Malone Rd, Belfast BT9 6RZ.

In recent years there has been a proliferation of **Forest Parks and Wildlife** sites throughout Ireland, many of them with nature-trails. A number of **National Parks** have also been inaugurated; in the south at **Killarney**, **Glenveagh** and **Connemara**, and in the north at **Glenariff**, **Glenshane**, **Gortin Glen** and **Tollymore**. Full details of their whereabouts may be obtained from the Forest Park and Wildlife Service (Department of Lands, 22 Upper Merrion St, Dublin 2), who also publish a number of informative booklets and leaflets on the natural history of the island, together with lists of bird haunts, etc. The Irish Wild Bird Conservancy is c/o The Royal Irish Academy, 19 Dawson St, Dublin 2.

The Forest Service, Department of Agriculture (Dundonald House, Upper Newtownards Road, Belfast BT4 3SF), the National Trust for Northern Ireland (Rowallane, Saintfield, Co. Down BT24 7LH), the Northern Ireland Tourist Board, the Royal Society for the Protection of Birds (Belvoir Forest Park, Belfast BT8 4QT) and the Ulster Society for the Preservation of the Countryside (Upper Malone Rd, Belfast BT9 6RZ) can provide comparable material for Northern Ireland.

Summer Schools

A hybrid type of gathering, related to literature and the arts, although not necessarily taking place during the summers, is the 'summer school', of which most counties have numerous on offer; they celebrate aspects of the Irish psyche, life and culture. The subject of a summer school is usually a notable poet, musician, scholar or local worthy, but it can in fact celebrate achievements and traditions of any kind. Dean Swift, Brian Merriman, William Carleton, W.B. Yeats, James Joyce, Oscar Wilde, are among those with a summer school in their honour. These encounters vary from highly serious academic discussions with a cast of international scholars, to more relaxed gatherings where the local life, liquor and landscape vies with the advertised topic for attention. The venue is normally an area of the country with which the hero in question is associated, credibly as in the case of Oliver Goldsmith at Ballymahon, Co. Longford, his native heath, or somewhat tongue-in-cheek in the Gerard Manley Hopkins gathering at Monasterevin, Co. Kildare. Gaelic and Anglo-Irish culture are equally represented, as are landscape, literature, language and folklore among the many strands addressed at individual venues. For the visitor with a desire to explore some aspect of Irish life in depth there is hardly a better way than through a Summer School. Bord Fáilte's booklets, *Cultural Courses in Ireland*, and *Literary Ireland*, are good although not exhaustive guides. Local tourist offices are the best source of information on occasional activities like festivals or summer schools. The importance of summer schools and festivals is the manner in which they allow the visitor instant and in-depth access to both the contemporary and historic cultural life of the country.

Public Holidays

1 January New Year's Day (RoI, NI); **17 March** St. Patrick's Day (RoI, NI); **Good Friday** and **Easter Monday** (RoI, NI) both moveable; **1 May** (RoI); **Last Monday in May** (NI); **First Monday in June** (RoI); **First Monday in August** (RoI); **Last Monday in October** (RoI); **25 December** Christmas Day (RoI, NI); **26 December** St Stephen's Day (RoI), Boxing Day (NI).

Festivals

The various festivals of grand opera (Wexford); oysters (Galway); theatre (Dublin), cinema (Belfast, Cork, Dublin); matchmaking (Lisdoonvarna); physical beauty (Tralee); traditional, choral, classical or early music (Belfast, Cork, Kilkenny); and the visual arts (Galway) have been an important feature of Irish life since the 1950s, they can vastly enrich a stay in any part of the country.

4 March (Dublin Film Festival); **17 March** (St. Patrick's Day Parade) (RoI, NI); **April** (Irish Grand National, Fairyhouse); **1 May** (International Choral Festival, Cork); **23 May** (Sligo Arts Festival); **6 June** (Festival of Music in Great Irish Houses); **16 June** (*Bloomsday*, celebration of James Joyce's *Ulysses*, Dublin); (Co. Wicklow Gardens Festival); (Irish Derby—the *Curragh*); **12 July** ('The Glorious Twelfth', start of the *Marching Season*) (NI); (Galway Arts Festival); (*Fleadh leadh Ceoil na héireann* traditional music festival, venue changes). **1 August** (O'Carolan Harp Festival, Keadue, Roscommon); **10 August** (Apprentice Boys March, Derry) (NI); (Puck Fair, Killorglin, Kerry); (Rose of Tralee Festival); (Galway Races); **17 August** (Kilkenny Arts Week); **Last Monday in August** (Royal Black Preceptory Marches); **12 September** (Clarenbridge Oyster Festival); **14 September** (All Ireland Hurling and (**28**) Gaelic Football finals, Dublin); **20 September** (Waterford International Festival of Light Opera); **6 October** (Dublin Theatre Festival); **17 October** (Wexford Opera Festival); **24 October** (Cork Film and Jazz Festivals); Belfast Arts Festival (NI); **30 October** (Lisdoonvarna Matchmaking Festival).

Place Names

Almost all Irish place names are topographical descriptions which have been anglicised (Derry or *Doire*; an oak wood), representing frequently in a garbled form the name of the place in Irish or on the eastern seaboard many are from Old Norse, the language of the Vikings (Leixlip or *Lax Hlaup*, a salmon leap). In either case some feature of the physical landscape, either still visible or submerged under later developments is recorded.

While every attempt has been made to achieve consistency with the spelling of surnames, place-names, etc, this has on occasions been impossible, as local signposting, local usage and the form approved by the Ordnance Survey Maps may not agree; these however are in the process of revision and codification. Signposts in the Republic, bear both Irish and English place names, in Northern Ireland only English language signs are in use.

Language

English, as it is spoken in Ireland, is a product of the particular historic circumstances which led the population in the course of the 18C–19C to exchange Irish for English as the mother tongue of the majority, a psychologically disturbing form of internal linguistic emigration involving a people undergoing one of the major traumas of emigrating without actually leaving home. Irish language structures and vocabulary inform the English commonly spoken in Ireland today as do archaic English and Scots usages derived from the centuries of plantation. The visitor with an ear for language will find even the most casual conversation rewarding.

English is the language of the vast majority of the inhabitants of Ireland, and in the Irish-speaking areas, all but small children are bilingual. The word *Éire* appears on the postage stamps and coinage of the Irish Republic and is the official name of the State, as defined in the Constitution; it is also a solecism—an offence against idiomatic usage—and is never spoken. Irish people are not pleased to hear their country referred to as *Éire*, preferring 'Ireland', 'the Irish Republic', or more briefly 'the Republic', (Northern Unionist politicians frequently refer to the south as 'Éire', conscious of its offensive potential). English, although the mother tongue of the majority, is the official second language of the Republic (a point brought home to visitors, who will see many public signs and placenames written up in both languages, although some are confusingly in Irish alone). Many words, however contrived, such as *aerphort*, will be immediately recognisable. The term Ireland or Irish may in different circumstances refer to the whole island, as in the Irish Rugby Team, or merely to the Republic as in the Irish Soccer Team. In Northern Ireland, the term 'Ulster', the historic name of the northern nine-county province, has been whittled down to mean the current six-county state; in contemporary usage it can refer to either (it depends on the politics of the speaker).

All Acts of Parliament and statutory instruments, agenda and proceedings of the Dáil and Senate are published bilingually, even if few use Irish in parliamentary debate. Some proficiency in the language is expected, even if standards are unexacting, in such bodies as the Garda; while it is obligatory in certain positions, a knowledge of Irish has no longer been compulsory in the Civil Service since 1974.

Although the campaign initiated late in the last century by Douglas Hyde to promote the language, then widely spoken only on the western seaboard, led to the establishment of the Gaelic League in 1893 and did much to foster interest in the vernacular (indeed it was for the first time taught in the primary schools) interest has never been widespread. In the 1950s it was estimated that merely 30,000 people used Irish as their first language, of whom only 3000 were ignorant of English, while perhaps 300,000 or 400,000 had a reasonable knowledge of it as the standardised second language. The census of 1981 optimistically claimed that there were some 1,018,000 Irish speakers (without indicating what degree of competence or use), but in the *Gaeltacht* itself (see below) there had been a decline. It has been estimated that of its population of 75,000 only one-third use Irish in everyday communication. These Irish-speaking districts, defined in 1956, are known as the **Gaeltacht** and the authority responsible for the *Gaeltacht* is now known as *Udarás na Gaeltachta*. Its main enclaves are located in north west of Donegal; north west of Mayo and on Achill Island; much of Connemara, and immediately north east of Galway city itself; on the Aran Islands; the Dingle peninsula; south west of Killarney, Cape Clear Island, Co. Cork, between Killarney and Macroom; and Ring, a small enclave south of Dungavan. It covers an area of 4800 sq km, less than 6 per cent of the total surface of Ireland, and has roughly the same borders as what were known as the Congested Districts.

Owing to the poverty of the soil and overpopulation—in spite of the inroads of actual starvation and emigration in the mid 19C—the economic problems here were so acute that the British Government set up a special administration to attend to them, which was thereafter known as the 'Congested Districts Board' (1891). On the purely material side it effected many improvements, and later merged with the Department of Lands, but as far as the preservation of the Irish language was concerned, it was less successful for while idealistic advocates for the revival live largely in English-speaking Ireland, those subsisting in the Gaeltacht often doubt its utility when it comes to their own economic survival. Indeed, the few numbers of native Irish speakers remaining brings it almost within measurable distance of extinction. It has been remarked that it is both ironic and symbolic that Maurice O'Sullivan's *Twenty Years Agrowing*, and *Peig*, by Peig Sayers—both with a wide circulation in their English translation— describe life on the Irish-speaking Blasket Islands off the Kerry coast, which have been uninhabited for over a quarter of a century.

The most significant late 20C development, outside the *gaeltachts*, has been the *Gaelscoileanna* movement, a parent-directed organisation devoted to establishing Irish language primary schools wherever there is a demand for them; the movement is growing rapidly.

Irish is a language of Indo-European origin belonging to the *Goidelic* development of Centic. Profusely idiomatic, its grammar is difficult, although there are only nine irregular verbs. There are slight dialectical differences peculiar to Ulster, Munster and Connacht, but these are of no great complexity. Yet such is its warmth of expression that it has been described as 'the language for your prayers, your curses, and your love-making'! The language has passed through the transitions known to scholars as Old Irish, Middle Irish (900–1200) and Early Modern Irish (1200–1650), to Modern Irish. The first (c 600–900) is practically a closed book to all but philologists, although a considerable body of literature from that period survives; indeed, Old Irish was the earliest vernacular literature in Europe after Greek and Latin. Middle and Early Modern Irish has attracted more general attention. Its literature is largely devoted to a vast mass of mythological and heroic saga; narrative, lyrical and elegiac poetry; hagiology, homilies and translations of foreign works of devotion; medieval works of philosophy, medicine, and science; native annals, histories, clan records and topographies; free Gaelic renderings of classical and medieval literature, and a mass of proverbial matter, epigrams, songs and folklore in general.

Bogs

Approximately one-seventh of the land area of Ireland is covered by bogs (from the Irish, *bog*=soft), which, forming such a noticeable part of the landscape, require some brief explanation.

There are basically two types of bog: the 'raised' or 'red' bog; and the 'blanket' bog. The raised bog, mostly sited in the central lowlands, requires a climate with less than 100cm of rain a year, being more dependent on ground water than the blanket bog, which is found further to the west of the country and in regions above 400m, including the Wicklow Mountains. The blanket bog thrives on higher rainfall—over 125cm annually—and general humidity. Intermediate conditions produce bogs with mixed characteristics.

The raised bogs develop above a fen, some having started to accumulate between 7000 and 5000 years ago (burying the skeletons of the giant deer and tree trunks such as 'bog oak'), the rising dome of peat formed by the hummocky growth of Sphagnum moss being frequently 8m deep. Plants such as the marsh adromeda, bog asphodel, deergrass, beak-sedge, with lichens, ling, and heaths on drier sites, are often present.

The blanket bogs, as their name suggests, cover much more extensive areas, even whole regions, as in north west Mayo, developing directly on the mineral soil. By filling in hollows (and sometimes burying archaeological sites, see Ceide Fields), and conforming to the contours, they also produce a general 'rounded' or streamlining effect. The peat formed is usually only 2–3m thick, although deeper in the hollows; Sphagnum moss plays a lesser role, and the vegetation is more grassy. Among the more common species are cotton grasses and low shrubs such as heathers and deer grass, while in lower lying districts they contain more purple moor grass and black bog rush.

Peat, or turf as it is called in Ireland, the natural resource thus produced, was long the only fuel available in rural areas, and until recently was cut by hand with the long-handled turf-spade. Only in 1934 did a State-directed board start machine-cutting, until superseded in 1946 by the State-sponsored Bord na Móna, which now employs some 5000 people. Massive machinery is used, but apart from producing peat briquettes for domestic use, milled peat and peat moss for gardeners and horticulturists; more than 25 per cent of Ireland's electricity is derived from 'peat-fired' generating-stations, supplied with fuel from these mechanical cuttings. In 1970 some 55,000 hectares, mostly from the raised bogs in level districts, were yielding 4,000,000 tonnes of peat per annum, although the undulating but shallower blanket bogs to the west were also being harvested. In remoter districts on the Atlantic Coast, the turf-spade, donkey-cart, and piles of peat on the road-side are still in evidence.

Admission to Monuments, Museums and Archaeological Sites

The principal monuments of Ireland are under the care of a government commission (partially protected by the National Monuments Acts 1930 to 1987); the majority are likewise 'in State care' in Northern Ireland.

The **Office of Public Works (OPW)**, established in 1831, is now responsible for over 600 individual or groups of national monuments in the Republic either by way of ownership or guardianship, together with numerous parks and gardens, inland waterways and 68 wildlife and wildfowl sanctuaries (the Wildlife Service was responsible for the Wildlife Act of 1976). Much work of conservation and restoration is constantly being carried out by the OPW, which has recently published *Heritage: a Visitor's Guide*, an attractively illustrated description of some 100 sites in its care.

Opening times may change periodically. Entrance to all the national collections is free; houses and musuems under the care of the OPW and those in other than State care generally charge admission (a '£' sign indicates that there is an entrance fee). An OPW '**Heritage Card**' is excellent value and entitles the holder to visit all sites under their care for a year (among them the most important historic sites in Dublin and throughout the Republic). It is available at OPW sites (Dublin castle is the most accessible).

In many cases—as at Cashel, Clonmacnoise, Jerpoint, Holycross, Cahir castle, monuments are in the charge of an official guide, in which case there is an admission fee, and tours provided. Where there is no regular guardian on the spot, and the object of interest is behind a locked gate, generally there is a notice announcing the whereabouts of the key, the holder of which can be a mine of local information.

Ruins

During the period 1919–23 alone, some 70 out of a total of at least 2000 country houses in Ireland were burnt. Although a number of these were subsequently rebuilt, the great majority of ruined buildings were merely dismantled and allowed to fall down. No trace remains of many more which were entirely demolished and their site ploughed over. As Mark Bence-Jones, editor of *Burke's Guide to Country Houses: Ireland* has emphasised, beware of approaching ruins too closely and to venture within their walls, for to do so 'is to court falling plaster on one's head and unexpected cellars opening up beneath one's feet'. He goes on to warn that should an accident occur, 'the ruin in question would almost certainly be bulldozed as being 'dangerous'; so that in the interests of preservation, as well as in their own interests, country house enthusiasts should treat ruins with respect'.

Over a decade ago an alarming number of those surviving were described as 'now derelict' or with an uncertain future, largely caused by the introduction of capital taxes in the Irish Republic at a time when the cost of maintenance was rocketing. The future of many more is increasingly precarious in spite of the strenuous efforts of preservation undertaken by the Irish Georgian Society, the Ulster Architectural Heritage Society, the Northern Ireland National Trust and Commissioners of Public Works, *An Taisce*, among other bodies.

One somewhat macabre sight frequently found among the ruins of churches and monasteries is evidence of their continued use as a cemetery, although the practice is officially deprecated. Often one will stumble across a recent burial mound, with its cross or wreath, plastic or otherwise. Some families have the hereditary right of burial within monastic precincts, and prefer to be interred in the most sanctified ground possible. With the current proliferation of tasteless bleached marble tombstones of surpassing vulgarity, the ambience of previously tranquil sites (Clonmacnoise, Co. Offaly and Clonmines, Co. Waterford) is seriously threatened.

Travellers wishing to visit country houses and castles are advised to acquire from any office of the Irish Tourist Board the latest list produced by the *Historic Irish Tourist Houses and Gardens Association* (otherwise known as HITHA; 3A Castle St, Dalkey, Co. Dublin), and likewise the brochure produced by The National Trust in Northern Ireland (Rowallane, Saintfield, Ballynahinch, Co. Down BT24 7LH), or from local tourist offices in Northern Ireland, which will give the times of admission, etc. Although the privacy of owners should be respected (in cases where admission normally applies only during the summer season, for example) the seriously interested visitors may be allowed in at other times. The local tourist office can usually advise, but it is always preferable to apply in advance. Several such mansions also hospitably accept guests, and tourist offices can supply lists of such establishments and other similar guest-houses.

Background Information

A History of Ireland

Prehistory (8000 BC–150 BC)

The earliest known human settlement of Ireland occurred in the Mesolithic c 8000 BC, when tribes from Europe crossed to Ireland by boat from Scotland, or possibly across a land-bridge from Britain or the Isle of Man, to the east coast of Ireland. Hunter-gatherer habitation sites and shell-middens have been found at **Lough Boora**, Co. Offaly (c 7030 BC), **Mount Sandel**, Co. Derry (c 7010 BC), and an increasing number of other sites which suggest a wide distribution of settlement. Most of the island was densely wooded, and it was not for a further four millennia that settled agriculture appears to have been practised. At **Lough Gur**, Co. Limerick (c 2740 BC), rudimentary Neolithic dwellings have been excavated, and at **Ceide Fields**, Co. Mayo (c 2270 BC), an organised farm-landscape has been excavated beneath blanket bog. These enclosed fields are quite extensive, up to 7 hectares; most probably they were used for cattle grazing, rather than grain crops. The impressive modern-looking planning of this settlement suggests a settled agricultural society, working co-operativly for the benefit of the extended family-unit or tribal sub-group.

The most substantial Neolithic remains are funerary architecture which indicates a hierarchical society, capable of investing considerable resources in the erection of tombs and ritual-sites to honour their dead. **Newgrange** (c 3100 BC), one of the major tombs of the Boyne Valley Necropolis, is both the burial place of a priest-king, a habitation for the spirit of the tribe, and, when the rays of the rising sun penetrate into its tomb-chamber during the mid-winter solstice, a monument to the spiritual beliefs, astronomical understanding, and engineering skills of the society. The geometric art with which the monoliths of Newgrange are decorated, confirm the accomplishment of this aesthetically sophisticated people, aware of the power of abstract symbolism, and skilled in using graphic form to record significant information.

From c 2000 BC, further waves of emigrants arrived in Ireland, bringing metal-working technology with them. Abundant sources of copper and gold enabled the Bronze Age peoples to produce the weaponry and body ornaments for which the period is famous, and which led to developments in agriculture, trade and warfare.

The Celts (c 5 BC–5C AD)

There is insufficient evidence as to when Celtic tribes migrated to Ireland from the European mainland, but it is most probably somewhere between 500–150 BC; an early date is now favoured. Between their arrival, and that of the Vikings in the 8C AD, Celtic culture absorbed and superseded the language and customs of all the peoples who had previously occupied Ireland. Celtic society was patriarchal, with a hereditary aristocratic caste, it venerated animist spirits of trees, water and rivers, and belief in an after-life. *Emain Macha,* (Navan Fort), Co. Armagh, associated with the Ulster Cycle, was one of the principal royal sites, and excavation of the hilltop have indicated that it was the focus of warrior-centred ritual.

Although there was contact between Ireland and Roman Britain, Ireland remained outside the Roman Empire, and was not significantly subject to its influence. Nonetheless classical historians who wrote about the Gaulish and British Celts (Diodorus Siculus, Strabo, Julius Caesar), describe the beliefs and behaviour of societies closely resembling that of the Irish Celts.

The great stone forts built by the Celts during the Iron Age, (**Grianan of Aileach**, Co. Donegal), are works of barbaric splendour, among the greatest monuments of their kind in Europe, a product of intense tribal rivalries and the continued significance of cult sites to a cattle-ranching localised society. Ogham, the only form of writing used in Ireland, (c 4C–10C AD), prior to the coming of Christian missionaries, is a crude and limited version of a twenty-word Latin alphabet.

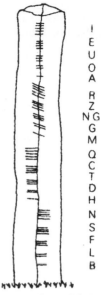

Ogham Alphabet

Early Christian Ireland (5C–11C AD)

The arrival of Christianity in Ireland in the late 4th–early 5C was achieved through a non-military conquest of the country by the culture and civilisation of the Roman Empire, bringing Classical scholarship, a nation-wide system of belief, and aspects of the social order of the Empire, as emphasised by monastic hierarchies. All that is now known from within Ireland of the Celtic oral tradition was recorded during the following centuries, in the monastic scriptoria. The tiny monasteries, established all over the country during the 6C–7C, became centres of learning, as well as adopting the asceticism of early Christianity. The religious authority of the priest-kings of Celtic Ireland was replaced by rulers whose role was purely political, the religious role being taken over by Christian bishops and abbesses many of whom were of aristocratic background, such as **Columba** and **Brigid**. Inter-tribal warfare between local kings was common, in a continuing struggle for the role of the High Kingship.

The Viking Age (8C–11C)

The first Viking sea-raiders appeared of the east coast of Ireland in AD 795, and in the following century they became a menace to the undefended Christian monasteries, repeatedly attacking, burning and pillaging them. Within half-a-century, the Vikings had established trading settlements on the east coast, their most enduring contribution to the development of Irish society; these settlements became the embryonic cities of Ireland. The Irish did not live in settlements, but were scattered about the landscape. Monastic sites were the closest the country came to any kind of proto-urban gathering. *Dyfflin*, *Vikingalo*, *Waesfjord, Vethra-fjorthr*, are the Old Norse names from which Dublin, Wicklow, Wexford, Waterford have derived.

The Medieval Period (12C–14C)

Fighting amongst themselves has long been an Irish weakness. The disputes between Dermot MacMurrough, King of Leinster, and O'Rourke of Breffni, a supporter of Rory O'Connor, King of Connacht, led MacMurrough to seek aid from Henry II in Britain. A small body of Anglo-Norman knights came to Ireland in 1169 to aid MacMorrough, an event which developed rapidly into the Norman invasion and conquest of Ireland, facilitated by superior armour and military strategy. Henry II landed with a substantial army in 1171, in order to claim Ireland as a Royal domain, rather than see his Barons set up a kingdom for themselves; he then presented *Dyfflin* 'to my men of Bristol.' Around the city, the **Pale** settlement developed as the only territory totally governed by English law. The Medieval period is characterised by an extensive building programme of fortresses, monasteries for the European orders of Cistercians, Augustinians, Franciscans (and many others) and walled towns with handsome parish churches and cathedrals. Although the Normans were always numerically at a disadvantage, Gaelic Ireland continued to flourish and adapt to the stimulus of Norman ideas. The issuing of the Statutes of Kilkenny (1366) was an unsuccessful attempt by English authority to forbid the mingling of Norman and Irish. Poyning's Law, enacted by the Irish Parliament in 1494, placed the Irish Parliament under English authority.

Disloyalty among the Irish lords led to 'plantations' of English settlers in Ireland. Offaly and Leix were planted under William and Mary, becoming King's and Queen's Counties, and thereby beginning the gradual English colonisation of Ireland. The Reformation had been declared in Ireland in 1536, introducing the strand of religious dissension to the already troubled Irish political scene. Gaelic and Anglo-Normans largely remained Catholic while the new settlers were of the Reformed Church.

The Reformation to the Enlightenment (1580–1820)

The Desmond Rebellion in Munster, led by the Earl of Desmond against the armies of Elizabeth I (1579) had left 30,000 dead. In 1581, the Corporation of Galway, composed of clannish families of Norman descent and antagonistic to their Gaelic neighbours, declared that *'neither O nor Mac shall strut nor swagger through the streets of Galway.'* Under Elizabeth I, the **Plantation of Munster** began in 1586. In parallel with military conquest and colonial expansion, ideas of Renaissance architecture, literature, music and art were penetrating Ireland.

The Gaelic lords, continually pressed by further English expansion, were never far from revolt. In Ulster, the Plantation seriously threatened the northern territories of the Earls of Tyrconnel, O'Neill and O'Donnell who, in desperation, joined with a Spanish force at Kinsale in 1601, and were defeated by an English army. This led to their departure to Europe in 1607, in search of support from the Catholic monarchs of Spain and Italy. The exodus, known as the *'Flight of the Earls'*, was followed by a further rebellion in 1641, during which large numbers of Protestant settlers in Munster and Ulster were massacred. Cromwell arrived in Ireland in 1649, and by a process of ruthless sieges and confiscation of land subdued the country and cleared the way for further Plantation. In 1690, the armies of William III and James II fought at **the Boyne** in respectively, the Protestant and Catholic interest. William's victory gave to his supporters a clarion cry in remembering this date, still emblazoned on walls all over Northern Ireland. The emigration of Gaelic leadership continued after the siege of Limerick in 1691, when the Jacobite garrison similarly took passage for Europe, becoming known as the *'Wild Geese.'* The consciously sectarian Penal

Laws, enacted in 1695 by the Irish parliament, were designed to inhibit the economic, educational, religious and political liberty of Catholics and Dissenters, and combined with the absence of their traditional aristocratic leadership, forced them into a position of subjection. During the 18C, these laws were relaxed but not removed from the Statutes.

The century of peace which followed the Protestant victory at the Boyne, was a period of widespread economic progress and population growth, during which the new owners of great landed estates built mansions on their demesnes. Fine town houses were built in Dublin for the Dublin Castle Viceregal season and parliamentary sessions. Because the Penal Laws disenfranchised Catholics and Dissenters and debarred them from professions, the law and the military, they concentrated on trade, beginning to establish an alternative power base to parliamentary representation. Inspired by the egalitarian principles of the French Revolution, and the failure of increasing demands for legislative reform, dissent continued to mount, not just among Catholics but also among Protestant intellectuals. An attempted French naval invasion in 1796, followed by the rebellion of 1798, led to the abolition of the Dublin Parliament, and in 1800, the Act of Union, which brought Ireland under direct control of Westminster. The political consequence was to transfer the seat of power to London, which resulted in a decline in the wealth and relevance of Dublin.

The Nineteenth Century

The century began with another failed insurrection, led by Robert Emmet in 1803, in this case confined to Dublin. An export trade in goods and food for the provisioning of the British Navy, and trans-Atlantic shipping, from the American War of Independence to the end of the Napoleonic Wars, contributed to economic expansion. Widespread population growth of the tenant-farmer population continued, with the sub-division of small plots into even smaller ones, in a system of single-crop subsistence agriculture based on the potato. Pursuing a repeal of the Penal Laws, **Daniel O'Connell**, won a parliamentary seat in 1825, although he was, as a Catholic, not entitled to sit in Parliament. Prime Minister William Pitt relented and O'Connell took his seat in Westminster; the **Catholic Emancipation Act** was passed in 1829. Having achieved his goal, O'Connell proceeded, by means of enormous public meetings, to democratically agitate for the repeal of the Union, a campaign which proved unsuccessful.

The Irish language, the mother-tongue of the majority of the rural population throughout the island, with the exception of those areas of the east coast long under English rule, and Plantation areas in Ulster, Leinster and Munster, began to be replaced by English, seen by all sectors of the population as the language of advancement. Prior to the establishment of the National School system in 1823, the only education available to Catholics was in 'Hedge Schools', private establishments providing only the most rudimentary education. The Queen's Colleges (1845), provided Universities in Belfast, Cork and Galway; tuition in the National Schools and Universities was in English.

Following a succession of bad potato harvests, the disaster of the **Great Famine** broke, and in the years 1845–47, over a million people died of starvation and cholera. British Government indifference and ineptitude, incompetence among local relief agencies, a *laissez-faire* attitude to trade which allowed grain to be exported from the country at the same time, and a moralistic attitude to relief, all contributed to transforming the natural disaster of crop failure into the greatest European social catastrophe of the 19C. Massive emigration followed the Famine; by the end of the century the population had been reduced by death and emigration from eight million to four. In 1848 the **Young Ireland** movement organised another abortive attempt to seize power; the failed **Fenian** rebellion followed in 1867. The last attempt to repeal the Union by political means during the 19C was the **Home Rule League**, founded in 1874, and subsequently led by **Charles Stewart Parnell**. The strength of the Home Rule party, and the pressure they exerted on the British Government began to achieve results with the passing a series of land acts, designed to grant security of tenure and ownership status to small farmers. The **Gaelic League**, founded in 1893, promoted a revival of interest in Gaelic culture, the Irish language, and Irish field sports.

The Twentieth Century

Ulster, the last area of Ireland to come under English rule, was also the most heavily planted by Anglicans or Presbyterians from English and Lowland Scots areas of Britain. This meant that the culture and loyalties of Ulster Protestants differed from those of the rest of the population. While both land and legislative reform were as widely supported by Ulster Protestants as by Catholics across the country, they opposed the campaign for Home Rule.

In the early years of the 20C, urban poverty in Dublin was another cause for discontent, a third of the population of the city were unskilled labourers with no security of employment. In 1913, a lock-out strike occurred, during which police brutality against strikers led to the foundation by the socialist **James Connolly** of the **Irish Citizen Army**, for their protection. In Ulster, **Edward Carson** organised an armed **Ulster Volunteers** force to oppose Home Rule, while in London a final Home Rule Act was passed in 1914, but its implementation was suspended for the duration of the 1914–18 war.

In the south, following the example of Carson's Volunteers, the armed **Irish Volunteers** were formed, and in combination with Connolly's Citizen Army, they launched the **1916 Rebellion** in Dublin. In the aftermath of the rebellion, sixteen of the nationalist leaders (including Connolly and **Patrick Pearse**, the leader of the insurrection), were executed by the British authorities. In the 1919 elections, the **Sinn Féin** party won 79 of the 105 seats, choosing to sit in Dublin rather than London, and establishing **Dáil Eireann**, the Irish Parliament. The British **Government of Ireland Act** (1920), partitioned Ireland into the twenty-six county **Irish Free State**, and the six county **Northern Ireland**, with respective parliaments in Dublin and Belfast. Following partition, **Civil War** (1922–23) broke out in the south between those who accepted or opposed the political two-state division of the island. The fact that c 40% of the population of Northern Ireland were nationalist, and that strong elements in the Free State rejected partition, continues to be a source of contention. In 1949 the Irish Free State, which had declared neutrality (while secretly on the Allied side), during the 1939–45 War, left the British Commonwealth to become **Éire**, the **Republic of Ireland**. The exceptionally conservative Catholic Church hierarchy, who represented the faith of 90% of the southern population, exerted undue influence over most aspects of public and private life in independent Ireland, strengthening northern Protestant opposition towards any rapprochement with the south.

In Northern Ireland, the Unionist majority saw **Stormont**, the new northern parliament, as '*a Protestant parliament for a Protestant people,*' (Sir Basil Brook, 1934) a definition which showed little interest in democratically representing the views and aspirations of the substantial Catholic nationalist sectors of the population. In 1932, the NI Prime Minister, James Craig stated '*Ours is a Protestant Government and I am an Orangeman.*' Behind the rhetoric lay long-standing and very real fears among northern Protestants of being overrun by the Catholic majority on the island. Between the1930s and the 60s, discontent, division and sectarian bigotry continued as unresolved factors in Northern Ireland political and social life; sectarian riots occurred in Belfast in 1935, as they had in 1857, 1864, 1876, 1878, 1886, 1898 and 1912.

Recent History ~ from 1960

Long overdue economic regeneration in the Republic was heralded in a 1958 by a Government White Paper on planned economic development, and following membership of the European Economic Community in 1973, the country began to benefit, as it still does, from Community-funded development projects. Throughout the island, improvements in the standard of private housing, health-care and material wealth continued, with less reliance on agriculture, as diversification into service-industries absorbed a better-educated population. The last quarter of the 20C has been a period of continued economic growth. The rural poverty and deprivation which characterised Ireland in the past was replaced by a rapidly dwindling rural population and urban unemployment on a dangerously large scale, a problem to which all Irish political parties claim to have the answer, but none the solution.

In 1967 the largely Catholic, **Northern Ireland Civil Rights Association's** attempts to campaign for reform of local government, housing and employment (areas in which discrimination was widespread), ended in an upsurge of violence and the beginning of the phase of sectarian warfare, close to Civil War, which has prevailed over the succeeding thirty years. Between 1968, when the **RUC** baton-charged peaceful demonstrators in Derry, and the outbreak of wide-spread rioting in Belfast the following year, the divisions in Northern society moved beyond the ability or willingness of Stormont to deal equitably with the problems of sectarian strife. The British Government suspended the Stormont Parliament in 1972, following the killing by the British Army on '**Bloody Sunday**' of 13 Civil Rights marchers in Derry. Direct Rule from Westminster was re-introduced after only fifty years of legislative independence for Northern Ireland. Fear of 'Rome Rule' among bigoted Protestants, led by the **Rev. Ian Paisley**, and a determination among reasonable Unionists to maintain the link with Britain, formed a strong coalition of opinion opposed to any change in Northern Ireland. Continuing atrocities committed by the **IRA** and **UVF**, terrorists from both sides of the community, exacerbated the already pervasive climate of fear and division; politically motivated acts of arson repeatedly reducing the commercial heart of Northern towns and cities to ashes.

The **SDLP** (nationalist) leader **John Hume**, one of the founders of the Civil Rights movement of the 1960s, attempted with Gerry Adams (Sinn Féin) to negotiate a republican paramilitary cease-fire. In 1994 the ongoing IRA terrorist campaign against Protestants, the RUC and British Army in Northern Ireland, against economic targets in Britain, and British Army bases in Europe, which was intended to force a total British withdrawal from Ireland and the creation of a 32-county Irish Republic, was suspended by a cease-fire which lasted for eighteen months. **Sinn Féin**, the political wing of the republican movement, which represents the most radical section of Northern nationalists, campaigned openly for peace, while failing to distance itself from the IRA, still adhering to Republican pragmatism of achieving their aims with *'an Armalite in one hand and a ballot-box in the other.'* In 1996, sectarian strife returned to Northern Irish streets during the **'Marching Season'**, showing the depth of feeling which still prevails in a divided society.

At the time of going to press, a second IRA cease-fire, called in 1997, has led to the establishment of inclusive all-party talks between the majority of the interested parties in British-Irish relations (the UDF/UDA cease-fire, also called in 1994, had been maintained). These talks included for the first time Ulster unionists and loyalists; nationalists and republicans, as well as representatives of the British and Irish governments. Whatever the outcome of the negotiations may be, the fact that they are taking place at all represents significant progress in encouraging elements of the for-centuries-divided society of Northern Ireland to face each other across a conference table rather than hurl abuse and missiles in the streets.

Art and Architecture

Introduction

Although human habitation is recorded in Ireland from c 8000 BC, our knowledge of the Neolithic period and Bronze Ages is almost entirely confined to the funerary practices of these agricultural peoples; architecture during these periods means constructions of earth and unhewn stone, art implies the application of abstract geometric surface decoration to elements within these structures.

Within the loosely defined period of the Iron Age the first non-funerary stone architecture is found in Ireland, both defensive and domestic in purpose (*Dun Aenghus*, Aran Islands). Of the wooden architecture of this and earlier periods nothing survives beyond evidence from habitation sites of domestic dwellings and what are understood to be public buildings. Manuscript accounts and excavations at **Navan Fort** (*Eamain Macha*) and **Tara** confirm the existence of large timber public or Royal buildings. Prior to the advent of Christianity which eventually produced the first stone domestic and religious architecture, buildings, down to the late medieval period, continued to be of timber, wattle and thatch; crannogs—lake dwellings constructed on artificial islands—and earth-rampart ring forts continued to be inhabited as late as the 16C.

Personal body-ornaments of gold, superb expressions of native artistry and craftsmanship which were worn by both men and women and possibly also used to decorate animals, are, from the Bronze Age through to the early Christian period, the principal outlet for the fine arts. Christian and medieval metalwork, principally in silver augmented by gemstone settings, concentrates on church plate and dress ornaments.

Neolithic (3500–2000 BC)

Court Tombs (a cairn of stones enclosing a tomb-chamber, with a formal fore-court, found principally in Ulster), and Passage Graves (a cairn with a lengthy access passage leading to the tomb chamber, found east coast and north), are the major architectural monuments of this period. **Creevykeel**, Co. Sligo is an impressive and unusual example of the former. The **Boyne Valley Necropolis** which includes the tumuli of **Dowth**, **Knowth** and **Newgrange** as well as many smaller satellite tombs, is the most important early architectural site in Ireland. Newgrange, which has been carbon-dated to c 3100 BC, has an impressive tomb-chamber with corbelled roof, the access passage is precisely oriented towards the rising sun of the mid-winter solstice. It is almost equally important for the corpus of **Boyne Valley Art** which is displayed on the upright and recumbent monoliths of the tombs, both internally and externally. The significance of this art is unclear, but it amply displays the capacity of Neolithic peoples to produce complex and sophisticated abstract patterning of a high decorative order; it is possible that the decoration represents some form of astronomical notations, related to the cycle of the seasons. Smaller Passage Grave cemeteries are found at **Loughcrew**, Co. Meath, and **Carrowkeel**, Co. Sligo. Later in the Neolithic, burial practices changed, possibly as previously, with the influx of fresh waves of immigrants from the European mainland. The portal tomb or Dolmen (one or two large cover slabs supported by upright boulders surrounding an incinerated burial, found in the north and east), is a product of this change, and isolated examples are to be found in many part of the country, **Browneshill**, Co. Carlow, and **Knockeen**, Co. Waterford are among the most spectacular. These and later tombs are not decorated.

Bronze Age (2000 BC–500 BC)

During the Bronze Age, the emphasis changes from the architecture of funerary practices to the manufacture of superb weapons of war, agricultural and industrial tools and more sophisticated body ornaments. Widespread copper mining (**Mt. Gabriel**, Co. Cork), produced an advanced bronze working industry, the form and elegance of its products are among the finest of the period. Gold continued to be used, with greater elaboration of ornament and variety of objects. The collection of Bronze Age gold in the National Museum of Ireland in Dublin, is among the finest, world-wide, of gold from antiquity. Wedge-tombs (a burial chamber surrounded by a wedge-shaped cairn, wider at the entrance), are characteristic of the period. **Labbacallee**, Co. Cork is a good example.

Iron Age (5C BC–5C AD)

There is a dramatic shift away from the architecture of the dead, to that of the living, during the Iron Age. Stone Circles (circular arrangements of upright monoliths, often with one recumbent stone aligned with sunrise/sunset, and a burial at the centre, found in the extreme north and south west), which began in the Bronze Age, continue into the Iron Age. Large and impressive Hill Forts and Ring Forts (surrounded by an earthen or stone rampart), some enclosing extensive areas of land and usually sited in positions of strategic or defensive importance, become the principal building mode of the period. ***Dun Aenghus***, Inishmore, and **Baltinglass** Co. Wicklow are widely differing examples of the uses of the hill fort as a domestic, ritualistic or military complex. Applied art of the Iron Age, on horse trappings, personal ornaments, musical instruments and household goods is in the La Téne style, a curvilinear form of surface decoration derived from the Celtic culture of Europe. The **Turoe Stone**, Co. Galway, a large ornamented boulder, is a rare example of La Téne decoration on stone. Enigmatic figure sculptures from the Iron Age, are rare representations of Pagan cult imagery (**Boa Island**, Co Fermanagh).

Early Christian (6C–9C)

The Late Iron Age merges into the early Christian period. Small monastic settlements were established throughout the country, often on islands, both coastal and in the inland lakes, and these became the focus of the largest surviving group of non-funerary or defensive buildings to be erected in Ireland from the 7C. Many of the churches and oratories are of great architectural interest. On **Inishmurray**, Co Sligo, **Skellig Michael**, Co. Kerry, and many other sites, small monastic enclosures with stone-built residential beehive huts and minute oratories are preserved; these early Christian monastic remains are sited in some of the most beautiful landscape locations in Ireland.

From the sixth to the ninth centuries, the Irish monasteries produced an unrivalled body of illuminated manuscripts, such as The **Books of Durrow and Kells** (Trinity College, Dublin), altar vessels and metal work. Christianity flourished under aristocratic patronage and monastic foundations continued to grow throughout the succeeding centuries. Two other significant developments in art and architecture between the ninth and twelfth centuries are the **High Crosses** and **Round Towers**. The crosses are a group of sculptural monuments decorated with high-relief panels depicting scriptural scenes, or in the later groupings, scenes of the Passion. **Moone**, Co. Kildare and **Clonmacnoise**, Co. Offaly are scripture crosses. The Round Towers (**Devinish**. Co. Limerick; **Glendalough**, Co. Wicklow), are the only unique form of architecture found in Ireland. Built as bell towers, they also acted as repositories for the communities' treasures during times of trouble. Monasteries often fell victim to the continuous warfare between Irish petty-kings. Irish Romanesque, the finest flowering of Irish architecture before the Viking and Norman invasions, combined the small scale of Irish church building and local decorative ideas with forms from European Romanesque. The finest building of the period is **Cormac's Chapel**, Cashel, Co. Tipperary, which has rare examples of mural decoration.

The Viking Age (9C–11C)

The first Viking raid on the Irish coast took place in AD 795. This was the beginning of three centuries of contact and conflict between the Celtic peoples of Ireland and the Norse, first as pirates, subsequently as settlers, lastly as founders of Ireland's principal cities. Viking art styles of Urnes and Ringerike decoration influenced native decorative forms and contributed to the development of style in metalwork and manuscript illumination. No Viking architecture survives except in the remnants of town walls and remains of domestic buildings in the archaeological excavations of **Wood Quay** in Dublin, and isolated sites in Waterford and Limerick; **Reginald's Tower**, Waterford is possibly a Viking structure.

Anglo-Norman (12C–14C)

Cistercian and Augustinian monastic orders were established in Ireland during the 12C, bringing with them fundamental changes in monastic architecture. **Mellifont Abbey**, Co. Louth, and its dependencies introduced current European Gothic architectural style. However the profoundest change in the history of Irish architecture came after the arrival of the Normans in 1169. The earliest Norman fortifications of motte and bailey (an earth mound with timber turret and outworks), at **Knockgraffon**, Co. Tipperary, were succeeded by an ambitious castle-building program, and at **Limerick, Carrickfergus, Dublin, Ferns, Trim, Liscarroll**, substantial stone castles of curtain wall with circular corner towers and internal keep were built, the first of their kind in Ireland. Christ Church Cathedral in Dublin is a transitional building between Romanesque and Gothic. It was followed by many fine abbeys such as **Jerpoint** and **Graiguenamanagh**, Co. Kilkenny, and cathedral churches, St. Canice's Cathedral, Kilkenny, and **St Patrick's Cathedral**, Dublin. Irish medieval monasteries, small by European standards, nonetheless dwarf the even smaller religious enclosures of the early Christian period. Their ordered life was reflected in a precise architecture of church and cloistral complex, a total departure from the un-planned arrangement of native monastic settlements.

Late Medieval (15C–16C)

Three dimensional figure sculpture is a relatively late development in Irish medieval architecture, **St. Canice's Cathedral** in Kilkenny is one of many with fine recumbent tomb effigies of this period. Delicate window-tracery, finely carved hood-mouldings on tombs and incidental low-relief sculptural decoration are the fine points of late Gothic architecture, good examples of which can be seen in **Holy Cross Abbey**, Co. Tipperary. New forms in metalwork, processional crosses and reliquaries were produced. Few murals have survived the dissolution of the monasteries and the ravages of a damp climate, yet there are fragmentary examples at Holy Cross Abbey. The construction of Tower Houses (small castles with residential quarters on the upper floors), the dwellings of minor landowners, was widespread, and many well-preserved examples are scattered throughout the island.

Elizabethan and Jacobean Period

After the Plantations of Ulster and Munster, and the general conquest of the country during the late 16C, the Elizabethan manor house, fortified or otherwise, became the model for the future direction of Irish domestic architecture, among Gaelic, Anglo Norman and Planter landowners, although Tower Houses continued to be built as late as the mid 17C. The Ormonde manor house in **Carrick-on-Suir**, Co. Waterford (c 1565), a two storey, unfortified house with ample windows, internally decorated with stucco, is stylistically unlike any earlier Irish building, and marks the emergence of the country-house architecture which became prominent in the following centuries. Walled towns like **Galway, Kilmallock** and **Kilkenny**, developed a high standard of urban architecture in the late medieval period, good examples of which remain in these and other towns. **Rothe House**, Kilkenny (1594), is a substantial stone-built merchant's house with a street-level arcade with small courtyards and buildings occupying a long narrow plot running between the street and the town wall.

Other houses of the same period, **Coppinger's Court**, Co. Cork (1616); **Portumna Castle**, Co. Galway (1618); **Donegal Castle** (1623) and **Burncourt**, Co. Tipperary (1641), display transitional elements between fortified and un-fortified dwellings, and chart the gradual emergence of classical architectural principles. The century ends with the **Royal Hospital Kilmainham** (1680), the first truly classical public building in Ireland.

Classicism and the Georgian Period

A period rich in great public and domestic architecture begins in the late 17C and continues during the reign of the four Georges (1714–1830), encompassing all of the 18C and finally trailing off into the late 19C, long after the last of the Georges. This period transformed Irish ideas of building, introduced classical concepts of planning and created the architectural splendour of Dublin, in which a small walled medieval city became absorbed into a geometrically and spaciously planned city, entirely classical in conception. Many small towns and villages were reorganised on a classical plan, and fine Palladian country-houses were built on gentlemen's estates; many excellent examples survive, The period is dominated, early in the 18C century, by the work of a small group of talented architects, **William Robinson**, **Edward Lovett Pearce**, **Richard Castle**, and **Thomas Ivory**, with **James Gandon** and **Francis Johnston** towards its close. Between them they created a corpus of public buildings and private houses of great beauty. Among public buildings, **Trinity College**, the **Parliament House**, **Custom House** and **Four Courts** are of major importance, while **Castletown**, **Cashel Palace** and **Bellamont Forest**, are country-houses of distinction. The **Lafrancini** stuccodores from Switzerland and **Michael Stapleton** from Dublin, produced remarkable pasterwork. **James Tarbary** and **Richard Haughton** both woodcarvers, decorated numerous important buildings. Architecture, the applied arts and crafts of furniture, glass, metalwork, stucco, and the visual arts were seriously patronised for the first time since the decline of the medieval monasteries. Among painters, **Hugh Douglas Hamilton** and **George Barrett** produced work of exceptional importance. Household goods attained a new eminence, with the manufacture of glass in Dublin, Cork and Waterford, and silver in Dublin and Cork. Furniture making, book binding and tapestry weaving, all excelled.

The Nineteenth Century

Outside Dublin, the architectural appearance of most towns and villages in rural Ireland is representative of a great surge of building activity in the latter half of the 19C. The number of Gothic Revival churches and cathedrals of the mid to late 19C is the most significant development in public building of the period, with outstanding examples of the latter at **Cork**, **Cobh** and **Armagh**. John Semple produced many austerely beautiful parish churches, while **Benjamin Woodward** was the most innovative architect of Gothic Revival civil buildings, his **Trinity Museum**, established Venetian Gothic as a popular style, and banks and other public buildings continued to be built in this manner to the end of the century. Many country-houses and public buildings were designed by Sir Richard and William Vitruvius Morrison, **Kilruddery**, Co. Wicklow and **Fota**, Co. Cork, as well as fine Neo-Classical courthouses at Carlow and Tralee.

Workhouses and penal institutions of intimidating grimness were a prominent feature of Irish architecture of the 18C–19C and stern examples of the latter survive at **Kilmainham**, Dublin; **Cork**, and **Downpatrick**.

Of painters, **Daniel Maclise, Richard Moynan, Henry Jones Thadeus, Frederick William Burton**, and sculptors **John Hogan** and **Thomas Farrell** are important, although few Irish artists considered the political and social turmoil of the 19C appropriate subject-matter; genre, landscape and the senti-mental dominated their work.

Late in the 19C, most Irish artists pursued further study abroad, in Antwerp (Walter Osborne, Richard Moynan), Paris (Frank O'Meara, Henry Jones Thaddeus) and Brittany (J.M. Kavanagh, Norman Garstin), and many of the most prominent were influenced by successive waves of modernist ideas, Impressionism and Post Impressionism. **Nathaniel Hone**, a superb plein-airist landscape painter, was influenced by Corot. He worked principally in France and Fontainbleau, and later in Co. Dublin.

The foundation of the **National Gallery of Ireland** in 1864 was an impor-tant development in creating the first permanently available public art collection as a source for study and inspiration.

The Twentieth Century

The work of **Jack B. Yeats** (brother of the poet W.B. Yeats), the most significant Irish artist of the 20C, represents important phases in the development of Irish art during the first half of the century. His earliest work, recording west of Ireland life, is a product of the Celtic Revival (1880–1930), a movement which embraced all the arts, and derived its inspiration from the Celtic past and the lives of country people. His mature work developed in an accomplished expres-sionist manner approaching abstraction. The major figurative painters of the first half of the century are **John Lavery, William Orpen, Paul Henry** and **Sean Keating**. All were accomplished portrait painters with the exception of Henry, who painted archetypal images of west of Ireland landscape.

The Celtic Revival became the dominant style in progressive architecture, and antiquarian scholarship of the 18C–19C provided a stylistic source for the deco-ration of many buildings derived from the motifs of medieval illuminated manu-scripts and monastic architecture. From **Loughrea Cathedral**, Co. Galway (1903), the **Honan Chapel**, Cork (1916), to the **Church of the Four Masters**, Donegal (1931), the ideas and style of the Celtic Revival showed considerable adaptability in the hands of contemporary architects and artist-craftsmen. The establishment of stained glass studios in Dublin, *An Túr Gloine* (1903), founded by Sarah Purser, and **Harry Clarke Studios** (1930) founded by Harry Clarke, enabled contemporary artists to produce superb windows for churches throughout Ireland and abroad; **Clarke, Michael Healy, Wilhelmina Geddes** and **Evie Hone** all produced fine windows. As well as glass, metal-work, embroidery, tapestry weaving and woodcarving thrived during this period.

European Modernism was represented by a number of important Irish painters; **Roderic O'Conor, W.J. Leech, Mary Swanzy, Evie Hone** and **Mainie Jellett**. Jellett and Hone were abstractionist, working in a Cubist idiom. **Eileen Gray** became one of the most important 20C avant-garde furniture designers, while among sculptors, **Andrew O'Connor** produced expressionist work of great power. Working in the middle years of the century were many artists of interest, influenced by School-of-Paris and other Continental movements, **Harry Kernoff**, **Cecil ffrecnch-Salkeld**, **Norah McGuinness**.

Twentieth century architectural concepts were much slower to find followers in Ireland. Such major buildings as **Belfast City Hall**, the parliament building at **Stormont**, **Cork City Hall**, the rebuilding of **O'Connell St** Dublin, and **Patrick's St** Cork, after the destruction of the 1916–19 period, all ignore contemporary ideas and opt for some form of Edwardian classicism. The **Church of Christ the King**, Cork (1927), is a lone representative of modernist architecture, while **Dublin Airport** (1941) and the **Busaras**, Dublin (1947), are the first Modern Movement public buildings. The strength of contemporary art was not paralleled in building developments and Ireland produced few architects of distinction during the early 20C. More recently, individual buildings indicate a new vitality among younger Irish architects, although any type of experimentation is rare (Waterways Visitor Centre, Ciran O'Connor; Temple Bar Gallery, McCullough Mulvin; Curved Street, Temple Bar, Group 91).

Up to the 1940s, the **Royal Irish Academy** (established in 1823) continued to be the major exhibiting venue for the visual arts, and experimental developments in art were not encouraged. In 1943, the **Irish Exhibition of Living Art** was established as a forum for contemporary thought in the arts, and for the following thirty years, it acted as a focus for all artists working in a non-academic manner.

With the establishment in Dublin (1908) of the Gallery of Modern Art (now the **Hugh Lane Municipal Gallery of Modern Art**), founded by Sir Hugh Lane as the first public gallery in the British Isles devoted to contemporary art, the visual arts in Ireland received an important boost. Its holding of the art of the late 19C–early 20C art is significant, but it is not a gallery of modern art in any contemporary sense. The recently established **Irish Museum of Modern Art** (1991) in Dublin, is devoted to the display and promotion of contemporary international art, but has so far failed to fill the absence of a museum devoted to developments in Irish art since the 1930s. Commercial galleries and arts centres in Dublin, Belfast and throughout the country show contemporary work of considerable interest, which augurs well for the future of the visual arts in Ireland.

Literature

Celtic Epics

There are two parallel strands in Irish literature—writing in English and writing in Irish—the former is well-known internationally, the latter has only a small readership even within Ireland. Yet they are not so much two literatures as different facets of the same culture which have at various times drawn upon each other for inspiration, sustenance and enrichment. The earliest literature which has survived, transcribed from the oral tradition by medieval monks, is the **Ulster Cycle**, a sequence of heroic tales of the Iron Age, great imaginative literature by any standard, which combine elements of magic, humour and satire with excellent storytelling. The ***Táin Bó Cuailnge*** (the Cattle Raid of Cooley), the central saga, forms a fascinating introduction to the heroic world of Celtic Ireland.

Early Christian Monastic writing

The poems of the early Christian monks, as sparse and delicate as Japanese Haiku, were inscribed as occasional jottings in the margins of ecclesiastical manuscripts; as word-pictures about nature, they are among of the most succinct in Irish writing:

> Bees and beetles, music-makers,
>   Croon and strum;
> Geese pass over, duck in autumn,
>   Dark streams hum.

AD 7C, version Frank O'Connor

Medieval Poets

Writing in Irish had become by the late medieval period, reactive to political change, as the traditional role of the bards, formerly patronised by the Gaelic lords, became redundant. Much of this literature is concerned with lamenting the loss of their aristocratic patrons. These Irish poets, whose culture was under threat, were no democrats, seeing themselves as an adjunct of an aristocratic caste system. The decline of the native leadership plunged the writers into poverty and despair.

> All Ireland's now one vessel's company,
> And riding west by cliffs of Beare to sea.
> Upon the snowy foam of the ebbing tide
> Away in one frail barque goes all our pride.

Fearghal Óg MacWard, 17C, version Lord Longford

End of the Gaelic Order

Satire is, unsurprisingly, a prevailing mode among a people deprived of all but language. From the end of the 18C, **Brian Merriman's (1749–1805) *Cúirt an Mheán-Oíche*** (*The Midnight Court*, 1780) a comic satire on Irish masculinity, borrows from both Irish and English literary traditions:

> A starved old gelding, blind and lamed
> And a twenty-year-old with her parts untamed.
> It wasn't her fault if things went wrong,
> She closed her eyes and held her tongue.

The Midnight Court (18C) version Frank O'Connor

Eibhlín Dubh Ní Chonaill's (1743–1800) *Caoineadh Airt Uí Laoghaire* (*The Lament for Art O'Leary*, c 1773), is a lament for her murdered husband, composed in a traditional Gaelic form,

> There were parlours whitened for me,
> Bedrooms painted for me,
> Ovens reddened for me,
> Loaves baked for me,
> Joints spitted for me

Beds made for me,
To take my ease on flock
Until milking time
And later if I pleased.

> *The Lament for Art O'Leary*, 18C, version Frank O'Connor.

The Enlightenment

The work of 16C–17C English writers resident in Ireland represent the beginning of a native tradition in English. Edmund Spenser's (1552–1599) **The Faerie Queene** (1590–6), written in Ireland, is the most accomplished poetry of the period. Works in English by Irish-born writers only begin to achieve significance in the early 18C, with a sudden flood of important poetry, plays, novels, satires and polemics, from **Jonathan Swift** (1667–1745) *Gulliver's Travels* (1726); **George Farquhar** (1677–1707) *The Beaux Stratagem* (1707); **Richard Brinsley Sheridan** (1751–1816) *The School for Scandal* (1777); **Edmund Burke** (1729–1797) *Reflections on the Revolution in France* (1790) and **Oliver Goldsmith** (1728–1774) *The Vicar of Wakefield* (1766).

Anglo-Irish Writing

Maria Edgeworth's (1767–1849) *Castle Rackrent* (1800), celebrates with black humour, the tragic contradictions of Irish ascendancy life, seen from within the gates of the big house; a theme and perspective which has continued for 200 years to produce some of the finest and most poignant novels in the work of **George Moore** (1852–1933), *A Drama in Muslin* (1884), **Molly Keane** (1905–1996), *Good Behaviour* (1981), and **Jennifer Johnston** (1930–), *Shadows on Our Skin* (1977).

The Literary Revival

Antiquarian writers in English of the early 19C attempted to disinter the bones of the earlier Gaelic literature, providing source material for new work and versions of early texts which proved influential to a new generation of writers. **The Celtic Twilight** (c1893–1930), a literary and artistic movement dominated by **W.B.Yeats** (1865–1939), explored the richness of Gaelic storytelling, legends and folk-speech as a means of invigorating Irish writing in English. Yeats managed to create great poetry out of the events of both his personal life and the politics of his time. His poetry developed from an early concern with Gaelic mythology to embrace the nationalist struggle and *Easter 1916* is one of the central texts of the emergent Irish independence movement. The Abbey Theatre was founded jointly by W.B. Yeats and **Lady Gregory** (1852–1932) in 1904 as a platform for Irish drama and the plays of **J.M.Synge** (1871–1909), *The Playboy of the Western World* (1907) and Lady Gregory, *Gods and Fighting Men* (1904), who based much of their work on the spoken dialect of the west of Ireland, were performed here.

The Theatre of Manners

Near contemporaries, Oscar Wilde (1854–1900) and George Bernard Shaw (1856–1950) both left Dublin in their late teens and subsequently achieved dominance on the London stage, Wilde as a witty commentator on the manners of high society (*The Importance of Being Ernest*, 1895), and Shaw as a committed social reformer (*Saint Joan*, 1923). Wilde's imprisonment for homosexuality in 1896 contributed to his early death.

Modernism

Sean O'Casey (1880–1964) whose plays were first performed at the Abbey Theatre, produced works of stark urban realism. *The Plough and the Stars* (1926) is set in an atmosphere of political unrest in early 20C Dublin. **James Joyce** (1882–1941), the greatest Irish imaginative and experimental writer of the 20C, is paradoxically also the foremost realist in all of Irish literature, and a wry observer of the *comédie humaine*. His greatest work, *Ulysses* (1922), is a landmark both in international literature and Irish writing. He employs a cinematic approach to construct his narrative, describing the journey of Leopold Bloom, a Jewish Dubliner, over a 24-hour period. Bloom represents Everyman, and his journey, life itself. Joyce influenced the work of **Flann O'Brien** (1911–1966), *At Swim-Two-Birds* (1939), and **Samuel Beckett** (1906–1989), who expressed a profound pessimism concerning human existence in the cryptic dialogue of his plays (*Waiting for Godot*, 1948).

Northern Irish Writing

Ulster, now largely represented by Northern Ireland, has not in the past, produced many major writers. The poets Louis MacNeice (1907–1963) and John Hewitt (1907–1987) are the most significant early 20C northern Irish writers. **Seamus Heaney** (1939–), winner of the 1996 Nobel Prize for Literature, draws on his country background to provide metaphors for the strife of his homeland (*North*, 1975). **Brian Friel** (1929–), a playwright of the same rural culture, has written imaginatively out of the conflicts in the Irish experience, both within and outside Ireland (*Translations*, 1980).

Writing in the Republic

The best of writing in the second half of the 20C in the Republic has concentrated more on an emerging urban society than preoccupation with a rural past. **John Montague** (1929–) writes from a sense of personal history and passionate involvement (*Collected Poems*, 1995). The dark contemporary world in the work of the playwright **Tom Murphy** (1935–) (*Bailegangaire*, 1985), or the savagely surreal comedy of poet **Paul Durcan's** (1944–) image of contemporary Ireland (*A Snail in my Prime*, 1993), suggest a society gravely troubled in the conflict between self-image and experience. Prose writing in the early years of the State is firmly associated with the short-story, as practised by **Elizabeth Bowen** (1899–1973), **Sean O'Faolain** (1900–1991) **and Frank O'Connor** (1903–1966), with **William Trevor** (1928–) forming a bridge between a younger generation of novelists, who, like Murphy and Durcan, contemplate the claustrophobia, sexual repression and violence of Irish life.

A resurgence of women writers, and writing in modern Irish has begun in recent years. The poetry of **Nuala Ní Dhomhnaill** (1952–), *Rogha Dánta* (1988; bilingual edition) has brought an eroticism and sensuousness to Irish literature, often lacking in either language, and the feminist writer, **Evan Boland** (1945) writes about the Irish woman's domestic and inner world, and the restrictions of inherited concepts of Irish women *Outside History*, 1990.

Music

Traditional Music

In the 12C **Giraldus Cambrensis** (1146–1220), the Anglo-Norman chronicler, and no admirer of the Irish, wrote favourably of native music, commenting upon its '*ornate rhythms and profusely intricate polyphony*'. The description might aptly be applied to the present-day inheritors of this musical tradition, and although the instrumentation has changed, certain features of the music have survived the passage of eight centuries of political upheaval. A special respect is reserved for the position of traditional music in contemporary Irish life, its widespread popular survival is a distinctive phenomenon among the declining folk music of Europe, and its health is in dramatic contrast to the faltering state of the Irish language with which it is culturally associated. Despite competition from international popular music, Irish traditional music shows no sign of weakening and its rhythms have invaded both popular and contemporary classical compositions. At the end of the 20C, the music as played today shows evidence of many sources of influence, and has in its development absorbed Scots, English, Renaissance European and American folk influences. The harp compositions of the 18C composer **Turlough O'Carolan** (1670–1738) which are still performed within the canon of traditional music, although with alternative instrumentation, were heavily influenced by the 18C Baroque music of Vivaldi and Corelli.

Forms as widely differing as the conventional jigs and reels, slow airs, '*sean-nós*' (unaccompanied singing) and wordless '*pus beal*' (mouth music) are among the surviving modes of this very vigorous expression, representing the distant origins of the Celtic peoples, tragic elegies for glories lost, romantic and political ballads, love-songs, haunting laments, and the conviviality of rural gatherings, all still holding some meaning today for an urban audience, even if they are more used to concrete pavements than plowed fields. The principal instruments used are the fiddle, wooden flute, tin whistle, *bodhran* (skin drum), bones, button and piano accordions, concertina, *uilleann* pipes and harp. Regional styles and virtuoso performers with a repertoire of many hundreds of tunes have maintained a rural generative base for the music, while young performers continue to invigorate an ancient cultural tradition. Legendary performers are honoured in annual gatherings, such as **The Willy Clancy Summer School**, in Doolin, Co.Clare, and in the *Fleadh Cheoil na hÉireann*, the principal music and dancing competitions, held annually in different towns.

Traditional music can be heard in bars all over the country, but is best experienced in small informal gatherings; the finest musicians are those of the Clare and Sligo region. Competitive Irish dancing of the 'intense unsmiling little girls in Celtic outfits, arms glued to the sides' variety, is always a constituent part of music gatherings; great skill is often exhibited, but unlike the music, there is something joyless and fossilised about most performances. Well-known individual musicians and groups include **Dolores Keane**, **The Chieftans**, **Clanad**.

Popular Music

Rock music (**U2**, **The Cranberries**), blues (**Van Morrison**), and solo singers, (**Enya**, **Sinead O'Connor**, **Maura O'Connell**) all bear witness to the international success of Irish popular music. A compilation of Irish women solo singers and musicians, *A Woman's Heart,* which includes many of the most distinguished contemporary popular and traditional singers, has been among the most successful of Irish records ever, both in Ireland and internationally. The repeated success of Irish singers in Eurovision is another strand in the widening scope of contemporary musical activity in the country. The magazine, *Hot Press,* is the authoritative journal of music events; popular music is staged in clubs and major concert venues in the principal towns and cities.

Contemporary Classical Music

Perhaps the least known aspect of Irish music, although there has been a tradition of operatic and classical composition since the 18C. The opera singer, **Michael Kelly** (1764–1826), created roles in Mozarts's *Le nozze di Figaro* (1787); **John Field** (1782–1837), pianist and composer, developed the Nocturne in his piano concertos (perfected by Chopin); The *Bohemian Girl* (1843) by **Michael William Balfe** (1808–1870) is still in the opera repertoire, and **William Vincent Wallace**'s (1812–1845) opera *Maritana* (1845), also remains popular.

Thomas Moore's (1779–1852) *Irish Melodies* (1808), brought traditional Irish airs (with Moore's words), to a sophisticated audience abroad during the early 19C, and he was one of the few to work in the internationally popular mode of *lieder* (the parlour 'art-song'). The music of **Moore, Balfe** and **Wallace** is an accurate reflection of 19C Irish bourgeois taste which forms the background to Joyce's *Ulysses,* set in the Dublin of 1904. The composer **Charles Villiers Stanford** (1852–1924) used traditional Irish melodies in the *Irish Symphony* (1887).

In the 20C, **Brian Boydell, Seoirse Bodley**, and many others have been interested in contemporary avant-garde ideas, rather than interpreting the native tradition and display influences from Bartók to Stockhausen. **Seán Ó'Riada** (1931–1971) originally a classical composer, his traditional music group *Ceoltóirí Cualann* (1961) influenced the direction of the current revival of the folk tradition.

Further Reading

Archaeology
Harbison, Peter. *Guide to National and Historic Monuments of Ireland* (Gill & Macmillan, 1992).
Harbison, Peter. *Irish High Crosses* (Boyne Valley Honey Company, 1994).
Killanin/Duignan/Harbison. *The Shell Guide to Ireland* (McGraw-Hill, 1989).
Cooney. Gabriel ed. *Archaeology Ireland* quarterly, Dublin.

Architecture
Casey, Christine & Rowan, Alistair. *The Buildings of Ireland. North Leinster* (Penguin, 1993).
Craig, Maurice. *Dublin 1660–1860* (Allen Figgis, 1969).
Craig, Maurice. *The Architecture of Ireland* (Batsford, 1982).
McCutcheon, W.A. *The Industrial Archaeology of Northern Ireland* (HMSO, 1980).
O'Brien/Guinness. *Dublin, A Grand Tour* (Weidenfeld & Nicolson, 1994).
Rothery, Sean. *Ireland and the New Architecture 1900–1940* (Lilliput, 1991)
Rowan, Alistair. *The Buildings of Ireland. North West Ulster* (Penguin, 1979).
Williams, Jeremy. *Architecture in Ireland 1837–1921* (Irish Academic Press, 1994).

Art
Crookshank/Glin. *The Painters of Ireland 1660–1920* (Barrie & Jenkins, 1978).
Crookshank/Glin. *The Watercolours of Ireland 1600–1914* (Barrie & Jenkins, 1994).
Gordon Bowe, Nicola. *Harry Clarke* (Irish Academic Press, 1989).
Kennedy. S.B. *Irish Art & Modernism* (Institute of Irish Studies, 1991).
Potterton, Homan ed. *Irish Arts Review Yearbook*, Dublin.

Food, Drink, Accommodation
McKenna. J. & S. *The Bridgestone 100 Best Restaurant* s (Estragon).
McKenna. J. & S. *The Bridgestone Irish Food Guide* (Estragon).
McKenna. J. & S. *The Bridgestone 100 Best Places to Stay* (Estragon).
Colclough. John. *The Hidden Ireland, Private Country House Accommodation* (Kensington Hall, Grove Park, Dublin 6).
Friendly Homes of Ireland (71 Waterloo Road, Dublin 4).
Ireland's Blue Book (40 of the best in Ireland; Ardbraccan Glebe, Navan, Co. Meath).
Hotels and Guesthouses, Irish Hotels Federation.
Where to eat in Northern Ireland, Northern Ireland Tourist Board.
Where to stay in Northern Ireland, Northern Ireland Tourist Board.

History
Bardon, Jonathan. *A History of Ulster* (The Blackstaff Press, 1992).
Beckett. J.C. *The Making of Modern Ireland 1603–1923* (Faber and Faber, 1966).
Knox, Oliver. Rebels and Informers: Stirrings of Irish Independence (pub, date)
Lee, J.J. *Ireland 1912-1985: Politics and Society* (Gill & Macmillan, 1989).
O'Brien, Máire and Conor Cruise, *A Concise History of Ireland* (Gill & Macmillan, 1972).
Stewart, A.T.Q. *The Narrow Ground: Aspects of Ulster* (Ashgate, 1977).

Literature
Kinsella, Thomas, trans. *Táin Bó Cuailnge* (Dolmen, 1969).
Kinsella/O Tuama. *An Duanaire*, Poems of the Disposessed (Dolmen, 1981).
Kinsella, Thomas. *The New Oxford Book of Irish Verse* (Oxford, 1986).
Montague, John. *The Faber Book of Irish Verse* (Faber and Faber, 1974).
Welch, Robert., ed. *The Oxford Companion to Irish Literature* (Oxford, 1996).
Yeats, W.B. *The Poems* (Everyman Library, 1992).

Music
Breathnach, Breandan. *Folk Music and Dances of Ireland*; *Ceol Rince na héireann* (Dance Music of Ireland) (*Oifig an tSoláthair*, 1976).
Ó Canainn, Tomás. *Traditional Music in Ireland* (Routledge, 1978).

Travel
Böll, Heinrich. *Irish Journal* (Minerva, 1995).
Brennan, Éilis. *Heritage, a Visitor's Guide* (OPW, 1990).
Delany, Ruth., ed. *Shell Guide to the River Shannon* (ERA-Maptec), 1993).
Lalor, Brian. *The Laugh of Lost Men, An Irish Journey* (Mainstream, 1997)
O'Faolain, Sean. *An Irish Journey* (Longmans, 1941).
Praeger, R.L. *The Way That I Went* (Methuen, 1939).
Robinson, Tim. *Stones of Aran* (Viking, 1985).
Somerville-Large, Peter. *The Grand Irish Tour* (Hamish Hamilton, 1982).
Toíbín Colm. *Bad Blood* (Vintage, 1994).

Walking
Dillon, Paddy. *The Trail Walkers Guide to the National Trails of Britain & Ireland* (Cicerone Press, 1990); *The Mountains of Ireland* (Cicerone Press, 1992).
Walking World Ireland (monthly magazine; 288 Harold's Cross, Dublin).

Read Ireland Book News is a weekly newsletter listing reviews of the most important new books published on issues of Irish interest. For further information, contact Read Ireland, 342 North Circular Road, Dublin 7 Ireland, ☎ & Fax +353-1-8302997. To access the site (Irish Internet Bookstore) on the internet: http://www.readireland.ie

Chronology

BC	8000	Arrival of first settlers.
	3100	Newgrange Passage Grave, Boyne Valley.
	2270	Neolithic farming at Ceide Fields, Co. Mayo.
Celtic	5-300?	Arrival of the Celts.
	150	*Ulster Cycle,* heroic tales from Iron Age Ulster.
AD	c400	Introduction of Christianity.
Early Christian	432	Arrival of St. Patrick.
	795	First Viking raid. ⟩ *Viking Raids*
	841	Dublin founded by Vikings.
Medieval	1127	Cormac's Chapel, Cashel begun.
	1169	Anglo-Norman invasion. *1172 ── English Invasion*
	1172	Christ Church Cathedral, Dublin founded.
	1315	Edward Bruce invasion from Scotland.
	1366	Statutes of Kilkenny forbidding Irish and Norman intermarriage.
Reformation	1494	Poynings' Law places Irish Parliament under English authority.
	1536	Plantation of King's and Queen's Counties.
	1565	Ormond Manor House, Carrick-on-Suir begun.
	1586	Plantation of Munster. *─ Irish dispossed of Land*
	1588	Spanish Armada ships wrecked off Irish coast.
	1592	Trinity College Dublin, founded by Elizabeth I.
	1601	Defeat of Irish and Spanish by English forces at the Battle of Kinsale.
	1607	Flight of the Earls to Europe, seeking military aid against England.
	1609	Plantation of Ulster.
	1613	Derry City Walls built.
	1641	Desmond Rebellion in Munster.
	1642	Confederation of Kilkenny. Catholic assembly.
	1654	Cromwellian Plantation.
	1680	Royal Hospital Kilmainham, Dublin begun.
	1688	Siege of Derry, lasts 105 days.
	1690	Battle of the Boyne, between James II and William III.
	1695	Penal Laws against Catholics and Dissenters enacted.
	1712	Trinity College Library begun.
	1719	Castletown House, Co. Kildare begun.
	1726	Jonathan Swift's *Gulliver's Travels* published in London.
	1729	Parliament House, Dublin begun.
	1731	Royal Dublin Society founded.
	1762	Casino, Marino begun.
	1782	Grattan's Parliament establishes legislative independence.
	1791	United Irishmen founded, Belfast.
	1795	Orange Order founded, Co Armagh.
	1796	French invasion fleet wrecked in bad weather at Bantry Bay.
	1798	United Irishmen rebellion, principally in Wexford and Mayo.
	1800	Act of Union imposed direct rule from London.
	1803	Robert Emmet rebellion in Dublin.

1829	Catholic Emancipation.
1843	Balfe's *The Bohemian Girl* produced in London.
1845	Great Famine begins.
	Birr Telescope.
	Queens Colleges established (Belfast, Cork, Galway).
1848	Young Ireland rebellion rejected Daniel O'Connell's non-violent politics.
1858	Irish Republican Brotherhood founded.
1867	Fenian rebellion attempted to gain Irish independence by physical force.
1873	Home Rule League founded.
1879	Land League founded to protect tenant farmers.
1880	Parnell leads Irish Parliamentary Party.
1884	Gaelic Athletic Association founded.
1897	Bram Stoker's *Dracula;* Ethel Voynich's *The Gadfly* published.
1903	Wyndham Land Act allowed tenants to purchase land with Government aid.
1904	Abbey Theatre opens.
1905	Sinn Féin founded.
1909	*Volta Picture Theatre* opens in Dublin with James Joyce as manager.
1911	*Titanic* launched in Belfast.
1913	Ulster Volunteers, Irish Volunteers, Irish Citizen Army founded.
	Lockout Strike in Dublin.
	Jack B. Yeats, Armory Show, New York.
1914	Home Rule Bill signed but suspended.
	James Joyce's *Dubliners* published in London.
1916	Easter Rising in Dublin, Irish Republic proclaimed, 16 leaders executed.
	Celtic Revival Honan Chapel, Cork University.
1919	First Dáil sits in Dublin; War of Independence.
1922	Irish Free State established; Civil War; Michael Collins killed in ambush.
	James Joyce's *Ulysses* published in Paris.
1923	W.B. Yeats awarded Nobel Prize for Literature.
1926	George Bernard Shaw awarded Nobel Prize for Literature.
1948	Irish Republic declared.
1951	Ernest Walton awarded Nobel Prize for Physics.
	Jack B. Yeats retrospective, Tate Gallery, London.
1953	Samuel Beckett's *Waiting for Godot* first performed in Paris.
1967	Northern Ireland Civil Rights Association founded.
1969	Samuel Beckett awarded Nobel Prize for Literature.
1971	Internment without trial in Northern Ireland.
1972	'Bloody Sunday' in Derry, 13 die; Stormont Parliament suspended.
1974	Ireland joins EC; Sean MacBride awarded Nobel Peace Prize.
1975	Ulster Workers Strike in Northern Ireland.
1976	British Ambassador assassinated in Dublin.
1979	Earl Mountbatten assassinated in Sligo.
1980	Brian Friel's *Translations* first performed in Derry.
1981	Republican hunger strike in Northern Ireland, ten die.
1985	Anglo-Irish Agreement between British and Irish Governments.
1987	Enniskillen Remembrance Day bombing, eleven die.
1994	IRA/Combined Loyalist Military Command cease-fire (ends 1996).
1996	Seamus Heaney awarded Nobel Prize for Literature.

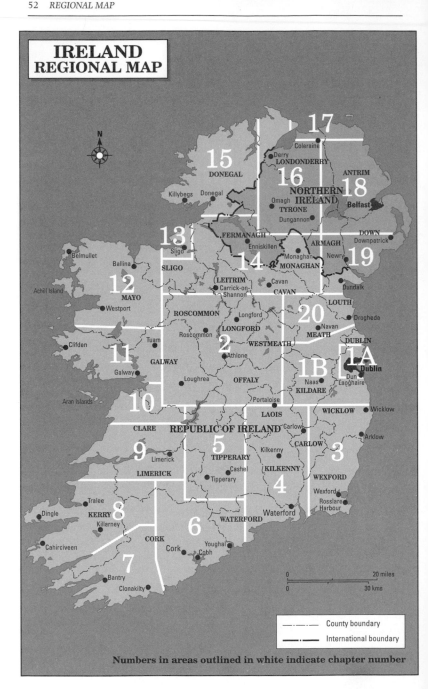

THE GUIDE

1a · Dublin City and Environs

Dublin, beautifully sited between sea and mountains, is the cultural, historic and sporting capital of Ireland; it has the greatest concentration of museums, theatres, concert venues, restaurants, pubs and urban tourist attractions of any part of Ireland. The premier sporting fixtures take place in Dublin or in the rich landscape of its hinterland. The city, at the centre of the road, rail and air network, is an ideal point from which to approach any other part of Ireland.

How to get there
- **Air**. Dublin International Airport is served by Aer Lingus, British Airways, British Midland, City Jet, Air France, Ryan Air, Sabena, Swiss Air, Lufthansa, SAS.
  Dublin Airport (☎ 705 6705/844 5387), 10km north of the city on the N1 Belfast Rd.
- **Sea**. Sailings to Holyhead are from Dublin Port and Dun Laoghaire. The less than two hour state-of-the-art catamaran service is the quickest (with a journey time of under two hours). Sailings for the Isle of Man leave from Dublin Port.
  Car Ferry Terminals at Port Centre, North Wall Rd (from city centre) (☎ 677 8271) and Dun Laoghaire (☎ 808 844), both for Holyhead.
- **Train**. Connolly Station for trains to the North and Northwest (☎ 363 333); Heuston for the South, Southeast and Southwest (☎ 366 222).
- **Bus**. Provincial services (Bus Éireann) from Busaras, Store St (☎ 302 222).

Travelling around the area
- **Train**. DART (Dublin Area Rapid Transit) (☎ 703 3633), a swift electric train service, links Bray to Howth via the city centre at Pearse, Tara St and Connolly Stations. Travelling mostly along the shore of Dublin Bay, the southern curve of which is a particularly attractive journey around the rim of Killiney Bay; it brings Howth and Dun Laoghaire within easy reach.
- **Bus**. City buses from various locations in city centre. **Dublin Bus**, 59 O'Connell St and 35 Lower Abbey St (☎ 734 222). Provincial services (see above).
- **Taxis**. Taxi ranks in prominent locations; O'Connell St, College Green, St Stephen's Green (Shelbourne Hotel), Jury's Hotel, Ballsbridge etc. Metered taxis good value for city centre.

Listings
Restaurants. **Chez Jules**, D'Olier St, French cuisine, chequered tablecloths (☎ 677 0499); **Commons Restaurant**, 85 St Stephen's Green, basement of an early

18C mansion, food as elegant as its surroundings (☎ 475 2597); **Cooke's Café**, 14 South William St, fashionable ambience, good food; Cooke's delicious breads are available opposite (☎ 679 0536); **The Elephant and Castle**, Temple Bar, popular middle-of-the-road (☎ 679 3121); **Restaurant Patrick Guilbaud**, 46 James Place, Baggot St, serious food, elegantly prepared, (☎ 676 4192); **Roly's Bistro**, 7 Ballsbridge Terrace, Ballsbridge, highly successful mixture of the extravagant and the standard (☎ 668 2611).

Pubs. **An Beal Bocht**, Charlemont St, current music pub (☎ 475 5614); **The Stag's Head**,1 Dame Court, Dame St, decor of 1911, younger clientele (☎ 679 3701); **The Long Hall**, 51 South Great George's St, Victorian clutter, lively crowd (☎ 475 1590); **Thomas Read's**, Parliament St, new-old pub, loud music (☎ 670 7220); **Toners** (☎ 676 3090), **Doheny and Nesbitt's** (☎ 676 2945), Lower Baggot St, blissfully un-improved old-style bars; **Davey Byrne's**, 21 Duke St, once a literary lounge, now lunge (☎ 677 5217); **The Dawson Lounge**, 25 Dawson St, smallest, most discreet bar in country (☎ 677 5909); **Horseshoe Bar**, Shelbourne Hotel, smart and lively (☎ 676 6471).

Traditional Music Pubs. **Hughes**, Chancery St (☎ 872 6540); **Slattery's**, Caple Street (☎ 872 7971); **Moran's Hotel**, Talbot St (☎ 836 5670); **The Piper's Club**, 15 Henrietta St (☎ 873 0093).

Cafés. **Bewley's**, Grafton St, a Dublin institution, Edwardian charm and chat (☎ 677 6761); **Leo Burdock's**, 2 Werburg St, fish and chips as Queen Victoria remembered them (☎ 454 0306); **The Irish Film Centre**, 6 Eustace Street; Temple Bar, pleasant pre-film cafe-bar (☎ 677 8788); **The Joy of Coffee**, Temple Bar, just that, good coffee (☎ 671 1110); **The Kilkenny Shop**, Nassau St, coffee and lunch overlooking College Park (☎ 677 7066); **The National Gallery Café**, Merrion Square, sustaining food for the visually weary (☎ 661 5133).

Hotels. **Westbury**, Grafton St, gracious elegance (for the internationally famous) (☎ 679 1122); **Buswell's Hotel**, Molesworth St, old fashioned, beloved of politicians and country clergy (☎ 676 4013); **Central Hotel**,1 Exchequer St, refurbished Victorian, now bright and cheerful (☎ 679 7302); **Clarence Hotel**, Temple Bar, the hippest hotel, (☎ 670 9000); **Georgian House Hotel**, 20 Lower Baggot St (☎ 661 8832), **Longfield's Hotel**, 9 Fitzwilliam St (☎ 676 1367); both attractive small hotels in 18C buildings.

Hostels. **Kinlay House**, Lord Edward St, convenient and friendly, in a Victorian industrial school (☎ 679 6644); **Isaac's Hostel**, Frenchman's Lane, Lower Gardiner St, on the doorstep of the Busaras (central bus station) (☎ 855 6215).

Shops. **Brown Thomas**, Grafton St, *the* department store, 'BT' to its customers (☎ 605 6666); **Design Yard**, East Essex St, Temple Bar, elegant contemporary jewellery and design objects (☎ 677 8453); **Crafts Council of Ireland**, Powerscourt Town House, South William St, showcase for Irish contemporary masters-craftsmen (☎ 679 7383); **Kilkenny Shop** (☎ 677 7066); and **Blarney Woollen Mills** (☎ 677 7066), Nassau St, crafts and fabrics.

Bookshops. **Fred Hanna's Bookshop**, Nassau St, excellent Irish writing section (☎ 677 1255); **Green's**, 16 Clare St, odd and antiquarian (☎ 676 2554); **Hodges Figgis Bookshop**, Dawson St, widest range in Dublin (☎ 677 4754); **The Winding Stair**, 40 Lower Ormond Quay, quirky, second-hand books, with café on four floors, overlooking the Liffey; soup and bread at their freshest, only the books are yesterday's (☎ 873 3292).

■ **Tourist Information**. Tourist Information Centre, Suffolk Street, D2 (☎ 605 7700); *Bord Fáilte*, Baggot St Bridge (☎ 284 4768; information); (☎ 284 1765; credit card reservations); Northern Ireland Tourist Board, 16 Nassau St (☎ 679 1977). A **Heritage Card** which provides admission for one year to all sites in OPW care (*see* practical information for further details), among them the most important historic sites in Dublin, is available at all OPW sites (Dublin Castle is the most accessible) and is excellent value.

■ **Post Office**. (☎ 728 888), O'Connell St Lower (open 09.00–18.00, every day except Christmas Day).

■ **Festivals and Events**.
January. Showcase (crafts), Royal Dublin Society.
March. 17th St. Patrick's Day Parade; International Film Festival.
April. Dublin Grand Opera Society (DGOS), spring season.
May. Spring Show (agricultural), Royal Dublin Society.
June. Dublin Street Carnival; 16th Bloomsday.
August. Dublin Horse Show, RDS; Antique Dealer's Fair.
September. All Ireland Gaelic Football and Hurling Finals.
October. Dublin Theatre Festival.
December. Dublin Grand Opera Society, winter season.

■ **Note**. **Street names** in Dublin are given in both English and Irish. The numbering of the houses in some of the older streets is consecutive, starting on one side and returning down the other so that No. 1 may be opposite No. 365. Many street names are prefixed by the designation Upper or Lower; lower always implies closer to the Liffey (Upper and Lower Mount St). Streets with identical names exist both north and south of the Liffey, the inclusion of North or South is therefore significant (North and South Great George's St).

Dublin

Dublin (*Dubh Linn*, a dark pool), population of Greater Dublin, 1,024,500, is both the administrative capital of the Irish Republic, the historic (until 1922) and cultural capital of the entire island. County Dublin, into which much of Greater Dublin extends, has been divided (January 1994) into three autonomous regions, Fingal (north and east of the Liffey), Dublin South (west and south of the river), and Dun Laoghaire and Rathdown (south east); the old historic city lies at the centre of Dublin South. A university and cathedral city with three universities and three cathedrals, it is an urbane and long established metropolitan centre of the arts and learning which celebrated (with debatable accuracy) its millennium in 1988. For seven and a half centuries the seat of English rule in Ireland, the relationship of Dublin to the wider island has been for lengthy periods both tenuous and ambiguous. In the last quarter of the 20C, the early history of Dublin has been revealed by extensive archaeological excavations and at the Undercroft in Dublin Castle the visitor is brought back to its origins in the Viking Age.

The 18C provided Dublin with its most formative period of growth and even today Georgian concepts of town planning and architecture dominate the city and many of the principal institutions of State and of learning are housed in Georgian buildings. The cultural institutions of theatre, museums, art galleries and libraries hold a position of international prominence and the permanent collections display an unrivalled variety of artefacts from the various 'golden ages' of native artistry and craftsmanship. Scrupulous restorations of important historic buildings have taken place in recent years; **Newman House, the Casino at Marino, Trinity College**, each of which superbly displays different aspects of 18C architecture and craftsmanship of the highest order. Unlike most European cities which suffered bombing raids during World War II, Dublin, except for two instances in January and May 1941 escaped unscathed. In consequence its holding of domestic 18C architecture and the characteristic internal decorative plasterwork which embellished virtually all buildings of the period remains the most extensive of any European city. Religion has always been a formative, if divisive, influence in Dublin and its seven hundred churches—from gospel halls to cathedrals—built over a period of a thousand years, vividly express a continuity of belief and ritual which has manifested itself in some of the most interesting, eccentric and bizarre buildings which the city possesses.

Dublin is a walkers' city with few hills of any significance; the compactness in the location of the major museums and historic sites facilitates the visitor with little time. The geographic location of the original city at the head of Dublin Bay has led to the gradual surrounding of the bay by the city, giving it a delightful maritime aspect. The Bay, mostly unseen by visitors, forms for Dubliners one of the most pleasing aspects of the city, while the Dublin and Wicklow mountains, rarely more than a half hour from the city and visible as the backdrop to the end of most south facing streets, are areas of unspoilt wilderness.

The development of the arts in Ireland since the 1940s has been phenomenal and at no period since the 18C has there been such vibrant and multifaceted cultural activity taking place in Dublin as there is at present. No visitor to the city should fail to experience the wealth of contemporary theatre, visual arts, music both traditional and classical, which is currently available. Contemporary Irish painting, sculpture and craftsmanship have emerged from the narrow isolation which the arts in Ireland experienced during the earlier years after the foundation of the State, and a lively intellectual atmosphere prevails. The work of classical and contemporary playwrights, both Irish and international, is constantly attracting the theatre-going public and contributing controversy and ferment to daily life.

Bloomsday, 16 June, the day in 1904 on which the events of James Joyce's *Ulysses* (the odyssey of Leopold Bloom) take place, is the only national festival devoted to a fictional character. It is commemorated annually, with events throughout the city at appropriate Joycean venues, with readings and dramatisations of Joyce's work. Bloomsday is among the most important days in the city's cultural calendar, celebrating as it does, Dublin as the focus of great literature, inextricably intertwined with Dublin as a living city.

Neither Dublin, nor any part of Ireland, can be discussed without reference to the social life of the multitudinous bars and cafés, an essential ingredient of social encounters in the city; most are of convivial interest while a small number preserve architecturally important interiors. Many have literary or historic associations.

The Georgian squares of the city are areas of parkland where one can experience a respite from the bustle of the city. The Phoenix Park is 'Rus in Urbe' on the grand scale with herds of deer first introduced during the reign of Charles II still grazing within walking distance of O'Connell Bridge.

Pre-Viking Dublin

The Dublin area was settled from the Mesolithic period, as excavations on Dalkey Island have demonstrated. The Neolithic portal tombs in Howth and the Phoenix Park show evidence of widespread and continued occupation, although the origins of the city belong to more recent times.

The city stands at the head of Dublin Bay (protected by the promontory of Howth on the north, and Dalkey Island on the south), bisected east–west by the river Liffey with the Dublin Mountains to the southwest, forming a natural barrier between the coastal region and its hinterland. River, bay and mountains are important factors in the genesis of the city which owes its urban origins to Viking raiders in the 9C. Settlement existed on the banks of the Liffey prior to the Norse invasion but this took the form of a number of separate small ecclesiastical foundations of the 6C–9C, principally scattered along the bank of the southern shore. Not even fragmentary remains of these survive today although an early Christian Round Tower belonging to the church of St. Mac Thail (west of St. Stephen's Green) stood until the 18C. This pre-Viking landscape is nonetheless still represented by the position of certain religious sites (St. Patrick's Cathedral) and other topographical features.

Dublin's current name in Irish, *Baile Átha Cliadh*, the town at the Hurdle Ford, records the existence of a river-crossing at a point on the river where four ancient pre-Christian trackways, the Slige Mor, Dala, Chualann and Midluachra from the west, southwest, southeast and north of the country converged. (Fr. Mathew Bridge on the Liffey is believed to represent this fording point).

The Viking settlers

Norse Vikings first made landfall in the Leinster coastal area when in AD 759 they raided Lambay Island to the north of Dublin Bay. In 837 a fleet of over 60 Viking longships landed at the mouth of the Liffey. Despite the firmly held conviction in Ireland that the Vikings were Danes, the majority of those who settled in Ireland were Norse (*Fingall*, is Irish for blond strangers, *fin* – blond, *gall* – foreigner; *see* 'gallowglass' in glossary), who left their homeland as a consequence of population explosion. It is probable that the earliest Norse Viking settlement on the Liffey, established in AD 841, was upstream of the river crossing in the Islandbridge area, where a substantial cemetery, including domestic and warrior burials, was discovered during railway cuttings in 1866 and excavations in the 1930s.

Local chieftains were frequently at war with the Vikings and the High

King Mael Sechnaill sacked Dublin in 849. The Vikings were driven out altogether in 902 and when they returned in 917 under Ivar the Boneless, they established the settlement which evolved into the present-day city of Dublin. This was on a high ridge of land south of the Liffey where the river Poddle joins it at a pool. The pool became the harbour for Viking longships and gave the city its Viking name *Dyfflin*, a corruption of the Irish topographical name, *Dubh Linn* (a dark pool) and hence Dublin. The settlement (700m east-west and 300m north-south) was originally protected by an earthen rampart and later enclosed by a stone wall; the principal street ran east-west along the ridge where Castle St—Christchurch Place—High St are today. The plots divided by wattle fences ran downhill from the street. These tenement boundaries remained constant for centuries despite continual rebuilding and the change in location of the wattle dwellings.

The adjacent coastal territory came under control of the Viking kingdom of *Dyfflin* and was known as *Dyfflinarskiri* (Dublinshire). It grew and prospered, stretching inland as far as Clondalkin and Leixlip. Intensive archaeological excavations carried on by the National Museum of Ireland and the Office of Public Works from the 1960s to 1980s have uncovered significant portions of Viking Dublin with its well preserved dwellings, rich in artefacts, and now regarded by medieval archaeologists as among the best-preserved Viking cities outside Scandinavia.

All the excavated strata date from c 920 to 1100, with no evidence of earlier occupation, leaving the question of the location of 9C Viking Dublin at Islandbridge or elsewhere, to be resolved by further excavation. It became evident from the nature of the settlement and quality of evidence recovered during the excavations, that Dublin was not merely a trading post but also a settled community within which a wide variety of crafts, metalwork, woodcarving, leatherwork, weaving and shipbuilding were practised by a technologically advanced society. The wattle dwellings, streetlines and pathways tightly occupied the land between the ridge and the riverbank where successive quay walls were built as the river channel narrowed with land reclamation on the southern bank.

Medieval Dublin ~ the rise of the Normans

By the 11C important public buildings were being erected. The forerunner of the medieval Christ Church Cathedral was a wooden cathedral of 1030 built by Sigtryggr Silkbeard (d. 1042), who also issued Ireland's first coinage in AD 997. At its maximum, the population of the settlement in the 11C did not amount to more than 5000. Nonetheless, the establishment of Dublin was a highly important departure from previous proto-urban Celtic ideas of community and to the Vikings is owed the origins of Ireland's first cities, mostly located along the eastern seaboard. The Viking kingdom of Dublin, Man and York, which flourished around the mid-10C stresses the trans-maritime bonds of Viking kinship. The Vikings never contemplated the conquest of Ireland, nor did they act as a coherent ethnic group, on the contrary, they frequently formed strategic alliances with other Norse or Irish leaders as the exigencies of local politics demanded. The Viking community started to integrate in the 11C, with gradual Gaelicisation caused by intermarriage, conversion to Christianity, the adoption of the

Irish language or bilingualism and they became as Hiberno Norse a permanent part of the Irish polity. At the battle of Clontarf on 23 April 1014, Brian Boru (Brian of the Tributes), High King of Ireland, together with a mixed force of Irish and Norse allies defeated a combined force of Norse from Dublin, Man and Orkney with their Leinster allies, significantly weakening Viking power which lasted for a further century and a half in Dublin.

Ecclesiastical foundations were established outside the city in the late 11C and early 12C, **St. Michan's**, 1096, **St. Mary's Abbey**, 1147, All Hallows and St. Mary de Hogge, 1163. The Anglo-Normans, who had landed in Co. Wexford in 1169, captured Dublin on 21 September 1170 and ejected the Norse occupiers who resettled on the north bank of the Liffey in what became known as Oxmantown (Eastmenstown). By the 14C the Vikings had been entirely assimilated into both Irish and Anglo-Norman society and disappear as a separate ethnic group. Their memory is principally preserved in the many Old Norse topographical names on the east coast, such as Strangford, Arklow, Wicklow, Waterford, Wexford, Helvick; the Norse artforms of Ringerike and Urnes decoration which contributed to the development of Irish medieval art, and in the establishing of important trading links with Continental Europe and the Mediterranean.

The layout of the Viking city was not altered by the change to Norman rule although in 1312 the walls were extended north to enclose the area between the city and the river and the town defences were augmented with towers. More importantly, the construction of **Dublin Castle** (which was to be the centre of British rule in Ireland until 16 January 1922) was begun by order of Henry II. Henry arrived in Ireland in 1172 in order to quell any attempt by Strongbow (Richard de Clare, Earl of Pembroke) and the Norman barons to set up an independent kingdom, and granted the city 'to my men of Bristol'.

The castle, begun in 1213, was a quadrilateral enclosure with drum towers at its corners, constructed at the southeast corner of the walled city with the River Poddle forming a natural moat on two sides, those most exposed to attack. Upper Castle Yard today represents the size and position of the original fortress. The remains of all four of the drum towers and some of the original curtain wall can be seen within the castle precincts.

The Anglo-Norman hold upon Dublin was subsequently bolstered by the creation of a defensive territory surrounding the city called the Pale, running roughly in an arc from Dalkey in the south to Drogheda in the north; this area was defended by a series of '£40.00 castles' (*see* glossary) occupied by the barons and designed to keep the native Irish at a distance, although they continued to harry the Pale for centuries from the safety of the Dublin Mountains. In 1316 the city was approached by the army of Robert and Edward Bruce but they failed to attack when the citizens burned the dwellings outside the walls.

The Normans completely rebuilt Christ Church Cathedral in stone in 1173, using masons from Gloucester. In the later medieval period many other small parish churches were built within the city walls, and a number of major religious foundations established outside its confines. The most significant of these are the Knights Hospitallers of Jerusalem at Kilmainham and St. Patrick's Cathedral which was raised from collegiate status in 1220 (creating the anomaly of Dublin being the only city in Latin Christendom with two medieval cathedrals). In 1486 the pretender Lambert Simnel was crowned Edward VI in Christ Church.

The Aftermath of the Reformation

The landholdings of the monasteries became a significant factor in the growth of the city. Following the Reformation, suppression of the monasteries freed this land for speculative re-use and it is from this development that the genesis of contemporary Dublin emerges. In 1591 Queen Elizabeth I founded the **College of the Most Holy Trinity** on former monastic lands of the Priory of All Hallows to the east of the city. This was followed by the dismantling, for building materials, of both St. Mary's Abbey, north of the Liffey and the Knights Hospitallers site at Kilmainham. Within the walled city cagework houses with gables facing on to the street were from the 14C, the most common form of building; the last of these was demolished during the early 19C.

In 1662, James Butler, Marquess of Ormonde, who had been Viceroy before the Commonwealth, returned to his post following the restoration of Charles II, bringing in his wake an awareness of the more sophisticated Continental architectural styles and fashions. He established the **Royal Hospital for Old Soldiers** at Kilmainham in 1688. Gradually, tracts of open land surrounding the medieval city were built upon, beginning the growth of residential areas northwards and eastwards, away from the narrow streets of the walled city.

The creation, during the 18C of a rationally planned urban layout began to display all the civic amenities of the Enlightenment. Dublin had moved from being a small, enclosed medieval city to becoming one of the significant modern cities of 18C Europe and the second city of the British Isles, all within a period of a century.

Georgian Dublin

Although Georgian Dublin (the reigns of the four Georges, 1714–1830) is now firmly associated with the architecture of the latter end of the century, the first 25 years were exceptionally fruitful and a small but important corpus of buildings survive from this period: **Marsh's Library** (1702), **The Tailor's Hall and Royal (Collins) Barracks**,(1706), **Trinity College Library** (1712), and **Dr Steevens' Hospital** (1720). This period is also the Dublin of Jonathan Swift (d. 1745). Eighteenth century growth was promoted by wealthy magnates, the Jervis, Beresford and Gardiner families. A national Parliament was established in College Green. Enlightened acts of Parliament promoted the improvement of the port, rationalised street planning and the creation of civic architecture and, most importantly, saw the residence in the city of those in whom power was vested. Following the revocation of the Edict of Nantes in 1685, the arrival of French Huguenot refugees (Tarbary, van Beaver, La Touche, etc) introduced into Dublin high standards of craftsmanship, and weaving, metalwork and other crafts flourished. But the destabilising influence of the French Revolution on British Government opinion and the outbreak of the 1798 Rebellion, in which members of the Protestant establishment were implicated, led eventually to the proroguing of the Dublin Parliament. The passing in 1801 of the Act of Union led to a decline in the type of aristocratic patronage which had created the wealth and development of the city.

A further Government alarm was caused by the abortive Emmet rising in 1803, and while this added another hero to the nationalist pantheon it had little popular support and was, unlike the rebellion of 1798, confined to Dublin and over in a matter of days. Union with Britain, and the consequent removal of the seat of Government to London spelt the end of a period in which grandees built palatial town houses (**Aldborough**, **Charlemont**, **Clanwilliam**, **Leinster**, **Powerscourt**, **Tyrone**), and the applied arts and trade flourished, but it did not set a pause to the growth of the city, merely changed the emphasis. The Georgian mode of town planning and architectural style remained dominant in Dublin into the mid-19C and the gradual democratising of society, encouraged by Emancipation Act (1829), caused a shift in the city's distribution of wealth and geographic development.

Economic Growth in the 19C

Brewing and distilling were the major industries in the city during the 19C. It hardly comes as a surprise that in the restoration of the two cathedrals, Christ Church was financed by the distiller Henry Roe and St. Patrick's by the brewer Sir Benjamin Lee Guinness. Behind the social, economic and political turmoil which characterised Irish life during the latter half of the 19C Dublin continued to expand, principally to the southeast, where elegant leafy suburbs (**Ballsbridge**, **Rathgar**) with enormous Victorian houses and sedate squares (**Belgrave**, **Dartmouth**, **Kenilworth**), became the residential focus of the city. The Georgian town houses of the landed gentry in St. Stephen's Green, Mountjoy and Merrion Squares became professional enclaves, business quarters and, ultimately, in many cases degenerated into tenements. As the wealthy moved further and further from the centre, the poor and deprived moved in to occupy the vacated mansions, squatting, many families to a room, under the surreal splendours of Baroque plasterwork cherubs. The Famine (1845–47) greatly increased their numbers as families from the countryside sought refuge in the city. The setting of James Joyce's early writings in the final years of the 19C, and *Ulysses* in the Dublin of 1904, are a true reflection of the manners and mores of the period.

The Twentieth Century and the Effects of Partition

The sedateness and complacency of professional life in Dublin was shattered early in the 20C by the eight-month-long **Lock Out Strike** of 1913 during which the poverty and exploited position of the unskilled labour force became a serious issue. This led to the establishment of the **Citizen Army** to protect the workers from the police. Social unrest had hardly been pacified when another and even more disturbing phenomenon occurred, the outbreak of the **1916 Rebellion**, in the middle of World War I. Such hostilities, given Ireland's position as an integral part of the United Kingdom, were seen by many as an act of treason.

The Proclamation of an Irish Republic was read from the portico of the **General Post Office** (GPO) on O'Connell St, and the city remained under curfew for some time. The rebellion caused considerable destruction to the fabric of the city. The GPO, headquarters of the rebellion, was shelled and it, as well as a large portion of O'Connell St destroyed. After the execution of the revolutionary leaders, public opinion became radicalised, and in 1919 the Sinn Féin Parliament (the First Dáil) met in the Mansion House and declared a Provisional Government for Ireland. Following the partition of Ireland in 1922 and the outbreak of Civil War in the south, further damage was done to the city with the gutting of James Gandon's two major buildings on the quays, the **Custom House** through the work of IRA incendiaries and the **Four Courts** through shelling by State Forces. The burning of the Public Records Office during the latter assault destroyed the principal archive of State Papers from the medieval period onwards. It was not until the 1930s that O'Connell St was rebuilt and the Four Courts and Custom House restored.

Architectural projects in the 20C

Civic development of Dublin from the 1930s was initially concerned with restoring the devastated areas of the city, sweeping away the slum and brothel quarter, (Joyce's 'Nighttown') and creating vast local authority housing schemes on the outskirts. This was followed by a tragic period of civic neglect of the Georgian core of the city. During the 1960s and 70s the largest housing stock of 18C terraces and squares in Europe came under serious threat from urban re-development of commercial projects, many of utter inappropriateness and insensitivity. Dublin's only high rise building, Liberty Hall (1964), which abuts the Custom House, was fortunately not seen as a direction to be followed.

The revival of the **Irish Georgian Society** in 1958 rallied public opinion concerning Georgian Dublin, but a generation of agitation was required before Government and developers became aware of the damage which was being done to the essential nature of the city. In 1976 the **Irish Architectural Archive** was founded to conserve records for all periods of Irish architecture. Although even today building interiors remain neither listed nor protected by law, the trend is away from wholesale destruction and many important buildings are being restored in an appropriate manner. More importantly, it has become accepted that preservation of individual buildings of great merit is further enhanced by maintaining their contemporary surroundings.

Little prominence has previously been given to the existence in Dublin of the architectural styles of the late 19C and early 20C; the Arts and Crafts Movement (Iveagh Baths), Art Noveau (Sunlight Chambers), the Chicago School (Market St, Store House), Beaux-Arts (Parnell Monument), Bauhaus (Scott House, Sandy cove), stripped Classicism (National Concert Hall), Art Deco (ETB offices, D'Olier St), and International Modernism (Busaras). Although Dublin is not notably rich in work of these periods such examples as exist are of individual merit, and interesting also for the manner with which they adapt to or ignore the classical and Victorian architecture which surrounds them.

Among the more famous citizens of Dublin are the following: in the realm of scholarship and literature: Jonathan Swift (1667–1745); Richard Brinsley Sheridan (1751–1816); Thomas Moore (1779–1852); Charles Robert Maturin (1782–1824), author of *Melmoth the Wanderer*; George Petrie (1789–1866), the antiquary; Joseph Sheridan Le Fanu (1814–73); W.E.H. Lecky (1838–1903), the historian; Bram Stoker (1847–1912), author of *Dracula*; Oscar Wilde (1854–1900); George Bernard Shaw (1856–1950); Katharine Tynan (1861–1931); William Butler Yeats (1865–1939); John Millington Synge (1871–1909); Seán O'Casey (1880–1964); James Joyce (1882–1941); Samuel Beckett (1906–89); Brendan Behan(1923–64) and Dame Iris Murdoch (born 1919).

The arts are represented by painters: George Barret (1732–84); Robert Carver (fl. 1750–91); Nathaniel Hone (1718–84); Hugh Douglas Hamilton (1739–1808); Thomas Hickey (1741–1824); Sir Martin Archer Shee (1769–1850); Sir William Orpen (1878–1931); Evie Hone (1894–1955); Francis Bacon (1909–1993); Albert Power (1882–1945) the sculptor and Rex Ingram (1893–1960) film director. Among composers: John Field (1782–1837); Michael William Balfe (1808–70); Sir Charles Villiers Stanford (1852–1924); and the singer and friend of Mozart, Michael Kelly (1764–1826).

Among Irish patriots: James Napper Tandy (1740–1803); Henry Grattan (1746–1820); Theobald Wolfe Tone (1763–98); Robert Emmet (1778–1803); John Dillon (1851–1927); Patrick Pearse (1879–1916); and Arthur Griffith (1872–1922).

And in their various fields: Edmund Burke (1729–97), statesman and orator; Arthur Wellesley, Duke of Wellington (1769–1852); Sir William Rowan Hamilton (1805–65) astronomer and mathematician; Dr Thomas John Barnardo (1845–1905), the philanthropist; Lord Carson (1854–1935), unionist politician; Ernest Walton (1903–95), nuclear physicist and Nobel Laureate.

Dublin Bay

The marine architecture and natural environment of Dublin Bay are of exceptional interest, and a number of separate areas are worth visiting for the combination of attractive coastal setting and impressive architecture. These harbourworks demonstrate both the importance of the bay to the life of the city and the quality of engineering. During the 18C-19C attempts were made to create safe shipping havens in its treacherous waters, and also to render navigable its capricious channel. So unpredictable was the position of the sandbars in the bay that Dalkey, on the south coast, acted as the port of Dublin up to the 17C; the problem was overcome in Viking and medieval times by using shallow draught ships. A prevailing theme in the history of the city is the loss of life through shipwreck, within sight of the shores of the bay. Captain William Bligh (1754–1817)—commander of the *Bounty* during the notorious mutiny—was commissioned to make a chart of the bay in 1800. The result was the most accurate produced up to that date.

Established in 1786, the **Corporation for Improving and Maintaining the Port of Dublin,** took the initiative and attempted to embank the river; by constructing a great harbour wall on the south side of the channel the tidal flow was re-directed so as to prevent the channel from silting up.

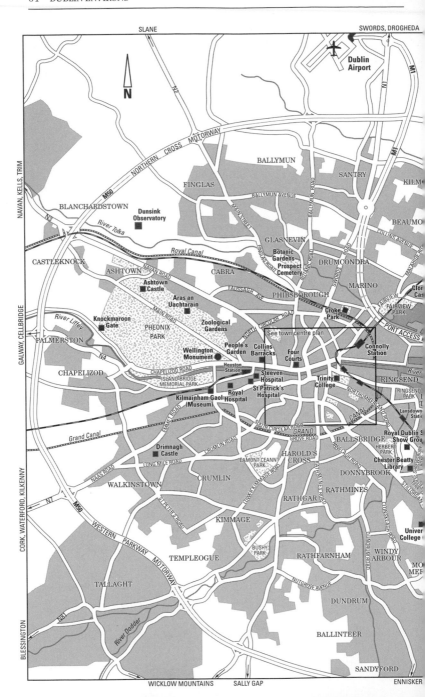

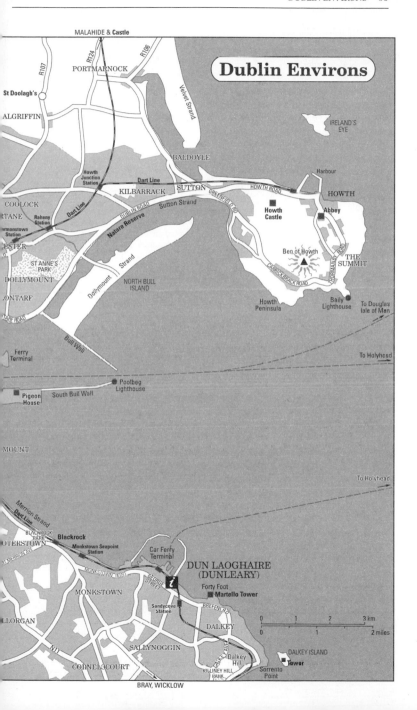

Dublin Environs

MALAHIDE & Castle
R124
R106
R107
PORTMARNOCK
St Doolagh's
ALGRIFFIN
Velvet Strand
IRELAND'S EYE
BALDOYLE
Howth Junction Station
Dart Line
KILBARRACK
SUTTON
Harbour
HOWTH ROAD
HOWTH
COOLOCK
Dart Line
Raheny Station
Dublin Road
Sutton Strand
GREENFIELD RD
Howth Castle
Abbey
RTANE
ermonstown Station
ESTER
Nature Reserve
Bull Island Strand
Ben of Howth
THE SUMMIT
NORMAN'S ROAD
ST ANNE'S PARK
DOLLYMOUNT
NORTH BULL ISLAND
Dollymount Strand
CARRICKBRACK ROAD
ONTARF
ARE ROAD
Howth Peninsula
Baily Lighthouse
To Douglas Isle of Man
Bull Wall
Ferry Terminal
To Holyhead
Pigeon House
South Bull Wall
Poolbeg Lighthouse
MOUNT
To Holyhead
Merrion Strand
Dart Line
BLACKROCK PARK
Blackrock
Monkstown Seapoint Station
Car Ferry Terminal
DUN LAOGHAIRE (DUNLEARY)
OTERSTOWN
MONKSTOWN LD
GEORGE STREET
i
Forty Foot
Martello Tower
MONKSTOWN
Sandycove Station
BREFFNI RD
LLORGAN
N11
DALKEY
SALLYNOGGIN
DALKEY ISLAND
Tower
0   1   2   3 km
0   1   2 miles
DALKEY HILL
Dalkey Hill
CORNELSCOURT
KILLINEY HILL PARK
Sorrento Point
BRAY, WICKLOW

Head of Dublin Metropolitan Police Constable, c 1915, Pearse St. Garda Station

At the east end of Pearse St is the **Grand Canal Dock** where the 18C navigational canal from the Shannon meets the Liffey. In this watery landscape of brick and stone canal warehouses is an imaginative modern building devoted to interpreting the history of the inland waterways, the **Waterways Visitor Centre** (09.30–18.30, June–Sept; 12.30–17.00, Oct–May; £; OPW).

The **South Bull Wall,** the most important single part of the harbour works, was begun in 1730 and under construction for most of the century. The Poolbeg Lighthouse was built at its eastern end in 1761 and the simultaneous building of the wall out from the city and backwards from the lighthouse, covered a distance of 4.5km of granite causeway. The city has encroached on most of the South Wall but the portion of it which is still surrounded by water is the most 'away-from-it-all' place to visit in Dublin. Here it is possible to walk right out into the very centre of the bay, surrounded only by sea and sky, and to observe the river traffic; the city with its backdrop of mountains curves around in the distance (see Dublin environs map). Paved in granite slabs and 10.00m wide, the causeway encompasses the Pigeon House Harbour with its defunct 18C hotel, and the 19C 'Half Moon' gun battery in its length.

To reach the South Bull Wall, approach through Ringsend (where Cromwell landed in 1646), turn left in Irishtown for the East Link Toll Bridge, then right at the roundabout (without crossing the river), and continue east past the tall stacks of the Poolbeg Power Station. A bus service from Tara St goes as far as the power station. By car you can drive slightly further. The walk is not recommended in gale-force winds for fear of being blown into the bay.

On the south coast, reached by the coast road or by DART, is **Dun Laoghaire Harbour**, one of the great harbours of the Victorian world, now a ferry-port and yachting centre. A journey by DART along the south coast of the bay to Bray travels along the most scenic coastal route in the region; Bray Head, the Wicklow Mountains and the sea surround the viewer, without ever leaving your seat.

Clontarf Promenade, on the northern shore of the Bay, continues east to **Bull Island** with its corresponding North Bull Wall, and the sand-dunes of Dollymount Strand. The island began to develop during the 1820s, caused by tidal action which deposited sand on the north side of the Bay. It is now an important nature reserve (see below).

Trinity College, Merrion Square, National Gallery & Museum

O'Connell Bridge, formerly Carlisle (1790) by Gandon, is the ideal point from which to begin a tour of the city and from here the extent of the Georgian city can easily be grasped. Upstream on the skyline to the west, the trees of the

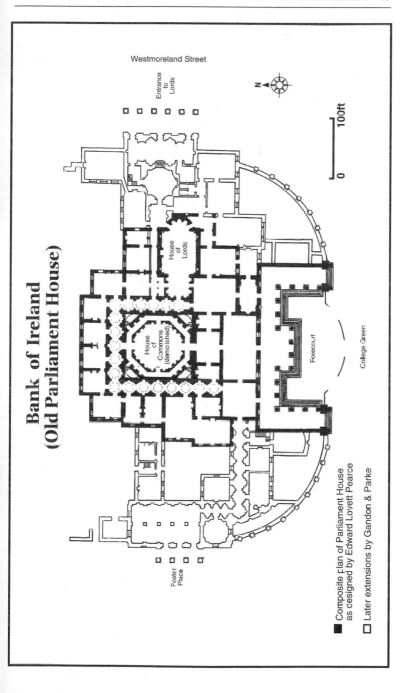

Bank of Ireland
(Old Parliament House)

Westmoreland Street

Entrance to Lords

N

100ft

0

House of Lords

House of Commons (demolished)

Forecourt

College Green

Foster Place

■ Composite plan of Parliament House as designed by Edward Lovett Pearce

□ Later extensions by Gandon & Parke

Phoenix Park and downstream to the east the Custom House, indicate the east and west limits of the 18C city. The extent to north and south are hidden from view but the city north of the Liffey did not extend very far beyond the top of O'Connell St as the Georgian city was roughly oval in shape, a similar distance south will give an idea of the overall limits of the city at the end of the Georgian era.

The most distinguished of the river bridges are those upstream . The nearest is the cast-iron singlespan '**Ha'penny Bridge**' by the Coalbrookdale ironmaster John Windsor, 1816. Erected by John Claudius Beresford as a toll bridge, the inflation-free fee remained one ha'penny (half an old penny), for a century, before the charge was abolished. Beyond this is Grattan Bridge (1874) and Queen Maeve Bridge (1764), the only one to survive from the 18C. From O'Connell Bridge a short walk up Westmoreland St leads to College Green (previously Hoggan Green, the site of the Viking 'Haugen', the burial-ground and meeting-place, levelled in 1682), and the hub of the city for the last three centuries. In Townsend St, to the right, stood the 'Thengmote', a stone set up by the Vikings to mark the point at which they first landed. In the adjoining axis (left) from O'Connell bridge, D'Olier St, is the Gas Company by Robinson Keefe (1927), the finest Art Deco building in Dublin, with most of its original features intact. Parliament House (now the Bank of Ireland) and Trinity College both flank College Green (with the castle further west) and formed the focus of public life, both politically and culturally, in the Georgian era. Monuments in College Green are Henry Grattan by Foley (1879), and Thomas Davis with the 'Heralds of the Four Provinces' fountain by Delaney (1966).

On the right, the **Parliament House** (now the Bank of Ireland) by **Sir Edward Lovett Pearce** (1729), the greatest Irish architect of the early 18C, is a complex building. The principal feature of the south front is the splendid classical Ionic colonnaded forecourt, with tall round arches at the ends of the flanking arcades. This is the entrance to Pearce's original bi-cameral Parliament House (the first-ever purpose-built parliament building) and needs to be imagined without the curved screen walls to east and west, in order to appreciate its original design. Directly behind the portico but separated from it by ante rooms was the octagonal Commons and to the right the smaller House of Lords. James Gandon added the Corinthian portico in Westmoreland St as an entrance to the Lords in 1785, and united this with Pearce's south front by a curved screen wall. A corresponding smaller Ionic portico was added on the west in Foster Place by Robert Parke in 1792, also united to the original front by a matching screen.

The Commons chamber was demolished in 1804 in order to emasculate the political significance of the building. The Parliament House, made redundant by the 1801 Act of Union (which removed Ireland's independent parliament, in existence since 1295), was purchased by the Bank of Ireland. The **Lords chamber** survived and still contains the tapestries by the Huguenot weaver, Jan van Beaver, depicting King William III at the Boyne, and the Siege of Derry (1728), for which they were woven. Under a segmented and barrel vaulted plaster ceiling it is panelled in oak with a remarkable carved fireplace (Houghton, 1748) and glass chandelier (1788). The Court of Requests is today the principal banking hall. A domed top-lit corridor from Pearce's building leads from the main courtyard around the now vanished Commons, to the Lords. The quality of the detailing shows Pearce's familiarity with classical antiquity (he was the first Irish born architect to make the Grand Tour and his annotated copy of Palladio's *I Quattro Libri* (1570) has survived). There is also rich sculptural decoration on the main façades; on the west portico, military trophies by Thomas Kirk; on the south front, Fidelity, Hibernia and Commerce (Edward Smyth, 1809); on the east portico, Wisdom, Justice and Liberty, also by Smyth (1787). The Parliament possesses a symbolic importance in the cause of Irish independence for although its membership was confined by the Penal Laws to Protestant representation, it was a first important step towards the achievement of national self-government by parliamentary means.

Mahogany head of a herm by John Houghton on the chimneypiece in the House of Lords, c 1730

Trinity College

The east side of College Green, occupied by the University of Dublin or **Trinity College**, familiarly known as 'TCD', or 'Trinity', a world within a world. Inside the confines of the campus, the traffic of the city is replaced by secluded calm, cobbled quadrangles and students carrying books. It comprises the most remarkable ensemble of 18th, 19th and 20C architecture in Ireland. The principal buildings are arranged in the form of a Greek cross around interconnecting areas of open space.

Trinity is the oldest university in Ireland, predating University College Dublin by two and a half centuries. It was founded by Elizabeth I in 1592 on the site of the Priory of All Hallows. The queen wrote that she had founded it for the 'reformation of the barbarism of this rude people', for many Irish had travelled abroad to attend foreign universities 'whereby they have been infected with Popery and other ill qualities, and so become evil subjects'. Long a bastion of the Anglican Established Church, it was freed of religious restrictions in 1873, and distinguished itself (before Oxford or Cambridge) by admitting women to take degrees as early as 1903.

Among those who have attended Trinity are James Ussher, Farquhar, Congreve, Swift, Berkeley, Burke, Samuel Molyneux (the astronomer), William Molyneux (the physician), Thomas Burgh (architect of the Old Library), the writers Thomas Moore, Maturin, Lever, Le Fanu, Oscar Wilde, Synge, Goldsmith, Robert Emmet, Isaac Butt, Bram Stoker, Edward Carson, Douglas Hyde, Samuel Beckett, Elizabeth Bowen (1900–73), William Trevor (b. 1928), Thomas Prior (philanthropist and founder of the Dublin Society) and Ernest Walton (b. 1903) nuclear physicist and Nobel prize winner (1951).

No buildings from the original foundation of 1592 survive, the earliest being the Rubrics of 1700, although even this has been much altered in the 19C. The external 90m long west front (1752) facing College Green and separated from the street by curved railings, is attributed to Theodore Jacobson. With central columned portico and end pavilions in granite dressed with Portland stone, it is the most important Georgian street façade in the city, dominating College Green, ending Dame St and providing a foil to the Baroque extravagance of the Bank of Ireland. Over the west entrance is a reception room known as the

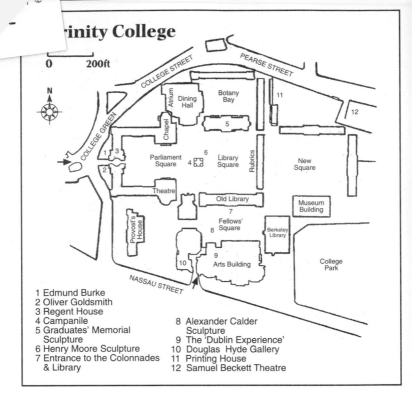

Trinity College

0 ——— 200ft

N

COLLEGE STREET

PEARSE STREET

COLLEGE GREEN

Atrium

Dining Hall

Chapel

Botany Bay

11

12

5

1 3
Parliament Square

2

4

6

Library Square

Rubrics

New Square

Theatre

Old Library

7

Fellows'
Square

8

Museum Building

Berkeley Library

Provost's House

10

9

Arts Building

College Park

NASSAU STREET

1 Edmund Burke
2 Oliver Goldsmith
3 Regent House
4 Campanile
5 Graduates' Memorial
  Sculpture
6 Henry Moore Sculpture
7 Entrance to the Colonnades
  & Library

8 Alexander Calder
  Sculpture
9 The 'Dublin Experience'
10 Douglas Hyde Gallery
11 Printing House
12 Samuel Beckett Theatre

Regent House, with plasterwork by Stapleton. The paired statues of Burke (1868) and Goldsmith (1861) inside the front railings are both by Foley. 19C wits claimed that the sculptor had cast the legs of both subjects and those of the nearby Grattan, from the same mould!

At the front of Parliament Square is a symmetrical composition with flanking projecting porticoes to right and left of the Theatre and Chapel, both by Sir William Chambers (1774). The Provost Baldwin monument in the **Chapel** is by Christopher Hewetson (1771). In front of the **Campanile** (Sir Charles Lanyon 1852), the square opens out with the Dining Hall (Richard Castle, 1745) on the north, the diminutive Music Library (1937) on the south. The **Dining Hall**— burned in 1989 and now totally restored—is decorated with a collection of immense brooding portraits of college worthies and noblemen. The **Atrium** (de Blacam and Meagher, 1986) to the left of the Dining Hall, uses timber and natural light to create an interesting interior court. Above the Dining Hall the Fellow's Bar is a re-creation of Adolf Loo's famous 'Kartner Bar' in Vienna of 1907 (private).

Beyond the campanile (right) is Library Square with the greatest building on the campus, Thomas Burgh's **Old Library** (1712) which vies with St. Patrick's

Cathedral in its claim to being the most majestic interior in Ireland (09.30–16.45 daily, 09.30–12.45 Sat, closed Sun & Bank Holidays; £). As designed by Burgh, it had a ground level open loggia (now enclosed) with the library above it. Known as the 'Long Room', it originally contained bookcases on only one level, and had a flat plastered ceiling. Benjamin Woodward (1852) introduced the second level of bookcases and timber barrel-vaulted roof which gives the interior its supreme sense of spaciousness. It has been one of the Copyright Libraries since 1801. Its collection was started in 1601; later acquisitions include the library of Archbishop Ussher (1581–1656) in 1661 and the Fagel collection in 1802. Ussher, one of the college's first students, entered at the age of 13. Among the results of his Biblical scholarship was the assertion that the world was created on 23 October 4004 BC! Divided between a number of buildings, the collection contains some 5000 MSS and two million printed books. The Old Library is confined to early material, the departments of Manuscripts and Early Printed Books.

Library Square leads into Fellows Square and the Library is reached (right) from here, through the Colonnades exhibition area, where the principal treasures of the College, 7C Book of Durrow, 8C Book of Dimna, and 9C Book of Kells, (for many years in the Long Room), are now on display in scientifically controlled conditions (which unfortunately do not make viewing any easier); in the high tourist season the manuscripts, protected by bullet-proof glass, are surrounded by a Rugby scrum of heaving bodies.

The **Book of Kells**, was described by Giraldus Cambrensis in the 12C as 'the chief glory of the western world', a judgement which for all its hyperbole, is still amply justified. It is a gorgeously illuminated Latin Gospel book, produced in Kells, or possibly in one of the Irish monasteries in the north of Scotland, around the year 800, and written in insular majuscule script. The 340 profusely decorated folios (680 pages) with 'carpet' (fully illuminated) pages of the evangelists, and lavish interlinear zoomorphic ornamentation, have retained a quite startling freshness of colouring despite its age and the vicissitudes it underwent. In 1007 it was stolen from Kells and found three months later in a bog, stripped of its metal covers; the loss of the beginning and end folios doubtless dates from this misadventure. In 1654, during the unrest of the Cromwellian wars, it was brought to Dublin, and presented to the college by Henry Jones, Bishop of Meath in 1661. It is considered by scholars to be among the most beautiful illuminated manuscripts in the world.

A stair rises from the Colonnade to the Long Room, where the dim filtered light entering through the tall windows illumines the serried rows of marble

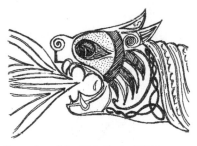

Beast from folio 124, Book of Kells, 9C

busts at the entrances to the book bays. The busts, by Scheemakers, Vierpyl, Cunningham and van Nost—the principal sculptors working in Ireland during the 18C—are of classical and later authors, including Swift by Roubiliac.

The Victorian Baroque **Graduates Memorial Building**, (1891), an extravagance by Sir Thomas Drew, faces the Old Library across a grassy quad with

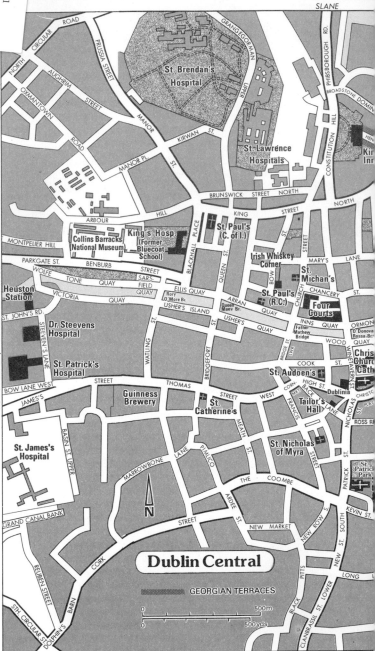

SLANE

St. Brendan's
Hospital

St. Lawrence
Hospitals

BRUNSWICK STREET NORTH

KING STREET

St. Paul's
(C. of I.)

Collins Barracks
National Museum

King's Hosp.
(Former
Bluecoat
School)

Irish Whiskey
Corner

St.
Michan's

St. Paul's
(R.C.)

Four
Courts

Heuston
Station

Dr. Steevens
Hospital

St. Patrick's
Hospital

Guinness
Brewery

St.
Catherine's

St. Audoen's

Dublinia

Tailor's
Hall

St. Nicholas
of Myra

St. James's
Hospital

THE COOMBE

NEW MARKET

Dublin Central

GEORGIAN TERRACES

0   500m

0   500yds

N

KILMAINHAM GAOL, IRISH MUSEUM OF MODERN ART,
ROYAL HOSPITAL, KILMAINHAM, PHOENIX PARK

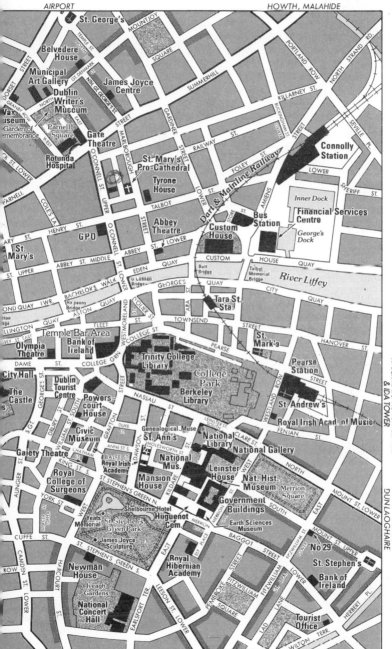

'Reclining Connected Forms' 1969 by Henry Moore, and the Rubrics on the east side. South of the Library is the Arts Block (Paul Koralec, 1980), in which are the Douglas Hyde Gallery (11.00–18.00, Mon–Thurs; 11.00–19.00 Fri; 11.00–16.45, Sat) (conceptual and avant garde art), and 'The Dublin Experience', an audio-visual presentation, rich in information and images on the history of Dublin from the Viking Age to recent times. The **Weingreen Museum of Biblical Antiquities** (top floor) contains an excellent and well displayed collection of antiquities from Egypt, historic Palestine, Greece, Rome and Mesopotamia, among which is a 9C BC Assyrian bas-relief from the palace of Ashurnasirpal II (appointment to view necessary). 'Cactus' by Alexander Calder (1967) is in the centre of Fellows Garden. Nassau St may be reached through the Arts Block. On the east side of Fellows' Square is the new **Berkeley Library** (Paul Koralec, 1967), one of the best modern buildings in the city, which manages the difficult task of sitting serenely between two of Trinity's most powerful buildings, Burgh's 'Old Library' and Dean and Woodward's Museum Building, 1853. On the forecourt of the New library is 'Sphere with Sphere' by Arnaldo Pomodoro (1962).

The Venetian Gothic Museum (1852), facing New Square, was much admired by Ruskin, and it has the greatest concentration of decorative stonecarving of any building in the city. Woodward allowed the masons to carve freely in the manner of medieval craftsmen. Its internal hall and staircase, decorated in polychrome marble is also of interest. Two skeletons of the extinct Giant Irish Deer stand guard over the hallway, and a small Geological Museum is on the top floor.

Behind the Museum is College Park, a delightful place to sit and while away some time watching a leisurely cricket match; here the arrangement of the buildings around the perimeter is less ordered. To the north of it and diagonally across New Square is the **Samuel Beckett Theatre**, a timber-clad pagoda by de Blacam and Meagher (1993). Also to the north is Richard Castle's earliest Dublin building, the tiny classical **Printing House** (1734), an exquisite small Doric temple of great refinement, visible from the back of the Rubrics.

At the extreme south-west corner of the College and seen from Grafton St is the **Provost's House** (by appointment only). Its design is attributed to John Smyth, (1759) but it is directly based on Lord Burlington's London house for General Wade, itself derived from a drawing by Palladio, and is the only 18C mansion in the city which has been continually lived in since it was built. The building, comprising a tall, cubical central block with superimposed arcades on the façade and pilasters on the upper floor, is flanked by low single storey wings with central pediment, and set back from the street by a courtyard entered through a rusticated gateway. It has a number of exceptional interiors; the hall and stairway have heavily articulated walls and the saloon on the *piano nobile* which has a notable coffered ceiling, runs the full width of the façade, with columned screens at either end; it has paintings by Reynolds and Gainsborough.

Continuing south, pedestrianised Grafton St—the smartest shopping area in the city—leads towards St. Stephen's Green. Half way up on the right is **Bewley's Oriental Café**, with an Egyptian mosaic façade (A.C.C. Miller, 1925), a product of the *Tutmania* which followed the discovery of Tutankhaman's tomb in 1922. It is the flagship of a group of Edwardian coffee-houses (founded 1894 by the Quaker Bewley family), and an important social institution in the city. The interior has windows by Harry Clarke (the four classical orders bearing cakes), and patrons sit on bentwood chairs among a clutter of small tables. On the top floor is **Bewley's Museum Café** (Museum: 10.30–17.00 daily) an intriguing mixture of family history, Danish pastries and antique catering equipment. Bewley's belongs with other famous survivals of European 'café society', the *Café Greco* in Rome, and Paris's *Café Flore*; it should not be missed.

Harry St, south and right off Grafton St, leads (left) to Balfe St, in which Michael William Balfe (1808–70), singer and composer of *The Bohemian Girl* (1843) and other operas, was born.

Passing down the north side of Bewley's is Johnson's Court, off which is the pre-Emancipation Carmelite church of St. Teresa (1793–1876) with Hogan's celebrated **Dead Christ** displayed below the altar (first version, 1829). The Court leads to the rear entrance of **Powerscourt Townhouse**, an 18C mansion with 19C extensions (now used as a shopping centre). The courtyard of what was the Stamp Office is now enclosed with cafés on three levels, and on the top floor the **Crafts Council of Ireland Gallery** (09.00–18.00, Mon–Sat) shows work by the leading craftworkers and designers in glass, ceramics, fabric, furniture and metalwork.

The main entrance to **Powerscourt House** (Robert Mack, 1771)—once the town mansion of Lord Powerscourt—is on south William St. It has Rococo plasterwork in the hallway by James McCullagh and Adamesque ceilings on the *piano nobile* by Michael Stapleton. The ornately carved staircase is by Ignatius McDonagh. Although the house is used for commercial purposes, it is one of a small number of fine 18C interiors (Newman House and 'Number Twenty Nine'), accessible to the public.

The adjacent building on South William St, is the **Dublin Civic Museum** (10.00–18.00, Tues–Sat; 11.00–14.00; closed Mon) occupying the Assembly House built for the Society of Artists in 1765, and after 1791 used for a time as the City Assembly (owing to the ruin of the old Tholsel). The main Octagon Room contains drawings, models and miscellaneous relics, including the shoes of the 'Irish Giant', Patrick Cotter O'Brien (c 1761–1806) who was some 8 feet 6 inches tall (2.59m). Other exhibits include Thomas Kirk's head of Lord Nelson, bruised and battered after the demise of the Pillar, a set of wax models of Edward Smyth's Riverine Heads from the Custom House, probably modelled by his son John; a set of James Malton's 1792 aquatints of Dublin. There are many good, small restaurants in the adjoining streets.

Return to Grafton St. Off its opposite, east side, in Duke St is *Davy Byrne's* (a pub rich in Joycean associations), with mysterious Neue Sachlichkeit (or 'New objectivity', a German art movement) murals by Cecil Ffrench Salkeld (1904–69). At the bottom of Grafton St is a statue of Molly Malone, a bronze

Stone carving of a mole playing a lute, by Charles Harrison (1859), Kildare St Club

costume-piece of a legendary 18C costermonger, complete with barrow of shell-fish (Jeanne Rynhart, 1988). Bear right along Nassau St (flanking the grounds of Trinity College), and pass the north end of Dawson St (on right), where Nassau St becomes South Leinster St. At this point, Kildare St leads south. On the corner here, at No. 2, in a brick Venetian-style palazzo (Benjamin Woodward, 1858) was the prestigious **Kildare Street Club**, the traditional refuge of Dublin conservatism. The spirited stone carving (William Harrison), which embellishes the exterior is in the best Ruskinian medieval-revivalist tradition. Part of the building, including rooms with important Woodward decoration, is now occupied by the **State Heraldic Museum** (10.00–16.30, Mon–Fri; 10.00–12.30, Sat) and the Genealogical Office, with an exhibition devoted to the use of heraldry.

Merrion Square

Continuing east along Clare St, you shortly reach the north-west corner of **Merrion Square**, a large quadrangle, once Lord Fitzwilliam of Meryon's land, lined completely on three sides, and partially on the fourth, by dignified Georgian mansions (1762 et seq.; mainly by John Ensor). The Georgian squares are best viewed at weekends when the traffic is absent; this is particularly so in Merrion Square. The view from the centre of the park gives a good impression of the grandeur and scale of the whole scheme, which represents Georgian urban planning at its zenith. The houses on the north side display the greatest variety of design (many have a rusticated stone ground floor), these are the earliest, gradually followed by those on the east and south. Those on the south are the most uniform; in many cases the houses were constructed in pairs or blocks. The characteristics of Dublin Georgian house are admirably displayed, with uniform roof lines uniting the otherwise uncoordinated private houses. External decoration is reserved for the doorcase and fanlight, and in some cases, wrought iron balconies on the first floor (19C additions). The brick façades of four storeys over basement, succeed in avoiding monotony by the variations which individual houses display. The main reception rooms are positioned on the *piano nobile* of the first floor and decorated with ornamental plasterwork ceilings and marble fireplaces. On winter evenings, a tour of the square reveals the lit up *piano nobile* of each house, with the stucco ceilings clearly visible.

The enclosed grassland which only became public in 1974, maintained until recently the appearance of open 18C parkland, with a screen of mature trees around its perimeter. (A scheme during the 1920s proposed building a Catholic cathedral in the centre of the square; fortunately the plan miscarried.) Now it is divided into groves and lawns of demented municipal planting and has a number of important sculptures; in the south-west corner the expressionist 'Les Debarqueme' by Andrew O'Connor (1874–1941); in the northeast the 'Kerry Poets Memorial' (1930) by Jerome Connor (1876–1943) and 'Tribute Head' (1975) by Dame Elizabeth Frink (1930–1993); erected as a tribute to Nelson Mandela and unveiled in 1983 while he was still in prison on Roben Island.

Originally built for the landed gentry, these town houses have now been divided up into offices. No.1, with its conservatory (on the north-west corner), was the home of Sir William and Lady Wilde ('Speranza') from 1855–1876. Their son, Oscar Wilde, was born (1854) around the corner at No. 21 Westland Row. Part of the Royal Irish Academy of Music has been housed at No.36 since

1871. Once the town house of Lord Conyngham, (Nicholas Tench, 1771), it contains good plasterwork, probably by Stapleton. Also in this street is the Greek Revival church of St. Andrew (James Bolger, 1832). The Farrell Memorial, a delicately carved bas-relief funerary stele by Hogan (1841) in the south transept is among his finest works.

Return to No. 39 on the east side of Merrion Sq. This was the British Embassy until 1972, when a mob burned it down in response to the 'Bloody Sunday' massacre in Derry. John Betjeman was Press Attaché here 1941–43. Sir Jonah Barrington, the diarist and politician (1760–1834), lived at No. 42. On the south side, Daniel O'Connell the politician (1775–1847) lived at No. 58. Ernest Schrödinger, the physicist (1887–1961) worked at No. 65 and the writer, Sheridan Le Fanu, died at No. 70 (now the Arts Council). The **Irish Architectural Archive** is in No. 73 and the **Irish Georgian Society** at 74. W.B. Yeats lived at No. 82, from 1922–28; the poet, painter, writer and economist, George William Russell, 'AE' (pen-name) worked at No. 84.

Lower Mount St extends from the north side of the square, passing the former **Sir Patrick Dunn's Hospital** (Sir Richard Morrison, 1816), following a bequest of Sir Patrick Dunn, the physician, 1642–1713. Based on the architecture of Gandon, it exhibits many of his mannerisms. Beyond the Grand Canal the street becomes Northumberland Rd, with St. Stephen's Schools by Benjamin Woodward (1856) on the corner; a charming Gothic Revival building with steep gables and tall chimney-stacks; J.M. Synge died at No. 130 (1909).

A short distance to the left, via Grand Canal Quay, are the wide waters of the L-shaped **Grand Canal Dock**, from which the canal traffic can enter the Liffey. Around the perimeter are good 18C and 19C warehouses, including the **IDA Tower**, a former sugar mill by the theatre architect Alfred Darbyshire (1862). Now converted into studios, and occupied by the largest concentration of designer-craftworkers in the Dublin area, it is open to the public. Opposite the Tower and standing on stilts in the waters of the canal is a 20C 'crannog', the **Waterways Visitor Centre**, (09.30–18.30, June–Sept; 12.30 17.00, Oct May; OPW), by Ciaran O'Connor (1993), an imaginatively conceived building which exploits maritime themes in its design, its sleek form contrasting totally with the rough stone of the warehouses. The display, using working models and documents explains the history of Ireland's inland waterways, the Royal and Grand Canal systems, which connect the Shannon to the Liffey.

Return to the west side of Merrion Sq. with the restored Rutland Fountain (1791) is Leinster Lawn. An 18m high obelisk (Raymond McGrath) commemorates Arthur Griffith, Michael Collins and Kevin O'Higgins (among the founders of the ' Irish Free State'). Beyond is the east front of Leinster House. The first balloon ascent in Ireland, by Richard Crosbie (1755–1800), took place here in 1783.

The National Gallery of Ireland

On the north side of Leinster Lawn, entered from Merrion Sq., is the **National Gallery of Ireland** (10.00–18.00, Mon–Sat; 10.00–19.00, Thurs; 14.00–17.00, Sun). Designed by Francis Fowke, it was opened in 1864, and owes its inception largely to the railway promoter, William Dargan (1799–1867), prime mover of the Exhibition of 1853, held on the adjacent Leinster Lawn. His statue (Sir Thomas Farrell, 1864) stands in the forecourt. The building was later enlarged. Further extended in 1968, it has recently undergone a major restoration program (1996). In recent years the collection has been extensively published in summary catalogues and monographs which for the first time make available a complete visual record of the gallery's holdings.

The foyer leads through the gallery shop to the central **Atrium** with James Hogan's *Hibernia with a bust of Lord Cloncurry*, and four panels by Felim Egan (b1941). The **Print Gallery** and **Print Room** can be reached from the Atrium, as can the restaurant. The building also accommodates an extensive Art Reference Library and Lecture Theatre (where free public lectures are regularly given).

Irish School. The Irish rooms (1–6), lead directly off the foyer, and are hung in chronological order, from the 17C–20C. Room 7 has a multimedia presentation of the collection. Some 18C portraits are of considerable interest; the superb double portrait by Hugh Douglas Hamilton of *the Earl-bishop of Derry with his granddaughter*; James Barry's intense *Self-portrait as Timanthes*, and Nathaniel Hone the elder's *The Conjuror* (in which he later painted out a naked figure of Angelica Kauffmann, which had caused scandal). Landscape artists include Thomas Roberts; George Barret, *Powerscourt Waterfall* and William Ashford, *A view of Dublin from Chapelizod*.

19C genre subjects include Richard Moynan's amusing *Military Manoeuvres*; Erskine Nicol's social document, *An ejected family*; Daniel Maclise's Victorian set-piece, much reproduced during the 19C, *Charles I and his family before Cromwell*; Thomas Hickey's beautiful *An Indian girl* and Francis Danby's, *Opening of the Sixth Seal*.

Irish followers of Impressionism and Post-Impressionism include Walter Osborne, *In a Dublin Park*, *Portrait of J.S.B. Macilwaine*; several works each by Nathaniel Hone, *Pastures at Malahide*; Roderick O'Conor, *Farm at Lezaven, Finistere*; and William Leech, *Convent Garden, Brittany*.

Outstanding among Irish academic painters of the early 20C are William Orpen's, *Self-portrait holding ptarmigan*; Sir John Lavery's enormous tribute to Velasques, *Lady Hazel Lavery with her daughter Alice and step-daughter Eileen*. John Butler Yeats was an accomplished portrait painter, *Portrait of W.B.Yeats, Miss Lilly Yeats* but the dominant figure in Irish 20C painting was his son, Jack B. Yeats, brother of the poet. *The Liffey Swim, About to Write a Letter, In memory of Boucicault and Bianconi, Grief* and *The Singing Horseman* are representative of his work.

Irish portraits (room 32) include Richard Moynan's *Taking Measurements*, which shows the Gallery in 1878. In the Shaw Room (41) is a statue (1927) of George Bernard Shaw by Paul Troubetzkoy (1866–1938); Shaw bequeathed one third of his estate to the gallery, which had given him so much pleasure in his youth. Also in the room is Daniel Maclise's major work, *The Marriage of Strongbow and Eve*. The Yeats room (8) has not yet been opened.

British School (rooms 33–36). Virtually all the major figures of British 18 and 19C painting are well represented. Among the most charming are J.M. Wright's, *Portraits of Catherine and Charlotte Talbot*, William Hogarth's, *the Mackinen Children*, and Phillip Reinagle's *Mrs Congreve with her Children*; works by Joshua Reynolds include the extrordinary *Portrait of Charles Coote, 1st Earl of Bellamont*. Interesting in an Irish context are Francis Wheatley's, *The Dublin Volunteers on College Green, 4 November 1779*, and portraits of the Marquess and Marchioness of Antrim in their coach.

National Gallery

UPPER LEVELS

Dargan Wing
9   Baroque Gallery
10-11   French 19th & 20th C.
12-13   French 19th C.

Milltown Wing
15   French 18th C.
16   French 17th C.
17   Italian 18th C.
18   Italian 17th C.
19   Caravaggio
    & Followers
20   Italian 16th C.
21   Italian 15th – 16th C.

North Wing
23-25   Early Renaissance
26   Later Flemish
27   Northern Renaissance
28-30   Dutch
31   Spanish

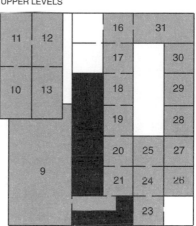

Dargan Wing   Milltown Wing   North Wing

Dargan Wing
41   Shaw Room
8   Yeats Gallery
14   Exhibition Gallery

Milltown Wing
1-6   Irish Rooms
7   Multimedia

North Wing
32   National Portraits
33-36   British
39   Print Gallery

LOWER LEVELS

Much of the gallery's strength lies in its small Dutch masters and works of the 17C French, Italian and Spanish Schools, of which some outstanding examples are listed below.

The Baroque Gallery (room 9) contains large-scale works, principally Italian 16C and 17C.

French School (rooms 10–13, 19C and 20C; 15–16, 17C and 18C). Claude Lorraine, landscapes; Poussin, *The Lamentation*, *The Holy Family*; David, *The Funeral of Patroclus*; Chardin, *Card Trick*; J.F. Millet, *Country Scene with Stile*; Jules Breton, *The Gleaners*; Monet, *Autumn Scene*; Sisley, *Bord du Canal du Loing a St. Mammes*; Picasso, *Still Life*; Juan Gris, *Pierrot*.

Italian School (rooms 17–21). The largest and best represented school in the collection. Includes Paolo Uccello's *The Virgin and Child*; Andrea Mantegna's small grisaille, *Judith with the Head of Holofernes*, one of the finest works in the Gallery; Giovanni Lanfranco, *The Last Supper*; Castiglione, *Shepherdess finding the infant Cyrus*; Giambattista Moroni, *Portrait of a Gentleman and his two children* and Gentileschi's, *David and Goliath*. A recent addition is Caravaggio's, *The Taking of Christ*, which hung for many years, unrecognised, in the house of study of the Jesuit community in Leeson St, not far from Merrion Square.

Gothic and Early Renaissance (rooms 23–25).

Flemish School (room 26). Jacob Jordaens, *The Veneration of the Eucharist*; Rubens/Breughel II, *Christ in the House of Martha and Mary*.

German and Early Netherlandish Schools (room 27). Master of St, Augustine, *Scenes from the life of St. Augustine*; two very fine portraits are Conrad Faber's, *Heinrich* and *Katherina Knoblauch*; Gerard David, *Christ Bidding Farwell to his Mother*.

Dutch School (rooms 28–30). This small collection has some very fine individual works, Rembrandt, *The Flight into Egypt*, *Portrait of a Lady*, and attributed, *Playing 'La Main Chaud'* ; Ferdinand Bol, *David's dying charge to Solomon*; Metsu, *A Woman Reading a Letter*; J. van Ruisdael, Castle at Bentheim; Cornelius Troost, *The Dilettanti*; Mytens, *Lady Playing a Lute*; Franz Hals, *A Young Fisherman*; Johannes Vermeer, *Lady Writing a letter, with her maid*.

Spanish School (room 31). El Greco, *St. Francis Receiving the Stigmata* ; Adam de Coster, *A Man Singing by Candlelight*; J.F. de Navarete, *Abraham and the Three Angels*; Luis de Morales, St. Jerome in the Wilderness; Murillio, *The meeting of Jacob and Rachel*. Diego Velazquez, *Kitchen Maid with the Supper at Emmaus*; Francisco de Goya, *Dona Antonia Zarate*.

On leaving the National Gallery turn right to skirt Leinster Lawn. Look along the south side of Merrion Sq., to the far end of Upper Mount St, where the pepper-pot cupola of **St. Stephen's** (1825; by John Bowden, and completed by Joseph Welland) can be seen. The façade is a collage of influences from Athenian antiquities based on three important buildings, the Erechtheion, the Horologium of Andronikos and the Choragic monument of Lysicrates. Although the exterior is in the Greek Revival style, the interior (containing a Snetzler organ-case designed for the Rotunda Chapel in 1754) is Victorian. Known colloquially as the 'Pepper Cannister', it is the best sited of any Dublin church, ending the vista of Upper Mount St in an exemplary classical manner; it is frequently a venue for concerts.

'Number Twenty Nine', (Tues–Sat 10.00–17.00; Sun 14.00–17.00 (closed Mon) on the corner of Upper Mount St–Lower Fitzwilliam St (at the south-east corner of the square), has been restored to the style of a professional family home as it would have been in c 1790–1820, with furniture from the National Museum of Ireland's collection. Entered through the basement at the street-corner, the visitor can walk through the house to the attic. Rooms have been decorated on all levels with the art and artefacts of the period.

At the end of Upper Mount St, Hubband Bridge (1791), the most attractive of the humpbacked canal bridges crosses the Grand Canal to Percy Place, a sylvan section of the late Georgian inner city.

Return to Merrion St. You now reach the entrance of the **Natural History Museum** (1856) (10.00–17.00 Tues–Sat; 14.00–17.00, Sun; closed Mon) its interior preserved, like a fly in amber, as it must have been at its inauguration. It contains a remarkably complete collection of Irish fauna, including three perfect skeletons of the prehistoric Irish elk, or, more correctly, Giant Deer (*Megaloceros giganteus*), which became extinct c 8000 BC. The museum, which has charmed children for many generations with its fascinating collection of plant and animal life, is in its 19C ambience a total contrast to modern ideas of museum display. On the upper galleries is the 19C Blaschka collection of glass models of marine plants, masterpieces of botanical accuracy and glass craftsmanship. In front of the Museum is an excellent statue of Surgeon-Major Park (Percy Wood 1896), who accompanied Livingstone to Africa.

Further south, on the opposite side of Upper Merrion St, No. 24, Mornington House was the birthplace of Arthur Wellesley, first Duke of Wellington (29 April 1769–1852), the fourth son of Garrett Wellesley (1735–81), first Earl of Mornington, who held the chair of music at Trinity College on its establishment in 1764.

Pass **Government Buildings** (Sat 11.00–16.00; tickets from National Gallery; OPW) on the right and Taoiseach's Office, built as the Royal College of Science (1904–22; by Sir Aston Webb and Sir Thomas Manley Deane). It is an overblown Edwardian-baroque 'palace', the last great classical building to be erected in Dublin; with its Merrion St façade it acknowledges a debt to Gandon's Custom House. The central courtyard is broken on the street side by a columned screen through which the dome over the main block can be seen; the cornice embellished with sculptural groups by Albert Power and Oliver Sheppard representing the arts and sciences. Above the main stairs in the front hall is Evie Hone's window 'My Four Green Fields' executed for the Irish Pavilion at the New York World Fair, 1939, it spent the following fifty years in a packing case. Conducted tours of Taoiseach's office, cabinet room, etc, take place on Saturday (tickets gratis from National Gallery).

You soon reach Baggot St; the artist Francis Bacon (1909–1993) was born at No. 63 Lower Baggot St; No. 67 (embellished with a bas-relief) was the home of

Thomas Davis (1814–45), leader of the 'Young Ireland' party. No. 134 was for many years the premises of the Cuala Press, run by Elizabeth and Susan Yeats, sisters of the poet, which published books written by W.B.Yeats and broadsheets illustrated by Jack B. Yeats, among others.

The southeast extension of Baggot St leads to the residential suburb of Ballsbridge. In Lower Baggot St, not far beyond East Fitzwilliam St, is the **Bank of Ireland Headquarters** (10.00–15.00 weekdays except Thurs, 10.00–12.30; 13.30–17.00) (Ronald Tallon, 1972), an arrangement of three slab blocks clad in bronze with dark glass. It is Dublin's most successful building in the Mies van der Rohe idiom. Between the blocks a courtyard opens to Baggot St. In the foyer—an exhibition venue—hangs an impressive Aubusson tapestry by Patrick Scott, entitled 'Blaze'.

Beyond, to the right, in Wilton Terrace, are the offices of **Bord Fáilte** (the Irish Tourist Board), with an information desk, overlooking the Grand Canal; while to the left is Herbert Pl. Elizabeth Bowen (1899–1973) was born and spent her childhood at No. 15, which she wrote about in *Seven Winters* (1942).

A short distance south is **Fitzwilliam Square**, the smallest, latest (1825), and best-preserved of Dublin's Georgian squares. It is now the Harley Street of Dublin, being almost entirely occupied by the medical profession. W.B. Yeats lived in a flat at No. 42 (1928–32). The central park still remains private, the only one to do so.

Opposite Upper Merrion St and directly south, across Baggot St is **Ely Place** (pronounced to rhyme with 'high'), a cul-de-sac preserving some interesting houses (c 1770). Long associated with the law, it was the home (No. 4) of John Philpot Curran (1750–1817) and of the unpopular Earl of Clare, an opponent of Catholic emancipation, derisively called 'Black Jack' Fitzgibbon (1749–1802). When Lord Chancellor he had to barricade his house (No. 6) against a hostile mob (1794). No. 8, **Ely House** is one of the finest Georgian mansions in the city, with a remarkable staircase depicting the Labours of Hercules, and Adam plasterwork by Michael Stapleton. Barry Yelverton, Lord Avonmore (1736–1805) lived at No. 3. No. 4 was also the residence of the writer, George Moore (1852–1933) from 1900–11 and is described in his trilogy, *Hail and Farewell*.

No. 25, the home of the politician and essayist John Wilson Croker (1780–1857), and later of Oliver St. John Gogarty, now occupied by the **Royal Hibernian Academy Gallagher Gallery** (Raymond McGrath, 1973) (11.00–17.00, Mon–Sat; closes at 21.00, Thurs) has the finest suite of modern exhibition rooms in the city. The Summer Show of the RHA has been an institution since 1826, surviving such traumas as having the entire exhibition of 1916 (as well as the then RHA building in Lower Abbey St) burnt out during the insurrection. The galleries are also used for a mixed programme of individual and group exhibitions throughout the year. The Academy was incorporated by charter in 1823.

No. 36 was briefly the home of the poetess, Mrs Felicia Hemans (1793–1835) perhaps best known for *Casabianca*: 'The boy stood on the burning deck' and 'The stately homes of England'. Turn west at the bottom of Upper Merrion St into Merrion Row, passing (right) the Huguenot cemetery (1693).

St. Stephen's Green, once surrounded by a 'dirty ditch...the recepticle of dead cats and dogs', according to Sir John Carr (1806) is now a park of nine hectares. It was an open common until 1663, although not finally encircled by buildings until the late 17C, and the scene of public hangings until the 18C. The gardens were laid out in 1880 as a public park at the expense of the brewer Lord Ardilaun (Sir Arthur Edward Guinness, 1840–1915). It is the most popular city-centre park in Dublin and contains a small lake with flocks of ornamental waterbirds, and also many political monuments. A statue of the leader of the United Irishmen who accompanied the French 1796 invasion, Wolfe Tone by Edward Delany (1967), stands at the north-east corner (known as 'Tonehenge'); it has lost its two wolfhounds. On the reverse of the granite screen wall is the most poignant monument in the city, *Famine*, also by Delaney. On the west of the gardens is *Knife Edge* (1967), a memorial to W.B. Yeats by Henry Moore. Here also are busts of the poet, James Clarence Mangan (1803–49; by Oliver Sheppard); Thomas M. Kettle (1880–1916), poet and patriot; Jeremiah O'Donovan Rossa (1839–1915), the Fenian; Countess Constance Markievicz, (1884–1927, by Seamus Murphy), a prominent member of the Citizen Army (1916) and a statue of Lord Ardilaun is by Thomas Farrell.

More than any of Dublin's squares, Stephen's Green has been subject to drastic re-development, and almost the entire west side has been replaced by modern buildings while substantial portions of the east side have been reduced by bogus Georgian office blocks.

On the east side, No. 21 is the headquarters of the Office of Public Works (OPW). No. 52, now the Ombudsman's Office, built in 1771, has ceiling panels on the *piano nobile* by the Swiss decorative painter, Anjelica Kaufmann (1741–1807) and a grisaille of Apollo and the Muses by Peter de Gree.

From the south east corner of the Green, Lower Leeson St leads east and Earlsfort Terrace south. On the west side of Earlsfort Terrace is a severe plain granite building reconstructed in 1978–81 to house the **National Concert Hall**, the main concert hall of the city. The long low stripped-classicism of the façade is (like Government Buildings) a discreet compliment to Gandon. It was formerly the home of University College Dublin (R.M. Butler, 1912) which in turn incorporates the hall of the Dublin International Exhibition of 1865 (Alfred Gresham Jones), University College was incorporated in 1909 as one of the constituent colleges of the National University, which succeeded the Royal University. Among eminent members of UCD have been Douglas Hyde (Professor of Modern Irish,1908–32, first President of the Irish Free State) and Eoin MacNill, co-founders of the Gaelic League; Brian O'Nolan (Flann O'Brien) 1911–66, novelist; Cyril Cusack (1910–93) actor (see Belfield campus).

Behind the Concert Hall and reached through an obscure gate in the rear (right) perimeter wall, is Dublin's least known park, the **Iveagh Gardens**. In a succession of incarnations this secret garden belonged variously to Clonmell House in Harcourt St (the first home of Hugh Lane's collection of modern art), Iveagh House, and now to UCD. Re-designed by Ninian Niven for the 1865 Exhibition as a pleasure ground, between the trees are scattered remnants of Niven's classical garden ornamentation; also reached from Clonmell Place off Harcourt St.

The author George Borrow stayed briefly at No. 75 St. Stephen's Green South in the summer of 1859, prior to a walking tour in Ireland. No. 80, Iveagh House, the earliest house in Dublin by Richard Castle (1730), but much altered, was built for Robert Clayton, Bishop of Cork, and was later the residence of

Lord Iveagh. It is now the Department of Foreign Affairs, incorporating No. 81. The extravagant Victorian ballroom (1863) was designed by William Young of London.

A few doors further on is **Newman House** (10.00–16.00, Tue–Fri, June–Sept; Oct–May groups by appointment; £) which incorporates two exceptionally fine 18C town-houses, comprising No. 85, **Clanwilliam House** (1738), and No. 86 (1765); the ambitious and scholarly restoration project currently in progress (David Sheehan for University College Dublin) is the finest undertaken in Ireland.

No. 85, of two storeys and three bays, is a miniature Palladian 'palazzo'. The first Dublin house to have a stone façade, it was designed by Richard Castle, architect of some of the city's greatest 18C buildings, including Leinster and Tyrone Houses, the Rotunda Hospital, and Russborough and Powerscourt Houses in Co. Wicklow.

Built for Captain Hugh Montgomery and conceived as a house for entertainment rather than for residence, Clanwilliam House is elegantly decorated in a refined Baroque manner. Off the entrance hall which preserves the original black and white marble floor paving and pine wainscoting, is the **Apollo Room**, embellished with high relief stucco panels by the Italian stuccodores Paul and Phillip Lafranchini. The walls have been restored to their original delicate colour scheme; the panels represent Apollo (after the Apollo Belvedere), surrounded by the nine Muses, derived from the antique after engravings published by Maffei (1704). Despite its small size (4.5 x 6m), the room is among the most remarkable stucco decorative schemes to survive from the 18C.

From the hall an arched screen leads into an arcaded space from which a Cuban mahogany staircase with Tuscan balusters rises to the *piano nobile*, where the **Saloon** occupies the entire frontage; here the ceiling, also by the Lafranchini brothers has panels of allegorical figures after Simon Vouet (1590–1649), in an elaborate manner hardly equalled in other Dublin houses. The panels on the coving of the end walls represent 'good government', those on the sides, the elements of earth, air, fire, water. The marble chimney-piece has been re-created from the design of the lost original, based on 1910 Georgian Society records. Early 18C houses retaining interiors of such quality are exceptionally rare in Ireland.

A mural staircase leads to the adjoining house, No 86. Also stone-faced but of five bays and four storeys, it dwarfs its neighbour, and was built for Richard Chapel Whaley in 1765 (he had acquired No. 85 years earlier), and probably designed by the stuccodore, Robert West. (Whaley was known as 'Burn-Chapel' for his priest-hunting activities; his son was the dashing eccentric Thomas 'Buck' Whaley (1766–1800) who for a wager of £20,000 travelled to Jerusalem and back in a year (1788). In contrast to the Baroque Saloon of No. 85, No. 86 is decorated with lavish Rococo plasterwork also by West. The decorative scheme of the spacious and lofty stair hall is based on musical allusions, with bas-relief groups of 18C instruments. The reception rooms await restoration. Over the Doric entrance portico is a lion couchant in lead by Van Nost.

In 1854, the **Catholic University** received its first students at No. 86, and by 1865 had acquired adjoining Clanwilliam House; the houses were later linked internally, the saloon being used as a chapel and the naked bodies of Juno and other figures on the ceiling were clothed with plaster 'bathing costumes' (one of these unfashionable garments has been retained). Associated with Newman House are the first rector of the Catholic University, John Henry Newman (1801–90), Gerard Manley Hopkins (1844–89), poet and Professor of Classics, and James Joyce who was a student here from 1899–1902.

Other rooms in No. 86 are restored to commemorate different periods in the complex history of the building. The **Bishop's Room**, used from 1851 as a meeting place for the committee of the Catholic University, is furnished in dark and ponderous Victorian ecclesiastical taste, and in the attic is the austere bedroom of Gerard Manley Hopkins, as well as a lecture theatre from the original Catholic University, furnished as in Joyce's student days. The *Commons Restaurant* in the vaulted basement is one of the city's most elegant eating places.

Newman's University Church (John Hungerford Pollen, 1855) adjoining No. 86 is a miniature Byzantine-Romanesque basilica, decorated in the manner of an Italian church of the 11C. Stylistically it is totally at variance with the Gothic or classical tradition of 19C Irish church building, and makes a fair claim to be the most eccentric church interior in Ireland. This Pre-Raphaelite curiosity was created while Pollen was Professor of Fine Art at the Catholic University. Entered through a brick porch which leads by a descending passageway from the street and through a forest of columns with variously carved capitals under the balcony, the building opens out into a tall narrow painted rectangle. The church perfectly reflects Newman's ambition—to 'build a large barn and decorate it in the style of a basilica'.

From the south-west corner of the Green, Harcourt St curves south, many of its brick houses retaining good 18C stucco work. No. 6, now a Celtic bookshop, became famous as the headquarters of Sinn Féin. This, together with other houses in the street, was occupied by various proscribed departments attempting to function surreptitiously with the government set up after the 1918 election had been 'proclaimed'. Edward Carson (1854–1935), the opponent of Home Rule, was born at No. 4. The former Harcourt St Station, at the far end of the street (left), built by George Wilkinson in 1859, has been converted into offices.

No. 33 (then No. 3) Synge St, four streets to the west of and parallel to the south end of Harcourt St, was the modest birthplace of George Bernard Shaw (1856–1950), restored as the **Shaw Birthplace Museum** (May–Oct Mon–Sat 10.00–17.00; Sun and BH 14.00–18.00; closed 13.00–14.00 daily; closed Nov–Apr; £) to house a collection of Shaviana, 'I am pure Dublin. We are a family of Pooh Bahs —snobs to the backbone. Drink and lunacy are minor specialities' (G.B.S., 1912).

Cuffe St lies to the northeast of Synge St and west from the south-west corner of St. Stephen's Green. No. 35 was the home of 'Honest Jack' Lawless (1773–1837) the intimate of many United Irish leaders. Shelley stayed here on his second visit to Dublin (1813).

On the west side of the Green, the only important building remaining is that of the **Royal College of Surgeons** (Edward Parke, 1806; extended in 1825 by William Murray), which became the HQ of the Citizens' Army during Easter Week, 1916. The Countess Markievicz, second in command of the garrison (the only woman in a position of authority), fought in a tailored uniform especially created for the occasion by her dressmaker. Nos 124–25 are the last 18C town houses on the west side. Robert Emmet, a spirited bronze of whom (Jerome Conor, 1917) stands on the opposite pavement, was born in an adjoining house, now demolished.

The **St. Stephen's Green Shopping Centre** (1989), on the corner of South King St is in Mississippi steamboat-gothic style. The interior—which contains a 28'6" diameter clock (6'6" larger than Big Ben) by the horologists Stokes of Cork—is spatially interesting.

In South King St is the Gaiety Theatre (C.J. Phillips, 1871) Dublin's oldest theatre, the interior is decorated in the Victorian music hall 'gilt and gingerbread' tradition. It is the venue for the twice yearly Dublin Grand Opera Society's seasons as well as pantomime and touring performances. At the northwest corner of the Green is the Fusilier's Arch, a miniature neo-classical triumphal arch (1907), in memory of the Royal Dublin Fusiliers killed in the Boer War.

Much of the north side of the Green was reconstructed in the 19C, although a few earlier houses remain, some with 19C façades, and there are several modern intrusions towards the east end. Nos 8, 9, 17 and 22 house club buildings, the 'gentlemen's' clubs of the past, which were themselves successors of the 18C coffee houses, now somewhat more egalitarian than when in 1887 George Moore observed of that bastion of landed conservatism, the **Kildare St Club**, 'This club is a sort of oyster-bed into which all the eldest sons of the landed gentry fall as a matter of course. There they remain, spending their days, drinking sherry and cursing Gladstone'. No. 9, the exclusive Stephen's Green Club, built in 1765, has Lafranchini plasterwork, including allegorical panels on the staircase.

Turn east along the north side of St. Stephen's Green, once known as 'Beaux Walk', shortly passing Dawson St to reach, on the corner of Kildare St, the **Shelbourne Hotel** (described in *A Drama in Muslin* by George Moore, one of many celebrated figures to have resided there). It is still a popular meeting place. Its interesting history has been written up by Elizabeth Bowen (*The Shelbourne Hotel*, 1951). During the 1930s, Aloys Hitler, half-brother of the more famous Adolf, worked here as a wine waiter—he was married to an Irishwoman. The present building dates from 1865–67; it was the earlier hotel on the site of Shelburne House (sic), opened in 1824, which had been patronised by Thackeray in 1842. A few doors further on the right is the **Earth Sciences Museum** (10.00–17.00, Tues–Sat; 14.00–17.00, Sun; closed Mon) 7–9 Merrion Row, houses exhibitions dealing with geology.

In Kildare St, we pass (left) the Department of Industry and Commerce, a stripped-classical building by J.R Boyd Barrett (1942), with socialist-realism bas-relief panels by Gabriel Hayes (1909–78). On the right we reach the main front of **Leinster House**, its quadrangle flanked by the **National Museum** and the **National Library**, two nearly symmetrical buildings by Sir Thomas Deane (1890), the main features of which are their massive colonnaded entrance rotundas.

Leinster House, (when Dail is not in session, apply to Kildare St entrance) occupied by the Royal Dublin Society (RDS) from 1815 to 1921, was the core from 1855 onwards of an interconnected cultural complex of National Museum, Library, Gallery, Natural History Museum and College of Art. With the conversion of the central block into the Dail, the cohesion of this inspired arrangement was lost (the orphaned Gallery and History Museum can only be reached from Merrion Sq.).

The National Museum of Ireland

The National Museum of Ireland (Tue–Sat 10.00–17.00; Sun 14.00–17.00; closed Mon) houses a remarkable collection of Irish antiquities, among them some of the finest examples of prehistoric, Early-Christian and medieval metal-work in Europe. The greater part of the collection was made by the Royal Irish Academy, and transferred here in 1891. It is now divided between two buildings, the main archeological collection (prehistoric–Medieval periods), much of which has been on display at Kildare Street for a century, and the new **Collins Barracks** (see p. 60) venue which holds the applied arts collections of glass and ceramics, silver, furniture, scientific instruments and folk-art.

From the entrance Rotunda (with bookshop) we enter the centre court containing the superb 'OR' (gold) exhibition, Irish Bronze Age gold objects of intoxicating richness, with bracelets, collars, dress-fasteners, earrings and other personal ornaments c 2200–700 BC. Surrounding this is an exhibition of func-tional and ritual objects from prehistoric Ireland (7000 BC–Iron Age), and equally fascinating, including the Dowris Hoard (c 500 BC), a set of trumpets, parts of an ancient wooden roadway (c 400 BC), a gruesome 'bog burial' (c 200 BC); the **Lurgan Longboat**, found in 1902, and carved from a single 15.25m long oak tree-trunk dates from c 2500 BC.

To the right is the **Treasury**, conceived as the treasury of a medieval cathe-dral, and containing the most famous ecclesiastical objects in the collection, remarkable both for their beauty and craftsmanship, as well as other individual pieces from the Iron Age to the late Middle Ages. In the outer room, among the more notable objects are those of the Broighter Hoard (Co. Derry; 1C BC) of gold lunules, torques, and gorgets; necklaces of hollow balls, and thin hammered discs; 'ring-money', a model boat, and amber beads.

In the main room—off which is an audio-visual show on Irish antiquities—are concentrated the master-works of the early-Christian period. One display case shows the development of the penannular brooch or fibula (6C–10C), a characteristic form of Irish ornament; others contain bronze articles—bucklers, cauldrons, trumpets, spear and axe-heads, the iron bell of St. Patrick and its shrine, also a buckler of leather, and two of alder-wood. Another case describes the development of the axe, spear, and sword from 2000 to 250 BC.

At the opposite end are the crosier-shrines, including those of St. Berach, St. Mura of Fahan and St. Dymphna of Tedavnet (all 11C); those of Clonmacnoise (also 11C), and Lismore (c 1100), and the crosier of Cormac MacCarthy, king-bishop of Cashel (died 1138), Limoges enamels (early 12C) are also displayed here.

Among outstanding items are the **Ardagh Chalice** (early 8C, found together with the adjacent cup and brooches, of a later date, in a rath at Ardagh, Co. Limerick, in 1868). This two-handled cup of silver, heavily alloyed with copper, is decorated with a variety of Celtic ornamentation; its bands and bosses, gold filigree work, studs of cloisonné and the names of the twelve apostles, should be closely examined. Another remarkable group of objects is the **Derrynaflan Hoard**, including a chalice and paten, found in Co. Tipperary in 1980. The finest of a notable series of processional crosses and crucifixes, mainly 13–15C (including the large Ballymacasey Cross made for Cornelius O'Connor of Kerry in 1479) is the **Cross of Cong** (1123), made of oak sheathed with silver and with panels of gilt bronze, richly adorned with interlacing patterns and jewelled bosses. It was made by order of Turlough O'Connor for the church at Tuam, and brought to Cong by Roderick O'Connor.

The **Shrine of St. Patrick's Bell** (12C) of bronze ornamented with silver-gilt, gold filigree and gems, is the finest of numerous bell-shrines; it was made to enclose the bronze-coated iron bell of St. Patrick, the oldest example of Irish metal-work known to survive. Other examples are the Clog n Oir, or Golden Bell of St. Senan, from Scattery, and the Corp Naoimh, another bell-shrine, preserving its leather satchel, from Temple Cross, Co. Meath.

Another case contains the *Breac Maodhog*, notable for details of costume, also with its leather satchel, made in the 11C for St. Moedoc of Drumlane (Co. Cavan); and the Lough Erne reliquaries (8C), one inside the other. Curious also are the shrines of St. Lachtin's arm (1118–27); of St. Brigid's shoe (1410; from Loughrea); the Fiacal Phadraig (1376; containing the tooth that fell from St. Patrick's head at Killespugbrone, near Sligo); the Domnach Airgid (8C, with an outer case of 1350); and other book-shrines, including that of the Stowe Missal (1045–52). Also displayed here is the **Tara Brooch** (700–750; found on the shore near Bettystown in 1850), the richest surviving example of the penannular type of brooch common in Irish art; it is of white bronze, decorated with patterns of great delicacy, and studded with glass and amber. Here too is the Moylough belt-shrine (8C) from near Tubbercurry, of silvered bronze with applied enamel decoration. An example from the collection of Sheila-na-gigs (grotesque medieval stone carvings of sexual significance) is on display.

To the left of the centre court is a historical collection dealing with the period 1900–23, tracing the background of the 1916 Rising, with memorabilia of the leaders and participants. The café is off this room.

Stairs ascend to the first floor, to all appearances a conservatory. The **Viking Rooms** display a remarkably fine collection of artefacts dealing with daily life, trade, craftsmanship and warfare during the Viking Age in Ireland, including many objects from excavations in Dublin.

The National Library

To the north of the museum is the **National Library** (10.00–21.00, Mon–Fri; 10.00–13.00 Sat; closed Mon). The main library or reading-room (in the upper part of the rotunda, matching that of the museum), on the first floor, was opened in 1890 to accommodate the collections of the Royal Dublin Society (founded as the Dublin Society in 1731), previously shelved in Leinster House, and purchased by the State in 1877. Among the library's items are printed and manuscript material relating to Irish history, topography, language, literature, folklore and the visual arts. This included the **Jolly Collection** of some 23,000 printed books and 6000 pamphlets, containing among its rareties Thomas Carve's *Lyra* (Vienna, 1651). There is also a representative collection of first editions of 17C Irish authors, and of Swift, Goldsmith, Yeats, Joyce, etc.; a collection devoted to the Napoleonic period; and the archives of the Ormond and O'Brien families, etc. Among its MSS are a 13C copy of Giraldus Cambrensis's *Topographia Hibernica* (c 1190); G.B. Shaw's early novels; a copy of Joyce's *Portrait of the Artist as a Young Man*; and the diary of Joseph Holloway (from 1895–1944), minutely describing the Irish theatre during this period; and more recent donations. It also contains an unrivalled collection of old Irish maps, topographical prints and drawings, etc. Among its newspapers is a run of the

Freeman's Journal (1763–1924). Since 1927 the library has been a legal deposit library for all material published in Ireland. A 35mm film is available, being a visual record from the 17C–19C of prints and drawings in the National Library and of the **Lawrence Collection of Photographs of Ireland** (1880–1910; some 25,000 plates). A recent feature is the valuable collection of microfilm copies of Irish documents and MSS in foreign archives and libraries.

Leinster House, is the seat of the *Oireachtas* or parliament of the Irish Republic, a bi-cameral executive, divided into Dáil (house of representatives) and Seanad (senate). Built as Kildare House by Richard Castle (1745) for the Earl of Kildare, but changed to its present name on his son being elevated to Duke of Leinster in 1766. Lord Edward Fitzgerald, son of the Duke of Leinster, grew up in the house, which he disliked. The third Duke sold the house to the RDS in 1815, from whom it was acquired by the government in 1922–24. The Kildare St façade, eleven bays with pedimented central projecting portico, influenced many other Dublin buildings such as the Rotunda (also by Castle), Trinity College west front, and Iveagh House, as late as the 1860s.

Although the interior has been altered to accommodate its varying functions, rooms designed by Castle, Sir William Chambers and James Wyatt remain. The chamber used by the Dáil was introduced by the RDS in 1897 as a lecture theatre; the Senate, however, is lodged in the picture gallery of the 18C house. The Royal Irish Academy occupies an extension of the original building, opened in 1897 as a lecture hall. Of more interest are the rooms of the Seanad, to the left of the entrance, with some good 18C mantelpieces, doorways, stuccoed and compartmented ceilings, etc.; the ceiling in the Senate chamber itself was designed by Wyatt in 1780. In his last speech here W.B. Yeats suggested that it was more desirable and important to have able men than representative men in the House! Note at the foot of the stair near the Library door the ensign of the 69th Regiment of Meagher's Irish Brigade (who fought at Virginia and Maryland). It was presented to the people of Ireland by John Fitzgerald Kennedy, then President of the United States, on his visit to Leinster House in June 1963.

Opposite the entrance to Leinster House, Molesworth St, retaining (left) some 18C houses with Georgian shopfronts, extends west. Left at No. 17 is **Freemason's Hall** (Edward Holmes, 1866), the most eclectic building in Dublin. Built as a Grand Lodge, its ponderous façade has three superimposed classical orders with Masonic symbols in the tympanum of the pediment. The interior combines every style available to a Victorian architect, with the Royal Arch Chapter Room in Egyptian manner, complete with sphinxes; the Grand Lodge Room in the style of Roman classicism, while the Knight's Templar and Prince's Mason Chapter Rooms exploit different medieval periods. The building also houses a good small museum of Masonic regalia. At the far end of Molesworth St is Dawson St. On the left of the north half of Kildare St is the building of the Royal College of Physicians, incorporated in 1667.

Turning left into Dawson St pass St. Ann's, a well-designed church (by Isaac Wills; 1720) hidden behind an uncompleted mid-19C façade by Sir Thomas Deane, but containing good woodwork (including shelving of 1723 used for the distribution of bread to the poor of the parish).

The Royal Irish Academy

The Royal Irish Academy, founded in 1785 (by the Earl of Charlemont), for the encouragement of science and learning is on the same side of Dawson St (No. 19). It has occupied these premises, with charming stuccoes in the vestibule, since 1852. The library contains some 2500 valuable MSS, either Irish or related to Ireland, including 58 leaves of the Cathach or MS Psalter of St. Columba, traditionally dating from 560; the Leabhar Breac ('the speckled book'; before 1411); and the 11C–12C *Leabhar nah Uidhre*, or Book of the Dun Cow. Among material brought from the Buckingham collection (c 1800–49) is the Stowe Missal (early 9C, and probably originating from Tallaght); the *Book of Ui Maine* (c 1390); the Book of Ballymote (early 15C); and the Annals of the Four Masters (1632–36; from Donegal). The library also houses over 30,000 volumes, the majority relating to Ireland, and other collections including Thomas Moore's library and early scientific books.

Adjacent is the **Mansion House** (1710, with a Victorian stucco façade), residence of the Lord Mayor and the oldest domestic building in continuous occupation in the city. The Round Room, or Rotunda, an addition by John Semple (1821) was built to accommodate a banquet held in honour of George IV's visit. The Declaration of Irish Independence was adopted here in 1919.

Dublin Castle, Christ Church & St. Patrick's Cathedrals

From College Green the old High St runs west under the successive names of Dame St, Cork Hill, Lord Edward St and Christchurch Pl. Dame St, once the principal resort of 'the goldsmiths, is now flanked by the largest assemblage of Victorian banks in the city. The AIB in Foster Place has an impressive banking hall by Charles Geoghan (1859), while the AIB on the corner of Dame St and Palace St, by Sir Thomas Deane (1872) is in his best Venetian manner. The composer, Francesco Geminiani (1687–1762), lived and taught for several years in Dame St, in a house with a concert-room attached. Dame St, inclining upwards towards the original Hill of Dublin, leads directly to the heart of the Viking and medieval city.

Temple Bar is on the right, between Dame St and the Liffey, which it parallels. The **Temple Bar Quarter**, an area of 17C–19C houses scheduled for demolition since the 1960s, when such modest architecture was anathema to town planners and developers. The area is now being restored as a cultural quarter. The city's 'Left Bank', it is the most successful example of urban renewal in Dublin. The narrow cobbled streets and small buildings represent Dublin streetscape before the improving hand of the 18C Wide Street Commissioners changed the appearance of the city. Excellent modern architecture has been added to the quarter in a manner which enhances the historic buildings; the **Curved Street**, **Art House** and the **Green Building** (a self-sustaining ecological apartment block), are all of interest. The central artery running east–west through the quarter, Fleet St, Temple Bar, Essex Streets East and West, have gathered around them numerous important cultural institutions; the Dublin Graphic Studio Gallery, the **Irish Film Centre** (cinema opening hours) and **National Film Archive** (in an early 18C Society of Friends Meeting House); the Photography Centre and **Gallery of Photography**

(10.00–17.00, Mon–Sat), **Temple Bar Gallery** and Studios; Project Arts Centre and Theatre; Design Yard and **Ark Children's Cultural Centre** (09.30–16.00, Mon–Sat; 09.30–19.00, Thurs) in a 1715 former Presbyterian Meeting House. Meeting House Square has an outdoor cinema screen. There are also many interesting ethnic restaurants, bars, small hotels and commercial art galleries. The **Viking Adventure** (09.30–16.30, Mon, Thurs–Sat; 11.00–18.00, Sun; £) in Lower Exchange St, presents an audio-visual programme on life in Viking Dublin.

Returning to Dame St, on the right the **Central Bank** (Sam Stephenson, 1978), a structurally daring office building in which the floors are suspended by external cables, conflicts with the scale of the street and is the dominant feature of its north side. Facing into the Bank piazza is the reconstructed and rotated façade of Edward Parke's Commercial Buildings (1796–99). On the opposite side of Dame St, through a narrow alleyway marked on the pavement with a mosaic of a stag, is the *Stag's Head*, a pleasant Victorian 'brown pub', and off Trinity St (on the same side) is, in Suffolk St, St. Andrew's church by Lanyon, Lynn and Lanyon (1873), successor to the medieval St. Mary de Hogges; Vanessa Vanhomrigh, a friend of Swift, is buried in the churchyard, now concealed beneath the street. The building now houses the main tourist facility of **Dublin Tourist Centre**.

North Great George's St (left) leads to the **South City Markets** (1878), a red brick and terracotta tile Victorian 'palace of trade', and opposite it *The Long Hall*, an atmospheric late Victorian bar. Further left on Dame St is the **City Hall** (10.00–13.00, 14.15–17.00; Mon–Fri) (Thomas Cooley, 1769), built as the Royal Exchange, a bulky neo-classical Corinthian temple with porticoes on the north and west fronts. The central rotunda, supported by 12 columns, shelters statues of local worthies, Daniel O'Connell, 1846, Thomas Davis, 1853, both by John Hogan and Dr Charles Lucas, by Edward Smyth, but it has been spoilt by the enclosure of the open aisles which originally surrounded it. Since 1852 it has been occupied by the Dublin Corporation except during its suspension in 1925–32. The City Archives contains charters dating back to 1172 and the ancient regalia of the corporation. Dr Barnado, founder of Barnardo's Homes, was born at No. 4 Dame St in 1845.

Opposite in Parliament St, cut through existing buildings by the Wide Street Commissioners to link up the north and south banks of the river over Essex (now Grattan) Bridge, No. 4 Thomas Read has been a cutler's business since 1670. The shop contains original 18C furniture and display cabinets; No. 27 was the premises of George Faulkner (?1699–1775), Swift's printer. To the right is Essex St East, the site (until 1815) of the Smock-Alley Theatre, founded in 1637 by John Ogilby, a Scottish printer. George Farquhar played his first part here in 1697 and Thomas Sheridan managed the theatre (rebuilt 1735) in 1745–59 (except for a brief interval). At the north end of the street, on the corner of Essex Quay is **Sunlight Chambers** by Edward Oud (1901), an Italianate palazzo with a two-tier polychrome ceramic Art Noveau freeze in high-relief, depicting the (pre-feminist) history of soap (men work and get clothes dirty, women wash them clean with soap!).

In Palace St is the curiously inscribed **Sick and Indigent Roomkeepers Association**, 1790, an 18C house with monumental external stucco inscription. In parallel Cork St is **Newcomen's Bank** (Thomas Ivory, 1781), added to in 1888 by doubling its size with a mirror-image of Ivory's building, both parts clipped together by an Ionic porch (the side which faces the castle is the original). Finished externally in Portland stone with delicate niches and swags in an Adam manner, it has a fine staircase and oval room on the first floor; now the offices of Dublin Corporation.

Dublin Castle

Dublin Castle (10.00–17.00, Mon–Fri; State Apartments: 14.00–17.00, Sat–Sun; closed daily 12.15–14.00; OPW). From Dame St there are two entrances to the Castle, from Palace St which leads into the Lower Yard and from Cork St into Upper Yard, which has been the principal entrance since the founding of the fortress.

'The Castle' (as it was both familiarly and derisively referred to during its long heyday as the centre of English rule), today resembles 18C collegiate architecture with two quadrangles, Upper and Lower Castle Yards, each surrounded by brick buildings, the last major public building in Georgian Dublin to be built in brick. Its Anglo-Norman origins are now only hinted at above ground by the Record Tower in Lower Yard. The building of the Anglo-Norman castle (1213–28) was ordered by Henry II on 30 August 1204 when he issued a commissioning mandate to his half-brother Meiler FitzHenry, Justiciar of Ireland.

'The King to his trusty and well-beloved Meiler, son of Henry, Justiciar of Ireland, greetings. You have given us to understand that you have no safe place for the custody of our treasure and, because for this reason and for many others we are in need of a strong fortress in Dublin, we commend you to erect a castle there in such a place as you may consider to be suitable for the administration of justice and if need be for the defence of the city, making it as strong as you can with good ditches and strong walls'.

What was actually built corresponds fairly closely to the King's instructions. The building itself was begun by Henry de Londres, Archbishop of Dublin.

Since the 13C, the Castle, which is on a high ridge of land with the terrain sloping away on all sides, has been the main defence of the city of Dublin. It was never successfully besieged and withstood an attack by Thomas Fitzgerald in 1534, as well as successive attacks in later rebellions, 1646, 1798 and 1803, culminating in that of Easter Monday 1916 when it was attacked by insurgents, some 50 of whom died and were buried temporarily in Castle Yard, but it was not taken by the attackers. The first Lord Deputy to make his residence here was Sir Henry Sidney (1565), and it remained the official seat of the lords lieutenant until the establishment of the Free State in 1922.

The Anglo-Norman fortress closely resembles other Norman castles built throughout Ireland during the 12th and 13C, Ferns, Roscommon, Trim and Kilkenny, the dominant characteristics of which are a large open quadrilateral keep surrounded by a curtain wall with massive circular drum towers at the corners and an entrance gateway protected by smaller D-shaped towers in one of the curtain walls. Dublin Castle was typical of this type of fortification with the additional safeguard of a moat on its two sides exposed to attack, provided by the waters of the Poddle river which still runs under the castle (the other two sides were within the city). Remains of all four towers and some fragments of the wall can still be seen, in varying degrees of preservation. From the 13C–16C the outward form of the castle hardly changed, as a late map of 1673 shows, though cluttered inside with a mass of disorganised buildings, and now surrounded by the growing city, it still in the 17C preserves the form which it was given in 1213.

It was not until the early 18C that the castle's present appearance began to develop. The development of **Upper Castle Yard** is attributed to the Surveyor General, Sir William Robinson, the arcaded appearance of which closely resembles his design for the Royal Hospital, Kilmainham. However, the architects of the other buildings are not known. Upper Castle Yard has on its south wing the **State Apartments**, built as residence for the viceroy and still used for State functions such as the inauguration of the Presidents of Ireland. Opposite, on the north side of the yard is the Palladian **Bedford Tower**, a small five bay building with an open loggia on the first floor, surmounted by an altogether out of scale cupola. The building is redeemed by a pair of robust Baroque entrances, flanked by broken pediments, surmounted by lead figures by Van Nost; Mars on the west and Justice on the east.

In **Lower Castle Yard** the medieval **Record Tower** is the dominant feature, re-faced and Gothicised by Francis Johnston in 1807, to which is adjoined the remarkable Gothic Revival **Chapel Royal**, now the Church of the Most Holy Trinity, embellished externally with over one hundred heads carved by Edward and John Smyth. It was the private chapel of the viceroys and is decorated with their armorials on the front of the gallery. The interior exploits the contrast of cream stucco and dark oak woodwork in a richly worked decorative scheme. Johnston shows his versatility in this building, he was also a master of the classical idiom as the GPO demonstrates.

The subterranean **Undercroft Excavations** reached in the north-east corner of Lower Yard which are beneath the Treasury Building, lead to the base of the Powder Tower, surrounded by a moat into which the Poddle river flows, with a postern gate and Viking rampart, all important elements in the genesis of the city. Through an arch in the west side of Upper Yard the moat and base of the Corke Tower are visible, and on an upper terrace are displayed the heroic bronze pendant figures from John Hughes' Victoria memorial (1908) which stood on Kildare St, now exiled to Victoria, New South Wales, where it is less likely to attract the attention of bombers.

■ **Note**. With the exception of the Chapel Royal which is open to the public, all internal parts of the Castle, the State Apartments and Undercroft can only be seen on a conducted tour. These begin in Upper Castle Yard at the State Apartments.

State Apartments. The Grand Staircase of the State Apartments ascends to the landing, off which (left) is St. Patrick's Hall, the former scene of investiture of the Knights of St. Patrick, with a painted ceiling of c 1778 (by Italian, Vincent Waldré, brought over from England by the Marquess of Buckingham, the Viceroy, for whom he had worked at Stowe House), and armorial bearings. From here you enter the Round Drawing Room, with its Gothick windows, in the drum of the Bermingham Tower (1411; reconstructed 1775–77). As a State prison, this tower has been the gaol of a number of famous Irishmen from Hugh Roe O'Donnell (1587, who escaped from here in 1592) to those who were

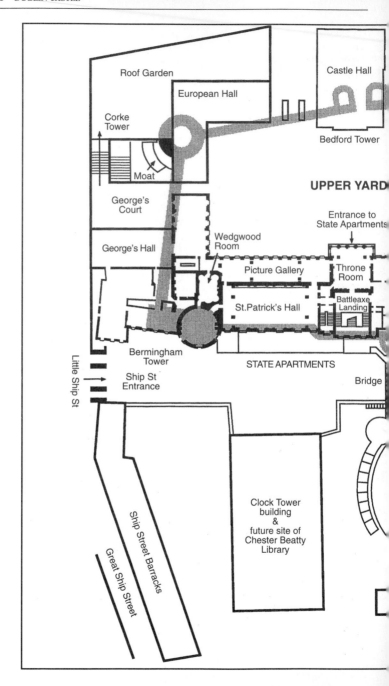

Roof Garden

Castle Hall

European Hall

Corke
Tower

Bedford Tower

Moat

UPPER YARD

George's
Court

Entrance to
State Apartments

Wedgwood
Room

George's Hall

Picture Gallery

Throne
Room

St.Patrick's Hall

Battleaxe
Landing

Bermingham
Tower

Little Ship St

Ship St
Entrance

STATE APARTMENTS

Bridge

Ship Street Barracks

Great Ship Street

Clock Tower
building
&
future site of
Chester Beatty
Library

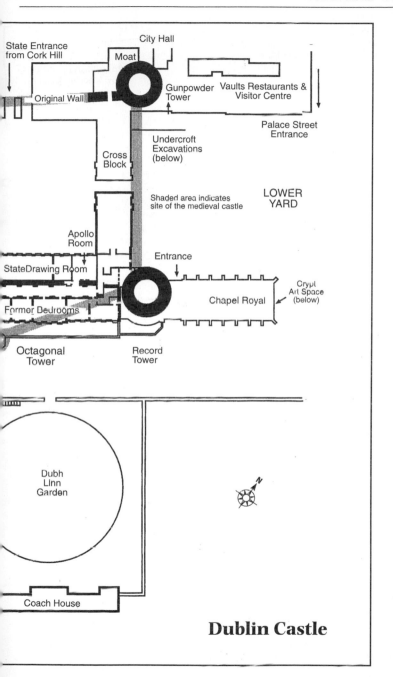

State Entrance
from Cork Hill

City Hall

Moat

Original Wall

Gunpowder
Tower

Vaults Restaurants &
Visitor Centre

Palace Street
Entrance

Cross
Block

Undercroft
Excavations
(below)

LOWER
YARD

Shaded area indicates
site of the medieval castle

Apollo
Room

StateDrawing Room

Entrance

Crypt
Art Space
(below)

Chapel Royal

Former Bedrooms

Octagonal
Tower

Record
Tower

N

Dubh
Linn
Garden

Coach House

Dublin Castle

incarcerated here during 1918–20. Adjacent is the blue Wedgwood Room, with paintings ascribed to Angelica Kauffman. Off an anteroom opens George's Hall, added to the apartments for the visit of George V and Queen Mary in 1911.

The regalia, known as the Irish Crown Jewels—in fact a diamond St. Patrick Star and Badge, together with other insignia—were mysteriously stolen from the Genealogical Office just before the state visit of Edward VII and Queen Alexandra in 1907, and have never been recovered (an 'inside job' was suspected at the time). Returning through the anteroom, you reach the Picture Gallery, with a series of 12 portraits of viceroys, to enter the richly gilt Throne Room (1740; redecorated by Francis Johnston), containing a throne possibly presented by William III. You next pass into the State Drawing Room, with its original furniture, re-upholstered; the paintings are by G.P. Panini (1740). The State Corridor, designed by Sir Edward Lovett Pearce leads (left) to the Apollo Room or Music Room, with a ceiling of 1746 incorporated here in 1964–68 from a drawing-room in Tracton House, Merrion Row. On the far side of the corridor is a series of drawing-rooms, formerly bedrooms, in the second of which is a ceiling transferred here in 1952 from demolished Mespil House (c 1751). The rooms display some outstanding stucco-work; note also the original door furniture. One of the rooms contains The Card Sharpers, by Matthew William Peters (1741–1814), and a portrait of the Countess of Southampton, by Van Dyck.

The **Austin Clarke Poetry Library**, a fine specialist collection based around the poet's own books, with reading room, is housed in the top floor of the Bermingham Tower. Access from the entrance to the State Apartments, it is the headquarters of Poetry Ireland. South of the State Apartments is the site of the original 'Pool of Dublin', the *Dubh Linn,* now called the Dubh Linn Garden.

A Tour of the Medieval City Walls

Only two substantial sections of the late medieval wall survive but it is possible to appreciate the extent of the medieval city by walking around the known perimeter. From south of the Record Tower (which marked the south-east corner of the town) proceed west towards the Bermingham Tower. Passing the projecting Octagonal Tower and the Bermingham Tower, the Castle Gate leads into Little Ship St, the wall is visible on the right with polygonal Stanihurst's Tower projecting. At the top of the street is the end of the longest single section of the wall, running back from here to the Record Tower. Cross Werburgh St into Ross Rd, then cross Patrick's St into Nicholas Place, turn right into John Dillon St and on the right in Power's Court the wall, now running north west can again be seen. This continues on the right side of the street as the wall of buildings to the end of John Dillon St. At High St cross the street and descend the hill of Bridge St Upper. At Cook St (right), the best preserved and least encumbered section of the wall is seen, running east. A small postern gate is followed by the only surviving city gate, **St. Audoen's Arch**. Inside the arch a narrow medieval street turns uphill to the medieval St. Audoen's church and High St from which the restored walkway on the top of the wall is accessible. East of the gate, the wall vanishes under the bulk of 19C Catholic St. Audoen's. At the end of Cook St cross St. Michael's Hill to the Corporation Offices. In the car park, under the east office block, is the last section of the wall, on the site of the Wood Quay excavations; this line was the northern limit of the Viking city.

Cross Fishamble St to into Essex St West and turn right into Parliament St at the top of which is Cork Hill. The **'Hellfire Club'** (see Montpellier Hill), founded in 1735 by the 1st Earl of Rosse, Col Jack St. Leger and James Worsdale, the artist, held its revels at the site of the Eagle Tavern in Cork Hill. Turn right into Lord Edward St then right again into Fishamble St where you will find Kennan's Iron Works. This is the site of the Neal's Music Hall where on 13 April 1742 the first performance of Handel's *Messiah* took place. Conducted by the composer, it was performed 'for the relief of the prisoners in the several Gaols and for the support of the Mercer's Hospital and of the Charitable Infirmary'. The event is commemorated annually by a performance in the street, of excerpts from *Messiah,* (the first Irish performance of his *Judas Maccabaeus* was also heard here, in 1748.)

In the same street the parliamentarian, Henry Grattan was born (1746–1820). The poet James Clarence Mangan (1803–49), passed his last years in abject poverty in neighbouring Bride St, dying of cholera in Meath hospital; and Archbishop James Ussher (1581–1656), at No. 3.

Werburgh St extends south from Fishamble St. Jonathan Swift was born at No. 7 Hoey's Court in 1667, now the site of a dismal Employment Exchange.

St. Werburgh's church (entered through Bristol Buildings, 7–8 Castle St), an ancient foundation, was rebuilt in 1715 by Thomas Burgh, and remodelled after a fire in 1759. Its Baroque façade has been much diminished by the removal of the spire. Unfortunately the Castle authorities had the spire taken down following the Emmet rising in 1803, in case some rebel might take a pot-shot at the viceroy.

The interior, by John Smyth, well-restored in 1960, has a sumptuously carved pulpit by Richard Stewart (originally in the Chapel Royal) and an organ-case of 1767. The stucco in the chancel is by Michael Maguire. In the west vestibule is a 16C Fitzgerald tomb; in the vaults are the remains of the revolutionary leader, Lord Edward Fitzgerald (1763–1798), who belonged to the United Irishmen and planned a French invasion of Ireland. The plot was discovered and he died of wounds received at his capture. His captor, Major Henry Sirr (1764–1841) lies in the graveyard.

Christ Church Cathedral

The cathedral (10.00–17.00) of the combined sees of Dublin and Glendalough (Church of Ireland), stands in a small green churchyard at the corner of Christchurch Pl. and St. Michael's Hill. It takes precedence over the city's other medieval cathedral, St. Patrick's, in seniority and being the seat of the Archbishop. Its external appearance is almost entirely due to the complete restoration of 1875.

The first cathedral was founded on this spot in 1038 by the Norse King of Dublin, Sigtryggr Silkbeard, in the most commanding position, on the brow of the Hill of Dublin and within the city walls. Nothing remains of this (probably) wooden structure. The present cathedral was begun in 1172 after the Anglo-Norman conquest of the city, at the instigation of 'Strongbow' Richard de Clare, 2nd Earl of Pembroke and Striguill, in conjunction with Archbishop Laurence O'Toole and Raymond le Grose. The Normans regarded the creation of magnificent church buildings as visual symbols of state power and ecclesiastical prestige. Working in the imported architectural styles current in England, the cathedral is a transitional building which reflects changes in style which were developing at the end of the 12C and in this way it differs from contemporary church building in Ireland, taking place in areas which were not influenced by the Normans. Native Irish cathedrals are very small by comparison with the scale of Norman church building (the Rock of Cashel has examples of both).

The 12C crypt is the least altered portion of the building, at the springing of its low arches can be seen the original timber ends of the formwork used in its vault construction, set into the stonework. The cathedral is cruciform with an aisled six bay nave, choir, sanctuary and short transepts following the plan of the 12C crypt. Both transepts and choir are part of the original structure begun in 1172 and have a combination of late Romanesque details, heavily chevroned round-headed window arches in the triforium, combined with a pointed but also chevroned arcade. The nave was begun in 1234 in an Early English Gothic style of pointed arches, the north wall of which is original and has an interesting arch formation. Above the nave arcade, the triforium and clerestory are combined in a repeat of the high arcade of the nave. In the transepts, choir and nave are a collection of 13C sculptured figural capitals which identify the masons as having come from Worcestershire, being remarkably similar to work in Glastonbury and Wells. The roof vaulting collapsed in 1562 bringing down the south side of the nave, which was rebuilt in the 17C. The choir and chancel were extended in 1358 and there are three chevet chapels with the Lady Chapel in the centre projecting east. To the north is the chapel of St. Edmund, to the south that of St. Laud. A chapel to St. Laurence O'Toole is on the east of the south transept.

The **Chapter House Cloister** and **Priory** were erected to the south of the cathedral in the 13C. Remains of the Chapter House are adjacent to the south transept. A fine Romanesque doorway visible on the outside of this transept was transferred here for decorative effect in 1826 from the north side of the building and is considerably above the actual internal floor level.

In 1871–78 the cathedral was so extensively restored by the English architect George Edmund Street with funds provided by the distiller Henry Roe that it now appears a 19C rather than a 13C building. Street's rather fanciful if scholarly restoration produced a lush Victorian interior of colour and surface ornament although through the glitter of his Victorian Gothicising the simplicity of the 12C transepts and grandeur of the 13C nave and choir are not altogether lost.

Externally, almost the entire building has been re-faced, giving it that smooth appearance of Victorian churches, totally out of sympathy with the more robust style of medieval masonry. Street also added the external buttresses and rebuilt the tower. The Synod Hall which is connected to the cathedral by a covered bridge crossing St. Michael's Hill was designed by Street. It incorporates the medieval church tower of St. Michael and All Angels.

Lambert Simnel, the imposter, was crowned as 'Edward VI' in the Cathedral in 1487. Until the 16C the Lord Deputy was sworn in here but the building of the Chapel Royal in Dublin Castle diminished the civic importance of the cathedral as the viceroys no longer felt obliged to attend service there; the Chapel Royal was less draughty!

On disestablishment St. Patrick's Cathedral was declared National Cathedral of the Church of Ireland, while Christ Church became the mother church of the united diocese of Dublin and Glendalough.

Cathedral Monuments

In the south aisle is the **Tomb of Strongbow** (died 1196) but the armoured effigy is actually that of an Earl of Drogheda. Strongbow's bowels (or Drogheda's) may be buried here in a probable visceral monument. The demi-figure beside the larger tomb is pointed out as being one of Strongbow's sons, cut in two by his own father for showing cowardice in battle! The transepts and choir are separated from the nave by a screen designed by Street. The brass lectern on the gospel side of the screen is a superb example of late medieval metalwork. In the south transept is the tiered tomb of the 19th Earl of Kildare (died 1734), by Sir Henry Cheere. In the Chapel of St. Laurence O'Toole are two ancient effigies, one of a prior (1212) and the other of a lady reputed to be the wife or sister of Strongbow.

The southeast chapel of the ambulatory is dedicated to St. Laud (a 6C Norman bishop) and contains a sinister heart-shaped iron box, enclosed in a cage in which the embalmed heart of St Laurence O'Toole (who died at Eu, near Dieppe, in 1180) reposes. This is one of the few relics to have survived the Reformation in its actual religious setting, along with some surviving 13C tiles, which were the model for the current floor.

Stairs descend from the south aisle to the **crypt**. The tabernacle and candle-sticks used at the Mass of James II in 1689 are in one of the east chapels of the crypt, and at the entrance to another are the battered figures of Charles II and James II (as Duke of York) by William de Keyser (removed from the old Tholsel in Christchurch Pl). Here also is the Sneyd Tomb, by Thomas Kirk (1777–1845) and the 17C town stocks.

Across St. Michael's Hill from the cathedral the Synod Hall is now occupied by '**Dublinia**', (10.00–17.00, Mon–Sat; 10.00–16.00, Sun, April–Sept; 11.00–16.00, Mon–Sat, Feb–Mar; 11.00–16.30 Sun; Nov–Jan shorter hours) a presentation with models, life size re-creations of street life, historical tableaux, and an audio-visual programme of Dublin from the Anglo-Norman conquest to the Reformation, 1170–1540, and an excellent model of the late medieval city. The most important individual aspects of the complex are an exhibition of Viking and medieval artefacts excavated at nearby Wood Quay from the National Museum of Ireland, and (in the café), a complete set of James Malton's (1760–1803), aquatints from his *Picturesque and Descriptive View of the City of Dublin* (1792), the definitive views of Georgian Dublin. The cathedral may be entered from 'Dublinia' across the bridge.

Immediately to the northwest of Christ Church rise the ugly stone clad tower-blocks of **Dublin Corporation Offices**, (10.00–13.00 and 14.15–17.00m, Mon–Fri) designed by Sam Stephenson, 1985, and the subject of much controversy regarding both the style of the architecture—next to the medieval cathedral—and the use of the site itself. The site, stretching from Christ Church to Wood Quay on the Liffey was excavated by archaeologists of the National Museum, 1972–78 and the Viking and medieval strata were uncovered, dating from the 10C–15C. The **Wood Quay** excavations revealed one of the most extensive and best preserved Viking sites to be found outside Scandinavia, and it was felt by medieval archaeologists internationally, that the whole area needed to be excavated and possibly preserved. Over 20,000 people marched in protest against the Corporation's determination to proceed with their plans. Wood Quay was the largest tract of land within medieval Dublin ever likely to become available for excavation but Dublin Corporation, despite widespread public protest, proceeded with the construction of the bunker-like offices, and the opportunity for large scale excavation was lost. A fragment of the 13C city wall which here runs east–west with a bend in the middle, can be seen under the eastern office block. The contour of Fishamble St follows that of the 10C Viking street, running down to the river. A later phase of Corporation Offices (Ronald Tallon, 1992), with cut-away corners to permit views of Christ Church from the quays flanks the river; it has a fine internal atrium and sculpture by Michael Warren on its Wood Quay façade, based on the prow of a Viking longship. Wood Quay was the waterfront of Viking Dyfflin.

Christchurch Pl. leads west to High Street and Cornmarket. At No. 22 Cornmarket Lord Edward Fitzgerald took refuge before his arrest (see St. Werburgh's). A short distance along High St you pass (right) steps descending to **St. Audoen's**, open for Sunday service. Dublin's only surviving medieval parish church, of which the 12C tower and west door and a 15C naive aisle remain intact. Beneath the tower is the tomb of Lord Portlester and his wife (1496), while the aisle contains a font of 1194 and some battered monuments of the Segrave family. An alley below the church leads down to an archway of the 13C city walls (restored), in a room above which the *Freeman's Journal* was founded in 1764.

A short distance south, on the opposite side of High St, in Back Lane, is the brick-built **Tailors' Hall**, (1703) the only remaining guildhall in Dublin (now the headquarters of An Taisce—the National Trust). It contains some interesting architectural details (the front door is dated 1707). In the Hall is a plaque bearing a list of masters of the tailor's guild from 1419–1841. It was used in 1792 by the '**Back Lane Parliament**', the Catholic Committee of the United Irishmen, led by Wolfe Tone, which petitioned Westminster for the repeal of laws which discriminated against the civil rights of Catholics and Dissenters. Christchurch Market, a flea market, is opposite the entrance (weekends). In Francis St, further west, centre of the city's antique trade, stands St. Nicholas of Myra (1829), by John Leeson. The portico is by John Byrne (1860) and the Pietà and attendant angels on the altar by John Hogan (1831).

From Cornmarket, Bridge St Upper and Lower leads downhill, near the bottom of which (left) stands the **Brazen Head Hotel** (1688), an interesting and ancient pub with rich political and literary associations. It became the headquarters of the United Irishmen, where 15 of them were arrested during 1798.

Beyond is Father Mathew Bridge (1816) by George Knowles, which replaced the first Dublin bridge (1210), and crosses the Liffey towards the Four Courts. The oldest surviving bridge is Queen Maeve Bridge to the west (formerly Queen's Bridge) by Gen. Charles Valance; 1764).

St. Patrick's Cathedral

Patrick St leads south from Christchurch Pl. to St. Patrick's Cathedral (running gradually downhill through the Liberties to the Coombe, a centre for the Huguenot weaving industry in the 18C). On the right are the Iveagh Buildings (1894), philanthropic flat blocks built by the Guinness family to replace an atrocious slum area, with Art Noveau decoration on the gables, and in Bride Road (left) is the **Iveagh Baths**, Joseph and Smithem (1904) an important Arts and

Crafts Movement building, its street-façade among the most original in Dublin (disused). The cathedral is adjoined by gardens laid out at the time of the 19C slum clearance. Like its sister cathedral, it too has been thoroughly restored, but in this case with much more respect for the historical fabric.

It is celebrated for its long association with **Jonathan Swift**, who served as dean 1713–1745, and in the city of his birth forms his most tangible memorial, there being in a city which has a superabundance of monuments, none to Swift, its greatest citizen. Always the champion of the poor of the Liberties and ready to rail at government corruption and stupidity, Swift promoted the idea of buying Irish produced merchandise in order to protect the livelihood of the Irish weaving industry, victim of the aristocratic fashion for buying foreign made goods.

'We'll dress in manufactures made at home,
Equip our kings and generals at the Coombe,
We'll rig in Meath Street Egypt's haughty queen
And Anthony shall court her in rateen'.

St. Patrick's also contains the largest and most interesting collection of church monuments in Ireland. The pre-Norman church of St. Patrick de Insula is believed to be the first predecessor of the present cathedral, marking the site of a holy well the dedication of which tradition ascribed to a visit from the patron saint. An early Christian cross slab found at the well is displayed in the north-west aisle corner of the cathedral, and is an important link with the pre-Viking period. In 1191, John Comyn established a collegiate church on the site, wishing to be removed from the monastic clergy of Christ Church. St. Patrick's was built in open land to the south of the city and was therefore free also of municipal restrictions. In 1213 St. Patrick's was raised to the status of cathedral by the new archbishop, Henry de Londres, who in 1220 decided to entirely re-build the cathedral. This building was consecrated in 1254 but was not actually completed until 1270. The two cathedrals were built concurrently, an extraordinary investment in wealth and craftsmanship for the Norman civil and ecclesiastical administration who had not been in Ireland much more than 50 years.

St. Patrick's Cathedral is the longest medieval church in Ireland and at 280 feet is over 80 feet longer than Christ Church; unlike its sister cathedral it has no crypt, as a result of being built on the banks of the Poddle river which formed an island around the site of the earlier church. The cathedral plan is remarkably harmonious and well proportioned, it has an aisled eight bay nave, the best preserved portion of the building, and the transepts are also aisled. The stone vault of the nave is a late replacement of the original which fell in 1544, a mere 18 years before the vaulting of Christ Church followed suit. Collapse of the vaulting was a recurring disaster in medieval cathedrals, due to land subsidence or straining the structural stability of the spans involved. The Lady Chapel is rectangular with projecting central bays, heavily buttressed on the east end. The architecture is 13C Gothic, without the evidence of earlier building except possibly in the baptistery in the south west corner which may remain from Comyn's original building. Externally, the most dominant feature of the cathedral is the **Minot Tower**, constructed by Archbishop Minot in 1370; its 30m spire was added in 1749 by George Semple. The tower is out of alignment with the cathedral.

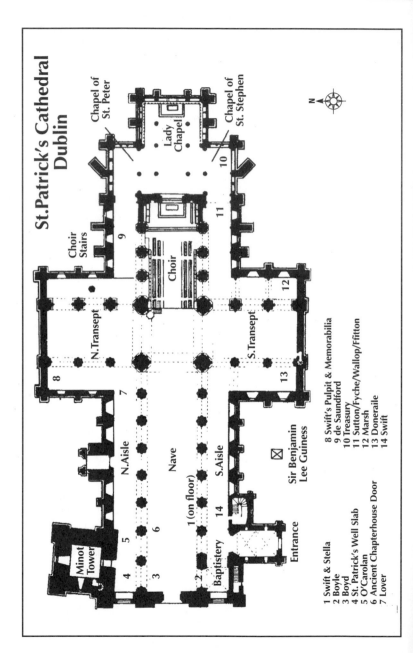

St.Patrick's Cathedral
Dublin

N

Chapel of St. Peter

Chapel of St. Stephen

Lady Chapel

Choir Stairs

Choir

N.Transept

S.Transept

Minot Tower

N.Aisle

Nave

S.Aisle

Baptistery

Entrance

Sir Benjamin Lee Guiness

1 Swift & Stella
2 Boyle
3 Boyd
4 St. Patrick's Well Slab
5 O'Carolan
6 Ancient Chapterhouse Door
7 Lover

8 Swift's Pulpit & Memorabilia
9 de Saundford
10 Treasury
11 Sutton/Fyche/Wallop/Ffitton
12 Marsh
13 Doneraile
14 Swift

1 (on floor)

Sir Thomas Drew was commissioned by the brewer Sir Benjamin Lee Guinness to extensively reconstruct the Cathedral 1864–1868, and he united the various parts of the cathedral which had been at that point used as the chapels of various communities and were in a state of serious disrepair. He also re-faced most of the external stonework. The Minot Tower seems to have received the least of Drew's attention. The cathedral is a remarkably dignified building, best viewed from across St. Patrick's Park where the stark massiveness of the tower suggests something of the defensive nature of the original settlement.

St. Patrick's retains more of the medieval spirit than Christ Church, a consequence of its interior being less lavishly restored. There is a much greater sense of the power of the stonework and the lofty nave is the most impressive in the country.

Cathedral Monuments

At the foot of the second column—half-right inside from the entrance—brass tablets mark the **Grave of Jonathan Swift** (1667–1745) and that of Esther Johnson (1681–1728); better known as 'Stella', the recipient of his letters which were later collected under the title *Journal to Stella*, and his companion (possibly his wife?), who lie side by side. On the left of the adjacent door is a fine bust of Swift by Patrick Cunningham (1775); on the tablet above is a Latin epitaph from his own pungent pen; 'He lies where furious rage can rend his heart no more'; while his simple record of Stella is on the other side of the doorway. W.B.Yeats summed up Swift's life and achievements in his own rendering of the epitaph,

'Swift has sailed into his rest;
Savage indignation there
Cannot lacerate his breast.
Imitate him if you dare,
World-besotted traveller; he
Served human liberty.'

In the south-west corner (left) is the dark, simply-groined **baptistery** with a 12C font. Against its outer wall is the huge **Boyle Monument**, remarkable for its profusion of painted figures. It was originally erected in 1633 by Richard Boyle, the 'great' Earl of Cork (1566–1643) at the east end of the choir, and its removal from there in 1635 by Strafford (when Lord Deputy, and at the instigation of Archbishop Laud) led to the enmity of Cork, the primary cause of Strafford's later impeachment and execution. The uppermost figures represent Dean Weston (d. 1573), Lord Chancellor of Ireland; below him are Sir Geoffrey Fenton (d. 1608) and his wife, the dean's daughter. Still lower are the Earl and his second wife (Catherine, d. 1630; a daughter of Fenton), with four sons, six daughters and an infant supposed to represent the physicist Robert Boyle (1627–91; see St. Mary's, Youghal). In the north-west corner is a **Cross Stone** that marked the site of St. Patrick's Well, and to the right is a bust of J.P. Curran (1750–1817). In the north aisle (eastwards) is the restored monument of Archbishop Thomas Jones (d. 1619) and Sir Roger Jones (d. 1620); then come memorials of **Turlough O'Carolan** (1670–1738), composer and itinerant harpist (John Hogan, 1824), erected by Lady Morgan, and just near the transept, of Samuel Lover (1797–1868), the novelist and miniaturist.

The north transept, for many years serving as the parish church of St. Nicholas Without, lay in ruins until 1830, and has been rebuilt twice since then. **Swift's Death Mask** and pulpit are in the north-west corner. The **choir** is also the Chapel of the Order of St. Patrick. Its knights were installed here from the institution of the order in 1783 until 1869, when the Church of Ireland was disestablished. Above the stalls hang the helmets, swords, banners and paraphernalia of members of the order. In the choir aisles are some of the most interesting monuments in the church; on the north side of the north choir aisle (restored 1902) is the marble effigy of Archbishop Fulk de Saundford (d. 1271), and opposite is a tablet marking the grave of Frederick Herman, Duke of Schomberg (1615–90), who fell at the Boyne. The epitaph, with its sarcastic reference to the indifference of Schomberg's family, is attributed to Swift. The Lady Chapel, built by Archbishop Saundford (c1256) resembles in the delicacy of its details the contemporary work in the Temple Church in London.

From 1666 to 1816 it was assigned to a Huguenot congregation, but by 1840 it was in ruins. The northeast and south east chapels retain Dutch brass candelabra (17C); in the latter is an effigy of Archbishop Tregury (d. 1471). In the wall of the south choir aisle are four interesting brasses, a form of memorial rare in Ireland; those of Dean Sutton (d. 1528), with an erasure—probably due to a change of doctrine at the Reformation—and Dean Fyche (d. 1537), with silver inlay, are especially noteworthy. That of Sir Henry Wallop (Lord Justice of Ireland, 1540–99) dates from 1608, and that of Sir Edward ffitton the Elder from 1579.

The south transept was for many centuries used as a chapter house. Leaning against a pier is an old door, pierced with a rough hole. A possibly apocryphal legend claims that in 1492 a fierce dispute took place in the nave between the Earls of Kildare and Ormonde over a matter of precedence, each supported with a band of armed retainers. Ormonde took refuge in the chapterhouse and a reconciliation having been effected, a hole was cut in the door so that the two earls might shake hands. Among the monuments are a canopied marble composition with paired Corinthian columns framing a lengthy inscription to Archbishop Narcissus Marsh (1638–1713), the finest surviving work by **Grinling Gibbons** in Ireland, and one to the poet Charles Wolfe (1791–1823) by Terence Farrell. In the south-west corner is the Baroque monument of Lady Doneraile, by Simon Vierpyl (c 1780), and above (right) is a plaque to Swift's 29-year-old servant, Alexander McGee, erected by the Dean; the inscription records 'his discretion, fidelity, and diligence in that humble station' (1722).

Opposite the cathedral, to the right, is the **Deanery** of 1781 (the earlier Deanery in which Swift lived burned down). It contains a portrait of Swift by Bindon in a remarkable carved frame by John Houghton. During his latter years (from c 1738) Swift suffered progressively from Meniere's syndrome, a form of vertigo, and his last three years were clouded by the mental deterioration, dying from the top like a tree, as he had earlier predicted.

To the left of St. Patrick's, a short distance along the street, is the entrance to **Marsh's Library** (10.00–17.00, Mon, Wed, Fri, closed 12.45–14.00; Sat 10.00–12.45; £), founded by Archbishop Narcissus Marsh (1638–1713) and built in brick from 1701 by Sir William Robinson (its west façade faced in stone in 1863–69). It was the first public library (open then to 'All Graduates and

Gentlemen') in Dublin. It consists of two wings at right angles, and its charming and well-maintained interior has remained almost untouched since the founder's time. In *Ulysses*, Joyce refers to the 'stagnant bay in Marsh's Library' where he read in October 1902. Note the three 'cages' in which readers were locked with their rare books to work undisturbed under the eye of the librarian. The library preserves some 80 incunabula (including a volume of Cicero printed in Milan in 1472) and 300 MSS. Part of the collection originated in the library (c 9500 volumes) of Edward Stillingfleet (1635–99), Bishop of Worcester, acquired by Marsh, and many later scholars made bequests of their books to the library. Swift was a governor, and it contains his annotated copy of Clarendon's *History of the Rebellion*. The library has its own conservation laboratory, the most advanced in the country, which cares for the 25,000 16C–18C books.

Continue up the street and turn left along Upper Kevin St and Lower Kevin St. To the south stood Swift's walled garden, which he called 'Naboth's Vineyard'. On Kevin St, the remains of the medieval archbishop's Palace of St. Sepulchre are now a Garda station.

Aungier St, the next crossroad, extends north towards Dame St. The poet **Thomas Moore** (1779–1852) was born at No. 12 Aungier St. Continue east along Cuffe St to reach the south-west corner of St. Stephen's Green.

Royal Hospital, Kilmainham Gaol, Islandbridge, the Four Courts

Thomas St is directly west of the route from Christchurch Pl. On the north side is the **Church of St. Augustine and St. John** (E.W. Pugin and G.C. Ashlin, 1860) the finest Gothic Revival building in Dublin. Its polychrome exterior of granite, limestone and sandstone, and 30m crocketed spire make it the most heavily textured of any of the city churches. Its dark and mysterious interior, lit by richly coloured stained glass and profusely embellished with metalwork and woodcarving, corresponds in spirit to the Ruskinian ideal. On the same side further along is the **National College of Art and Design** (NCAD), successor of the 18C Dublin Society Schools, now occupying the warehouses of the former Power's Distillery. Founded in 1796, it is, after Trinity, the second oldest educational institution in Ireland. Some distance along the south side of Thomas St rises the deconsecrated **St. Catherine's church**, a massive rusticated building of 1769, by John Smyth, with an imposing Roman Doric façade, the finest Georgian church front in Dublin. Its spire, like that of many city churches, was never completed. In 1803, Robert Emmet, a United Irishman who led an unsuccessful attack on Dublin castle, was hanged on a scaffold erected outside the church, and his head then struck off. It was near here that his adherents had shortly before murdered Arthur Wolfe, Lord Chief Justice Kilwarden (1739–1803). The executioner's block is on display in Kilmainham Gaol Museum.

A few steps beyond, at St. James's Gate, is the entrance to Guinness's Brewery. In 1759, the small Rainsford's Brewery on this site (one of 50 breweries then operating in the city) was purchased by Arthur Guinness, who began brewing 'porter' or 'stout', as it is still known by devotees. Approximately 60 per cent of the beer sold in the Republic is now brewed here. You are no longer able to tour the brewery, but visitors are welcome at the Hop Store in Rainsford St (left), where you can see an explanatory film about the manufacture of this world-famous stout, and are invited to sample their brew, bottled or draught. A brewing museum is in the **Guinness Hop Store**, Rainsford St (Mon–Fri 10.00–15.00; closed Sat, Sun, BH; £) and it usually hosts a range of contemporary art exhibitions.

Off Rainsford St, is the **Market St Store House** (Arrold and Hignett, 1903) the earliest 'Chicago School' steel frame building in Britain or Ireland and a pioneering example of early 20C architecture. It is clad in brick with a heavy machicolated cornice.

At the end of James St, passing on the south the main entrance to the Guinness Brewery, Bow Lane leads downhill to the right. At the corner is **St. Patrick's or 'Swift's Hospital** (George Semple, 1749) the first psychiatric hospital in Ireland, built with a bequest from Jonathan Swift. 'He gave the little wealth he had, to found a home for fools and mad, showing by one satiric touch, no nation wanted it so much.' The Swift Museum is a small but interesting collection of the Dean's personal possessions and documents relating to him. At the bottom of Bow Lane turn right and uphill to the gates of the Royal Hospital Kilmainham.

Royal Hospital Kilmainham and Irish Museum of Modern Art

Royal Hospital Kilmainham (RHK; Sir William Robinson, 1680), now the Irish Museum of Modern Art (IMMA). The RHK was the first major classical public building to be erected in Ireland. Modelled on the Hôtel des Invalides in Paris (Liberal Bruant, 1671), the enormous rectangular block with slate roof, stucco walls and limestone window surrounds presents a fairly sober aspect to the visitor, but inside the quadrangle the ambience is enlivened by an arcade which runs around three sides of the court, while on the north wing are a central clock tower with spire and the tall windows of the **Chapel**, **Dining Hall** and **Master's Residence**. The Chapel has woodcarving by James Tarbery and the Baroque Caroline floral ceiling (a partial replica) is without parallel in Ireland; also by Tarbery are the carved tympanum of the axial entrance doors. The **Great Hall**, panelled in pine, is now used for concerts, and hung with a collection of portraits of monarchs and viceroys. Built as a home for army veterans who wore a Chelsea Pensioners style of uniform, it continued this function until 1922. Subsequently used as a Garda training depot it gradually fell into total disrepair and was extensively restored in 1981–90 (John Costello), but the restorers unfortunately opted for returning the building to its 19C stucco rather than 17C brick appearance. The classically-planned Formal Gardens on the north side of the building are being restored to the style of the late 17C-early 18C when they were known as the Master's Gardens.

The **Irish Museum of Modern Art** (IMMA) (10.00–17.30, Tue–Sat; 12.00–17.30, Sun and BH), established in 1991, is devoted to avant-garde art of the late 20C. The permanent collection includes the Sidney Nolan Bequest, and somewhat of an anomaly, the Madden-Arnholtz Collection, a collection of European master-prints, representing, among others, Callot, Daumier, Dürer, Goya, Hogarth and Rembrandt. The rooms in enfilade arrangement around the courtyard are admirably suited for the display of exhibitions. The museum has a first-class visual arts bookshop and small café.

The tree-lined main avenue leads west to a Gothic gateway by Francis Johnston (1820) which was removed from 'Bloody Bridge' on the Liffey Quays in 1844.

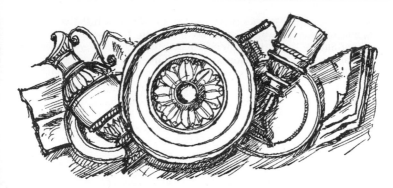

Pine bas-relief c 1688 by James Tarberry, Royal Hospital Kilmainham

Inside the gate on the right is Bully's Acre, an ancient burial ground in which is the shaft of an early cross. Outside the gate is **Kilmainham Gaol** (Sir John Traile, 1792), now a museum of Irish political history (11.00–18.00 daily, Jun–Sept; 14.00–18.00, Sun & Wed, Oct–May; £; OPW). The cells occupied by Parnell, Emmet and many other patriots can be seen as well as the yard in which the leaders of the Easter Rising of 1916 were executed. Tours of its bleak and chilly interior are not for the faint-of-heart; the excellent and dynamically presented new **Museum** deals with Irish political history, 1796–1924.

Northwest of Kilmainham at **Islandbridge** on the south bank of the Liffey is the **Irish National War Memorial** by Sir Edwin Lutyens (1921) finally completed 1994, which commemorates the 49,000 Irish soldiers killed while serving in the British Army during World War I. The memorial, one of Lutyens' masterpieces, is a late classical composition of pavilions, fountains, pergolas and sunken rose gardens on a sequence of descending terraces, planted with holm oaks and myrtles. The Liffey, which flows at the bottom of the hill, is incorporated into the design, symbolising the Styx, river of the Underworld.

Return towards the city centre via **Heuston Station** at Kingsbridge (Scranton Wood, 1845), a heavily decorated Italianate palazzo which fronts the train sheds, by Sir John McNeill. Opposite the John's Road side of Heuston is the recently restored **Dr Steevens' Hospital** (Thomas Burgh, 1720) built as a private hospital and in use until 1980. The plan resembles the Royal Hospital with an internal arcaded courtyard although on a much smaller scale. It is now the headquarters of the Eastern Health Board.

Cross the Liffey at the pedestrianised King's Bridge (or by car on Liam Mellows Bridge). Directly west is the entrance to the Phoenix Park (see above). The philosopher Ludwig Wittgenstein (1889–1951) lived from 1947–49 in what is now the Ashling Hotel. Return along Wolf Tone Quay to the city, passing (left) the **National Museum** at **Collins Barracks** in Benburb St. (10.00–17.00, Tue–Sat; 14.00–17.00, Sun). Built as the Royal Barracks in 1700 by Sir William Robinson and capable of accommodating six regiments, it was until its takeover by the National Museum, the oldest continuously occupied military complex in Europe. Two wings of this vast and impressive classical building are now occupied by the applied arts collections of the National Museum. There are displays of 16C–18C furniture, folk furniture, glass and ceramics, metalwork, costume and scientific instruments. The 14C Chinese **Fonthill Vase** and the extensive display of **Georgian silver** are among the highlights of the Collins Barracks collection.

In Blackhall Pl. left off the quays is the **Bluecoat School** (Thomas Ivory), now the Incorporated Law Society. This is one of the most elegant and least known of Dublin's 18C buildings, a composition of central block with chapel and dining hall linked by curved screen walls; the central block was intended to have a tall spire, the ovoid cupola was finally added as a compromise. Behind the building is a small open area, the last visible remnant of **Oxmantown Green** the quarter to which the Vikings migrated when expelled from the city in 1172.

The Four Courts

Further east, on Upper Ormond Quay is the Four Courts (open when courts are sitting) seat of the High Court of Justice of Ireland, and the second masterpiece of James Gandon, who, incorporating work (the west wing) by Thomas Cooley (1776), completed it in 1786–1802. The central block, entered through an imposing Corinthian portico (with weather-worn statues of Moses and the Legal Virtues, by Edward Smyth) is surmounted by the copper-covered dome on a tall colonnaded drum which gives the building its distinctive outline. The curve of the dome as restored is higher than the original. The upper rotunda provides a fine view over the city. It is flanked by two wings enclosing quadrangles. Off the circular central hall open the halls that contained the original four courts: Exchequer, Common Pleas, King's Bench and Chancery.

The original Law Courts stood on the south side of the Liffey, to the west of Christ Church. A society of lawyers, or Inn of Court, was established in the time of Edward I in Exchequer St, and known as Collett's Inn. It was succeeded by Preston's Inn, on the site of the present City Hall. On the assumption of the title of King of Ireland by Henry VIII in 1541, the Society took the name of King's Inn, and the confiscated lands of the Dominican convent of St. Saviour (founded 1224), where the Four Courts stood, were granted to it. It was in the building erected here that James II held his last parliament in 1689. In the 18C the Law Courts were transferred to their present site, and the Society of King's Inn took a new site in Henrietta St (see below); the old Law Courts were finally abandoned in 1796. In 1916 the Four Courts were temporarily occupied by the insurgents, with little damage being caused. However, in 1922, during the Civil War, the building was put in a state of defence and garrisoned by 150 anti-treaty men under Rory O'Connor, a civil engineer. On 28–30 June it was heavily shelled by Michael Collins, mindless of the priceless archives in the adjoining Public Record Office, which were largely destroyed, although the shell of the Four Courts stood up to the explosions. Fragments of charred medieval parchment fell on the city for days afterwards. Among the archives were the 149 volumes of *Manuscript Journals* (1613–1800) of the Irish Parliament, mostly full red morocco folios, which have been described as 'probably the most majestic series of bound volumes in the world'. The earlier volumes were bound up in the 1730s, the 'golden years' of Irish book-binding. The Law Courts were eventually re-installed here in 1931 and the restoration was completed the following year, with a number of minor but noticeable variations in the façade, such as the trimming of the flanking wings by one bay (to facilitate traffic).

Behind the Four Courts is the Green Street Courthouse (1792), by Richard Johnston. Immediately west of the Fourt Courts, opposite the Father Mathew Bridge; Church St leads away from the Liffey to (left) **St. Michan's church** (pronounced Mikan). A Viking foundation of 1095, the present building, except for its medieval battlemented tower and the tomb of Bishop O'Haingli, is an early 19C restoration of a church rebuilt in 1685–86. Some of the furniture, including a moveable litany desk, dates from 1724; a wreck of a keyboard is pointed out as that of an organ used by Handel, whose *Dettingen Te Deum* was performed here; the carving of the organ-case has been ascribed to Cuvilles, and the high-relief panel of musical instruments on the organ-loft to Henry Houghton. Edmund Burke was probably baptised at the font.

In the sheltered graveyard, near the path, lie Dr Charles Lucas (1713–71), founder of the Freeman's Journal, and, according to one tradition, Robert Emmet (1778–1803; see below). In the vaults lie the brothers Henry and John Sheares (1753–98 and 1766–98, respectively), executed as rebels, and several mummies of so-called 'crusaders' (but probably 17C) preserved by the moisture-absorbing magnesian limestone of the vault. No. 12 Arran Quay (demolished), to the west of the Four Courts, was the birthplace of **Edmund Burke** (1729–97); St. Paul's (RC), just beyond, is a striking building of 1835–37, by Patrick Byrne, its slender cupola a foil to the weight of the Four Courts dome.

Return to city centre along North Quays; opposite the 'Ha'penny Bridge' is the **Winding Stairs Bookshop** (secondhand), on three floors, with café tables overlooking the river.

Abbey Theatre, O'Connell St, Hugh Lane Gallery, James Joyce Centre

The Custom House
Before ascending O'Connell St, turn east along Eden Quay, passing below the loop line railway bridge which joins Pearse and Connolly stations (both give access to the DART as well as main line) to reach the Custom House, fronting the Liffey, and built here in the face of the opposition of 18C merchants who did not wish to see trade move downriver from where they were established. Its exterior has recently been restored.

Externally this is one of the most impressive buildings in Dublin, and the first masterpiece of James Gandon (1743–1823), an English architect of Huguenot extraction, born in London and invited to Dublin by John Beresford. Gandon had been apprenticed for seven years in Sir William Chambers' office and there learned the Roman neo-classicism which was Chambers' passion, emphasising rigorous attention to proportions and fine workmanship. When the offer came for a commission in Dublin, he had been contemplating going to St. Petersburg to work for Catherine the Great.

Begun in 1781, the building of the Custom House took ten years and cost £200,000. The main south front—best seen from the far bank—has a fine Doric portico, with statues by Edward Smyth and Agostino Carlini. Classical heads, personification of the rivers of Ireland, known as the 'Riverine Heads', also by Smyth are on 14 keystones, distributed around the building. The central block is linked to end pavilions by deeply shadowed arcades which, with the main portico, give relief to the considerable length of the south front. The flanking pavilions, with a columned recessed central bay, are surmounted by the arms of Ireland. These corner pavilions are an important link in uniting the east and west façades with the main ones north and south.

The north front has a smaller pediment-less portico bearing statues of the Continents, by Thomas Banks (1735–1805) one of the first British sculptors to be influenced by Neo-Classical ideals. The central copper dome is 38m high, topped by a statue of Commerce. The drum (following the 1921 destruction) was replaced in grey Ardbraccan limestone, rather than Portland stone, striking a false note in an otherwise delightfully harmonious building. Set alight by a party of Republicans on 25 May 1921, it blazed for five days, and its extensive records were destroyed. It now houses government offices. Gandon's two great buildings, the Custom House and Four Courts are considered to embody the female and male principles in architecture—the delicacy and refinement of the former contrasted with the robustness and strength of the latter!

Immediately northeast of the Custom House, in Store St, is the central bus station or **Busaras** (1947) by Michael Scott (1905–89). An important example of International Modernism, it shows the influence of Le Corbusier, and was the first public building erected in central Dublin which was not designed in the historic styles of the past. Immediately to the right are the cubical glass blocks of the **Financial Services Centre** (Burke, Kennedy, Doyle, 1985), arranged around the basins of the Royal Canal Docks.

A short distance beyond, on the east side of Amiens St, is **Connolly Railway Station** (1844–46), previously Amiens St Station. Charles Lever, the novelist, was born in a house on its site; *Charles O'Malley* (1841)—his most popular novel—is a comic account of his student days at Trinity College during the 1820s. North west of the Custom House are the imposing offices of the Irish Life Assurance Co, within the Talbot St courtyard of the complex the *Charioteer of Life* (Oisin Kelly, 1982), the closest Dublin gets to an equestrian monument.

The Abbey Theatre

From the Custom House we may make our way west along Lower Abbey St, passing (left) the Abbey Theatre. The theatre opened in 1904 and W.B. Yeats and Lady Gregory were its first directors. It (accidentally) burnt down in 1951. The present theatre was designed by Michael Scott in 1966 and houses two auditoria, the **Abbey** (638 seats) and the **Peacock** (157 seats). As the National Theatre of Ireland, the Abbey devotes part of its annual programme to productions of Irish theatrical classics by Boucicault, Richard Brinsley Sheridan, Yeats, O'Casey, Synge and Lady Gregory. Plays by contemporary playwrights—Brian Friel, Tom Murphy, John B. Keane, Frank McGuinness—form the remainder of the production. The Peacock is a venue for new playwrights.

O'Connell Street

O'Connell Street was originally laid out in the mid-18C as an elongated 45m wide residential square by Luke Gardiner and known as 'Gardiner's Mall', a precursor of the later Georgian squares. It once had a promenading walk in the centre. In 1790, the square was extended to the Liffey, connected to the south side by a bridge (the predecessor of O'Connell Bridge) and named Sackville St after the viceroy. It takes its present name from Daniel O'Connell (1775–1847), 'the Liberator'. Shelley lodged at No. 7 in 1812, where he wrote *An address to the Irish People*.

Almost the whole of the east side of the street, from the Liffey to North Earl St was destroyed by shelling or fire during 1916, as well as the blocks surrounding the Custom House. It remained a ruin for nearly 20 years. In July 1922 it was the scene of the last stand of the 'Irregulars' of the anti-treaty party against the Free State government. Cathal Brugha, a leader of the Irregulars, who counselled surrender, but with the courage of fanaticism refused to do so himself, was shot down as he rushed out at the government troops.

Rebuilt to follow the rooflines of the Georgian street with large cut-stone blocks blending into organised façades composed of department stores, shops, banks, and cinemas, it is still the centre of the busiest shopping area in the city. Despite its tawdriness at street level, it maintains the grandeur of a Parisian boulevard. Clery's (1918) department store on the east side of the street is a scaled-down replica of Selfridges on Oxford St, London.

The Monuments
The Liffey end of the street is dominated by the **O'Connell Monument** commemorating Daniel O'Connell, (Foley, 1882) with allegorical figures; Erin casting off her fetters and four winged victories. Those on the north side bear bullet holes from 1916. O'Connell, known as 'the Liberator' was the first non-Anglican to sit in Westminster; he promoted the Emancipation Act of 1829 to repeal the Penal Laws which discriminated against Catholics and dissenters. The monument was once overlooked by the Nelson Pillar—a 40.2m Doric column built 32 years before its counterpart in Trafalgar Square, London (designed by William Wilkins, its statue by Thomas Kirk)—but it was blown up by the IRA in March 1966 (50th anniversary of the Rising). Nelson's head is in the Civic Museum. Other monuments are those to William Smith O'Brien (1803–64), leader of the Young Ireland party; Sir John Gray (1816–75), proprietor of the *Freeman's Journal* and organiser of Dublin's water-supply; Jim Larkin by Oisin Kelly, 1981; Father (Theobald) Mathew (1790–1856), the 'apostle' of Temperance; and Charles Stewart Parnell (1846–91), the advocate of 'Home Rule'. Among recent attempts by the municipality to embellish the street has been the erection of the **Anna Livia Fountain** (Eammon O'Doherty, 1988), an allegorical figure representing Anna Livia, personification of the Liffey, which wits have since dubbed 'The Floozie in the Jacuzzi'. The **Parnell Monument** (Augustus Saint Gaudens, 1911) is the finest of those on the street; the obelisk is by the American Beaux-Arts architect Henry Bacon (1861–1924), best known for the Lincoln Memorial (1917), Washington DC. In North Earl St. (right) is an untidy figure of the characteristically dapper **James Joyce** by Marjorie Fitzgibbon (1990).

The Proclamation of the Republic
Half-way up the west side of the street is the **General Post Office** (Francis Johnston, 1814), retaining its granite façade and fine Portland stone Ionic portico which spans the pavement. Headquarters of the Volunteers during the Easter Rising, 1916, it was commanded by Patrick Pearse and James Connolly. The Proclamation of the Republic was read by Pearse from the

steps. Set alight by shelling, the building was abandoned by its garrison, and both Pearse and Connolly and 13 of their co-conspirators were executed at Kilmainham Gaol soon after, providing additional martyrs for the movement. Statues of 'Fidelity', 'Hibernia' and 'Mercury' (Thomas Kirk) top the pediment. The building was re-opened in 1929, and within the main hall is a small commemorative statue, the 'Death of Cuchulainn' (pronounced *Coo-hu-lin*) by Oliver Sheppard (1934). Erected as a memorial to 1916, it symbolises both the image of a tribal hero and the idea of the blood-sacrifice espoused by Pearse and his followers. The GPO is regarded as an Irish political Valhalla and birthplace of the Republic, a site sacred to every shade of Nationalist opinion and still a rallying point for all forms of civil and political protest. The columns of the portico bear the bullet marks of the Rising. The Philatelic Office is to the right of the main hall.

From the opposite side of the street you can turn east to Marlborough St—parallel to O'Connell St—and then bear left, passing **Tyrone House** (right), built by Castle in 1741 for the Marquess of Waterford, and occupied since 1835 by the Education Department. It contains good stucco work by the Lafrancinis. A replica of the house was later erected to the left to replace the stable block.

On the left stands **St. Mary's Pro-Cathedral** the principal Catholic church of Dublin. Attributed to the French architect, Louis Hippolyte le Bas (1815), but the actual author of its design, which was sent from Paris, is a mystery. It is a Greek Revival building of great power and confidence, although poorly sited. The Doric portico—based on the Temple of Theseus in Athens—faces the street and is surrounded by exceptional ironwork. The interior has not been helped by the insertion of a dome, but still remains the finest neo-classical church interior in the city, although its narrow columned aisle is cluttered by large monuments, among which are Archbishops Cullen and Murray (Sir Thomas Farrell). Of interest is the architectural model of the building by John Sweetman (to whom the design is also credited), and the vaults, which are used for burials. Its Palestrina choir (with which the tenor John McCormac sang as a young man) was endowed by Edward Martyn and still performs sacred music; the high altar (recently whittled down) is by Peter Turnerelli.

Return to O'Connell St, where you will find the offices of Bus Éireann and Dublin Bus, the national and city bus services, while a few steps further north (No. 40) are those of Aer Lingus.

At the end of the street is the **Rotunda** of the Assembly Rooms designed by John Ensor (1764) and embellished by Gandon who added the portico and a Coadstone frieze by Edward Smyth in 1786. Among those who performed here in its heyday were the pianist and composer, John Field, the singer and friend of Mozart, Michael Kelly (1764–1826) and Franz Liszt.

Immediately behind it is the **Gate Theatre**, accommodated in an extension of the Assembly Rooms built in 1784–86 by Richard Johnston. The theatre was founded in 1928 by Hilton Edwards (1903–82) and Michel Mac Liammoir (1899–1978), and transferred to these premises in the following year. Orson Wells and James Mason performed with the company when still unrecognised. The theatre was shared with Lord Longford's company for many years (see Tullynally Castle). The Gate is the leading exponent of contemporary international theatre in Dublin, and also promotes the work of living Irish playwrights.

Adjoining the Assembly Rooms to the west is the **Rotunda Hospital** (1748), designed by Castle and later much extended. This, the first purpose-built 'lying-in' or maternity hospital in the British Isles was founded by Dr Bartholomew Mosse (1712–59), who had already opened a provisional one on smaller premises in 1745. He also established the Assembly Rooms, the profits of which were devoted to the hospital. The façade closely resembles Castle's Leinster House. Of particular interest is the **Chapel**, reached from the main entrance on the west (modern) side of the hospital. It is notable for its exuberant Rococo figurative plasterwork (Barthelemy Cramillion, 1757–58) which swarms with putti and cherubs. The gallery, entered from the floor above, affords a closer view of the ceiling.

Turn left behind the Gate Theatre into Parnell (formerly Rutland) Sq. in which there is the **Garden of Remembrance** (1966). Embellished with a monument 'The Children of Lir' by Oisin Kelly (1971) it is dedicated to those who gave their lives to the cause of Irish freedom. In the pool at the centre of the garden, a mosaic depicts the broken armaments of Bronze Age warriors

The square contains dignified mid-18C mansions, many of them designed by John Ensor. No. 11 was once the town house of the Earls of Ormonde; the poet and author, Oliver St. John Gogarty (1878–1957) was born at No. 5. The **Dublin Writers' Museum** (11.00–17.00 Fri & Sat, 13.00–17.00, Sun; closed Mon–Thurs, Oct–Mar; 10.00–17.00, Tue–Sat, closed Mon, Apr–Sept; £) is housed at No. 18 and is devoted to the lives and work of the city's many famous poets, playwrights and novelists. It contains a fledgling collection of books, manuscripts and memorabilia of Beckett, Behan, Gogarty, Kavanagh, O'Connor and many others; reading rooms, a café and bookshop. Built in 1755 the principal feature of the house is the salon (Alfred Darbyshire, 1891) now the Gallery of Writers, decorated with a collection of Irish literary portraits. The adjoining No. 19 is the **Irish Writers' Centre** (10.00–18.00, Mon–Sat; £). Both houses are the frequent venue for literary readings and conferences.

Hugh Lane Municipal Gallery of Modern Art
In the centre of the north side of the Square is Charlemont House, a graceful building designed by Sir William Chambers (1762) for the 1st Earl of Charlemont. It is now the Hugh Lane Municipal Gallery of Modern Art (09.30–18.00, Tue–Fri; 09.30–15.00 Sat; 11.00–15.00 Sun; closed Mon) founded in 1908 largely through the generosity of Sir Hugh Lane (1875–1915), a nephew of Lady Gregory. It contains a notable Bossi fireplace on the first floor. The original home of the Lane Collection was 17 Harcourt St, but after Lane's death by drowning (when the *Lusitania* was torpedoed), the collection was held in safe-keeping in London pending a decision on the 'legal' interpretation of the unwitnessed codicil to his will. Agreement between the British and Irish governments was reached only in 1959 (and renewed in 1993) since when half the collection has alternated quinquennially between the two capitals.

The gallery's extensive collection is rotated, so the accompanying list is representative of the works which may be on view. Its holding of Continental, British and Irish art of the late 19C and 20C is comprehensive, and includes seminal works by Corot, Monet, Manet and Renoir.

The Gallery also hosts an annual and highly regarded winter series of **free classical music concerts** on Sundays at noon, with performers of international reputation.

In the **Entrance Hall** is a heroic Socialist Realism portrait bust of 'Michael Collins' by Seamus Murphy, a small reclining figure by Henry Moore and equestrian figure of 'General Lafayette' by Andrew O'Connor. Off the foyer are the café, bookshop and the stained glass room, with 'The Eve of St. Agnes' by Harry Clarke and works by Wilhelmina Geddes, Evie Hone and James Scanlon.

Oval room. August Rodin, *The Age of Bronze*; Jacob Epstein, *Man of Aran*. **Room 8** (to the right) Josef Beuys, *Blackboards*; Christo, *Wrapping of St. Stephen's Green*, leading to **Room 9** Edward McGuire, *Francis Stuart*; Patrick Hennesy, *Exiles*; Tony O'Malley, *Mid-Summer Window with Moths*. Opposite is **Room 6**. Edward Burne-Jones, *The Sleeping Princesses*.

Room 1. Roderick O'Conor, *Breton Girl*; Vuillard, *Mantlepiece*; Vlaminck, *Opium*; Utrillo. **Room 2**. Corot, *Rome from the Pinico*; Lavery, *Sutton Courtenay*; Walter Osborne; Frank O'Meara; Norman Garstin; George Clausen. **Room 3**. Gwen John, *Study of a young girl*; Augustus John, *Miss Iris Tree*; Sean Keating, *Men of the West*; de Segonzac; Mary Swanzy; Mannie Jellett; Jack B. Yeats, *There is no night*; Walter Sickert, *The old Church, Dieppe*. **Room 4**. Michael Farrell, *Madonna Irlanda*; Patrick Scott, *Chinese Landscape*; Phelim Egan. *Sound Reference II*. **Room 5**. Mancini, *Sir Hugh Lane*; Gerome, *A cadet*; Courbet, *In the forest*, and *Snowstorm*; Honoré Daumier, *Peasant Woman*, and *Summer morning*; Forain, *Law Courts*.

From the north-east corner of Parnell Square walk along Great Denmark St, to **Belvedere House** (1785) which contains Adamesque stucco-work by Michael Stapleton. The stair hall is as patterned as a Pompeian villa. James Joyce attended the Jesuit school here between 1893 and 1898, as recorded in *Portrait of the Artist as a Young Man*.

The James Joyce Cultural Centre

The James Joyce Cultural Centre (Tues–Sat 10.00–16.30, Sun 12.30–16.30, £) has been established at 35 North Great George's St which runs steeply downhill from the front of Belvedere House. The Centre, in the town house of Lord Kenmare (1784), is devoted to promoting Joycean studies, and organises high quality tours of Joyce's Dublin, guided by descendants of the writer. Many of the houses in this street have been restored and it is one of the few streets of 18C houses which has returned to residential use after a century of tenement or institutional occupation. J.P. Mahaffy, Provost of Trinity and early patron of Oscar Wilde lived at No. 38.

Temple St North, the next left-hand turning, leads to Hardwick Crescent and **St. George's church** (deconsecrated) built by Francis Johnston (from 1802), with a fine steeple over 60m high, adapted from the design of that of St. Martin-in-the-Fields, London. The future Duke of Wellington and Kitty Pakenham were married here in 1806.

To the northwest, the street crosses Dorset into Eccles St, in which No. 64 was the home of Francis Johnston architect of the General Post Office and Chapel Royal, Dublin Castle, and later of Isaac Butt, founder of the Home Rule Movement (1870). No. 7 (demolished in 1982) was the fictional home of

Leopold Bloom, in Joyce's *Ulysses*. Its site is now covered by a modern extension of the Mater Misericordiae Hospital (John Bourke, 1855) a monumental classical composition.

Parallel to and east of Temple St is Gardiner St, in which stands the Jesuit church of St. Francis Xavier (1832), by Joseph Keane, with a tetrastyle Ionic portico based on Notre Dame de Lorette (L.H. Le Bas). Off Gardiner St opens **Mountjoy Square**, the centre of a fashionable quarter of Dublin during the greatest period of the 'Ascendancy', but no longer so, although some improvement in the sad condition of its remaining mansions has taken place. The south side of the square was largely demolished in the 1970s, but has been rebuilt.

In his *Excursions through Ireland* (1820), Thomas Cromwell described this district, as seen from St. George's church, as one which 'taste and opulence have united to embellish; the streets in the vicinity are all built on a regular plan; the houses are lofty and elegant; and neither hotels, shops, nor warehouses, obtruding upon the scene, the whole possesses an air of dignified retirement— the tranquillity of ease, affluence and leisure. The inhabitants of this parish are indeed almost exclusively of the upper ranks...' By 1894 Somerville and Ross could write of the same area 'few towns are duller out of season than Dublin, but the dullness of its north side neither waxes nor wanes; it is immutable'. This area of the 18C city has yet to be 'discovered' and rescued from further decline.

Some distance northwest of Mountjoy Square, between the North Circular Rd and the Royal Canal (commenced 1789), lies **Mountjoy Prison** (1847), scene of the incarceration of many insurgents in 1916–21 and of opponents of the Free State government in 1922–23. Thomas Ashe (1885–1917) died there after forcible feeding during a hunger-strike. It is the setting of Brendan Behan's play *The Quare Fellow*.

From the north-west corner of Parnell Sq. turn right into Granby Row before turning left along Dorset St. Opposite Granby Row, is St. Mary Place and the deconsecrated **Black Church** or St. Mary's Chapel of Ease (1829–30). It is the ingenious masterpiece of John Semple, built of black Dublin calp, and roofed internally by one huge parabolic vault. There is no relationship between internal and external design; the conventional exterior masks its revolutionary concept (it is now used for commercial purposes).

The **National Wax Museum** (10.00–18.00 Mon–Sat, 12.00–18.00, Sun) in Granby Row (not a National institution), is a conventional collection of wax-work tableaux of poor-quality, representing personalities from Irish life and international figures; the heads rarely seem to belong to the bodies. Leonardo da Vinci's 'Last Supper' is an unintentionally comic representation of this masterpiece.

Dorset St is historically important if now undistinguished. The dramatist Richard Brinsley Sheridan (1751–1816) was born at No. 12 and No. 85 stands on the site of the birthplace of Seán O'Casey (1880–1964). Arthur Griffith (1872–1922), architect of Irish independence and first president of the Dail, and Sir William Rowan Hamilton (1805–65), the mathematician, were born in Dominick St, the next cross street, in which stands St. Saviour's (J.J. McCarthy, 1858). No. 20 Lower Dominick St is the masterpiece of the stuccoer Robert West (1755), it is embellished with his characteristic Rococo birds in high relief.

Dorset St runs downhill to the southwest and is continued as Bolton St, off which leads (right) **Henrietta St**. Laid out by Luke Gardiner in 1730–40, and the first street in Dublin to contain enormous aristocratic residences, it remained a most fashionable address up to the 1800s. Among its important residents were the Earls of Thomond, Bessborough, and Kingston, the Bishops of Limerick and Ferns and the Speaker of the House of Commons. The houses were sumptuously decorated and a few still retain their interior decoration. Nos 3–7 are by Nathaniel Clements and Nos 9 and 11, by Sir Edward Lovett Pearce. Others were gutted of their staircases and marble fireplaces by Alderman Meade earlier this century and converted into grotesque tenements. More recent owners have done much to restore the mansions to their former splendour, assisted by the Irish Georgian Society. Among them, notably, is No. 13 (1740), once the residence of Bishop Richard Pococke, and earlier of Viscount Loftus. Nos 9 and 10 are occupied by the Sisters of Charity and some of the interiors may be visited.

At the top end of the street stands **King's Inns**, the Dublin Inns of Court, an impressive classical building designed by Gandon in 1795, begun seven years later, and completed by Henry Aaron Baker. This is among the last and most original of Gandon's buildings and its narrow courtyard and twin projecting wings come as a surprise after the width and openness of Henrietta St. Its cupola was added by Francis Johnston in 1816. It contains a fine dining-hall, the only significant interior by Gandon which is still intact, and an extensive library, with Gothic Revival plasterwork by Frederick Darley (1827). Wings were added in the mid-19C. On the far side of the courtyard is a small park (for history, see under Four Courts).

To the northwest is the neo-Egyptian Broadstone Station (disused since 1937), by J.S. Mulvany (1850), now a bus depot. The roof of the passenger sheds is by the ironmaster Richard Turner. From Bolton St you can bear south along Capel St towards the Liffey. In St. Mary's St, to the left, is what remains of deconsecrated St. Mary's church (from 1697), by Thomas Burgh, where in 1747 **John Wesley** preached his first sermon in Ireland (where he was later to travel some 40,000km). Richard Brinsley Sheridan, Lord Charlemont, and Wolfe Tone were baptised here. Adjacent is Wolfe Tone St (formerly Stafford St), where Theobald Wolfe Tone (1763–98), founder of the United Irishmen, was born.

The next left-hand turning off Capel St leads to **St. Mary's Abbey** (10.00–17.00, Wed only, June–Sept; OPW), incorporating part of the chapter-house and slype (late-12C) of the Abbey of St. Mary Ostmanby (*Ostman*, Vikings), a Benedictine foundation of 1139 transferred to the Cistercians in 1147. Here 'Silken Thomas' Fitzgerald, appointed Lord Deputy, threw off his allegiance to England in 1534, only to be captured and, in the following year, executed. The dependencies of the abbey were later quarried for their stone; in 1676 the remaining stone was used in the construction of Essex Bridge. Return to Liffey Quays via Capel St.

Following a recent government initiative, the quays which were in a sorry state of dilapidation are being rebuilt with apartment blocks and commercial developments. Although these maintain the Georgian roof lines, the unity of the quays has been seriously eroded by a century of neglect. Beyond the Ha'penny Bridge you reach Bachelors' Walk, known for the affray that took place there on 26 July 1914 after the Howth gun-running, a party of British troops (the King's Own Scottish Borderers) fired on a crowd of jeering, missile-hurling citizens, killing three and wounding thirty-eight.

The Phoenix Park

Phoenix Park may be approached from the O'Connell Bridge (bus from Aston Quay) or by walking along the quays on the north bank of the Liffey past the Four Courts.

The main entrance is in Parkgate St although there are entrances from numerous points around the perimiter. *Ryan's Pub* in Parkgate St has an excellent Victorian interior. The Phoenix Park is one of the largest and most attractive enclosed public parks in Europe (808 hectares), with a wall c 11km long. The route indicated here proceeds along the main northwest road through the park and return by way of the woods and valleys to the south.

The name of the park is believed to be a corruption of *Fionn Uisce* (clear water), from a spring that rises not far from the Phoenix Column (erected by Lord Chesterfield in 1747) which stands in the middle of the main roadway.

The layout of the park is mainly due to Chesterfield, although the original grant of Crown land confiscated from the priory of St. John at Kilmainham was made by Charles II; it was enclosed in 1662 at the suggestion of the Duke of Ormonde. Many landscape and architectural features of the park and the main boulevard which runs southeast–northwest through the park were introduced from 1834 by Decimus Burton, but the landscape is better appreciated by travelling the circuitous side roads which meander through the richly wooded parkland. A herd of 300 fallow deer, introduced by the Duke of Ormonde in the 17C roam freely and may usually be seen in the south-western area of Oldtown Wood or the 'Fifteen Acres'.

Immediately to the right of the entrance is the People's Garden, a colourful flower garden, adjoining buildings of the Irish Department of Defence, designed by Gandon, but carried out from 1787 by W. Gibson. Nearby are the *Garda Síochána* headquarters, containing a small **Police Museum**.

This south-east corner of the park is dominated by the **Wellington Testimonial**, a 60m-high obelisk, the largest in Europe, designed by Sir Robert Smirke in 1817 to commemorate the Duke of Wellington, a Dubliner, and the victor at the battle of Waterloo. The plinth is decorated with bas-relief panels. Cast from cannons captured at Waterloo, 'Civil and Religious Liberty' (Hogan), 'Indian Wars' (Kirk) and 'Waterloo' (Farrell), and a grandiloquent inscription.

To the right and north of the Main Road are the **Zoological Gardens** (Dublin Zoo; 09.00–18.00, Mon–Sat; 10.30–18.00, Sun; closes at sunset in winter) opened in 1830 and famous for their lions and other large carnivores, and the breeding of endangered species; the MGM lion was born here. The cottage orné near the entrance is by Burton (1847); the grounds contain two natural lakes and numerous waterfowl, pelicans and flamingos.

Beyond the Polo Ground is the *Aras an Uachtaráin* (Residence of the President), the former Viceregal Lodge, of 1751–54, by Nathaniel Clements (1705–77; who built it for himself). The Ionic portico was added in 1816 by Francis Johnston, and the lodge contains a fine plaster ceiling from Mespil House. Queen Victoria, writing from here in 1849 while on her first visit to Ireland, makes no mention of the Famine still raging! Winston Churchill spent almost three years of his childhood (until early 1879) at 'The Little Lodge', a stone's throw away. His father was then secretary to his own father, the Duke of Marlborough, appointed Lord Lieutenant in 1876. Opposite, in the Main Road, Lord Frederick Cavendish, the Chief Secretary, and his Under-Secretary

Thomas Burke, were stabbed to death in 1882 by members of the 'Invincibles'. Cavendish and Burke are commemorated by a small plaque set in the ground on the roadside of the Polo Grounds, while their assassins are remembered by a florid monument in Glasnevin Cemetery.

Ashtown Castle (10.00–17.00 daily; OPW; £) (right). Formerly the Under-Secretary's Lodge, then the Apostolic Nunciature until recently demolished, this is now the site of Ashford Castle, a small and previously unknown 17C tower house which was discovered within the Nunciature during demolition. The **Phoenix Park Visitor Centre** next to the Castle is devoted to the history and reconstruction of the building, as well as the wildlife and history of the Park.

To the left of the main road is the **American Ambassador's Residence** (formerly the Chief Secretary's Lodge, 1776; for Sir John Blaquiere).

Turn left at the first main crossroads west of Ashtown Castle. On the right are the offices of the Irish Ordnance Survey (previously the Mountjoy Barracks). Follow the road through Oldtown Wood where the deer may be seen. The towering Papal Cross marks the place where Paul VI celebrated Mass in 1977. The road skirts the south edge of the park passing through more rugged terrain.

Near the centre of the south side of the park is St. Mary's (Chest) Hospital, formerly the Hibernian Military School, with a chapel by Thomas Cooley (1771). Joseph Sheridan Le Fanu (1814–73) was born here, his father being the chaplain. There is a fine portal dolmen in the grounds.

The building of the **Magazine Fort** (1734) on a hillock between this point and the main entrance, caused Swift to write 'Lo, here's a proof of Irish sense. Here Irish wit is seen. Where nothing's left that's worth defence, they build a magazine'. The fort, set into the ground, is hardly visible from a distance. Inside its star-fort defences are a group of diminutive 18C houses, and powder magazines.

Return to the Parkgate St entrance. The Wellington Testimonial is well worth closer inspection. The sheer monumentality places it among the great follies of the 19C. An equestrian statue was planned as part of the memorial but it got no further than the plinth, which was later removed. Equestrian statues have a very poor survival rate throughout Ireland, attracting the particular ire of nationalist bombers (in such a horse-loving country there is probably a deeper significance to the matter). Return to the city along the north quays.

For a longer return to the city centre, leave Phoenix Park by the Knockmaroon Gate (south-west corner), and bear left through the now suburban village of Chapelizod, traditionally taking its name from Isolde (or Iseult), daughter of Aengus, King of Ireland, and beloved of Tristan. It was also the scene of Sheridan Le Fanu's story *The House by the Churchyard*, and the birthplace of the newspaper magnate Alfred Harmsworth, later Lord Northcliffe (1865–1922).

From Chapelizod return to the centre of Dublin by skirting the south wall of Phoenix Park, later passing the Islandbridge Gate, and continuing along the North Quays to city centre.

National Botanic Gardens, Glasnevin

National Botanic Gardens, Glasnevin (09.00–18.00 Mon–Sat; 11.00–18.00 Sun, in summer; 10.00–16.30, Mon–Fri, 11.00–16.30, Sun in winter). Bus from O'Connell Street.

The best approach is to drive due north along Church St (from the east side of Four Courts) and its extension through the suburb of Phibsborough, and take the right-hand fork shortly beyond the Royal Canal.

These delightful gardens (20 hectares) contain a remarkable collection of 20,000 species and varieties and the arrangement is botanical rather than geographical, skirted to the north by the river Tolka. Founded in 1795 by direction of the Irish Parliament—largely the work of the Hon. John Foster (1740–1828) the last Speaker of the Irish House of Commons—the gardens were under the care of the Royal Dublin Society; until 1899, when the Department of Agriculture took charge. The demesne originally belonged to Thomas Tickell (1686–1740), the poet; and Swift, Steele, Delany, and Thomas Parnell all at one time lived in the vicinity. The Yew Walk (c 1740) is the only 18C part of the gardens; it is also known as 'Addison's Walk', although his connection with the district is entirely apocryphal.

The cast-iron glass houses are early and important examples of their genre. The **Curvilinear Range** (1843) is by the Dublin ironmaster Richard Turner, and the **Great Palm House** (1884) was prefabricated by Boyds of Paisley in Scotland. The garden's collections of conifers, rhododendrons, orchids and shrubberies are all of importance and it was at Glasnevin that in 1844 the earliest attempt to raise orchids from seed is recorded. The cedars in the garden are notable, Cedrus atlantica 'Pendula', was planted in 1875.

'Delville', the home of Mrs Delany (1700–88), the celebrated diarist and letter writer, was demolished in the 1940s. Her most significant work, a collection of botanical collages, done when in her 80s, are in the British Library.

Immediately to the southwest is **Glasnevin** (or Prospect) **Cemetery**. Tours of Glasnevin take place at 11.30 on Sundays; the guides usually of strident republican inclination. It is the national cemetery in which are buried many of the advocates of Irish liberty. The O'Connell Monument (George Petrie, 1790–1866), a 51m Round Tower (considerably taller than the originals which average 30m) is the centrepiece of a forest of Celtic crosses which express the nationalistic aspirations of those buried here. Among them are J.P. Curran (brought here from London in 1834), Daniel O'Connell (brought from Genoa, and reburied in 1869 in the crypt under the Round Tower), C.S. Parnell, Arthur Griffith, Michael Collins, John Blake Dillon, Charles Gavan Duffy, Constance Markicvicz, Thomas Ashe, William Dargan, James Larkin, Jeremiah O'Donovan Rossa, Maud Gonne Macbride and her son, Sean MacBride (recipient of the Lenin and Nobel Peace Prizes), Eamon de Valera and (since 1965, from Pentonville Prison), Sir Roger Casement. Among writers and musicians Brendan Behan, Gerard Manley Hopkins (in the Jesuit Plot), Margaret Burke-Sheridan.

Casino Marino, Howth, Malahide Castle

To the left of Amien St. in Portland Row stands Aldborough House, an imposing building (1792–98) in the style of Sir William Chambers and the last of the 18C mansions to be built in Dublin.

The road crosses the Royal Canal and the river Tolka. On the north bank, to the west, is **Croke Park**. Named after Archbishop Croke (1824–1902), an advocate of athletics and temperance, it is the national stadium for 'Gaelic

Games' (hurling, Gaelic football, camogie and handball) and venue for the All-Ireland finals. The new stand, built in 1995, is architecturally interesting. The Gaelic Athletic Association (GAA) which owns Croke Park, does not permit its grounds to be used for 'foreign games', ie, anything not believed to have been played by the ancient Gaels.

The road to the right skirts Fairview Park, on land reclaimed from the sea. Bear left on Howth Rd for a short distance for the 18C Casino at Marino (bus from city centre).

The Casino Marino

The charming little Casino, (09.30–18.30 daily, June–Sept; £; OPW) stands in the grounds of Lord Charlemont's old estate of Marino (the house was demolished in 1921 but the original entrance gates have been re-erected). Built by Sir William Chambers (1759–71), this building represents the finest achievement of 18C antiquarian research into the architecture of the Roman period in Ireland. Charlemont and Chambers were both deeply imbued with a love for and scholarly understanding of classical architecture. The Casino is the culmination of a life-long collaboration of the leading intellectual figure of Georgian Dublin with the principal English architect of the classical revival.

Designed in the Franco-Roman neo-classical style, it is a building of considerable complexity. Set on rising ground, externally it appears as a single-storey, small rectangular classical temple with porticoes on four faces, topped by a balustraded cornice with ornamental urns on an attic storey. At the base, between crouching (although un-leonine-looking) lions at the corners, steps rise to the ground floor terrace level. What lies behind the façade is a three storey villa, a Greek cross in plan (enclosed in a circular colonnade), containing 16 rooms, all interlocked and so ingeniously arranged that their presence is unsuspected. Entered from the north, a vestibule (with a reproduction of Pompeo Batoni's portrait of the young Charlemont) leads into the main suite of reception rooms. Here the original plasterwork and parquet floors are the main decorative treatment. A library and music room approached through concealed gib doors adjoin the central saloon.

From the vestibule a hidden staircase leads to the bedroom floor with canopied bed in the state room, entered through a columned screen. Dressing rooms and the valet's bedroom are on either side. Another flight leads to the roof terrace. From here there is a view of the bay, as there would have been from all south and east-facing rooms when the Casino was built. The stone urns are chimney pots. Below the ground floor are kitchens, wine and ale cellars, and storerooms. The hollow Doric columns at the corners act as drainpipes for the roof. The cornice soffit is the most richly ornamented area of the whole building.

Chambers brought Simon Vierpyl from Rome to do the stonecarving on the Casino and Edward Smyth, the Irish sculptor, worked as his assistant. Joseph Wilton executed the lions, and Cipriani the panels beneath them. The carved decoration of the Casino is without parallel in Ireland for its richness and quality of classical ornament.

Taken into State care in 1930, the restoration (Dunphy/Redmill/O'Connell)

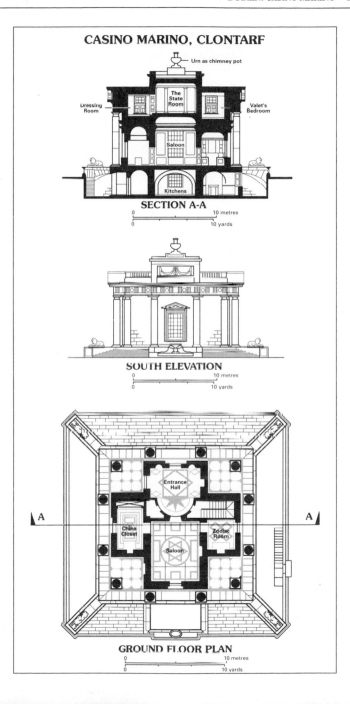

CASINO MARINO, CLONTARF

Urn as chimney pot

The State Room

Dressing Room

Valet's Bedroom

Saloon

Kitchens

SECTION A-A

0   10 metres
0   10 yards

SOUTH ELEVATION

0   10 metres
0   10 yards

A   A

Entrance Hall

China Closet

Zodiac Room

Saloon

GROUND FLOOR PLAN

0   10 metres
0   10 yards

1974–84, has by scientific analysis of the wall surfaces attempted to reproduce the original colour scheme. As all Charlemont's art and furniture collection were dispersed in the 19C, the furniture comes from the National Museum collection. Adjoining the entrance is a charming memorial inscription to Neptune, the 2nd Earl's dog, the text is attributed to Byron.

Return to the coast road, skirt Dublin Bay and Clontarf (*Cluain Tarbh*, bull's meadow), the scene of the battle of Good Friday, 1014, when the Irish under Brian Boru, mortally wounded in the combat, broke the power of the Vikings.

Clontarf Castle (1835) was built on the site of an ancient fortification of the Pale, which had belonged successively to the Templars and to the Knights of St. John.

Beyond Dollymount and before you pass (left) St. Anne's Park (500 acres) with its fine rose gardens, offshore (right) and approached by a long and narrow timber bridge is **North Bull Island**, a UNESCO Biosphere Reserve and the largest overwintering site for migratory birds on the east coast. This causeway is the northern counterpart of the South Bull Wall, but its stretch above water does not project so far into the bay; on its length are a number of attractive Modern Movement (c 1930) bathing shelters.

The 6km-long island, which has been created by the action of sand-bearing tides in the bay since 1820, is a combination of dune grassland and salt marsh. **The Bull Island Interpretative Centre** (10.00–18.00 daily) runs a programme of information on the wildlife habitat. It is possible to drive on to the island, continuing along the beach and return to the shore by the modern bridge at the east end.

The two roads to Howth converge at Kilbarrack, with a ruined 13C church said to be a votive chapel of the mariners of Dublin Bay, and a short distance beyond, at Sutton, you reach the narrow isthmus of the **Howth Peninsula**. Whistler occupied a villa here in 1900, and caused consternation by papering over half its north-facing windows.

The road skirts the northern shore of the peninsula, passing (right) the main entrance to Howth Castle demesne. The peninsula (virtually an island) was acquired in 1177 by Sir Almeric Tristram, a Norman noble, and the lands have remained without a break in the possession of the St. Lawrence family. Their change of name to St. Lawrence is attributed to a vow of Sir Almeric's, made at a battle fought against the Vikings on St. Lawrence's Day, to assume the name if victorious. Howth was also the childhood home of Maude Gonne MacBride (1866–1953) and W.B.Yeats lived there in 1880.

Howth

Howth (DART from central Dublin) itself, a resort of steep streets (the *King Sitric Restaurant* is noted for its seafood) has an unexpectedly large harbour, and commands a view of Ireland's Eye. The name of Howth is derived from the Old Norse 'hoved' (a cape) and is pronounced to rhyme with 'both'; the Irish name, *Binn Eadair*, recalls the legendary hero, Edar. It was the Dublin packet-station from 1813 until it was superceded by Kingstown (see Dun Laoghaire). Its harbour, constructed in 1807–09, and frequented by both yachts and fishing-boats, was the scene of the gun-running incident of 26 July 1914 (following the success of the Larne gun-running shortly before, arming the Ulster Volunteers). Only 900 rifles and 25,000 rounds of ammunition were landed here from Germany in Erskine Childer's yacht the *Asgard* similarly to arm the Irish Volunteers. The *Asgard* is on display in Kilmainham Gaol.

Another notable landing was that of George IV who disembarked here drunk on 12 August 1821. In honour of the event the imprint of his dainty feet was carved in a granite slab at the end of the west pier where they are still visible.

The offshore quartzite rock of Ireland's Eye, now a seabird sanctuary, bears the over-restored remains of Cill Mac Nessan, an early medieval church. On its north facing cliffs nest the peregrine falcon, shearwater, guillemot, fulmar, petrel and puffin which can be observed at close quarters. Many species of tern frequent the Malahide estuary. Boat services to Ireland's Eye from the east pier.

St. Mary's Abbey, (10.00–17.00, Wed only, June–Sept) above the harbour is a Viking foundation of 1042, perhaps built by Sigtryggr, but nothing of this building survives. The present remains of the collegiate church of the Virgin Mary (14C–17C) consists of two parallel aisles divided by an arcade of crude pointed arches, with a triple lancet window in the south aisle and a triple 17C bellcote on the west gable. Near the south-east corner is the fine medieval recumbent double-figure tomb of Sir Christopher St. Lawrence, 13th Baron Howth (d. 1462) and his wife, Anne Plunkett of Ratoath, with the St. Lawrence and Plunkett arms. Facing Abbey St is the 'College of Howth', a small 15C ecclesiastical residence.

Howth Castle

A few minutes' walk west of the village, is an irregular battlemented structure dating from 1564, but much restored by Francis Bindon in 1738 (his portrait of Swift hangs in the Castle) and by Morrison and Lutyens (1911) who added the pseudo-medieval west tower. Seat of the Earl of Howth until the death of the 4th Earl and 30th Baron in 1909, it is still lived in by the Gaisford-St. Lawrence family, and the oldest inhabited house in Ireland. The castle is not open to the public although the grounds are; there is a rather cluttered Transport Museum in the stables.

The gardens are famous for their 400 species of rhododendrons which crowd the slopes of adjacent 'Mud Rock' (and for the early 18C formal garden with its, 9m-high beech hedges). In the grounds are the ruins of Corr Castle, a tall square 16C edifice guarding the isthmus and Aideen's Grave, a magnificent portal dolmen in the rhododendron grove, it was the inspiration for the eponymous poem by Sir Samuel Ferguson (1810–1886).

> They heaved the stone; they heap'd the cairn:
> Said Ossian.'In a queenly grave
> We leave her, 'mong her fields of fern,
> Between the cliff and wave'.

Standing beside the huge portal tomb, this does not sound quite so fanciful.

For many years the castle door was open to all comers at mealtimes, a custom dating, it is said, from 1575, when Grace O'Malley, the uncrowned queen of the West (see Clare Island), passed by on her return journey to Ireland after visiting Queen Elizabeth. Inhospitably refused admittance to the castle on the excuse that the family was at dinner, she abducted the heir of Howth to her castle of

Carrigahowley, and kept him there until she had wrung a promise from Lord Howth to keep his gates open at mealtimes in the future. The story is apocryphal.

The road climbs southeast from the village centre to make the circle of the peninsula. From The Summit you may climb to the Ben of Howth (171m), with a cairn said to cover the remains of King Crimhthan Niadhnair (AD 90). A cliff walk approaches the Baily lighthouse (1814) on the south-east point, erected on the site of an old stone fort or baile, and replacing the older hill-top beacon. Cliff walks extend from the Summit north to Howth village and west towards Sutton. The road returning to Sutton around the south side of the peninsula, providing extensive views towards Dublin, passes at Carrickbrack Rd, the minute Early Christian church of St. Fintan (9C) in Shielmartin graveyard.

If travelling by car from Sutton, bear northwest, and then turn through Portmarnock, skirting the coast near a sandy peninsula known as the Velvet Strand before entering the village of Malahide, a resort on the estuary of the Broad Meadow river. Its parish church retains some of the few surviving hatchments in Ireland (bus from central Dublin or train from Conolly station).

Malahide Castle

Malahide Castle, southwest of the village (10.00–17.00, Mon–Thur, April–Sept, 14.00–18.00, Sat, Sun & BH) was the seat of the Talbot de Malahide family (except during the years 1653–60, when it was tenanted by the regicide Miles Corbet) since Richard Talbot received a grant of land here in 1174. The Malahide and Talbot families managed by remarkable political dexterity and a fair degree of luck to hold on to the lands for 800 years, until the late Lord Talbot's death in 1975, when it was acquired by Dublin County Council. In the turmoil of Irish history, such survivals are rare. Paintings from the family collection hang in the Great hall of the the castle.

Considerably altered over the centuries, the core of the building is medieval with 17C–19C additions. The 16C panelled **Oak Room** is the earliest to retain its decoration, with Old Testament subjects carved in low relief. The reception rooms contain Rococo plasterwork by Robert West; in the small rooms of the corner turrets are Gothick ogee windows.

It is said that on the morning of the Battle of the Boyne (1690) some 14 Talbots, all first cousins, breakfasted at Malahide before sallying out to their death in that contest, which is depicted in a painting by Jan Wyck hanging over the fireplace in the Great Hall.

The **hall** is the only surviving medieval great hall in Ireland to retain its original form and, until quite recently, to remain in domestic use. Among the more notable paintings which may be on display here are: after Van Dyck, *The Concert*; after Maratti, *Luke Wadding* (founder of the Irish College in Rome; see Waterford); Kneller, Portraits of General Godert de Ginkel, and of Richard Steele; after Batoni, the Earl-Bishop of Derry; George Barret, several landscapes; anon. Irish School, *William Conolly and Adam Loftus*; Lely, *James Butler, 1st Duke of Ormonde*; Longhi, *Portrait of General Christopher Nugent*; attrib. Thomas Hickey, *Portrait of Joseph Hickey*; Romney, *The artist's wife*; John Lewis, *Portrait of Thomas Sheridan*; Frank Reynolds, *Coursing enthusiasts*; Hogarth, *Portrait of Lord Wade*; after Hogarth, *2nd Viscount Boyne*.

Between 1928 and 1948 many of the papers of James Boswell (great-grand-father of Emily Boswell, who married the 5th Lord Talbot) came to light in the castle, including the original version of the *Tour to the Hebrides* and an early draft of the *Life of Johnson* (including suppressed passages), which were acquired by Yale University, as described in *The Treasure of Auchinleck* by David Buchanan (1975). *The Malahide Papers* have been published by Yale.

North of the castle which is set in 268 acres of parkland is the **Talbot Botanic Gardens** (20 acres). Created by Milo Talbot in the early 20C, it has 5000 species and varieties adaptable to an alkaline soil, with a concentration on the Southern Hemisphere; Australia, Chile, New Zealand and Tasmania.

The 14C–15C Abbey beside the castle was unroofed by Corbet (see above), but contains the 15C tomb of Maud Plunkett, 'maid, wife, and widow in one day', who survived to marry Sir Richard Talbot as her third husband. The east gable has a three lancet window and triple bellcote. There is a *Shiela-Na-Gig* on the west gable.

The **Fry Model Railway**, installed in the old Corn Store at Malahide features a remarkably extensive collection of 'O' gauge model trains (working layout 32' x 72', 2.8 miles of track) made in the 1920s and 1930s by railway engineer Cyril Fry, based on Irish railway history and the Dublin, Cork and Belfast transport system.

St. Doulagh's church is the oldest church still in use in Ireland, its external appearance is a complex arrangement of shapes. The east end is probably 12C; the high-pitched roof and sturdy square tower with stepped battlements 15C and 19C additions. Inside are two chambers lighted by Gothic windows with trefoil heads; in the smaller of which is the so-called tomb of St. Doulagh. Three stair-cases lead to vaulted upper chambers, once used as anchorites' cells. To the north is an octagonal stone-roofed building which probably served as a baptistery. A stone cross stands on the roadside. Nathaniel Hone the Younger (1831–1917), the landscape painter, lived nearby during the latter part of his life, and many of his paintings depict the landscape of North Co. Dublin

Ballsbridge, Dun Laoghaire, Maritime Museum, Killiney Hill

The continuations of Lower Mount St (leading southeast from Merrion Sq.) and Lower Baggot St (near the north-east corner of St. Stephen's Green) converge a short distance beyond the Grand Canal near Jury's Hotel at Ballsbridge, one of the most pleasant residential suburbs of Dublin. On the right is the cylindrical **American Embassy** (John Mc L. Johansen, 1964), the exterior treatment inspired by Celtic interlace.

Crossing the river Dodder by a bridge of 1791, you reach the premises (right) of the **Royal Dublin Society** (RDS), behind which are their extensive Show Grounds (1881). The Spring Show is held here in early May and the Horse Show takes place in August. The buildings include a restaurant, bar, library and concert-hall. The Society, founded in 1731 by 14 Dublin gentlemen (among them Thomas Prior and Sir Thomas Molyneux), and incorporated in 1750, occupied Leinster House from 1815 until 1925. It has specialised in the appli-cation of the arts and sciences for the country's use, among its activities were the establishment of the Botanic Gardens at Glasnevin, the National Library and Museum, and the National College of Art. Since 1877 it has been more particularly concerned with the encouragement of scientific agriculture and stock-breeding.

Opposite is the **A.I.B. Bankcenter** (1979; Andrew Devane), a successful office complex of long low blocks with a recess central court. 'Freedom' by Alexandra Wejchert (1985), in the forecourt is the finest piece of contemporary public sculpture in Dublin.

Follow Merrion Rd, shortly passing (right) the **British Embassy**, transferred here after the previous premises in Merrion Sq. were burnt out in the riots which followed 'Bloody Sunday', 30 January 1972 when British paratroopers in Derry fired on an unarmed Civil Rights march and killed 13. The new building (1995) is an unfortunate late-flowering example of the 'New Brutalist' British architecture of the 1960s, utterly inappropriate in redbrick Ballsbridge.

W.B. Yeats (1864–1939) was born at 'Georgeville', Sandymount Ave, a short distance northeast, off the corner of Sandymount Green; there is a bust of the poet in the Green by Albert Power (1925).

Shrewsbury Rd diverges immediately to the right where at No. 20, set back from the road, is the Chester Beatty Library. Anthony Trollope lived at No. 5 Seaview Terrace, a short distance to the south, in 1854–59.

Chester Beatty Library and Gallery of Oriental Art

The Chester Beatty Library and Gallery of Oriental Art (10.00–17.00, Tues–Fri; 14.00–17.00 Sat) is one of the world's more important collections of Oriental art and MSS—and of Western books and MSS—presented to the State by Sir Alfred Chester Beatty (1875–1968), a Canadian mining millionaire, who in 1953 chose to make Dublin his home. The collections were assembled over a period of 60 years by his agents throughout the world. Most objects are associated with the propagation of the written word but the Gallery's collection of European old master prints is also extensive, including a major holding of woodcuts of Albert Dürer. The collection is to be moved to larger premises in Dublin Castle.

The building nearest the entrance houses the **Garden Library**, containing European MSS displayed in furniture designed by Hicks of Dublin (1950–53). Among the illuminated works are a 12C Bible from Walsingham; a '*Speculum Historiale*' (French; 1360–80) of the Duc de Berry, and numerous fine 15C examples, among them the Coetivy *Book of Hours* (before 1445) and a prayer-book belonging to Philip II of Spain, with miniatures attributed to Simon Bening. Here too are the early printed books, and representative bindings of every period, notably an 18C Irish masterpiece (bound by Michael Wills) and icons.

On the far side of the garden is the **New Gallery** (Michael Scott, 1957) and lecture theatre (seating 100). It accommodates the Oriental treasures, only a selection of which are on display at any one time, being periodically changed. To the left of the vestibule is the Far Eastern Gallery, with a selection of the 800 Chinese snuff-bottles in the collection; hand-scrolls; Chinese rhinoceros-horn cups (11C); Chinese carved seals; two (of 18) Chinese imperial robes; and jade books.

In an adjacent section are shown Japanese woodblock colour-prints—the collector had scruples at the inclusion of any of an erotic nature—Japanese and Chinese lacquer (the sap of the Rhus Venicifera tree); Nara-e (paintings); Tsuba (sword guards); Inro (pill-boxes, etc.); and Netsuke.

Stairs ascend to the **Islamic Collection**, with a representative selection of early Korans, largely from Persia, Egypt and Turkey; Arabic bindings; Sanscrit MSS (12C–13C) on palm-leaves; Persian lacquer-work; Indian miniatures, with a particularly fine collection from the Mughal period; Tibetan miniatures; Batak MSS from Sumatra; Burmese Parabaiks (18C–19C) and 'concertina' books, 90m long, a curious example of folk art.

Among other precious items in the collections are the Babylonian clay tablets (2500–2300 BC); and Egyptian and Greek papyri, notably the Biblical texts. Here also are the near-Eastern MSS—Arabic, Syriac, Coptic, Hebrew, Turkish, Persian, Armenian, and Ethiopic—and medieval Greek, Serbian and Bulgarian texts.

At **Booterstown Marsh** (DART to Booterstown station), between Rock Rd and the bay, is a small bird sanctuary of 4 hectares, combining salt and freshwater habitats. **Blackrock** (*An Charraig Dhubh*) was the birthplace of John Dillon (1851–1927), the Nationalist politician and the statesman Kevin O'Higgins (1892–1927) was assassinated here.

St. Mary's Church (C of I) at Monkstown is John Semple's eccentric master-piece (1831), with its chessmen-like turrets and fanciful skyline in his eccentric interpretation of Gothic Revival. It greets the traveller on the coast road, in the middle of 19C suburbs, like a setting for the *Lord of the Rings*.

Dun Laoghaire

Dun Laoghaire (DART to Dun Laoghaire; Tourist Information, St. Michael's Wharf, ☎ 280 6984/5/6), (pronounced 'Dunleary'), was known as Kingstown from the embarkation of George IV (who had disembarked at Howth in an undignified state of inebriation) in 1821 until the establishment of the Free State a century later, when all such memorials of the British Rule were enthusi-astically swept away (Queenstown reverting to Cobh at the same time, as did King's and Queen's Counties to Laois and Offaly). Its magnificent granite harbour, long the Irish terminus for the mail-boat, and now of the Sealink cata-maran ferry to Holyhead, was designed by John Rennie, and under construction from 1817 to 1859. It is one of the greatest harbour-works of the Victorian age. Both piers end in a lighthouse, that on the east surrounded by a battery. Dun Laoghaire is Ireland's principal yachting centre and the HQ of several clubs, of which the Royal St. George and the Royal Irish are the oldest (designed by J.S. Mulvany; 1832 and 1846, respectively).

The Dublin–Kingstown Railway, the first in Ireland (Charles Blacker Vignoles, 1793–1875, chief engineer), which in 1834 connected Kingstown to the city, established it as the premier Victorian township of the county. Clarinda Park, Crosthwaite Park, De Vesci Terrace, the Town Hall and the yacht clubs are among a wide array of good 19C architecture in the town. The **East Pier** of the harbour is an invigorating walking area and is punctuated by interesting monu-ments, including the Greek inscribed Anemometer (1852), invented by Thomas Robinson of TCD to check wind speeds, and the Boyd Obelisk (see St. Columb's Cathedral Derry, and St Patrick's Cathedral, Dublin). The artist Sarah Purser (1848–1943) was born here.

Irish National Maritime Museum Haigh Terrace, (14.00–17.30, Tue–Sun, May–Sept; weekdays only, Apr, Oct & Nov; £) appropriately in the former Mariners' Church, records many aspects of local and national seafaring and seamanship. Its display consists of historical models, artefacts of the lighthouse and lifeboat services, Irish naval history, memorabilia of Charles Halpin, captain of the Great Eastern (the cable-layer) and a ship's boat from the *Résolue*, captured during the French invasion of Bantry in 1796. The still-rotating 'optic' (1902–72) from the Baily lighthouse in Howth, blinks like a Cyclops from among the flotsam and jetsam of marine heroism and disasters commemorated in the exhibits.

At the northern end of the terrace, overlooking the harbour is the Expressionist *Christ the King* by Andrew O'Connor, (Paris 1926), intended as a memorial to the fallen of World War I. Erected in total seclusion in 1978 after a 20 year controversy concerning its 'appropriateness'. It is the finest public monument of the early 20C in Dublin.

The **James Joyce Museum**, (10.00–17.00, Mon–Sat, Apr–Oct; 14.00–18.00, Sun & BH, closed daily 13.00–14.00; £) to the east, at **Sandycove**, is a granite pepper-pot-shaped martello tower in which James Joyce and Oliver St. John Gogarty ('Buck Mulligan') resided briefly during September 1904. It provides the setting for the first chapter of *Ulysses*. The museum was opened in 1962, by Sylvia Beach, the first publisher of his masterpiece, 40 years previously. This small building, overlooking Dublin Bay and built by the War Office in 1804 as part of a scheme of coastal defences is now a shrine of pilgrimage for admirers of Joyce's writing. On display are some of Joyce's personal possessions, books, letters and photographs, and a collection of editions of his work. Adjacent to the martello is 'Geragh', Michael Scott (1937), a fine exercise in the Bauhaus manner, which Scott built for himself (private). Sir Roger Casement (1864–1916), colonial reformer and revolutionary was born at Sandycove.

Nearby is the **Forty-foot** gentlemen's bathing place, a cove popular with male nude swimmers, although its sanctuary is occasionally invaded by women, to the great indignation of the 'gentlemen'. The name comes from the 40th Regiment of Foot, which was stationed in the gun-battery above.

From Sandycove the road passes restored Bullock Castle (with a small museum), a 13C battlemented tower above a little boat harbour, and enters **Dalkey** (pronounced 'Dawky'), a residential resort beneath the north slope of Killiney Hill. In the main street are remains of two fortified warehouses, Archbold's Castle (now the Town Hall) and Goat's Castle (both 15C–16C) and the ruined St. Begnet's church (15C); relics of its earlier importance when Dalkey roadstead was the principal port for Dublin and landing-place of passengers from England.

From the town centre you can ascend to Sorrento Point for the view south towards Bray Head and the two Sugar Loaf Mountains.

From here the Vico road follows the coast, skirting the parkland and shrubberies of Killiney Hill before descending to Killiney Bay.

Below is **Dalkey Island** (frequent boat service from Colimore Harbour) with a small ruined early-Christian church, martello tower (1804) and gun battery. Excavations have shown Mesolithic to Bronze Age occupation. It was a Viking base, and notorious in the 18C for the periodical elections of the 'King of Dalkey', originally a student prank, but later invested with political significance until suppressed by Lord Clare in 1797. The last 'king' was a bookseller, named Armitage; the practice has been revised.

Dalkey Ave climbs south to Dalkey Hill, with its park, from where a path leads to the summit crowned by an old telegraph tower (view). Torca Cottage, on the hill, was the boyhood home of G.B. Shaw in 1866–74. On the east side is a quarry—now popular with rock-climbers—which supplied granite for the construction of Dun Laoghaire harbour.

On adjacent **Killiney Hill**, from which are panoramic views of the bay, is an obelisk erected as a famine relief work in 1741, in order to provide work during a particularly sever winter. Further south, off Killiney Hill Road is *Cill Inghena Lenine* (Church of the Daughters of Lenin), an 11C church with later additions.

Clondalkin, Donnybrook, Bray

From Dame St drive due west to Kilmainham (or by bus from city centre) shortly after bearing southwest, passing near (left) Drimnagh Castle (see p 202). The main road later by-passes (right) **Clondalkin**, with remains of a medieval church, and a Round Tower, 25.5m high with its original conical cap; the stair-case is early, though not part of the original construction. The episcopal see of *Cluain Dolcin* was established in the 7C by St. Mochua, but the only traces remaining are the tower and a granite cross in the churchyard.

Donnybrook was famous for its fair, founded by King John in 1204; but too much noise and fighting led to its suppression in 1855. Barrington, the diarist, was told by a priest that more marriages were celebrated in Dublin during the week after the fair than in any other months of the year. It is now the site of the Irish Radio and TV Centre, which has some buildings of interest; the Television (1962) and Radio (1973) Buildings, both by Ronald Talon are elegant and sophisticated essays in the International Modernist style. Sir Edward Lovett Pearce (c 1699–1733), the architect, is buried in Old Donnybrook churchyard.

The road passes (right) the extensive **Belfield Campus**, dotted with the modern buildings of **University College** (UCD), 1964–94, now the largest complex of 20C civic architecture in the State. The master plan, by A. and D. Wejchert (from Warsaw), organises a number of interesting buildings around an artificial lake in a parkland setting. The Restaurant (Robin Walker, 1970), Administration Building and the Water Tower (a dodecahedron, Wejchert, 1972) are the best individual examples. The University is attended by over 10,000 students.

Stillorgan was the birthplace of the painter Sir William Orpen (1878–1931). The slight remains of the demesne of the Viscounts Allen (left), include an obelisk of c 1732 by Sir Edward Lovett Pearce. Shortly beyond are (right) Galloping Green and a road leading to the Leopardstown racecourse, with the Wicklow hills rising beyond.

Southeast of Dalkey, on the N11 is the village of Carrickmines, with a ruined church said to be of Viking foundation; at Brenanstown, nearer the main road, in the private grounds of Glendruid, is a fine portal dolmen. You soon reach **Loughlinstown**, with a 12C–13C church and a tall cross in a nearby field, and as the road descends the Shanganagh vale the Little Sugar Loaf comes into view on the right. To the east lies Killiney Bay, a crescent of sandy beach extending all the way to Bray.

On the flank of Carrickgolligan Hill (left; 278m) are the ruins of the old church of Rathmichael and the stump of a Round Tower. You pass the ruins of

Kilturk church (left), and crossing the river Dargle, enter **Bray** (Bré), now by-passed, an attractively sited dormitory town and resort, popular since the mid-19C. It was the birthplace of singer Harry Plunkett Greene (1865–1936), and was James Joyce's family home from 1888 to 1891 (No. 1 Martello Terrace, north end of the esplanade). The town is sheltered by Bray Head to the south-east, its summit with a close view of the Little and Great Sugar Loaf. The **Oscar Wilde Autumn School** takes place here in October.

Ranelagh, Rathmines, Harold's Cross, Drimnagh Castle

Cross the Grand Canal at Charlemont Bridge for the suburb of **Ranelagh**, the site of the 'Bloody Fields', scene of a massacre of the early English colonists by the men of Wicklow on Easter Monday, 1209. It was later the site of a pleasure-garden like its London namesake. On the (left) is **Mount Pleasant Square** (c 1830) an excellent late Georgian development. The R117 soon turns right through **Milltown**, on the Dodder, and **Dundrum** with its castle ruins. This was the home of William Dargan (1799–1867) largely responsible for laying the Irish railways and establishing the National Gallery of Ireland. Roebuck Lodge, at Clonskeagh, was once the home of Maud Gonne MacBride (1866–1953), the Nationalist, and friend of Yeats.

Continue through Stepaside, at the foot of the Three Rocks Mountain (450m), with a tall (12C?) cross by the roadside at **Kilgobbin**, its church in ruins. Some distance to the right of the next village, **Kiltiernan**, with an attractive little timber clapboard church (1937), is a large dolmen with a capstone almost 7m long.

For **Rathmines**, cross the Grand Canal at Portobello Bridge, with Portobello House on the right (Thomas Colbourne, 1807), formerly the Grand Canal Hotel, now well restored as a private college. The **Irish Jewish Museum** (11.00–15.00, Tues, Thurs, Sun) in nearby Walworth Rd, off Victoria St, which incorporates a 19C synagogue, presents the history of Jewish life in Ireland. The surrounding streets were the centre of the Dublin Jewish community. Continue through the suburb of Rathmines, like Ballsbridge and Dun Laoghaire, a pros-perous independent township in the 19C and scene of Ormonde's defeat by Michael Jones in 1649. Lr Rathmines Rd, and the church of Our Lady of Refuge (Patrick Byrne, 1850), show the late survival of the Georgian idiom. Next to the church is the Blackberry Market, a flea-market (weekends), while opposite, No 41, is the Art Deco former Kodak Building (c1930), as much a period piece as bakelite radio. Palmerstown Rd runs parallel (left) and leads to Palmerstown Park, at No 20 is the **Museum of Childhood** (14.30–17.30 Sun, throughout year; Wed during July–Aug; £) a fascinating private collection of 18C-20C chil-dren's toys and dolls. An essential ingredient of enjoying this treasure trove of nostalgia is the company of a small child.

Returning to Rathmines Rd, No 21 Leinster Sq, (right) was the childhood home of the pioneering Japanese folklorist, Lafcadio Hearn (Koizumi Yakumo; 1850-1904), who was of Irish extraction. The campanile of the Italianate Town Hall (Sir Thomas Drew, 1897), admirably closes the vista towards the Dublin Mountains. Continue through **Rathgar**, there bearing right along Terenure Rd, East. The first street to the right, Brighton Rd, leads to the triangular Brighton Sq. where at No 41 James Joyce (1882–1941), was born. J.M. Synge (1871–1909), lived from 1872–90 at No 4 Orwell Park, to the left of Orwell Rd, leading southeast from the junction at Rathgar; his birthplace was No 2 Newton Villas, on the far side of the Dodder. Continuing southwest through Terenure, you reach Templeogue, once the home of Charles Lever, and the Wicklow Mountains come into view on the left.

From Terenure turn due south along the R 115 across the Dodder to **Rathfarnam Castle** (10.00–16.00; closed 13.00–14.00 daily, £, OPW) built by Archbishop Loftus c1580 as a fortified manor house, it was later the residence of the Marquess of Ely, who erected the triumphal arch at the north entry. The square house with corner towers has fine 18C interiors by Sir William Chambers and James 'Athenian' Stuart; recently opened to the public, it is undergoing extensive restoration.

The **Pearse Museum** at St. Enda's (10.00–16.00 daily, closed 13.00–14.00, Nov–Jan; 10.00–17.00, Feb–April; 10.00–17.30, May–Aug; £, OPW) Rathfarnam, in a late 18C house, is devoted to the memory of Patrick Pearse, a progressive educationalist. Pearse ran his school here from 1910 until his execution after the Rebellion of 1916. **Marlay Park** is the parkland of Marlay House, in the courtyard of which is a collection of craft studios. **Evie Hone** had her studio here up to her death.

Further west along the Grand Canal at Harold's Cross is **Mount Jerome Cemetery** (09.00–17.00 daily), the Protestant equivalent of the Catholic Glasnevin, although such sectarian divisions were never rigorously observed. It is Ireland's 'Père Lachaise', with an outstanding array of funerary monuments in a state of romantic disorder. Those interred here include an impressive list of 19C intellectuals and merchant princes; J.S. Le Fanu, William Lecky, William Carleton, Edward Dowden, 'AE', J.M. Synge, George Petrie, Sir William Wilde, John Pentland Mahaffy, and Thomas Davis, as well as the architects Mulvany and the Morrisons.

Return to the Grand Canal and again turn west for the Long Mile Rd. Shortly before the junction with the N7 to Naas is **Drimnagh Castle** (12.00–17.00, Wed, Sat & Sun), a recently restored miniature medieval tower house (Peter Pearson, 1986) is entered through the Christian Brother's school (right). Built by the Anglo-Norman Barnwell family in the 13C, it was inhabited until 1954. The 16C **Great Hall** has been restored using only techniques available to medieval craftsmen. A water-filled moat surrounds the castle.

Continue through Terenure, after 3km enter Tallagh. By the church is a crenellated tower, part of an abbey which stood here until the 13C. On a hill to the southeast, Mt. Pellier, are ruins once thought to be the country headquarters of the 'Hell Fire Club', actually a hunting-lodge of Castletown House, Celbridge. The road circles to the west before climbing the valley to Brittas, beyond which a branch road (left) affords access to the east side of the Lacken Reservoir (1938).

1b · The Pale: Dublin, Meath, Kildare & North Wicklow

This region covers the immediate hinterland of Dublin City and County, including parts of counties Meath, Kildare and Wicklow, and small portions of Westmeath, Offaly and Laois. **The Pale** refers to a district spreading westwards from Dublin during the 12C–16C, its varying frontier fortified by castles, circumscribing the area under effective Anglo-Norman control; the expression 'beyond the Pale' refers to the unsegregated rest of the country, later having a deprecatory connotation. It is a region of abruptly contrasting landscape, with Dublin City hemmed in on the west and south by the Dublin and Wicklow Mountains, accessible areas of wilderness, forest, lakes and bogland, ideal for hill walking or driving, within half an hour of the city centre. **The Wicklow Way** (132km), a long-distance waymarked walking route through the Wicklow Mountains can be reached from Rathfarnam in the Dublin suburbs; less strenuous are the **Royal** (122km), and **Grand Canal** (130km), Ways which link Dublin with the Shannon. There are exceptional gardens at **Mount Usher** in Ashford, Co. Wicklow and the **Japanese Gardens** in Kildare town; **Pollardstown Fen** at Milltown is an important nature reserve (see Bogs, General Information).

To the north and west are the flat grazing lands of Meath and Kildare, the centre of the Irish bloodstock industry, and the Curragh in Co. Kildare is a broad heathland which has been a centre for horse racing for centuries. Northeast of the Curragh, on the edge of the Region is the **Bog of Allen**, one of the largest expanses of open bogland in the country.

To the north and south of Dublin Bay, the coastal region has many attractive sandy beaches and golf links, small harbours for sailing and a variety of facilities for land and sea angling.

Among the most beautiful and historic sites are the early Christian monastic settlement at **Glendalough**, the 18C landscaping of the **Powerscourt** demesne and **Castletown House**, the greatest early-18C mansion in Ireland.

The principal motorways of the country radiate from Dublin, designated in an anti-clockwise manner. The N1 follows the east coast, north to Belfast, while the N2, N3, N4, N7, N9, N81 and N11 fan out through the region, linking Dublin to the midlands, west and south coasts. All the important towns of the region, **Maynooth**, **Kildare**, **Leixlip**, were established as Anglo-Norman settlements during the 13C, and form part of the defences of the Pale.

Among the museums and heritage centres of the region are the **Lusk Heritage Centre**; **the National Stud** and **Military Museum**, Kildare; **the Peatlands Centre**, Lullymore; **Straffan Steam Museum**; and **the Ecclesiastical Museum**, Maynooth.

Getting to the area
■ **Train**. Connolly Station (Dublin) for east coast north; Heuston Station (Dublin) for east coast south and inland, north and southwest.
■ **Air**. Dublin International Airport.
■ **Sea**. Holyhead from Dublin Port and Dun Laoghaire; Isle of Man from Dublin Port.

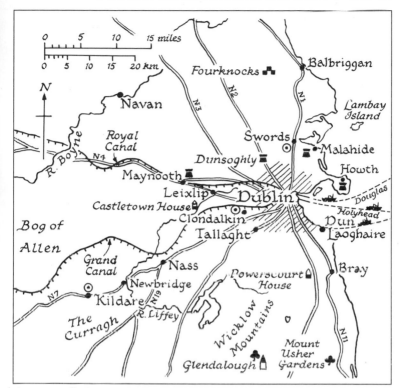

Accommodation

Ashford. Bel-Air Hotel, country-house hotel and riding school (☎ 0404-40109).

Blessington. The Manor, Manor Kilbride, mid-19C Tudor Gothic country house. B&B and restaurant (☎ 01-582105).

Bray. The Tree of Idleness, Strand Rd, Greek Cypriot, long-established, one of the best regional food restaurants in Ireland (☎ 01-2863498).

Dunlavin. Rathsallagh House, long and wandering 18C country-house, facilities from helipad to horse riding, B&B (☎ 045-403112).

Edenderry. Creidim House Hostel, Kishavanna (☎ 0405-32166).

Glendalough. Glendalough Hotel, popular family hotel next to lakes and antiquities (☎ 0404-45135).

Kildare. Lord Edward, B&B, pub-restaurant (☎ 045-522232).

Maynooth. Moyglare Manor, Moyglare, luxurious country house B&B (☎ 01-628635).

Roundwood. The Roundwood Inn, fine pub-restaurant (☎ 01-281 8107).

Skerries. Pier House Hotel, seaside hotel in sailing watersports area (☎ 01-849 1708).

Straffan. Barberstown Castle, fine restaurant and country-house accommodation in attached 13C tower house and 18C mansion (☎ 01-628 8157); **Kildare Hotel and Country Club**, hotel restaurant in lavish surroundings (☎ 01-627 3333).

Swords, Lambay Island, Lusk, Newbridge House

North of Dublin, the N1 passes west of several seaside towns, of which only Malahide is of interest. For Drogheda and the north, the N1 is more direct, passing Dublin Airport before reaching Swords.

Swords was formerly a town of importance, with an abbey founded by St. Columba in 550 for St. Finan the Leper. It became so rich that it was called 'the Golden Prebend' (held by William of Wykeham in 1366). Among the ancient buildings of Swords are a Round Tower of the earliest type, with a restored cap (entrance at ground level, a short distance west of the main street), the 14C tower of the abbey church and the extensive remains of the Archbishop's Castle (c 1200), many times burned by the Vikings, within which the bodies of Brian Ború and his son rested on their way to Armagh on the night after the battle of Clontarf (1014).

3km northwest is **Rathbeale Hall** (c 1710; extended in c 1740, perhaps by Castle), restored after being derelict for years. Crossing the mouth of the Broad Meadow Water, a right-hand turn leads 3km to **Donabate** with a ruined castle. The Cobbe gallery, in the Church of Ireland church is decorated with exuberant stucco-work by Robert West. **Portrane**, 2.5km beyond, was once the home of Swift's 'Stella' (Esther Johnson; his companion or possibly his wife). Offshore is **Lambay Island**, a porphyry rock 127m high. It was the scene of the first Viking raid, in 795, and is now a bird sanctuary. The curious defence-works were built in 1551. The island, which is private, has a house by Sir Edwin Lutyens (1907), with gardens by Gertrude Jekyll.

The right-hand fork at **Donabate** rejoins the N1, passing (left) **Newbridge House** (c 1737) (10.00–17.00, Tue–Fri, Apr–Oct; 14.00–18.00, Sat & Sun; Sat & Sun only, Nov–Mar) which has recently been opened to the public. The mansion was probably designed by Castle for Charles Cobbe (1687–1765), later Archbishop of Dublin. Charles Cobbe, his grandson, was one of the few members of the Irish Parliament who 'voted for the Union and yet refused either a peerage or money compensation for his seat'. Set in parkland, the house contains a fine ceiling by Robert West, and some good 18C furniture, paintings, a 'cabinet of curiosities', and working farmyard.

The right-hand fork at the next road junction leads to (3km) **Lusk**, where the **Lusk Heritage Centre** (10.00–18.00 Fridays only, Jun–Sept; £) incorporates a church with an ancient battlemented square tower supported on three sides by slender round towers with stepped battlements; on the fourth side is a Round Tower. Within are 16C–18C monuments. To the east is the resort of Rush. The road continues past the ruins of Baldongan Castle (13C) to the resort of **Skerries**. Offshore lie the rocks of that name, and the Rockabill lighthouse, on an island which is the breeding site for roseate terns.

The N1 can be rejoined at Balbriggan. The road passes through **Balrothery**, where the church has a square tower (c 1500) before reaching the coast at **Balbriggan**. Here, on 21–22 September 1920, there was extensive destruction of property and indiscriminate barbarity by a drunken rabble of 'Black and Tans'; a plaque on the bridge commemorates the incident in which local nationalists were 'brutally done to death by British Forces while in captivity'.

8km inland is The Naul, to the northwest of which, on **Fourknocks Hill** (*Fornocht*, bleak place), are barrows which were excavated in 1950–52, yielding a quantity of Bronze Age artefacts (not on display), and revealing a **passage-grave** with a pear-shaped chamber and three recesses. Some of the monoliths are decorated with Boyne Valley art.

The N1 veers away from the coast, north at Balbriggan, passing (left) **Gormanstown Castle** (1786, now a Franciscan house), which gives a title to the premier viscount of Ireland (the family vault adjoins the ruined church of **Stamullen**, further west). Evelyn Waugh, when considering buying the place in 1946, described it as 'a fine, solid, grim, square, half-finished block with tower and turrets'. Cross the river Nanny at **Julianstown**, on the bank of which stands the restored castellated 17C mansion of **Ballygarth**. The 'Tara Brooch' (National Museum, Dublin) was found on the shore at Bettystown to the north-east, in 1850.

Dunsoghly, Ashbourne (for Slane and Newgrange)

Fork left (N2) after crossing the Royal Canal to Finglas, with an old cross and church, reputedly founded by St. Patrick. In 1171, the Normans surprised and defeated Roderick O'Connor, the High King here.

8km northwest on the N2, to the right of the main road, stands the 15C **Dunsoghly Castle** (open by appt.). It retains its original roof-timbers, and has been an example for the restoration of other medieval buildings (see Drimnagh Castle, Ch.1). The long straight road continues northwest to (21km) **Ashbourne**. This is near the site of a five-hour battle during the Easter Rising in 1916, after 40 members of the Royal Irish Constabulary had been ambushed by insurgents led by Thomas Ashe, the local schoolmaster. The following year Ashe was arrested and died after being forcibly fed during a hunger strike in Mountjoy Prison. 6.5km beyond. The R152 forks right, passing (left) **Athcarne Castle** (1519), and **Annesbrook House**, with its huge Ionic portico, and Georgian-Gothic 'banqueting room' hastily added in 1821 to impress George IV when visiting Slane (not open to public). As he preferred dining out of doors, the effort was wasted.

Detour to Dunboyne & Summerhill

After 14.5km from Dublin city centre (N3) you reach the junction of the R156 (diverging left) for the detour to Trim (also reached more directly by the less interesting R154 from Black Bull, 5km further northeast on the N3). You first enter **Dunboyne**, the birthplace of Colonel Thomas Blood (1618–80), who attempted to steal the Crown Jewels from the Tower of London in 1671 (he managed to steal the Crown and globe and was arrested, although later pardoned). After 22km you enter **Summerhill**, with its pleasant village green. In the demesne of the Langfords are the remains of a castle destroyed in August 1647 when Colonel Michael Jones's victory over General Thomas Preston at Dungan Hill made Dublin safe for Oliver Cromwell. Ambrosio O'Higgins (1720–1801), viceroy of Peru and Chile, and father of Bernardo O'Higgins (1778–1842) the liberator of Chile, was born on the estate of Summerhill, near Dangan Castle.

Lucan, Celbridge, Castletown House, Maynooth

Following the N4, drive due west from Dublin through Palmerstown, the suburban village giving its name to the Temple family, among whom the 3rd

Viscount, Lord Palmerston, Foreign Secretary in 1840–51, was the most famous. The steep slopes of the north bank of the river are known here as The Strawberry Beds. About 2.5km to the north, originally a fortress of the Pale, stands **Luttrellstown Castle**, elaborately Gothic-ised after 1800 by Luke White (not open to public). The beautiful demesne borders the Liffey.

Lucan (by-passed), was much frequented after 1758 when the medicinal properties of its waters were discovered. It was also the venue for meets of the Kildare and Meath foxhounds and the Ward Union staghounds. The extensive riverside demesne of Lucan House (since 1944 the residence of the Italian ambassador), was once known as Sarsfield House, after Patrick Sarsfield (born in Lucan; d. 1693), titular Earl of Lucan (created by James II in 1691). The present mansion, containing very fine decoration by James Wyatt and Michael Stapleton, was not built until c 1776. James Gandon, the architect, died in 1824 at Canonbrook, to the southeast; he is buried at Drumcondra.

Turn left immediately west of Lucan onto the R403 for (5km) Celbridge, via the hamlet of **St. Wolstan**, where a 14C bridge spans the Liffey. Fragmentary remains of an abbey founded by Adam de Hereford c 1202 can be seen. **Celbridge** was the residence of Esther Vanhomrigh (1690–1723), Swift's 'Vanessa' (Swift's play upon her real name; he devised the name Cadenus for himself, an anagram of his latin title as Decanus or Dean of St. Patrick's Cathedral, Dublin).

> *Vanessa* not in years a score,
> Dreams of a gown of forty-four;
> Imaginary Charms can find
> In Eyes with Reading almost blind;
> *Cadenus* now no more appears
> Declined in Health, advanced in Years.
> She fancies Musick in his Tongue,
> Nor further looks, but thinks him young.'
>
> 'Cadenus and Vanessa', Jonathan Swift (1713)

She inherited Celbridge from her father, the Williamite mayor of Dublin (of Dutch descent, see Drogheda). Her unrequited passion for the dean is said to have hastened her death. A seat by the riverside below her home, **Celbridge Abbey** (not open to public), is erroneously pointed out as her favourite retreat, but in fact this was on an adjacent island. Also of architectural interest is **Oakley Park** (1720), and **Celbridge College** (1730), both possibly by Thomas Burgh. A house on the left of the Clane road was the boyhood home of Admiral Sir Charles Napier (1786–1860) and his brothers. In the disused Protestant church is the splendid monument to Speaker William Conolly and his wife, by Thomas Carter the Elder (1730).

Castletown House

To the northeast of the village, approached by a lengthy avenue, stands the imposing mansion built for William Conolly (c 1660–1729), speaker of the Irish Parliament from 1715–1729. **Castletown House** (10.00–17.00, Mon–Fri; 11.00–18.00, Sat; 14.00–18.00, Sun & BH; OPW; £) was designed in 1722–32 by Alessandro Galilei and (internally) by Sir Edward Lovett Pearce. It consists of a central block flanked by curved colonnaded quadrants with pavilions added by Pearce. It remained in the Conolly family until 1965. Saved from demolition by the Irish Georgian Society, and opened to the public, it was taken into state care in 1994, but its enormous interior has a ghostly air, shorn of most of its original furnishings. It nonetheless remains one of the 18C houses most worth a visit.

Plasterwork of 1759–60 by the Lafranchini brothers embellishes the walls of the slightly later cantilevered staircase, with brass banisters. The **Long Gallery** on the first floor is decorated in a style based on wall-paintings discovered during the excavation of Pompeii, the work of Thomas Riley. Portraits in the house include those of William Conolly by Jervas, of 'Speaker' (of the Dublin Parliament) Boyle, Ginkel and Charles James Fox. Also note-worthy is the **'print room'**, papered with 18C engravings by Lady Louisa Conolly (c 1770), the only one to survive in Ireland. At the end of a vista north of the house is a folly of superimposed arches topped by an obelisk, prob-ably designed by Castle in 1740. To the east is the 'Wonderful Barn', an example of 18C archi-tectural whimsy, a conical struc-ture with an external stair (1743), which functions perfectly as a grain barn, despite its extraordi-nary design.

The main road from **Lucan** re-crosses the Liffey at **Leixlip**, a large village on one of the most attractive reaches of the river. Above the modernised castle, built for Adam de Hereford after 1170, was the famous Salmon Leap (in Old Norse, *Lax Hlaup*), replaced by a 24m-high dam, part of the Liffey hydro-electric works, (provided with an ingenious fish-pass).

Continue west between the Royal Canal and the Rye Water, before skirting (right) the walled demesne of **Carton** where Lord Edward Fitzgerald (1735–98), the United Irishman, was born. This former seat of the Fitzgeralds, dukes of Leinster and earls of Kildare, is no longer open to the public. Richard Castle rebuilt the

'The Wonderful Barn', 18C folly to the east of Castletown House

earlier mansion in 1739–45 (and died there in 1751, being buried in Maynooth church). In c 1815 it was radically re-modelled by Sir Richard Morrison, who added a Regency dining room. Other rooms retain stuccowork by the Lafranchini brothers, including, the Courtship of the Gods (1739) in the great saloon. In the grounds there are several follies and a bridge by Thomas Ivory (1763).

Maynooth

The **castle** was probably built in 1176 by Maurice Fitzgerald, a companion of Strongbow. It remained a Fitzgerald stronghold until 1535, when the rebel Lord Thomas Fitzgerald (known as 'Silken Thomas' from the silk fringes worn on the helmets of his retainers) was betrayed to Sir William Skeffington by his foster-brother Christopher Paris. Although restored to the 11th Earl in 1552, it was taken by Owen Roe O'Neill in 1647 and dismantled. A massive keep remains, surrounded by several other towers and fragments of outworks.

Adjacent is **St. Patrick's College**, a constituent college of the National University of Ireland, and no longer exclusively a clerical university. Founded in 1795, largely through the good offices of Edmund Burke, as a seminary for the Irish priesthood (whose continental schools were inaccessible during the Napoleonic wars) it succeeded a previous establishment of 1521, endowed by the 8th and 9th Earls of Kildare and suppressed in 1538.

Of the two quadrangles, the first dates from 1795; the second, by A.W.N. Pugin, from 1845. The chapel, with its tall spire, was designed by J.J. McCarthy (1875). The Library contains some illuminated MSS, old Irish printed books and MSS, and books from Burke's library. The **Maynooth Ecclesiastical Museum** (open by appt.) contains church plate and vestments (including Geoffrey Keating's) used during 'Penal' times and the 19C scientific instrument collection of the Rev N.J. Callan, electrical pioneer and inventor, which is of considerable interest.

Aghadoe Round Tower, 4km south, although imperfect, is of unusually large dimensions. At Kilcock you pass the ruined church and barrow of **Cloncurry**, before reaching Enfield.

A minor road (R402) winds southwest beside the **Bog of Allen** to **Carbury**. Its conspicuous ruined castle was the original stronghold of Sir Pierce de Bermingham (early 14C), enemy of the O'Connors. The existing 16C building has moulded chimneys and mullioned windows, and belonged to the Cowleys or Colleys, ancestors of the Duke of Wellington. **Newberry Hall**, east of the town, dates from 1760. **Mylerstown Castle**, a ruined tower to the north, was another fort of the Berminghams.

The road continues across the Bog, which extends south for some distance, to **Edenderry**, on the edge of the **Pale**, defended by a castle of the Blundell family whose descendant, the Marquess of Downshire, was lord of the manor. The flora and fauna of the bogland is interpreted in the **Peatlands Centre** (10.00–17.00 daily, Mar–Sept) southeast at Lullymore.

4km north, on **Carrick Hill**, are the ruins of the church and castle or *Carraig Fheorais*, where Sir Pierce de Bermingham treacherously killed 32 of the O'Connors of Offaly, including Muirchertach O'Conor, King of Uí Faílght (Offaly) who were his guests. To the west of Edenderry lies **Monasteroris** (*Mainistir*

Fheorais, the monastery of Pierce), with a ruined church, dovecot, and monastery founded by Sir John de Bermingham in c 1325. Beyond lies another of their strongholds, Kinnafad Castle.

Continue west until you reach **Daingean**, formerly Philipstown. It was once the main town of Offaly (King's County), with an 18C Court House (now a fire station). It was named after Phillip II of Spain (husband of Mary Tudor) in who's reign Offaly became shire land, or settlement land, to be distributed to tenants sympathetic to English rule and the Protestant Reformation. The castle was erected in the 16C by Lord Justice Sir William Brabazon (d. 1552). In an otherwise dull landscape, **Croghan Hill**, on which there are several ruins, is prominent to the north.

At Geashill, 3km south of the adjacent village of Ballingar, is an Anglo-Norman motte.

Beyond **Enfield** you twice cross the Royal Canal before entering (13km) **Clonard** (*Cluain Ioraird*, Erard's meadow), once the most famous bishopric in Meath, founded by St. Finian (520), an immediate successor of St. Patrick. It was the seat of a school that numbered St. Kieran and St. Columba among its pupils, but nothing remains of its buildings except the curious panelled font of grey marble in the church and two mounds nearby, one sepulchral, the other (further northwest) of military origin.

To the left of the road, 3km southwest, is an extensive earthwork of low profile known as **Ticroghan Castle**, the defenders of which made a stubborn resistance to the Roundheads in 1650. At **Ballyboggan**, further south, survives the large plain church (near the river) of an Augustinian priory founded in the 19C. Beyond Kinnegad, the road divides; the N4 continuing towards Sligo, the N6 to Galway.

Naas to Kildare

At **Rathcoole**, the N7 skirts the foothills of the Wicklow Mountains rising to the southeast. **Newcastle**, Co. Wicklow, 3km northwest, has a 15C church with a fortified tower, and an attractive mid-18C rectory. **Lyons House** (1797) to the west, with a large artificial lake, lies in the valley through which the Grand Canal runs. It was the home of Lord Cloncurry (1773–1853), a United Irishman, and friend of Lord Anglesey, Lord-Lieutenant of Ireland (1828) and celebrated in John Betjeman's poem *Sir John Piers*. It is now part of the University College, Dublin, and an arch from Browne's Hill has been re-erected at one of its entrances. After 6.5km a right-hand turn leads shortly to **Oughterard**, where a stump of a Round Tower is all that remains of a 6C monastery burnt in 1094. The ruined 16C–early 17C church was the burial-place of the Ponsonbys of Bishopscourt, and of early members of the Guinness family, including Arthur Guinness (1725–1803), founder of the brewery. On the hill to the southwest the famous duel between O'Connell and D'Esterre (a Dublin merchant who challenged him and was fatally wounded) was fought in 1815. Drive through **Kill**, birthplace of John Devoy (1842–1928), the Fenian. Adjacent is **Bishopscourt House** (c 1788), possibly designed by Gandon, and the site of an important stud farm. South of Kill lie the remains of Hartwell Castle.

Naas (pronounced Náce; by-passed), the county town of Kildare is a very ancient centre (*Nás na Riogh*, meeting-place of the kings), and once the residence of the Kings of Leinster. The States of Leinster formerly assembled in a rath outside the town. Naas is now a hunting and horse-racing centre; Punchestown Racecourse is particularly attractive at the April meeting when the gorse is in bloom. At **Oldtown**, in the northern suburbs, one pavilion remains from the first Palladian house built in Ireland, designed by the architect Thomas Burgh (1670–1730) as his country seat. There is a 7m-high standing stone—the tallest in Ireland—south of Kilcullen on the N9. Immediately beyond it fork right, passing (right) the large circular royal fort of Dun Ailinne. Beyond (13km) Fontstown is Ardscull, with a conspicuous old fort or motte almost 17m high, planted with trees. It was here that Edward Bruce defeated Sir Edmund Butler in January 1316. To the south is Inche Castle, enlarged by the Earl of Kildare c 1420.

From Naas on the N7, are the remains (left) of **Jigginstown House** (c 1637), a huge unfinished brick-built mansion with a frontage of 115m, erected by Strafford for himself or possibly as a residence for Charles I. It is the earliest substantial brick building in Ireland.

Newbridge (*Driochead Nua*), Co. Kildare; on the Liffey, arose around a cavalry barrack built here in 1816. It has a cutlery factory and Board na Mona's experimental peat station. Because of the presence of the barracks, the housing of the main street developed on only one side. Downstream, on the right bank of the river, are the ruins of **Great Connell Abbey**, built in 1202 by Myler Fitzhenry, and peopled with Augustinian Canons from Llanthony. The table-tomb of Walter Wellesley (d. 1539), Bishop of Kildare and Prior of Connell with a recumbant figure, formerly in the graveyard, was transferred to Kildare Cathedral in 1971 (see below).

You shortly reach **the Curragh** (*Currach,* a racecourse), one of the finest and long-established stretches of racing turf in Ireland (2000 hectares). It has many training stables, and its **racecourse** is the venue of the Irish Derby in late June or early July, when the district is entirely given over to the racing fraternity.

Although mainly devoted to pasturage—St. Brigid's flocks are said to have grazed here—the Curragh has also been known as a military training centre since 1646. In March 1914 it came into prominence when General Sir Hubert Gough (1870–1963), Commander of the Cavalry Brigade at the Curragh, and 59 other British army officers (although only 57 was the figure officially cited) threatened to disobey if ordered to fire on Carson's 'Ulster Volunteers', a decision euphemistically referred to as the 'Curragh Incident'. The **Military Museum** (open by appt.) contains an interesting collection of militaria and oriental weapons.

Kildare

Kildare (*Cill Dara,* the church of the oak-wood) (Tourist Office, Market House, ☎ 045-22696, June-August) is a small but ancient town, owing its origin to St. Brigid, who in 490 founded the first of several religious houses here. The oak mentioned in the name was probably the Celtic cult of the sacred oak and it has been suggested that Brigid was previously a priestess of this cult. Her 'fire' was kept burning in her church despite Viking and other raids until the Reformation, except for one short break in 1220 when it was extinguished by order of De Londres, Archbishop of Dublin.

The physical origins of the town can be traced in the likely existence of a double rampart or ring fort enclosing the ecclesiastical centre. The roughly oval form of the graveyard wall surrounding the cathedral probably follows the line of the original inner enclosure and in the street plan of the town can be seen the contours of the outer ring (the beginning of Station Rd off the Market Square and Priest's Lane represent part of its circumference). The town has a triangular market square with a small arcaded **Market House** (1817) which has a number of medieval carved stones on display; a naïve statue of St. Brigid commemorates the 300 who died at Gibbet Rath in 1798. A tower of the 15C Fitzgerald castle is off the east end of the square, behind the Court House.

The present **Cathedral of St. Brigid** was begun by Bishop Ralph de Bristol in 1229, which, enlarged and embellished by Bishop Lane in 1482, was ruined in the Confederate War of 1641, when the north transept and choir were razed. In 1683–86 Bishop Morton rebuilt the choir in the prevailing classical style, while in 1875 G.E. Street (who also 'restored' the cathedral of Christ Church in Dublin) undertook what amounted practically to a rebuilding, although more sympathetic to the original design. The west front, choir and north transept are entirely new, but the unusual buttresses and merlons of the nave walls, connected by arches which support a defensive parapet, and the simple but effective south transeptal façade are original.

At the west end is a primitive font, and in the south transept and choir are medieval monuments; one of a 13C bishop, several sculptured stones, and the excellent effigy of Bishop Walter Wellesley (d. 1539), moved here from Great Connell in 1971 (see above). In the churchyard to the southwest is an early cross (reconstructed). To the north the 12C Round Tower is notable for its unusually elaborate doorway, 4m from the ground; the incongruous battlements are an 18C addition. It has an internal staircase and can be climbed to the top (seasonal). To the northwest, the foundations of a building now identified as the 'fire-house', is an early oratory.

St. Brigid's church (RC), 1823, south of Main St, with a classical front and unusually tall lantern, has been skilfully modernised and among its excellent contemporary fittings are a window by Patrick Pye (1974) and a door by Imogen Stuart. In the **Carmelite church** (Michael Hague, 1884), northwest, the west transept has a collection of late medieval carved slabs including an Ecce Homo. Lord Edward Fitzgerald lived in a house on Dublin Road in 1794. To the south of the town are the ruins of a Franciscan friary.

1.5km northeast of Kildare, at **Tully House** is the **National Irish Stud and Horse Museum** (combined ticket to Museum, Stud and Garden; 09.00–18.00 daily, Feb–Nov; £) a horse-breeding centre presented to Britain in 1916 by Lord Wavertree (Colonel Hall-Walker, a brewing millionaire). It retained extra-territorial rights until 1944 when the British establishment was moved to Wiltshire, and the Tully stud was vested in the Irish government. A fine (0.6 hectare) **Japanese Garden**, laid out in 1906–10 by the Japanese garden designer Tassa Eida for Lord Wavertree, can also be visited; the garden symbolically charts the passage of life.

Conspicuous from their position on the edge of the great central plain are the **Red Hills**, a low sandstone range to the north of Kildare. The highest of them is

Dunmurry Hill (231m; just to the right of the Rathangan road); adjoining that and further north is **Grange Hill** (with the curious outcrop known as the 'Chair of Kildare'); while on the Robertstown road, to the northeast, is the **Hill of Allen**, where a monument marks the site of a residence of the Kings of Leinster (the erection of which damaged the old fort).

South and West of Kildare

At Milltown is **Pollardstown Fen**, the largest spring-fed fen in Ireland, with many rare species of plants. The road soon enters the dreary expanse of the **Bog of Allen**, a vast peat-bog, now mechanically cut for fuel and peat moss. In 1946 the Bord na Móna (the Turf, or Peat Board) was set up, a corporation devoted to the production of machine-cut turf for use both as domestic fuel and in power stations. Its experimental station is at Newbridge, and 'turf villages' have been built near the bogs to house both permanent and seasonal workers.

At **Robertstown** is the former Grand Canal Hotel, originally erected for the accommodation of 'express' canal passengers, and now again open to visitors. There is a small canal museum here, and a 'Falconry' in the neighbourhood.

Monasterevin, 10.5km south of Kildare, is a small canal-town, dominated even on its principal street by vast 19C warehouses. A 19C aqueduct carries the Royal Canal over the River Barrow. Beside the canal to the south is a Palladian complex of neglected buildings, originally the Charter School (c 1740).

Moore Abbey, built by Lord Drogheda (1767), was later the home of the singer John McCormack (1884–1945). Its name commemorates a monastery founded in the late 12C on the site of a 7C foundation, by Dermot O'Dempsey, Lord of Offaly. It had the reputation of being a very cold house, and the story is told that when the 4th Earl of Clonmell visited the place, an abnormally heavy portmanteau among his luggage burst open when being carried up the stairs, and was found to be full of coal! The plain Drogheda family chapel can be seen in the **Protestant church** (1820).

Gerard Manley Hopkins (1844–89), experimental poet, who was Professor of Classics at the Catholic University, Dublin, from 1884 to his death, frequently stayed in Monasterevin and is commemorated in Main St by an impressive pair of figures in stone (James McKenna, 1990). A Summer School is held here in his honour in June.

At **Kildangan**, southeast of the town, is an extensive demesne, and an old tower.

Follow the R424 to the west, crossing the Grand Canal, and shortly pass (right) **Lea Castle**, the remnant of a De Vesci stronghold of which the gateway and a round bastion have survived. Razed by Cromwell's order in 1650, it was last inhabited by a noted horse-stealer, 'Cathal na gCapall' ('Charles of the Horses'), who used the vaults as stables, and carried on a flourishing trade.

10km **Portarlington** takes its name from Sir Henry Bennet, afterwards Lord Arlington, to whom the neighbouring country was given, having been confiscated from the O'Dempseys in 1641. A colony of Huguenot settlers was established here by the French Williamite, General Ruvigny, Earl of Galway, when he founded the town in 1667. The Market-House (c 1800) now houses a garage and betting shop. The first Irish power-plant to be driven by peat was built here in 1948.

15km northwest (R420) is the village of **Geashill**, with remains of Digby Castle, an O'Dempsey fortress, which was later occupied by the Lords Digby, and an Anglo-Norman motte. Tullamore (see chapter 2), lies 12km beyond.

To the right, southwest of **Ballybrittas** on the N7, in fine parkland lies **Emo Court** (10.00–18.00 daily, Jun–Sept; £) the seat of the Earls of Portarlington. Its domed porticoed mansion was designed c 1790 by Gandon and completed c 1810 by Sir Richard Morrison. The north front portico was added in 1834 by Lewis Vulliamy. There is a remarkable sculptured font, originally in the church which stood in the park and now in the church at adjacent **Coolbanagher** (1786; also originally by Gandon). To the south of the main road is **Morretta Castle**, an ancient stronghold of the Fitzgeralds, on a stretch of open moorland known as the Great Heath of Maryborough.

Detour to Sallins, Straffan, Ballintore, Dunlavin

The R407 leads north from Naas to (3km) **Sallins**, a village on the Grand Canal. 1.5km west of Sallins is the **Leinster Aqueduct**, by which the canal crosses the Liffey. Cross Bodenstown (right), where a monument marks the grave of Theobald Wolfe Tone (1763–98); annually the scene of commemorative rallies (on discreetly separate dates), by the different strands of Irish nationalist opinion. After 3km pass (right) **Blackhall House**, birthplace of Charles Wolfe (1791–1823), the poet; (see Cobh). At **Clane**, where a six-arched bridge crosses the Liffey, are the ruins of a Franciscan friary founded in the 13C by Sir Gerald Fitzmaurice. Northeast of Clane at **Straffan** is the **Straffan Steam Museum** (14.30–17.30, Sun & BH, Easter–May; 14.00–18.00, Tue–Sun & BH, June–Aug; 14.30–17.00, Sun & BH, Sept), housed in the 19C church of St. Jude, transported from Inchicore, Dublin (home of the Inchicore Works, where many Irish trains have been built). There are important early examples of steam tech nology in the collection, including the Richard Trevithick (1771–1833) third model of 1797, beam and horizontal engines from the early 19C, and a display of historic models of important train engines, one of the most impressive of which is the 1831 *Planet*, successor to Stephenson's *Rocket*.

To the right of the Maynooth road, some 3km north, is the Jesuit College of Clongowes Wood, containing stained glass by Evie Hone and Michael Healy in its chapel. James Joyce was a pupil here in 1888–91.

Returning to Naas, fork left for **Kilcullen** (11km), a rambling village whose bridge dates from 1319. Some 3km southwest are remains of the old walled town, with parts of an Observantine abbey, a Round Tower, and shafts of 9C crosses.

Dunlavin, 10km southeast of Castlemartin (with its restored 15C church, and mansion, 1730), retains its notable domed Court-House, tentatively attrib- uted to Richard Castle (1743, restored) and a church of c 1816. Southwest of Dunlavin is **Killeen Cormac**, an early-Christian site with ogham and pillar stones, which mark the reputed grave of King Cormac of Munster. **Ballitore**, (16km south) is a village just west of the road, founded by the Quakers. Edmund Burke received his early education at the hands of Abraham Shackleton (1697–1771), a Yorkshireman, who established the school here in 1728. It is now the **Quaker Museum** (12.00–17.00, Tue–Fri, 11.00–17.00, Sat; 14.00–16.00, Sun). Mrs Mary Leadbeater (1758–1828), the authoress of *Annals of Ballitore* (1862), and Shackleton's grand-daughter, also lived here.

Nearby is the **Rath of Mullaghmast** (171m), once a stronghold of the Kings of Leinster. In 1577 it was the scene of the treacherous massacre of the chiefs of Leix and Offaly by the English and their allies, the O'Dempseys, who had invited them to a friendly conference. The 'Wizard Earl' of Kildare is said to be buried in the rath in an enchanted sleep.

East of Naas ~ Brittas to Blessington and the Sally Gap

3km beyond Brittas, the R759 turns through Manor Kilbride and climbs steadily, parallel to the headwaters of the Liffey, with the Kippure massif to the north (752m; with TV mast) to the **Sally Gap**, a mountain cross-road a short distance south of a bog forming the source of the Liffey. The Dargle, which descends towards Powerscourt, has its source in the same bog. From the Sally Gap a rough road bears south along the side of the main range and descends past the Glenmacnass Waterfall before following the river to Laragh. The main road offers magnificent views of **Lough Tay** (on the shore of which, at Luggala St. Kevin is said to have had a cell, now graced by a rebuilt Gothic 'cottage'). Towards Lough Dan it skirts the south side of War Hill, and Djouce Mountain (724m). and crosses over into the Vartry Valley, joining the R755, just north of **Roundwood**.

Just beyond the village of Brittas a turning (right) leads to **Kilteel** where the chancel arch of its church (re-erected) has figure sculpture. To the left of this junction is one of three castles in the neighbourhood dating from the early 14C. Gravel works in the area have scarred the landscape.

The road from Brittas to **Blessington** offers fine views of the mountains to the southeast. Blessington has one long street and a church built by Archbishop Michael Boyle in 1669. Austin Cooper's late 17C house, with its important gardens, was burnt and demolished in the 'troubles' of 1798. Dame Ninette de Valois, (her real name was Edris Stannus, b. 1898), founder of the Sadler's Wells Ballet (now the Birmingham Royal Ballet), was born at neighbouring **Baltiboys**.

A short distance beyond Blessington, a left-hand turn leads up to the **Lacken Resevoir**. The Liffey used to descend here in a series of waterfalls and the 'pool of the Pooka', the haunt of the malicious water-sprite of Irish fairy-tale was at the foot of the principal fall. But the waters have been much reduced by the construction of the dam at Poulaphuca, further south.

Russborough House

To the right before reaching Poulaphuca is **Russborough House** (10.30–17.30 daily, June–Aug; Easter–Oct, Sun & BH only 10.30–17.30; £), the former Palladian seat of Joseph Leeson, later the Earl of Milltown. Built in 1741 by Castle and Francis Bindon, its ceilings richly decorated by the Lafranchini brothers, it was described in 1748 as 'a noble new house forming into perfection'. Alfred Beit (1853–1906; pronounced 'Bite'), uncle of the present owner, founded the De Beer Diamond Mining Company at Kimberley with Cecil Rhodes, and started collecting works of art in the 1880s. Sir Alfred Beit acquired the house in 1952, and it now accommodates the treasures of the Beit Foundation. Unfortunately it has twice been the object of theft. In 1974, 16 paintings were stolen in an armed raid (organised by Bridget Rose Dugdale, in an attempt to raise funds for the IRA), but they were recovered undamaged. In May

1986, art thieves struck again, however some of the paintings have recently been recovered in Istanbul and Amsterdam. In 1988, the cream of the remaining collection was donated to the National Gallery of Ireland, but some paintings, together with these listed below, are usually on display. Among those stolen was Vermeer's *Woman writing*.

The **Dining-room** has a notable marble fireplace. **Hall** Paintings by Oudry, and Magnasco, and two busts by Pajou. **Drawing-room**. Four Marine scenes by Joseph Vernet, were commissioned especially for this room; Van Steenwijk the elder, *Church Interior*. **Bedroom**. Works by Bonington and Boucher; W. van der Velde, *Marine view*; a copy of a section of Velázquez's *The tapestry weavers* by Sargent. A Soho chinoiserie tapestry by John Vanderbank of 1720 and an early 18C bed. **Music Room**. A mantlepiece depicting Leda and the Swan, probably by Thomas Carter; Vestier, *Portrait of the Princesse de Lamballe*; Gainsborough, *Sketch of the dancer Giovanna Bacelli*; two small *Views of Florence* by Bellotto and two paintings by Guardi. Note the Serpent clock. **Saloon** (with its original floor). David Teniers, *Village Dance*; Palamedez, *Musical Party*; Rubens, *Head of an Abbot*; Metsu, *Man Writing*, and *Woman Reading*. Note the chairs by Pluvinet with Gobelin tapestries, and the blue ceramic water-spaniel once belonging to Mme du Barry, mistress of Louis XV, guillotined during the Revolution, (1793). **Library**. Reynolds, *Thomas Conolly of Castletown*; Morelsee, *A Huguenot Lady*; and a microscope and its case (1772; by Gozzi of Parma). The plasterwork in the **staircase** is attributed to Irish pupils of the Lafranchini brothers.

From **Hollywood**, 5km south of Russborough, the R756 crosses the mountains via the Wicklow Gap to Glendalough and Laragh. From the Gap you can easily ascend Tonelagee (816m), to the north, for the splendid comprehensive panorama of the Wicklow Mountains.

North of Hollywood lies Ballymore Eustace, an old Pale town on the Liffey. It was burnt in 1572, but there are some old houses to be seen in the district. On nearby **Broadleas Common** is a large stone circle known as the **Piper's Stones**.

South of Dublin

3km beyond **Rathfarnham** the road (L 94) forks right and climbs, passing (left) Mt Venus, with a large dolmen, probably never roofed. Higher up you cross the side of Killakee, behind which rises Glendoo Mountain (587m). To the right lie the Glenasmole valley (entered by a road circling to the west of the one described), with its reservoir.

Crossing the shoulder of a ridge ascending south to **Kippure** (752m; the highest peak in Co. Dublin) you descend to **Glencree**. On the left is the beautiful **German cemetery** (1961) in which are interred c 100 German servicemen, who died either in Ireland or off the coast, during both World Wars. Two roads descend the Glencree valley; one to the north of the river—with a view of Powerscourt—leading directly to **Enniskerry**, passing at **Parknasilloge** a small but perfect dolmen. The other road bears left further south (along the side of Tonduff), from which you can approach the Powerscourt waterfall. It continues south from Glencree, shortly passing (right) Lower and Upper Lough Bray, and climbs to the Sally Gap.

Pass through Stepaside, at the foot of Three Rock Mountain; a tall (12C) cross by the roadside at **Kilgobbin**, its church in ruins. Some distance to the right of the next village, **Kiltiernan**, with an attractive little wooden church, is a large dolmen with a capstone almost 7m long.

The road to Enniskerry now climbs a hill to the defile of The Scalp before descending into the Glencullan valley past the site of a monastery (left) to Enniskerry. It is a charming village, with a copper-spired church, and a good centre for excursions into the hills. Nearby is **Charleville House**, rebuilt by Whitmore Davis c 1820 after a disastrous fire in 1792; the interior may have been designed by Sir Richard Morrison.

Powerscourt House

Less than 1km south is the entrance (right) to the demesne of Powerscourt House (09.00–17.30 daily, Mon–Oct), magnificently situated, the gardens of which are open to the public. A beech avenue leads up to the house, an imposing granite building (1731–41) by Castle, encasing an earlier house, with two arcades connecting the central block to two-storied pavilions. The main block was virtually gutted by fire in November 1974 which destroyed many of its valuable contents. It has recently been restored.

The **gardens**, although laid out in the 18C, were radically transformed between 1843 and 1875, and are entered through fine wrought-iron gates (c 1770) brought here from the cathedral of Bamberg, Bavaria. The view from the 244m-long terrace looking across the Dargle valley towards the Great and Little Sugar Loaf, is very striking. According to Maurice Craig, Daniel Robertson, designer of the upper terraces 'was wheeled about the place in a wheelbarrow grasping a bottle of sherry. When the sherry was finished Mr Robertson ended his designing for the day'. Also of interest is the armoury. Plants may be bought at nurseries near the entrance. A walk of c 6km through rhododendron woods will bring you to the Powerscourt Waterfall, but this is also easily approached by car from the main road (see below).

On regaining the main road, turn right. After crossing the Dargle by the **Tinnehinch Bridge**, Co. Wicklow, one of the more attractive spots in the district, the next right-hand turning leads to the entrance of the deer-park (left) in which the **Powerscourt Waterfall** hurls itself obliquely across a rock-shelf 120m high. Above it rise the summits of War Hill and Douce Mountain (724m). Only the outer walls of **Tinnehinch House** survive (it was presented to Henry Grattan by the Irish Parliament in 1782).

Returning to the main road, bear right towards (11km) **Roundwood**, also approached by a minor road parallel to it to the west. To the east rises the Great Sugar Loaf (503m), a steep but simple climb from the highest point of the main road and rewarded by one of the finest views in the area.

Inland is the great mass of the Wicklow Mountains, with Douce, War Hill, and Maulin in the foreground, and Tonduff behind, while away to the southwest is Lugnaquillia 924m. To the northeast, the coast can be followed from Bray to Howth, with the Mourne Mountains in the far distance, while on a clear day the Welsh hills are visible to the east. Before entering Roundwood pass (left) the **Vartry Reservoir**, part of Dublin's water supply.

A lane to the right beyond Roundwood leads to (3km) Oldbridge, from where the **Lough Dan** area can be explored. In the hills above the lough, Joseph Holt, the insurgent, held out for three months after the disasters of 1798 before surrendering to Lord Powerscourt and being transported to Botany Bay (returning in 1813).

To the north is Lough Tay, set in a rocky basin, which may also be approached from the Sally Gap road. Descend the Annamoe Valley. Annamoe itself was the scene of the remarkable escape of Laurence Sterne, aged seven, who was staying at the parsonage at Annamoe with Mr Fetherston—a relation of his mother's—when he fell into the mill-race. Although the mill (now ruined) was working he escaped unharmed. From here the road winds steeply down to **Laragh**, a small village at the confluence of the Annamoe and Avonmore, where you turn right for the important early-Christian site of **Glendalough** (3km).

From Laragh the main road veers southeast down the Vale of Clara, and through the hamlet of Clara Bridge, to Rathdrum, a pleasant village perched on the steep side of the wooded Avonmore valley; **Clara-Lara Adventure Park** (10.00–18.00 daily, all year; £) is very popular with children. Just south of Laragh the road climbs to the right across the east side of the hills, into the Avonbeg Valley, before climbing again to Aghavannagh.

The Vale of Glendalough

The Vale of Glendalough (*Glean-da-lough*, glen of the two lakes) soon divides into two valleys, the Vale of Glendasan, to the north, being followed by a road from the Wicklow Gap. The left-hand fork continues along Glendalough itself, its Lower and Upper Lakes flanked to the south by Mullacor and Lugduff, and to the north by Camaderry. The best view up the valley, with the flat-topped mass of Table Mountain in the distance (699m), may be obtained from the hillside above the neighbouring hotel.

A lane continues up the valley to a car-park close to the shore of the Upper Lake.

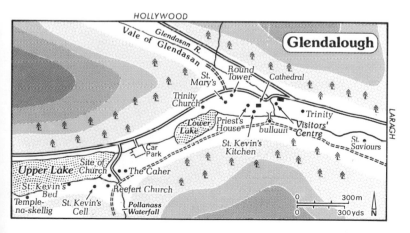

The foundation of Glendalough as an ecclesiastical site is ascribed to St. Kevin (*Coemhghen*, the fair-born), a scion of the royal house of Leinster, who built a church on the south bank of the upper lake some time in the 6C. Later he removed to the opening of the valley and died there at an advanced age in 618. The monastery which his disciples built flourished until the 11C, when it was ravaged by the Vikings. In 1398 the English of Dublin sacked it, and by the 16C the destruction was almost complete. The first group of buildings lie in a cemetery enclosure approached through a medieval gateway of two arches above which once stood a tower, standing just behind the hotel.

The **cathedral**, the nearest ruin, was probably erected at the beginning of the 9C, although the chancel, constructed of less massive masonry than the nave, is 11C–12C. The chancel arch has been partly rebuilt. Note the clustered shafts of the north doorway, the ornamental east window (of an oolite foreign to the neighbourhood) and the grave slabs. To the south is **St. Kevin's Cross** (c 1150), a granite monolith 3.3m high, perhaps unfinished, for the ring enclosing the cross is unpierced. Near it is the **Priest's House** (12C), partly reconstructed in 1875–80, above the door of which is a carved figure of St. Kevin (?) between two ecclesiastics (damaged).

The most interesting building, known as **St. Kevin's Kitchen**, is slightly further down the slope. It is in fact a fine example of a two-storied oratory, 7m by 4.5m in area, with a steeply pitched stone roof. Within, it consists of a barrel-vaulted lower chamber and a loft above. A chancel (since demolished) and sacristy were later added at the east end, and a round bell-turret at the west. The present entrance is the chancel arch; the original square-headed west entrance is now blocked up. Note that the 'arch' is in fact formed merely by cutting away the horizontal courses of stone. A collection of stone cross-slabs and other remains may be seen.

To the northwest rises the **Round Tower**, its conical cap reconstructed with the original stones. The doorway, over 3m from the ground, is without ornament. To the west, outside the enclosure, is **St. Mary's church**, believed to have been the first building in the lower valley, and marking the site of St. Kevin's grave.

West door of St. Mary's church and Round Tower

Also of interest, and best approached by crossing the stream south of St. Kevin's Kitchen and following a path to the left, is **St. Saviour's**. Here, there is an artificially hollowed stone or bullaun into which—according to legend—St. Kevin used to milk a mysterious white doe, to feed a child he had found abandoned at this hermitage. St. Saviour's church (12C) preserves the best Irish Romanesque decoration in the valley, but some stones were incorrectly replaced when the building was restored in 1875. Returning to the ballaun, continue east along the bank of the Lower Lake, to approach the

Upper Lake. A few steps to the left, overlooking the Upper Lake, are the remains of **Reefert church** (later the burial-place of the O'Tooles), behind which a path ascends the Lugdaff Glen to the Pollanass Waterfall. In a cliff on the south bank of the Upper Lake is the so-called **St. Kevin's Bed**, a rocky edge only approachable by boat. It was visited by Sir Walter Scott and Lockhart in 1825, among earlier tourists. Legend relates that the hermit chose this inaccessible haunt as a refuge from the persistent attentions of a beautiful woman, until one morning, awakening to find her standing beside him, St. Kevin pushed her into the lake, which presumably cooled her ardour; the incident is the subject of a popular 19C ballad. Further west are the slight remains, partly reconstructed, of *Teampull na Skellig* (the 'church of the rock'), probably the earliest building in the glen. **St. Kevin's Cell** is traditionally associated with the foundations of a beehive hut between his 'Bed' and Reefert church. Between Reefert church and the car-park to the north are five 'termon' or boundary crosses. The view from this point up the valley is outstanding. From here you may return to the hotel via the road skirting the north side of the Lower Lake. On the road returning to Laragh you pass (right) Trinity church (11C–12C), with a round-headed east window and chancel arch. The **Glendalough Visitor Centre** (09.30–17.00, Oct–Mar; 09.00–18.00, Mar–May; 09.00–18.30, June–Aug; 09.00–18.00, Sept–Oct; £) provides guided tours of the site and an audio-visual programme.

Bray to Wicklow by the Coast Road

Following the R761 south, you pass (right) **Killruddery**, the Tudor-revival seat (c1820, Sir Richard Morrison) of the Earls of Meath, famous in hunting annals. Its formal gardens date from the late 17C, with twin canals and pond. Above it rises the Cnoc Gilspir or Little Sugar Loaf (341m). A little further south the Great Sugar Loaf comes into view again (both named for their resemblance to the shape of the 18C loaf-sugar), while to the left are the ruined church and castle of Rathdown. After 6km you pass (right) the remains of Kindlestown, a 13C hulled castle. To the east lies the resort of **Greystones**; to the southwest is **Delgany** with a prominent church of 1789 containing the imposing monument to David La Touche, by John Hickey (1751–95).

Continue through **Kilcool** and **Newcastle**, Co. Wicklow, named after a fort of the Pale, where the Palladian house of Colganstown (attributed to Nathaniel Clements), is notable, before regaining the main road at Rathnew.

From **Little Bray**, on the north bank of the Dargle, ascend the valley and shortly enter **Kilbride**, where the Dargle and Glencullen streams meet. Just to the southwest, in the grounds of **Killcroney**, are the remains of the old church. From here a by-road climbs due west up the deep wooded Dargle Glen in the Powerscourt demesne, the grey mass of the great house is visible from View Rock. Better views are provided by taking the improved road (R761) forking right in Bray, which rejoins the main road near the demesne of **Hollybrook**, with its holly, arbutus, and ilex shrubs. A former house here was the home of Robin Adair (c 1737), made famous by the song set to the old Irish air *Eileen Aroon*.

The road continues to **Kilmacanoge**, at the foot of the Rocky Valley, through which a lane leads up to join the R755 west of the Great Sugar Loaf.

A gorge between the Great and Little Sugar Loaf, known as the Glen of the Downs, is an ancient river-bed, now a wooded ravine. The road descends through a series of demesnes to Newtown Mountkennedy. **Mount Kennedy**, designed in 1772 by James Wyatt and built in 1782 by Thomas Cooley and Richard Johnston, contains elaborate plasterwork by Stapleton. Beyond Dunran, the village of **Ashford**, in its rocky glen, is by-passed to the right. From here a by-road ascends the valley near the **Devil's Glen**, a romantic gorge with its waterfall, and the remains of Glenmore, a castellated pile erected by Francis Johnstone for Francis Synge, a great-grandfather of J.M. Synge (partly rebuilt).

Just beyond Ashford are **Mount Usher Gardens** (Mon–Sat, Mar–Oct ; £), laid out in 1868 by the Walpole family on the banks of the Vartry. It is one of the most beautiful and important gardens in the country, comprising 20 acres and 5000 species, arranged in the romantic, informal style of Robertson, and utilising the natural topography. The gardens are noted for their eucalyptus and tree-high rhododendrons.

At **Rathnew**, the R752 diverges southwest to (14km) Rathdrum, and southeast to adjacent Wicklow.

2 · The Shannon and Central Plain

Athlone is at the centre of this region, as well as being in the very centre of Ireland, although there are a number of claimants to the precise geographic centre—Birr, Glassan, and historically, the Hill of Uisneach. The town spans the **River Shannon** at an early fording point, and from here the principal internal waterways of the country are accessible; the Shannon and its extensive lake system, as well as the 18C **Royal** (145km) and **Grand** (132km) **Canals** which enter the Shannon on its eastern bank, respectively at Tarmonbarry and Shannon Harbour, above and below Athlone, linking Dublin with the central plain. North of Lough Boderg is the **Shannon–Erne Waterway**, and via the Grand Canal, access to the **Barrow Navigation** in the southeast of the country.

Excellent facilities for watersports, angling, sailing and cabin cruising are available in the Shannon region with 285km of cruising waterway, and 2000 sq. km of uncrowded open water. It is possible to cross Ireland from south to north and east to west on the waterways, totally avoiding road traffic. Two waymarked walking routes are the **Slieve Bloom Way** (77km) and the **Offaly Way** (29km).

The flat central plain which surrounds Athlone is bounded on the east by the **Bog of Allen**, and to the southeast and southwest by the **Slieve Bloom** and **Slieve Aughty Mountains**.

The '**Goldsmith Country**' which occupies a triangle north of Athlone, consists of the villages and countryside associated with the poet and playwright Oliver Goldsmith. The Goldsmith Summer School is held in June (☎ 043-41030). **Edgeworthstown** was the home of the remarkable Edgeworth family, the most notable of whom was Maria Edgeworth, novelist and educationalist.

Athlone has for over forty years been the venue for the annual **All-Ireland Drama Festival**, held in early May. **Coralee Bog**, an important Iron Age site lies north of Athlone, while to the south on a majestic sweep of the Shannon is **Clonmacnoise**, among the most important early-Christian monastic sites in the country.

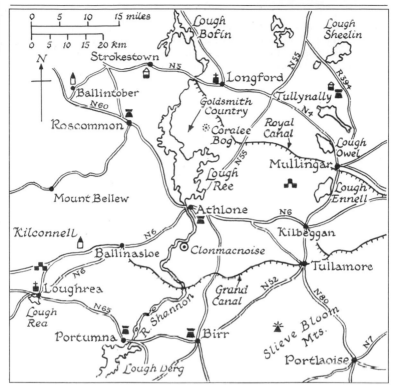

In a circle, more-or-less equidistant from Athlone, are the towns of the central plain, Ballinasloe, Roscommon, Longford, Mullingar, Tullamore and Birr; further distant are Portlaoise, Loughrea and Castlerea. Longford, Loughrea and Mullingar are cathedral towns. **Birr Castle**, **Belvedere** and **Strokestown** are important 18C houses, and good museums are to be found at Athlone and Mullingar (military history), Loughrea and Mullingar (ecclesiastical history) and Strokestown (the Famine). Birr Castle has the remains of the famous 19C Rosse Telescope.

This region comprises, west of the Shannon, parts of Counties Roscommon, Mayo and Galway, and on the east bank, parts of Cavan, Longford, Westmeath, Offaly and Laois.

How to get there
- **Train**. Direct from Dublin and Galway.
- **Air**. Equidistant from Galway, Knock, Shannon International airports.
- **Water**. Shannon waterways.

Listings
Athlone. **Left Bank Bistro**, Bastion St, adventurous, imaginative cooking (☎ 0902-94446); **Hodson Bay Hotel**, on Lough Ree; superb views, fine fish restaurant (☎ 0902-92444).

Ballinasloe. Hynes Hostel, Aughrim (☎ 0905-73734).

Ballycumber. Heartland Holiday Hostel (☎ 0506-36102).

Banagher. Brosna Lodge Hotel, Main St, small country-house hotel (☎ 0509-51350); **Crank House Hostel** (☎ 0509-51458).

Birr. Birr Castle Kitchen, good, not-so-simple food (☎ 0509-20985); **Spinners Town House**, Castle St, bistro, adaptable accommodation (☎ 0509-21673); **Tullanisk**, Banagher Road, croquet, bicycles, fishing, good cooking, B&B (☎ 0509-20572).

Carrick-on-shannon. Bush Hotel, modernised country town hotel (☎ 078-20014).

Castlerea. Clonalis House, Victorian mansion on lands continuously occupied for 1500 years by Gaelic aristocracy, the O'Conor Don family, B&B (☎ 0907-20014).

Glassan. (0902), **Grogan's Pub** and **Nannie Murph's**, attractive seafood bar (☎ 0902-85158); **Glassan Village Restaurant**, simple, and good (☎ 0902-85001).

Longford. Camlin Court Hotel, Great Water St, modern, comfortable (☎ 043-47190); Carriglass Manor (5km northeast of Longford, restaurant, B&B and Gardens & Costume Museum (☎ 043-45165).

Moate. 'Temple', Horseleap, 19C farmhouse, fine cooking, welcoming atmosphere, B&B (☎ 0506-35118).

Mullingar. **Crookedwood House**, Crookedwood, superlative cooking in 18C Rectory (☎ 044-72165); **Mearescourt House**, Rathconrath, classic Irish Georgian mansion, B&B (☎ 044-55112); **Greville Arms Hotel**, old-fashioned, attractive gardens (☎ 044-48563).

Portlaoise. *Chez Nous*, Kilminchy on the Dublin Road, one of those B&Bs which save the culinary reputation of the species (☎ 0502-21251); **Jim's Country Kitchen**, Church St, unassuming but good (☎ 0502-32616).

Roscommon. Abbey Hotel, Galway Road, Georgian Gothick, pleasantly refurbished (☎ 0903-6240).

Tullamore. Shepherd's Wood, Screggan, 1930s country house by Michael Scott, in extensive woodlands, B&B, outdoor heated pool (☎ 0506-21499).

North of Athlone ~ Kinnegad to Mullingar

To the east of Athlone, the N4 and N6 divide at Kinnegad where you enter Westmeath, and run northwest and southwest. Bear northwest at Kinnegad. After 6.5km a right-hand turning leads to **Killucan**, with three 16C–17C wayside crosses; nearby are remains of Rathwire Castle and traces of a Bronze Age barrow.

Mullingar

Mullingar, (Tourist Information, Dublin Rd, ☎ 044-48650) with its 18C Court House is the county town of Westmeath. Long a garrison town, it is still an important agricultural and angling centre.

The town is contained by the Royal Canal. The Catholic **Cathedral of Christ the King** (W.H. Byrne, 1936), is a curious building, belonging neither in style nor date to any Irish tradition of church building; it is a late classical basilica with twin west towers, showing in its various parts the influence of Renaissance church architecture, combined with that of Gandon and Lutyens.

The nave which has a coffered roof and double columned arcades, has considerable dignity. There are mosaics by Boris Anrep (1883–1969) who provided the floor mosaics for the National and Tate Galleries in London) in the side chapels of St. Patrick and St. Anne. The disappointing exterior has panels by Albert Power in the tympanum of the pediment, and a much-too-small dome at the crossing. Of the former cathedral (1836), only the clock tower survives. The three museums are of interest; adjoining the cathedral is the **Ecclesiastical Museum**, with a concentration of vestments and penal crosses; the **Town Museum** (10.00–17.00, June–Sept, £) at the Market House (William Caldbeck, 1867) deals with social history and archaeology, while the **Military Museum** in Columb Barracks (by appointment) has an extensive collection of militaria, local history and Iron Age log canoes. The attractive railway station is by the railway pioneer J.S. Mulvany (c 1850). All Saints church (C of I; 1733–1888) has good 19C stained glass including the Swift window (s. transept) acquired from the 1890 Paris exhibition.

Lough Ennell (4.5km south on the Tullamore road), **Lough Owel** (4.5km north west on the Longford road), and **Lough Derravaragh** (8.5km north on the way to Castlepollard), all provide good fishing.

In the 17C–19C, Mullingar was almost the exclusive domain of the Rochforts. The former mid-18C family mansions are between the main road to Kilbeggan (N52) and Lough Ennell. **Belvedere**, with its splendid stucco ceilings of 1745, has a remarkable sham ruin (1760) in the grounds—known as the 'Jealous Wall'—to screen it from another mansion, **Tudenham Park** (attributed to Castle). A ruin since 1958, it belonged to a brother of Lord Belvedere, whose wife had run off with another brother with whom he had quarrelled. She was later incarcerated for almost 30 years at his seat at Gaulston.

Castlepollard and Lough Sheelin

Turning north off the N4, 1.5km east of Crookedwood (10km northeast of Mullingar on the R394), is the 15C fortified church of St. Munna. At Castlepollard, a neat village, **Castlepollard Museum** (14.00–18.00, Sat, Sun & BH; also by appointment) displays agricultural and craft material. Just southwest is the wooded demesne of **Tullynally Castle** (formerly Pakenham Hall), (10.00–16.00, April–Oct, £) a grey castellated pile, originally a 17C house, classicised in 1775–80 by Graham Myers, and in 1803–6 transformed into a Gothick castle by Francis Johnston. Additions were made by James Shiel in 1825 and further extensions by Sir Richard Morrison (1842). It contains mementoes of the Duke of Wellington, whose wife was Catherine (or Kitty) Pakenham. It is the home of the Longford family; Edward Longford (1902–61) 7th Earl, directed a Dublin theatre company which toured the provinces for many years, bringing European drama to country towns.

At **Fore**, in a valley 5km east of Castlepollard, are the remains of an abbey founded by St. Fechin in 630 and refounded early in the 13C as a Benedictine house by Walter de Lacy. The ancient cell on the hillside was occupied by a hermit until 1764, while lower down are remains of fortifications and the church, remarkable for its massive doorway. 3km north of Castlepollard a well-preserved bawn with motte and bailey can be seen on the right. To the left, a ruined church crowns a height while further north, to the east of the road to Finnea, on **Lough Sheelin**, is the abrupt crag of the **Hill of Máel**.

Northeast of Lough Sheelin is Ballyjamesduff, which takes its name from General Sir James Duff (1752–1839), commander of the Limerick district in the troubles of 1798.

Mullingar to Edgeworthstown

Beyond Mullingar the N4 skirts **Lough Owel**, in which it is said that Máel Sechnaill, King of Meath, personally drowned the Viking chieftain Thorgestr (845). On the north bank is the demesne of Clonhugh, long connected with the Nugent family.

Multyfarnham (3km north of the N4) is a village noted for the partial ruins of a once-powerful Cistercian abbey, founded in 1306 by William Delamere. Its most remarkable feature is the slender tower 27m high. It was saved from spoliation by the Nugents at the time of the dissolution of the monasteries, but the friars were driven out in 1641 during the Civil War; the precincts are now occupied by Franciscans.

Northeast of Multyfarnham is **Lough Derravaragh**, 9.5km long, with low and boggy banks except at its southeast end. On the far bank is Faughalstown, a retreat of Mortimer, 5th Earl of March, in the reign of Henry IV. The road enters Bunbrosna, where to the right are the grounds of **Wilson's Hospital** (1760–70, now a school) built by John Pentland.

At Ballinalack (16km from Mullingar) you cross the Inny, to the southwest of which is **Lough Iron**, with the remains of the 12C abbey of Tristernagh, destroyed in 1783, and Templecross church (15C).

Edgeworthstown (13km) or Mostrim (*Meathas Truim*), on the Cavan–Athlone crossroads, has long been associated with the Edgeworth family, who became established in the neighbourhood in 1583 when the first Irish Edgeworth was appointed Bishop of Down and Connor. Richard Lovell Edgeworth (1744–1817), was a benefactor to the village, improving landlord, inventor, and father of 22 children. 'I am not a man of prejudices. I have had four wives'. Among his children was Maria Edgeworth (1767–1849), who lived there from 1782 until her death and is buried in St. John's churchyard. After the publication of her satirical Anglo-Irish novel, '*Castle Rackrent*' (1800), in 1825, she was visited here by Sir Walter Scott, who acknowledged her influence, and by Wordsworth in 1829. Some of her admirers in Boston, Mass., sent 150 barrels of flour during the famine of 1846, addressed to 'Miss Edgeworth, for her poor'. The Edgeworth's house is now a convent. Firmount, to the north, was the family home of the Abbé de Firmont (1745–1807), alias Henry Edgeworth—he changed his name because the French could not pronounce Edgeworth—who attended Louis XVI to the scaffold as his confessor; Maria's half-nephew was the mathematical economist Francis Ysidro Edgeworth (1845–1926). Oliver Goldsmith attended school in Edgeworthstown in 1741–45 (building demolished).

Currygrane, 9.5km northwest, was the birthplace of General Sir Henry Wilson (1864–1922), assassinated in London for his part in attempting to crush the Irish independence movement.

At Edgeworthstown the N55 turns northwest towards **Granard**. The town is commanded by the huge motte (disfigured by a shrine), of Hugh de Lacy's castle of 1191. The fine Catholic church (1861), is by John Burke.

A ruined medieval church (1214), with a Sheila-na-gig on its 15C tower is 4km southeast, at **Abbeylara**. This is all that remains of its Cistercian abbey, founded by Richard de Tuit, pillaged by Edward Bruce in 1315, and demolished in 1540. The road continues to Cavan with **Lough Gowna** to the left.

Goldsmith Country, Glassan, Lough Ree, Roscommon

Many of the places associated with Oliver Goldsmith's (1728–1774), youth are in the Lough Ree area. 'Sweet Auburn,' the village of his long poem *'The Deserted Village'*, which deals with the destructive effect of depopulation on rural communities, caused by 18C land enclosure, is possibly a recollection of an idyllic childhood in Glassan. Most of the buildings associated with Goldsmith have either been replaced or demolished, yet the pretty countryside is evocative of the world which he describes. Road signs in the area indicate the sites of 'Goldsmith Country'.

'Sweet was the sound, when oft at evening's close
Up yonder hill the village murmur rose.
There, as I passed with careless steps and slow,
The mingling notes came softened from below;
The swain responsive as the milk-maid sung,
The sober herd that lowed to meet their young.'

Ardagh 8km southwest on the N55, an ancient bishopric united to Kilmore and Elphin in 1833, shows little trace of antiquity, except for a small ruined church, and abandoned deanery. It is fabled as being the scene of an adventure of young Goldsmith, who mistaking the manor house (now a convent) for an inn, later based the plot of *She Stoops to Conquer* (1773) on his error. The **Ardagh Heritage Centre** (09.00–17.00 daily, £), in a schoolhouse of 1898 expands on the history of the region.

Ballymahon (19km south of Ardagh) is a large village pleasantly situated on the Inny, was Goldsmith's last home in Ireland, which he left for good in 1752. He was probably born (c 1730) at **Pallas** (4km east; house demolished), where there is a monument commemorating the writer, and baptised at Forgney (4km southeast).

Decayed **Ledwithstown House** (1749; by Castle), at Ballymahon, is being restored by the Irish Georgian Society. At **Corlea Bog Visitor Centre** (09.00–18.00 daily, June–Sept; £), near **Keenagh**, west of Ballymahon, an Iron Age wooden trackway of oak (148 BC) was excavated and a portion of this important and impressive structure has been preserved. **Castlecor House**, 2.5km northeast of Ballymahon, and now a convent, is a very curious building of c 1765, possibly based on *Clemenswerth*, Saxony. It contains an octagonal ballroom with a square central column incorporating four fireplaces.

The main road shortly passes the *Three Jolly Pigeons*, which preserves the name only of the inn of *She Stoops to Conquer*. The site of the village of Lissoy (another claimant to 'Sweet Auburn'), where Goldsmith's father was incumbent, and where the poet was brought up, is at the crossroads 2.5km further on.

At **Glassan** strike the shore of Lough Killinure, a bay of **Lough Ree**, on the bank of which, 5km northwest, stands **Portlick Castle** (14C–17C), and (7km beyond) bypass Athlone on its north side; Waterston House (1749; by Castle), south of Glassan, is derelict.

From Athlone turn northwest skirting the west bank of Lough Ree (for Athlone, see below) one of the larger of those irregular island-studded lakes that are characteristic of the Shannon valley. It is 25.5km long from north to south and 11km across at its widest, and provides trout fishing in the may-fly season, and coarse fishing at all seasons.

After 8km pass (left) **Moyvannan Castle**, and after another 8km reach (right) Lecarrow. From here a lane turns towards Lough Ree to (3km) the fortified promontory on which rises **Rinndown Castle**, built by John de Grey c 1227 on the legendary site of a stronghold of Thorgestr. It is sometimes called St. John's Castle, having at one time passed into the possession of the Knights of St. John. The massive keep, 15m in diameter, is overgrown with ivy.

Knockcroghery lies 8km north on the N61. On the summit of a hill to the west is a ruined observatory. To the east is Galey Castle (14C). In the middle of Lough Ree at this point is the island of Inchcleraun, or Inis Clothrann, named after Clothra, sister of that Queen Maeve who is said to have been killed here, when bathing, by a stone from the sling of Forbaid, Prince of Ulster. Its alternative name of Quaker Island recalls a 19C resident. The church here is notable as having a square tower of pre-Gothic date.

There is a good view of Lough Ree from a small promontory 4km north on the east bank, with wooded Hare Island offshore, on which are the ruins of a church said to have been built by St. Kieran before Clonmacnoise. This is one of many islets in the lough, some of them with ecclesiastical ruins, such as on Saints' Island (in fact a peninsula) near the head of the east lobe of the lough.

Roscommon

Roscommon is an old wool-town, deriving its name (Coman's wood) from a monastery founded here by St. Coman in 746. (Tourist Information. ☎ 0903-26342, June–September).

The most conspicuous building is the huge **Roscommon Castle**, immediately north of the town, to the left of the road. It was erected by Sir Robert de Ufford, justiciar of Ireland, in 1280 but suffered considerably in the wars of the 16–17Cs. It was partially dismantled by General John Reynolds in 1652, but is thought to have been inhabited as late as 1691. The mullioned windows were added c 1580. The outer enclosure, entered through a fortified gateway, is defended by a drum-tower at each angle; in the inner court is the building that contained the state apartments.

The **Dominican priory** in the lower part of the town, founded by Phelim O'Conor, King of Connacht, in 1257, and rebuilt in 1453, has a very long and narrow church with a fine west window. On the north side of the choir is a tomb with a damaged figure, said to be that of the founder; the four armed gallow-glasses that guard it appear to be of later workmanship.

The classical **Court House** (1736) in the town centre, has a tower and dome. About 5km northeast is the demesne of Hollywell, taking its name from a well dedicated to St. Brigid. The Gunning sisters, Maria and Elizabeth, daughters of the poverty-stricken James Gunning of Castlecoote (6.5km west of Roscommon), whose beauty was the toast of London in the 1750s, are said to have owed their complexions to its water; they became respectively, Countess of Coventry, and Duchess of first Hamilton, and later Argyll. The foolish Maria died aged 23 from cosmetic poisoning due to excessive use of white lead.

At **Athleague**, 9km southwest of Roscommon, is the 'Fort of the Earls', divided by a trench across the middle after a series of indecisive contests between two rival nobles. The **Castlestrange Stone**, 2.5km north west of Athleague, is a good example of Late Iron Age decoration. The mansion of Castle Strange was accidentally burnt.

Mount Bellew and Abbey Knockmoy

The N63 leads southwest from Roscommon to Galway via the demesne of **Mount Bellew** (landscaped by Hely Dutton; mansion demolished), shortly passing the battlefield of **Knockdoe**, where in August 1504 Gerald Fitzgerald, the Great Earl of Kildare, defeated his son-in-law Ulick de Burgh. **Abbey Knockmoy** (15km beyond this turning to the left) was founded for Cistercians by Cathal O'Connor 'of the Red Hand' to commemorate his victory over the English under Almeric St. Lawrence (see Howth) in 1189 (*Cnocmuaidhe*, hill of the slaughter). There is a Romanesque three-light window in the choir, and important remains of frescoes on the north chancel wall, and elsewhere. The canopied tomb of Malachy O'Kelly (d. 1401) and his wife is also notable. The isolated hill of **Caherpucha** (the 'Hill of the Fairies') rises prominently to the southwest.

15C mail-clad gallowglass on the O'Conor altar tomb, Dominican Friary, Roscommon Town

Roscommon to Ballyhaunis

The N61 leads north from Roscommon to Tulsk (18km), and beyond to Boyle (26km). The main route continues northwest from Roscommon on the N60 (passing the remains of a Round Tower) to Ballymoe(10km). The ruins of Glinsk Castle (17C) are 6.5km to the south. A little west of Glinsk, in the churchyard of Ballynakill, is a fine effigy of a late 15C armoured gallowglass. 6km northeast of Ballymoe at **Ballintober**, is an extensive castle, built before 1315, the headquarters of the O'Conors of Connacht until the 18C. The plan is similar to that of Roscommon, but the towers are polygonal instead of cylindrical. **The Old Schoolhouse** (1929) has been restored to represent a schoolroom of the period. The road turns north at Ballymoe to **Castlerea** on the river Suck.

The Victorian **Clonalis House**, (11.00–17.00, Tues–Sun, June–Sept; £) (1878–80, Pepys Cockerell) was the first mass-concrete house to be built in Ireland, and unusually, it is still in possession of an hereditary Gaelic family (the O'Conor Don family, descendants of the last Irish High King). It preserves the papers of the antiquary, Charles O'Conor (1710–91) in its large library, together with other family possessions, portraits, and furniture. The harp of Turlough O'Carolan last of the great 18C harpists, stands in the billiards-room. Castlerea was the birthplace of Sir William Wilde (1815–76), the antiquary and surgeon, and father of Oscar Wilde.

Bearing west, you enter **Ballyhaunis** after 20km with remains of an Augustinian priory and restored church. 8km to the northwest is Loughglinn, with an 18C mansion and circular fort. The Mosque was built in 1990 to serve the growing Islamic community, involved in the export of halal meat.

Northeast of Roscommon on the N63 is Lanesborough, a fishing centre at the north end of Lough Ree, where boats can be hired.

Towards Sligo ~ Longford, Strokestown and Frenchpark

The county town of **Longford** (Tourist Information, Main St. ☎ 043-46566, June–August) 14km west of Edgeworthstown, was once a fortress ('long-phort') of the O'Farrels, but no trace remains either of their castle or of the priory they founded in 1400.

St. Mel's Cathedral, by Joseph B. Keane, with its lofty belfry, is in the Italian Renaissance style of 1840–93. The **County Museum and Heritage Centre** (10.00–16.00 daily, June–Sept) is devoted to local history. The Clinton family, famous in Longford annals, included George Clinton (c 1686–1751), first governor of New York, and his nephew De Witt Clinton (1769–1828). Also born here was Pádraic Colum (1881–1972), the poet and dramatist.

5km northeast is **Carrigglass Manor** (1837), (14.00–18.00, Gardens & Costume Museum, £; B&B (see listings), restaurant) a Tudor-Revival house with original contents, rebuilt by Daniel Robertson, with stables and entrance arch by Gandon (1790).

Continue west and then northwest from Longford on the N5, through Cloondara, western terminus of the old Royal Canal, crossing the Shannon at Termonbarry, before veering north over the ridge of Slieve Bawn (263m).

Strokestown (22.5km) is a planned market-town with a wide tree-lined street, to the east of which is the mansion of the Mahon family, **Strokestown Park** (11.00–17.00, Tues–Sun, May–Sept; £). The 17C building was extended c 1730, possibly by Castle, and altered c 1819; the house, with original contents is open to the public. The important **Famine Museum**, housed in the stables, uses present-day documentation to commemorate the Irish Famine, (1845–47), the consequences of which, through death by starvation and disease, followed by massive emigration, led to the reduction of the Irish population by half at the end of the 19C. The displays draw parallels with similar present-day disasters. Strokestown became notorious in 1847 when Major Dennis Mahon, the landlord, was murdered, after the forced eviction of 3000 of his tenants at the height of the Famine.

Extensive remains of Neolithic settlement have been found between Strokestown and Tulsk.

Elphin 10.5km northwest, the seat of a bishop since the time of St. Patrick, also claims (with Pallas) to be the birthplace of Oliver Goldsmith (1730–74). He was certainly educated at the diocesan school here before moving on to Athlone. His grandfather, the Rev. Oliver Jones, curate of Elphin, lived at Smith Hill, northeast of the village.

The N5 is regained at **Tulsk** (9.5km southwest on the N5), once a place of importance because of its abbey. Only slight remains of the 15C abbey, perhaps founded by Phelim O'Connor, can be seen. The road passes (left) the Hill of Rathcroghan, the site of the palace of the pagan kings of Connacht. The curious enclosure to the south is known as the *Reilig-na-Riogh* (Cemetery of the Kings); near it is a small sandstone pillar said to mark the grave of Dathi, the last pagan king of Ireland.

At **Frenchpark** (16km) the Protestant rectory, was the birthplace of Douglas Hyde (1860–1949), the poet and Gaelic scholar, and first President of the Irish Republic (1938–45). He is buried at Churchstreet, on the road northwest (see Fermoy). The **Dr. Douglas Hyde Interpretative Centre** (14.00–17.00, Tues–Fri; 14.00–18.00, Sat–Sun, May–Sept) is housed in the church. The mansion of Frenchpark (c 1729), possibly by Castle, and recently demolished, was the former seat of the Lords De Freyne. To the southeast are the slight remains of the Dominican abbey-church of Cloonshanville (1385).

Continue northwest to Ballaghaderreen (13km), which has a broad market square and an inordinate number of pubs. It was the birthplace of John Blake Dillon (1814–66), the politician and joint-founder of the nationalist newspaper, *The Nation*.

Longford to Newtown Forbes and Dromod

From Longford drive northwest roughly parallel to the east bank of the Shannon, after 5km passing Newtown Forbes, which is separated from Lough Forbes, an expansion of the river, by Castle Forbes, the estate of the Earl of Granard, with a castellated mansion of c 1830 replacing that built by Sir Arthur Forbes c 1619.

A right-hand fork just beyond the village leads 16km northeast to **Ballinamuck**, where General Humbert's French invading force, which hoped to coordinate with insurgents in other parts of the country, finally surrendered to Cornwallis on 8 September 1798. Some 884 French officers and men were than transported back to France, but c 400 of some 900 Irish rebels then cornered at Killala were killed, and another 90 (including Wolfe Tone's brother) were later executed.

14km back along the N4, **Dromod**, on the shore of Lough Bofin. **The Cavan and Leitrim Railway**, runs steam and diesel trains on a restored portion of the narrow-gauge track. Dromod was once noted for its ironworks; it is now visited for trout fishing both on this lough and its western extension, Lough Boderg. Continue up the N4 for Carrick-on-Shannon.

South of Athlone ~ Kinnegad to Athlone

Bear left on to the N6 from Kinnegad, and skirting the northern edge of the Bog of Allen, approach (15km) **Rochfortbridge**, named after Robert Rochfort (1652–1727), MP for Westmeath, Speaker of the Irish Parliament, and a friend of Swift. 8km beyond is **Tyrrellspass**, laid out around a semicircular green, where the church contains a monument by John Bacon Jr, to the Countess of Belvedere (d. 1814). Just beyond that is Killavally, birthplace of General Wade (1673–1748), the road-builder, with a 15C castle.

Kilbeggan, at the crossroads between Mullingar and Tullamore (12km south), has an old harbour on the Grand Canal, a market-house and courthouse; **Locke's Distillery** (09.00–18.00, Apr–Oct; 10.00–16.00, Nov–Mar; £), which flourished from 1757 to 1957, is now a museum of industrial archaeology.

The mansion of Newforest, 5km northeast was built in 1749, while to the north stands Middleton House, nearer Castletown Geoghegan, with remains of a medieval priory and an Anglo-Norman motte and bailey.

Further northwest rises the **Hill of Uisneach** (or *Ushnagh*, 181m), the summit of which was an ancient assembly-place, and which commands a good view over the undulating plain. Adjacent, to the south, is the lower hill of Knockcosgrey, another contender for the geographical centre of Ireland, on the west slope of which are the ruins of Killeenbrack Castle. Between the two hills, but slightly to the west, is Killare, the site of a 12C motte and bailey, and of an ancient monastery.

4km south of Kilbeggan, to the right of the Tullamore road, is **Durrow Abbey**, founded by St. Columba, where the *Book of Durrow* was written in the 7C. A copy of the Gospels, it is now in Trinity College Library, Dublin. The late 10C High Cross and St. Columba's Well may be seen in the churchyard, and the present house (c 1837; rebuilt 1924), formerly occupied by the earls of Norbury (the 2nd earl was murdered here in 1839), stands on the site of a castle built by Hugh de Lacy, who was murdered in 1186 by one of the workmen. The main road from Kilbeggan leads west to (6.5km) **Horseleap**, said to take its name from an exploit of Hugh de Lacy, beyond which you enter **Moate**. The **Moate Museum**, has a good local history and folklore collection. To the southwest rises the Motte of Grania. Some 8km northeast, on the hill of Knockast, is a large cairn, probably a pre-Celtic cemetery (c 2000 BC).

Athlone

Athlone (*Baile Atha Luain*, the Ford of Luan) straddles the Shannon just below its outflow from Lough Ree (Tourist Information. Athlone Castle, ☎ 0902-94630 May–October)

It was of military importance since 1129 when Turloch Mor O'Conor built a fort to protect the bridge. Its importance grew in 1210 when a castle was built by John de Grey, Bishop of Norwich and Justiciar of Ireland. As the key to the west it was strategically placed, and in 1641 Viscount Ranelagh was besieged here for almost six months by the men of Connacht. In 1690 it was held successfully for James II by Colonel Richard Grace; but in the following year, after a violent bombardment of ten days, Godert de Ginkel (1644–1703) William III's Dutch commander, took the town by assaulting the bridge (replaced by the present structure in 1844) despite a brave defence by the Irish army under Colonel Nicholas Fitzgerald and General St. Ruth. Ginkel was rewarded with the Earldom of Athlone.

Athlone is a busy and thriving town and railway junction, now by-passed on the north by the N6 Dublin-Galway road. On the west bank is **Athlone Castle** (11.00–16.30 Mon–Sat; 12.00–16.30, Sun; June–Oct) repaired in 1547 and defaced since, but incorporating earlier work, also damaged sections of the town walls (1576) which have survived the bombardment of 1691 and the explosion of a magazine in 1697. The Castle contains the **Museum**, dealing with the folklore and history of the region, military history and Count John McCormack, a native of the town. **St. Peter and Paul's Church** (RC; Ralph Byrne 1937), is a substantial neo-Renaissance building.

On the east bank are the remains of a Franciscan abbey, built by Cathal O'Connor and completed in 1241. A house at the corner of Church St and Northgate St is said to have been the residence (now modernised) of Ginkel after the siege. Other buildings of interest are **St. Mary's Church** 1826 (C of I), which has some interesting monuments, including the de Renzi tomb, and the ruins of St. Peter's Abbey. Off Church St is the ruined Jacobean **Court Devenish House**. From The Strand, boats make the delightful upriver journey to Lough Ree, and downriver to the famous monastery of Clonmacnoise, probably the most attractive way in which to visit the site.

Tullamore, Clara Bog, Boher

From Kilbeggan, due south is **Tullamore** the county town of Offaly and an important agricultural and distillery centre (Tourist Information, ☎ 0506 52617, July–August). It was the original terminus of the Grand Canal, and has some interesting canal architecture remains.

Tullamore has an 18C Market-House, a porticoed Court-House (c 1835) by J.B. Keane, and a Protestant church (1818) by Francis Johnston, containing the Charleville monument by Van Nost. Castellated Charleville Forest (1800–12, also by Johnston), to the right of the Birr road, leading southwest, retains some interesting Gothic Revival details, and has been restored. Srah Castle (1588) and Ballycowan Castle (1625), both west of the town on an extension of the canal (1804), are typical of the many fortified houses in the vicinity. To the south rise the Slieve Bloom Mountains (20km).

From Tullamore drive northwest through Clara, a Quaker foundation, with flour mills and jute works, to (22km) Moate. South of Clara (2km) is **Clara Bog**, one of the largest and best preserved raised bogs in Ireland, its acid nutrient conditions form an ideal habitat for a wide range of plant and moss species.

An interesting detour lies west via (7km) the church at Boher, with its shrine of St. Manchan, probably made at Clonmacnoise c 1130 for the abbey of Lemanaghan. The gabled yew-wood box is adorned with metalwork and cloisonné enamel, with later crude copies of figures from European Romanesque models. Continue west via the Doon crossroads to Clonmacnoise.

Tullamore to Cloghan, Clonmacnoise

At 9.5km southwest of Tullamore turn right off the N52 on to the R357 at Blue Ball. At **Rahan** (5km north of this junction) are the remains of an abbey founded in the 6C by St. Carthach, Bishop of Lismore, the 12C church of which still survives. The piers and capitals of the chancel arch are perhaps earlier; the rose-window, unique in Ireland, is late Romanesque. Nearby is a small ruined church (15C), with details from an older building. Pass through **Cloghan** 19.5km, a neat village, 6.5km north east of which lies **Gallan Priory**, a Georgian building 'Gothicised' and retaining only a few relics of the former monastery said to have been founded in the 5C by St. Canoc. To the east is **Kilcolgan House** (Jacobean), and to the south ruins of a 15C church. Remains of a monastery survive at Lemanaghan about 5km further northeast. 3.5km northwest of Cloghan you pass the keep and bawn of Clonony Castle, in a fair state of preservation. To the southwest lies **Shannon Harbour**, once important as standing at the junction of the Grand Canal and the navigable Shannon, with old warehouses, barracks, and a grand Hotel (1806).

At **Shannonbridge** with a power-station, and some massive fortifications of 1804 on the west bank, is the **Clonmacnoise and West Offaly Railway** which gives a 8km tour of the Blackwater raised bog.

Clonmacnoise

Clonmacnoise (OPW), (*Cluain Moccu* (or *Mhic*) *Nóis*, the meadow of the sons of Nós) is one of the most rewarding ecclesiastical sites in Ireland to visit (10.00–17.00 daily, except Mar–May to 18.00, May–Sept to 19.00; OPW; £).

The first church here was founded by St. Kieran in 548 on ground given by King Dermot. The saint died the following year, but the abbey grew in importance. It was sent a present by the English theologian, bishop Alcuin (AD 730–840) on behalf of Charlemagne in 790 and continued to flourish in spite of attacks by the Vikings, the men of Munster, and the Normans. Abbot Tigernach (d. 1088) composed his *Annals* here and Maelmuire (d. 1106) wrote the *Book of the Dun Cow* (in the Royal Irish Academy Library, Dublin). It was plundered in 1552 by the English from Athlone, and in 1568, on the death of Bishop Peter Ware, the see was merged with that of Meath.

From the **Visitor Centre** (OPW, opening times as above), which contains the originals of the High Crosses and grave slabs, now replaced on site by replicas, you enter the enclosure. To the left is O'Rourke's Tower', a large roofless Round Tower, almost 19m high, with a doorway 1.5m from the ground, and eight bell-windows (later). It was completed, according to the *Annals of the Four Masters* in 1124, but was struck by lightning in 1134. Teampull (church) Connor, to the north on lower ground, founded c 1010 by Cathal O'Connor, was converted into a parish church c 1780 and retains only one round-headed doorway.

Inscribed early Christian cross slab in the monastic enclosure; 'a prayer for Dainéil', 8C–9C, Clonmacnoise

Beyond stand Teampull Finghin, on the northern edge of the enclosure, believed to have been erected by Fineen MacCarthy Mór, with its chancel, and the round MacCarthy Tower. The tower is an unusually perfect example, retaining its conical top, but with its entrance at ground level, and with only two bell-windows.

Walking up towards the cathedral you pass the much-worn shaft of the North Cross, while opposite the west door stands the Cross of the Scriptures (early 10C), a monolith over 4m high, with votive inscriptions, now illegible, but said to commemorate King Flann and Abbot Colman. Of the elaborate

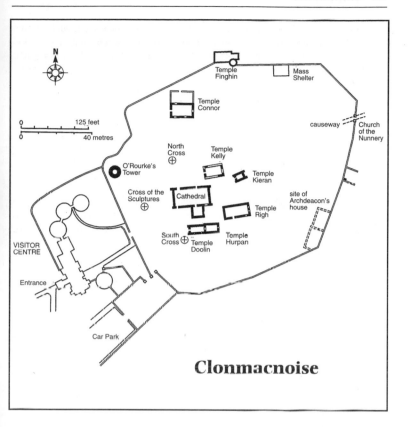

Clonmacnoise

sculptures, those on the east side depict the foundation of Clonmacnoise by St. Kieran, who is represented with King Dermot holding a maul. On the west side are Passion scenes, from which are derived Tigernach's alternative name for the cross (*Cros na Screaptra*, Cross of the Scriptures).

The Cathedral or Great Church (*Daimhlaig Mór*) was built in 904 by King Flann and Abbot Colman Conailleach, and rebuilt in the 14C by Tomultach MacDermot, from whom comes its later name of Teampull Dermot. The sandstone capitals of the west doorway, different in style and material from the rest of the building, were probably incorporated from the original 10C church; the choir vault and the elaborately ornamented north doorway, surmounted by a figure of St. Patrick between SS Francis and Dominic, were built c 1460 by Dean Odo.

To the south is the South Cross (9C), with a Crucifixion, and floral and zoomorphic ornamentation, beside the entrance to Teampull Doolin (12C or earlier), restored in 1689, and abutted to the east by Teampull Hurpan (17C). Behind the latter stands Teampull Righ (*Ri*; or Meaghlin's Chapel; c 1200), to the north of which lie Teampull Kieran, with a good two-light east window, and, nearer the cathedral, fragmentary Teampull Kelly (12C).

A causeway leads from Teampull Kieran out of the enclosure to a track. Cross a style (right) to reach the ruined Church of the Nunnery, founded in 1167 by Devorguilla O'Meaghlin, wife of O'Rourke, Prince of Breffni. It has a good Romanesque door and chancel arch (restored 1867). To the southwest stood the castle (c 1212), built by John de Grey on the site of the Abbot's House (burnt 1135), and destroyed by the Cromwellians.

Turning east at Clonmacnoise, after 6.5km you pass (right) Esker Hill, on which is a slab with carvings related to the Neolithic wall-paintings of Spain, showing rudimentary figures perhaps engaged in battle. The N62 at Ballynahown bears northwest for Athlone. East of Clonmacnoise (2km) is Mongan Bog, an An Taisce nature reserve and roosting site for Greenland white-fronted geese.

Ballinasloe, Aughrim, Loughrea for Galway

Ballinasloe (*Beal Atha na Sluiaghe*, mouth of the ford of the hosts) is a busy agricultural centre on the river Suck, a tributary of the Shannon (Tourist Information, ☎ 0905 42131; July–August). The town is known for its great livestock fair, held in early October partly on the Fair Green, and partly in the grounds of Garbally Court, west of the town (1819–24, by Thomas Cundy, and now a school). Seamus O'Kelly (1880–1918) the playwright was born here.

In 1856, a peak year, almost 100,000 sheep and 20,000 head of cattle were sold here; it was Europe's largest horse fair in the era of Cavalry regiments and horse transport, declining after World War I and the terminus (abandoned in 1961) of a branch of the Grand Canal. Ivy Castle, a modern residence, has been built around the shell of the original fortress guarding the river crossing. Several 18C buildings survive, and the former mental hospital, with its domed tower (1839, by Francis Johnston) is the finest building in the town. On Dunlo Hill, overlooking the Fair Green, is a classical monument to Archdeacon Charles Trench (d. 1839), benefactor of the town. St. Michael's church (1846–58) by J.J. McCarthy (revised by Pugin) has a *Dead Christ* by Albert Power under the reordered High Altar; in the north aisle is a tabernacle in gold, silver and enamels by Mia Cranwill (1926), an important work of the Celtic Revival movement. There are also two windows by Harry Clarke, 1926 (east and west aisles) and two by Patrick Pollen 1958 (west aisle).

The main road veers southwest through (8km) **Aughrim** (*Each Dhruim*, horse hill), where on 12 June 1691 General St. Ruth was defeated and killed by the Williamites under Ginkel. Although the Jacobites were superior in position and numbers, the day was lost owing to the reluctance of St. Ruth to take his lieutenant (Sarsfield), into his confidence; and to the fact that his troops in the castle of the O'Kellys had been supplied with ammunition which would not fit their muskets. The well documented **Battle of Aughrim Interpretative Centre** (10.00–18.00 daily, Easter–Oct, OPW; £), presents an overview of the battle.

The R348 drives due west from Ballinasloe through (13km) **Kilconnell**, with a charming ruined abbey, founded in 1400 by William O'Kelly for Franciscans on the site of an earlier church of St. Canal. Its best features are the slender tower (high up under the crossing of which is a carved owl), the fine window-tracery, and part of a little cloister, only 14.5m square, with arcades springing from a low wall. It contains some interesting monuments, including a Flamboyant tomb of c 1475, and was probably the burial-place of General St. Ruth.

22.5km beyond, you enter **Loughrea**, sited on the northern bank of its Loughs, to which the town turns its back. It retains its water-filled medieval moat and there are crannogs in the lake. The principal ruins are those of the Carmelite friary c1300 and a castle, built by Richard de Burgo.

Cathedral of St. Brendan

This cathedral (RC) by William Byrne (1897–1903) is one of the most interesting 19C churches in Ireland, not for its exterior, which is bland, although the spire is tall and dignified, but for its interior furnishings. Between the inception of the building and its completion, the Celtic Revival movement had begun to influence ecclesiastical taste, and Loughrea became a repository for the work of the finest artists of the movement over the next fifty years. It has the largest number of windows (best viewed in the morning or evening) in any church in Ireland by *An Túr Gloine*, with work by Sarah Purser, Patrick Pye (porch), Evie Hone (rose window and west aisle), A.E.Child (apse), Michael Healy (west transept, west aisle, east and west side chapels), and Hubert McGoldrick. Healy's *Ascension* (1936) and *Last Judgement* (1940), west transept, are among the masterpieces of Irish 20C glass. Healy contributed 14 windows to the cathedral between 1904 and 1940.

The carvings of the capitals, corbels and altar table are by Michael Shortall, the reredos bas-relief in the apse and the Virgin in the Lady Chapel are by John Hughes, the opus-sectile stations of the cross are by Ethel Mary Rhind, metalwork, woodwork and the floor tiling was designed by W.A.Scott. With the exception of the glass, the decorative work all dates from the first 20 years of the century.

The **Clonfert Museum of ecclesiastical art** in the cathedral yard (09.00–17.00, Mon–Fri; ask in church for attendant if museum closed) has a good collection of church vestments, including a 15C English chasuble reworked from earlier vestments; a collection of chalices, the most notable of which is the 'Matheus Macraith' c 1500; the figures of the 13C polychrome 'Kilcorban Virgin' have excellent expressions; and banners by the Dun Emer Guild (embroidered by the Yeats sisters after design by Jack B. Yeats). The surviving town gate is incorporated in the grounds.

On the summit of a hill to the north is a good stone circle, while several crannogs have been discovered in Lough Rea. About 5km north, then west of the village of **Bullaun**, is the **Turoe Stone**, with its richly ornamented carvings in the *La Tène* style (Late Iron Age), moved here from a nearby ring fort.

At St. Cleran's (right of the Galway road, 6km from Loughrea) Robert O'Hara Burke (1820-61), the explorer of Australia was born. He starved to death at Cooper's Creek on his return journey, having been the first European to cross the continent.

There are a number of ruined mansions in the area, including **Roxborough House**, off the Gort Road, the birthplace of Lady Gregory (see Ch. 10).

The country becomes bleaker and stonier as you approach Athenry (27km). **Athenry** (*Baile Atha an Ri*, ford of the king), on the Clarin, contains several memorials to its past importance. The town was walled in 1211 and became the principal seat of the De Burghs and the Berminghams who, a century later (in 1316) held out against Phelim O'Connor, King of Connacht (a partisan of Edward Bruce). In 1596 the town was was burned by Red Hugh O'Donnell (1571–1602) chief of the Ulster O'Donnells, from which destruction it never recovered. Considerable fragments of the wall survive, including the North Gate Tower and restored **Athenry Castle** (09.30–18.30 daily, June–Sept; OPW; £) has a rectangular keep (1238) with outworks. The Dominican priory, founded in 1241, dates mainly from the 15C, and contains tombs of the Berminghams, De Burghs, and other Galway families. Of the Franciscan friary (1464), the Protestant parish church occupies the site of the chancel and crossing; the nave and transepts are in ruins.

Portlaoise to Mountmellick, Birr

South and west of Tullamore lies Portlaoise on the N7, Dublin to Cork route. **Portlaoise** (pronounced 'Portleesha', and sometimes spelt as two words) (Tourist Information. James Fintan Lalor Ave. ☎ 0502 21178) is the county town of Laois (Leix), formerly Queen's County and is notable today as the home of Ireland's **maximum security prison** for IRA terrorists, situated on the N7 Dublin Road and shrouded in defensive screens. The prison dates from 1830 (G. and J. Pain). It has been the scene of some spectacular escapes. Opposite it is the former **Lunatic Asylum** by Francis Johnston c 1830.

Nothing remains of the castle erected during the reign of Mary Tudor to hold in check the powerful O'Mores except part of the curtain-wall, north of the Main St. There are a number of distinguished 18C buildings, the **Protestant church** has a fine spire by Gandon and windows by A.E. Child (1938). The **Court House** (Sir Richard Morrison, 1805) on the Main St has a delightful floating staircase and at its rear is the old county gaol, with heavy rusticated classical pilasters and fine central carved armorial panel. Bartholomew Mosse (1712–59), philanthropist and founder of Dublin's Rotunda Hospital, was born here.

9km northwest of Portlaoise lies **Ballyfin House** (1822), perhaps the grandest early Classical mansion in Ireland, designed by Sir Richard and William Vitruvius Morrison for Sir Charles Coote (now a school).

Turn southwest of Portlaoise onto the N8, is **Ballyknockan House**, the site of the Pass of the Plumes, the marshy level where the Earl of Essex was defeated in 1599 during the Elizabethan conquest by Owen MacRory O'More. Its name is said to derive from the plumed helmets left on the battlefield.

North of Portlaoise (on the N80) you enter **Mountmellick** (at 11km) once a busy manufacturing town founded by the Society of Friends, where the first Quaker school in Ireland was established in 1677, but now only its 18C houses recall its prosperous past. 3km west stands the demesne of **Summer Grove** (c 1760), and some 5km beyond, a charming stretch of the river Owenass known as Cathole Glen, with cascades and troutpools.

This pleasant road (R422 and R421) skirts the afforested northern slopes of Slieve Bloom, reaching (5km) **Rosenallis**, a pretty village with the oldest Friends' burial-ground in Ireland (c 1700). About 13km beyond lie the ruins of **Castle Cuffe**, one of the strongholds of Sir Charles Coote. Kinnitty (12km) is an attractive village. On its outskirts is the demesne of **Castle Bernard** (1833, by the Pain brothers), now a forestry centre. It contains the shaft of a High Cross, a relic of St. Finan's 6C monastery, destroyed in 839. At Sierkieran, 3km south, are remains of a monastery founded by St. Kieran (5C), with some curious sculptures on the 19C church.

From Mountmellick, the N80 continues northwest via (14.5km) **Killeigh**, with the church of a Franciscan friary and an old churchyard, to Tullamore.

Birr

Birr, known formerly as Parsonstown from an earlier Laurence Parsons to whom the land was granted in 1620, was described from its very approximate central position as '*Umbilicus Hiberniae*' in Sir William Petty's Survey of Ireland (known as the Down Survey from the fact that 'he plotted everything down'). It is regularly built, and has a couple of attractive malls. Both Catholic and Protestant churches are large early 19C Gothick buildings. An Ionic temple (1828), designed by Lord Rosse, serves as a school house.

Birr Castle, (09.00–13.00, 14.00–17.00, Jan–March & Nov–Dec; 09.00–18.00, Apr–Oct; £) on the northeast side of the town, the seat of the Earl of Rosse, was built in 1620–27 by Sir Laurence Parsons on the site of the keep of the O'Carrolls (the foundations of which survive). It was twice besieged in the 17C, in 1643 and 1690, and the fortified outworks were removed in the 18C. The façade was altered after c 1801 by John Johnston (d. 1812) and his successors for Sir Laurence Parsons, 2nd Earl of Rosse, who added a battlemented third storey after a fire in 1832. The Vaubanesque outworks were constructed in 1846–48 as a famine relief project. The **gardens** (open to the public daily) were laid out by the 2nd Earl (1757–1841), and are not only noted for their box and yew hedges, but also for their magnolias, maples, conifers and Eucryphia (from Nymans, Sussex), among a large variety of trees, shrubs and flowers, some of them rare. A number of species are propagated for commercial purposes. An informative booklet is available at the entrance lodge.

Of additional interest is the shell of the **Rosse Telescope** (1845), 16.5m long, which stands half-left from the entrance. Built by the 3rd Earl (1800–67), the instrument was used by the 4th Earl (1840–1908), assisted from 1880 by Dr Otto Boeddicker of Göttingen University, to make the first accurate measurement of the heat of the moon and to survey the spiral nebulae. The 183cm-diameter speculum was dismantled and removed to the Science Museum, London, in 1914. The telescope tube has been replaced (1996), as part of a restoration project, and a small exhibition of optical flats, lenses, eye-pieces, etc. is on display. There is a campaign to restore the telescope.

Sir Charles Parsons (1854–1931), the engineer and younger brother of the 4th earl, and renowned for his development of the steam turbine, spent much of his childhood at Birr. His turbine-propelled vessel, *Turbinia*, which made rings around the British fleet at the naval review of 1897, led to the general adoption by 1905 of this method of propulsion for ships.

Immediately southwest of Birr turn right onto the R489, after 13km passing near (left) **Lackeen Castle**, a 16C tower-house standing in its bawn, and further west, to the left, the ruins of the Priory of Lorrha (13C). The Protestant church and St. Ruadhans (15C), east of the village crossroads, are also of interest. 5km northwest is the restored castle of Redwood, burned in 1640. Cross the Shannon by a long bridge before entering Portumna.

Clonfert, Ballinasloe, Portumna

Follow the R439 northwest, passing (right) before (9km) Taylor's Cross, Hill House, where the Rev. Arthur Nicholls, husband of Charlotte Brontë, died in 1906. They spent their honeymoon (in 1854) at neighbouring Cuba Court an early 18C building ascribed to Sir Edward Lovett Pearce, now demolished.

4km beyond lies **Banagher**, celebrated for its fairs, its distillery, and its bridge (1843) across the Shannon. It was Trollope's first residence in Ireland as a Post Office surveyor, and here he wrote some early, unsuccessful novels (1841–44). **Cloghan Castle** (1249) 5km southwest, damaged in 1595, with a Georgian wing added in 1800, is now partly restored.

Cross the river, fork right, and turn right at the crossroads (7km) to **Clonfert**. Although now no more than a hamlet, it still holds the title of the bishop of the united sees of Killaloe, Clonfert, Kilmacduagh and Kilfenora. The partly ruined cathedral, the successor of the monastery founded by St. Brendan in 558 at *Cluain Fhearta* (the field of the grave), is notable for its very fine Irish Romanesque doorway (mid–late 12C), with its six recessed orders and grotesque capitals, below a tall triangular pediment, as at Roscrea. The innermost order, in limestone, was added in the late 15C. The chancel (early 13C) has quaintly carved corbels and beautiful twin lancets at the east end; the south transept and slender tower were added after 1414 (the parapet is an incorrect restoration).

7km southwest of the crossroads stand the ruins of **Eyrecourt Castle**, a Dutch-inspired house (c 1660), which has been allowed to decay since 1920. Its rare staircase was extracted and sold to the Detroit Institute of Arts. 3km beyond to the southeast, at Meelick, are a ruined castle of 1229 and the re-roofed church of a Franciscan friary founded in 1479.

Continuing northwest from the crossroads, pass **Laurencetown** on the left (8km) with a tower-house, and after 6.5km pass the well-preserved ruins of Clontuskert Abbey, an Augustinian house on the site of a monastery founded in the 9C. It has a remarkable west door of 1471, on which St. Michael, St. Catherine and St. John the Baptist are depicted, together with a carved mermaid, pelican, griffin.

There are two routes to Athlone from Birr; the direct road via Cloghan Ferbane and Ballynahown, near which is long derelict Ledwithstown (possibly by Castle, recently restored), and the more interesting road via Clonmacnoise, best approached by turning left at (16km) Cloghan for (13km) Shannonbridge, and there turning right for 7km.

Lord Castlemaine's demesne lies to the east at **Moydrum**. The battlemented castle (1821; by Sir Richard Morrison), burned down in 1921. 3km further east, at Bealin, is a 9C sculptured and inscribed High Cross of the Clonmacnoise type; note the hunting scene.

Portumna, lying at the northern end of Lough Derg, retains the imposing ruins of a huge semi-fortified **Portumna Castle** (c 1618) (09.30–18.30 daily, June–Sept; OPW; £), formerly the seat of the earls of Clanricarde and built for Richard Burke, the 4th earl. Accidentally burnt in 1826, it is currently undergoing restoration. The main approach (from the north) is through three aligned gates and formal gardens. Also within the demesne are arches of an early 13C Dominican convent, and two walks of a cloister; also the shell of the last earl's residence (1862: by Sir Thomas Newenham Deane), burnt in 1922, six years after the death of the unpopular and reactionary earl, whose extensive estates were compulsorily transferred to the Congested Districts board in 1915.

Derryhivenney Castle, (6.5km northeast) one of the last castles to be built in Ireland, retains its four-storey tower of 1643 and most of its bawn.

3 · The South East: South Wicklow and Wexford

This region consists of south Counties Wicklow and Wexford, with portions of Kilkenny and Carlow. The **Wicklow** and **Blackstairs Mountains** define the character of the region as a coastal strip running from Wicklow Town to the Ferryport of **Rosslare** in the south-east corner of Ireland. The Region, known as 'the sunny south-east' has the highest average temperatures and the lowest rainfall in Ireland, no guarantee however, against downpours.

The southern part of the region is associated with the United Irishmen rebellion of 1798 which was led by both Catholics and Protestants and **Vinegar Hill**, Enniscorthy, is the site of one of the most significant battles of the period. The River **Slaney**, which flows south throughout the region, passes through **Enniscorthy** and enters the sea at Wexford where the sheltered harbour attracted Viking settlement in the 10C; Wicklow, Arklow and Wexford all derive from Old Norse topographical names.

The N11 runs south from Dublin, close to the coast as far as Wicklow, then diverts inland in a southwest sweep before returning to the coast at Wexford. From here the N25 turns west towards Waterford, Cork and the west coast.

Avondale Forest Park in south County Wicklow and the adjacent countryside of **Avoca** offers some of the most scenic areas of the south east, and **Collatin Woods** near Shillelagh is one of the few surviving indigenous oak-woods. At Clongall, north of Bunclody, the Wicklow Way (132km; from Rathfarnam, Dublin) meets the South Leinster Way. Further west around **Baltinglass** are an impressive series of Iron Age hill forts, antiquities which remain enigmatic. At Ferrycarrig, outside Wexford is the **Irish National Heritage Park**, with reconstructions of antiquities from 7000 BC to the 12C AD.

Anglo-Norman influence can

be seen in the very well-preserved medieval remains in **Ferns** and **Baltinglas**. Gorey, Enniscorthy and Wexford have good Gothic Revival churches and at Wexford in August the **Grand Opera Festival** is held, a platform for the revival of neglected masterpieces.

How to get there
- **Train**. Belfast-Dublin-Wexford line, connecting to Rosslare Harbour.
- **Air**. Waterford Airport.
- **Sea**. Rosslare Harbour to Fishguard, Pembroke, Le Havre, Cherbourg; sailings to Saltee Islands.

Listings
Arklow. **Bridge Hotel**, Bridge St, small country-town hotel (☎ 0402-31666).
Avoca. **Avoca Handweavers**, Kilmacanogue, clothes and fabrics, fine café (☎ 0402-351 05).
Ballydesmond. **Eugene's Restaurant**, fine pub-restaurant (☎ 054-89288).
Bunclody. **Bunclody Holiday Hostel**, Ryland Road (☎ 054-76076); **Clohamon House**, Clohamon, country-house, B&B, Connemara ponies, fishing (☎ 054-77253).
Enniscorthy. **Ballinkeele House**, Ballymurn; country-house of undisturbed charm and comfort (☎ 053-38105); **Salville House**, delightful country-house cooking, B&B and self-catering wing (☎ 054-35252).
Glendalough. **Wicklow Way Hostel**, Laragh (☎ 0404-45398).
Gorey. **Marlfield House**, the absolute luxury of a Regency country-house, noted for fine food, sumptuous surroundings (☎ 055-21124).
Kilmore Quay. **Kilturk Hostel and Studios** (☎ 053-29883).
Rathdrum. **The Old Presbytery**, hostel (☎ 0404-46930).
Rathnew. **Hunter's Hotel**, coaching inn with gardens on the Vartry River, old-world ambience (☎ 0404-40106); **Tinakilly House**, built by Captain Halpin, Commander of the trans-Atlantic cable-laying Great Eastern, relaxed and sumptuous country house, B&B, dinner (☎ 0404-69274).
Rosslare Harbour. **Kelly's Resort Hotel**, fine family-run hotel (☎ 053-32114).
Wexford. **Broade's**, South Main St, attractive music pub; **Ferrycarrig Hotel**, Ferrycarrig Bridge, modern, stunning location on Slaney Estuary (☎ 053-20999); **McMenamin's Town House**, 3 Auburn Terrace, Redmond Road, B&B (☎ 053-46442); **The Raisin**, Paul's Quay, traditional pub (☎ 053-20982).
Wicklow. **The Old Rectory**, pretty 19C house, food includes organic vegetables, seafood, vegetarian and edible-flower based dishes, B&B (☎ 0404-67048).

Wicklow, Ferns, Enniscorthy
The county town of **Wicklow** of Viking foundation (*Vikingalo*, Viking's loch), lies on a long creek or 'wick' through which the Vartry enters the sea, flanked by a grassy strip of land known as The Morrough. (Tourist Information, Fitzwilliam Square, ☎ 0404-69117).

Near the town entrance are the ruins of a Franciscan friary founded in 1279 by the O'Byrnes and O'Tooles after defeating the Fitzgeralds; a statue in the town commemorates Miles Byrne (1780–1862) and leaders of the 1798 insurrection. The 18C church, with a square tower and dome, preserves a Romanesque door of a medieval church. As a child, Laurence Sterne spent a year in the barracks at Wicklow, where his father was serving. On the cliffs to the south are the remains of Black Castle, begun c 1175 by Maurice Fitzgerald.

Beyond Wicklow Head, and as far as **Brittas Bay** and Mizen Head, extends the Silver Strand, spoilt by caravans, and seen only intermittently from the road. The main road (N11) may be regained south west of Wicklow, to approach **Arklow** (Tourist Information, ☎ 0402-32484, seasonal) a boat-building centre at the mouth of the Avoca, with an imposing stone domed church of c 1840, and the tower of an old castle. It was the scene of General Francis Needham's defeat of the insurgents in 1798. The **Maritime Museum** (summer, 10.00–13.00, 14.00–17.00 daily; winter, same times, Sat & Sun) deals with the maritime and political history and folklore of the area.

From Arklow drive southwest, passing (left) the isolated hill of Tara (253m; not to be confused with that in Meath) before entering **Gorey** (Tourist Information, ☎ 055-21248; seasonal) was strongly associated with the 1798 rebellion. It was once an important cattle market, but is now the centre of a coastal holiday resort area. The Protestant church has windows by Clarke and O'Brien and opus-sectile by Rhind. The Loretto convent and church are by A.W.N. Pugin.

There are two direct roads south to Wexford, that nearer the coast (R742) passing through **Courtown**, a small resort on a sandy strand backed by dunes, some 6.5km south of which a track leads left to Glascarrig Abbey, with the ruins of a Benedictine house.

The parallel road (R741) crosses dull farming country but passes (right) **Oulart Hill**, after 22km, the scene of an insurgent victory on 27 May 1798 under Fr John Murphy, before the disaster of Vinegar Hill (see below). Cross the Slaney by a bridge after 19km, to enter Wexford.

The main road from Gorey continues southwest, parallel to a range of hills, including Slieveboy (421m) to **Ferns**, a small village which has a number of interesting ecclesiastical buildings, as well as the ruins of an important Norman castle. It was once the capital of the Kingdom of Leinster, and still shares a bishop with Ossory and Leighlin. Ferns was plundered many times by the Vikings, and suffered similarly at the hands of Dermot MacMurrough's rivals, being a refuge of that chieftain. The first monastery here was built after 598 in memory of St. Mogue (Maedoc-Edan) of Clonmore (d. 632).

The **cathedral** (1816–17), to the left of the road, incorporates the central part of the chancel of an older building (1223–43; burnt in 1577) containing the monument of an ecclesiastic, perhaps Bishop St. John (d. 1243). To the east are the remains of the Augustinian priory, founded by MacMurrough c 1160, where a cross-shaft covered with a key pattern is said to mark his grave. The tower (23m high), with a square lower stage, is round above. There are some plain High Crosses in the churchyard. On the hill to the right, approaching the village, are the ruins of St. Peter's (17C), apparently reconstructed with fragments from two older buildings.

Ferns Castle (early 13C), on the site of the stronghold of the Kings of Leinster, was partially dismantled in 1641 by Sir Charles Coote, but retains a cylindrical angle-tower and a beautifully vaulted oratory. The bishop's palace is 18C. A hill just to the west commands a good view of Mt Leinster (surmounted by a wireless mast) and the Blackstairs range. Just beyond Ferns you meet the N80, and bear left, descending to Enniscorthy.

Enniscorthy

Enniscorthy (Tourist Information, ☎ 054-34699; seasonal), built on a steeply sloping site above the valley of the Slaney, the town has fine 19C industrial buildings along the river; it has since the 17C been a centre for the manufacture of earthenware pottery from local clays, and there are interesting potteries at Carley's Bridge and Kiltrea Bridge a few kilometres outside the town. The 1798 monument in the Market Square is by Oliver Sheppard (1907).

The principal antiquity is the **Norman keep** with drum towers at its corners, which commands the crossing point of the river. It was rebuilt in 1586–95 by Sir Henry Wallop on the site of the mid-13C original, and restored by his descendant the Earl of Portsmouth in the 19C. It was taken by Cromwell in person in 1649 and now houses the **Wexford County Museum** a cabinet of curiosities (10.00–13.00, 14.00–18.00, Mon–Sat, 14.00–17.00 Sun, June–Sept; 14.00–17.00, Oct–Nov & Feb–Mar; 14.00–17.00, Sun only, Dec–Jan). There are many items of interest in this vast and disorganised collection, ranging across a broad spectrum, from Early Christian cross slabs to maritime and transport history, relics of 1798 and the social history of the county.

St. Aidan's Cathedral, by A.W.N. Pugin (1843) is a severe building placed on an awkward site at the top of the town. It has a later tower built with stones from an old Franciscan monastery; it was constructed around its predecessor, which was then demolished. The interior is tall, long and narrow with a fine east window. There is a ruined church, Templeshannon, at the north end of the town.

Vinegar Hill (121m) overlooks the town on the east bank of the Slaney. The shell of its windmill was the final position occupied by the Irish insurgent forces after the capture and sacking of the town in 1798. As a defensive position it is exposed on all sides; here on 21 June some 500 men were killed when the hill was assaulted by General Lake with 13,000 men. The remainder of the motley army rapidly dispersed.

Eileen Gray (1878–1976), the avant-garde furniture designer and one of the pioneers of 20C design was born in Brownswood House outside Enniscorthy; her work in architecture, lacquered furniture and carpet design brought her into collaboration with Le Corbusier and the De Stijl movement.

West from Enniscorthy, the R702 passes Kiltealy, at the entrance of the Scullogue Gap (240m), the main and once the only pass across the Blackstairs Mountains, with Mt Leinster (793m) to the north and Blackstairs (732m) to the south. You make a winding descent to Ballymurphy, and keep right for Borris, crossing the Barrow at Goresbridge for Gowran; Kilkenny lies 14.5km further west.

Enniscorthy Castle and museum, Co. Wexford

Avondale, Avoca, Shillelagh

To reach the Glenmalure valley, bear right just south of Rathdrum on the R752, to Ballinaclash, there turning right and following the road north west, parallel to the Avonbeg river. The valley is remarkably straight because it lies along the line of a large fault. It contains numerous glacial moraine-boulders, which lie in piles on either side. Here, in 1573, the crushing defeat of Lord Grey de Wilton by Fiac MacHugh O'Byrne took place. In later years it was the resort of fugitives from the English, such as Red Hugh O'Donnell (1591) and Michael Dwyer. At Derrynamuck the reconstructed **Dwyer/McAllister Cottage** (14.00–18.00 daily, June–Sept) contains a folk museum which commemorates Michael Dwyer's refuge here, and escape from encircling British troops in 1799.

The main road south from Rathdrum (R752) passes **Avondale Forest Park** (10.00–18.00, Mon–Fri, 12.00–18.00, Sat & Sun; all year)and **Avondale House** (11.00–18.00 daily; £) (1779, possibly designed by Wyatt, and built by Samuel Hayes), birthplace of Charles Stewart Parnell (1846–91). It now contains memorabilia of his political career and period furniture. Some distance beyond (left) is **Castle Howard** (early 19C), finely placed, with a view down the **Vale of Avoca**, near '**The Meeting of the Waters**' (the confluence of the Avonmore and Avonbeg), immortalised in the lines of Thomas Moore (1807):

> 'Sweet vale of Avoca! how calm could I rest
> In thy bosom of shade, with the friends I love best,
> Where the storms that we feel in this cold world should cease,
> And our hearts, like thy waters, be mingled in peace.'

Unfortunately some stretches of the valley are now marred by mine workings (gold-bearing and sulphur-bearing pyrites, etc.; in 1745 a gold nugget of 22 ounces was discovered, but the mother lode has never been found).

A good view of the Wicklow Mountains is commanded by the ridge of Cronebane, above Castle Howard, reached by a road from Lion's Bridge. On the summit is the 4m-long Motta Stone, traditionally reputed to be the 'hurling-stone' of the legendary Celtic hero, Finn MacCoul. Another meeting of the waters—those of the Aughrim and Avoca rivers—takes place at Woodenbridge among pinewoods. The demesne of **Shelton Abbey** lies to the south. Built in 1770, it was transformed into a Gothic Revival building c 1819 by the Morrisons and is now a remand prison. Glenart Castle, former residence of the Earls of Carysfort and now a convent, is passed on the right as you enter Arklow.

The R 753, southwest of Rathdrum, passes through Ballinaclash to Aughrim, and from there roughly follows the Derry Valley. Aughrim is pleasantly situated in a valley just below the point at which the Ow and Derry meet. The old 'military road' leads north west from Aughrim to **Aghavannagh**. A group of barracks was built here in the post-1798 period; one was later used as a shooting-box by both Parnell and Redmond.

After 8km a by-road leads right to **Moyne**, birthplace of Edwin L. Godkin (1831–1902), founder of the New York *Nation* in 1865. Shortly beyond this turning fork left for **Tinahely**, then we follow the R749 past Coolattin Park demesne (left) to enter **Shillelagh**, famous for its oak-wood, which gave its name to the 19C stage-Irishman's cudgel (in later years the name was applied to the more modern 'blackthorn'). The king of Leinster is said to have sent oak from here to William Rufus for the roof of Westminster Hall; it was also used in St. Patrick's Cathedral, Dublin.

To reach the primitive church of **Aghowle** (early-12C) turn left off the Tullow road, leading north west behind a hill. The church is well preserved but for the south wall, with a massive doorway like that at Fore, in Westmeath.

The main road continues northwest towards Tullow, off which a right-hand fork leads past the Iron Age ring-fort of Rathgall, with its four circumvallations. The road from Shillelagh continues down the valley before bearing left and then right for Bunclody (on the N80). Turn left here for Enniscorthy.

Baltinglass, Tullow, Clonegal

Descend through **Castleruddery** (N81) with its stone circle and by-pass the planned village of **Stratford-upon-Slaney**, founded for a weaving community before 1780 by Edward Stratford, 2nd Earl of Aldborough; few of its 18C houses remain unaltered. Shortly afterwards **Baltinglass** is reached. It has been described as the 'hillfort capital of Ireland', and has on the surrounding hilltops a number of significant defensive settlements dating from the Iron Age, or earlier. **Rathcoran**, a bivallate fort surrounding three chamber tombs, is immediately northeast above the town. **Rathnagree**, a trivallate fort a few hundred meters further north, and northeast of **Brusselstown-Spinans** on adjoining hills, the largest hillfort in the country, enclosing 130 hectares within its perimeter. This remarkable settlement consists of a stone enclosure on the summit of Brusslestown hill and a lengthy rampart encircling field boundaries, house sites and the opposing Spinans hill (about 2km in extent). Two-three hours are required for the steep climb to Rathcoran or Brusslestown, but it is really worth it as the views of the surrounding countryside are superb.

In the town of Baltinglass, which is of peculiar 'Y' form, are the remains of the Cistercian abbey of **Vallis Salutis**, founded by Dermot McMurrough in 1148. The alternating sequence of round and square Romanesque piers in the south arcade of the nave is of interest; the crossing tower is late medieval. There is a 19C neo-Egyptian family tomb (J.G. Mulvany?) in the churchyard and a Coade stone memorial to the Earl and Countess of Aldborough (John Bacon, 1796) in the adjoining Protestant church.

Hacketstown, 14km southeast, was the scene of two battles in 1798. At **Clonmore** (3km further south), a monastery was founded by St. Maedhoc (or St. Mogue; 6C). The northeast tower, known as 'the Six Windows', of the late 13C castle of De Lacy, is well preserved. Cross the Slaney to reach **Rathvilly** (*Ráth Bhile*, the fort of the trees) leaving two roads leading to the right for Carlow. The large ringfort represents the royal stronghold in which the King of Leinster was in residence on the arrival of St. Patrick, by whom he was baptised. The summit of the fort (171m) commands a view extending from Lagnaquillia to the northeast to Mt Leinster to the south, to distant Slievenamon southwest, and to the Slieve Bloom range to the northwest. Haroldstown portal tomb, 5km south east, with two capstones, was inhabited during the last century by a hermit.

Tullow, a pleasant agricultural town on the Slaney, retains only a battered cross (in the abbey burial ground) of its Augustinian priory. Fr John Murphy, a leader of the 1798 rising, was hanged at Tullow, and his body burned in a tar barrel. There is a large rath at **Castlemore** (1.5km west) and at **Rathgall hill fort**, (5km east), adjacent to the road and easily accessible, is a trivallate enclosure with a stone inner circle, enclosing 7.30 hectares. Three Late Bronze Age (7C BC) cremated burials, the first to have been excavated in Ireland, were uncovered here during the 1960s, together with numerous Iron Age clay moulds for bronze swords and spearheads, indicating occupation over a lengthy period.

A by-road leads southwest from Tullow to (20km) Leighlinbridge on the main road to Kilkenny. 8km south of Tullow turn left onto the N80, and descend past the confluence of the Slaney and Derry, and enter Bunclody (also known as Newtownbarry). An older road, further east, passes the once-beautiful riverside demesne of **Ballintemple** (house demolished), famous for its rhododendrons, and **Clonegal**, overlooked by Huntington Castle (partly 17C). To the right Mt Leinster (793m) is conspicuous, as you descend the valley to Enniscorthy and Wexford.

Irish National Heritage Park, Ferrycarrig

Skirting the east bank of the Slaney (N11), after 4km you pass (right) Black Castle, once a Franciscan Abbey, the lands of which were later held by Edmund Spenser. At the next main junction either bear right to cross the river by the Ferrycarrig Bridge, the scene of a skirmish in 1798, and overlooked by the ruined castle of Robert Fitzstephen (the first built by the Anglo-Normans in Ireland, in 1169), or left through Castlebridge, to approach Wexford from the north, passing near (left), **Raven Nature Reserve** and **Wexford Wildfowl Reserve** (open for access) in the sloblands and sand dunes of the harbour. The estuary is crossed by a new bridge commanding a view of the town, which is by-passed to the west by a ring-road circling to the south and on to Rosslare Harbour.

Cross the bridge and turn right for the **Irish National Heritage Park** (10.00–19.00 daily, Mar–Nov). The Park, a well-wooded site. has been developed by Wexford County Council, using expert archaeological and scholarly advice to provide a series of accurate reconstructions of the habitation sites, technology, ecclesiastical and military architecture from the Mesolithic period to the Norman Conquest. Arranged in chronological order from a 7000 BC campsite to a 12C AD Norman fort, the reconstructions go as far as archaeology and artifice can to make the past tangible without departing from the discipline

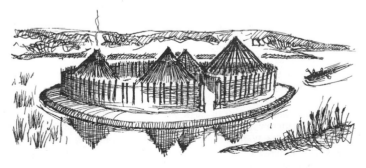

Reconstructed crannog lake settlement with houses, National Heritage Park

of serious research. The Park also contains an actual historic site, that of the first Norman fortification in Ireland, a 'ditch and bank' constructed by Robert Fitzstephen in 1169, which was excavated in 1984, and with utter incongruity, an 1857 memorial to Wexfordmen killed in the Crimean War (1854–55), in the form of a replica Irish Round Tower, the only touch of kitsch on the site.

Wexford, Rosslare Harbour, Kilmore Quay

Wexford (*Waesfjord*, the ford of the mud-flats) is a town with a distinctly old-fashioned air, at the centre of which is its long narrow meandering main street, flanked by innumerable bars. Of considerable interest are its 19C churches and the extensive remains of the medieval city wall. The **Grand Opera Festival** (September–October), in the Theatre Royal, is among the country's premier cultural events, specialising in the revival of neglected operas.

■ **Tourist Information**. Crescent Quay, ☎ 053 23111.
■ **Train**. Railway Station at Redmond Place (north end).

Associated in legend with the pre-Christian Queen Garman (its Irish name is *Loch Garman)*, the genesis of the town is in the combination of a fortified 9C Viking settlement to the south, and a more dispersed Gaelic one to the north, which dictated its linear form. In 1169, Dermot MacMurrough and his Anglo-Norman allies Robert Fitzstephen and Maurice Fitzgerald captured it. In 1172, Henry II spent the Lenten season in Waterford doing penance for instigating the murder of Thomas à Beckett and in 1174 Strongbow celebrated the marriage of his sister Basilia de Clare and Raymond *'le Gros'* Fitzgerald here. The walling of the entire settlement was carried out by the Normans during the 13C.

Cromwell took Wexford in 1649, destroyed the churches and massacred the garrison (he occupied No. 29 South Main St). Some 80 'Defenders' were killed here in July 1793 and in 1798 it was held by the United Irish insurgents.

A plaque marks the songwriter Thomas Moore's residence in 1851, in the Cornmarket. The landscape painter Francis Danby (1793–1861) was born here; also Sir Robert McClure (1807–73), discoverer of the North-West Passage (in what is now part of *White's Hotel)*. Jane Elgee, later Lady Wilde and mother of Oscar (1826–96); who wrote militant political poems under the pseudonym of Speranza, was born in the old rectory, Main St.

The historic town was composed of a long narrow rectangle on rising ground above the river Slaney, first crossed by a bridge in 1794 (many of those who subscribed to the bridge were executed on it during the insurrection of 1798). Most of the buildings of interest are west of the Main St, and dominating the skyline are two tall identical spires. These are the Twin Churches, both by Robert Pierce, 1851 (a pupil of Pugin), the Church of the Assumption (south) which has a two-light window by Harry Clarke, and (north) the Church of the Immaculate Conception (Rowe St), full of old-fashioned devotional clutter and shrines. Between these is the **Franciscan friary**,(open for access) a 19C building which incorporates 13C walls, with a gracefully modernised interior and interesting contemporary lectern and tabernacle. At the rear is a bizarre 19C shrine containing a life-size wax effigy of a Roman child martyr, St. Adjutor; his grisly experiences are recounted above the shrine. It was presented to Richard Devereux, a local philanthropist, by Pius IX.

To see the best preserved section of the city wall start from the Methodist church (1835) with its slender Gothic lancet windows, also in Rowe St. The wall runs north, to the remains of Selskar (Holy Sepulchre) Abbey, a priory founded by the Roches, Lords of Fermoy, at the end of the 12C, and the **West Gate Heritage Centre**, (09.00–13.00, 14.00–17.00 daily; 14.00–17.00 Sun, July–Aug; 11.00–13.00, 14.00–17.30 Mon–Sat, Mar–June & Oct–Nov) which consists of the restored c 1300 city gate and 18C stable buildings in which is presented an audio-visual programme on local history. The roofless 19C church with a medieval tower adjoining it stands on the spot where the first treaty between the Anglo-Normans and the Irish was ratified in 1169. In West Gate St, north, is (left) the Scots Baronial façade of the County Gaol, 1812, now the offices of the County Council.

On Main St is **St. Iberius church** (C of I) 1775, with a restrained 19C Venetian Gothic façade. The fine Georgian interior has galleries on three sides and an arcaded screen with Corinthian columns separates the nave from the shallow bowed chancel; it contains some interesting monuments.

Parallel to Main St in the even narrower and unobtrusive High St is the **Theatre Royal** (William Taylor, 1830) its small box-like auditorium, gloriously decorated in 'peasant baroque' (extravagant folk-art) manner, hidden behind the domestic buildings of the street. It is a most unlikely venue for the annual extravaganza of the opera season. At the south end of the street is St. Patrick's churchyard and ruins of a small 15C chapel. In Cornmarket is the arcaded former **Market House** (1775), which had the Assembly Rooms on the upper floor, the building is now the **Wexford Arts Centre**.

Close to the waterfront, in the Bull Ring are Oliver Sheppard's 1905 figure of a 1798 pikeman, and at Crescent Quay a monument to **Commodore John Barry** (1745–1803), known as the 'father of the American Navy' by American sculptor N.A. Wheeler Williams (1955). Commanding the *Lexington* in taking *HMS Edward*, Barry effected the first capture of the US Navy in 1776, during the American War of Independence (although he subsequently suffered defeat and lost his ship).

St. Peter's College above the town is by A.W.N. Pugin (1840). The chapel interior has an openwork wooden rood screen and ornate gilded Gothic triptych above the altar.

From Wexford, the New Ross road (N25) bears almost due west, passing the road to **Taghmon** (left) where a rude cross in the churchyard is all that remains of the monastery founded in the 6C by St. Munna (Teach Munna). The hymn writer Henry Francis Lyte (1793–1847) was curate here in 1815. After 15km you pass (right) **Carrickbyrne Hill**, with a monument to Sir Ralph Abercromby (1734–1801), commander of the British troops in Ireland prior to March 1798; and (left) **Scullabogue House**, scene of the massacre of c 200 Protestants in June 1798, when a barn in which they had sought shelter was set alight.

Wexford Harbour

Wexford Harbour, an extensive bay over 13km wide and 6.5km long, famous for its swans, is safe but shallow. Cross-channel ferries from Fishguard and Le Havre now berth at Rosslare Harbour, c 19km south east (N25). The resort of **Rosslare**, with a sandy strand, is approached from Killinick, about half-way between Wexford and Rosslare Harbour. Some 4km south of Rosslare Harbour stands **Ballytrent House** (closed to public), birthplace of John Redmond (1856–1918), for many years leader of the Irish Party in the Westminister parliament after the eclipse of Parnell. A ring-fort lies within the grounds. Out to sea rises the Tuskar Rock, with a lighthouse built in 1815 (improved in 1885). To the north are the cliffs of Greenore Point; to the south is Carnsore Point, the sandy south eastern extremity of Ireland. Nearby are remains of St. Vogue's church, built by St. Veoc, who died in Brittany in 585.

One of the few remaining windmills in Ireland may be seen (1846; reconstructed 1952) 6km south east of Killinick at **Tacumshin**. To the east of Tacumshin is a lagoon known as **Lady's Island Lake**. On the island itself, connected by a causeway with the mainland, are the ruins of a monastery, castle keep (both c 1237) and a later tower. The two islands in the lake have the largest breeding colonies of terns in the Republic.

7km south of Wexford fork to the right off the Rosslare road, shortly passing (right) **Rathmacknee Castle**, probably erected by John Rosseter in 1451. It has a five-sided bawn and a five-storey tower with stepped battlements. A short distance beyond (right) lies **Mayglass**, with a church ruined in 1798 but retaining its Norman arches, and further south (left) **Bargy Castle**, another tower-house (converted to a hotel), once the property of Bagenal Harvey (see below).

The 'English Baronies' of Bargy and Forth were colonised by Anglo-Norman adventurers from South Wales in the 12C, and may be reckoned as the part of Ireland where the English language has been spoken the longest; the local dialect of 'Yola' contains many early usages, derived from Anglo-Norman Wales.

At adjacent **Tomhaggard** is a late 14C church near the Tacumshin Lake. Continuing south west, at Forlorn Point is the hamlet of **Kilmore Quay**, known to deep-sea fishermen for its bass and pollack. The **Maritime Museum** (12.00–18.00 daily, May–Oct), is aboard the Lightship 'Guillemot', commissioned in 1922 by the German Government to replace one destroyed during WWI.

Boats may be hired to visit the offshore reef-girt **Saltee Island**, (half-hour trip) once the terror of navigators. Two leaders of the Wexford insurrection, Beauchamp Bagenal Harvey (1762–98) and John Henry Colclough (1769–98), were discovered hiding in a cave on the outer Great Saltee after the rout of Vinegar Hill and were escorted to Wexford, where they were beheaded. The island is now a bird sanctuary. The return trip may be made by driving due north past (right) Ballyteige Castle (15C), and after 6km forking right for Murntown, shortly beyond which (right), we pass **Johnstown Castle**, a massive building designed by Daniel Robertson in a Norman and Gothic-revival style, encasing the 13C stronghold of the Esmonde and Fitzgerald families. It now accommodates an agricultural college, working farm and the excellent **Irish Agricultural Museum** (09.00–17.00, Mon–Fri, 14.00–17.00 Sat–Sun, June–Aug; 09.00–12.30, 13.30–17.00, Mon–Fri; 14.00–17.00, Sat & Sun, Apr–May & Sept–Nov; £), with important collections of early country furniture, farm equipment and rural transport.

4 · Waterford: the Suir, Nore and Barrow

This region is dominated by the river valleys of the Suir, Nore and Barrow which enter the sea at Waterford. The principal towns on their banks, **Waterford**, **Kilkenny**, **Carrick-on-Suir** are among the historically most interesting and attractive in Ireland. There are well preserved and beautifully sited medieval abbeys at **Dunbrody, Graiguenamanagh, Jerpoint** and **Kilcooley**, and an important group of early Christian High Crosses (9C–12C) at **Ahenny, Killamery, Kilkieran** and **Moone**.

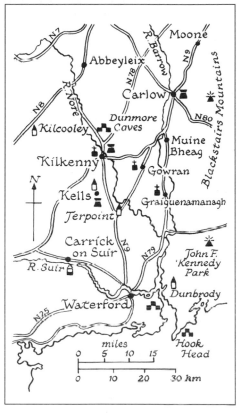

At **Ardmore** is the finest surviving early Christian Round Tower, an architectural form unique to Ireland, and there are further examples at **Kilkenny, Kilree, Fertagh** and **St. Mullins**. Kilkenny's 13C cathedral, (after St. Patrick's in Dublin the largest in the country), is a venue for recitals during **Kilkenny Arts Week** (Aug/Sept).

Although the natural landscape of the area is its principal attraction, there are outstanding gardens at **Abbeyleix** and the **John F. Kennedy Memorial Park** at Dunganstown. **The Leinster Way**, from Kildavin to Carrick-on-Suir (110km/62 miles), is a waymarked walking route that climbs the slopes of Mt. Leinster and follows the Barrow valley; it is linked on the north to the Wicklow Way. **Dunmore Caves** were historically known as among the darkest places in Ireland.

The **Barrow Navigation** allows travel by inland waterways from New Ross via the Grand Canal to the River Shannon (see Ch. 2).

How to get there
■ **Train**. Dublin or Waterford, via Athy, Carlow, Kilkenny.
■ **Air**. Waterford Airport.
■ **Sea**. Rosslare Harbour (see Ch. 3).

Listings

Abbeyleix. Morrissey's, the Sistine Chapel of Irish country pubs, not an item changed since 1904, spacious, austerely welcoming (☎ 0502-31233); **Quinn's Tea and Coffee Room**, small and unpretentious roadside café (☎ 0502-31020).

Annestown. Annestown House, country-house restaurant in quiet coastal village (☎ 051-396160).

Butlerstown. The Coach House, Butlerstown Castle, restaurant, B&B in grounds of 13C castle (☎ 051-384656).

Carlow. The Beams Restaurant, 59 Dublin St, restaurant and wine shop concentrating on a fine balance of food and wines (☎ 0503-31824); **Otterholt Riverside Hostel** (☎ 0503-30404).

Carrick-on-Suir. Carraig Hotel, small hotel, dance bands at weekends, (☎ 051-641444); **The Gables**, B&B, former convent, conventual comfort (☎ 051-641400).

Dungarvan. Gold Coast Golf Hotel and Leisure Centre, Ballinacourty, excellent recreational facilities (☎ 058-42249).

Dunmore East: Dunmore Lodge, charming 19C house, B&B, ☎051-83454.

Graiguenamanagh. The Waterside, good restaurant in 19C riverside mill with hostel (☎ 0503-24246).

Inistioge. Cullintra House, The Rower, Kilkenny Rd, pretty 18C country-house, dining in Somerville and Ross style, B&B (☎ 051-23614).

New Ross. Mac Murrough Farm Hostel (☎ 051-21383).

Thomastown. Kilfane Glen, Kilfane, cottage orné in magical grounds, teahouse (☎ 056-24558); **Kilmurry House**, former home of the painter, Mildred Ann Butler, dinner, B&B (☎ 056-24130).

Tramore. Monkey Puzzle Seaside Hostel, Upper Branch Rd (☎ 051-386754).

Abbeyleix, Durrow, Urlingford, Kilcooley Abbey

14km **Abbeyleix** north of the Durrow on the N8, is a charming village of tree-lined streets, and takes its name from an abbey founded by Conogher O'More in 1183 (of which nothing remains). The tomb of Melaghlin O'More, a 13C Prince of Leix, may be seen in the demesne of **Abbey Leix House**, built in 1773–74 for the 1st Viscount de Vesci by Wyatt, and refaced in the 19C; the gardens are open to the public.

It is a planned village, laid out in the mid-18C by the de Vescis with a crescent-shaped square and a **Market House** (1836) with arcaded ground floor (which houses the fire brigade). The de Vesci monument (1855) commemorates the 2nd Viscount. The **Protestant church** (by John Semple, c 1830) is approached by an avenue of mature trees and has windows by A.E. Child (1907 and 1929); and C. O'Brien (1942). A Gothic **fountain** (1873) at the south end of Main St, which commemorates the 3rd Viscount was erected predictably 'by a grateful tenantry'. **Morrissey's pub** on Main St is an exceptional example of a country town spirit-grocery. Sir Jonah Barrington (1760–1834), the diarist, was born at adjacent Knapton.

Cross the river Block on Portlaoise–Cashel road at **Durrow**, and turn north-west just north of the village. 14.5km **Aghaboe** (*Achadh Bhó*, the land of the cow), where St. Canice founded a monastery c 550. Of the church preserving the saint's relics little remains, although it served as the cathedral of the see of Ossory (c 1050–1200), when it merged with Kilkenny. A small chapel and part of one aisle have survived from the Dominican church founded at the end of the 14C by the Fitzpatricks. Attached to the Protestant church is an old tower of the cathedral; the walls and barns in the area are largely made up of re-used medieval material.

At **Ballinakill**, 6km south east, are fragmentary remains of a castle that stubbornly resisted Cromwellian troops in 1649. A by-road regaining the N8 passes (left) **Rosconnell**, with a 13C church rebuilt in 1646.

Durrow (9km), built around a green, lies at the crossroad from Kilkenny to Roscrea. To the west is the demesne of **Castle Durrow** (1716–18); built by the Fitzpatricks, who likewise erected the (ruined) priory and castle of Aghmacart, some 6.5km beyond. After 6.5km you pass (right) the Round Tower of **Fertagh** (restored), 27.5m high, burnt by O'Loughlin, King of Ireland, in 1156, beside which is a chapel surviving from a 14C Augustinian priory, containing the MacGiollaphadraig tomb, with traceried decoration. **Johnstown** is soon entered, its church with a font from Fertagh, and in its churchyard a well incorporating a crucifix from the same site. To the west is Foulkscourt Castle (c 1450) in the demesne of a ruined mansion of 1715. You next approach Urlingford.

Kilcooley Abbey

Kilcooley Abbeystands 5km south of Urlingford, and is approached by a long drive through 18C parkland, passing two adjacent (C of I) churches, 18C and 1825. The ruins of the Cistercian abbey, founded from Jerpoint Abbey by Donal Mór O'Brien in 1182, and rebuilt after 1445 (when it was almost destroyed by fire), are unusually well preserved, especially the choir and transepts; the roofless nave lost its aisles in the 15C restoration.

Enter by the north transept, which retains its vault and contains a font with interlaced pattern. In the choir is the tomb of Abbot Philip (d. 1463), restorer of the abbey, and the finely carved effigy of Piers Fitz Oge Butler (d. 1526), signed by Rory O'Tunney, with excellent 'weepers' below (a row of guardian figures on the face of the tomb, frequently soldiers of saints), as well as other tombs carved by the O'Tunneys.

The late-14C **decorated screen** in the south transept leading to the sacristy is unique, with motifs of a Crucifixion, St. Christopher on the right, and lower down a vigorous figure of a bishop surmounted by a censing angel, all in high relief; note also the mermaid holding a mirror, on the doorway. Cut into the west piers of the tower are two uniquely placed stalls, that on the south, probably for the abbot, is elaborately decorated, and surmounted by the Butler arms. The traceried east window was added at the 15C restoration. Substantial remains of the claustral buildings survive, although altered, while some of the chambers have been fitted up with fireplaces and ceilings. A dovecote survives northeast of the church.

Some 3km south, at **Clonamicklin**, is a 17C gabled Butler castle with a fortified bawn. Close by rises Slieve Ardagh (333m).

The two churches of **Leigh**, or *Liathmore Mochoemog*, are passed (left) 8km beyond Urlingford one an 8C structure with a high-pitched roof (partly restored); the other a 12C–15C building containing 13C–14C tomb slabs. A monastery was founded here before 650 by St. Mochoemog. The main road continues southwest direct to Cashel (22.5km, see region 5), passing at the next crossroad, the Turnpike, **Grallagh Castle** (left), with a 16C tower-house. It was to the south of Littleton, on this road, that the **Derrynaflan hoard** was unearthed in 1980 (now in the National Museum), consisting of a decorated silver chalice, a bronze liturgical strainer, and a silver paten on its stand, all covered by a bronze bowl (8C–9C).

Athy, Dunmore Caves, Kilkenny, Kells

Athy (pronounced with the accent on the last syllable, (*Baile Atha h-I*, town of the ford of I), on the N78, (Tourist Information ☎ 0507-31859; seasonal), is a busy agricultural centre in the fertile valley of the Barrow. A branch of the Grand Canal joins the navigable river here. It has a pleasing Market House (c 1780) in its square (where in 1798 the first wooden triangle was set up on which United Irishmen were spreadeagled and flogged by the militia). Standing on the borders of Kildare and Leix, it was the scene of many battles. **White's Castle**, built by the 8th Earl of Kildare in c 1500 and repaired in 1575 by a certain William White defends the bridgehead. In a field north of the town is **Woodstock Castle**, (c 1290); though remarkable for the thickness of its walls, it was severely damaged during a siege by the Confederates under General Preston in 1649.

5km northwest lies **Kilberry**, with a peat-moss factory and ruined abbey, while on the opposite bank of the Barrow stands **Reban Castle**(by Richard de St. Michel, builder of Woodstock Castle). Cross the Carlow-Portlaoise road towards **Castlecomer** (18km), a pleasant country town built by the Wandesforde family after 1637, and the centre of the defunct Leinster coalfield (once noted for the production of smokeless anthracite). The motte of the first Anglo-Norman castle (which gave the town its name) lies to the east. A later castle was besieged in 1641–42, and the town suffered at the hands of the insurgents in 1798.

Dunmore Caves

Dunmore Caves (7km) is a series of limestone caverns opening from one to another, the second of which contains a huge stalactite pillar known as 'the Market Cross'. Here, according to legend, the monster Luchtigern, 'Lord of the Mice', was slaughtered. It may possibly be the site of a massacre of some hundreds trapped here by Vikings on a plundering expedition in 928. Continue to descend the Dinin Valley, which shortly joins the Nore, and enter Kilkenny, the county town.

Kilkenny

Kilkenny (*Cill Chainnigh*, the church of St. Canice), one of the oldest and most interesting towns of Ireland, which has grown rapidly in the last decade, is attractively situated on the Nore. It has been called the 'Marble City' from the fine and long-quarried limestone in the neighbourhood.

Topography contributes to the dramatic appearance of the town, with the two centres of ecclesiastical and civic power, St. Canice's Cathedral and the castle, linked along a ridge by the main street, above a gentle curve in the river valley. The rich assemblage of historic buildings which range from the early and late medieval to the 18th and 19C, give it a character different from many other Irish towns, and it combines the intimacy of a market town with the formality of the seat of the Butlers, earls and dukes of Ormond, who occupied the castle for 550 years.

Culturally it has always been a vital place and has a vibrant contemporary existence, with a strong local craft tradition; in the town and its hinterland are the studios of some of the country's most prominent artist-craftsmen, working in glass, ceramics, gold, silver and other disciplines. The Crafts Council of Ireland's Crescent Workshops occupy the castle stables.

■ **Railway and Bus Station**. Carlow Road (☎ 056-22024).
■ **Tourist Information**. Shee Alms House, Rose Inn St (☎ 056-21755).
■ **Post Office**. 73 High St (☎ 056-21879).
■ **Festivals**. Kilkenny Arts Week, a music festival of international calibre devoted to classical music with a visual arts fringe, is held August–September.

Kilkenny was the ancient capital of the Kings of Ossory. A fortress seems to have been established here by Strongbow as early as 1172, and the episcopal see of Ossory was transferred here from Aghaboe in 1202. In the 14C Kilkenny was at the height of its fame, and was the scene of many parliaments, that of 1366–67 passing the notorious 'Statutes of Kilkenny', penalising the descendants of the Anglo-Normans for excessive Hibernisation, making it a treasonable offence for them to marry any man or woman of the Irish race.

The lordship was purchased from Strongbow's descendants in 1391 by James Butler, 3rd Earl of Ormonde. In 1642–48 it was the headquarters of the Confederates, and a great assembly of Catholic clergy was held here in 1645, presided over by Lord Mountgarret and Rinuccini, the Papal legate. The former came to terms with his relative Ormonde, the viceroy, after the Irish victory at Benburb in 1646, but the intransigent legate issued an edict of excommunication on all who desired peace with Cromwell. In 1650 the Protector himself succeeded in storming Kilkenny, and the garrison under Sir Walter Butler marched out with full military honours.

The novelists Michael and John Banim (1796–1874, and 1798–1842 respectively) were born here, as was James Stephens (1825–1901), the Fenian; and also, probably (her father was a local lawyer) the 'matchless actress' Kitty Clive (1711–85). The expression 'fighting like Kilkenny Cats' derives from the long-standing antipathy between the citizens of High Town (the Castle and the English), and Low Town (Irishtown), for each other.

The Town spans the Nore which was bridged in the 13C, the medieval walls originally only included the west bank, but were later extended to encompass both sides. The best preserved sections are on the west.

On the east bank, approached by the Dublin road, is St. John's, a parish church incorporating part of a hospital founded by William, Earl of Pembroke c 1220, with its original Lady Chapel, although the choir is in ruins. In adjacent Maudlin St are traces of town walls; these may also be seen in the grounds of the former Kilkenny College (1780), to the left in John St, now the offices of Kilkenny County Council. This is the successor (now on a new site) to St. John's College, founded in 1666 (in the cathedral close), where Swift, Congreve, Berkeley, Farquhar, and many other eminent men, were educated.

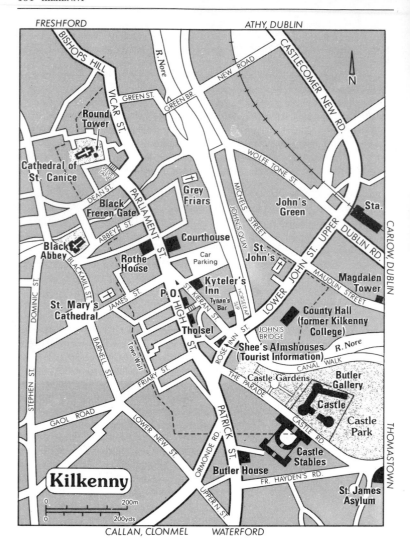

Cross the river at John's Bridge (Alexander Burden, 1910)—a pioneering single-span reinforced concrete structure—with an oblique view of the castle to the left, and pass *Tynan's*, (right) a particularly attractive bar, climbing Rose Inn St, on the right of which are **Shee's Almshouses** (1594) (09.00–18.00, Mon–Sat, May–Sept; 09.00–21.00 daily, July–Aug; 09.00–17.00 Tues–Sat, rest of year). The **Tourist Office** has an informative model of medieval Kilkenny on the first floor, and an uninspired audio-visual presentation. You then reach The Parade, a broad street with 18C houses on the left. Turn left here to approach **Kilkenny Castle** (10.30–17.30 daily, Apr–May; 10.00–19.00 daily, June–

Sept; 10.00–12.45, 14.00–17.00, Tues–Sat; 11.00–12.45, 14.00–17.00 Sun, Oct–March; OPW) which occupies a prominent position overlooking the Nore.

The castle occupies three sides of a quadrilateral; the fourth side was demolished in 1659. With its grey stone round towers and battlements, it still maintains a martial air, although it has gone through a number of metamorphoses, masquerading successively as 17C French chateau and 19C country-house, (extensively rebuilt in 1826–35 by William Robertson). The castle was first built in 1192, being erected by William Marshal, Earl of Pembroke, son-in-law of Strongbow, probably on the site of an earlier fortress commanding this river crossing. In 1392 it passed by purchase to James, 3rd Earl of Ormonde, the descendant of Theobald FitzWalter, who had received lands from Henry II and the appointment of Chief Butler of Ireland; his son took the title of Butler or Botiler as a surname. The Butlers played a prominent part in Irish history and waged a bitter feud with the Fitzgeralds of Kildare. The Dukes lost lands and fortune in defence of the Stuart cause, and the 2nd Duke was attainted in 1715. The earldom was revived in 1791 in favour of John Butler, and survived until 1935 when the contents of the castle were dispersed and the Ormonde archives transferred to the National Library. In 1967 the castle was given to the town by Arthur Butler, 6th Marquess and 24th Earl of Ormonde (the 7th and last Marquess—he has no heirs—is an American citizen).

The main entrance is a fine classical composition by Sir William Robinson, 1685, leading between the 13C drum towers into a grassed courtyard, open to the southeast with a view of the 23 hectares of parkland. Opposite the entrance is the new wing by Benjamin Woodward (1858); it contains the **Long Picture Gallery** on the first floor, which has a hammer-beam roof decorated in Pre-Raphaelite style by John Hungerford Pollen (1861), who also designed and decorated Newman's University Church, Dublin, and a double fireplace in Carrara marble by Charles Harrison which has low relief carved panels depicting Ormonde family history. Although only 43 of the over 200 family portraits survived the sale of the castle's contents, many of these are of interest; *Elizabeth Poyntz* by John Michael Wright c 1690; Sir Anthony Van Dyke, *Self Portrait*, 1633, probably a copy; *21st Earl of Ormonde* by Henry Richard Graves c 1845; *Susan Wandsford* by Hugh Douglas Hamilton; *Barbara Villiers* by Sir Peter Lely (Charles II gave her a present of the Phoenix Park but the 1st Duke of Ormonde scuppered the deal); *James Stuart,'the Old Pretender'*, by Antonio David. The **Butler Gallery** in the basement shows contemporary art and the old kitchens house a restaurant. The south wing has recently been totally restored, and contains the 19C domestic apartments.

The **castle stables** (1780), opposite the entrance, now accommodate the showrooms of the Crafts Council of Ireland, with studios in a semi-circular range of buildings to the rear, beyond which stands Butler House (1780), a dower house of the Butlers.

The Parade is continued to the south east by Castle Rd, at the far end of which is St. James's or Switsir's Hospital (1803), an almshouse embellished with an agreeably pompous statue of its founder.

At the bottom of the Parade (left) is Patrick's St (houses on left have Tudor chimneys) and on the right (No. 26) is the old Kilkenny Theatre (1902–62). This leads (right) to Ormonde and College Road in which is St. Kieran's College (W.D. Butler, 1836) an excellent Gothic Revival building with some unfortunate modern additions.

From the Parade, the High St runs uphill, passing (right) the **Tholsel** (1761), by the amateur architect William Colles, an attractive building with an arcade projecting over the pavement with the council chamber above, and an octagonal clocktower. The building (*Tholsel*, a toll stall), is of a type commonly found in Irish towns, but rare in the fact that it still fulfils its original function as the Corporation Rates office.

Behind the Tholsel stands St. Mary's (13C; disused), containing fine monuments; Richard Rothe (Patrick Kerin, 1637), the Maude tomb (Stanton and Horsnaile, 1703); and in the churchyard the tombs of John Rothe (north side; 1612), and Sir Richard Shee (1608), with sculptured figures at the base. The *Marble City Bar* on the same side of the street is a fine traditional premises. Stepped and arched medieval lanes called Slips (*slype*, a passage; a Norman-French survival) descend to St. Kieran St, in which stands *Kytler's Inn*, associated with the dame Alice Kytler witchcraft trials in 1324, but now reconstructed and housing a restaurant. Beyond the Tholsel, on the left of Parliament St, is **Rothe House** (1594; restored in 1966), (10.30–17.00, Mon–Sat, 15.00–17.00, Sun, Apr–June/Sept–Oct; 10.00–18.00, Mon–Sat, 13.00–17.00, Sun, July–Aug; 13.00–17.00, Mon–Sat, 15.00–17.00 Sun, Jan–Mar/Nov–Dec) an important stone-built merchant's house, which is now a good museum of local history, with a section on historic costumes. The house (which is roughly contemporary with the Butler manor house at Carrick-on-Suir), is a succession of three individual houses, built behind each other in a narrow plot and separated by courtyards. The arcade at street level was originally open and the pavement ran beneath it. In the upper room of the main house the fine timber roof is visible. The Rothe family supported the Confederacy and in 1653 the house was forfeited and the Rothes transported to Connaught.

Almost opposite, a tablet marks the site of the Confederation Hall, where the Irish Confederation Parliament met in 1642–48. In the car park at the rear, on the bank of the Nore, is a small pavilion, a rare example of an 18C teahouse.

Towards the end of the street, inside the entrance to Smithwick's Brewery (right) are the ruins of a Franciscan friary (1331), retaining a beautifully graduated seven-light window, and a graceful tower, inside which are six unusual sculptures of lay-figures bearing the springing of the groined vault.

Crossing the stream of the Bregagh into Irishtown, Velvet Lane leads to St. Canice's Steps (1614) and steep approach the **Cathedral of St. Canice** (C of I), the second largest medieval cathedral in Ireland (after St. Patrick's, Dublin) which, despite the damage done by Cromwell's troops, is one of the finest churches.

When the Cromwellians occupied Kilkenny they engaged in wanton destruction of the cathedral, as described by Bishop Griffith Williams, 'They have utterly defaced, and ruined, thrown down all the Roof of it, taken away five great and goodly Bells, broken down all the windows, and carried away every bit of the Glass, that they say was worth a very great deal; and all the doors of it that Hogs might come, and root, and Dogs gnaw the bones of the dead'. The havoc committed by the Cromwellians was temporarily repaired, but the church remained in a deplorable state until the time of Bishop Richard Pococke (1756), when the choir was refitted in classical style and the monuments rearranged (a phenomenon which has caused some of them to be re-assembled with the wrong parts!). The bishop himself (1704–65), who in 1741 'discovered' Chamonix, has been described by Mary Delaney, one of the 18C's great letter-writers, as 'the dullest man that ever travelled'.

The central tower fell in 1332, but was reconstructed by Bishop Ledrede (d. 1360), who also installed the stained glass, while the fan-vault was instituted by Bishop Hacket in 1465.

The present edifice is cruciform with an aisled nave, transepts and a partially aisled chancel—69m long by 37.5m wide—and was begun probably by Bishop Hugh de Rous (1202–18), continued by his successor Hugh de Mapilton in 1251–56, and completed by Bishop Geoffrey St. Leger after 1260.

The most notable features of the exterior are the low and massive central tower, the characteristically Irish stepped battlements of the parapet (a restoration except on the transepts), and the unusual quatrefoil windows of the clerestory. The quatrefoil motif recurs on the west front, which has the finest surviving early Gothic doorway in Ireland. The master mason of the 13C work is known as the 'Gowran Master', he worked extensively in Kilkenny, Gowran and Thomastown, and was the leading mason and sculptor of the period.

The south apse is abutted by a Round Tower (c 10C), 30m high, capless and slightly tilting but otherwise in a good state of preservation. It is fitted inside with timber stairs from which the viewing platform on top can be reached; this vertiginous perch is not for the squeamish.

The aisled nave, of five bays, is noteworthy mainly for its monuments and other furniture. Used as the main venue for recitals during Arts Week, the nave acoustics are excellent. The traceried gallery above the west door was probably used for the exhibition of relics. The fine internal stonework was revealed during Thomas Newenham Deane's restoration of 1866.

Cathedral Monuments

The first tomb in the **south aisle** is that of Bishop Hacket (1478); the second is of Honorina Schorthals (née Grace; d. 1596). Next comes a female effigy wearing the old Irish or Kinsale cloak. The 13C font of black limestone has incised patterns in the corners. Against the wall beyond the south door are the tombs of the 1st Viscount Mountgarret (1571), with a good armoured effigy, and of Bishop Walsh (1585).

Corbel in tower of the 14C
St. Francis Friary, Kilkenny

In the **north aisle**, between the pillars opposite the font, is the grave-slab of the son of Henry de Ponto of Lyra, perhaps the oldest memorial in the church (1285). By the wall is the fine figure of James Schorthals (1508). In the floor further east, opposite the mutilated effigy of Sir John Grace (1552), is the gravestone of Edmund Purcell (d. 1549), captain of Ormonde's gallowglasses, with a mailed half-figure, the Emblems of the Passion, and St. Peter's cock crowing on the edge of the High Priest's pot in which he was cooking it. In the next bay are the tomb of Adam Cottrell (1550), with a base appropriated from a 13C monument, and the wall-slab of the Bourchier brothers (1584–87), with an elaborately carved escutcheon.

The central lantern is roofed with Bishop Hacket's vault. In the west corner of the north transept is St. Kieran's Chair (13C; seat modern), and on the north wall is a large aumbry adorned with male and female heads; here also are the tombs of the Pack family, including that of the Peninsular War veteran, Sir Denis Pack (Sir Francis Chantrey, 1828). In the east chapel is a piscina of curious design, possibly a survival from the earlier church.

The **south transept** may be regarded as the Ormonde Chapel but with so many recumbent figures, it is more like a dormitory. It contains numerous tombs of the Butler family: in the centre lies the 2nd Marquess of Ormonde in calm repose (Edward Richardson, 1855, executed in Caen stone); to the south, the splendid double tomb of **Piers Butler**, 8th Earl (d. 1539) and his wife **Margaret Fitzgerald**; and against the south wall, the 9th Earl (d. 1549), with a remarkably good effigy bearing a sword. The tomb of Archbishop Cox (builder of Castletown Cox) and his wife is by Peter Scheemakers, 1779, for which he charged the bishop the then exorbitant sum of £240. By the east wall is displayed 'Ireland's Memorial Records', volumes listing the dead of World War I, decorated by Harry Clarke.

The **choir**, flanked by chapels, has a modern floor of Irish marble. The east window (in memory of the 2nd Marquess of Ormonde) replaces the magnificent stained-glass for which the papal nuncio Rinuccini offered £700 only a few years before it was smashed by Cromwell's soldiers. By the north wall is an episcopal crosier gnawed by a serpent, probably that of Bishop Ledrede.

In the south wall of the **nave** are windows by artists of the important Dublin-based stained glass revival movement, the Loftus window is by A.E. Child (1931); the Connellan window by Sarah Purser and Ethel M. Rhind (c 1918).

Adjacent is **St. Canice's Library**, containing some 3000 16–17C volumes, bequeathed by Bishops Otway and Maurice, including among its rarities the MS Red Book of Ossory. The Bishop's Palace dates from 1735–36.

To the northeast, the Nore is spanned by Green's Bridge (1764; by George Smith), a Palladian design with five arches.

On regaining Parliament St turn right along Abbey St and under Black Freren Gate, the sole surviving town gate, to reach the **Black Abbey**, a Dominican church. Dissolved in 1543, the building went through various civic uses and was ruinous in the 18C when it was again used for worship. The church incorporates the slender tower and several good early windows of the 14C abbey; the five-light window in the south apse is particularly fine. It also contains a number of interesting medieval figures; in the south transept is a large alabaster image of the Trinity, probably English, it is inscribed 1264 but is more likely c 1400. The priory museum (open by request) houses a 14C Irish figure of St. Catherine of Alexandria in limestone and a mutilated penal period painted oak figure of a Dominican monk. In the forecourt are a collection of rare mid-13C stone coffins and lids, three of which are inscribed in Norman French or Latin, including one of a woman (unusual for the date) Isomein del Marmpole.

At the north projection of Abbey St, in Dean St is St. Canice's church (RC) a Tudor Gothic 19C church with fine confessionals and vaulting.

Blackmill St (in which James Stephens, the Fenian, was born), ascends in a graceful curve to St. Mary's Cathedral (RC; W. D. Butler, 1843), its disproportionately large grey limestone tower (60m high) is a conspicuous feature of the town. Kenny's Well Rd is at the bottom of Blackmill St, on the banks of the Breagagh river. Here you will find **Kenny's Well**, a diminutive, possibly early medieval steep roofed building from which the well associated with the founder of Kilkenny bubbles.

6.5km northeast of Kilkenny stands the five-storey tower-house of **Clara Castle**. Some 6.5km northwest of Kilkenny is **Freshford**, with a central square, and incorporated into the 18C Protestant church are relics of the original church, rebuilt early in the 12C, with a richly decorated porch; over the inner arch are some early Irish inscriptions. 4km further southwest is **Rathealy**, a trivallate ring-fort with a souterrain. **Ballylarkin** church (13C), has good carved stonework.

6.5km east of Freshford is **Ballyragget**. It has a large square and retains the large keep of its 15C–16C castle, once the headquarters of the Mountgarret branch of the Butler family, but used as barracks in 1798. Beyond Ballyragget you reach Ballyconra, a seat of Viscount Mountgarret. Cross the river Block on the Portlaoise-Cashel road at Durrow, and turn northwest just north of the village onto the R434.

The N76 leads southwest of Kilkenny, passing near (right) **Desart**, birthplace of James Hoban (1762–1831), who emigrated to America in 1785 and was the architect of the White House, Washington. 1.5km to the left of the main road is the tower-house of Burnchurch (15C–16C; open to the public). **Callan** (16km) is an ancient town whose present fame is mainly derived from its ruins, most notably the Augustinian friary, built in 1467–70 by Sir James Butler, to the northeast. On the riverbank are traces of a castle, bombarded by Cromwell in 1650. The choir of the parish church has survived south of the centre.

9.5km southwest is **Mullinahone**, home and burial-place of Charles Kickham (1828–1882), the Young Ireland revolutionary and writer (see Tipperary). At **Killamery** pass a richly sculptured 9C cross of the local type, before skirting (right) Slievenamon (719m) and descending into the Suir valley near **Kilcash**, celebrated in one of the most well known Gaelic poems of the 18C, which laments the decline of the Anglo-Norman Catholic aristocracy:

> The courtyard's filled with water
> And the great earls where are they?
> The earls, the lady, the people
> Beaten into the clay.
> (version Frank O'Connor)

Margaret Butler, Viscountess Iveagh, the woman whose grace and hospitality are mentioned in the text is buried in the Butler tomb in the nearby medieval chapel. The ruins consist of a tower house c 1544, 17C domestic buildings, and two chapels, one with a fine Romanesque south doorway. The road bears west for Clonmel.

For Kells, follow the N10 south from Kilkenny and cross Kings river at (11km) Stonyford. **Kells** (3km west), is formerly known as Ceanannus Caraighe (Kenlys-in-Ossory) to distinguish it from the greater Kells (*Ceanannus Mor*) in Meath. It preserves important remains of **Kells Augustinian Priory**, founded by Geoffrey de Marisco in 1193, although the existing remains are 14th and 15C. The site—the most extensive monastic enclosure in Ireland—is an impressive one, resembling a medieval walled town. The curtain wall, interspersed with five intact battlemented tower houses (one has a dovecote in its upper storey and another was lived in during the 18C by a cobbler-hermit) encloses five acres, divided into an outer quadrant which was probably used as an enclosure for livestock, and an inner area on the banks of King's river, in the centre of which is the church and claustral complex. The church has suffered more than the defensive walls. Originally cruciform in design, it has a nave and choir with a single transept, Lady Chapel and two towers. A mill-race (now dry) ran through the outer enclosure to drive a mill and act as a moat.

Further west is **Newton Castle** (early 16C). 3km south of Kells, at **Kilree**, in an overgrown graveyard is a Round Tower, 29m high, which has lost its cap. The monolithic cross, in a field beyond, similar to those at Ahenny, is said (incorrectly) to commemorate Niall Caille, King of Ireland (845) who drowned trying to save a henchman who had fallen into Kings river. Southeast of Stonyford is **Mount Juliet**, with a house of c 1780, a golf course, fox-hunting centre, with stud farm and the kennels of the Kilkenny hunt.

Castledermot, Carlow, Browneshill, Old Leighlin

South of Ballitore on the N9, is the **Rath of Mullaghmast** (171m), once a stronghold of the Kings of Leinster, and the scene of the treacherous massacre of the chiefs of Leix and Offaly in 1577 by the English and their allies, the O'Dempseys,

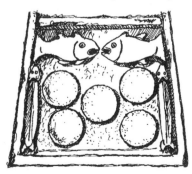

The Multiplication of Loaves and Fishes, base of the south face of the Moone High Cross (8C–9C)

who had invited them to a friendly conference. The 'Wizard Earl' of Kildare (see below) is said to be buried in the rath in an enchanted sleep.

The road next runs through the villages of Timolin and **Moone**, the former with a 12C effigy of a knight in its churchyard. In the garden of Moone Abbey are the ruins of a 14C Franciscan friary and a re-erected 9C **Moone High Cross**, over 5m high, with sculptured panels of stylised and naïve figures, it is among the finest of the 'scripture crosses'. 18C Moone House is also of interest.

You soon enter **Castledermot**,

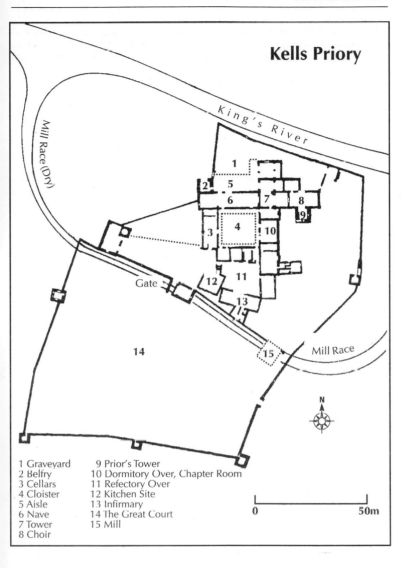

Kells Priory

King's River

Mill Race (Dry)

1
2
5
6
7
8
9
3
4
10
12
11
Gate
13
14
15
Mill Race

N

1 Graveyard
2 Belfry
3 Cellars
4 Cloister
5 Aisle
6 Nave
7 Tower
8 Choir
9 Prior's Tower
10 Dormitory Over, Chapter Room
11 Refectory Over
12 Kitchen Site
13 Infirmary
14 The Great Court
15 Mill

0   50m

taking the second half of its name from St. Diarmuid, who founded a monastery here in c 800. The castle was that of Walter de Riddlesford, built in 1182, where Sir Edmund Butler defeated Edward Bruce in 1316. A parliament was held here in 1499.

From the main street a short but attractive tree-lined avenue forms an axis with St. James's Church (C of I) which has significant early medieval remains in the churchyard. The Round Tower (20m), erected by Abbot Cairbre (d. 919) and built of uncoursed granite, is rare in having what appears to be its original door at ground level. The battlemented top is medieval although it lacks 'Irish battlements'.

There are also two fine 9C **High Crosses** with scripture panels; a freestanding Romanesque doorway (of which the modern church's doorway is a copy); many medieval gravestones and the base of another High Cross. Further south, on the other side of the main street, are the remains of a Franciscan friary, founded in 1302, with a simple nave, a single north apse and adjoining tower house, both 15C.

North of the village is the so-called **Pigeon House**, the square tower of a house of Crutched Friars, founded by Walter de Ridlesford in c 1200. **Kilkea Castle** (1180) lies 4km northwest. A seat of the Fitzgerald family and now an hotel, it is notorious for being haunted by the 'Wizard Earl' (Gerald, 11th Earl of Kildare; d. 1585), who rides every seventh year into his former study on a white charger shod with silver. Battered in the 1798 rebellion, the castle was 'restored' in 1849. Hermione, Duchess of Leinster (then Marchioness of Kildare), bored with her husband and her home, composed the couplet: 'Kilkea Castle and Lord Kildare, Are more than any woman can bear'. Sir Ernest Shackleton (1874–1922), the Antarctic explorer, was born at Kilkea House.

Carlow

Carlow (*Ceatharlach*, the four-fold lake, perhaps from the meeting of the Burren and the Barrow rivers). (Tourist Office, Community Office, town centre (☎ 0503-31554).

Standing on the edge of the Pale, it was a place of great strategic importance, and was walled by Lionel, Duke of Clarence, in 1361, but taken and burnt in 1405 by Art MacMurrough, and again by Rory Og O'More in 1577. On 25 May 1789 several hundred Irish insurgents were ambushed and killed in a fierce battle in its streets, and buried in the gravel-pits at Graiguecullen on the opposite bank of the river. Some 200 more were hanged or shot in retribution.

Carlow Castle, probably built by William Marshall c 1208, the earliest of the typically Anglo-Norman four towered keeps, is positioned overlooking the crossing of the river Barrow, it retains only two of its drum towers. Although it suffered during the sieges, much of its ruinous condition is due to the enterprising Dr Middleton, who in 1814 fixed upon the old fortress as being a suitable site for a lunatic asylum, and in using an excessive charge of gunpowder with the idea of reducing the thickness of the wall, succeeded in demolishing three quarters of the structure.

The **Cathedral of the Assumption** (RC), an early Gothic Revival building (1828) by Thomas Cobden, with west tower and highly distinctive openwork octagonal lantern, has a bright and restrained interior with minimalist decoration. There is a fine monument (north apse) to its founder (Hogan,1839), Bishop James Doyle of Kildare and Leighlin, a polemicist and champion of Catholic emancipation (1786–1834), who wrote under the initials J.K.L. The monument was carved in Rome and shows J.K.L. raising the stooping Hibernia from her suffering. Hogan gained election to the Institute of the Virtuosi of the Pantheon in 1837; the first native of the British Isles to win admission to that learned Roman Society.

The elaborately decorated pulpit was carved in Brugge, 1899, with figures of SS Victor, Condleath and Laserian (see Oldleighlin) has been transferred to the Heritage Centre next to the Cathedral. William Thackeray in 1842 was not impressed with the cathedral, remarking, 'nor were its innumerable spires and pinnacles the more pleasing to the eye because some of them were quite off the perpendicular'.

The **Court House** (William Vitruvius Morrison, 1830), at the junction of the Athy and Dublin roads, is one of the finest 19C classical buildings in Ireland, it has an unique octastyle Ionic portico raised on a high plinth and polygonal wings; the surrounding railing with military emblems and the siting at a wide street junction both contribute to the building's great air of dignity. The artist Frank O'Meara (1853–88), an important Symbolist, was born at 37 Dublin St (see Hugh Lane Gallery, Dublin). 'The Cigar Divan' at No.50 has a fine 19C shopfront.

St. Mary's church (C of I), a Gothic building (18C–19C), has some monuments to local dignitaries, of interest; Bagnel Gurly (Richard Morrison, c 1796), Jane Verdon (J.R. Kirk, 1827) and two windows by Catherine O'Brien c 1930. **Carlow Museum** (open all year 09.30–13.00, 14.00–17.00, Tue–Sat; Sun 14.30–17.30; £), at the town hall in Centaur St. has sections dealing with natural history, country life, technology, and local history.

In the demesne of Browne's Hill, 3km north of Carlow, is the impressive **Browneshill Dolmen**, its capstone (weighing 1000 kilos and the size of a small car), is the largest in Ireland.

At **Sleaty** (*Sleibhte*), 3km north of Carlow, on the west bank of the Barrow, are the ruins of a monastery with a 5C cross, founded by St. Fiach, a disciple of St. Patrick. **Killeshin**, 4km west of Carlow, within a girdle of limestone hills surrounding the disused Leinster coalfield, retains a remarkable ruined Romanesque chapel. Its parti-coloured doorway with four recessed arches has sculpted heads as capitals; above runs a votive inscription in Irish, its decoration in part obliterated. The east window is a late-Gothic insertion.

Heading south from Carlow, you pass near the site of **Clogrenan Castle**—on the far bank of the Barrow—built by Sir Edward Butler and held by eight men against the besieging force of Sir Peter Carew in 1568. At 10km the by-pass veers to the right across the Barrow just before **Leighlinbridge** (pronounced Lock-lin-), where the first bridge over the river was constructed in 1320. On its east bank lie the ruins of the 'Black Castle', erected by partisans of Hugh de Lacy in 1181, and later the residence of Sir Peter Carew. Not much more than a 16C tower remains and the 14C bridge has been widened. The physicist and mountaineer John Tyndall (1820–93) was born in the village. To the south is the Dinn Righ rath, marking an ancient seat of the Kings of Leinster.

Old Leighlin (3km due west) is the site of a monastery founded in the 7C by St. Laserian/Molaise, and the see of both a Catholic and Protestant bishop (combined with Kildare, and with Ossory and Ferns respectively). **St. Laserian's Cathedral** (C of I), built after 1248 and altered and enlarged in 1529–49, is one of the least known cathedrals in Ireland. Situated on the main street of a village of a few houses, its impressive 18C gates frame a small building of considerable interest. The cathedral consists of a nave and chancel, separated by a screen, a north transept and Lady Chapel, now used as a chapter house. The virtually windowless nave has a font (c 1225) and 16C altar-tomb, with a design of vault-ribbing on its side. In the chancel there is another font (11C, taken from St. Mary's, Gowran), and monuments to the vigorous Vigors family, who produced High Sheriffs of the county in the late 17 and early 20Cs. There is a window by Catherine O'Brien and monument by J.R. Kirk in the chancel, and set in the floor a slab dated 1555, commemorating 'John the dumb, son of William, son of David Roe O'Brien, and his wife Mabel Cavanagh daughter of Wilbomona'.

The saint's well (signposted as St. Molaise well), which incorporates an early cross, is west outside the walls of the churchyard and is bedecked with votive offerings, indicating the continued veneration of the saint.

Leighlinbridge to Graiguenamanagh, Inistioge

From Leighlinbridge follow the east bank of the Barrow (R705) past (left) **Dunleckney Manor** (c 1850), former seat of the Bagenal family, who settled here in the 16C. Beauchamp Bagenal Harvey, commander-in-chief of the Wexford insurgents in 1798, had raised a regiment of Volunteers at Carlow, and Sir Jonah Barrington the diarist was present when he reviewed them on his estate in 1780. After the inspection so much claret and whiskey was apparently consumed that the party spent the night on the ground, surrounded by empty bottles. We enter Muine Bheag (or Bagenalstown), a fine court house with Ionic portico, and an imposing railway station of c 1850. 3km east is the massive square ruin of Ballymoon Castle (early 14C), retaining some interesting features; its plan is unique.

12km further south, cross the Barrow, leaving on the left the demesne of the Kavanagh family, the lineal descendants of the MacMurroughs, Kings of Leinster; while from the Georgian village of **Borris**, further east, you can reach the Sculloge Gap in the Blackstairs Mountains, the highest of which is Mt Leinster (793m).

Borris House (late 18C, and modernised by R. and W.V. Morrison c 1820) was formerly the home of Lady Eleanor Butler (1739–1829; later one of the celebrated intellectual gay couple, the 'Ladies of Llangollen'. It then became the residence of Arthur MacMurrough Kavanagh (1831–89), the politician and sportsman. Although born without arms or legs, he became a Westminster MP and an accomplished sportsman. On visiting Abbey Leix he remarked to his hostess 'It's an extraordinary thing—I haven't been here for five years, but the station-master recognised me'.

Passing Ullard, a little further south (R705), with a 9C Cross and a 12C Romanesque church (in ruins) you enter **Graiguenamanagh** ('the granary of the monks'). It is an attractive town on the west bank of the Barrow, here crossed by a mid-18C seven-arched bridge with ornamental niches, (by George Semple) and overlooked to the south by gracefully shaped Brandon Hill (516m). **Tinnahinch Castle**, on the far bank, was a Butler fortress. The river-front has good 19C warehouses, above which rises the dignified outline of the Cistercian abbey–church, the largest in Ireland in its day. The town was built among the ruins of the abbey of Duiske (*dub-uisce*, black water) founded in 1204 by William the Marshall, earl of Pembroke. The Catholic church consists of the choir and transepts—where parts of the 13C glazed tiled floor can be seen—and part of the nave of the abbey, which have been excellently restored, although many other parts of the cloistral complex are still in use as part of the domestic buildings of the town. A fine processional arch which led to the cloisters is in the south aisle. **Duiske** originally had a 200 foot nave and octagonal crossing tower (which fell in 1774); what remains still retains much of its original dignity; the rough stone walls are limewashed which contrasts well with the window dressings of Dundry stone from Bristol.

The **church** contains an effigy of 'Alan Beg' an armoured knight (c 1300), in a coat of mail, surcoat and arms grasping his sword. In the churchyard are two 9C High Crosses, removed here from the nearby monastic sites of Ballyogan and Akylthawn in 1820, the former is a scripture cross, its panels illustrating David the Psalmist and the Sacrifice of Isaac. A small museum and heritage centre is opposite the church.

The main road from Graignamanagh runs parallel to the west bank of the river via Ballyogan, with the ruins of Galmoy Castle and a churchyard cross with spiral ornaments. A more interesting road follows the east bank, passing (right) **St. Mullins**, named after St. Moling, Bishop of Ferns (d. 696), who is buried here in the monastery he founded, a plan of which is drawn in the 7C MS *Book of Mulling*. Adjacent to the present church are the ruins of several medieval churches, a 9C High Cross, and a Norman motte. Continue south to New Ross (12km) via Mountgarret Bridge, defended by an old keep.

New Ross

New Ross is a small port on the Barrow, said to have been founded by Isabella de Clare, a daughter of Strongbow. Due to its strong fortifications, it was long a rival of Waterford, and was formerly of commercial importance, notably for the export of beef, butter and wool.

Originally called *Ros Mhic Treoin*, in the 16C it took the name Rossponte, and was so known to Spenser. The bridge was destroyed by its Irish defenders in 1643, but in 1649 it was replaced with a bridge of boats by Cromwell, the first to be seen in Ireland. In 1798 the Irish insurgents under Bagenal Harvey made a determined attack on the town, and were only repulsed after a stubborn struggle, in which Lord Mountjoy was killed. Charles Tottenham (1685–1758) was MP for New Ross from 1727 until shortly before his death. He is alleged (by Sir Jonah Barrington) to have ridden 60 miles overnight to Dublin, entering Parliament House in his muddy boots in time to give a casting vote against an unpopular measure (the event is commemorated in a painting of *Tottenham in his Boots* by Latham (1731), in the National Gallery.

Today, the most attractive feature of New Ross is the river front which has 19C warehouses. The steep and narrow streets of the town have some buildings of interest. The Tholsel (1749), was rebuilt in 1806; in South Street is Trinity Hospital (1772); of the fortifications little is left but a tower and fragments of gates. Overlooking the town is the large ruined 13C **church of St. Mary**, with the 19C (C of I) parish church inserted into its nave, which contains monuments by Van Nost to Vicount Loftus (d. 1768). It is among the earliest Gothic buildings in Ireland; the ruins contain an interesting collection of medieval tombs, including that of Peter Butler (d. 1599), and in the graveyard a slab claimed to be the cenotaph of Isabella de Clare, founder of the abbey (d. 1220) and wife of William Marshall.

The adjacent **church of SS Mary and Michael** (RC), has a pietà by John Hogan and a fine timber roof. All trace of the great Dominican abbey of Rosbercon, on the west bank of the Barrow, has vanished.

At New Ross turn north on the R700 to **Mountgarret Bridge**, with its old keep, before veering northwest, skirting heather-covered **Brandon Hill** (516m), providing extensive views. As you descend towards the Nore through **Clonamery**, with an 11C–12C church with a massive west door, you see on the left a hill crowned with an ornamental tower. Beneath is the beech-wooded demesne of **Woodstock**, where the 1740s house by Francis Bindon, burned c 1920, was once the seat of the Tighe family. The Hon. Sarah Ponsonby (1755–1831) was living here with her cousins in the late 1770s, and it was from here that she left for Wales with her friend Eleanor Butler (see above), where the eccentric couple were known as the 'Ladies of Llangollen'.

Inistioge (Teoc's or Tighe's island; pronounced Inisteeg) is charmingly situated on the west bank of the Nore (16km), crossed here by a ten-arch bridge (18C). The village square is planted with lime trees. Two ancient towers, one of them incorporated in the parish church, recall the Augustinian friary that was founded here in 1210. A neo-Classical mausoleum has some Tighe monuments, including the effigy by Flaxman of Mrs Mary Tighe (1772–1810), the author of *Psyche*. A ruined Norman fort stands on a rock overhanging the river.

Ascending the Nore valley (N77), shortly forking left, you pass **Foulksrath Castle**(right) after 11km. A 16C structure on 13C foundations; it is now a Youth Hostel.

Kennedy Memorial Park, Dunbrody, Tintern Abbey

Across the New Ross bridge, the main road (N25) to Waterford, (23km) climbs above the well-wooded banks of the Barrow. Beyond Glenmore a steep ascent commands retrospective views of Brandon Hill (left) and the Blackstairs range, before the road descends into the Suir valley to Waterford (excursions to the south may be made conveniently from New Ross, or alternatively from Wexford).

Take the R733 along the east bank of the Barrow, shortly forking right, and passing (right) **Dunganstown**, a hamlet from where US President J.F. Kennedy's grandfather emigrated to Boston; the **John F. Kennedy Memorial Forest Park** and Arboretum were opened here in 1968.

Dunbrody Abbey

Dunbrody Abbey (13km), is an impressive ruin on the banks of the river Barrow, founded in 1175 by Hervé de Montemarisco, seneschal of Strongbow, but the early Gothic church was not erected until c 1210–40. The plain but graceful building (it is one of the longest Cistercian churches in Ireland, (at 59m) is fairly complete (although the south wall of the nave fell in 1852) and retains a massive low 15C crossing tower. The chapels opening off the transepts and the east window in the Early English style are its most noteworthy features. The night stairs (leading originally to the monk's dormitories) in the south apse is intact. Although the cloister has disappeared there are considerable remains of the conventual buildings, including the **refectory** to the south. A 15C abbot's residence was built on top of the chapels of the south apse, the groin-ribs of the tower crossing are composed of alternative red and white stone.

If you continue to skirt the estuary you will see **Ballyhack Castle** (OPW), a substantial tower house which was originally a preceptory of the Knights Templar c1450. Opposite the castle lies Passage East; a car-ferry which provides a convenient and continuous service to Waterford. At **Duncannon** is an old fort, on a promontory, taken by Lord Castlehaven in 1645 and held by him against Ireton in 1649. James II sailed from here for Kinsale after his defeat at the Boyne, and later William III embarked here for England.

The fishing village of **Slade** lies towards the end of the peninsula. The village has a well-preserved late-15C or early-16C castle with a 17m-high tower adjoining an early 17C house. Beyond lies **Hook Head**, its lighthouse surmounting a circular keep of 1170–84. In 1834 the last great auk (a now extinct flightless seabird) to be captured alive in the British Isles was brought ashore by fishermen in Waterford Harbour.

Returning along the same road, fork right past **Baginbun Head**, where the first Anglo-Norman expeditionary force—300 men under Robert FitzStephen and Maurice FitzGerald—landed in May 1169. The earthworks on the neck of the headland probably date from this period.

Keeping to the right through Fethard and Saltmills, you shortly reach **Tintern Abbey** (OPW), in a pleasant wooded demesne running down to a creek of Bannow Bay, crossed by a battlemented 19C Gothic bridge. The Abbey was founded in 1200 by William Marshal, Earl of Pembroke, in thanksgiving for his rescue from drowning off the coast, and peopled by monks from Tintern in Gwent. Nothing of the conventual buildings remain, but the nave, tower and chancel, having been used as a dwelling by the Colclough family from the mid-16C until 1963, are currently being restored. The nave and south transept aisle were excavated in 1982–83. Note the numerous corbel heads. Bearing north-west you can return directly to New Ross.

The trip can be extended to include **Bannow**, on the far side of its bay, founded by the Normans, but later buried by drifting sand. It was a ruin as early as the 16C, although it returned two Members of Parliament until 1798, when the Earl of Ely was paid £15.000 in compensation for the loss of the seat. A ruined church survives above the bay.

Bannow may be approached on by-roads circling the north side of the bay via **Clonmines**, a 'rotten borough' which sent two members to parliament until it was disfranchised in 1800. It is a fascinating medieval ghost town, with four churches and four castles; relics from its days as a wealthy port—silver and lead were mined nearby until the Elizabethan period—which declined when the harbour silted up in the 16C. The building known as the Town Hall (on the right of the approach road), a fortified tower c 1400, has a chapel on the ground floor with unusual vaulting. Nearby is another 15C church with a west tower. The nave is still used for burials but the modern tawdry tombstones are in danger of destroying the beauty of the site. There is a charming little late 16C castle at **Coolhull**, some 5km southeast, a crenellated two-storey structure.

Gowran to Thomastown, Jerpoint Abbey, Waterford

14C tomb slab of Cantwell Fada, Kilfane

Just west of Leighlinbridge, the main Waterford road (N9) continues southwest. The N10 shortly diverges (right) for Kilkenny. After another 7km you reach **Gowran** (pronounced Gawran), one of the chief seats of the Lords of Ossory. The chancel of the old collegiate Church of the Blessed Virgin of the Assumption (c 1275) retains a massive 14C square crossing tower to which is attached the 19C Protestant parish church, occupying the position of the chancel, which has an Ogham stone on its north wall and monuments to Viscount Clifden and the Countess of Brandon (by Edward Smyth). Now associated with 'the Gowran Master' to whom the design of St. Canice's Cathedral and Thomastown church are also attributed, the quality of the decorative carving and church monuments (14C–17C) is exceptional; in the tower are two 16C table tombs, one baring two male recumbent figures and the Agar tomb 1711. In the roofless nave in the north aisle are two early 14C slabs with beautifully carved male and female figures, possibly James, first earl of Ormond (d. 1327) and Eleanor his wife, and the Kealy cadaver (1626) and mural (1646) tombs, the latter commemorates James Kealy and his wives Ellen and Mary with the verse, 'Both wives at once alive he could not have/Both to enjoy at once he made this grave'.

Immediately west of the next village of Dungarvan is **Tullaherin**, with a ruined church and Round Tower, 22m high. The name (*Tulach Chiarain*) signifies that it was the burial place of St. Kieran. Pass (left), 8km beyond, the church of **Kilfane**, a 14C church with adjoining domestic building, and the over life-size effigy of 'Cantwell Fada' (long Cantwell), a mailed knight c 1320 (doubtless regarded as a giant in a period when people were considerably shorter than they are today), and a strikingly graphic image of the individuals who ruled Ireland during the medieval period. Further along the road, on the same side, is **Kilfane Glen** and **Waterfall**, a restored 18C wild garden with authentic planting, a delightful Cottage Orné with billowing thatch, and a hermit's grotto in the midst of a wood. **Thomastown**. It was named after Thomas FitzAnthony Walsh, seneschal of Leinster, who built a castle and the town walls, but few remnants of its former importance remain except the defence towers near each end of the bridge and a large ruined church (13C) within which a modern church has been erected. The Catholic church contains the old high altar from Jerpoint Abbey. Below the town, on the opposite bank of the Nore, is the ruined **Grenan Castle**. George Berkeley (1685–1753), Bishop of Cloyne and philosopher, may have been born at Dysert Castle, 3km southeast of Thomastown.

Jerpoint Abbey

Cross the Nore and bear right for Jerpoint Abbey (10.00–17.00, Tue–Sun, Apr–June & Sept–Oct; closed Mon except BH; 09.30–18.00, June–Sept; OPW).

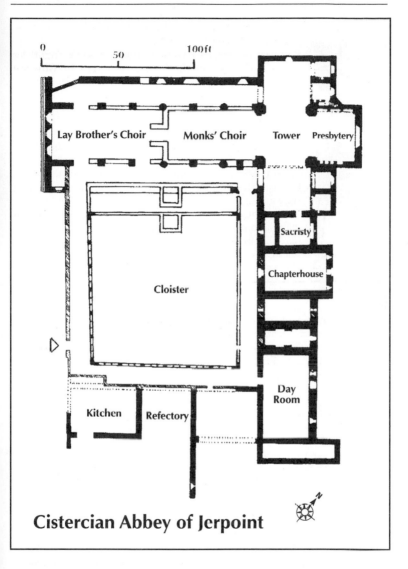

Cistercian Abbey of Jerpoint

Founded in 1180 (possibly 1160) for Cistercians, probably by Donal MacGillapatrick, Lord of Ossory, the abbey gained renown under its first abbot, Felix O'Dullany (d. 1202), founder of St. Canice's Cathedral, Kilkenny. At the Dissolution in 1540 its lands passed to James Butler, Earl of Ormonde. The cloister, restored in 1953, dating from a 15C rebuilding, retains some interesting carving, including a St. Christopher, an armed knight, and a lady with a pleated gown. The south side of the nave has vanished, but on the north a row of six wide pointed arches on low piers

Jerpoint, 15C
figure of a woman
in pleated gown
and pointed cap in
the cloister arcade

separates it from the aisle. The clerestory windows and the triple west window are round-headed. There is no west door, the only entrance to the church having been a fortified porch on the north side of the nave. The nave appears to be of a later date than the choir and transepts, which are in the Irish Romanesque style, the former retaining its stone barrel vault, but the east window is a 14C insertion.

The **tower** with its characteristic Irish battlements, is probably 15C. The south transept contains Walsh and Butler tombs of the late 15th and early 16C, and in the choir is the early 13C tomb of O'Dullany, with his crosier gnawed by a serpent. There are two more carved tombs in the north transept. The **chapter-house** contains objects found among the ruins.

At Newtown Jerpoint, to the northwest, is a ruined church with an unusual gallery, and a 15C tower. The road shortly joins that from Kilkenny at Knocktopher (*Cnoc an Ttchair*, the hill of the causeway), still retaining traces of an ancient causeway crossing the marshy valley, and a medieval tower and other remains of its Gothic church. To the right as you turn south are also the considerable remains of a Carmelite priory founded by the 2nd Earl of Ormonde in 1356. To the west, at Sheepstown, is a very primitive (11C?) church.

Passing Ballyhale, you cross the Slieve Brenach hills before descending into the valley of the Suir, briefly skirting its northern bank to approach the bridge spanning the river, providing a view across to Waterford.

Waterford

Waterford (*Vethra fjorthr*, the ford of the father, (ie. Odin), or weather-haven). The view of the town from the north bank of the Suir is striking and has been described by Mark Girouard as 'the noblest quay in Europe'. Indeed, its half mile length seen from the Kilkenny bank of the river displays the finest urban prospect in Ireland. A painting of Waterford by William van der Hagen (1736) which hangs in the Town Hall shows the same view, its essentials hardly altered since the 17C. The concept of the town in its earliest Viking form of a walled enclosure strategically hugging the south bank of the Suir, established the shape of Waterford which in an expanded form it still holds today. The 200m width of the river (not bridged until 1794) and the fact that the far bank is in a different province, county and diocese has promoted historic and contemporary growth to occur into its hinterland to the southwest, giving Waterford a linear and composed waterside, like a late medieval town. With the exception of Derry, more of Waterford's medieval walls are intact than any other Irish city.

As the regional capital of the southeast, it is a busy commercial and industrial centre with two cathedrals; the town today has an important container port (located on the north bank of the Suir), and has been since 1947 the site of the major producer of Irish crystal, Waterford Glass, which has its factory in the southeastern suburbs at Kilbarry. This is a revival of a craft tradition for which Waterford was noted in the 18C and 19C.

- **Tourist Office**. 41 The Quay (☎ 051-75788).
- **Post Office**. Keyser St, the Quay (☎ 051-74321).
- **Railway and Bus Stations**. North end of the bridge (☎ 051-73401).
- **Airport**. Killowen (☎ 051-75589).
- **Festivals**. A festival of light opera takes place in September–October in the Theatre Royal (☎ 051-74402).

Listings

Chapman's Pantry, 61 The Quay, excellent café-restaurant behind delicatessen (☎ 051-71142); **Dwyer's**, 5 Mary Street, imaginative cooking, good sea-food (☎ 051-77478); **Granville Hotel**, Meagher Quay, fine long-established hotel overlooking the River Suir (☎ 051-55111); **Prendiville's**, Cork Road, good restaurant, B&B (☎ 051-78851); **Viking House**, Coffee House Lane; **The Quay**, hostel (☎ 051-53827); **The Wine Vault**, High St, food with wine, wine with food, a glorious combination (☎ 051-53444).

The establishment of Waterford as a Viking settlement and trading port in the 9C–10C is attributed to Sigtryggr, and to his son Ragnvald, the fortification of the town. This was in the form of a triangle, stretching along the quay front from Reginald's Tower, and inland, occupying an area of eight hectares. The building of the first church on the site of Christ Church cathedral dates to c 1050. In the two centuries of Viking occupation the town developed into a well-defended fortress with numerous churches and public buildings. St. Olaf's church commemorates a Viking foundation.

On 25 August 1170 Raymond le Gros and Strongbow captured the city after a three day siege, and in 1171 Strongbow was married to Aoife, daughter of Dermot MacMurrough, King of Leinster, establishing an important dynastic and political alliance (Maclise's enormous painting *The Marriage of Strongbow and Eve* (1854), is in the National Gallery). Henry II arrived in 1171 with a flotilla of 400 ships, carrying 4000 infantry and cavalry, intent on preventing his barons from establishing an independent kingdom in Ireland. Other than Dublin, Waterford remained the principal seat of English authority throughout the medieval period. King John, when Earl of Morton, established a mint at Waterford in Reginald's Tower, which continued to issue coins for 200 years. The Normans extended the fortifications to the west, more than doubling the area within the walls.

Waterford showed its loyalty to Henry VII by refusing to admit the Pretender, Lambert Simnel, and by sustaining a siege of 12 days by Perkin Warbeck and the Earl of Desmond. Accordingly, in 1493, it was given the right to the device *'Urbs Intacta Manet Waterfordia'* (the unconquered city of Waterford), a motto still born by the city arms.

Marmaduke Middleton, Bishop of Waterford from 1579, was accused of plundering the cathedral, but was acquitted. An enviable distinction was won in 1649 when the town forced Cromwell to abandon its siege (the only Irish city to repulse the Lord Protector) but in 1650 it was stormed by Ireton. James II received a welcome on his flight from the Boyne (1690), but the town surrendered soon after to William III.

Glass was being manufactured in Ireland from c 1590 when George Longe established a glassworks near Dungarvan, and from the 1720s flint glass tableware was being produced in Waterford. In 1746 an English Act of Parliament forbade the export of Irish glass which forced native manufacturers to compete for the local trade with English producers. With the relaxation of restrictions in the 1780s, Irish glass entered its period of greatest development and was exported all over the world, creating many new forms and styles of cutting. George and William Penrose established a factory in the centre of Waterford in 1783, which under various managements produced the now much sought after 'Old Waterford Crystal', its greatest period being 1780–1810. Excise taxes of 1825 again affected glass manufacture which by 1851 had ceased in Waterford. Examples of Waterford Glass can be found in decorative arts museums in many countries and in locations as unexpected as the Topkapi Museum in Istanbul.

To visit the **Waterford Glass Factory**, some 2km down the Cork road, apply at the Tourist Office. Tours take place on weekdays, when you can see certain stages in its manufacture, cutting, and polishing, etc. Children are not admitted, nor is photography allowed. Glass is not sold at the factory, although most shops in the town sell it.

Waterford was the birthplace of Luke Wadding (1588–1657), Franciscan scholar, historian, and professor of theology at Salamanca; Michael Wadding (1591–1644), missionary to the Mexican Indians; Dorothy Jordan (1762–1816) and Charles Kean (1811–68), actors; William Vincent Wallace (1813–65), the composer of *Maritana*; Thomas Meagher (1823–67), a member of the Young Ireland party, who, transported to Tasmania, escaped to fight in the American Civil War at Fredericksburg; and William Bonaparte-Wyse (1862–92), the philologist and grandson of Lucien Bonaparte. John O'Donovan (1806–61), topographer and historiographer, was born at Slieveroe, to the northeast. Lord Roberts (1832–1914), although born in India, came of a distinguished Waterford family. John Redmond, who succeeded Parnell as leader of the Home Rule party, was MP for Waterford for 26 years.

Any exploration of the town should begin at the broad quay which fronts the river; most of its buildings are 19C. At the east end is **Reginald's Tower** (10.00–17.00, Mon–Fri, Apr–May & Sept–Oct; 14.00–17.00 Sat & Sun; 08.30–20.30, daily, June–Aug; £) the distinctive pepper-pot form of which is unique among Ireland's historic buildings. It is a fine early medieval drum tower (possibly dating from 1003) with conical roof and battered walls, the best preserved fragment of the original defences and one of the earliest mortared defensive towers to survive in Europe. It now contains the **Civic Museum** (£), which displays a rich collection of historic documents, including the Charter Roll of Richard II, illuminated with royal and other portraits and a schematic view of Waterford; ceremonial swords of King John and Henry VIII and the Waterford Maces; and a cannon of c 1497—a rare example of early artillery—probably from Perkin Warbeck's fleet. In the adjacent 'Reginald Bar' can be seen the sallyports of the medieval wall.

Turn into the Mall for the **Town Hall** designed by Waterford's most prominent 18C architect, John Roberts (1783), with a selection of the municipal art collection on display. The building also contains the **Theatre Royal**, one of the few surviving 19C theatre interiors in Ireland, with three-tiered horseshoe balconies.

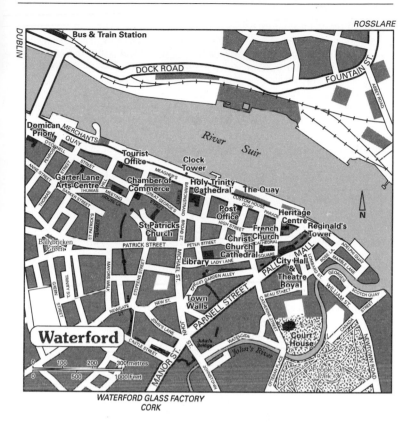

ROSSLARE

DUBLIN

Bus & Train Station

DOCK ROAD

FOUNTAIN ST.

ABBEY ROAD

Domican Priory

MERCHANTS QUAY

O'CONNELL STREET

PLUNKETT STREET

ANNE STREET

THOMAS STREET

River Suir

Tourist Office

MEAGHER'S QUAY

Clock Tower

Garter Lane Arts Centre

Chamber of Commerce

Holy Trinity Cathedral

The Quay

HILL STREET

THOMAS STREET

HILL STREET

MEETING HOUSE LA.

BARRONSTRAND

GREAT GEORGE'S ST.

CUSTOM HOUSE QUAY

PARADE

Ballybricken Green

ST PATRICK'S TERRACE

St Patricks Church

BROAD ST

Post Office

HIGH STREET

French Church

Heritage Centre

Reginald's Tower

ADELPHI QUAY

PATRICK STREET

MICHAEL ST.

PETER STREET

Christ Church Church Cathedral

CATHEDRAL SQUARE

ROSE LANE

MARBLE LANE

Library

LADY LANE

PALL MALL

LOMBARD ST.

City Hall & Theatre Royal

GEORGE'S STREET

WILLIAM ST.

SCOTCH QUAY

TRINITY SQ.

GREEN STREET

MAYOR'S WALK

STEPHEN STREET

SPRING'S GARDEN ALLEY

Town Walls

PARNELL STREET

BEAU STREET

CATHERINE STREET

NEWGATE

NEW ST.

JOHN'S LANE

CASTLE STREET

John's Bridge

WATERSIDE

URBAN PLACE

Court House

CANADA STREET

NEWTOWN ROAD

Waterford

MANOR ST.

JOHN ST.

JOHNSTOWN

John's River

People's Park

0   100   200   300 metres
0   500   1000 Feet

N

WATERFORD GLASS FACTORY
CORK

Beyond is Palace Lane leading up into **Cathedral Square**, an attractive urban space with buildings of varying character surrounding **Christ Church Cathedral** (C of I; John Roberts, 1773), on the south of which is the Bishop's Palace, a fine stone-built classical town house by Richard Castle (1741) on the west side are restored Clergymen's Widows' Apartments (1702), and on the east the 18C Deanery, with medieval undercroft. Christ Church replaced a medieval cathedral (demolished in 1771) which resembled that of the same dedication in Dublin. The principal features of the exterior are the Doric portico and the spire, the lower section of which has rather heavy detailing. The bright and spacious interior is entered through a vestibule which leads into the nave separated from the aisles by rows of tall and slender Corinthian columns, the galleries have been removed. There are many interesting church monuments, the Rice monument (1469) with a *memento mori* representing a decomposing cadaver; Bishop Foy by William Kidwell (1707) and the Fitzgerald memorial by Van Nost (1770).

To the north in Greyfriars St is the **Waterford Heritage Museum** (08.30–20.30, June–Aug, daily; 10.00–17.00, Apr–May & Sept–Oct, Mon–Fri;

14.00–17.00, Sat & Sun; £), which contains an excellent display of Viking and medieval artefacts from recent excavations, demonstrating local craftsmanship, trade links with the Continent, personal ornaments and lathe-turned vessels. The 19C 'Munster Bar' has attractive panelled interiors. Also in Greyfriar's St are the remains of the 'French church', the nave, chancel, crossing tower and Lady Chapel of a Franciscan priory, founded in 1240. Its choir was used 1695–1819 as a chapel for a Huguenot colony (hence the 'French' association) and the nave as a hospital. John Roberts, the architect, is buried here.

In parallel Lady Lane are good Georgian houses. West in Olaf St is the deconsecrated St. Olaf's church (C of I), a prebendary chapel on the edge of the cathedral close, dedicated to the Viking, Olaf the Holy. The present building dates from 1734 but its fine 18C furnishings have recently been dispersed.

From Henrietta St, pass through Arundel Square to Blackfriars in which are the tower and ruins of Blackfriars priory, a Dominican foundation of 1226 dissolved in 1541; from 1617 it served for a time as the assize court.

Turn right into Barronstrand with the **Cathedral of the Holy Trinity** (RC) by John Roberts (1793). Unusually, both Protestant and Catholic cathedrals, built 20 years apart, are by the same hand, the latter designed when Roberts was in his 80s. The west façade has an Ionic portico with balustrade surmounted by statues of saints, which was not completed till 1892 when the cathedral was consecrated, a century after its inception. The ornate interior retains its galleries and is a hybrid between the 18C design of the building and its protracted 19C execution. The unobtrusive location of the cathedral (like St. Patrick's church, see below) was determined by the penal strictures against non-Established Church religious buildings. The modern chandeliers are Waterford Glass.

Off Great George's St is the diminutive **St. Patrick's church** (1764), a rare example of a mid-18C pre-Emancipation Catholic Church; the charmingly unaltered interior which has a U-shaped timber gallery is of exceptional interest. Ironically, it is now the earliest surviving place of worship in Waterford still in use, pre-dating both cathedrals.

Great George's St leads into O'Connell St, both parallel to the river front. Facing down the broad Gladstone St (off George St) is the **Chamber of Commerce** Building (John Roberts, 1795), a superbly sited 18C town house. The four storey, six bay façade with fanlighted doorcase is best viewed from the quay. The house contains a majestic oval staircase, surmounted by a dome, decorated by the Waterford stuccodore Patrick Osborne with Adamesque plasterwork. Through an archway (left) in O'Connell St, is the **Garter Lane Arts Centre**, which presents a regular programme of theatre, recitals and exhibitions. Opposite is the Trustee Savings Bank with a restrained classical façade (Thomas Jackson,1841).

In Bridge St, at the very end of O'Connell St is St. Saviour's Dominican church (George Goldie,1874), the west front has a fine classical campanile which commands the approach across the bridge, but the interior (which contains a 17C Spanish figure of the Virgin), is very gloomy. Turn right at the end of the street to return to the quays.

Return to the Mall from where a separate tour may be made of the **medieval city walls**; proceed south along the Mall, prolonged into Parnell St, at John St the road breaches the walls, here with three towers. Turn right to follow the best preserved and accessible sections of the wall line with four surviving towers (see map) which runs northwest in an arc, back towards the Suir.

Further south, the Mall leads to (right), the excellent Presentation Convent by A.W.N. Pugin (1842), in sandstone with limestone trimming, it has the appearance of medieval almshouses.

At Reginald's Tower cross the Mall, in the middle of which is a monument to Luke Wadding (Gabriel Hayes, 1957), and down Catherine St to the People's Park in which is the Greek Revival **Court House** by J.B. Keane (1849), replacing an earlier one by Gandon. It has an excellent Ionic portico but the interiors have been modernised. The John's river meanders through the park.

Waterford Castle, on an island at Ballinakill, 5km south of the town, is a medieval building, enlarged in the 19C.

Some 12km southeast of Waterford, passing Little Island (R683), with an old castle of the Fitzgeralds, lies **Passage East**, with a 15C–16C castle, from where a passenger ferry crosses the estuary to Ballyhack. Perkin Warbeck took ship here after his failure to storm Waterford in 1491. On the coast further south is the site of New Geneva, a colony of Genevese Protestants established here in 1785 by Lord Temple with a grant of £50.00 from Parliament. They were unreasonable in their demands, however, and soon returned to their own country. Their dwellings were converted into barracks, and in 1798 used as a prison.

Further south, opposite Hook Head, is Dunmore East, named from the 'great dun', remnants of which can still be traced. It was formerly of importance as the terminus of the mail-packet service from Milford Haven to Waterford, and still possesses a long pier. To the south is the cliff of Black Knob, beneath which is Merlin's Cave.

The N25 leads west from Waterford, skirting the glass factory, towards the Comeragh Mountains, after 7km passing (right) the demesne of **Mount Congreve**, an early 18C mansion ostentatiously refaced and remodelled in 1965, when some of its interesting decoration was wantonly destroyed. Its gardens, which display a large rhododendron plantation, may be visited (by appointment only). Shortly beyond (right) are the ruins of **Kilmeaden**, a castle of the Le Poers taken by Cromwell in 1649, who in anger at having to raise the siege of Waterford, hanged the owner out of hand.

Cross the river Mahon at **Kilmacthomas**, birthplace of the Irish comedian Tyrone Power (1787–1841). Sir Tyrone Guthrie (1900–71) theatrical producer and Tyrone Power (1914–58), Hollywood film star, were two of his great-grandsons. Beyond Kilmacthomas the road winds around the south side of the Monavullagh Mountains, commanding a good view of Dungarvan (also by-passed) on the final descent.

Northwest of Waterford

Leaving Waterford by the N25, you turn right for Portlaw, passing the ruined Ormonde keep of **Grannagh Castle**, where the Suir makes a bend to the south. The river is met again at Fiddown.

A long bridge crosses an islet to the far bank below wooded Mt Bolton. Just south of this hill, and west of **Portlaw**—once a busy cotton-spinning village of

Quaker foundation (1825–1904), its wide streets and peculiarly sober, ellipti-cally-roofed workers' houses suggesting its former activity—lies **Curraghmore**. This is the imposing seat of the Marquesses of Waterford, its forecourt commanded by a remodelled medieval entrance tower surmounted by a stag, the crest of the De la Poer family. It was built by John Roberts of Waterford in 1742–50, and contains interior decoration by Wyatt. To the right of the mansion is a shell house sheltering John van Nost's statue of Lady Catherine Power. It was the birthplace of Admiral Lord Charles Beresford (1846–1919). The demesne is regarded as one of the most beautiful in Ireland.

Shortly beyond Fiddown you reach **Piltown**, an attractive village with the seat of the Earl of Bessborough, restored since burnt in 1923. Several Bessborough and Ponsonby monuments may be seen in the remains of the 13C church at **Fiddown**.

A lane leading uphill to the right ascends to the *Leac an Scáil* portal tomb at **Kilmogue**, the largest in the region; other prehistoric remains are scattered around the village of Owning, to the west of this lane. Nearby stands **Castletown Cox**, built in 1767 for Michael Cox, Archbishop of Cashel, the masterpiece of Davis Ducart and the finest small Palladian house in the country; the central block is linked by arcaded wings to domed pavilions; it contains fine plasterwork by Patrick Osborne.

Carrick-on-Suir

The R680 continues to Carrick-on-Suir situated at the foot of a beautiful stretch of the river, here crossed by a narrow medieval bridge (c 1356), retains its medieval plan, but the walls have disappeared. At the east end is **Ormonde Castle** (09.30–18.30, June–Sept, daily; OPW; £).

Ormonde Castle, a 15C tower built by Sir Edward MacRichard Butler, with a gabled Elizabethan three-storey, seven-bay manor house forming three wings of a courtyard with the earlier building. Built by 'Black Tom', 10th Earl of Ormond in 1565, the stucco decoration of its principal rooms is unique in Ireland.

On the ground floor is a room with the arms of the Ormonds, and upstairs the Long Gallery (30m) has an elaborate ceiling and frieze with alternating portrait medallions of Edward VI and Elizabeth I, and figures of Equity and Justice; a fireplace with a magnificent carved overmantle and another with one in stucco. In contrast to other Elizabethan mansions built during the 16C, Carrick is unfortified, a testament to Black Tom's confi-dence. As a young man he had spent eight years at the court of Elizabeth I, and returned with ideas of Renaissance style allied to an Irish tradition for lavish hospitality. The Gaelic poet Flann MacCraith wrote enthusiastically of the Ormond court in Carrick,

Court without grief, the court of lights,
A court of wax-tapered glitter,
A palace food-filled, stuccoed, monstered,
Gabled, sunny, wall adorned.

It has been claimed that Anne Boleyn (1507–36; grand-daughter of the 7th Earl and mother of Elizabeth I) was born here.

In the Main St is the Tholsel, with a clock tower and lantern and the deconsecrated St. Nicholas church, now the **Heritage Centre** (10.00–17.00, Mon–Fri, Jan & Dec; 10.00–17.00, Mon–Sat; 14.00–17.00 Sun, June–Sept). Dorothea Herbert (1768–1829), driven mad by unrequited love, is buried in the Herbert family plot; most of her writing has been lost. A steep, narrow street opposite the Tholsel leads to the medieval bridge, across which, in the suburb of Carrickbeg, are the remains of a 13C friary, incorporated into St. Molleran's church (1827).

On the south bank of the Suir and overlooking the new Dillon Bridge (east of the old one), is a monument by Cliodhna Cussen, commemorating the Irish language pioneer, Michael O'Hickey (1861–1917), who though he published nothing in the language, also died of a broken heart when his proposals for its promotion were rejected by the Irish hierarchy.

At **Ahenny** (7km north), on the monastic site of Kilclispeen, are two 8C high crosses, carved with spirals and reticulated patterns, instead of panels which were common at this time; remains of similar crosses may be seen at **Kilkieran** on the right before the road starts to climb.

Tramore, Dungarvan, Ardmore, Helvick Head

From Carrick to Dungarvan (37km) the road (R676) climbs steeply onto the lower slopes of the Comeragh Mountains. After some 9km you reach a col, from where a climb to the right brings you to **Lough Coumshingaun**, a gloomy tarn set in a deep corrie with rock walls 300m high. Above it the mountains rise to 789m. Further north is **Crotty's Lake**, in a smaller corrie, named after a local Robin Hood of the 1750s. The road soon joins the N25, bearing right for Dungarvan.

Between Carrick and Clonmel, the Suir makes its way between Slievenamon to the north and the Comeragh Mountains: the views on both sides are attractive. The minor road, skirting the thickly wooded south bank, passes Glen Poer (a seat of the De la Poer family), **Gurteen Le Poer** (formerly the home of the statesman Richard Lalor Sheil, 1791–1851) and birthplace of Gen. Sir Hubert Gough (see the Curragh), with a mansion of 1830–66 in a mixture of 'Revival' styles, and Tikinor (17C), built for Sir Richard Osborne.

The main road enters Kilsheeland Bridge, to the east of which the ruined church has a 12C arch with traces of delicate carving. Northwest of the village lies late Georgian **Newtown Anner**, a seat of the Duke of St. Albans.

For an alternative to the main road from Waterford to Dungarvan take the R675 due south (passing near **Knockeen**, to the right, with a perfect portal tomb) to **Tramore** (13km), a popular resort on a sandy but exposed bay between **Brownstone Head** and **Great Newton Head**, both surmounted by 19C towers; on the latter is a painted cast-iron figure of a costumed sailor known as the 'Metal Man'. Immediately east of the town a sand spit known as **The Burrows** almost cuts off the lagoon of Back Strand from the sea. The road west reaches the sea again at Annestown, behind which are the ruins of **Dunhill Castle**, the original stronghold of the Le Poers. Some 14km further west, at **Drumlohan** (right), several Ogham stones may be seen (re-erected). Stradbally, on the coast, was once the site of an Augustinian friary. Regain the main road at Dungarvan.

Dungarvan

Dungarvan (Tourist Information, ☎ 058-41741; seasonal). The 5th and 6th Dukes of Devonshire re-planned the town in the early 19C, and a grid layout surrounds the spacious Grattan Square. It lies at the head of its fine harbour, and is the capital of the district of The Decies. It was saved from Cromwell's bombardment in 1649, it is said, by the Protector's pleasure at seeing a woman affecting to drink his health at the town gate. **King John's Castle**, early 13C, at Davitt's Quay, is a polygonal keep with twin towered gateway. Opposite the castle is **St. Garvan's church**, actually a 16C merchant's house. In the grounds of **St. Mary's church** (C of I) is the gable of a medieval building with circular windows. **Old Market House** on Lower Main Street houses a museum of local history. **St. Mary's church** (RC), by G.R. Pain (1828) altered by George Ashlin (1890) is impressive, with a fine set of stained glass windows, and a *pietà* under the altar.

At Abbeyside, a suburb on the east bank of the Colligan, spanned by a bridge of 1815, are the ruins of the **MacGraths' Castle** and an **Augustinian friary** founded by the same family in the 13C and now incorporated in the Catholic church.

Ardmore

Beyond the summit of the Drum Hills (14km from Dungarvan) a road forks left for Ardmore(8km), a small resort where a monastery is said to have been founded in the 6C by St. Declan. His oratory, with its original door blocked and with a slate roof added in 1716, is still standing.

The **cathedral**, or its remains, is a very ancient structure many times repaired and altered, with an 11C nave in the Irish-Romanesque style, and a Gothic choir, probably 13C. Note the capitals of the chancel arch. The north wall of both nave and choir show traces of much earlier craftsmanship, including a course of rude Cyclopean masonry and some unusual arcading; the north door, originally round-headed, has a pointed arch inserted. Two Ogham stones—one very worn—may be seen within the church.

More remarkable is the west front, where within two blind arches below a blind arcade are an important group of bas-relief sculptures, including Adam and Eve, the Judgement of Solomon, and the Adoration of the Magi, most probably re-used from an earlier building. Adjacent is a tapering **Round Tower**, 29m high, one of the latest and finest in Ireland (late 12C), unusual in being decorated externally by string-courses. Its conical roof is a restoration.

Romanesque relief of Adam and Eve on west wall, Ardmore Cathedral

To the east is another group of buildings, including St. Declan's Well and ruined Temple Disert (12C–14C). The vanished castle, nearby, was occupied by Perkin Warbeck, and destroyed after a siege in 1642 when 117 of its defenders were summarily hanged by Lord Broghill. To the south stands **Ardo**, a turreted 18C 'folly' house near the cliffs, abandoned 1918 and now derelict.

The best approach to the **Comeragh Mountains** (789m), the highest in Co. Waterford, and their southern extension above Dungarvan—known as the **Monavullagh Mountains** (725m)—leads northwest from Dungarvan. The road commands a fine view of the Galty range to the northwest on the descent into the Suir valley.

The N25 bears southwest, skirting Dungarvan harbour and climbs steeply, leaving to the left a lane leading to **Helvick Head**—its name betraying its Viking origin—between it and Ardmore is the small *Gaeltacht* (Irish speaking area) enclave of **Ring**.

Regaining the main road, turn due west, and cross the estuary of the Blackwater north of the long iron bridge of 1880, before bearing south to Youghal. Near the north entrance of the town you pass some fragments of **St. John's Abbey**, a 14C Benedictine house converted into an ammunition store by Charles II, and remains of **North Abbey** (Dominican) founded in 1268. South Abbey (Franciscan), of 1224, has entirely disappeared.

Higher up, on the opposite bank, in the beautiful grounds of **Dromana Castle**, is a delightful 'Hindu-Gothick' gate lodge, topped by a green onion dome, designed by Martin Day (1849) and based on a gateway at Nash's Brighton Pavilion; it has been restored by the Irish Georgian Society. Here are also the ruins of a keep of the Fitzgeralds of Decies, the birthplace of the 'Old' Countess of Desmond (1500–1604) who, according to legend, died when falling out of an apple tree!

5 · Tipperary: the Golden Vale

The '**Golden Vale**', one of the richest farming landscapes in the country, runs northwest–southeast across this region, with the town of Tipperary at its centre. To the north and south are the **Silvermines** and **Galty** mountain ranges, with the **Comeraghs** in the south-east corner, all of which provide superb countryside for walking, cycling or driving. The **Ballyhoura Way** (80km), a walking route in the heart of Munster, crosses the Golden Vale and Glen of Aherlow.

At the heart of the region is **The Rock of Cashel**, the most spectacularly sited and important historic site in Munster; around it are grouped the historic towns of **Cahir, Clonmel** and **Roscrea**, and scattered throughout the area are further medieval remains including the abbeys of **Holycross** and **Athassel**. South of Cahir are the **Mitchelstown Caves**, the finest accessible cave-system in Ireland. At Clonmel is the excellent **Tipperary South Riding Museum**, and at Cahir the charming Regency **Swiss Cottage**. The region includes most of county Tipperary, as well as portions of Cork, Kilkenny, Laois, Roscommon and Limerick.

How to get there
■ **Train**. At Limerick Junction, Dublin/Cork and Limerick/Rosslare lines meet.
■ **Air**. Shannon International Airport.
■ **Water**. Lough Derg for Shannon Navigation.

Listings

Ballinderry. Brocka on the Water, Kilgarvan Quay, small eccentrically special restaurant (☎ 067-22038).

Cahir. Kilcoran Farm Hostel, organic farm (☎ 062-41906); Lismacue House, grand early-19C mansion with spectacular lime avenue, lavish country-house atmosphere, B&B (☎ 062-54106).**Cashel**. Cashel Palace Hotel, early-18C Bishop's Palace off the Main St, refurbished in elegant and comfortable manner, restaurant and brasserie (☎ 062-61411); O'Brien's Farm Hostel, sitting under the great Rock of Cashel (☎ 062-61003); *Chez Hans*, also below the Rock, long-established, excellent stylish restaurant (☎ 062-61177).

Clonmel. Angela's Wholefood, restaurant (☎ 052-26899); Knocklofty House, stately home hotel (☎ 052-38222).

Fethard. McCarthy's, atmospheric old pub and country hotel (☎ 052-31149).

Montrath. Roundwood House, distinguished Palladian house, B&B (☎ 0502-32120).

Nenagh. Country Choice, small restaurant attached to one of the most interesting fine food shops in the country (☎ 067-32596).

Roscrea. Grant's Hotel, fine old coaching inn (☎ 0505-23300).

Templemore. Cranagh Castle, self-catering, hostel (☎ 0504-53104).

Thurles. Ballynahow Castle Farm, working farm with 16C tower house on lands, dark room and studio facilities, B&B (☎ 0504-21297); O'Gorman's, old-fashioned pub, music sessions; Inch House, fine country-house B&B and restaurant (☎ 0504-51348).

Tipperary. Royal Hotel, family run, good restaurant (☎ 0504-33596).

Portlaoise to Roscrea, Nenagh

From Portlaoise drive west (N7) across rather boggy country, shortly bearing southwest parallel to the extensively reafforested **Slieve Bloom Mountains**, the highest summit of which is Arderin (527m). At 7km you pass Concourse Bridge, where a few mounds are the only trace of the Churches of Clonenagh, a once-famous monastery founded by St. Fintan. Drive through (7km) **Mountrath**, a market town on a tributary of the Nore, and the village of Castletown, built around a green, before reaching the Pike of Rushall, above which rises the ruined castle of Rushall, built for Sir Charles Coote. Roundwood House, an 18C Palladian villa (attributed to Francis Bindon), now restored by the Irish Georgian Society (B&B available, see Listings), lies 5km northwest of Mountrath.

Just beyond the Pike you enter **Borris-in-Ossory**, with its long main street, once a place of importance and known as 'The Gate of Munster', defended by a ruined castle of the Fitzpatricks.

Roscrea

Roscrea is pleasantly situated on a tributary of the Bosna, with the fine ruins of its Augustinian Priory, founded c 1100 on the site of a 7C foundation of St. Cronan. The main doorway of the church with its typical steep gable is flanked by arched and gabled niches; within is a mutilated image, and in the churchyard is a cross with a rude carving of the Crucifixion. The Round Tower opposite has lost its cap, but is otherwise well preserved; both are endangered by heavy traffic. The tower is said to have been reduced in height by the English in 1798 after a sentry at the castle had been sniped at.

Roscrea Castle (OPW; £) c 1285 and once moated, was a stronghold of the Butlers until 1703. Now being restored as the Roscrea Heritage Centre (09.30–18.30, June–Sept), the square keep still retains its stone roof. It stands within a 13C curtain wall; with two of its original D-shaped towers intact. Also within the enceinte is the nine-bay, three-storey early 17C Damer House which has a fine Queen Anne brick façade with scroll pedimented doorway, and (internally) one of the finest staircases in the country. It was purchased by John Damer in 1722 as a residence, was subsequently used as a military barracks and school, and it is now used for exhibitions.

On the south side of the town, at the approach to a modern church, is the square tower and part of the church of a Franciscan friary of 1490. Some 5km southeast are the remains of the abbey of Monaincha, notably a cross, damaged and repaired, and a ruined church with a fine Romanesque archway and 13C south and east windows. According to Giraldus Cambrensis, no one could die on the island on which the abbey was built, in the midst of a lake (now drained). Some 300 standing-stones may be seen on the Timoney Hills, c 8km southeast of Roscrea. To the southwest of the town is the ruined castle of **Ballynakill** (c 1580), with a huge bawn.

Some 6km north is Leap Castle, an ancient and much-haunted stronghold of the O'Carrolls. Although rebuilt, it was burned in 1922. It commands a good view of the Slieve Bloom range to the northeast.

From here bear northwest (N62), descending the Little Bosna valley towards the Shannon, with the Slieve Bloom range to the east, and passing (right) after 8km the demesne of Gloster (or Glasterrymore; now a convent); in 1749 Wesley preached in the mansion of Sir Laurence Parsons here. Beyond, you pass (right) Rathmore Castle.

South of Roscrea, a range of hills to the left rises to the **Devil's Bit Mountain** (479m). The N62 leads to Templemore(19km) where in the demesne of the priory are the ruins of a castle of the Templars and a gable-end of their church. The writer George Borrow spent a few months here as a boy in 1816, and recorded the scenery later in his book, *Lavengro* (1851). 10km southwest, at Borrisoleigh, is another ruined castle. The road descends the Suir valley, passing (left) Loughmoe, with a ruined castellated mansion (15C and 17C) of the Purcells to the east of the railway. Thurles is 8km beyond.

From Roscrea the N7 continues southwest. At Moneygall, turn northeast for **Cloghjordan**, with a Protestant church, (probably by James Pain), in the main square; it was the birthplace of the poet Thomas MacDonagh 1878–1916, executed as one of the leaders of the 1916 Rising. Continuing southwest the Devil's Bit Mountain rises to the left. After 21km the main road bears right at Toomyvara, (with a ruined 15C church). The left-hand fork leads to Silvermines (16km) recalling the old mines of silver-bearing lead once worked here. Nearby are the Silvermine Mountains (489m), beyond which rises Slievekimalta (693m).

Nenagh

Nenagh, an important agricultural centre, still preserves one of the three large cylindrical keeps of the castle of the Butlers (early 13C), dismantled in the 17C. It stands in the grounds of St Mary's Church (RC; 1894) with fine Gothic Revival interior. Also of interest is the octagonal Governor's House of the former Gaol, now occupied by the **Heritage Centre**, and remains of a friary, founded c 1250, south of the centre. The Courthouse is by J.B. Keane (1843). John Desmond Bernal (1901–71), the scientist, was born here.

Turn right off the N52 just north of Nenagh and skirt a range of low hills. The highest (21km; right) is **Knockshigowna** (213m), famous in the fairy legends of Ireland, its summit commanding a view of Lough Derg and the surrounding hills.

A minor road (K493) skirts the eastern bank of Lough Derg, passing a number of pleasant demesnes, among them **Terryglass Castle** (early 13C), of quatrefoil plan, near the site of an early monastery. Regain the main road at Carrigahorig.

Approaching the Shannon, continue north along the east bank of the lake, passing (left) Derry Castle. On the right rises **Tountinna** (461m), the highest of the Arra range, with some barrows known as the 'Graves of the Leinster Men' on its north flank. Turn east away from the lough and through the slate-quarrying village of Portroe. At Rathurles, to the northeast, is a trivallate ring-fort, in the centre of which is a 15C church.

The main road skirts the south slope of the Arra Mountains, off which a right-hand turning leads to (5km) Killaloe, while some 12km beyond this junction you pass (right) Castleconnel, a village on the Shannon and a spa in the 18C. The castle, standing on an isolated rock, was a seat of the O'Briens, Kings of Thomond, and was later granted to Richard de Burgh, the Red Earl of Ulster. It was blown up by General Ginkel during the siege of Limerick (1690).

Thurles to Holycross Abbey, Cashel, Athassel Priory, Cahir

Thurles

Thurles is an ancient episcopal market town, where in 1174 Strongbow met his match at the hands of Donal O'Brien and Roderick O'Connor. The **castle** (12C) guards the bridge over the Suir, and there is another smaller fort near the square.

The handsome **Cathedral of the Assumption** (RC) in Lombardo Romanesque style (1865–72) by the 'Gothicist' J.J. McCarthy is the main architectural attraction and provides a strong contrast to the prevailing Gothic of the period. Inspired by the Duomo of Pisa, the polychrome façade has tiers of blind arcading and a rose window, with a campanile and circular baptistery flanking the façade. Internally the plan is basilican with a sustained use of coloured marbles, and an ambulatory connecting the aisles. The general effect is of the height being insufficient for the width of the building. It contains an original Baroque tabernacle from the *Gesù* in Rome by Giacomo della Porta c 1600, adapted for this setting.

The square has an indifferent 1798 pikeman. In **St Mary's church** (C of I) is the fine tomb of Edmund Archer (c 1520) and surgeon William Bradshaw VC (d.1861) by J.R. Kirk. The pretty Gothic Revival railway station is by Sancton Wood (c1845).

3km north of the town is **Brittas Castle**, the remains of a moated medieval-revival edifice with an impressive barbican tower by W.V. Morrison, on the site of an earlier fortress; its completion came to an abrupt halt in 1834 when the owner was killed by a piece of falling masonry.

Holycross Abbey

From Thurles drive about 6km southwest on the R660 via Holycross Abbey, a Cistercian house attractively placed on the bank of the Suir (OPW). The Abbey of Holycross was founded c 1182 by Donal Mór O'Brien, King of Thomond, as a shrine for a relic of the True Cross given to his father Murtogh O'Brien in 1110 by Pope Paschal II. On account of its relic, Holy Cross was the most important place of pilgrimage in medieval Ireland. A medieval Gaelic poem suggests the esteem in which it was held:

> A sanctuary inviolable hung with gold variegated tapestry,
> a bright castle with carved doorways,
> a house full of books and light and music of psalms.
> The Lord's Cross is our treasure, every stone of its wall being marble;
> the wood of it has surpassed all others; I marvel at its wood-work.

It was almost certainly enlarged after c 1431, but it has not been spoilt by 19C or more recent additions. The church, in a fine state of preservation, was restored by the OPW in 1971–77. In 1969 over 100 graves, mostly dating after 1750, were cleared from the fine interior, now crowded with devotional shrines.

The abbey is approached across the Suir by a late medieval bridge. The arch over the west end of the bridge (removed to facilitate traffic in the 19C) bore a dedicatory inscription which is now built into the left-hand parapet. The pub on

Medieval mural of a stag hunt, Holycross Abbey

the right occupies domestic buildings of the abbey, and the mill which retains its 19C wheel represents the position of the abbey mill.

The most striking feature of the exterior of the church is the beautiful reticulated window-tracery, that of the east and west windows and the south transept being especially notable.

Enter through the cloister, its north range restored, with the cellarium and dorter on the west side, and the sacristy, **chapter house** (with a doorway of unique design) and monk's parlour on the east. The **nave**, with its wooden roof, is of grey stone, set off by whitewashed walls, with one row of round-headed and one of pointed arches. It is a good example of transitional work. Note the sculpted owl on the wall of the northwest pier of the crossing.

The **south transept** is the finest area of the church, with its two east chapels; the pier separating them is pierced by the **'Monk's Waking Place'**, a small open space surrounded by eight barley-sugar columns bearing elaborate groined vaulting, probably designed for the display of the relic which was returned to the abbey at its restoration and is now shown in a modern shrine by Richard King over the O'Fogarty tomb in the chancel. The 15C reliquary is adorned with symbols of the Evangelists, which is reflected by the sharp metalwork 'M. M. L. J' monogram (Mathew, Mark, Luke, John) surrounding it.

The vaulted **choir**, extended at a later date some distance west of the squat central tower (which contains a bell c 1250), is remarkable for its carving, and excellently preserved owing to the durable quality of the local limestone. Noteworthy is the late 14C sedilia, bearing the arms of England, Ormonde and Desmond, with foliated crockets and elaborate carved valance. The north transept also has two chapels, and traces of mural painting depicting a stag hunt; such murals although once common are now, due to exposure, exceptionally rare in Ireland.

On the banks of the river is a modern oratory and stations of the cross for large outdoor gatherings. Nearby is **St Michael's church** (1834) a 'barn church' which was used for worship up to the restoration of the abbey.

Skirt **Boherlahan**, where Charles Bianconi (born in 1786 in Lombardy, d. 1875), the Irish transport entrepreneur, is buried in a mortuary chapel at the roadside. His home from 1850 was at **Longfield House** (c 1760), a short distance to the west. It is in the care of the Irish Georgian Society, and open to the public.

Cashel

Cashel (*Caiseal*, stone fort). (Tourist Office, Town Hall, ☎ 062-61333). 30km from Thurles, was the ancient capital of the Kings of Munster, and long a famous ecclesiastical centre. The attractive town is rich in antiquities and around its main street are buildings from the 15C onwards, some of considerable distinction.

Rock of Cashel

Distant prospects of the Rock of Cashel (09.00–16.30, Sept–Mar; 09.00–17.30, Apr–June; 07.00–19.30, July–Sept; £; OPW) from the Cork or Dublin directions, present the viewer with one of the most striking historic sites in Ireland, unusual for its acropolis-like quality as well as for possessing the aura of a Gothick romantic ruin. 'Bare ruined choirs' beckon the visitor from afar and even close-up the overpowering atmosphere of the site is compelling. Irish ecclesiastical and monastic ruins tend to be found on the banks of rivers in fertile valleys, not as here, up in the air like a fantasy castle of Ludwig of Bavaria. The challenge of the site has produced one of the masterpieces of Irish medieval architecture, Cormac's Chapel, but that is not inappropriate to a settlement known for centuries as 'Cashel of the Kings'.

Cashel was fortified at a very early date, and was certainly a stronghold of Brian Ború (926–1014), and later of the O'Kearneys. The first church was founded here by St. Declan, a 6C disciple of St. Patrick. The bishop's see, founded soon after, is now united with Emly, Waterford and Lismore. In 1127 the King-Bishop Cormac McCarthy built a fine Romanesque chapel on the Rock which was superseded in 1169 by Donal Mór O'Brien, King of Thomond, who built a larger building onto the north side of Cormac's Chapel. In 1171 Henry II received here the homage of Donal O'Brien and lesser nobles but his church too was superseded by the now ruined 13C cathedral which still dominates the Rock. In 1315 Edward Bruce summoned a parliament here.

In 1495 the cathedral was set alight by Gerald, Earl of Kildare, who, when he was arraigned by Henry VII for his action, alleged in extenuation that 'he thought the archbishop was in it'. Enchanted by the candour of the reply, Henry immediately reappointed him in the office of Lord Deputy. The town was plundered in 1647 by Lord Inchiquin (1614–1674) ('Murrough of the Burnings').

The lead roof of the cathedral was probably removed in 1749 by Archbishop Arthur Price (d. 1752)—or his successor—who, it was said, was too lazy to climb the hill to his church. The Protestant archbishopric was reduced to a bishopric in 1839; the Catholic Archbishop's cathedral is at Thurles.

The rocky escarpment itself, rising abruptly to c 30m above the plain, is stated in legend to be due to the Devil, who, in some great hurry to cross the mountains to the north, bit out a huge block and spat it onto the plain below, the measurements taken of the gap in the Devil's Bit Mountain (of Silurian grits) corresponding exactly—it is said—to the dimensions of the Rock. Glacial scratchings on the rock offer the more prosaic explanation that it is a fold of carboniferous limestone.

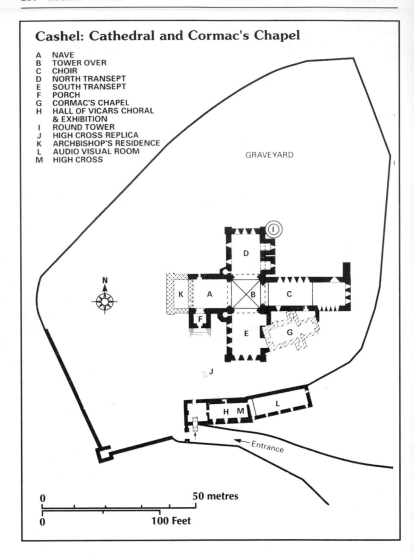

Cashel: Cathedral and Cormac's Chapel

A   NAVE
B   TOWER OVER
C   CHOIR
D   NORTH TRANSEPT
E   SOUTH TRANSEPT
F   PORCH
G   CORMAC'S CHAPEL
H   HALL OF VICARS CHORAL
    & EXHIBITION
I   ROUND TOWER
J   HIGH CROSS REPLICA
K   ARCHBISHOP'S RESIDENCE
L   AUDIO VISUAL ROOM
M   HIGH CROSS

GRAVEYARD

N

Entrance

0   50 metres

0   100 Feet

Properly known as St. Patrick's Rock the stone-walled enclosure is entered from the south through the restored 15C Vicars Choral and dormitory which contains an audio-visual presentation on the Rock's history and small museum. This includes the unique 12C St. Patrick's Cross (a replica of which now stands in the original location in front of the Archbishop's Castle), and a fine 13C tomb-fragment from Athassel showing four armed knights. The relatively oval line of the medieval and later boundary wall most probably follows the contour of the early Christian enclosure, from which only the Round Tower now remains; this wall is broken by the Vicars Choral and a single projecting tower in the south-west corner.

Cormac's Chapel

Directly to the right and abutting the south side of the cathedral, but not structurally connected with it, is the Romanesque Cormac's Chapel (*Teampull Mór Chormaic*). The earliest Romanesque church in Ireland, its external and internal decoration appear to have originated from Murbach, in Alsace, and Bavaria. The aisleless and apseless plan, however, is more conventionally Irish.

Its most remarkable feature is the external blind arcading and steep stone roof, the latter the traditional covering of the early saints' cells (as at Glendalough, Kells and Killaloe). The chapel, the building of which is recorded in the Annals of Lough Ce for the year 1134, is of a browner stone than the cathedral, and was built by Cormac MacCarthy, King of Desmond and Bishop of Cashel. An unusual aspect of its plan are the square towers on either side at the junction of nave and chancel; the north tower is 15m high to the top of its pyramidal roof; the other, which is slightly higher, has lost its roof, and has been finished by a later straight coping. The present south entrance is notable for its carving, while the later west door, giving access to the south apse of the cathedral, has been blocked.

Four superimposed bands of blind arcading entirely cover the external walls of the **nave**, with the motif continued by a single band on the towers and chancel. The large windows above the south door are later insertions, and evidently the interior would always have been exceptionally dark.

The main entrance on the north side is now obstructed by the cathedral, but you can see its elaborate chevron arch-mouldings, and the tympanum displays vigorous sculpture of a centaur shooting a lion with a bow; the origin of this motif is probably Norman Britain, as the bow and arrow was not current in Ireland prior to the Normans. The interior is likewise embellished by blind arcading. The ribbed barrel-vaulted roof of the nave rests on massive pilasters, the bases of which are level with the capitals of the chancel arch, which is not quite central. The chancel arcading is surmounted by round-headed three-light windows. The square altar recess is decorated with twisted columns, and lighted by two oblique windows; the arch above it bears a row of heads. Fragments of high quality fresco, the earliest to survive in Ireland, depicting figures and architecture, were also recently revealed on the vault of the chancel and the whole interior was most probably brightly painted. Above the vault are two lofts approached by a stair in the south tower; that over the nave has a fireplace.

Romanesque fresco of King Solomon meeting the Queen of Sheba before the walls of Jerusalem, Cormac's Chapel

The 11C stone **sarcophagus**, decorated in the Hiberno-Norse Urnes style, was placed at the west end in the 19C; it had previously been in the north transept of the cathedral. Tradition associates it with Cormac. A 13C crosier found in the sarcophagus is now in the National Museum.

The relative sizes of Cormac's Chapel and the cathedral aptly demonstrate the change which occurred in church building after the Anglo-Norman conquest; the most obvious differences are the altered orientation and greater scale, but the 13C cathedral also represents more sophisticated concepts of planning, engineering and lighting and, perhaps most significantly, the political decision to invest vastly greater resources of finance and manpower. The silhouette of the Rock in the pre-Norman period would have been dominated by the Round Tower and Cormac's Chapel rather than as now by the cathedral, the mass of which absorbs both its predecessors.

The Cathedral

The largest building on the summit, which commands panoramic views, is the shell of the cathedral. Erected in c 1235 it was restored following a fire in 1495, and again after its desecration in 1647. The castle of the archbishops was added to the west end by Richard O'Median, archbishop in 1406–40, at the same time as the central tower was raised and the parapets battlemented, giving it a defensive character. It is entered on the south side by a massive porch with a Gothic doorway leading into the nave which is less than half the length of the choir. The transepts, containing some good 16C tombs, have imposing windows, and in the north transept is a series of sculptures representing the Apostles and various saints, and the Beasts of the Apocalypse, with the Butler and Hacket arms; also a tomb of the O'Kearney family (that of Nicholas O'Kearney, 1460) is in the nave.

The long **choir** is flanked by lancet windows, with a blank wall on the south where the choir abuts Cormac's Chapel; the large east window has vanished. On the **south side** is a recumbent figure of Archbishop Myler Magrath (1523–1622; by Patrick Kearin) the notorious (and long-lived) pluralist who apart from being archbishop for 52 years, held three bishoprics and no fewer than 77 other livings!

An **octagonal staircase** turret ascends beside the central tower to a series of mural passages in the thickness of the transept walls, those on the north side give access to the Round Tower. The view from the top of the central tower is even more extensive: to the north is seen the Devil's Bit; to the east, Slievenamon, with the Comeragh range further south; to the southwest are the Galty Mountains; to the northwest towards Limerick rises the dark mass of Slievefelim; while to the west lies Tipperary and the 'Golden Vale'. Adjoining the north transept of the cathedral is the 11C Round Tower, 24m high, with its perfectly preserved conical cap.

Bru Ború, a modern building near the foot of the Rock, is dedicated to Brian Ború, and vulgarises the surroundings of what is one of the most important sites in the country. Just below the Rock are the well-preserved ruins of **Hore Abbey**, founded for Cistercians in 1272 by Archbishop MacCarville, and at one time fortified.

The town has considerable but dispersed antiquities. These include Quirke's Castle, a tower house (15C) in the main street, probably a relic of an O'Kearney castle erected in 1199; the Catholic church, which retains some relics of Hacket's Friary, a Franciscan house of c 1250; and the ruins of the Dominican Priory (1243), rebuilt 15C, founded by Archbishop MacKelly; a simple nave and chancel church with south aisle, transept and crossing tower.

Cashel Palace Hotel, separated by a forecourt from the main street, is a superb early Georgian brick mansion of c 1731 by Sir Edward Lovett Pearce, built for Archbishop Theophilius Bolton. From the garden front of the house, a winding walk follows a path used by the more agile archbishops, which leads to the Rock. From the palace gardens the Rock assumes the role of grandiose garden folly, in keeping with the best 18C romantic ideas of landscape design.

The cathedral of **St. John the Baptist and St. Patrick's Rock** (C of I) hardly lives up to its dual dedication, and its construction spelled the final abandonment of the Rock for religious purposes. It is a plain classical building with projecting porch and tower and dates from 1784, with a spire added in 1812; the interior has been considerably altered and a museum of local interest is housed in the vestry. Of much greater interest is its **chapter-house** (1835) in the cathedral close, now styled the **GPA Bolton Library** (10.00–14.00, Mon–Fri & by appointment; £) which contains a notable collection of early printed books and incunabula with many unique printings. The books were presented by Archbishop Bolton in 1743. The churchyard is bounded on two sides by the **town walls** (temp. Edward III), in which are inserted four tomb-effigies of members of the Hacket family (c 1260).

Athassel Priory

The N74 runs west, after passing Golden. Just beyond the Suir Bridge, with its defensive tower (7km) is **Athassel Priory** (7km) (open all hours) (open all hours), founded for Augustinian canons in 1192 by William de Burgo and the largest medieval priory in Ireland. The important and extensive ruins on the bank of the river Suir, covering 1.6 hectares, consist of a well-preserved church, fragmentary cloister and domestic buildings, dating variously from the 13–15C. The outer defensive walls on the north have a central gate tower with the original three-arch bridge over the dry moat. The church has a lengthy nave, apses, a very fine west doorway, and tall crossing tower as well as a smaller tower in the north-west corner (a 13C tomb-slab from the church is now in the Vicars Choral in Cashel). Richard de Burgh (d. 1326) is buried here. Nothing remains of the town, burnt twice in between 1319–29.

Regaining the main road, you shortly pass Thomastown Castle, founded by Augustinian canons in 1192 by William de Burgo and the largest medieval priory in Ireland. The important and extensive ruins on the bank of the river Suir, covering 1.6 hectares, consist of a well-preserved church, fragmentary cloister and domestic buildings, dating variously from the 13C–15C. The outer defensive walls on the north have a central gate tower with the original three-arch bridge over the dry moat. The church has a lengthy nave, apses, a very fine west doorway, and tall crosssing tower as well as a smaller tower in the north-west corner (a 13C tomb slab from the church is now in the Vicars Choral in Cashel). Richard de Burgh (d. 1326) is buried here. Nothing remains of the town, burnt twice between 1319–29.

Regaining the main road, you shortly pass **Thomastown Castle**, a 17C

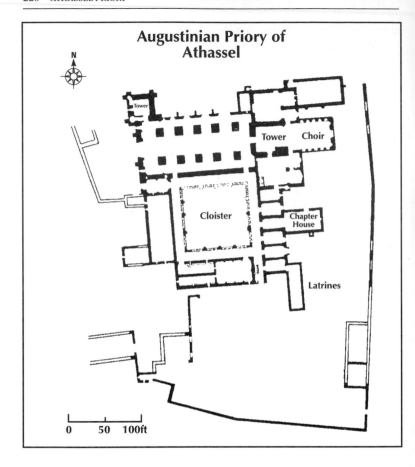

Augustinian Priory of Athassel

house refaced and embellished by Sir Richard Morrison in the Gothick taste in 1820, and now an ivy-clad ruin. It was formerly the seat of the earls of Landaff, and the birthplace of the advocate of temperance, Fr Theobald Mathew (1790–1856). Swift was an earlier visitor to the house, which once had extensive gardens. The road continues to Tipperary.

From Cashel drive due south (N8), with occasional views of the Galtee or Galty Mountains to the southwest, after 9km reaching Newinn, immediately beyond which a road leads right to Knockgraffon, with a fine Norman motte, c 1192, a ruined 13C church and a 16C tower house. Descend the valley to Cahir (Cathair, a fortified town).

Cahir

Although the island in the Suir was occupied from the 13C, the town itself was laid out during the 18C on the Dublin–Cork and Waterford–Limerick crossroads. It contains important remains and is at the centre of an area rich in historic buildings (Tourist Office, Castle car park, ☎ 052-41453).

Cahir Castle (10.00–18.00, Apr & May; 09.00–19.30, June–Aug; 10.00–18.00, Sept & Oct; 10.00–13.00, 14.00–16.30, Nov–Mar; OPW) on an island commanding the Suir bridge, the largest of its period in Ireland, was built in the 15C by successive members of the Butler family, lords of Cahir, on the site of a 13C Norman fortress, restored in 1840 and 1964. It comprises an elaborate curtain wall between round and square towers, enclosing a tall keep in the restored rooms of which is a collection of early oak furniture and a working portcullis. Cahir was besieged by Essex in 1599 and Inchiquin in 1647. The castle was regarded in the 16C as 'the bulwark of Munster and a safe retreat for all the agents of Spain and Rome', but Cromwell was not to be deterred and when encamped below its walls in 1650 issued an acerbic reminder to its garrison, 'if I be necessitated to bend my cannon upon you, you must expect the extremity usual in such cases'. The inhabitants took his point, capitulated, and the garrison marched out with banners flying.

There is a worthwhile audio-visual programme in Cahir Cottage in the outer ward of the castle.

A half-hour walk along the riverbank leads to the **Swiss Cottage**, (10.00–13.00, 14.00–16.30, Mar–Apr; 10.00–18.00, May–Sept; OPW; £) a cottage orné by John Nash c 1810, for Richard Butler, 12th Baron Cahir, and later Earl of Glengall. Lavishly restored to its original form as an aristocrat's play-house, it forms the perfect antidote for the traveller, exhausted from a surfeit of ruined friaries and sad castles. The heavy all-encompassing thatch encloses rustic balconies and pretty reception and bedrooms conceived for an idyllic rural life. The music room has original Dufour wallpaper depicting scenes on the Bosphorus.

Opposite the castle and overlooking the river is the 18C **Mall**, and in the town square are good 18C houses. Cahir House Hotel was the home of the Earl of Glengall. The **Market House** which was arched on the ground floor has unfortunately been 'improved' with plate glass windows. On the Clonmel Rd are the remains of the medieval parish church, and east of the square is the exceptionally spiky Gothick **St. Paul's church** by John Nash 1817. Remains of an early 13C **Priory of Augustinian Canons**, abutted by a 17C tower, lie off the Tipperary road.

Driving due south from Cahir on the R668 immediately west of the town, you shortly pass Tubbrid (left), where the historian Geoffrey Keating (c 1570–c 1644) is buried. Further south, is **Clogheen**, to the east of which is **Castle Grace**, a fine ruin of c 1250. The road climbs steeply southeast into the hills in a series of hairpin bends to reach the **Gap** at 339m between Sugarloaf Hill (655m) to the west and, to the southeast, Knockmealdown (*Cnoc Mealdomhnaig*, or Mealdowney's Hill), the summit of the range (793m). Samuel Grubb, once owner of Castle Grace, chose to be buried here in an upright position, which has since been known as 'Grubb's Grave'.

Southwest of Cahir, the N8 runs along a wide valley commanding superb views, flanked to the north by the Galty Mountains, and with the Knockmealdown range to the south.

Slievefelim and Slievekimalta Mountains

Follow the R503 almost due west from Thurles, keeping to the left on passing the racecourse (right) and at Rosmult, bear right to ascend the Owenbeg valley, with Knockalough (457m) on your left, and continue to climb through desolate scenery until just beyond Milestone (22km). Above **Rear Cross** (12km) you pass a remarkable two-chambered dolmen on the flank of Mautherslieve (542m). The road descends the valley of the Clare, with its cascades, and Cullaun (463m), one of the Slievefelim Mountains to the left; the more distant Slievekimalta (693m) to the north.

Galty Mountains, Burncourt, Tipperary, and the Glen of Aherlow

The Galty Mountains (Galtymore, 917m) are among the loftiest in southern Ireland, occupying a triangle between Tipperary, Cahir and Mitchelstown, and are prolonged to the west by the Ballyhoura range. On every side they rise steeply, and on the south side the old red sandstone is cut up by deep gullies into bold escarpments. The usual ascent is via Mountain Lodge and the saddle between Galtybeg and Galtymore. The ridge walks command extensive views, including the mountains above Killarney (southwest), the distant Slieve Bloom range (northeast), and the nearer Knockmealdown and Comeragh ranges to the south and southeast.

9km southwest of Cahir, off the N8, you pass (left) the remarkably complete shell of the late Elizabethan mansion of **Burncourt** (1641), with its bawn wall, built for Sir Richard Everard, and in 1650 set alight perhaps by Cromwell, or by Lady Everard to prevent it falling into Cromwell's hands. On the right at the next bridge is the approach road to Mountain Lodge; beyond and northwest of Kilbeheny is a ruined castle.

Turning right immediately beyond Cahir (N24), ascend the Ara valley, shortly passing Toureen Peakaun, a monastic site with a 12C church. To the left is the Glen of Aherlow (views). The road crosses the wooded outlying ridge of Slievenamuck (rising further west to 368m) before descending into the rich plain known as the 'Golden Vale'.

Tipperary

Tipperary, made famous by the World War I marching song, and taking its name (*Tiobraid Arann*, the well of Ara) from the nearby source of the river Ara, is a manufacturing and dairying centre. (Tourist Information. James' St, ☎ 062-51457). There are hardly any remains of antiquity, except a gateway of a 13C Augustinian priory. A statue (1898, by John Hughes) commemorates Charles Kickham (1826–82), the scholar, novelist and patriot.

Tipperary played a prominent part in the 'Land League' agitations, when the tenants of Mr Barry Smith established a temporary settlement ('New Tipperary') outside the town. The scheme, called 'The Plan of Campaign', was unsuccessful as a boycotting measure, and was soon abandoned. James O'Neill, father of the American dramatist Eugene O'Neill, was born on a farm on the outskirts of the town; and the Fenian leader John O'Leary (1830–1907) was also a native, while John Burke (1787–1848), the genealogist and founder of Burke's Peerage, was born at neighbouring Elm Hall.

The outbreak of the Anglo-Irish war in 1919 is commemorated by a monument at Sollohod Cross, north of Tipperary (where Brian Ború beat the Munster Vikings). Just beyond at Donohill (8km), is a fine Anglo-Norman motte.

The N24 continues northwest, passing (left) the Tipperary racecourse, to Oola(9km), to the southwest of which Patrick Sarsfield surprised and destroyed William III's siege-train destined for Limerick, at the same time blowing up the fortified Tudor castle of Oola. To the north rise the Slievefelim Mountains (Cullaun, 463m being conspicuous), on the west foothills of which stands Glenstal Abbey (now a school), a 19C building with a cylindrical keep, a modern church (1956), and an old terraced garden, now restored. A church with a Romanesque doorway and later additions, and remains of an early monastic settlement, lies further west, at Clonkeen.

Travelling southeast on the R 516 from Tipperary town you reach the ruins of Elizabethan **Kenmare Castle** (32km), on the outskirts of Hospital, a village which once belonged to the Knights Hospitallers. The early 13C church retains a figure of a knight.

At **Knockainy**, to the west, at the foot of the isolated hill of the same name, are the remains of a Fitzgerald castle and traces of a 13C Augustinian priory. Further west, on either side of the Bruff road, are the mansions of **Baggotstown** (left; early 17C) and (right) **Kilballyowen**, rebuilt, and incorporating an old tower of the O'Gradys.

Emly, 7km to the east, is a village of ancient importance. The see founded here by St. Aibhe (Albeus), a shadowy contemporary of St. Patrick, was amalgamated with Cashel in 1568, and the old cathedral was demolished in 1828; a large rude **cross** survives in the churchyard.

Continuing south from Hospital (R513), drive through **Knocklong**, with the ruins of the O'Hurly's castle, and an old church on a hill to the west. The road approaches the Galty Mountains to the southeast and the Ballyhoura range, their western outliers.

At **Pinker's Cross**, a lane R683 to the left leads shortly to **Galbally**, beautifully situated at the head of the **Glen of Aherlow**, where the pass from Tipperary into north Cork was for many years in dispute between the Fitzpatricks and the O'Briens. Near the bridge rises the lofty tower of **Moor Abbey** (15C), a Franciscan house burnt down in 1569.

On the south side of the glen is **St. Berrihert's Kyle**, a mysterious enclosure in a coppice containing a remarkable number of early cross-slabs, and a fragmentary high cross; it is still a place of pilgrimage. Outside the enclosure is a *turas* or path used by pilgrims on the saint's day.

At **Duntryleague** (or Cush), nearby, is a fine passage-grave. Continuing south from Pinker's Cross, you reach **Ballylanders**, with a ruined church and abutting 17C tower, before crossing the upland below the Galty range, to descend to Mitchelstown.

Fethard to Clonmel

Between Carrick-on-Suir and Clonmel, the Suir makes its way between
Slievenamon to the north and the Comeragh Mountains: the views on both sides
are attractive. The minor road, skirting the thickly wooded south bank, passes
Glen Poer (a seat of the De la Poer family), and Gurteen Le Poer (formerly the
home of the statesman Richard Lalor Sheil, 1791–1851) and birthplace of Gen.
Sir Hubert Gough (see the Curragh), its mansion of 1830–66 in a mixture of
'Revival' styles, and Tikinor (17C), built for Sir Richard Osborne.

The main road enters Kilsheelan Bridge, to the east of which the ruined
church has a 12C arch with traces of delicate carving. Northwest of the village
lies the late Georgian Newtown Anner, a seat of the Duke of St. Albans.

The R706 leads northwest from the N24, with **Slievenamon** (719m; view)
rising steeply from the valley on the right. The name of this sandstone hill is a
corruption of *Sliabh na nBán Fheimheann*, the mountain of the women of
Feimhinn. Legend relates that the redoubtable Finn MacCoul, unable to choose
a wife, seated himself on the summit, while all the suitably nubile and agile who
wished to do so, raced up the slope, the winner securing his hand. The race was
won by Grainne, daughter of King Cormac, who then eloped with Diarmuid. The
hill is also celebrated by Ossian as the hunting-ground of the Fianna, the hero-
army of Finn. At 9.5km you pass (right) Kiltinain Castle, a fortified quadrangle
with corner towers, and with ruins of a medieval church nearby, and shortly
beyond, enter Fethard.

Fethard (*Fiodh Ard*, high wood) is the most important medieval small town in
Ireland. Built on the banks of the river Clashawley, its14C town walls are virtually intact (enclosing 5.5 hectares), including the north gate. There is more to
see in this small space than there is in many major towns. The Town Hall in the
wide Market Square was once a merchant's house (1640) and bears the Everard
coat of arms. Behind the Town Hall is Holy Trinity church (C of I) which occupies the nave of a 15C building. It has a fine battlemented west tower and many
interesting monuments; 16C–17C memorial slabs to local families, on with the
royal arms of Edward VI, its churchyard bounded by the town wall, with
walkway and corner tower. There is an early 19C neo-classical Catholic Church
with tower-house off the east end and to the east of the town is a 14C
Augustinian friary which was returned to use in 1823. The Presentation
Convent (1862) is by Pugin and Ashlin. Fethard pragmatically surrendered to
Cromwell in 1650, and thus avoided siege and massacre.

At 4 km northeast stands the 16C tower-house and extensive bawn of
Knockelly. About 2km west of Lisronagh (5.5km south of Fethard, on the
Clonmel road) is Donaghmore, where the ruined church of St. Forannan has a
fine doorway carved with elaborate Romanesque patterns.

From Fethard continue northwest (R692), after 6km passing (right) Knockbrit,
the birthplace of Margaret Power, Lady Blessington (1789–1849), the
authoress, and friend of Byron.

Clonmel

Clonmel (*Cluain Meala*, the honey meadow) is a busy and well-sited town, with many buildings of interest. It retains well-preserved portions of the city wall and fine 17C–19C classical buildings. (Tourist Information, Nelson St, ☎ 052-22960).

A place of ancient importance, Clonmel received its charter as a borough and its fortifications from Edward I. As an Ormond possession it was besieged by Kildare in 1516. In 1650, under Hugh Dubh O'Neill, it withstood for a time the assaults of Cromwell.

Perhaps the most charming feature of the town is the Suir, here flanked by riverside walks and old warehouses. The pivot of the town is the **Main Guard**, or Tholsel 1674 (from which Gladstone and O'Connell Streets radiate); the Palatinate Court House, built by order of the Duke of Ormonde and bearing his arms (doubtfully attributed to the Surveyor General, Sir William Robinson) which occupies an imposing west-facing position. Its 19C conversion into shops at street-level with two floors of rooms overhead, conceals the original design of a massive five bay street-arcade, carried on circular columns, over which a large single chamber contained the Palatinate court. The pedimented roof is topped by an octagonal lantern; a recent study of the building suggests its original facade may have resembled the Royal Hospital Kilmainham's courtyard elevations.

The West Gate, a mock-Tudor replacement (c 1831) of the medieval town gate, faces the Main Guard from the end of O'Connell St. A plaque on an adjoining building commemorates Laurence Sterne(1713–68). The author of *Tristram Shandy*, was born in Clonmel (his mother's home town), his father, Ensign Roger Sterne, having just arrived with his regiment from Dunkerque. Sterne remained sporadically in Ireland, largely in Dublin, until 1723. George Borrow was a pupil at the old grammar school (1815), near the West Gate (now the county engineering HQ). Here, his young friend Murtagh taught him Irish in exchange for a pack of cards. Anthony Trollope also lived here in 1844–45, after his marriage.

Outside the town gate the street (west) narrows into Irishtown, the original quarter of the non-Anglo-Norman inhabitants of the walled town, in which is St. Mary's church (RC; George Goldie 1836). It has a fine Corinthian portico and excellent interior; the belltower is c 1880.

Turn right into Wolfe Tone St which follows the west line of the town walls passing the small Greek-Revival former Wesleyan chapel by William Tinsley, (1843), to the churchyard of St. Mary's (C of I). The church occupies the north-west angle of the town's defences, here well preserved with three mural towers and a substantial rampart supported on pointed arches.

Of the 13C church nothing remains, the present 19C building (J. Welland, 1857) incorporates portions from the 14C–16C, most notably the west and east windows c 1500 (the latter with glass by Catherine O'Brien, 1931), the vestry and an 18C octagonal west tower. There are numerous 17C gravestones in the church and churchyard. Among the church monuments are Joseph Moore (d. 1795) by Sir Richard Morrison and Michael Shanahan, and the Bagwell memorial by Michael Taylor c 1812.

William St leads into Gladstone St and back to the Main Guard. In adjoining Abbey St is the Franciscan church, remnant of a 13C friary which unusually was within the town walls; only the 15C tower and north choir wall survive, with, in the northwest corner the double recumbent tomb of Thomas Butler, 1st Baron Cahir and his wife Ellen, c 1530. The tomb front with crucifixion symbols is 17C.

In Mitchell St is the **Town Hall** 1881, which has a collection of municipal regalia and documents. Further east in Parnell St is the **South Riding County Museum** (10.00–13.00, 14.00–17.00, Tue–Sat, all year), formerly the Court House (Sir Richard Morrison, 1803), which contains a well displayed and interesting local history collection and a small but worthwhile art gallery including a portrait of John O'Leary by John B. Yeats and landscapes by W. J. Leech and Nathaniel Hone. Charles Bianconi lived in what is now Hearn's Hotel from where he ran the first public horse-drawn service from Clonmel to Cahir, in 1815.

South, in Anglesea St, is the former Scots church (1838) with an imposing Ionic portico by William Tinsley, and at the end of the street, the quays. No. 1, the slate-hung John Christian House, c 1770, has very unusual cut slate armorial panels. Quay House, with its fine fanlighted doorcase, is an excellent example of an early 19C merchant's house. Arthur Young refers to the worsted trade in the south of Ireland being then 'in the hands of the Quakers of Clonmel, Carrick, Bandon, etc.' They also monopolised the export of flour from the area. Race-meetings are held at Powerstown Park to the northeast.

West of Clonmel, by-pass Marlfield where the Protestant church incorporates a Romanesque door from the former Cistercian abbey of Inislounaght, founded here in 1148. The R665 bears west, passing Knocklofty (left), the imposing 18C seat of the Earl of Donoughmore. At Ardfinnan (14km) is the site of a monastery founded in the 7C by St. Finan the Leper. The castle, built by King John when Earl of Morton, stands on a steep rock overlooking the Suir. Two of the square towers are well preserved; the rest was battered down by Cromwell. Crossing the river by a three-arched bridge, you can regain the main road at Cahir by shortly turning right.

6 · Cork City and County

Beautifully situated on the River Lee, Cork City is, after Dublin and Belfast, the third city of Ireland, with long-established Choral, Film and Jazz Festivals. The rich farm-land of Cork (the largest of the thirty-two counties) is separated by the **Ballyhoura**, **Galty** and the **Knockmealdown Mountains** range from Tipperary to the north, and two parallel river-valleys noted for their angling, the **Blackwater** and the **Lee**, cross the county, flowing west-east to enter the sea at Cobh and Youghal. The seaport towns of **Cobh**, **Youghal** and **Kinsale** are historically and architecturally interesting, with the latter being also noted for its **Gourmet Festival** in November, and the well preserved 17C **Charles Fort**.

The Georgian layout and architecture of **Mitchelstown** are a surprise among country towns. **Fota Arboretum and Wildlife Park**, south of Cork City, combines a historically important garden with African, Asian and other wild animals in a demesne parkland setting. The **Crawford Gallery** in Cork has a distinguished art collection and gourmet restaurant. There are regional museums in Cork, Kinsale and Youghal. **Blarney Castle** and the ritual of kissing its 'gift of the gab' granting magical stone, is a bizarre and popular attraction.

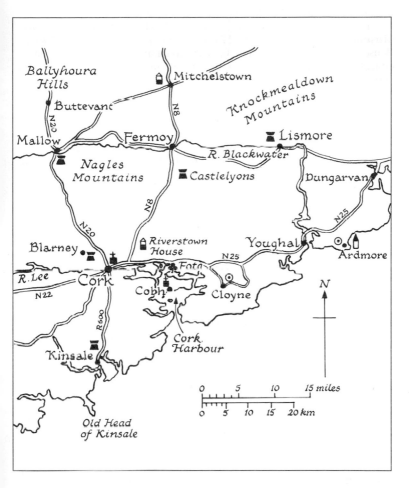

This Chapter covers most of north and east County Cork, with fragments of the adjoining west Waterford and south Tipperary.

How to get there

- **Train**. Cork is linked to Dublin by the main-line service, and via Mallow to Killarney; via Limerick Junction for Limerick, Galway; via Portarlington for Westport.
- **Air**. Cork Airport.
- **Sea**. Ringaskiddy Ferryport for Swansea, Cherbourg, Le Havre, Roscoff and St.Malo.

Listings (except Cork City)

Kanturk. Assolas House, a 17C mansion with celebrated garden, great food, luxurious rooms (☎ 029-50015).

Kinsale. Regarded as the **Gourmet Capital of Ireland** for the quality and number of its restaurants, the annual Gourmet Festival is held in October. **The Vintage**, delicious and atmospheric (☎ 021-772502); **The Blue Haven**, small, luxurious town centre hotel, excellent seafood its forte (☎ 021-772209).

Mallow. **Longueville House**, 18C mansion, spacious accommodation, superlative cooking, home-grown ingredients (☎ 022-47156).

Shannagarry. **Ballymaloe House** and the **Ballymaloe Cookery School**, renowned for its fine cuisine on the one hand and excellent instruction on the other. For thirty years Ballymaloe has been the finest and most enjoyable of Irish eateries and places to stay; its founder, Myrtle Allen, was a pioneer in the use of the best local food, cooked with great inspiration. Darina Allen, chef-chancellor of the academic department, is a popular TV cook and food writer (☎ 021-646785).

Mitchelstown, Fermoy, Castlelyons, Riverstown, Dunkathel

Just south of the Galty Mountains and on the main Dublin-Cork road (N8) is **Mitchelstown**. Superficially similar to other country towns with its long main street of shops and houses, it was in fact planned in the 18C grand manner, with a grid of wide streets and squares; the principal buildings placed at the ends of vistas.

The axis from the main street (on the left, coming from Cork) which once led to the (now demolished) castle passes through dignified **Kingston Square**. The north range of the square (1771), with almshouses for 'decayed Protestant gentlefolk' has a central chapel and is of great interest. Known as Kingston College, it was designed by John Morrison of Cork (father and grandfather of the architects, Sir Richard and William Vitruvius Morrison). At right angles to the castle 'axis' is a tree-lined avenue leading to the Protestant church (G.R. Pain, 1823) with its needle spire.

Market Square, on the east side of which passes Main Street, is also bisected east-west by an axis which leads east to the Catholic church, of which only the spire remains from the original building. Police fired on a crowd here in September 1887 during Land League agitation, killing three. A statue of John Mandeville (1869–88), agrarian agitator and leader of the local campaign of tenant resistance, and three crosses in the pavement commemorate the period. An open market has been held on Thursdays in the square since 1640.

The vanished castle (on the site of which is a large dairy products factory), founded by the White Knights of Desmond, passed by marriage c 1660 to the Lords Kingston. This was replaced by a Gothic mansion (G.R. Pain, 1823) later demolished, its masonry being used to construct the church at Mount Melleray; the castle gardens are being restored.

The town's most famous resident was the feminist Mary Wollstonecraft (1759–97), who in 1786 came as governess to the many children of the capricious Lord and Lady Kingsborough. Lady Kingsborough considered that Wollstonecraft's libertarian ideas and emancipated behaviour had a bad influence on her children. Wollstonecraft's opinion of the aristocracy was deeply coloured by the experience.

The town is associated with the **Mitchelstown Caves** (actually in Co. Tipperary), perhaps the finest group of limestone caverns in Ireland, with impressive rock formations, stalactites and stalagmites. They are best approached via **Ballyporeen**, 11km to the east, where a turning north leads to a house marked 'The Caves'. The caves are divided into two groups, the Old Caves (for spelaeologists only), and the New (discovered in 1833). The caves are not for the arachnophobic, being home to *Porrhomma myops*, a rare spider. It was here that the 'Sugán' Earl of Desmond, was hiding when run to ground by Edmund Fitzgibbon, the last of the White Knights, in 1601 (he fought against the English for three years in Munster, was defeated, and died in the Tower of London in 1608).

The main road from Mitchelstown to Fermoy (N8) ascends due south across the Kilworth Mountains, a continuation of the **Knockmealdown** range. The mountains rise to 297m, offering fine retrospective views. The road passes the lonely tower of Caherdinney, and further down, the village of **Kilworth** (left), and the demesne of Moore Park, through which flows the river Funshion.

Alternatively, an older road leads southwest from Mitchelstown past Killeenemer, with a 12C church, before turning left to **Glanworth**, with its 13C church, part of a Dominican friary founded by the Roche family, their ruined castle, and a 13-arched bridge. Turning southeast the road passes a wedge-shaped passage-grave at Labbacallee.

Fermoy, long a British garrison town, owes its origin to the enterprise of John Anderson (d. 1816), a Scottish merchant, who in 1789 built a hotel and some houses here and entered into a contract with the government for the erection of barracks, which lie on the north bank of the Blackwater. The College, an impressive sandstone with limestone dressing Gothic Revival building on a ridge above the town, was formerly a military school.

The **Blackwater** bisects the town, with a fine bridge and quays on the south bank, which open out into a small square. The Protestant church (Abraham Hargrave, 1802) is at the north end, effectively dominating the wide street. Close to the south end of the town is the Catholic church (reconstructed by E.W. Pugin and G.C. Ashlin, 1867), with a good interior by the Pain brothers (c 1825).

Castle Hyde, an imposing late-Georgian house by Abraham Hargrave overlooking the river to the west of the town, was the ancestral home of Douglas Hyde (1860–1949; first President of Ireland), although he was born at Frenchpark (see Ch. 2).

Castlelyons, a small village of considerable interest, lies off the N8, just south of Fermoy. The Franciscan Abbey, is on the main street. Founded by John de Barry in 1307, it is a simple nave and chancel church with cloister and domestic buildings. At the end of the broad main street (which formed its avenue), are the massive ruins of the 16C Barrymore Castle, accidentally burned in 1771.

On the outskirts of the village in the graveyard of Kill St. Ann (which has rare 17C tombstones) is a roofless 15C church, the ruin of the 18C parish church standing inside it. In the classical Barrymore mausoleum the fine monument by Richard Houghton incorporates a white marble bust of the Earl of Barrymore by David Sheehan (1747). The Irish language writer, Peadar O'Laoighre, served as parish priest here, 1890–1920.

Beyond (8km) Ratcormack on the N8, you pass the fine Georgian mansion of **Kilshannig** on the left (1765; by Davis Ducart). It has some outstanding plasterwork by Paul and Philip Lafranchini and with a fine cantilevered staircase. It was built for Abraham Devonshire (1725–83), a Quaker banker of Cork.

Climbing out of the valley you reach **Watergrasshill**. Francis Mahony (see Shandon below) adopted the pen-name of Father Prout from its former parish priest. Descending the N8 towards Cork, pass **Riverstown House** (left). Built in 1742 for Jemmett Browne, Bishop of Cork, it has important Lafranchini plasterwork, some fine furniture, etchings by James Barry and a collection of original objects, recently returned to the house. The stucco panels in the Salon were executed in 1745, the same period as the Lafranchini brothers produced the Apollo Room in Newman House, Dublin, 20 years before their embellishment of nearby Kilshannig.

Dunkathel House (10.00–18.00, Wed–Sun, May–Oct; £) approached either from Glanmire village or the Glanmire roundabout, was built at the end of the 18C in the Palladian style, and was the home of the Gubbins family in the 19C. There is a permanent exhibition of the work of the Edwardian watercolorist, Elizabeth Gubbins, one of five mute sisters. She travelled widely and recorded her visits in small watercolours. In the front hall is a working Victrolla which plays music of the 1890s.

Castletownroche, Mallow, Kanturk, Buttevant, Charleville

North of the Nagles Mountains and west of Fermoy (N72) lies **Castletownroche**, in the Awbeg glen. The old keep of the Roches, later incorporated in Castle Widenham, was gallantly defended by Lady Roche against the Cromwellians in 1649, but her outlawed husband was neglected by Charles II and became dependent on the charity of the Duke of Ormond. Its gardens are well worth visiting, as are those at neighbouring **Annes Grove**. At the mouth of the Awbeg is 13C Augustinian Bridgetown Abbey, founded by FitzHugh Roche in the reign of King John. Further west is Mallow.

Mallow

During the 18C and 19C, Mallow was 'the Bath of Ireland', an aristocratic junketing place with a famous mineral-water spa, raucously commemorated in a 19C ballad

> Beauing, belle-ing, dancing, drinking;
> Breaking windows, damning, sinking;
> Ever raking, never thinking;
> Like the Rakes of Mallow.

A 19C medical 'opinion' on the spa was that 'if the water was boiled twice, it was no longer dangerous.' Today Mallow is a more sober, though not quite somnolent place. It is a prosperous country town and its importance as a centre for angling, fox hunting and horse racing suggest that the Rakes may still be in residence.

Mallow was granted to Sir Thomas Norreys, Lord President of Munster in 1584 after the Desmond rebellion, and it remained in the ownership of the Norreys and the Jepsons, their descendants, until 1975. The castle, which incorporates the stables of the previous castle (1584; burned in 1689) has a fragment of the older Desmond fortress in its grounds. Sir John Norris (c 1547–97) died here. Thomas Davis (1815–45), poet and patriot, and William O'Brien (1852–1928), Nationalist leader, were natives of Mallow.

On Spa Walk stands the original **Spa House** by G. and J. Pain, (1828) (private), which encloses the Spa Well, and nearby, the public water fountain, known as 'the Dog's Heads' (c 1850); both remain from the period of the town's heyday. **The Clock House** (1860), which commands the south Main St, is an impressive limestone Tudor Revival town house, built for Denham Jepson Norreys, who also owned the Spa House. There are some 18C houses at the east end of the town.

Off the Main St are St. Mary's Church (RC); the excellent interior (1822) has a Corinthian nave arcade, the Romanesque Revival façade dates from 1900. St. James (C of I), approached by an avenue from the street, is by G. and J. Pain (1824). It has a fine pointed spire, and windows by Catherine O'Brien. To the east is the ruined medieval St. Anne's, used for worship until 1817. Thomas Davis was baptised here.

The rebuilt railway viaduct over the Blackwater to the west of the town was blown up by 'Irregulars' in 1923.

South of Mallow the road descends the Clyda valley, passing the castle of Ballynamona, with unusual gable-shaped recesses and **Mourne Abbey** (right), a preceptory of the Knights Templar. The mid-13C tower of **Castlemore** (to the left) was built by John de Cogan. It was in Fitzgerald hands in 1439–1601, when a Barrett purchased it, and was also known as Castle Barrett. After a brief climb, descend the valley of the Martin towards Cork.

Mallow lies some 29km southwest of Mitchelstown, approached via the N73, passing through Kildorrery, near which stood **Bowen's Court** (1776), home until 1959 of the novelist Elizabeth Bowen (1899–1973). It was demolished in 1961 (a pathetic little signpost announces 'Site of Bowen's Court', as though the disgrace of its demolition might be lain at Cromwell's door, rather than an event of recent years).

The N72 continues west up the river valley, passing (left on the far bank) the burnt-out Tudor residence of Dromaneen, with extensive bawn, belonging to the O'Callaghans. Behind it are the Boggeragh Mountains, a stony and uncultivated range which rises further west to 644m (Musheramore). To the right is Longueville House (1740), now a noted hotel (see Listings).

It is well worth making a detour north to the old town of **Kanturk** (*Ceann Tuirc*, the boar's head), with an attractive market-house, and the birthplace of Barry Yelverton, 1st Viscount Avonmore (1736–1805), the lawyer.

7km further northwest is the village of **Newmarket**, birthplace and residence of John Philpot Curran (1750–1817), patriot, orator and wit, who lived in the Priory. His daughter Sarah, betrothed to Robert Emmet, is buried in the churchyard. To the north rise the desolate Mullagharierk Mountains (408m).

The main road is regained to the southwest of Kanturk, passing (right) the huge uncompleted Elizabethan castle known as MacDonough's Folly (before 1609). The plans were so grandiose that the government took alarm, and placed a veto on its completion.

Drishane Castle is some distance south, near Millstreet (R583). There is a tower-house dating from 1450, with later additions and a modern top. South of Millstreet is Kilmeedy Castle, a ruined O'Keefe fortress.

The scenery improves once you cross the Blackwater at Duncannon Bridge (N72), on the boundary of Co. Cork and Kerry. To the south rises Caherbarnagh (682m), and further west, the prominent and characteristically shaped hills known as The Paps (694m and 691m). On the next descent you have a good view (left) of the mountains overlooking the Vale of Killarney, **Crohane** (657m) and **Mangerton** (838m).

The ruins of **Ballybeg Abbey** lie to the north of Mallow on the N20. Founded 1229 by Philip Barry, they are now incorporated in a farmhouse. Just beyond this is the town of **Buttevant**, on the Awbeg river (called the Mulla by Spenser). The town allegedly derives its name from the Norman-French cry '*Boutez en avant*' (push forward), or more plausibly, from '*botavant*,' an outwork.

The ruins of the Franciscan abbey (late 13C) are worth seeing; the nave contains some good canopied tombs of the 14C, while on the east side of the south transept is a small chapel with Barry, Fitzgerald and Butler monuments. Beneath the choir is a crypt vaulted from a single massive pier of four columns. A tower of the Desmonds has been incorporated in the Catholic church. The Protestant church (1826), by J & G Pain, is notable. The earlier fortification of Buttevant Castle, overlooking the river, the old seat of the Barrys, was made into a home in the early 19C by John Anderson (see Fermoy, above).

Liscarroll, 11km northwest of Buttevant (R522) was the scene of a battle in 1642, when David, 1st Earl of Barrymore, was fatally wounded. A later notable inhabitant was Sir John Purcell of Highfort, who, armed only with a carving-knife, allegedly slew eight armed robbers single-handed as they forced their way into his bedroom. The massive bawn wall of **Liscarroll Castle** (13C)—one of the most extensive in Ireland—with circular towers at its corners, is impressive but its keep has not survived.

7km east of Buttevant is **Doneraile** (pronounced Dunerale), once owned by Edmund Spenser, and sold by his son in 1636 to Sir William St. Leger, ancestor of the Viscounts Doneraile. Their seat, Doneraile Court (rebuilt c 1730), is being restored by the Irish Georgian Society. The tomb of the first Viscount (d. 1727), by Sir Henry Cheere, can be seen in the church. The demesne is now a forest park (OPW).

Some 4.5km northeast of Buttevant stand the ruins of Kilcolman Castle, thought to have been Spenser's home for several years, where he wrote the first three books of the Faerie Queene. The castle is ruined above the ground floor, but the top of the walls can be reached by a turret stair. As secretary to Lord Grey de Wilton, the Lord Deputy, Spenser came into possession of the property in 1586 after the forfeiture of the Earl of Desmond's estates, and took up residence in 1588. In the following year a visit by his friend Sir Walter Raleigh persuaded him to publish his poem, and he moved to London where he stayed until 1591.

He reluctantly returned to Kilcolman—during the period of 'Colin Clouts come home againe' (1595)—and remained here until 1598, when the house was burned down during Tyrone's rebellion.

Skirt the Ballyhoura Hills to the east before entering **Charleville** (or *Rath Luirc*, Lorc's Fort) founded c 1659 by Roger Boyle, first Earl of Orrery, and named in honour of Charles II. Boyle's mansion was burnt down by the Duke of Berwick in 1690. A charming little 18C market-house remains, but it has lost its cupola.

12km west is ruined Kilbolane Castle (early 16C; but in a 13C style), partly moated, and with two circular towers.

Blackwater Valley, Lismore

Beyond Cappoquin the road follows the Valley of the Blackwater, a beautiful stream, famous for its trout and salmon. You shortly cross it by a bridge (1775, by Thomas Ivory) largely rebuilt after floods in 1853, with a fine view of Lismore ahead.

Lismore

Lismore is a pleasant cathedral town and the Irish seat of the dukes of Devonshire. (Tourist Information, the Interpretative Centre, ☎ 058-54646; seasonal.) The non-vernacular quality of the buildings in the centre proclaim the influence of an 'improving' landlord.

The monastery and bishopric founded by St. Carthage in the 7C became a centre of monastic learning, and the retiring-place of kings, despite the incursions of Vikings and the men of Ossory (a territory now corresponding to Co. Kilkenny). Henry II visited the Papal Legate here in 1171. The castle (originally built by King John when Earl of Morton, in 1185) was the residence of the bishops until Bishop Magrath generously presented it to Sir Walter Raleigh in 1589. In 1602 he sold it to Richard Boyle, the 1st or 'Great' Earl of Cork (1566–1643) one of the more successful of the English adventurers who sought their fortune in the exploitation of Ireland in the 16C–17C. His sons Roger Boyle (1621–79) statesman and later Earl of Orrery, and Robert Boyle (1627–91) 'father of British chemistry', were born here. According to the antiquarian, John Aubrey, the latter was 'nursed by an Irish Nurse, after the Irish manner wher they putt the child into a pendulous Satchell (instead of a Cradle) with a slitt for the Child's head to peepe out'. Roger Boyle held the castle for the king in 1641, but it fell to Lord Castlehaven in 1645, and in 1753 passed by marriage to the Duke of Devonshire.

Lismore Castle (private) is dramatically poised on a scarp overlooking the river, and was largely rebuilt in 1812–21 by the 'Bachelor Duke', and remodelled by Sir Joseph Paxton and Henry Stokes in 1850–58. There is, however, a fine yew walk, said to be 800 years old and the gardens can be visited. In 1814 a remarkable discovery was made; the 13C 'Lismore Crosier', and the 15C 'Book of Lismore' which contains lives of the saints and an Irish translation of the travels of Marco Polo were found built into a wall of the castle, presumably hidden during the Reformation.

The attractive **Cathedral of St. Carthage** (C of I) is the result of rebuilding in 1679 by Sir William Robinson (the original building was almost entirely destroyed by Edmund the White Knight c 1600). Alterations were made c 1810 by Richard Morrison and a spire added in 1827, probably by G.R. Pain. An aisleless cruciform church, it has a tower at the west end; the north and south transept arches are 13C. In addition to many early Christian cross-slabs of the 9C–11C, in the nave, with its Georgian glass and Gothic vaulting, there is a sumptuous monument to the Magrath family (1557), and the grave of Archbishop Myler Magrath (1523–1622). In the south transept is a window designed by Sir Edward Burne-Jones and made by William Morris, his only window in Ireland.

The early 19C **Courthouse** (Thomas Ivory) is now the **Lismore Heritage Centre** (09.30–18.30, Mon–Sat, 10.00–17.00, Sun; June–Aug; 09.30–17.30, Mon–Sat, 10.00–17.30, Sun; Apr–May & Sept–Oct; £) which has a good audio-visual introduction to the development of the town. Nearby is the Celtic revival Carnegie Library (George P. Sherridan, 1900). St. Carthage's church (RC) by W.G. Doolin (1881) is a Lombardo Romanesque red sandstone building, dressed with limestone; the well-composed west front has a rose window and campanile. To the east is the Great Rath (Lios Mór, the great fort), which gives Lismore its name. Further west (23km) along the north side of the Blackwater valley, the R666 passes near the remarkable Gothick gates and bridge of Ballysaggartmore, (1834), gates to a mansion never completed. In the Forest Park are other gate lodges and features of the scheme. Beyond Ballyduff, (with a fortified manor of 1628) you pass (left) Mocollop Castle, (left) a ruined drum-tower of the Desmonds, and further west, the ruins of Carrigabrick Castle.

The main road N72 runs southwest from Lismore to (7km) Tallowbridge, where Lisfinny, a square tower of the Desmonds, is incorporated in a modern house. **Tallow**, just to the south on the far bank of the Bride, was the birthplace of the sculptor John Hogan (1800–58; see Carlow). From Tallowbridge bear west, shortly passing near (left) the impressive 16C castle of Conna, which resisted Cromwell in 1650, to enter Fermoy.

Youghal to Cloyne, Midleton Fota Arboretum & Wildlife Park, Cobh

Youghal

Youghal (*Eochaill*, the yew-wood, pronounced 'yokel'; the English word 'yokel' may be a corruption of *Eochaill*) is an important walled medieval town and seaport on the estuary of the river Blackwater, where it opens out into Youghal Bay. Today it is also a fine resort town with excellent beaches.

Founded by the Anglo-Normans c 1250, the early history of the town is unclear. It was long a Fitzgerald stronghold, and in 1579 was beseiged by Ormonde during the Desmond rebellion. On entering it, according to some reports, Ormonde hanged Coppinger, the mayor, for failing to protect the place. The town was (very briefly) owned by Sir Walter Raleigh, and was the residence of Sir Richard Boyle, later Baron Youghal and Earl of Cork, to whom Raleigh sold it. Cromwell, well-received here, established his head-quarters in the town in 1649. General Michael Jones, his lieutenant, died of a fever here, and is buried in the Cork transept of the Protestant church.

William Lithgow, the traveller, embarked from here for St. Malo and Spain in 1620. William Congreve spent his infancy here. Claud Cockburn, journalist (1904–81) is buried in St. Mary's churchyard and Liam O' Leary (1910–93), film historian, was born here.

The long and narrow Main Street, lined with 19C shops and houses, runs parallel to the harbour and is extended by the Strand. There are a number of medieval buildings of importance on the street and at the south end, spanning the street, is the massive four-storey **Clock Tower** (William Meade, 1771). One of the more attractive features of the town, it now contains a small museum. Further along (left) are fragments of a Benedictine Abbey (right), the remains of 15C Tynte's Castle, and (left) the '**Red House**' (1706–15) by Leuventhan, a Dutch builder, a brick house with a steep roof and pedimented central bay. On the corner of Church Street is a fine and well-restored group of medieval **Almshouses**, still inhabited.

St. Mary's Church

Church St ascends right to St. Mary's church, c 1250, which (with St. Multose in Kinsale) is among the few medieval churches in Ireland still in use. Rebuilt in 1461 and over-restored in the 1850s after lying in partial ruin since the rebellion of the Earl of Desmond in 1579, it is cruciform with an aisled nave and has fine three-light lancet window in the west end and transepts. A massive detached belfry tower stands at the north west corner, 19m high; another at the west end was demolished in 1792. The west front is a good example of the Early English style.

The **interior** is notable for the nave roof, the provost's stall, the pulpit and the font cover, all of oak; and the font itself is unusually elaborate in design. In the nave hangs a rare example of a carved cradle (1684) for holding the sword of the Corporation. In the south aisle are the tombs of the 8th Earl of Desmond (1468), who founded the college, and Matthew Le Mercier (13C). The south transept contains the tomb with painted figures (restored by the Earl of Cork in 1619), of Richard Bennet and his wife, founders of the chantry that stood here.

Here also is the **Cork Tomb** (1620; compare his monument in St. Patrick's Cathedral, Dublin) of the great Earl of Cork (1566–1643) with his two wives and nine of his 16 children, presenting with its copious inscriptions 'a series of heraldic and genealogical memoirs'. It is said to have been designed by the earl, and was executed by Alexander Hills of Holborn. The choir contains the 15C tombs of the Flemings.

The churchyard is abutted by part of the 15C–16C town walls, with four projecting half-round towers, respectively south-north. Banshee, Montmorenci and Half Moon Tower, the fourth is 19C. These walls, among the most extensive medieval town walls in the south of Ireland, surround Youghal to the northwest and south and can be walked around. The section around the churchyard has an accessible parapet. A flight of steps leads down from the south end of the wall, back to the Clock Tower.

Just northeast of the church stands **Myrtle Grove**, a much altered Elizabethan mansion retaining carved oak wainscoting and contemporary chimneypieces; the story that Sir Walter Raleigh lived in Myrtle Grove and planted the first potato here is without foundation. To the southeast is New College House (1781–82), with a fine 17C chimneypiece. On the opposite side of the harbour lies Ferry Point, from which Lord Castlehaven, a supporter of Charles I, tried to bombard Youghal in 1645 (where there was local resistance to the Crown).

A pleasant trip can be made by following the lanes, more-or-less skirting the west bank of the Blackwater. Turn left at the west end of the Bridge north of the town, and round Rincrew Hill, where Raymond le Gros built a preceptory for the Templars. You next pass **Templemichael**, with a keep of the Fitzgeralds, at the mouth of the Glendine, facing Molana Abbey(ruined), approached by a causeway. An urn in one of the chapels commemorates Raymond Fitzgerald ('le Gros'), possibly buried here in 1186. Some distance upstream on a crag stands Strancally Castle, blown up by Ormonde in 1579. New Strancally Castle, further north, near the mouth of the Bride, is a large castellated building by Pain of Cork (c 1830).

From Youghal, the Cork road (N25), circling around the harbour entrance, bears due west towards Killeagh and Midleton. Alternatively, the road (R633) forks left shortly after leaving Youghal, bearing southwest directly to Cloyne(c 25km). On approaching Cloyne the road passes the demesne of Ballymaloe House (see Listings), noted for its fine cuisine and cookery school.

Cloyne

Cloyne (*Cluain Uamha*, the meadow of the cave), now only a village, was the seat of an ancient bishopric, founded by St. Colman in the 6C and now joined to Cork. The philosopher George Berkeley (1685–1753) lived here from 1734; the artist Philip Hussey (1713–83) was born here.

Cloyne Cathedral, a 13C cruciform building with aisles has been much altered during the 18C–19C. The church contains some monuments of interest, a 17C Fitzgerald family tomb, and memorials to a brace of bishops, Berkeley (by Bruce-Joy, 1890); Bennett (by James Heffernan; d. 1820); Warburton (by Samuel Manning; d. 1826); and Brinkley (by John Hogan). A window in the choir is by Patrick Pye. Other features to look out for are the carvings on the small north door representing pagan symbols of life, and the heavy cubic masonry blocks from which the nave-arches spring. In the north-east corner of the churchyard are the ruins of a small early Chrisitan oratory, called a 'fire house', probably after a similar building in the grounds of Kildare Cathedral in which, according to legend, a fire was continually maintained in honour of St. Brigid; in both cases, the assocation is spurious.

Opposite is a Round Tower, used as the cathedral belfry (30.5m high). The castellated top was added in 1683, the conical roof having been struck by lightning; it displays an almost entire absence of taper.

Southwest of Cloyne are a number of sandy strands and small resorts, popular for the sea-fishing on offer; among them Ballycotton, reached via Shanagarry. The ruined castle, once the home of the Penn family, was visited by William Penn, the Quaker, in 1666 and 1698.

Killeagh (pronounced Killa) lies at the foot of Glenbower, in which, on the Dissour, is the demesne of Aghadoe. Until 1932 it was known as the 'maiden estate', having remained in the hands of the Capell family for almost 700 years; it is now a forestry centre.

Further west is **Castlemartyr** the home of Henry Boyle, 1st Earl of Shannon (1682–1764), and of Roger Boyle, 1st Earl of Orrery (1621–79), who died here. Some 3km southeast stands the castle of Ightermurragh (c 1641). On one of the many fireplaces is a commemorative inscription by the builder Edmund Supple and his wife 'whom love binds in one'.

Midleton

Midleton (8km) was founded c 1670 by the Brodrick family, Earls of Midleton. On the Main St is an 18C arcaded Market-house with cupola bearing the Midleton Arms (E.W. Pugin, 1981). The Protestant church (J. and G. Pain, 1825) completing the street.

The college (built in 1829), was founded in 1696 by Elizabeth Villiers (c 1657–1733), mistress of William, Prince of Orange, and later Countess of Orkney. John Philpot Curran (1730–1817), who distinguished himself as an advocate and as an opponent of the Union with Britain, and dualist was a student here. His daughter, Sarah, was engaged to Robert Emmet before his execution. The architect, Sir Richard Morrison (1767–1849) was born here.

Midleton Distillery, an extensive and well-preserved complex of 18C–19C industrial buildings, has been converted to the **Jameson Irish Whiskey Heritage Centre** (10.00–16.30, Mar–Oct; £) which contains unique examples of early technology; the Fairbairn waterwheel (1852) with a diameter of 6.6m was in use until 1975; among the enormous sculptural copper wash stills is one with a capacity of 143.827 litres, reputedly the largest in the world. Whiskey distilling remains a major industry in the town, now in a modern plant.

On a creek to the south is Ballynacorra. Sir Walter Raleigh, an Elizabethan planter, claimed to have held the ford here single-handed against an insurgent band (followers of the local clan leader, the Earl of Desmond) until rescued by his own men (he was supported by English soldiers). You shortly reach Carrigtohill, with its limestone caves, and (left) Barryscourt Castle (11.00–17.00 daily; OPW; £), a well-preserved 15C tower house with intact bawn.

Immediately beyond the castle the R625 (and then 624) leads left onto Fota Island and Fota Arboretum and Wildlife Park (10.00–17.00, Mar–Oct; from 11.00, Sun; £) to the estate of Fota House, famous for its arboretum of sub-tropical trees and shrubs from the southern hemisphere. A Wildlife Park, established by the Royal Zoological Society of Ireland was established in 1983. The entrance at the south end of the estate leads to Fota House, a Regency mansion, built in 1825 by Sir Richard and William Vitruvius Morrison for the Smith-Barry family. The road then crosses a strait to Belvelly, with a 14C castle and martello tower, circles the west side of Great Island—the largest in Cork Harbour—to Cobh.

Cobh

Cobh (pronounced Cove), was originally known as the Cove of Cork, but between 1849—when Queen Victoria disembarked here—and 1922, it was called Queenstown. An exceptionally attractive town, hugging the north slopes of the harbour, it developed rapidly throughout the 19C; and very few buildings pre-date 1800. Most of its houses face out over the water and give the impression of a Victorian watering-place in aspic. Topography dictated the shape of the town and the streets follow the contours, with houses generally only on the seaward side.

The land-locked harbour first attracted notice in the 18C, being a convenient naval base and place of concentration for the huge convoys of transport required during the French and American wars. Up to 300 vessels could anchor in the harbour. Gen. Charles Vallancey (1721–1812), an amateur antiquarian (and the father of 43 children by three wives), was the engineer responsible for its late 18C fortifications. In 1838 the *Sirius*, the first steamer to cross the Atlantic, set sail from here, taking 18 days. During the famine years it was the last Irish soil trodden by many thousands of emigrants before being crowded onto the waiting hulks known as 'coffin ships' because too often they were unseaworthy.

On 22 April, 1916, the *Aud*, carrying a cargo of arms ordered from Germany by Sir Roger Casement in readiness for the Easter Rising, was intercepted by the Royal Navy and scuttled as it approached the port. In the old graveyard north of the town are buried the Rev. Charles Wolfe (1791–1823), author of *The Burial of Sir John Moore*, and numerous victims of the *Lusitania* disaster (see Old Head of Kinsale, below). Cobh was the *Titanic*'s last port-of-call in Europe before she sank on her maiden voyage to America. Jack Doyle (b. 1913), the 'Gorgeous Gael', pugilist, was born in Cobh.

The town is dominated by the superbly sited **St. Colman's Cathedral**, by E.W. Pugin and G. Ashlin dating from 1868; but not completed until 1919. It is built of Dalkey granite in a French Gothic style, decorated with Irish marble, and surmounted by a 90m spire, with a carillon of 47 bells in the tower. It rises out of the middle of Cobh in the best spirit of a European medieval cathedral, and is among the finest Gothic Revival buildings in the country. It cost £235,000 to build, a remarkable figure for the time; there is a tragic irony in the simultaneous expenditure on the cathedral, and the massive exodus of destitute emigrants from the harbour which it overlooks. Below the cathedral at **West View** there is a picturesque terrace of 23 gabled houses with oriel windows, descending a steep slope and known as the 'Pack of Cards'.

The waterfront runs the full length of the town, with at the centre two indentations, Casement and Pearse Squares. In the former is the Town Hall (c 1850), a small break-fronted classical building, and the **Lusitania Memorial** by Jerome Connor. It is the finest public monument in the south of Ireland and shows a figure grouping with the Angel of Peace on a plinth and at the base, two sailors, (reminiscent of Rodin's *Burghers of Calais*). The carving on the surrounding seat is by Seamus Murphy.

Projecting from the Promenade is the former premises of the Royal Cork Yacht Club, the oldest in the world, founded here in 1720. It is a fine building on a massive granite terrace (Anthony Salvin, 1854) and now houses the **Sirius Centre**, devoted to maritime exhibitions and the contemporary arts. Nearby is another charming Italianate building, the offices of Cobh UDC.

The '**Queenstown Story**', can be absorbed at the railway station, now a heritage centre. It emphasises Cobh's role in 19C emigration, merchant shipping and naval history.

Immediately opposite the beach at **Haulbowline Island** are the headquarters of the Irish Navy, with steelworks, and Spike Island, a convict prison in 1847–85. Both islands have interesting naval architecture. Rocky Island is uninhabited.

Cork harbour is approached by a curved channel (c 3km long and 1.5km wide), with a lighthouse at Roche's Point. At the inner entrance are Camden and Carlisle forts, the 18C harbour defences.

Back on the mainland, continue due west from Carrigtohill and you will shortly enter the north-east outskirts of Cork, below the wooded suburbs of Tivoli and Montenotte, place-names evocative of Cork gentlemen and merchant-princes on the Grand Tour in Italy.

Cork City

Cork (*Corcaig*, a marsh), the second city of the Republic and the cultural and economic capital of the south of Ireland, is a university city with the most important public art gallery (the Crawford) outside the capital.

- **Tourist Information.**, 35 Grand Parade, ☎ 021-273251.
- **General Post Office**. Oliver Plunkett Street.
- **Festivals**. January, Film; May, Choral and Folkdance; October, Jazz.

Listings

Cafés
Crawford Gallery Cafe, Emmet Place; gourmet food in artistic surroundings (☎ 021-966777); **Triskel Arts Centre Café**, Tobin St, arty ambience, informal food (☎ 021-272022); **The Gingerbread House**, Paul St (☎ 021-276411).

Restaurants
Arbutus Lodge, Montenotte; famous restaurant in the grand manner (☎ 021-501237); **Café Paradiso**, Western Road, attractive and imaginative vegetarian cooking (☎ 021-277939); **The Ivory Tower**, 35 Princes St, uniquely imaginative food (☎ 021-274665); **The Quay Co-Op**, 24 Sullivan's Quay, excellent vegetarian with Tuscan-red walls (☎ 021-317660); **Scoosi**, Winthrop Ave, pizzas and continental cuisine (☎ 021-275077).

Pubs
The Long Valley, Winthrop St, old-times bar, the genuine article, ham sandwiches which would satisfy Cuchulainn (☎ 021-272144); **Henchy's**, St. Luke's Cross, modernised Victorian, popular among conversationalists (☎ 021-507833); **The Phoenix** (☎ 021-964275) and **The Lobby**, Union Quay (☎ 021-311113), both traditional music venues, spit and sawdust style.

Hotels
Arbutus Lodge, Montenotte (see under restaurants above), wallowing in comfort; **The Metropole**, MacCurtain St, sedate (except during the Jazz Festival) and convenient (☎ 021-508122).

Hostels
Isaac's, MacCurtain St, attractive Victorian Gothic conversion, hostellers café and fancy restaurant under one roof (☎ 021-500011); **Kinlay House**, Upper John

St, in the heart of the Shandon district, Himalayan climb to backpacker's world
(☎ 021-508966).

Bookshops

Collins Bookshop, Carey's Lane, excellent general and Irish interest (☎ 021-271346); **Lee Book Store**, Lavitt's Quay, secondhand and antiquarian, treasures to be found (☎ 021-272307).

Cork as it now appears is substantially a 19C merchant city, beautifully sited at a precipitous point of the Lee valley where the river opens out into Cork Harbour, the largest in the island. Spenser's phrase for the twin channels of the River Lee, the 'divided flood' is as apt today as in the 16C, and the city-reaches of the river make Cork among the most attractive of Ireland's urban centres in which to walk about. Above the flatland of the city centre, divided east–west by the Lee, rises the steep terrain of the 19C suburbs where the finest assemblage of church spires in Ireland emphasise the Victorian city's piety and prosperity.

The buildings of Cork have a distinctive character. The majority of the city's public buildings, quay walls and bridges are constructed in a beautiful silvery-grey local limestone and often used in dramatic contrast to brick or red and green sandstone, combined in an abstract manner. Nowhere in the Republic is there as interesting a selection of 19C architecture as in the Cork area (see also Ballincollig, Cobh, Midleton), representing important aspects of urban and social history, trade, industrial archaeology, military, penal, educational and religious institutions.

With the exception of the traditional industries of brewing and distilling, all major industry is now located outside the city. Pharmaceutical, petrochemical and steel manufacturing plants are sited around the harbour.

Famous natives of Cork were artists James Barry (1741–1806), buried in St. Paul's Cathedral, London; Robert Fagan (1745–1816); Daniel Maclise (1806–70); Patrick Hennessy (1915–81); Henry Jones Thaddeus (1859–1929); John Hogan (1800–58) sculptor; Robert Gibbings (1889–1958) author and wood-engraver; Seamus Murphy (1907–1975) sculptor; architects Thomas Ivory (1720–86); William Atkins (1812–87); Sir Thomas (1792–1871) and Kearns Deane (1803–47); the poet Francis Mahony (1804–66; pseud. Father Prout); novelists Frank O'Connor (1903–66); Sean O'Faolain (1900–91); Patricia Lynch (1898–1972); novelist Ethel Voynich, née Boole (1867–1947), famous in Russia but not in Cork; and the orientalist and pioneer in the deciphering of Egyptian hieroglyphics Edward Hincks (1792–1866).

In the late Iron Age-early medieval period the Lee valley was one of many broad stretches of marshland bisected by the delta-like arteries of the river (occupied by the area of downtown Cork today), with two principal channels. Settlement all around the harbour area is indicated by the presence of many ringforts, *fulacht fiadha* and standing stones, indicating a pastoral community. In the 6C–7C St. Finbar established a monastic settlement in the area, probably on the site now occupied by St. Fin Barre's Cathedral. A round tower stood on this site until the early 18C, but no buildings of this early foundation now survive.

Historical manuscript sources suggest that the marshland was not occupied until the Viking raiders established a trading settlement here in the 9C. In 820 and 838 they attacked the monastery of Cork and by 846 had founded a trading post in the area, but a permanent settlement was not established until 917 on an island in the marsh to the south of the main channel of the Lee. From here they initially fought with the indigenous population, but subsequently established trading links and converted to Christianity. So far none of the excavations within the area of medieval Cork has exposed the Viking occupation levels, although numbers of individual artefacts, coins, personal ornaments and gaming pieces clearly indicate a Viking presence. The importance of this settlement is in the initial establishment of Cork as a city and its emergence as a trading harbour with widespread links to neighbouring countries and the Mediterranean.

Viking hegemony came to an end with the arrival of the Anglo-Normans in the 11C. The city, already under the rule of King Dermot MacCarthy, was besieged and captured in 1177, and Henry II granted it to Milo de Cogan and Robert Fitzstephen; the Vikings were banished from Cork and their presence as a political force in local life ceased. In the topography of Cork harbour, some place names derive from the Viking Age, Dunkettle (*Dun Ketil*) on the outskirts, and Keyser's (ship-quay) Hill, close to the South Gate Bridge.

After the Norman conquest, the nucleus of an urban settlement was transformed into the medieval walled city which occupied a narrow strip of land between the north and south banks of the river delta. The city was connected to the mainland by two bridges, (in the position of the North and South Gate Bridges). The present Main Street running between them follows the line of the medieval high street (an instructive model of late medieval Cork can be seen in the Public Museum). Various medieval foundations grew up within and outside the walls, on other islands in the marsh and on the north and south banks of the river. These were followed by the growth of suburbs on the roads leading from the two city gates.

In 1491 Cork supported the claim of Perkin Warbeck to the English throne, an inept move for which the mayor, John Walters, was hanged. It was the English headquarters during the Desmond rebellion of 1590–1600. In 1649 it offered no resistance to Cromwell, but showed resistance to the Crown by holding out for five days against Marlborough and the Duke of Würtemburg in 1690.

It was not until the 17C that the city began to spread eastwards towards the harbour. In the following century the streets which now form Patrick St, Grand Parade and South Mall were actually canals, lined by quays with merchants' houses. The streets were later formed by filling in the navigable channels, thus ending the Venice-like, sea-girt aspect of the city. The marshy terrain defied the creation of a Georgian grid plan, but terraces of 18C houses were built in isolated locations (North and South Malls, Washington St).

In the 19C Cork Harbour became an important manufacturing centre and provisioning port for trans-Atlantic shipping and the British Navy; local industry and agriculture received much encouragement. Brewing, distilling, sail making, munitions, glass, silver and butter manufacture, all flourished, leading to the establishment of large industrial complexes in and around the city. This prosperity was followed by the growth of affluent residential suburbs and villas on the slopes to the north of the city and over-looking the harbour.

During the early 20C and in the aftermath of the 1916 rebellion, nationalist opposition to British rule was active in Cork and the Lord Mayor, Thomas MacCurtain, was murdered by the Royal Irish Constabulary in 1920. Further atrocities followed and as a reprisal for the ambush of British 'Black and Tan' forces in 1921, the centre of the city was burned by them. Most of the south side of Patrick St, the City Hall with its archives and Carnegie Library were destroyed. During the 1930s many of the traditional industries failed, but brewing and distilling continue as important sources of employment, on sites in continuous use since the 18C.

The Quays

St. Patrick's Bridge, spanning the north channel of the Lee—the wider of the two arms of the river—is a good point from which to begin a tour of the city, with the hills to the north rising steeply from the quays. There is a panoramic view of the city from the top of the exceptionally steep St. Patrick's Hill (gradient 1:72) A statue of Fr. Theobald Mathew, the *Apostle of Temperance*, by Foley, stands at the head of St. Patrick's Street. Lavitt's Quay, to the west of the bridge, leads into Emmet Place. The river front is dominated by the **Opera House** (Michael Scott, 1965), a cube of glass and graceless blockwork. It replaced an earlier, although unfinished, neo-classical building, destroyed by fire. Opposite, on Popes Quay, is the impressive Ionic portico of St Mary's church (Kearns Deane, 1832), the most successfully sited neo-classical building in Cork, with a fine Queen Anne brick merchant's house adjoining it.

Crawford Art Gallery

Next to the Opera House is the Crawford Art Gallery (Mon–Sat, 10.00–17.00; closed Sun). It is the finest purpose-built 19C art gallery in Ireland and incorporates the Old Custom House (1724), its elegant brick façade skilfully blended by an octagonal turret into the later building of 1884 (by William Hill). The Crawford, which developed from the Royal Cork Institution of 1807, was established as a drawing academy in 1832 and has the finest public art collection outside Dublin, its strength being in 18C–20C British and Irish schools (the art college moved to another building in 1980). The diverse collection is also strong in prints, stained glass and sculpture.

To the left of the entrance are the lofty former sculpture galleries, now used for major contemporary exhibitions, with Hogan's monumental statue of William Crawford (1843), and opposite, the bookshop. At the end of the hall is the Crawford Gallery Café, a superlative eating place and the only first-class gallery café in Ireland.

An ornate mahogany staircase rises to the (first floor) Gibson Rooms which contain the Irish 19C and 20C paintings and to the right English paintings with works from the Newlyn and St. Ives schools. On the second floor are the stained glass rooms with work by Harry Clarke, James Scanlon and Maud Cotter; another suite of rooms is used for smaller contemporary exhibitions and the 19C and 20C watercolour rooms.

ROSSLARE , DUBLIN   THE MARINA

Cork

MALLOW, LIMERICK

AIRPORT, KINSALE

BALLINCOLLIG

BLARNEY   MACROOM. KILLARNEY

Kent Station

R. Lee

Custom House

City Hall

Collins Barracks

Everyman Palace Theatre

Bus Sta.

Parnell

G.P.O.

Holy Trinity

Cork Arts Society Gallery

St. Finbarr's South

Red Abbey

St. Mary's Cathedral

Skiddy's Almshouses

St. Mary's

Opera House

Crawford Art Gallery

St. Peter & Paul's

English Market

Tourist Office

St. Ann Shandon

Firkin Crane Building

Butter Exchange

Market Craft Centre

Cork Archives Inst.

Elizabeth Fort

Triskel Arts Centre

St. Peter's

Court House

St. Fin Barre's Cath.

Mercy Hosp.

Lee Maltings (UCC)

Episcopal Palace

Honan Chapel

University College

Cricket Ground

Fitzgerald Park

Cork Public Museum

Cork Gaol

Gaol Portico

Daly's Bridge

R Lee

N

300m

300yds

Among individual Irish painters represented are exceptional examples of work by James Barry, *Portraits of Barry and Burke in the Characters of Ulysses and his Companions*; Daniel Maclise, *The Falconers*, and *Lear and Cordelia*; J.B. Yeats, *The Small Ring*, and *Off the Donegal Coast*; William Orpen, Sean Keating, William Leech, Louis Le Brocquy, Tony O'Malley and Barrie Cooke.

The English school is well represented, particularly by Frank Brangwyn, *The Vineyard*; Frank Bramley, *Domino!*; Norman Garstin, *Sunshine in the Béguinage*; George Clausen, as well as sculptures by Michael Ayrton and Jacob Epstein.

Opposite the Gallery is a small Queen Anne house. From Emmet Place, Paul St leads west through a web of narrow streets with many cafés, bookshops and restaurants. French Church St (left) is the centre of the old **Huguenot Quarter**. Further left is SS Peter and Paul (E.W. Pugin and G.C. Ashlin, 1866), a fine interior in a high Gothic Revival manner, with much good woodcarving.

From St. Patrick's St Grand Parade leads to the south channel of the Lee. On the right is Bishop Lucy Park. Inside the gates is the only visible fragment of the medieval city wall; the fountain is by John Behan. At the west end is the Cork Archives Institute (11.00–13.00, 14.00–17.00, Mon–Fri) in the deconsecrated Christ Church (Coltsman, 1726), and the Triskel Arts Centre 10.00–17.00, Mon–Sat) for the contemporary arts. The Triskel has an attractive gallery, small theatre and café. Directly opposite the Parade entrance to the park is the English Market, a covered arcade of food stalls, with fine Victorian fountain at its Lombardo-Romanesque Princes's St entrance (Sir John Benson, 1840).

At the river end of the Parade are three conjoined bow-fronted and slate-hung 18C houses, and opposite, the 'Maid of Erin' monument commemorating 19C nationalist leaders, and the World War I Cenotaph.

There is an excellent view (west) of William Burges' ecclesiastical masterpiece, St. Fin Barre's Cathedral (1862; C of I) and looking east, the Holy Trinity church (G.R. Pain, 1832) from the Nano Nagle footbridge. At the east end of the South Mall are a pair of excellent neo-classical buildings, the Provincial Bank (W.G. Murray, 1865), and Cork Savings Bank (Kearns Deane, 1837) and across the river, the City Hall (Jones and Kelly, 1935), the last classical public building to be erected in Ireland.

Turning left into Parnell Place, you reach the north channel of the Lee, with a view of the spires of St. Luke's and Holy Trinity church as well as the classical campanile of St. Patrick's church (J. and G. Pain, 1836). Holy Trinity church (G.R. Pain, 1832), approachable from the South Mall, is the most individual-looking church in the city with its openwork neo-Gothic portico and spire. Crossing Trinity footbridge with the humped-back Parliament Bridge (1806) to the right and a group of unusually steep-roofed 18C houses on George's Quay to St. Finbarr's South Chapel (1766), where Hogan's *Dead Christ* (second version, 1832) is displayed beneath the altar. The only standing remnant of Cork's medieval buildings is the crossing tower of the Augustinian Red Abbey, nearby in Red Abbey St. It was commandeered by the Duke of Marlborough during the five-day siege of 1690.

Returning to Sullivan's Quay, the **Munster Literature Centre** presents a pictorial exhibition on the writers of the region, including Elizabeth Bowen,

Sean O'Faolain, Frank O'Connor and William Trevor. A short walk past the South Gate Bridge (1713) leads to the grounds of St. Fin Barre's Cathedral, passing below the walls of the 17C star formation Elizabeth Fort(accessible from Barrack St). Opposite the churchyard in Bishop St is an exotic brick and tile Arts and Crafts Movement building by Houston and Houston (1900).

St. Fin Barre's Cathedral

William Burges' cathedral (10.00–17.00 daily)—a competition-winning design of 1861—is deceptively proportioned; the shortness of the nave comes as a shock after the grandeur of its exterior. Built in a 13C French Gothic style with three spires and elaborately carved west front, the whole building is richly ornamented with sculptural decoration. Internally, among a wealth of precious materials and ornamentation, the single most impressive feature is the Bishop's Throne. In the perimeter wall to the south is the 13C chapter house door from the nearby monastery of St. Mary of the Isle, and there are some fine late medieval sculpted heads set into a wall outside the east end of the cathedral.

In adjoining Dean St are interesting early 18C stone-fronted houses. A short distance south of the cathedral, off the Bandon Road and approached by Hartland's Avenue is the oval Cork Lough, a bird sanctuary and nature reserve. A short walk north of St. Fin Barre's via Sharman Crawford St leads to Washington St, dominated by the Ionic portico of the **Court House** (J. and G. Pain, 1835). Following Washington St west is the entrance to University College Cork.

University College Cork

was founded in 1845 as Queen's College. The most interesting parts of the large campus are the Old Quad (Kearns Deane and Benjamin Woodward (1846), a fine example of Gothick college architecture in limestone, based on Magdalen College, Oxford. Queen Victoria visited the university in 1849 and a bust of the young queen was set up on the gable end of the Aula Maxima. During the 1920s, for fear of nationalist reprisals, the statue was buried in the college grounds. It has recently been dug up and put on display. The college has an important collection of Ogham stones, and the **Honan Chapel** (☎ 021-276871) (J.F. McMullen, 1915) which, with Loughrea Cathedral, represents the finest achievement of the Celtic Revival Movement in the applied arts. The profusely ornamented interior of the small chapel has 12 windows by Harry Clarke (some of his finest work), and eight by An Túr Gloine, (Child, O'Brien and Rhind) as well as original decoration in opus sectile, mosaic, enamelwork, illumination and embroidery. An Túr Gloine, or 'Tower of Glass' was the important stained glass studio established in Dublin in 1903 which led the artist/craftsman revival of stained glass in Ireland and contributed windows to churches all over Ireland in Britain and the US. A.E.Child, C. O'Brien and Ethyl Rhind were prominent members.

The **Boole Library** (named after George Boole (1815–64) professor of mathematics at Queen's College and creator of 'Boolean algebra', the precursor of modern computer systems) has a collection of Sir Arnold Bax memorabilia (Bax, under the influence of Patrick Pearse, and with the alias 'Dermot O'Byrne' wrote nationalist ballads during the 1920s).

Adjacent to UCC in Gaol Walk is the fine Greek Revival Doric portico of the **Cork County Gaol** (G.R. and J. Pain, 1818). A memorial plaque (right) commemorates the dead of the War of Independence (1919–21).

Walk up to the north side of Western Road and cross over (right) to the Mardyke. The riverside Fitzgerald Park and **Cork Public Museum** (11.00–13.00, 14.15–17.00, Mon–Fri; 15.00–17.00, Sun; closed Sat) are on the left. The museum concentrates on Cork's social, economic and political history. A strong representation of archaeology includes a number of unique exhibits, most notably the Cape Clear Stone, an example of 'Boyne Valley Art', c 3000 BC; the Iron Age La Tène 'Cork Horns', c 200 BC; and the Garryduff Bird, a minuscule wren of the Early Christian period in gold filigree, excavated in Garranes, Co. Cork. A working model of a medieval water mill relates to important finds of early industrial technology in the harbour area. Other exhibits of importance are collections of 18C Cork silver and glass, municipal regalia, and mementoes of Cork's turbulent 20C political history.

From the west end of the Park, Daly's Bridge, a charming suspension foot-bridge of 1929, crosses the river to Sundays Well. Above this residential quarter is **Cork City Gaol** (09.30–18.00, Mar–Oct; 10.00–15.00, Nov–Feb; daily; £) recently restored and of both architectural and historical interest. Designed by Sir Thomas Deane in 1824, it represented the 'enlightened' penal ideas of the time. The history of the building and its residents is presented in a socio-historical context. Research has enabled the identification of actual inmates, their crimes, sentence, diet and punishment. An audio-visual programme complements a visit to the building. The **Radio Museum Experience**, housed in the Gaol, incorporates the actual 6CK 1927 broadcasting studio from the building and includes an important collection of radio memorabilia.

Leaving the city, follow the N22 west to the Lee fields where the north channel of the Lee again becomes visible. On the north bank is the finely composed complex of the Water Works in polychrome Lombardo-Romanesque style, by Sir

The Cork Horns, La Tène period crown, Cork Public Museum

John Benson (1888). Above, and to the west of it is the most remarkably sustained Victorian façade in Ireland, the 330m-long former Lunatic Asylum, now St. Patrick's Hospital by William Atkins, disparagingly described in the National Gazetteer of 1868 as 'a hideous structure like an overgrown cruet-stand'. On the left is County Hall (P.L. McSweeney, 1977), the only significant high-rise building in the south of Ireland, at the base of which is Oisin Kelly's humorous bronze figure group, *Men Watching* (1975) originally intended to stand below Liberty Hall in Dublin, but denied planning permission!

Shandon Steeple and Firkin Crane

Starting at Popes Quay, Cathedral St leads north to the Shandon area, in which are concentrated a number of interesting buildings. St. Anne's Shandon (09.30–17.00, Mon–Sat), Skiddy's

Almshouse, the North Cathedral, and the Firkin Crane and Buttermarket buildings are surrounded by an area of attractive small streets of 19C vernacular architecture. **St. Anne's Shandon** (1722) steeple is the most significant feature of Cork's north side; curiously the east and south faces (those facing the city) are of limestone, the others of red sandstone. The steeple was added in 1749. Shandon steeple may be climbed to the top viewing gallery and its notable peal of bells can be played. Shandon has been immortalised by Francis Mahony, writing under the name of 'Fr. Prout', in his song *The Bells of Shandon.* From the balcony is an unparalleled view of the surrounding hinterland, as well as a bird's-eye view of Skiddy's Almshouse (1718), an L-shaped building with arcaded courtyard (the south side, completed by the Greencoat School (1715), has been demolished).

St. Mary's North Cathedral (G.R. Pain, 1820; RC) is among the least successful of the city churches, having been altered a number of times and now possessing no unified style. An early (1820), set of lime-wood statues of church fathers, carved by Hogan for the Cathedral, have recently been recovered after a long absence; also on display is an arm-bone of Saint Oliver Plunkett (see Drogheda, Ch. 20).

The circular **Firkin Crane,** now a performing arts centre, opposite the portico of the former Buttermarket (1796) represents the era of Cork's importance in provisioning the trans-Atlantic shipping routes.

Church of Christ the King

From the city centre the Church of Christ the King in Turners Cross is worth a visit and within walking distance of the City Hall.

The church was designed in 1927 by Barry Byrne, Chicago architect and student of Frank Lloyd Wright (he supervised the construction of many of

Wright's most important buildings). This is the only early Modern Movement church in Ireland, its Expressionist design probably inspired by Jensen Klint's (1853–1930) Grundtvig church in Copenhagen (1913).

Built of concrete with an open elliptical plan, it anticipates church design of the post Vatican II era. At the time, however, it exerted no influence on contemporary architecture among Ireland's conservative architects and churchmen. Although shabby, with a few minor exceptions the exterior and interior of the church are unaltered. The opus-sectile crucifixion is by Hubert McGoldrick and the integral monumental sculpture on the façade by American sculptor John Storrs.

The Custom House (William Hargrave, 1818) at the seaward prow of the island (see plan), has a restrained classical façade; the royal arms have been replaced by those of Cork (Seamus Murphy).

Monumental head of Christ over the entrance, Church of Christ the King

Blackrock Castle, opposite Dunkathel, on the south bank of the river is approached east along the riverside Marina. Dramatically sited where the river opens out into the harbour, it is a 17C fort, converted to a miniature Scots Baronial folly (G.R. Pain, 1829); it is now a restaurant. On the Marina is the 'quarter-to-one gun', which was fired every day at 12.45pm between 1876–1920 to set the city's clocks by GMT; Cork is 8°30' west of Greenwich.

Cork Heritage Park (10.30–17.00, May–Sept) in the Old Pike Estate at Bessboro, Blackrock, illustrates Cork's maritime history, the burning of Cork, and other historical events.

Ballincollig Royal Gunpowder Mills, Lee Maltings

Follow the N22, 4km west is Ballincollig, formerly a garrison town, where a road to the right at the entrance to the village leads to the **Ballincollig Royal Gunpowder Mills** (10.00–18.30 daily; Apr–Sept) the most extensive surviving historic munitions complex in Europe. From 1794 until 1903 the mills produced gunpowder for the British Empire. After an intensive industrial archaeological survey, a number of the small individual buildings have been restored to working order and there is a museum with a display of artefacts of the manufacturing process, set in riverside Ballincollig Regional Park.

Return to the city or cross the Inniscarra bridge at the far end of the site and travel back on the north bank of the river, arriving at the North Mall with a terrace of early 18C houses. The **Lee Maltings** (1796–1880) viewed from across this wide stretch of river, where many swans congregate, is the most important complex of historic industrial buildings in the city. Opposite the Maltings, now a campus of UCC, is the **Mayoralty House** (Davis Ducart, 1765), with a fine staircase and plasterwork by Patrick Osborne, now incorporated into the Mercy Hospital. The public areas of the building may be visited.

Blarney Castle

9km NW of Cork (approached by forking left off the N20 onto the R617) is the village of Blarney with woollen mills, but charmingly situated in wooded country and famous for the 'Blarney Stone'.

The **Blarney stone** is actually a sill of one of the machicolations of its large 15C Castle, (09.00–19.00, Mon–Sat; 09.00–17.30 Sun, June–Aug; 09.00–18.30, May & Sept; 09.00–sunset, Mon–Sat; 09.30–sundown Sun, Oct–Apr); built by Cormac Laidhir MacCarthy, Lord of Muskerry, on a rock overlooking the river Martin. It consists of a tall tower and a stouter and later battlemented keep, and retains some Jacobean brickwork. It is apt to be crowded during the holiday season, being a popular excursion on the track beaten by organised tours.

The legend of the stone's properties is relatively modern, being unknown in the early 19C. However, the association of the name Blarney with persuasive talk possibly dates from the protracted negotiations between Queen Elizabeth I (or her Lord Deputy, Sir George Carew) and the MacCarthy Mór (the Great MacCarthy) of that time, concerning a mundane matter of land tenure. The queen herself is said to have coined the phrase, exclaiming petulantly after a succession of evasive answers from

MacCarthy, 'This is more Blarney!' The well-known lines of Fr Prout (Francis Mahoney) describing the stone are a supplementary verse to Richard Milliken's song *The Groves of Blarney*. Difficult to reach, the 'stone', when kissed, is said to endow the speaker with extraordinary powers of eloquence. (Winston Churchill kissed it in 1912!). To perform this feat properly the candidate must be hung head downwards below the battlements on the south side of the castle, which has resulted in a number of fatalities. The gabled and turreted **Blarney House** (Lanyon, 1874), with original furnishings, is also open to the public (12.30–17.00, Mon–Sat, July & Aug).

Passage West, Myrtleville Bay

The R610 circles a peninsula to the east of the city, via (7km) Passage West. It was extolled by Father Prout, and once famous for its dockyard on the south shore. Regain the main road by skirting the narrow estuary to **Monkstown**, with ruins of a fortified mansion (1639). To the southwest, at Ringaskiddy, opposite Cobh, is a martello tower. This is the current Ferryport. Turning left on reaching the R611, you enter Carrigaline on the Owenboy river and at the end of a long creek and Drake's Pool (where Sir Francis Drake reputedly took refuge with his ships when hard-pressed by a superior Spanish fleet in 1587), to (7km) **Crosshaven**, a popular resort with good bathing at Church Bay to the east, or Myrtleville Bay, southeast on the Atlantic. The R611 continues southwest over a range of low hills, and at Ballyfeard bears west to meet the R600 at Belgooly, some 6km northeast of Kinsale.

To reach the airport follow the R600 (due south), or the N71 (west) from the city. Climb over a ridge before making your descent to Fivemilebridge, there crossing the Owenbeg river to skirt the river Stick to Belgooly at the head of **Oyster Haven**. On the east side of the estuary are the ruins of Mount Long Castle (1631), built by Dr John Long, hanged for his part in the rising of 1641. At **Tracton**, 7km northeast of Belgooly, the Protestant church of 1817 stands on the site of a Cistercian abbey church, founded in 1228.

Kinsale

Kinsale (*Ceann Saile*, a head of the salt water) is a picturesque fishing harbour on the estuary of the river Bandon; its great attraction is its position, the charm of which is well appreciated from Compass Hill. (Tourist Information. Pier Road, ☎ 021-772224; seasonal). The crooked streets, slate-hung houses, bow-fronted shops and oriel windows are all characteristic of an individuality in the style and form of the town. An exceptional number of 18C houses survive, distinguishing Kinsale from many towns of similar size. Today it is a popular yachting centre.

Settlement dates from c 1200; John de Courcy was created Baron of Kingsale in 1181. The Barons Kingsale are the premier barons of Ireland and had the right of remaining with head covered in the presence of the sovereign.

Kinsale was the scene of the landing in September 1601 of Don Juan del Aguila with a Spanish force of 3814 infantry. The Spaniards, and their allies, the Earls of Tyrone and Tyrconnel, held out until January 1602 against Mountjoy and Carew, but when the time came for a united attack, the plan miscarried and only the Irish, under the leadership of Tyrone and Tyrconnel, took the field. They were routed, and their allies surrendered. It was the last decisive battle in the south of Ireland. The town subsequently became a naval station and was colonised with English settlers, remaining an important bastion of English authority to the end of the 18C.

In the Parliamentary War, Kinsale declared for Cromwell, but in 1689 it welcomed James II when he landed in an attempt to regain his crown. Defeated, he sailed from here the following year, and shortly after it was besieged and occupied by Marlborough (supporting William III of Orange). Admiral Sir William Penn was Governor of James Fort and Captain of the Foot Company in 1660–69; Lord Ligonier was Governor in 1739–42. No Irish or Catholic was allowed to live within its walls until the close of the 18C, and the first post-Reformation Catholic church was not built here until 1809.

The most interesting building is **St. Multose** (C of I), one of the small number of Irish medieval churches still in use. Erected c 1200, it retains much of its 13C cruciform plan and character despite 19C alterations. The ruined Galway Chapel (1520) adjoins the south transept, the sculptured reredos and tombs from which are in the south aisle. The north transept, and a font probably contemporary with the foundation, are notable. The massive west tower is in two stages, the lower part, also c 1200, has a substantial batter, the smaller upper stage is 18C. Some hatchments, rare in Ireland, have also been preserved. The north nave arcade and roof were rebuilt in 1835, and in 1951 a more judicious restoration took place. In the north transept, the five-light window 'Crossing the Bar' (1933) as well as two other windows are by Catherine O'Brien, and there are two fine tombs, dated 1682 and 1697.

Nearby is **Desmond Castle** (10.00–17.00, Tue–Sun, Apr–June; 09.00–18.00 daily, June–Sept; 09.00–17.00, Mon–Sat, 10.00–17.00 Sun, Sept–Oct; OPW; £) c 1500, also known as the 'French Prison', a good example of a small late 15C town castle built as a custom house by the Earl of Desmond. The Geraldine arms (bees on a quartered shield) are over the finely moulded doorcase. The asymmetrical façade has graceful ogee-headed lancet windows on the first floor, above which are the royal arms. Used as a prison during the 17C–19C, 54 captive French seamen died here in 1747 when huts in which they were incarcerated at the rear, caught fire. The building was used as an auxiliary workhouse during the famine of 1847.

The **Tholsel** or Old Court House (1706) is of exceptional interest for its attractive design; slate-hung, it has a ground floor arcade and triple curvilinear Dutch gables, with a Venetian window over the central bay of the arcade, the earliest in Ireland. The rear section of the building may date from c 1600. It now houses a small museum which contains relics of the siege of 1601 and other objects of local history.

The **Southwell Gift Houses** (1682), a group of almshouses built by Sir Robert Southwell, President of the Royal Society, are arranged around a small courtyard, with the main building flanked by two rows of smaller ones. The moulded brickwork of the porch to the central block is rare in Ireland.

On the east side of the harbour is **Charles Fort** (1677) (09.00–17.00, Mon–Sun, Apr–June; 09.00–18.00, June–Sept; 09.00–17.00, Sept–Oct daily; OPW; £) a remarkably well-preserved star-fort designed by Sir William Robinson, modelled on the French military engineering of Sebastien de Vauban. It is the largest fortress of its kind in Ireland and effectively commands the defences of the harbour, although it is quite vulnerable from adjacent high ground. A feature of the fort are projecting corner turrets overlooking the outer defences. Charles Fort was attacked in 1690 by Williamite forces under Marlborough and Würtemberg and, after a 13-day siege, the landward bastion was breached. The garrison were allowed to depart in safety for Limerick. Inside the fort are some finely detailed roofless 18C and 19C barrack buildings; these were destroyed by Republican Irregulars in 1921. On the opposite west shore are the remains of James Fort, a smaller star-fort.

On the east side, lower down, is the pretty village of **Summer Cove**, with good bathing. On the south bank is the ruin of Ringrone Castle, approached by a bridge. In 1973 an extensive field of natural gas was discovered offshore, which now supplies a large part of the island.

The road (R60) skirts the Bandon river, shortly crossing the estuary by a new bridge, to Barrel's Cross Road. The left-hand fork here leads to the Old Head of Kinsale, a promontory which, although only 80m high, commands a fine coastal view, especially of Seven Heads and Galley Head to the west. 190 were drowned off the Old Head in 1816 when the troopship *Boadicea* was wrecked. It was here that on 7 May 1915 the *Lusitania* was torpedoed by a German submarine, with the loss of 1198 lives (including Sir Hugh Lane; see Cobh). The main road continues to Ballinspittle, southwest of which is a trivallate ring-fort, occupied in the early 7C.

7 · West Cork and South Kerry

The southwest coast is an area of rugged and dramatic landscape, with finger-like promontories stretching out into the Atlantic; Mizen Head is the southernmost point of the Irish mainland. While West Cork is an area of poor land and rough rocky fields, its coastal islands and bays are among the most beautiful of the west coast. Bantry and Dunmanus Bays probe deep inland, and the largest of the offshore islands, Sherkin, Cape Clear (the only Gaeltacht in the southwest), and Bear, are inhabited and accessible by ferry.

Gougane Barra, the island hermitage of St. Finbarr, surrounded by the Sheehy Mountains, is a place of remoteness and majestic natural beauty, and **Ilnacullin** (Garinish Island) in Glengarriff Bay has a stunning tropical island garden created earlier this century; both are remarkable and among the most special places in the region. **Lough Hyne**, west of Skibbereen, is a unique marine habitat and nature reserve. The **Beara Way** (196 km) runs in a loop from Glengarriff along the Beara peninsula to Kenmare and covers the best landscape, villages and antiquities of the area.

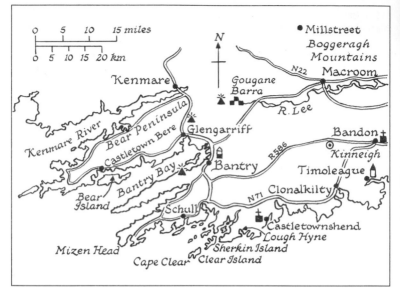

Bantry House, overlooking Bantry Bay, is one of Ireland's great 18C houses, and the only one in West Cork. The history of Bantry Bay, and the attempted invasion by French fleets in 1689 and 1796—unsuccessful on both occasions— are commemorated at the **French Armada Exhibition Centre** at Bantry House.

The **Great Famine** of the 1840s is the historic event most associated with the region, **Skibbereen** and **Schull** were at its epicentre. In the 20C, the area was heavily involved in the **War of Independence** (1919–1922), and at Crossbarry, General Michael Collins was killed in an ambush during the subsequent **Civil War** (1922).

The towns of the region, **Bandon**, **Bantry**, **Clonakilty**, **Macroom** and **Skibbereen**, are thriving market towns with good vernacular architecture. 20C modern movement architecture is represented by early suspension bridges at **Mizen Head** and **Kenmare** and the Corbusian **Bantry Library**. In the visual and performing arts, and the contemporary craft movement there is plenty of activity, the **West Cork Arts Centre** in Skibbereen, and **West Cork Music Festival** at Bantry House are its highlights. Antiquities and field monuments are abundant throughout the southwest, with outstanding monuments at **Drombeg**, **Kinneigh Round Tower**, **Coppinger's Court**, **Timoleague Friary**.

Pubs and quality restaurants located in attractive seacoast villages are a significant local feature, with **Schull** and **Ballydehob** central to a charming combination of seacoast landscape and abundant facilities.

How to get there
- **Air and Train**. As for Cork City and County.
- **Bus**. Service to region from Busaras, Cork.
- **Sea**. Sailings to Sherkin Island, Cape Clear from Baltimore.

Listings

Ahakista. Shiro Japanese Dinner House, East meets ultima Thule, small restaurant, classical Japanese food (☎ 027-67030).

Ballydehob. Annie's Restaurant (☎ 028-37292) and Levis' Bar (☎ 028-37118) opposite each other, are an unbeatable combination, the charming Levis sisters dispensing pints and pounds of butter, Annie's following up with rich and ample food; just what one need at the end of a hard day's idleness. **Coughlan's** *Dun An Oir*, friendly family-run B&B (☎ 028-37272).

Baltimore. *Chez Youen*, Breton chef, seafood (☎ 028-20136); Rolf's Hostel (☎ 028-20130).

Bantry. Bantry House, family home of the Earls of Bantry, with a wing of comfortable modernised rooms for B&B, one of the most spectacularly sited houses in the country, overlooking Bantry Bay (☎ 027-50047); from the sublime to the impecunious, the 5A Café, a vegetarian heaven, more brown rice than you knew existed; Bantry Independent Hostel (☎ 027-51050); Ballylickey Manor House, 17C luxury hotel in exotic setting (☎ 027-50071).

Castletownshend. Mary Anne's, bar and restaurant, busy and convivial (☎ 028-36146).

Clonakilty. *An Sugan*, popular pub-restaurant (☎ 023-33498); Kicki's Cabin, considered menu of attractive dishes, local and seafood (☎ 023-33384).

Durrus. Blair's Cove Restaurant, church-like interior, buffet to graze upon, excellent imaginative cooking (☎ 027-61127).

Goleen. Heron's Cove Restaurant, fine food in attractive setting (☎ 028-35225).

Kenmare. The Park Hotel, celebrated 5-star, award winning hotel in rambling Gothic building (☎ 064-41200).

Leap. Connolly's of Leap, the most interesting music pub in the region (☎ 028-33784).

Schull. Adèle's, Viennese fin-de-siècle style coffee shop, home baking, restaurant (☎ 028-28459); The Courtyard, a hidden speakeasy with concert room (☎ 028-28390); Schull Backpacker's Lodge (☎ 028-28681); The East End Hotel (☎ 028-28101).

Skibbereen. Baby Hanna's, small, basic and charming pub; Island Cottage Restaurant, Heir Island, sea-girt sea-food, salivating! (☎ 028-38102); West Cork Hotel, traditional country hotel (☎ 028-21277); Russagh Mill Hostel and Adventure Centre (☎ 028-22451).

Timoleague. Lettercollum House and Hostel, distinguished restaurant with great specialities (☎ 023-46251).

Cork to Macroom, Ballyvourney

The main road from Cork keeps to the south side of the Lee valley through **Ballincollig**, with the Royal Gunpowder Mills (see Ch. 6), southwest of which is the 14C keep of the Barretts' stronghold, and other ruins. James Thomson, the Scottish poet, taught here in 1851 where he met Charles Bradlaugh, in whose *National Reformer* Thomson's melancholy poem 'The City of Dreadful Night' was first published in 1874. To the north, on a cliff overhanging the Lee, are the remains of Carrigrohane Castle (14C–17C; restored in the 1840's by Benjamin Woodward).

Beyond **Ovens**, with several limestone caves, you pass (left) **Kilcrea Friary**. Here are the ruins of a Franciscan foundation (1465), a lofty tower, and the grave of its founder Cormac MacCarthy (d. 1494/5) and also the keep of a castle of the MacSweeneys. Also buried in the friary is Art O'Leary (d. 1773), subject of Eibhlín Dubh Ní Chonaill's (b. 1743) lament and love-poem in Irish for her murdered husband, *'Caoineadh Airt Uí Laoghaire'*, ('Lament for Art O'Leary'). It is one of the last great poems of the dying Gaelic society and among the finest 19C love poems in any language (see Irish Literature).

The road continues to skirt the river past (left), near which are two more MacSweeney strongholds.

At **Bealnablath**, 4km southwest, a monument marks the spot where in August 1922, during the Civil War, General Michael Collins, Commander-in-Chief of the Irish Free State forces, was killed in an ambush by Irregulars' of the Republican army. It has never been conclusively established whether the ambushing forces had prior information of Collins' presence. Near Templemartin, 5km southeast, at **Garranes**, is a large ring fort, 106m in diameter. Excavations have revealed the workshop of 6C bronzesmiths and enamel workers; the Garryduff Bird (Cork Public Museum) was excavated here. It has also been identified with Rath Raithleann, the birthplace of St. Finbarr. Beyond Crookstown the road (N22) bears northwest into the Lee valley with its reservoir. 3km short of Macroom, the R584 turns off to the left for Ballylickey, on Bantry Bay.

Macroom is a prosperous market town retaining some late Georgian houses, and an early 19C market-house. The castle, the demesne of which is entered by a castellated gate in the middle of the main street, dates from c 1200. Unsuccessfully defended by the Bishop of Ross against Lord Broghill, it is said to have been the birthplace of Admiral Sir William Penn (1621–70), father of the founder of Pennsylvania. The 15C castle, later enlarged and admired by Swift, was burnt in 1921.

Just south of Macroom town turn left, passing (left) on the R584 **The Gearagh**, a small delta-like region of oak, ash and birch, the only alluvial-soil forest in Europe west of the river Rhine. Access depends on water levels and the ground can be treacherous. A central causeway is the best position from which to view the abundant birdlife.

Alternative route from Cork to Macroom

An alternative road from Cork to Macroom (R618) follows the north bank of the Lee and its reservoir, after some 13km passing the ruined church of **Inniscarra**, founded by St. Senan. Beyond it is the main dam (244m long) and hydro-electric station; there is another dam and power station at **Carrigadrohid**, further west. To the northeast on the first dam is the demesne of Ardrum, while on the far bank of the reservoir stands the square keep of Inch Castle. Ascend a side valley at **Inishleena**, with another church founded by St. Senan, before reaching Dripsey, on a cliff, above which perches the ruins of dry-moated Carrignamuck Castle (15C).

Carrigadrohid is named after a ruined castle ('the rock of the bridges') built in the 16C on an islet in midstream, on a site said to have been chosen to gratify the whim of the beautiful Una O'Carroll by her lover, Diarmuid

MacCarthy. In 1650 it was besieged by Lord Broghill and taken by a stratagem. An attempt to persuade the captured Bishop of Ross to urge the
garrison to surrender was unsuccessful; on the contrary, the Bishop advised
them to hold out at all costs, for which act he was hanged on the spot. The
entrance to the castle from the bridge was built by Cromwell's men.

Pass (left) the 16C tower of **Mashanaglass Castle** before meeting the N22 just
short of Macroom.

From Macroom, the Killarney road (N22) ascends the Sullane valley, passing
(right) **Carrigaphuca Castle**, a ruined MacCarthy tower, the haunt of a malicious elf (Carraig-a-phuca, the rock of the faries). You now cross into the principal *Gaeltacht* area of Munster.

Ballyvourney, with a number of early Christian remains, a Sheila-na-gig,
and three Ogham stones, is overlooked to the north by Mullaghanish (648m),
the east summit of the Derrynasaggart Mountains, which the road shortly
crosses at its summit level of 291m, entering Co. Kerry.

The descent provides a good view of The Paps (to the right) and of Crohane
(657m; left). At Poulgorm Bridge, where you cross the Clydagh, take the road to
the left (R569) which leads down via **Kilgarvan** to Kenmare, some 27km
southwest. Continuing on the N22 you soon enter the valley of the Flesk, and
descend alongside the stream to Killarney.

From Macroom cross Toon Bridge, to meet the river Lee again at Inchigeelagh,
with the commanding tower of Carrynacurra or Castle Masters to the left, a
former O'Leary stronghold. The village is frequented by anglers on **Lough
Allua**, a winding extension of the Lee, the north bank of which you now skirt,
before crossing and climbing south.

From Lough Aulla descend the lonely valley of the Owvane towards Bantry,
later passing (right) Carriganass Castle, an O'Sullivan stronghold. At Ballylickey
you reach the head of Bantry Bay (spectacular views). Turn south for (5km)
Bantry, or north for Glengarriff.

Bandon to Dunmanway

Follow the N71 southwest from Cork, at the summit of the first ascent passing
(right) the ruins of **Ballymacadane Abbey**, an Augustinian house founded c
1450. To the left as you bear west in the next valley is **Ballyhassig**, scene of a
desperate fight between Florence MacCarthy and the English in 1600. You skirt
and soon cross the Owenboy river. **Inishannon**, established as a Huguenot
weaving community in the 18C and once a fortified town, stands at the upper
limit of navigation of the Bandon river, it has good 18C houses on the main
street and fine churches, one of 1828 (RC) by G. & J. Pain, and the other of 1856
(C of I) by Welland. The ruined castle of Poulnalong, built by the Roches, lies on
the east bank, on the road to Kinsale.

Crossing to its south bank, briefly bear west, passing on its far bank the ruins
of **Dundaniel** and Kilbeg castles, before entering **Bandon**.

A bridge was established in Bandon by 1594, and by 1611 a private enterprise settlement developed as part of the plantation of Munster. The land
was purchased by Richard Boyle, Earl of Cork, the largest landholder in
Munster, who walled the town c 1620. During the Jacobite rebellion of

1689 the walls were seriously damaged and possibly never fully restored. Although Boyle wished to establish an entirely Protestant town and Cromwell described it in 1649 as 'a fine sweet town and an entire English plantation without any admixture of Irish', a census of 1659 indicated that the population was one-third Irish. Boyle's ambitious plans for the plantation scheme in Bandon mirror those of Derry. However, its defences were less well built and only partially survive. The ownership of Bandon passed by marriage to the dukes of Devonshire in 1753, who contributed to the construction of most of its public buildings.

The town spans the Bandon river, with a main street on either bank, a result of its beginnings as two separate settlements in the 16C. On the North Main St is the deconsecrated **Christ Church** (1610), the first post-Reformation church built in Ireland. The town wall runs around the churchyard. Slightly beyond this is the Town Hall, a small Palladian building (Robert Brash, 1862), and the Court House (1802). The street widens here into a broad green around the interesting 15-sided **Shambles**, a meat market of 1815. The 'Maid of Erin' monument (removed here from south of the river), a tall and slender Corinthian column with an allegorical figure (of Erin or Hibernia), commemorates the rebellions of 1798, 1848 and 1867. Kilgoban Hill (right) has some good 18C houses. William Hazlitt (1778–1830), the essayist, spent three years of his early childhood here.

The approach from Cork on the south bank is dominated by the Georgian Methodist chapel (1821), and at the west end of the South Main St is **St. Peter's church** (C of I) by George Welland (1949), also surrounded by a portion of the town wall. It has some fine monuments, including a Baroque memorial to Judge Bernard by Peter Scheemakers (c 1731), an excellent recumbent tomb of this 2nd Earl of Bandon by Edward Richardson (1859), his coronet resting by his feet. St. Patrick's church (RC) on Bridewell St is by George Goldie (1861). Shippool Castle, a 17C tower-house, lies to the northeast.

West of Bandon the river skirts the demesne of Castle Bernard, the extensive ruins of a Gothic-Revival mansion of the Earl of Bandon, burned in 1921. Northwest of Ballineen (R588) is Kinneigh Round Tower, the only one surviving in the southwest of Ireland, is all that remains of a monastery founded by St. Mo-Cholmog. Almost 21m high, but minus its cap, it is unique in that its lowest 5.5m are hexagonal, not round. The square-headed doorway is some 3m up.

The main road (586) continues past (right) Fort Robert—residence of Feargus O'Connor (1794–1855) the Chartist—to the interesting and well-preserved ruins (left) of **Ballynacarriga Castle** (1585), (11km beyond Enniskean) a seat of the MacCarthys, on the wall of which a Sheila-na-gig may be seen. The top floor room, used as a chapel to 1818, has fine low relief stone carving (in imitation of plaster) in the window embrasures, with the figure of Catherine Cullinane, the earliest representation of an actual person in the region.

Dunmanway to the southwest, borders on some hilly country. A road runs directly west to Bantry, but the better (main) road (R586) runs parallel to it to the south via (13km) Drimoleague, 13km beyond which you reach the N71 and turn right for Bantry, with Whiddy Island to the west.

Bantry, Gougane Barra, Glengarriff

Bantry Bay, a deepwater harbour between the Beara and Dunmanas peninsulas, is a setting of great natural beauty. Free from rocks and sandbanks, and thus providing secure anchorage it has from its remoteness twice attracted invading fleets. In 1689 a French squadron was engaged here by Admiral Herbert in an indecisive battle, after which he was created Earl of Torrington. Again in December 1796, General Hoche (1768–97), with a fleet of 47 ships and 14,000 troops, and Wolfe Tone on board the *Indomitable*, attempted to enter the bay but were unable to land due to adverse weather conditions. They eventually abandoned the invasion in January 1797, and headed for home. The *Surveillante*, too badly damaged to sail, was scuttled off Whiddy Island.

Bantry is a small town at the head of Bantry Bay (*Beanntráighe,* hilly strand), with a large market square (fair-day, first Friday of month). During the **Bantry Mussel Fair** (early May) mussels from Bantry Bay are served free in all local bars and hostels. Tim Healy (1855–1931), the first governor-general of the Free State (1922–28), was born here, as was William Martin Murphy (1844–1919), newspaper baron and unrelenting opponent of the Dublin labour movement during the 1913 lockout strike.

The '**St. Brendan the Navigator**' monument (I. Stuart, 1968), in the square perpetuates a legend that the saint set off on his voyages (ultimately to America) from here, a feat replicated in 1976 by Tim Severin in a hide boat, now preserved at Cragganowen (see Chapter 9). The **County Library** (east of the square), by P.L. McSweeny (1974), around which a mill-race swirls, echoes the form of a portal dolmen; it is a fine example of 20C sculptural architecture, rare in Ireland.

Bantry House

Bantry House (1700, with a south front of 1840), stands in dramatically sited Italianate gardens just west of the town, overlooking the magnificent bay (10.00–18.00, Apr–Oct daily; £). It contains centuries of bric-a-brac, as well as items of real interest. The Library (venue for the West Cork Music Festival and other concerts), Rose Drawing Room with Aubusson tapestries (made for Marie Antoinette), Gobelin Drawing Room, and Blue Dining Room with portraits by Ramsey of George III and Queen Charlotte, are the finest rooms in the house.

This is the ancestral home of the White family, ennobled by George III, who still live in the house. Richard White (1765–1851) was ennobled in December 1796, after he alerted Government forces to the imminent French invasion by General Hoche and Wolf Tone (leaders of the invasion hoped to defeat the British Forces and establish a Republic in Ireland).

A longboat captured from Le Rèsolue remained in the house until 1944 (it was sailed in the Bantry Regatta until 1900, and is now in the National Maritime Museum, Dún Laoghaire). In the east stable-block is the French Armada Exhibition Centre (see Bantry House for opening times) a presentation of the events of 1796 with models, tableau, earls of Bantry family memorabilia and artefacts from a marine archaeological excavation at the Surveillante.

West of the town (turn left at West Lodge Hotel) stands the **Kilnaruane Pillar Stone**, a 9C early Christian pillar, embellished with figurative and interlaced panels, and including one of a boat with oarsmen—identified as St. Brendan—sailing up its slender shaft. To the north of the town is ruined Reenadisert, an early 17C house.

Offshore in Bantry Bay lies **Whiddy Island**, on which stand the battered remains of Reenabanny Castle, built by the O'Sullivans in the 15C. Regrettably the island has been disfigured by an unsightly petrol dump established, in the face of considerable criticism, by Gulf Oil in 1968, who took advantage of the depth of the bay to accommodate their giant tankers. Following the explosion of the tanker *Betelgeuse* in January 1979, when 50 people were killed, operations were suspended.

From Bantry drive north, to circle the head of the bay, crossing the Mealagh river at a charming little cascade, to reach Ballylickey (fine coastal views).

Turn right for Kealkil where the road climbs to the **Pass of Keimaneigh** (*Céim ab Fheidh*, pass of the deer) a defile between (right) Doughill Mountain and Foilastockeen, where many unusual ferns and alpine plants grow in the rock crevices.

To the left beyond the pass lies **Gougane Barra**, the source of the Lee, a small deep tarn walled in on three sides by precipices which after rain are veiled by cataracts. The oratory of St. Finbarr was founded here, on an island in the tarn. It is said that the saint drowned a hideous dragon—overlooked by St. Patrick, who banished snakes and reptiles from Ireland—in its depths (see Croagh Patrick, Ch. 12). An 18C courtyard with eight cells now stands there; a romantic re-creation of an early Christian monastery, built by the Rev. Dennis Mahony in the style of a garden folly. The summits around the lake—among them Conicar (572m)—command fine views towards Glengarriff and Bantry Bay, best reached from the mountain road between Glengarriff and Kilgarvan.

Return to the main road at Snave Bridge; the right-hand road, a winding mountain road, leads up the Coomhola valley, rising to 355m near Lough Nambrackderg, before descending to Kilgarvan.

Passing (left) N71, the demesne of Ardnagashel, veer northwest, skirting Glengarriff Harbour (views), backed by the Caha Mountains. In the bay lies Illnacullin or Garinish Island (15 hectares) (10.00–16.30, Mon–Sat, 13.00–17.00, Sun, Mar & Oct; 09.00–18.30, Mon–Sat, 13.00–19.00 Sun, Apr–June & Sept; 9.00–18.30, Mon–Sat, 11.00–19.00 Sun, July & Aug; OPW; £), accessible by boat, with its beautiful tropical gardens, landscaped in 1910–13 by Harold Peto. G.B. Shaw visited the place in 1923, and reputedly wrote part of Saint Joan here. As you enter the village, the boatmen will practically hurl themselves under your car, touting for business.

Pass (left) Glengarriff Castle before entering the village. Glengarriff has a particularly mild climate (mean annual temperature 11°C), making it a pleasant winter resort. Arbutus, fuchsia, yew and holly luxuriate here, their foliage extending down to the water's edge, and the sea, warmed by the Gulf Stream, affords excellent bathing, boating and fishing. At the back of Glengarriff is the 'rough glen' (Gleann Garbh) where trees and shrubs fill the crevices between the tumbled glaciated boulders; above rise the bare summits of the Caha Mountains, the graceful Sugarloaf prominent to the west.

The best of the nearer climbs are Cobduff (east; 376m), reached from the Bantry road, and the Sugarloaf (west; 574m), reached either from the coast road at Furkeal Bridge or by a track on the north side of Shrone Hill. To the north of the Sugarloaf, between it and the Glengarriff river, is a wilderness of tiny lakes (allegedly 365 in number), and the larger **Barley Lake**.

Just beyond the village on the left is Cromwell's Bridge, a half-ruined structure built, it is said, by order of Cromwell at an hour's notice. Exploration of the numerous creeks, further on, off the Castletownbear road, is a worthwhile trip.

Circuit of Bear Peninsula to Kenmare

There are other routes across the Bear Peninsula via the Healy Pass (55km, R574), or via Castletownbear (82km), also known as the 'Ring of Bear' (in emulation of the more promoted 'Ring of Kerry'). Driving southwest from Glengarriff, pass below the Sugarloaf to skirt Bantry Bay and the south side of the Bear Peninsula, the rocky ridge of the Caha range worn smooth by glaciation.

At (19km) Adrigole Bridge turn right for the winding ascent of the Healy Pass, begun as famine relief work and completed in 1931 under the aegis of the governor-general, Tim Healy. You enter Co. Kerry at its summit (330m), with Knockowen (659m) to the east. Below (left) lies the dark green islet-studded **Glanmore Lough**, and further north an extensive and beautiful view embracing the Kenmare river, the Iveragh Mountains, and the **MacGillycuddy's Reeks**. At Lauragh Bridge turn right into the Glantrasna valley, descending again to sea level past (left) Ormond's Island and (right) the lower of the Clonee Loughs. The upper lakes and Lough Inchiquin are approached by a lane to the right of Cloonee. Beyond this village skirt the narrowing estuary before turning left across the suspension bridge for Kenmare.

Alternatively, continue west beyond Adrigole, passing beneath the cliffs of **Hungry Hill** (684m; the highest of the Caha range) with a cascade over 200m high, most impressive after heavy rain. Bear Island (9.5km long, to the left); once strongly fortified to protect the natural harbour and former naval base of Bear Haven. **Castletown Bearhaven** is the only village of any size on the peninsula, with a sailing school and fishing port.

> **Dunboy Castle**, to the southwest (ruined), is the ancient seat of the O'Sullivan Beare (the title given to the head of the O'Sullivan clan). It is famous for its stubborn resistance, under MacGeoghegan (a subsidiary chief), to the assault of Sir George Carew, following the surrender of Del Aguila (leader of the Spanish forces) at Kinsale (1602), when MacGeoghegan tried (unsuccessfully) to blow up the fortress before it was stormed. The survivors of the garrison were hanged on the spot. Donall O'Sullivan Beare (1560–1618) with 1000 followers, soldiers, women and children, attempted to escape to Ulster in December 1602, but only 35 survived the journey. Beare went into exile in Spain and was murdered in Madrid.

Continue further west towards Dursey Island (24km from Castletownbear), along some impressive cliffs, beyond which rise the rocks called the Bull, Cow and Calf.

From Castletownbear take the road which ascends north before climbing down to **Eyeries**, passing (right) below Maulin (621m). An Ogham stone over 5m high stands to the left, on a hillock; the tallest known. Beyond, is Ballycrovane Harbour. You approach the sea again beyond a low ridge, at Ardgroom Harbour, before meeting the 'Healy Pass' road at Lauragh Bridge. To the left is the wooded demesne of Derreen, with ancient oaks, exotic tree ferns, rhododendrons. The house was burned down in 1922 and has since been rebuilt. The historian J.A. Froude wrote most of *The English in Ireland in the 18C* (1872) and his Irish historical romance, *Two Chiefs of Dunboy* (1889) here. There is an old church and a cell of St. Cinian at adjacent Kilmakillogue village.

The main road from **Glengarriff to Kenmare** is impressive, providing extensive views as it climbs out of the thickly wooded rock-strewn valley, and winds up its east side and over heather-covered hills. At the summit level (304m) you cross the watershed into Kerry through a tunnel. To the east rises Knockboy (706m). There are three more short tunnels on the descent into the Sheen valley before the road bears round to the west and crosses the Kenmare river by its suspension bridge (1934).

Kenmare, an attractive village at the head of a long inlet, was founded in 1670 by Sir William Petty (1623–87), who was responsible for the 'Down Survey'. It was planned in 1775 by the Marquess of Landsdowne and its attractive layout, pubs and shops make it a popular halting point between Cork and Kerry. It is a good base for local trips, and frequented by anglers. **Kenmare Heritage Centre** in the town centre, bases its programme on walking tours of local antiquities (10.00–18.00, Easter–Sept; £).

Along the Coast from Timoleague to Cape Clear

The R600 from Kinsale passes south of the partly restored Gothick castle of **Kilbrittain**, around a 16C MacCarthy tower. Follow the attractive tree-lined inlet to (25.5km). **Timoleague** (*Teach Molaga*, St. Molaga's House), taking its name from a church founded by a 7C disciple of St. David. This was replaced in the 14C by Franciscan **Timoleague Friary** founded by Donal Glas McCarthy, Prince of Carbery (d. 1366) and added to by Bishop Edmund de Courcy (d. 1518). The friary was famous for its Spanish wine; its splendid position on the shore of a creek made it easy to land. The best features of the ruined church are De Courcy's graceful tower, the south transept and the east and west fronts, all with lancet windows, and the south nave arcade. Two tomb recesses survive and, in the extensive ruins of the friary, three bays of a cloister. 4km southeast, facing the estuary, is **Courtmacsherry**, a village of some charm. Cross the neck of a peninsula to (10km) Clonakilty.

Clonakilty

Clonakilty (Tourist Information, Rossa St, ☎ 02333226; June–Aug) was founded by the Earl of Cork in 1614. The town, which at the east end has one of the narrowest main streets in any Irish country town, has many well-preserved 19C shopfronts. The Catholic church in the early 19C Emmet Square is a fine Gothic revival structure with a good interior (George Ashlin, 1869), adjacent to which is the **West Cork Regional Museum**, housed in a 19C school building on the Main St. There are some fine 19C industrial buildings; the former Distillery is now the West Cork Craft Centre, and another mill houses the County

Council Offices. Also worth a visit is **Lis-na-Gun Ringfort** and **Conakilty Animal Park** (at Darrara Agricultural College). The Ringfort has been restored to its original condition as a 10C farmstead, after archaeological excavations of the site.

5km west at Woodfield, is the birthplace of Michael Collins (1890–1922). He is commemorated by a monument at Sam's Cross (Seamus Murphy, 1965).

Some 9.5km southwest is **Galley Hea**d, a conspicuous promontory with a light-house and the ruined castle of Dundeady. Around the headland is **Castle Freke** (Richard Morrison, 1820) a Gothick mansion in a state of romantic decay in the former demesne of the Barons Carbery. Just beyond here you can regain the main road. At (13km) **Rosscarbery** you again meet the sea. The beautifully sited village, approached across a long causeway contains a small cathedral, rebuilt in the 19C, with a re-set 13C window and a tower of 1612. It is an aisle-less cruciform church, distinguished by the gracefulness of the west tower and 18C spire which commands the estuary. The nave is divided from the narthex which contains some interesting memorials, including a marble statue of the 6th Baron Carbery looking ridiculous in Elizabethan fancy-dress, (Guillaume Greefs,1848), and the Townsend memorial (Thomas Kirk c 1837). Ross was the site of St. Fachtna's monastery, and the fragmentary remains of his church lie to the south. To the east are remains of a commandery of the Templars. Jeremiah O'Donovan Rossa (1831–1915), the Fenian, was born here. Patrick Pearse, delivering Rossa's funeral oration at Glasnevin, declared, 'The fools, the fools, the fools—they have left us our Fenian dead'.

The main road to Skibbereen (17.5km west) now turns inland via **Leap** (pronounced to rhyme with step), picturesquely situated on a narrow ravine.

The more interesting **coast road** forks left just west of Ross Carbery, passing (left) the tall, gabled and machicolated ruin of **Coppinger's Court**, built by Sir Walter Coppinger, who surrendered his estates in 1616 to James I, and had them re-granted. The house is an impressive 17C semi-fortified mansion, the central block defended by two attached towers on the east and another in the middle of the west side. The road then reaches Glandore, a sheltered village, with a bridge crossing the harbour to **Unionhall**. Jonathan Swift either stayed here or at Castletownshend, further southwest during the summer of 1723 (after Vanessa's death), and wrote *Carberiae Rupes*, a poem describing the scenery of the district (later translated from Latin into English by William Dunkin). The O'Donovan fortress of Rahine Castle lies ruined to the south. On the west side of the next inlet is Castletownshend.

Castletownshend

Although a village, Castletownshend is remarkable for the fact that there are numerous 18C mansions on and around the Main St, the landed families living in close proximity as in an English country town, rather than in the Irish manner of building on widely separated estates. This was the scene of a naval engagement in 1602 between English and Spaniards.

Edith Somerville (1858–1949), who collaborated with her cousin Violet Martin ('Martin Ross'; 1862–1915) in writing (among other things) *Some Experiences of an Irish R.M.* (1899) and *The Real Charlotte* (1894), lived much of her life at Drishane House, at the upper end of the village, and died at Tally Ho House (she performed every local role from Master of Foxhounds to church organist). In 1936 Admiral Boyle Somerville, Edith's brother, aged 72, was murdered here by IRA gunmen.

The village houses line a steeply descending street, which divides around an Eros-like stone enclosure with sycamore trees, in the middle of the street. From here the Mall turns right, and the street descends further to the castle at the harbour where there are fine views from the cliffs. The castle is the home of the Salter-Townshend family (Charlotte was the wife of George Bernard Shaw).

St. Barrahane's church (C of I), sited on an outcrop above the castle, contains important windows by Harry Clarke, and a long-winded family history of the Townshends, inscribed on massive marble slabs. Edith Somerville and Violet Martin are buried in the churchyard.

Returning on the Skibbereen road you pass (left **Knockdrum Fort**, a stone-built cashel 29m in diameter, containing a cross-slab, souterrain and house ruins, and right, on the opposite side of the road, the 'Five Fingers', an impressive stone alignment, before entering Skibbereen, 9km north west.

Skibbereen
Skibbereen is a busy and enterprising market town, attractively situated on the Illen just above its estuary. (Tourist Office, North St, ☎ 028-21766). In North St is the former Cathedral of St. Patrick, a small pre-emancipation Greek Revival building of 1826, once cathedral to the diocese of Ross, now amalgamated with Cork. The chancel, separated by a screen from the nave, is the most impressive part of the church; there is a monument by Hogan on the nave wall (1832). Next to St. Patrick's is the **West Cork Arts Centre**, which has excellent exhibition facilities, and presents an interesting annual programme of visual and performing arts; it is a focus for the thriving artistic community of the area. The Post Office (1904) has an Art Nouveau brick façade.

The R595 skirts the south bank of the Illen, in the estuary of which are the islands of Inishbeg and Ringarogy. **Baltimore**, the ancient seat of the O'Driscolls—whose ruined 15C castle crowns a rock overlooking the pier—is a small fishing port, with a good harbour protected from the Atlantic by Sherkin Island.

Contrary to assumptions, the American city is not named after this village, but after the Earl of Baltimore's estate in Co. Longford. In 1537 Baltimore was burned by the men of Waterford in revenge for the seizure of one of their vessels in the harbour, and in 1631 it was sacked by Algerian pirates, who carried into slavery over 100 of its inhabitants. Its fishing industry was revived in 1887 by Baroness Burdett-Coutts, who founded a fishery training school.

Trips to the Islands
Regular boat ferries from the harbour serve Sherkin and Cape Clear Islands, both of which are inhabited. There is also a ferry service from Cape Clear to Schull. Both Sherkin and Cape Clear make good day trips, the terrain of the latter being more rugged and challenging.

Sherkin Island (8km long and 3km wide).
Extensive ruins of a Franciscan friary (founded by the O'Driscolls in 1460), lie by the harbour. A 16C crossing tower and domestic buildings survive, although the cloister has vanished. To the east stands one of the towers of Dunalong Castle. The **Sherkin Island Marine Station** is engaged in research into the marine habitat of the area and organises study tours of the underwater environment.

Cape Clear Island

The Cape, with its imposing south-facing cliffs, is the southernmost point of Ireland, except for Fastnet Rock, further southwest, a lonely reef with a light-house 45m high, familiar in the past to transatlantic passengers, and to yachtsmen as the turning-point of the long-distance Fastnet race.

Cape Clear island is a *Gaeltacht* (Irish-speaking community), the only one on the southwest coast. It is believed to be one of the sites of pre-Patrician Christianity, and an Early Christian cross slab can be seen on the road at the head of the pier. An important example of Boyne Valley-style passage grave art was found here in the 19C (now in Cork Public Museum), and a tumulus, its possible source, has also been identified on the island.

The island is renowned for its variety of birds. An important seabird observatory was established here in 1959 and it is now considered one of the best sites in Ireland.

On the return to Baltimore, you can fork right to pass **Lough Hyne**, a sea lough with a narrow tidal channel just wide enough to admit a boat. It is the country's most important marine nature reserve and has a combined salt water/fresh water habitat with many Mediterranean and native species. There is a marine biology station, and the island in the middle bears a ruined tower.

Skibbereen to Ballydehob, Schull, Mizen Head

On leaving Skibbereen you pass (right) **Abbeystrewery**, a small 15C chapel with a mid-19C mass grave—a result of the Great Famine—in the churchyard. Skibbereen was one of the areas worst hit during the period. Skirt the head of Roaringwater Bay, with its many islets, and (left) Ballydehob, a copper-mining centre in the 19C, at the head of the longest creek.

Ballydehob, its Main St rising up from the tidal reaches of the estuary which is crossed here by an impressive 12-arch railway viaduct of the defunct Schull and Skibbereen Light Tramway. The colourfully painted houses of this pretty village have (other than in colour) hardly changed since the 1890s. Dan O'Mahony, world heavyweight wrestling champion (1934), known as the 'Irish Whip', was born here, a pub is named in his honour. Ballydehob has for many years been associated with a community of artists and craftworkers whose studios are in the surrounding countryside.

A longer route, skirting the shores of the two peninsulas jutting out into the Atlantic, may be made from Ballydehob, following the R592 to the south west via (7km) **Schull**, a fishing harbour at the foot of Mt Gabriel (407m), a village of remarkable sophistication in the variety of its facilities. It was an important centre for Bronze Age copper mining and many of these mines, recently excavated, are situated on the slopes of Mt Gabriel. The Durrus road (north) passes through a glacially polished gap in the mountain. The ruined workhouse, (burned 1921), scene of 19C famine-relief, is (left) at the entrance to the village. Shortly beyond this (left) is Mill Cove, with a small restored water-mill. **Schull Planetarium**, the only one in the Republic, is at the Community College on Colla Road. Restaurants abound in the village and adjacent countryside.

Continuing west past (left) Spanish Cove, you reach **Crookhaven**, once well described as the 'ultima Thule' of civilisation in southern Ireland, but with a safe harbour, its entrance facing east and protected from Atlantic gales. Gugliemo Marconi (1874–1937) set up a telegraph station here in 1902, later moving it to Brow Head where you can still see the remains) and subsequently to Knightstown, Valentia. There is also a Napoleonic watch-tower (1804) on the headland.

Mizen Head lies at the extreme south west point of the mainland, passing Barley Cove, with extensive and attractive beaches and dunes. At the cliff edge, **Mizen Head Signal Fog Station** is approached by a 172ft early concrete suspension bridge (1908), spanning an impressive chasm. From 1910–70 it operated as a signal station; the last keeper left in 1993. As **Mizen Vision**, its living quarters, archives and complementary exhibitions have been opened to the public. The summit of the head (233m) commands a view of Three Castle Head, named from the ruined promontory fort of the O'Mahonys.

Now follow the south shore of Dunmanus Bay, with the lower Seefin hills on the parallel peninsula to the north passing ruined Dunmanus Castle and Dunbeacon, yet another stronghold of the O'Mahonys. At Durrus, at the head of the inlet, either turn west, or continue north to Bantry direct.

The tour of the peninsulas may be extended by following the north shore of Dunmanus Bay from Durrus to (15km) Kilcrohane. Sheep's Head at the extremity of the peninsula lies 10km beyond. From Kilcrohane turn north over the flank of Seefin (345m), the summit of which enjoys some of the finest views in the area, with a splendid panorama of the Caha Mountains on the north side of Bantry Bay. Follow the north side of the peninsula to reach Bantry.

8 · Killarney and the Ring of Kerry

County Kerry, with **Killarney** and its lakes, contains the most celebrated, and consequently the most visited scenic attractions in Ireland; the reputation of its landscape is amply justified but the town of Killarney is not of comparable interest. Among the mountain ranges are **Carrantouhill** (1038m), the highest peak in Ireland, **Macgillycuddy's Reeks**, and the **Slieve Mish Mountains** with Brandon (953m) the highest peak. Waymarked walking routes, the **Kerry Way** (Killarney-Kenmare via Glenbeigh; 214km), and the **Dingle Way** (from Tralee around the Dingle peninsula; 153km), explore the best of the region, the Kerry Way allows the traveller to experience all the joys of the region's stunning landscape, but away from the crowds. The peninsulas of Dingle and Iveragh—the latter also known as the **Ring of Kerry**—are particularly worth visiting for their rugged landscape, antiquities and attractive villages.

The islands of the region, the **Blaskets**, **Valentia** and the **Skelligs** are of considerable interest. The Great Skellig is celebrated as the site of the most remarkable early Christian monastic site in the country. **Staigue Fort**, **Ardfert** and **Gallarus** are other important sites, and Derrynane is the family home of Daniel O'Connell, 'the Liberator'. Museums include the **Kerry County Museum**, Tralee and there are heritage centres at Dunquin and Valentia.

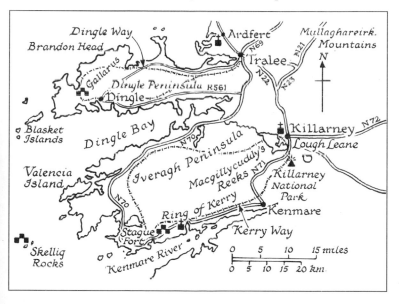

How to get there

■ **Train**. Tralee, Farranfore and Killarney are connected via Mallow to Cork, Dublin and Rosslare.

■ **Air**. Farranfore Airport, Tralee (internal flights only).

■ **Sea**. Ferry to the Skelligs, Blasket Islands.

Listings
Annascaul. Lios Dana Natural Living Centre, holistic accommodation (☎ 066-58189).

Cahirciveen. The Old Schoolhouse, Fine sea-food in relaxed surroundings (☎ 066-2426); Ocean View Farmhouse, B&B.

Dingle. *An Cafe Liteartha*, exceptional cafe-bookshop (☎ 066-51388); Doyle's, seafood bar-restaurant with accommodation (☎ 066-51174); *An Droichead Beag*, music pub (☎ 066-51723); Ballintaggart Hostel and Equestrian Centre (☎ 066-51454); Dick Mack's, atmospheric pub (☎ 066-51960).

Glenbeigh. Caragh Lodge, Caragh Lake, small Victorian hotel-restaurant in magical landscape (☎ 066-69115).

Killarney. Carriglea House, B&B (☎ 064-31116); Sugan Kitchen Hostel (☎ 064-33104); The Strawberry Tree, bar-restaurant, free-range food (☎ 064-32688); Gaby's, sea-food restaurant, sophisticated cuisine (☎ 064-32519).

Tralee. Larkin's Restaurant, excellent and informal (☎ 066-211300).

Waterville. Butler Arms Hotel, sportsman's Grade A hotel (☎ 066-74144).

Valencia Island. Lavelle's, B&B (☎ 066-76124).

The Ring of Kerry: Sneem, Derrynane House, Valencia, the Skelligs, Castlemaine

The fine scenic road around the Iveragh Peninsula is apt to be overcrowded at the height of the tourist season, but is nevertheless well worth following.

Immediately north of Kenmare turn left onto the N70, skirting the thickly wooded north bank of the estuary, with only intermittent glimpses of the water, passing (right) Dunkerron Castle (1596) near an old keep of the O'Sullivan Mór, and, further on, the demesne of Dromore Castle, before reaching **Blackwater Bridge**. From here a minor road climbs up through the beautiful and densely wooded Blackwater valley to the **Ballaghbeama Gap** (259m).

The main road, skirting the flank of Knocknagullion (412m) and passing Ross Island, shortly enters Parknasilla, a small resort established in the former demesne of Dr Charles Graves (1812–99), Bishop of Limerick. The wooded grounds of the main hotel are intersected by a labyrinth of salt-water channels; the bathing is good both in the sheltered waters here and from the open strand beyond. The original 'Fr O'Flynn' in the song of Alfred Percival Graves (1846–1931, son of Charles Graves and grandfather of the poet Robert Graves) was the local priest of this parish (Fr Michael Walsh).

To the south lies **Rossdohan Island**, whose sandy coves are a haunt of the Atlantic seal.

Sneem

At the head of the estuary lies Sneem, a charming village lying below an amphitheatre of mountains, with Mullaghanattin (772m) to the northeast, and the peak of Coomcallee to the west. The village is ranged around two opposing triangular greens, with the small and attractive Protestant church on the eastern green. South of the bridge are intriguing stone *faux-naïf* sculpture by James Scanlon (1990).

Descend towards the sea and enter Castlecove. A narrow lane (right) beyond the church climbs to **Staigue Fort**, one of the most perfect examples of a Iron

Age stone fortress in Ireland. It is a circular dry-stone wall 34.5m in diameter, and originally 5.5m high, varying in thickness from 4m to 1.5m, the only entrance to which is on the south side. Within the walls are two small chambers; a series of steps in the walls ascend to a defensive platform providing splendid seaward views.

Further along the coast lies Derrynane, with an Ogham stone found below the waterline and re-erected here.

Derrynane House

Derrynane House (09.00–18.00, Mon–Sat, 11.00–19.00, Sun, May–Sept; 13.00–17.00, Tue–Sun, Apr–Oct; 13.00–17.00, Sat & Sun, Nov–Mar; OPW) dating back to c 1702, was long the residence of 'the Liberator', Daniel O'Connell (1775–1847), and contains some of his personal possessions. O'Connell was the first Catholic to take a seat in Westminster and was responsible for introducing the Emancipation Act of 1829 which removed legal restrictions against Catholics and Dissenters. Among the portraits is one of Eibhlín Dubh Ní Chonaill, author of the *Lament for Art O'Leary* (see Kilcraea). The demesne is part of Derrynane National Park.

On offshore **Abbey Island**, reached dryshod at low tide, are the battered ruins of a small abbey founded in the 6C by St. Finan Cam; it commands a good view of Deenish and the Scariff Islands to the west, and of Dursey Island to the south.

You shortly climb north over the Coomakesta Pass (208m), with a retrospective view of the Slieve Miskish range south of the Kenmare River, and west— very briefly—of the Skelligs. The road now winds downhill round the mountain backbone of the Iveragh Peninsula, passing a stone circle, **Eightercua Stone Alignment**, the ruined church of Templenakilla, before entering Waterville, a small resort between Lough Currane and Ballinskelligs Bay.

The lough (c 27km in circumference) provides good fishing, while further up the valley of the Cummeragh river are several mountain tarns abounding in sea-trout and brown trout. **Church Island**, in Lough Currane, has a ruined house (6C) and church (12C) of St. Finan Cam; the former has an intriguing design being almost circular without and rectangular within; the latter is a good but defaced example of Irish Romanesque.

In the wide valley of the Inny to the north, a rough road ascends northeast to Bealalaw Bridge, but it is very narrow and winding when crossing the Ballaghisheen Pass (304m).

Pass through the Inny valley circling the bay to Ballinskelligs, a sheltered village on a fine strand, with remains of an abbey practically eroded by the sea, and a castle. In the nearby village of Dun Geagan, the **Cill Rialaig Centre**, an interesting complex of workshops and gallery is devoted to the revival of craftsmanship and display of fine art and craft in glass, wood and ceramics. **Cill Rialaig** itself, on Bolus Head, is a deserted pre-Famine village which is being restored as an international centre for the visual arts and literature.

To the southwest rise Bolus Hill (410m) and Bolus Head, which you leave on your left as you bear northwest. Towards St. Finan's Bay a lane to the right leads to **St. Buonia's Chapel**, a very primitive oratory, with a well, several cells and two standing-stones. Following the line of the bay you shortly zig-zag uphill, passing the small Romanesque ruin of St. Finan's Chapel (12C), with views out to sea towards Puffin Island, and the Skelligs. You can regain the main road 11km to the east, or alternatively cross the bridge to Valentia Island and take the ferry from Knightstown to Reenard.

Valentia Island

Valentia Island—also known as Valencia—(*Daibhre*, the oak-wood, or *Béale Inse*) with its dramatic cliffs at Bray Head, is separated from the mainland by a tortuous sound with narrow entrances. It is 11km long and 3km broad, and was once famous for its slate (no longer quarried). The original Atlantic cable was finally laid by the cable ship *The Great Eastern*, from here to Trinity Bay, Newfoundland, after several unsuccessful attempts to lay it between 1857 and 1865 (the first message was finally sent bt cable later that year).

A road on the north side of the island skirts **Glanleam**, with its subtropical gardens and enormous fuchsias. Offshore is the smaller island of **Beginish** with the sheer cliffs of Douglas Head. Geokaun, the highest point on the island, (268m), ending in the Fogher Cliff, provides a good view of the Dingle mountains and the Blaskets.

The Skelligs

In calm weather boat trips to the Skelligs and the Blaskets are available from Knightstown, Portmagee and Reenard (takes half-an-hour). Boats may also be hired for deep-sea fishing, etc. There are some interesting early Christian remains on both Beginish and adjacent Church Island.

If the weather is too bad to take a boat to the Skelligs, the bunker-like **Skellig Heritage Centre** (10.00–18.30 daily, Apr–Sept; 09.30–18.00 daily, Jun–Aug; £) opposite the pretty fishing village of Portmagee, provides information on the flora, fauna, and history of the Great and Little Skelligs.

'The Priests' Stone', The Skellig Michael; early-Christian cross slab with Little Skellig in the distance

The boat to the Skelligs passes Lemon Rock and the higher **Little Skellig**, the haunt of some 18,000 gannets. **Great Skellig** or **Skellig Michael** (with its two lighthouses) is a huge double peak of rock (186m and 217m high). It is among the most remarkable historic sites in Ireland, and the utter improbability of its location distinguishes it as the most daring and inspiringly sited of all the early Christian settlements.

Perched on the edge of a dizzy precipice and approached by a flight of over 500 steps, is the monastery of *Sceilg Mhichíl* (partly restored), possibly founded by St. Finan in the 7C. It consists of a group of cells, two oratories—all of dry rubble—and two early crosses, together with the ruins of a medieval church. All are enclosed by an unmortared wall of perfect construction. For many years a visit to the Skelligs was a penitent's pilgrimage; after visiting the ruins, it was required to make the tortuous ascent to the summit. Although considerably more inaccessible than the associated Mont St.-Michel in Brittany, it was raided by Vikings in 823, and its monks are said to have eventually emigrated to Ballinskelligs on the south side of the Iveragh peninsula in the 12C.

On the mainland near Valencia Island is **Cahirciveen**, the birthplace of Daniel O'Connell (1775–1847) 'the Liberator' (the house is now an ivyed ruin, east of the town to the left of a bridge on the bank of the Carhan river). On the opposite side of the narrow estuary (about 3km) is **Leacanabuaile Fort** (accessible only from the east) and one (of three) beehive huts occupied in the 9C–10C.

Pass through the wide valley between the isolated hill of Knocknadobar (689m) and a range to the east—the highest peak of which is Coomacarrea (772m)—regaining the sea at **Dingle Bay** almost closed by two ridges of dunes behind sandy strands. Go round Drung Hill and follow the coast road, with extensive views towards the Dingle mountains, and the Blaskets beyond. The glen of the Behy, enclosed to the south by mountains called the Glenbeigh horseshoe, surrounds three lakes—**Coomnacronia**, **Coomaglaslaw**, and **Coomasaharn**—the last and southernmost lying in a gloomy cirque at the foot of Coomacarrea.

Passing Wynne's Folly (1867, right), you reach the village of Glenbeigh, a small resort with excellent fishing and noted for its seafood, before crossing the Caragh. The **Kerry Bog Village Museum** (08.30–19.00 daily, Mar–Nov; f.) explores rural domestic life c 1800 in a collection of six dwellings.

A road to the right skirts **Lough Caragh**, a long sickle-shaped lake fringed with woods below steep hills, before opening out into a wider valley around Glencar; it continues south to Bealalaw Bridge.

The main road continues northwest across dull bogland to **Killorglin**, a salmon-fishing centre, with 'Puck Fair' in mid-August, during which a goat is raised on a platform in the town and crowned with garlands. The fair is nominally for goats, but in fact caters for all kinds of livestock. There are good views towards MacGillycuddy's Reeks. Some 5km southeast of Killorglin, at **Kilcoolaght East**, are six Ogham stones (some broken; a seventh has been stolen!).

From Killorglin to Castlemaine the road passes the ruins of Killagh Priory, (known also as the 'White Church'), an Augustinian priory founded in the reign of King John. Beyond Milltown, cross the Maine river and enter **Castlemaine** by a medieval bridge. The town was once defended by its castle; hence its name. It is now a derelict port, ruined by the silting up of its estuary and river.

From Killorglin the R582 leads to Killarney, passing the fine ruin of the 16C Ballymalis Castle, (near the right bank of the river Laune), with an increasingly closer view of the Reeks, dominated by **Carrantuohill** (1038m), Ireland's highest peak.

Killarney, Muckross Abbey, the Lakes of Killarney

Killarney

Killarney (*Cill Airne*, the church of the sloe). (Tourist Information, Town Hall, ☎ 064-31633) owes its justifiable reputation to the beauty of its surroundings. The town stands in the valley of the Flesk on the side of Lough Leane, the lowest of the three lakes. The **Cathedral of the Assumption**, an elaborate Gothic-Revival building (1842–55), and among the best works of A.W.N. Pugin, is the most significant building in the town. In the early 1970s, at the cost of

£278,000, it was 'restored', and adapted to the modern liturgical practice. The plasterwork was unfortunately removed to expose the natural stone; nonetheless its interior remains impressive. St. Finian's Hospital (built as the lunatic asylum) is by Benjamin Woodward (1848). The traditional local industry of lace making has been replaced by the wider net of tourism; Killarney is the single most visited tourist attraction in Ireland and in high summer its streets become impassable.

Its climate is mild, its vegetation rich, and for the energetic (and the less agile) there are innumerable walks and climbs in the adjacent mountains. The neighbouring loughs and rivers are delightful, especially for anglers, and have been praised by travellers in search of the sublime and beautiful since the mid-18C, Richard Pococke, Sir Walter Scott, Maria Edgeworth, Tennyson and Thackeray among them. Sir Julius Benedict's opera *Lily of Killarney* was first performed in 1862 and Tennyson's poem *Blow, Bugle, Blow*, was inspired by his visit here:

> The splendour falls on castle walls
> And snowy summits old in story:
> The long light shakes across the lakes,
> And the wild cataract leaps in glory.
> Blow, bugle, blow, set thy wild echoes flying,
> Blow, bugle; answer, echoes, dying, dying, dying.

Nineteenth century visitors to Killarney were often accompanied by musicians who demonstrated the quality of the acoustics by sounding their trumpets in the mountains or on the lakes.

Most of the more interesting trips are some distance from the town, and may be reached by car, bicycle, on foot or on the local horse-drawn sight-seeing 'jaunting cars', with lateral back-to-back seating; the routes they follow are the outcome of generations of experience. Jaunting cars charge a minimum per person, or per car for, say, two and a half hours. The **Tourist Office** (at the south end of the main street), has all the details for day trips to the Gap of Dunloe by jaunting car, or pony and trap returning by boat through the lakes. Cars and boats may also be hired at Ross Castle.

Opposite the cathedral is the demesne of Killarney (or Kenmare) House, the former residence of the earls of Kenmare, accidentally destroyed by fire in 1913. A new house was built on the site in 1956, and another further west in 1974.

Facing the Franciscan church (1860) in College St is a memorial by Seámus Murphy to four Kerry poets of the 17C–18Cs: Pierce Ferriter (d. 1653), Geoffrey O'Donoghue (d. 1677), Aodhagan O'Rahilly (d. 1728) and Eoghan Ruadh O'Sullivan (d. 1784). It is, alas, quite inferior to the original commissioned monument by Jerome Connor (1932) which was rejected by the Kerry committee because it lacked religious symbolism (a late casting of the monument is in Merrion Square, Dublin).

At Scotts Hotel Gardens is the **Museum of Irish Transport** (10.00–17.00 daily, all year; £) with a fine collection of veteran and vintage cars, motorcycles, bicycles and transport-related exhibits, including a 1930s working garage.

The most obvious natural feature in the immediate vicinity of the town is **Lough Leane** the largest of the Lakes of Killarney, at approximately 2000 hectares in extent and 8km long by 3km wide. Also known as the Lower Lake, it is divided into roughly equal parts by a wooded peninsula known as Ross Island (see below). There are over 30 small islands in the lake, of which the largest is **Innisfallen**, formerly covered by trees, particularly ash and holly. Perhaps the best general view of the lake may be had from Aghadoe.

Close to the landing-place on Innisfallen are the ruins of an **abbey**, founded in the 7C by St. Finan Lobhar (the Leper), famous for the *Annals of Innisfallen*, an historical compilation of the 13C, the only copy of which is now in the Bodleian Library, Oxford. The abbey church is of no architectural beauty, but the smaller church to the north, has a good Romanesque west door.

A number of the islets between here and the landing at Ross Castle are associated in name with O'Donoghue, a chieftain who, it is claimed, holds eternal court beneath the water, and—with luck—may be seen emerging every year just before sunrise on May Day.

Lake Cruises. From Ross Castle on Lough Lean, the M.V. 'Pride of the Lakes', sails at 11.00/12.30/14.30/16.00/17.15, subject to weather conditions (£). East of Ross Island, on the shore south of the town, is Muckross Abbey.

Muckross Abbey

Muckross Abbey is set in **Killarney National Park**, (10,000 hectares), also known as the Bourn-Vincent Memorial Park, after its donors. The Franciscan foundation of Muckross Abbey (1340), was refounded by Donal MacCarthy in c 1440, and most of the present buildings belong to this period. Suppressed by Henry VIII, it was revived for a while in 1626 only to be ruined by General Ludlow in 1652. Its best features are the strong square tower and its east window, but it is principally interesting as the burial-place for many generations of four notable Kerry families: the MacCarthys, MacGillycuddys, O'Donoghues and O'Sullivans; the modern tomb in the centre of the choir commemorates MacCarthy Mór, created Earl of Clancarty by Elizabeth I in 1565.

On the north side are the cloisters, a vaulted quadrangle, the arches of which are round-headed on the south and west sides and pointed on the other two. On the sill of the central arch on the north is a sundial; at the corners, staircases ascend to the domestic apartments. The cloister surrounds a large yew tree.

From the abbey you can cross part of the gardens with their fine rhododendrons to **Muckross House** (1843), (09.00–17.30, Nov–Mar; 09.00–18.00, Apr–June; 09.00–19.00, July & Aug; 09.00–18.00, Sept & Oct; OPW; £), and descend to the peninsula between the Lower and **Middle Lake** (or **Muckross Lake**, 275 hectares) to the south. The mansion was built for Henry Arthur Herbert, a local landowner, by William Burn, with rooms furnished in period style and a collection of family portraits; it also contains a folk museum dealing with local life and crafts. **Muckross Traditional Farm** preserves the farming traditions of the area.

To the west rises Sheehy Mountain (557m); to the south beyond the Middle Lake is Torc Mountain (538m). Continuing west you pass tiny **Doo Lough**. Cross the thickly wooded **Dinis Island**, and regain the mainland at the so-called 'Meeting of the Waters' (where the river from the Upper lake enters the Lower lake).

To visit the **Torc Waterfall**—a cascade 18m high between wooded banks—take the ascending path beside a bridge across the Owengarriff. There is a beautiful view from the summit.

Professor Rudolf Erich Raspe (1737–94), the creator of 'Baron Münchhausen' (1785) died in the next hamlet of Muckross. He masqueraded to the end, being employed as a mining expert and investigating local copper lodes on behalf of the Herbert family.

Lakes of Killarney

The **Upper Lake** (175 hectares), is the smallest but perhaps the most beautiful of the three, on the shores of which the Kerry arbutus (*Arbutus unedo*) flourishes (best seen in October and November when its red fruit is at its prime). The lake may be approached by the N71, narrow in places, ascending to the south of the 'Meeting of the Waters' roughly parallel to the Long Range. The Upper lake's banks are likewise covered with arbutus and royal fern, while beyond rises the Eagle's Nest (335m), where the golden eagle was once a common sight.

Further west is Purple Mountain (835m), beyond which rear the **MacGillycuddy's Reeks** a huge mass of sandstone and the highest mountain group in Ireland, with Carrantuohill rising to 1038m (the last wolf in Ireland was killed here in 1700). This was the haunt of the eponymous clan, the head of which still holds the title of The MacGillycuddy of the Reeks (pronounced Mác-licuddy). Mangerton (838m), is to the left while further southwest the N71 climbs to Moll's Gap (263m), some 9km northwest of Kenmare.

Among **walks from Killarney** the following four are recommended, although expeditions may be made in almost any direction south of the town, preferably in clear weather.

Walk One (3–4 hours; strenous)

Much of the route to the **Gap of Dunloe** is also followed by organised tours or routine excursions. Leave Killarney by the Tralee road (N22) bearing north, and ascend a steep lane to the left as the main road turns right. The first turning on the left leads up along a ridge overlooking the north bank of the Lower Lake to **Aghadoe** (120m; *Achadh-da-eó*, the field of the two yews). A church built here in the 7C by St. Finan the Leper soon after became the seat of a bishopric (now united with Limerick and Ardfert). The present church perhaps retains part of the original building in the nave, which has a fine but damaged west door; the choir, an addition of the 13C, has an Ogham stone built into its south wall. To the northwest is the stump of a Round Tower. Below the graveyard is a round castle, with walls over 2m thick, perhaps once part of the episcopal residence, and possibly as early as the 9C. The view from here towards Lough Leane is very fine; above its glistening surface rises a range of mountains from the Reeks to the southwest to Mangerton on the southeast.

Continue west and make your way downhill to the main road from Killarney (R562), there turning right before forking left parallel to the lakeside, and crossing the Laune. On the right is Dunloe Castle (1215, now an hotel), with attractive gardens. In the grounds is a group of Ogham stones, mostly discovered in an underground chamber (since destroyed). Now turn south towards the savage defile known as the Gap of Dunloe, passing **Kate Kearney's Cottage**, where a bar replaces the cabin of an early 19C beauty who dispensed 'mountain dew', or poteen—otherwise known as illicitly distilled whiskey—to the thirsty tourist. Ponies or traps may be hired here.

From here the track shortly crosses the stream and skirts **Black Lake**, **Cush Valley Lake** and **Auger Lake**, beyond which the pass narrows between the steep slopes of Purple Mountain (835m; left) and the MacGillycuddy's Reeks. The landscape has inspired many folktales and legends; the boulder-strewn gorge is fabled to have been cleft by Finn MacCoul with a blow of his sword, while the absence of fish in an adjacent tarn is said to be due to the fact that St. Patrick drowned the last snake in Ireland there.

On the right is the so-called **Black Valley** or **Cummeenduff Glen** (*Cum ui Dhuibh*, O'Duff's Valley), which penetrates the heart of the Reeks and ends in a series of tarns, beyond which a fine walk ascends to **Curraghmore Lough**, below Carrantuohill. Purple Mountain, on the left of the road, is an easy but boggy climb from the Head of the Gap, rewarded by a fine view.

The road zig-zags down into the Gearhameen valley, where you turn left and, keeping to the left, follow the north bank of a stream. After 1.5km cross to skirt the south shore of the Upper Lake, gaining the N71 c 13km southwest of Killarney, not far north of Galway's Bridge, and adjacent to the cascade of **Derrycunnihy** ('oak-wood of the rabbits'). Follow the N71 back to Killarney.

Walk Two (1 hour; easy)

A much shorter excursion is that to **Ross Castle** (14C)(11.00–18.00, Easter & April; 10.00–18.00, May; 09.00–18.30, Jun–Aug; 10.00–18.00, Sept; open daily; 10.00–17.00, Tue–Sun, Oct; £) 3km southwest of Killarney, at the neck of the peninsula of Ross Island. The graceful castle keep (restored) is surrounded by outworks with cylindrical corner-towers; a spiral stair of 94 steps ascends to the top. This principal residence of O'Donoghue Mór, the chief of one of the three divisions of his sept or clan, was the last place in Munster to be taken by the Cromwellian forces (1652), being gallantly defended by Lord Muskerry. General Ludlow, reminded of the tradition that 'Ross Castle could not be taken until a ship should swim upon the lake', had ships bearing ordnance sent up the Laune from Castlemaine. The garrison promptly surrendered. Shelley spent a few weeks in a cottage here with Harriet in 1813.

Walk Three (2 hours; strenuous)

Follow the N22 southeast towards Lough Guilane, passing a stone circle at Lissivigeen (3km), known as **The Seven Sisters**. Further on cross the railway and the river Flesk, and the ruins of **Killaha Castle**. Shortly beyond this, at Glenfesk chapel turn right to skirt the north shore of the bleak-looking **Lough Guitane**, famous for its trout. You shortly descend to meet the N71 at Muckross village, and turn right to regain Killarney.

Walk 4 (3–4 hours; stiff climb)

The Ascent of Mangerton, which dominates the lakes from the south, offers magnificent views from its summit. This rounded mountain is an easy climb (838m) from Muckross. Take the Lough Guitane road from Muckross, after 1.5km ascending south by a bridlepath, which later commands a good view of the Lough on the left. After about three-quarters of the ascent you reach the crater-like hollow in which lies the tarn known as the **Devil's Punch Bowl**, the principal feeder of the Torc Waterfall and source of Killarney's water supply. On approaching the summit you pass, on the left, a large and deeper combe,

Gleann na gCapall (the Horse's Glen), at the bottom of which are three gloomy tarns: Lough Erhagh, Lough Managh and Lough Garagarry. From the summit you can see mountains and more lochs: due west are the Torc and Purple Mountains, with the Reeks beyond; further northwest, beyond Lough Leane, is the distant Slieve Mish range, above Tralee. The silver thread of the Shannon can be seen to the north; to the east are Stoompa and Crohane, with The Paps, Caherbarnagh and the distant Galty Mountains beyond. The Caha Mountains are to the south and southwest, and the hills above Kenmare, with Kenmare River on the right.

Walk 5 (for keen walkers; half a day needed)

Energetic walkers may approach Killarney by following the old track (c 30km, now part of the Kerry Way), which climbs due north from Kenmare via Windy Gap, descending to Galway's Bridge on the new road (see below). On the descent to the bridge bear right, keeping on the old road, over another high pass into the Esknamucky Glen, and along the west side of Mangerton mountain to Torc Waterfall, 7km from Killarney. E.J. Moeran (1894–1950) who composed choral and chamber music and arrangements of English folk songs, was drowned here.

From Kenmare (N71) the well-engineered road to Killarney ascends the Finnihy valley (northwest), crossing the stream at Sahaleen Bridge, with superb retrospective views. At Moll's Gap (263m), between Boughil (left; 627m) and Derrygarriff, you begin the descent. MacGillycuddy's Reeks are seen across the valley to the north, while beyond (right) Looscaunagh Lough the **Vale of Killarney** suddenly comes into view, in striking contrast to the bare uplands you have just crossed. The prospect on the left shortly beyond is one of the finest in Ireland, with the Gap of Dunloe on the left behind the Upper Lake, Muckross Lake and Lough Leane closing the vista ahead. Passing between the Long Range and Torc Mountain, you enter the woods on the lake shore.

The road leading north from Killarney via Farranfore (airport) to Tralee (N22) is of little interest apart from its retrospective views on leaving Killarney. At Farranfore the N23 diverges northeast direct to Limerick, and a minor road (R561) leads due west via Castlemaine towards the Dingle Peninsula.

Three mountain excursions (day trips)

Trip One

Skirting the north side of Lough Leane, fork left across the river Laune, as if approaching the Dunloe Gap, then bear west along the north slope of the Reeks, cross the river Gaddagh, and ascend the valley of the Cottoners river. On the left you can see the corrie of Coomloughra. An alternative ascent of Carrantuohill, (*Corrá n Tuathail*, the left-handed reaping-hook) can be made from the upper end of Lough Acoose (the usual approach is via the Gaddagh valley). It should not be attempted in bad weather, as mists are frequent. The ascent, easy at first, follows the Gaddagh to its head in a deep combe (the Hag's Glen) in which are two unattractive lakes (Lough Gouragh and Lough Callee). Some rocks on the mountainside on the right are known as the **Hag's Teeth**. A very steep climb leads up the west side of the combe to the topmost ridge, a narrow horseshoe covered with slippery grass. The view is disappointing, except for the fine silhouette of the mountains above Dingle to the north west, and the coasts of Dingle Bay and Kenmare River. **Lough Caragh** is well seen immediately below to the north west. The descent may be made into Glen Cummeenduff on the south side, and down the valley road to the Upper Lake, or west by the summit of Caher (973m) and the south ridge of Coomloughra corrie to Lough Acoose. From the lake, the Kerry Way can be followed to the N71 for Killarney.

Trip Two

A right-hand turning west of Lough Acoose leads to **Glencar Hotel**, delightfully situated among woods near the south end of Lough Caragh, and a favourite angling centre. Continuing southwest you shortly reach Bealalaw Bridge, on the Caragh. From here a mountain road climbs southwest over the Ballaghisheen Pass (304m) between Knocknacusha (left; 547m) and Knocknagapple (686m), beyond which, at Lissatinnig Bridge, the road divides, the left-hand branch descending the Inny to Waterville, and the right fork crossing a pass towards Cahirciveen. The road ascending to the left at Bealalaw Bridge is actually a very rough track, keeping left up the Bridagh Valley (the upper valley of the Caragh) and crossing a high pass into Glen Cummeenduff.

Trip Three

An alternative route south from Bealalaw Bridge (rough, but improving) turns sharp right at (6km) the entrance to the Bridagh Valley, leaving on the right the track to Cloon Lough. The road then climbs the north side of Mullaghanattin (right; 772m), and crosses the ridge at the Ballaghbeama Gap (259m), a wild and stony defile, beyond which a track on the left leads to Lough Brin. Follow the west side of the Kealduff valley to join the inland road (R568) from Sneem to Killarney at Gearha Cross. From here, descend through Derreendarragh to Blackwater Bridge, about half-way between Parknasilla and Kenmare, or alternatively turn left (for some wonderful views) to join the Kenmare-Killarney road at Moll's Gap.

Tralee is about 20km to the west of Castleisland, the road passing below Desmond's Grave, the burial place of Gerald Fitzgerald, 15th Earl of Desmond (d. 1583), murdered in his mountain refuge by the soldiers of Ormond.

Tralee and Ardfert Cathedral

Tralee

Although Tralee is the busy county town of Kerry (Tourist Information, Ash Memorial Hall, ☎ 066-21288) it is devoid of any trace of antiquity (although some Georgian houses survive in Day Place). As the headquarters of the earls of Desmond, the town suffered when the 15th earl was murdered in the mountains and the castle was awarded to Sir Edward Denn. Although retaken by the Irish in 1641, its citizens were once again driven to defend themselves against Lord Inchiquin in 1643. They set fire to the place, thus denying him his usual pleasure. The Jacobites followed their example in 1691 when the Williamite troops advanced on the town.

The Court House, by William Vitruvius Morrison, has a typical Ionic portico. The Ash Memorial Hall (1928) in the town park is built of red sandstone, unusual in this limestone country (although the ancient church of Ratass is also an exception). It contains the Kerry County Museum (10.00–18.00, daily, Jan–Oct; 12.00–17.00, Nov; 14.00–18.00, Dec; £) with an excellent archaeological collection. The Geraldine Experience presents Kerry history in an audio-visual tour with reconstructed streets. Siamsa Tire, the National Folk Theatre of Ireland, also in the Park, is home to an exciting dance-theatre company, which uses material from Irish folk culture in its work.

Tralee Steam Railway has revived the Tralee-Blennerville section of the 1891 railway (a scenic journey of 30 minutes, leaving Tralee on the hour and Blenerville on the half-hour), with Loco No5 brought back from exile in a US railway museum. Tralee Harbour, at the mouth of the little river Lee (Tralee, Tráigh Li, the strand of the Lee) is so shallow that the town was once connected by a ship-canal with Blennerville, to the southwest. A beauty contest, known as the Rose of Tralee Festival takes place in August.

12.5km due west of Tralee is **Fenit**, the birthplace of St. Brendan (483–578).

Ardfert Cathedral

The imposing ruins of a 13C Ardfert Cathedral (09.30–18.30 daily, May–Sept; OPW; £) lie 9km northeast of Tralee at Ardfert, famous as the episcopal see founded by St. Brendan (now united with Limerick and Aghadoe). Built of red and grey stone, the choir of is lighted by a good east triplet, while in a niche beside the altar is the effigy of a bishop. The west door is a good example of Irish Romanesque; the south transept and sacristy are of the 14–15C. The cathedral was finally abandoned in 1641, when the castle, to the east of it was destroyed. Adjacent are two small churches, Temple-na-Hoe (12C) and Temple-na-Griffin (late Gothic).

In the grounds of Ardfert Abbey, (described in the 18C as 'an old-fashioned place in a very bleak country'), are the ruins of a Franciscan friary, founded by Thomas Fitzmaurice in 1253, with a good choir, a south chapel of 1453, and part of a cloister and refectory.

The ruins of a 14C–15C Cistercian abbey (founded in 1154) can be seen just north of Abbeydorney.

The coast near Abbeydorney is called Banna Strand. It was here, on Good Friday 1916, that Sir Roger Casement (1864–1916) landed from a German submarine only to be arrested some hours later in the rath, called MacKenna's Fort. He was convicted of treason, having attempted to raise support for the 1916 Irish rebellion in Germany, and was hanged at Pentonville Prison on 3 August that year.

Dingle Peninsula, Slea Head, the Blaskets, Gallarus Oratory

The promontory of Dingle (or Corkaguiny) is the most northerly of the five peninsulas that extend into the Atlantic from the southwest of Ireland like the fingers of a hand, each with its ridge of mountains. The Dingle peninsula is particularly notable in that, apart from possessing the highest peak in the country after MacGillycuddy's Reeks (and some of the most magnificent coastal scenery in Munster), it contains an unequalled series of Early Christian monuments, Iron Age fortifications, and beehive huts, most of which are now in state care. Its western half is part of the *Gaeltacht*.

From Tralee, the direct road (R559) leads to **Dingle**, passing **Blennerville Windmill** (10.00–18.00 daily, Apr–Oct; £) the largest working windmill in the British Isles (a heritage centre surrounds it). Beyond is the ruined church of Annagh (to the right), with a sculptured stone in its enclosure. The Slieve Mish Mountains rise steeply from the coast.

At **Camp**, the main road starts to climb above the valley of Glengalt, known as 'the valley of the madmen'—so called from a healing spring that was alleged to cure madness—to the top of the pass. This village is a good base for the ascent of **Caherconree** (825m), the track climbing Glen Fas before bearing left to the summit. The *cathair* or fort of King Curol MacDaire that gives the peak its name stands at 625m, and is probably the highest point for a fort in Ireland. To the north on the ridge is a dolmen called 'Finn MacCoul's Table' or 'Chair'. Further to the east is the highest summit of the Slieve Mish Mountains, **Baurtregaum** (850m). The more gradual descent to Anascaul provides good views across the bay.

The coastal road then passes the little resort of Castlegregory. Here in 1580 Raleigh and Spenser were entertained in a castle by Black Hugh, son of Gregory Hoare, a local chieftain. Offshore are the **Magharee Islands**, otherwise known as the Seven Hogs; on **Illauntannig**, the largest, are the ruins of a small monastic establishment built within a cashel.

Passing beneath the double peaks of Beenoskee (825m), between which, in a crater-like hollow, lies gloomy Lough Acummeen, with the peak of Mt Brandon (251m) ahead. Bear away from the sea, climbing steeply to the **Connor Pass** (456m) for some fine views and three lakes, lying in the Owenmore valley. To the left nestles tiny Lough Doon. The rapid descent to Dingle provides extensive views of Dingle Bay and the Iveragh Peninsula beyond.

The road bears west parallel to the coast, on which stood Minard Castle, a stronghold of the Knights of Kerry, largely destroyed in 1650 by Cromwell's troops. Croaghskearda rises above, on the right. At Ballintaggart, in a circular burial ground, are nine **Ogham stones**, three of them bearing incised crosses. Some of the inscriptions, notoriously difficult to translate, may be read as 'Sual Grandson of Dochar'; 'The three sons of Mailagnos'; 'Conmac grandson of Coirpre'.

Dingle enjoys a superb situation on its almost land-locked harbour at the foot of Ballysitteragh (623m). The village still possesses a fishing-fleet and has some excellent restaurants.

Although once walled (*Daingean ui Chuis*, the fortress of O'Cush) nothing much has survived in Dingle, except the Desmond tomb of 1540 in the churchyard. However, the area is exceptionally rich in archaeological remains, a few of the more interesting and important antiquities are described in the following trips.

The R559 leading due west from Dingle passes three standing stones before reaching **Ventry** (*Fionn Trágha*, white strand), its harbour, more exposed to Atlantic gales than that of Dingle. This area is traditionally the last occupied by the unassimilated Vikings in Ireland, and legend tells of a Homeric-style battle fought here by Finn MacCoul.

Beyond, to the left, is the Iron Age cliff-edge promontory-fort of Dunbeg (approach dangerous), guarded by a massive stone rampart 4.5m to 7.5m thick, and provided with a souterrain to allow a safe exit for the defenders in case of surprise. Between Ventry and Slea Head, on the lower slopes of Mt Eagle over 400 *clochans* or 'beehive' huts have been discovered in various states of preservation, the best of which are at Fahan.

Slea Head

Slea Head (17km) commands a magnificent view of the Iveragh Peninsula to the south, with the Skelligs in the distance, and of the Great Blasket. Rounding the promontory you approach the hamlet of Coomeenoole, beyond which protrudes Dunmore Head, the westernmost point of the Irish mainland. On the summit is an Ogham stone with an unusually long commemorative inscription (obscure). A little further north is the village of **Dunquin**, where *currachs*, light but seaworthy boats of tarred canvas stretched on a frame, are still to be seen.

The Blaskets

The Blaskets (reached by boat from Dunquin or Dingle; information on boat-hire and sailings to Blaskets from Kruger Kavenagh's pub in Dunquin) are a group of rocky islands, uninhabited since 1953. Life there earlier in the century has been graphically described in Maurice O'Sullivan's *Twenty Years Agrowing* ; Peig Sayers's *Peig*; Tomás O'Crohan's *The Islandman*, and Robin Flower's *The Western Island* (all but the last-mentioned translated from the Irish).

On the **Great Blasket** stood the castle of Piaras Ferriter, the last Irish chieftain to surrender to Cromwell. His safe-conduct after his capitulation was dishonoured, and he was later hanged. The westernmost is **Tearaght Island**, with a lighthouse 83m high; and to the north is Inishtooskert, with a ruined oratory of St. Brendan. *Ionad an Bhlascaoid Mhóir* (10.00–18.00, Easter–June; 10.00–19.00, July & Aug; 10.00–18.00, Sept & Oct), the Blasket Centre at Dunquin celebrates the language, culture and writers of the Blaskets. Facilities include exhibitions, research room, bookshop and concert facilities. Audio-visual show in five languages. Guided tours available (visit takes about one-and-a-half-hours).

The road passes an attractive little cove below the north slope of Croaghmartin. Here there are fine views across to the cliff ridge of Sybil Head, The Three Sisters, and Ballydavid Head to Smerwick Harbour (from the Old Norse).

The *Corca Dhuibhne* **Regional Museum** at **Ballyferriter** has a good display on the archaeology, geology and flora of the peninsula.

The Dingle road turns south, passing by a low ridge the castle of Rahinnane before regaining Ventry.

The fate of the Fort del Oro

A lane running northwest from Ballyferriter passes the remains of the castle where Piaras Ferriter (a local chieftain) was born, and leads to Ferriter's Cove. Here, in 1579, a Spanish force landed, accompanied by Dr Nicholas Sanders, the Papal Nuncio. Crossing the isthmus, they built a fort, the Fort del Oro, to the west side of Smerwick Harbour, as a base for operations against the English forces. Although reinforced in the following year, this fortified settlement was taken by Lord Deputy Grey and the garrison was butchered, as was common practice at the time, on the orders of Macworth and (perhaps) Raleigh. Sanders escaped, but died a fugitive in 1581; Macworth was murdered by the O'Connors of Offaly. The episode has been described in Kingsley's *Westward Ho!*

An alternative road back from Ballyferriter is that continuing east, which shortly climbs the far side of the valley to a small hamlet, where it bears left. At the next crossroads, the hamlet of Ballynana,—having first visited the Oratory of Gallarus (for directions, see below)—you turn right over a ridge and drive southeast towards Dingle Harbour.

The Oratory of Gallarus

Just west of Dingle and immediately beyond Milltown turn right and shortly ascend a low pass to the hamlet of **Ballynana**. Fork left downhill along a lane. After a short distance the road widens (parking space), and a path leads across to the field in which stands the Oratory of Gallarus, one of the most perfect relics of early Irish Christianity (8C). This curious little building, resembling in part an upturned boat, is a development of the clochan or corbel-roofed style of construction, but rectangular instead of circular in plan (6.5m long, 5.5m wide and almost 5m high). The dry rubble masonry is almost perfect, except for a slight sag in the roof-line. It is entered by a low square-headed doorway with slightly inclined sides, and is lit by a small arched and deeply splayed window in the east wall. The two-holed flagstones above the door were doubtless sockets for wooden door-posts. In the churchyard is an inscribed cross.

Continuing down the lane, a right-hand turn leads to Gallarus Castle (15C), just short of which is a group of ruined beehive huts (one restored).

The hamlet of **Kilmalkedar** has an interesting 12C church, consisting of a roofless nave with a good doorway and ornamented chancel-arch; inside is the 'Alphabet Stone', on which the letters of the Irish alphabet are incised. In the churchyard is an Ogham stone, several inscribed stones. St. Brendan's House, a rude 12C structure, probably a priest's residence, is beyond a lane to the north.

Early-Christian boat-shaped oratory, Gallarus, Co. Kerry

The road now descends towards Smerwick Harbour and the village of Murreagh, where you turn right for Feohanagh, and the cliffs of Ballydavid Head (244m). The road bears northeast towards Mt Brandon and the hamlet of Ballycurrane, to the left of which is Brandon Creek, the starting-point for the steep ascent of (6km) **Brandon Head**, where the cliffs rise to 377m.

For the easy ascent of **Mount Brandon** (at 951m the second highest peak in Ireland), which rises directly from the sea, park in the hamlet of Tiduff. A broad green path leads up to the crest of the ridge, where you turn right to reach the summit, on the north and south sides of which are small **stone circles**. The superb view extends from Loop Head to the MacGillycuddy's Reeks (southeast), and south towards the Inveragh mountains beyond Dingle Bay. Immediately to the southeast is the slightly lower Brandon Peak (840m), below which nestles Lough Cruttia.

The descent of the east side, down a wild and precipitous glen towards Cloghane at the head of Brandon Bay, is very impressive but not easily found without a guide.

Descending to Tiduff, regain the road, and drive almost due south, crossing a low coll and down the Milltown valley to Dingle.

Other points of interest in the neighbourhood are **Temple Monachan** (5km northwest), where there are remains of an oratory and the well of St. Monachan, with an Ogham stone, and a 'Killeen' (or little church; a cemetery for suicides and unbaptised infants; but frequently an early Christian site); and the **Coomanare Lakes** (8km northeast). These are approached by a road ascending Connor Hill, and bearing east for just over a kilometre before reaching the summit of the pass. The number of arrow-heads found on the hillside bears out the tradition of a great battle fought here in ancient times.

Return from Dingle to Tralee, by following the R559 east towards Anascaul, just before which bear right to follow the line of Dingle Bay, with a good view ahead of the sandy 'inch' or peninsula, 4.5km long, separating and sheltering **Castlemaine Harbour** from the Atlantic. Beyond this magnificent strand is the village of Inch, with the Slieve Mish Mountains, rising on your left, and the MacGillycuddy's Reeks prominent to the southeast.

At Castlemaine you join the N70 from Tralee (16km north) to Milltown and Killorglin (9.5km southwest), and the start of the Ring of Kerry.

9 · Limerick and Clare

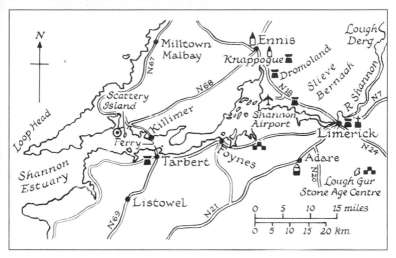

The **Shannon estuary**, dividing Counties Clare and Limerick, winds its way deep into the country, only narrowing below Limerick. Above the city, the major inland waterways and lake systems of the country begin with the broad expanses of **Lough Derg**, at the southern end of the Shannon Navigation. The lough has abundant boating facilities in the towns and villages on its shores. There are marinas at Killaloe, Dromineer, Williamstown and Portumna, and pubs and restaurants at most of the landing points around the lake. *The Shell Guide to the Shannon* by Ruth Delaney is an excellent introduction and guide to the waterway from Limerick to Lough Erne, north of Eskillen. The **Lough Derg Way** (52km) follows the beautiful eastern shore of the lake from Limerick to Dromineer.

Limerick City, at the centre of the region is of considerable historical interest, with the Anglo-Norman **St. Mary's Cathedral**, **King John's Castle** and the the **Hunt Museum** which has an important collection of medieval art.

Ennis, **Kilmallock** and **Adare** are interesting and attractive historic towns, and there are numerous sites of antiquity throughout the region; **Creggaunowen**, the **Lough Gur Stone Age Centre**, and early Christian sites on **Scattery** and **Holy Islands**.

Bunratty, **Dromoland** and **Knappogue Castles** all host medieval banquets which are an entertaining if superficial introduction to Irish music and traditions. For a more authentic and vital experience of Irish culture, visit the pubs and villages of the Clare Coast such as **Milltown Malbay** which is also home to the **Willie Clancy Summer School**, and an important centre for traditional music, as is much of County Clare.

Curragh Chase Forest Park (north of Adare) 18C **Glin Castle** and the 19C **Adare Manor** are all worth a visit as is the **Flying Boat Museum** at Foynes.

How to get there

■ **Train**. Via Limerick Junction on the Cork-Dublin line.
■ **Air**. Shannon International Airport on the Clare bank of the Shannon.
■ **Water**. Shannon Waterways.

Listings

Adare. Adare Manor, 5-star Gothic splendour (☎ 061-396566); The Wild Geese, French cuisine under enveloping eaves (☎ 061-396451).

Ballingarry. Mustard Seed, Echo Lodge, virtuoso cooking in a demure country house (☎ 069-68508).

Ballyvaughan. Gregans Castle, away-from-it-all country-house hotel, seafood restaurant (☎ 065-77005); The Tea Junction Café, glorious fresh and wholesome food (☎ 065-77174); Hyland's Hotel, a country hotel with satisfying, generous meals and friendly bar (☎ 065-77037).

Bunratty and **Knappogue Castles**. Medieval banquets, hearty tourist attraction with harpists while you swill, both (☎ 061-61788); MacCloskey's cellar restaurant at Bunratty, excellent food in old-world ambience (☎ 061-364082).

Ennis. Derrynane House, B&B (☎ 065-28464); The Cloister, first-class bar-restaurant (☎ 065-29521); Old Ground Hotel, traditional country-town hostelry (☎ 065-28127); Abbey Tourist Hostel (☎ 065-22620).

Limerick. Belltable Arts Centre, informal basement café (☎ 061-319866); Green Onion Café, attractive, good quality (☎ 061-400710); Limerick Holiday Hostel, Barrington's Lodge, George's Quay (☎ 061-415222); Railway Hotel, old fashioned, convenient, comfortable (☎ 061-413653).

Milltown Malbay. The Flowing Tide, music hostel.

Newmarket-on-Fergus. Thomond House B&B, this is bungalow bliss; luxurious modern home of the 18th Baron Inchiquin, Gaelic lord and *the* O'Brien of Thomond (☎ 061-368304).

Limerick City

Limerick (*Hlymreker*, bare marshland), the fourth largest city in Ireland and capital of the Shannon region, straddles the waters of the Shannon at the point where the lower reaches open out into the estuary. The medieval castle and cathedral are of great importance and the **Hunt Museum** has the finest collection of medieval antiquities and art objects in the Republic, outside the National Museum. East of the city, at Plassey, is the University of Limerick, which houses the **National Self-Portrait Collection** and the **University Concert Hall**.

Although the major part of the city is late 18C, many of its public buildings, including a group of High Victorian city churches, date from the 19C. Always of commercial importance, Limerick regained its prominence in the 1920s after the construction of Ireland's first hydro-electric power station at Ardnacrushna, harnessing the energy of the Shannon. The opening of the Shannon International Airport at Rineanna in 1945, and surrounding trading estates, further increased its prosperity.

Among natives of the town were the artist and architect Francis Bindon (c 1690–1765), dramatists and novelists Gerald Griffin (1803–40) and Kate O'Brien (1897–1974). Catherine Hayes (1825–61) the operatic soprano, known as 'The Swan of Erin', and Ada Rehan (1860–1916), Shakespearean actress, were also born here.

- **Railway station**. Colbert Station, Parnell St (☎ 061-315555).
- **Bus station**. Colbert Station, Parnell St (☎ 061-313333).
- **Shannon Airport**. (☎ 061-414444).
- **Hovercraft**. Shannon Cruising, Derg Marine, (☎ 061-376364); **HoverEire** (☎ 061-394413).
- **Tourist Information**. Arthur's Quay (☎ 061-317522).
- **General Post Office**. Henry St (☎ 061-315777).

The origins of Limerick lie in a Norse settlement of c 922 on King's Island. It was sacked in 967 by Mahon of Thomond and his brother, BrianBorú, although it continued for two centuries as a Viking trading post under the patronage of the kings of Thomond. Muirchertach Mor O'Brien, King of Munster and High King of Ireland, made it his principal seat. The city constantly changed hands in the **Middle Ages**, being captured by the Anglo-Norman, Raymond le Gros, in 1175, re-taken by Donal Mór O'Brien and again seized by the Normans in 1197 when Prince John granted it a royal charter. In c 1210 King John's castle was built and entrusted to the stewardship of the Anglo-Norman, William de Braose. The city was occupied for some months by Edward Bruce in 1316, during his unsuccessful campaign for the Irish kingship.

During the **Civil War** the town was besieged twice: in 1642 it was taken by the Catholic Confederacy, and in 1651, Hugh O'Neill held it for six months, before falling to Cromwell's son-in-law, Henry Ireton, (who died here of the plague in the same year). Anthony Hamilton (c 1646–1720), the Jacobite satirist, and author of the French classic, *Mémoires du Comte de Grammont*, was governor of Limerick in 1685.

The most famous **siege of Limerick** was that of 1690. Held by the Jacobite leader Tyrconnel as the last Jacobite bastion in Ireland, it had already been unsuccessfully assaulted by William III with 26,000 men. However, Lauzun, the commander of James's French troops, returned to France, abandoning the city to its fate. The defenders were waiting for the arrival of William's siege-train from Dublin but, unbeknown to them, Patrick Sarsfield (the titular Earl of Lucan), had crossed the Shannon at Killaloe and surprised the siege-train, blowing it up and capturing the cannon and ammunition. More ordnance was brought up from Waterford by the Williamites and a breach made in the walls; the defenders, both men and women, repulsed the assault with heavy loss of life. Tyrconnel succumbed to an untimely apoplectic stroke and William's commander, Godert de Ginkel (later created Earl of Athlone) launched a violent attack; 600 of Limerick's garrison were butchered.

To save further slaughter, Sarsfield (Tyrconnel's successor) surrendered on honourable terms, and on 3 October 1691 a treaty was signed, allegedly on the **Treaty Stone**. The two-part treaty was divided into military and civil articles. The military part allowed all those who wished to leave for France to do so, and this was honoured. Some 12,000 Irish soldiers (with their women and children)—later known as the 'Wild Geese'—left the country to enlist abroad (Sarsfield himself died in 1693 at the battle of Landen, c 60km from Brussels). Here also, on the adjacent river bank, Sarsfield's troops were given the opportunity of enlisting in the English army, of which one-tenth took advantage.

Under the civil articles, Catholics were promised that the privileges they had enjoyed under Charles II would be honoured. However, this part of the treaty was largely repudiated, particularly with regard to land tenure and religious toleration.

The **18C** proved to be a century of peace and growth for Limerick, during which, through the influence of Edmund Pery, member for Limerick. The Irish Parliament voted £17,000 towards its improvement between 1755 and 1761. The fortifications (of which many fragments still stand) were dismantled in 1760. By then its population was c 25,000. A theatre was built here in 1770, at which Garrick and other leading actors played.

Following the Emancipation Act (1829), many new Catholic churches were built, including St. John's Cathedral but the early 20C witnessed another outburst of religious intolerance. In 1904, an **Anti-Semitic Pogrom** took place in Limerick, when a Catholic priest incited his congregation against the Jewish community who were driven from the city.

During the war of independence against the British forces in Ireland, the city experienced a radicalisation unique in Irish political affairs, when the Trades Council, under the banner of the '**Limerick Soviet**' (a Marxist collective) took over the city from the civic authorities in 1919 in protest against British military actions. In 1921 both the Mayor, George Clancy, and Michael O'Callaghan, ex-mayor, were murdered by Royal Irish Constabulary auxiliaries.

Edward Lear and the Limerick

The origin of the Limerick, a nonsense verse-form popularised by Edward Lear, is disputed. One explanation claims that it comes from the chorus 'Will you come up to Limerick' following an extemporised 'nonsense-verse' sung at convivial gatherings. Another more plausible explanation is that it derives from the satirical verses of the 18C Gaelic poets of Croom, Co. Limerick, also known as 'the Poets of Maigue', whose work was translated into English in the mid-19C. Lear's limericks closely resemble these poets:

I sell the best brandy and sherry
To make my good customers merry
But at times their finances
Run short as it chances
And then I feel very sad, very.
Sean O'Tuama. (Trans. James Clarence Mangan)

For anyone with an interest in urban development, Limerick is an excellent example. Emerging from a Norse foundation, there are clearly defined, separate medieval quarters for Anglo-Norman and Irish inhabitants linked in the shape of an hour-glass across the Abbey river at Baal's Bridge. Subsequent post-Reformation growth occurred on a new site, free from the restrictions of fortifications.

The historic town, on the east bank, is divided into three districts: **English Town**, on King's Island just north of where the Abbey river meets the Shannon and the old fortified port; **Irish Town**, on the south bank (not fully walled until 1495) and the 18C Georgian suburb of **Newtown Pery**, further south.

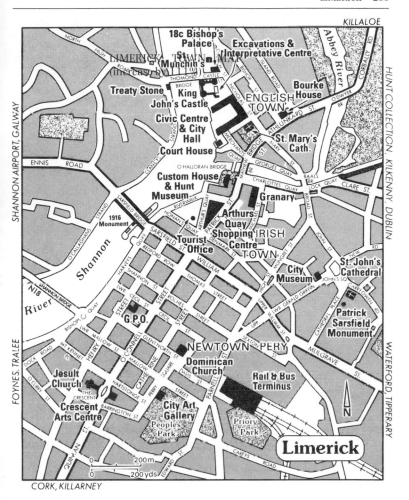

The Shannon, 220m wide at Sarsfield Bridge, is an important element in the origins and character of Limerick and is best appreciated by a tour which crosses three bridges in close proximity, linking Irish Town, English Town and the west bank.

Irish Town

The Palladian **Custom House** on Charlotte's Quay (Davis Ducart, 1765) has an excellent stone breakfront façade with Corinthian pilasters and flanking arcades facing the Shannon. It now houses the Hunt Museum.

The Hunt Museum

This extraordinary collection (10.00–17.00, Tue–Sat; 14.00–17.00 Sun; £), formed by John and Gertrude Hunt between 1930 and 1950, was presented to the State in 1976. It ranges from the Neolithic to the 19C, but concentrates on European medieval art, with an emphasis on items of superb craftsmanship, design and historical significance. All the applied and decorative arts are included with examples of ivories, panel-painting, metalwork, jewellery, enamels, ceramics and crystal. Bronze Age to early Christian periods are represented by bronze, iron and gold objects some, such as the 8C **Antrim Cross**, are unique. Individual items from later periods, works by Picasso and Modigliani emphasise the wide range and great interest of the collection.

The finest objects, which are displayed in the 'Captain's Room', include a bronze horse, cast from a maquette by Leonardo da Vinci (c 1495). The lower ground floor display covers the development of the medieval crucifix and other rooms contain a display of religious art through history. 'The Cathedral' contains the principal liturgical art exhibits, including the 15C Shrine of St Patrick and the Beverley crozier.

The finest early 18C architecture in Limerick is in **John's Square**, further east. The cut stone houses comprise three sides of the square (Bindon, 1751) two sides of which are occupied by the excellent **Limerick City Museum** (10.00–13.00, 14.15–17.00; Tues–Sat) which has a display of artefacts from the Neolithic to the 19C, including objects from the Lough Gur excavations, the Civic Sword of Elizabeth I and the charter of Charles II.

St. John's Cathedral (RC) (10.00–17.30), a Gothic Revival church by Philip C. Hardwick and Maurice Hennessy (1856–61), has an exceptionally tall and slender spire (85m high). The nave and apses have tall, thin stepped lancets, with 19C glass from the Mayer factory in Munich. Its treasury contains a mitre and crosier of c 1418, which are among the very few examples of medieval ecclesiastical regalia to remain in church hands. The spirited **Sarsfield monument** in the grounds is by James Lawlor (1880). Adjacent is **St. John's Hospital**. Just inside the entrance is the **Citadel** (c 1600), defence headquarters during the siege of Limerick, and the most extensive portion of the city wall (best seen from Leila St).

On Charlotte's Quay is the **18C granary** with a restaurant and library, the finest of the city's many stone warehouses. **Mathew Bridge** leads to English Town and St. Mary's Cathedral.

English Town

The O'Halloran footbridge (1987) spans the river to the restored **Potato Market** (1843), built on the site of one of the earliest ship quays.

St. Mary's Cathedral

The cathedral (C of I) (10.00–17.00 daily), founded by Donal Mór O'Brien in 1172 but many times altered since, was extensively restored in 1857–60. The most prominent external features are the square west tower (the upper part restored after 1690), the parapet with Irish battlements, and the riotous confusion of windows of the south façade; the 12C west doorway was ineptly restored in 1895.

The 12C church was cruciform with aisles and transepts. Of this, the impressively austere **nave** with clerestory and north transept remain intact; the north and south aisles have been expanded to contain individual chantry chapels with many interesting monuments. At the west end of the south aisle is the **Pery Chapel**, with tombs of the earls of Limerick. The recumbent effigy of Lord Glentworth is by Richard Westmacott (1845); in the south transept are the Bullingfort Galway tomb (1414) and the Budstone tomb (c 1400) and a 4m-long pre-Reformation stone altar-table, with five consecration crosses. The brass candelabra date from 1759.

The **choir** is notable for its 23 **misericords**, a unique survival in an Irish church, and for its tomb slabs. The oak misericords (mercy seats) which consist of carved oak panels on the underneath of the choir seats, were used to support the body when standing during lengthy services. They represent a bizarre bestiary of real and mythical creatures including the cockatrice (a cock with a serpent's tail), griffin (lion with eagle's head and wings), lindworm (wingless dragon), manticora (human head, lion's body with porcupine quills and scorpion's tail) and wyvern (winged dragon with barbed tail), as well as angels and human figures. They probably date from c 1490, when the cathedral was enlarged by Bishop Folan. The reredos in the chancel is by James Pearse (father of **Patrick Pearse**, leader of the 1916 uprising).

To the left of the altar is the elaborate polychrome monument of Donough O'Brien (erected 1678), Earl of Thomond, and his wife; the effigies are from an earlier monument of 1621, wrecked by the Cromwellians. Below this is the alleged tomb of the church's founder, Donal Mór O'Brien (d. 1194). The north transept contains the arcaded monument of Geoffrey Arthur, treasurer (d. 1519). In the Jebb chapel the Bishop Jebb monument is by E.H. Baily (1836).

The small two-light windows are by Catherine O'Brien; the Dowd window (1912), shows a cleric carrying a model of the cathedral. The O'Brien Chapel commemorates the notorious 'Murrough of the Burnings' (d. 1647), the pyromaniac Earl of Inchiquin, noted for his propensity to burn his opponents' towns and fortresses. His tomb was desecrated by his enemies.

Opposite the cathedral entrance is the old **Court House** (1764) where the celebrated 19C murder trial of Scanlan and Sullivan was held. They were accused of murdering 16-year-old Ellen Hanley, the 'Colleen Bawn' ('fair haired girl'). The case subsequently formed the subject of Gerald Griffin's well-known novel, *The Collegians* (1828), on which Dion Boucicault based his play *The Colleen Bawn* (1860) and Sir Julius Benedict, his operetta, *The Lily of Killarney* (1862).

Forming the churchyard wall of the cathedral in Nicholas St is the classical arcade of the **Exchange** (1777). Little remains of **Bourke House** (c 1654), further up the hill in Athlunkard St. Around the corner in Mary St is **Fanning's Castle**, the remains of a 15C town house with an interesting array of windows.

Returning to Merchant's Quay, between the cathedral and the river, on which is the classical **Court House** (N. & W. Hannan, 1809), pass through the City Hall precincts and Civic Centre into Nicholas St. The 17C '**Forty-shilling Almshouses**', lead to Castle St and **King John's Castle** (c 1200), one of the most impressively sited Norman castles in the country.

King John's Castle

Much of the castle has been preserved; its quadrilateral form, with curtain walls and drum towers survives. The west side stands in the river and presents an unspoilt view from the opposite bank. On the north side, still bearing traces of the bombardment of 1690, is the original gateway with D-shaped towers. Archaeological excavations have been taking place in the castle since 1990. The architecturally intrusive **Visitor Centre** (Murray O'Laoire, 1991) (09.00–17.30, Apr–Oct; rest of year 12.00–17.30, Sat & Sun only; £) occupies the space of the missing east curtain-wall and straddles the site of three Viking Age houses which pre-date the castle (these can be seen in the undercroft). An inept and clichéd multi-media programme using models and audio-visual presentation, gives an introduction to the history of the castle and surrounding area. Reconstructed half-scale examples of medieval war machines, battering ram, mangonel and trebuchet are in the courtyard; there is a café in one of the corner towers.

North of the castle in Church St is the **Bishop's Palace**, the oldest domestic building in English Town (headquarters of the Heritage Trust). It was the residence of the Protestant bishops, 1661–1784, its 18C façade attributed to Bindon. Its interior is entirely modern. Adjacent is **St. Munchin's**, a 7C foundation, entirely rebuilt in 1827 (J. & G. Pain), with a fragment of the town wall behind it; it is believed to occupy the original cathedral site. The charming courtyard of **Villier's Alms Houses** (also by Pain, 1830) adjoins the church.

At the corner of Castle St and Verdant Place is the **Toll House**, a miniature castle in contrast to the authentic one opposite. West of the castle is **Thomond Bridge**, with a tower towards the west bank. It was rebuilt by James Pain in 1836, replacing the 14-arch medieval bridge. At its far end, on the site of Thomond Gate, is the **Treaty Stone**, a battered cube of limestone raised on a pedestal, on which it is alleged the violated treaty of 1691 was signed.

Before crossing back over the Shannon, it is worth making a small detour to the timber **Church of Our Lady of the Rosary** (RC; Corr and McCormac, 1949) in Ennis Road. This has a fine collection of 20C church art; a single-light window in the baptistery by Evie Hone (1950) sculptures by Oisin Kelly (on the bell tower); a suite of paintings by Jack Hanlon; and the remarkable *Deposition* by Andrew O'Connor (c 1930).

The Arts and Crafts style **Shannon Boat Club** (Clifford Smith, 1902) is approached from **Sarsfield Bridge** (Alexander Nimmo, 1824–27). The monument (Arthur Power, 1956) on the bridge is to Tom Clarke and Limerick's involvement in the 1916 rebellion. Cross the bridge to Newtown Pery.

Newtown Pery

Rutland St (in which is the former **Town Hall**, 1803), prolonged into Patrick's St and O'Connell St, is the central artery of the planned Georgian quarter of Newtown Pery. It was laid out by Davis Ducart for Edmond Sexton Pery (1719–1806), Speaker of the Irish House of Commons from 1771–85.

In Upper Cecil St (left) is the Theatre Royal and further south, at 69 O'Connell St, is the **Belltable Arts Centre** with gallery, theatre and restaurant; an important venue for the visual and performing arts (10.00–17.00, Mon–Sat).

The Crescent (statue of O'Connell, by Hogan, 1857) at the south end of O'Connell St, has been well restored. The façade of the **Jesuit Church of the Sacred Heart** (RC, 1862), forms part of the west side. In the parallel Upper Henry St, further south, are the Pery's town houses, the Bishop's Palace (both 1787) and the **Church of the Immaculate Conception** (RC) by W.E. Corbett (1876) which has a Corinthian portico and fine basilican interior.

Returning to The Crescent, Barrington St (right), leads to Pery Square and the **People's Park**. A classical column commemorates the liberal lawyer and Chancellor of the Exchequer, Thomas Spring-Rice (1790–1866), by Alexander Nimmo (c 1866), and the **City Art Gallery** (10.00–13.00, 14.15–17.00; Tue–Sat) in the park, houses a small but worthwhile collection of 19C and 20C Irish and international contemporary art. In the adjacent streets are good 18C houses; in Hartstonge St is the tudor revival **Leamy School** (1843) and further north, in Glentworth St, **St. Saviour's church** (RC; Goldie & McCarthy, 1860), with a 17C Flemish figure of the Virgin over the lady altar, and the extremely attractive small Doric temple in the same street (now the Savings Bank) by W.H. Owen (c 1860).

Upper Gerald Griffin St, William St and Mulgrave St (Kate O'Brien was born in Ború House), lead to the N24, passing (right) the classical portico of **Limerick Gaol** (J. Pain, 1821), and **St. Joseph's Hospital**, the former lunatic asylum, (Francis Johnston & William Murray). At the junction where the Kilmallock road diverges south is a curious monument to the world champion weight-thrower, John O'Grady (1892–1934), in the form of a giant weight on a pedestal, an athletic parody of the Treaty Stone.

By following the Dublin road (N7), turning left for Plassey (after 3km) just beyond a ruined tower, you soon approach the buildings (Arthur Gibney, 1972) of the **University of Limerick** in a parkland setting. The Foundation Building contains the 18C–20C **National Self-Portrait Collection**. Head for the front of the Schrödinger Building, to see James McKenna's complex limestone monument *Resurgence* (1979).

Askeaton, Foynes, Glin, Listowel

Head south, leaving Limerick by Dock Road. At first the road follows the south bank of the Shannon, and after 8km passes the fragmentary ruins of a monastery founded by St. Patrick at Mungret. Despite repeated Viking raids it was regularly rebuilt and flourished until the Dissolution, first under Canons Regular and then under Dominican rule. Besides the 15C church, there is also a castle, nearer the road.

The isolated towers of **Carrigogunnell** castle (known as 'the Rock of the O'Connells') can be seen on the right. Built on a crag near the Shannon in the 14C–16C it surrendered to General Ginkel in 1691, and was later blown up. Cross the river Maigue, passing more ruined castles, the minute 10C church of **Killulta**, and the demesne of **Dromore Castle**, a fantastic Victorian Gothic-Revival confection (1867–70). It was partially dismantled in the 1950s, but plans are afoot to re-roof and restore it. **Shannongrove** (c 1709–23), an imposing mansion, lies near the river beyond Pallaskenry, (3km).

Curragh Chase, further on the left, is the birthplace of the poet, Aubrey de Vere (1814–1902), his grave is in the Protestant churchyard at Askeaton. The demesne is now called Curragh Chase Forest Park.

Askeaton (*Eas Géphtine*, Gephtin's waterfall) was defended by a strong **castle** (1199) belonging to the earls of Desmond, the ruins of which stand on an island in the Deel. The **great hall** is well preserved, but the rest was destroyed in Cromwell's wars. It was the final home of Gerald Fitzgerald, the last great earl of Desmond, who fled here after the failure of his revolt against Ormond in 1570. The castle surrendered in 1580, although the earl held out for four years in the Kerry hills.

The parish church incorporates part of a commandery of the Templars (13C). The **Franciscan Friary**, on the bank of the Deel north of the town, retains its cloister (completed c 1420) with black marble arcading. This was the burial-place of James Fitzgerald, 14th Earl of Desmond (d. 1558), the Lord Treasurer of Ireland. The Limerick 'Hell Fire Club', a well-known 18C drinking and carousing society, is said to have met at Askeaton (as painted by James Worsdale, where the group includes Mrs Celinda Blennerhassett, their alleged only female member).

At **Foynes** you regain the south shore of the Shannon estuary. This was the former trans-Atlantic seaplane base (1939–45), now superseded by Shannon airport. If you are interested in flying, the **Foynes Flying Boat Museum** (10.00–18.00, Mar–Oct; £) explains the history of flight in the area and its displays include original equipment.

Towards the Shannon and east of **Shanagolden** are the tree-lined ruins of **Old Abbey**, an Augustinian house retaining its dovecot, and a fine west door in the ruined church. Over 2km south (on the Ardagh road) is the ruin of 13C **Shanid Castle** (Seanad, or Council), a former Desmond fortress.

The hill between Foynes and Shanagolden, **Knockpatrick** (172m), commands **fine views** of the estuary. The hill is named after a ruined church, said to have been built by St. Patrick.

The village of **Glin** is adjacent to the seat of the 29th Knight of Glin, a scion of the Fitzgerald clan, whose family has held it in succession for 700 years. During the Desmond rebellion of 1641, the old castle was besieged by Sir George Carew and surrendered after a fierce hand-to-hand fight. The then Knight survived, only to fall at Kinsale a year later (the ruined keep is near the stream). The present battlemented **Glin Castle** (1789–1812), with later Gothick embellishments and lodges, lies to the left of the road just west of the village (10.00–12.00, 14.00–16.00 daily, May & by arrangement; £).

You enter Co. Kerry before reaching **Tarbert**, a village protected by a wooded hinterland but now disfigured by a power station. Tarbert Bridwell (10.00–18.00, Apr–Oct; £) an 1830 Courthouse and jail complex, emphasises the grimness of 19C prison conditions with a series of tableaux. This is the south terminus of the car ferry to Killimer on the Clare coast. The crossing averages 20 minutes to Killimer and sails on the hour from 10.00–18.00 (or 19.00, depending on tides), (09.00–22.00, May–September).

Tarbert to Tralee via Ballybunnion

A rather dull road leads west. Earl Kitchener (1850–1916) was born at Ballylongford (8km). Nearby are the ruins of a Franciscan monastery, **Lislaughtin Abbey** (1477), with three finely carved sedilia and a good east window. At the mouth of the creek, protected by Carrig Island, stands **Carrigafoyle Castle**, with vaulted tower, once a stronghold of the O'Connors of Kerry, now uninhabited.

Continuing west, you pass **Knockanore Hill** (267m), with views across the Shannon estuary, to **Ballybunnion**, a small seaside resort with good bathing and surfing and 4km of sandy beach. To the north are caves and the rocky scenery of Doon Bay, with Lick Castle beyond. These cliff forts were presumably erected to guard the entrance to the Shannon.

Just beyond the village of Ballyduff. A lane on the left leads to the **Round Tower of Rattoo**, one of the most perfect extant (cap restored). Nearby is a 13C Augustinian priory church.

On the coast west of Ballyduff are the ruins of the Cromwellian fort of **Ballingarry**. From Ballyduff roads continue south to Tralee.

The direct road leads southwest from Tarbert to (11km) **Listowel** (*Lios Tuathail*, the fort of King Tuathal), a thriving country town, with remains of a Desmond fortress. The Lartique monorail train, unique in Britain and Ireland, ran to Ballybunnion. **Writers' Week**, a literary festival, is held during May.

Adare, Newcastle West, Abbeyfeale

Drive southwest from Limerick to (10km) Patrickswell, just beyond which the N20 bears left for Mallow and Cork. The right-hand fork leads shortly to **Adare**, an unusually neat village, with thatched cottages, a 19C improvement for which the Earl of Dunraven (1812–71) was responsible. It stands on the river Maigue, and is noted for its trees (*Ath Dara*, ford of the oaks), and for its monastic remains.

Cross a long bridge of fourteen 15C arches and pass (right) the **Augustinian Friary**, probably built by John, 1st Earl of Kildare—Adare was ancestrally associated with the Fitzgeralds, earls of Kildare, and the O'Donovans, later becoming the seat of the Dunravens—in 1315. On the north side are the cloisters, converted into a mausoleum by the Earl of Dunraven (1826) and in the church (restored 1852) are memorials to other members of the Wyndham-Quin family.

Further down the main street is the Catholic church, occupying that of the **White Abbey**, a Trinitarian friary founded in 1230, and saved from being turned into a market-house in 1811 by the 2nd Earl of Dunraven (1782–1850).

The well-wooded demesne contains, in addition to the mansion itself, both **Desmond Castle** and a Franciscan friary. The 14C castle, built by the O'Donovans and rebuilt by Thomas, 2nd Earl of Kildare (d.1328), consists of a keep within a moated inner ward, the whole surrounded by a spacious quadrangle. In the adjoining churchyard are the ruins of the parish church and a 14C chapel.

The **Franciscan friary** was founded in 1464 by Thomas, 7th Earl of Kildare (d. 1477), who is buried in the choir. The beautiful ruins consist of a graceful tower, two attractive little chapels in the south transept and, in the choir, some carved niches sheltering the tombs of the Fitzgeralds. On the north side are the well-preserved cloisters, with an old yew in the centre of the garth, the refectory and infirmary, among other dependencies.

18C **Adare Manor** (now an hotel) was enlarged in the Tudor-Revival style between 1832 and 1876, after the original designs by James Pain. A.W.N. Pugin and P.C. Hardwick were responsible for some of the later reconstruction (1846–50).

The road now passes through a district once known as 'The Palatine', owing to the settlement here of a colony of Lutherans from the Rhenish Palatinate, who had been expelled by the French in the early 18C. Traces of these families survive in local surnames such as Switzer and Teskey. **Croagh** (4km) has a ruined tower (right), and the remains of an old church, beyond which you by-pass Rathkeale, a straggling village with a tall church spire, incorporating fragments of a 13C Augustinian priory. Just outside **Rathkeale** there is a restored and furnished keep of the Earl of Desmond, known as **Castle Matrix** (10.00–17.00, Sat–Thurs; May–Sept; £). Here, in 1580, Edmund Spenser met Sir Walter Raleigh.

4km beyond Rathkeale the right-hand fork leads direct to Listowel via **Ardagh** where the 'Ardagh Chalice' was found in a neighbouring rath; (see National Museum, Dublin).

Bear left for **Newcastle West**. The castle (under restoration) was built by the Knights Templar in the 12C. The road descends to **Abbeyfeale** where part of a Cistercian abbey is incorporated in the Catholic parish church. The **Mullaghareirk Mountains** rise in the distance.

Lough Gur Stone Age Centre, Kilmallock, Bruree

Leave Limerick by the N24 (southeast for Tipperary), immediately diverging to the R514 (right) to approach the north-west corner of **Lough Gur**, a pretty lake where the last of the Desmonds, according to legend, holds eternal court beneath its waters, emerging every seventh year on a silver-shod steed. Of more historical interest is the remarkable concentration of **stone circles** and other monuments to be seen on its banks, from **Neolithic dwellings** (2000 BC) to those of the early Christian period.

Lough Gur Stone Age Centre

The centre (10.00–18.00 daily, May–Sept; £) (approached by the R514) has been set up on the banks of **Lough Gur** and is devoted to explaining the antiquities of the site. Among these sites are those between the road and the north-west corner of the lake. They include **two stone circles**; one, at Grange, is among the most impressive in the country. a large standing stone, a *crannóg* (not a good example, and now too close to the shore) a small stone circle, and a ring-fort.

If you walk clockwise around the lake, starting at its northeastern end, you will pass the foundations of early Christian huts; two stone forts (probably occupied until the 10C) and on **Knockadun hill** beside the lake, a **Stone Age house**, burial-place, and enclosure. Skirting the south-east corner of the lough, you reach the ruins of **Black Castle**. Return to the main road by following the south bank, passing a wedge-shaped gallery-grave (see introduction to Art and Architecture).

Kilmallock, now a village, was once one of the most important places in Munster, and the headquarters of the earls of Desmond. Foundations of Neolithic dwellings dating from the fourth millennium were excavated a short distance north west of the village in 1986.

The White Knights of Kilmallock

Kilmallock's history is interwoven with the annals of the earls, a branch of the great Fitzgerald family, (which dominated the greater part of Munster from the 14C to the 16C). The 1st Earl died in 1356. Gerald Fitzgerald, the

15th Earl, was killed in 1583, a fugitive from the Earl of Ormond backed by the power of Queen Elizabeth. The last White Knight, Edmund Fitzgibbon (?1552–1608) defeated James FitzThomas Fitzgerald, Earl of Desmond, (the 'Sugan' or straw earl) after he had assumed the title in 1604. His tomb is in the Dominican abbey north of the town.

The White Knights were a sept (Irish term for a division of a clan) of the Fitzgerald family. who made their headquarters at Kilmallock. The first of these knights won his nickname at Halidon Hill in Britain (1333). He was knighted by Edward III for services against the Scots and his glittering armour was so conspicuous in the fray that he became known as the White Knight.

Lord Blakeney (1672–1761), the defender of Stirling Castle and Minorca, and Sir Eyre Coote (1726–83), who defeated the Indian ruler Haidar Ali, were natives. Kilmallock now presents a picture of fallen greatness. Of its fortifications (razed by Cromwell's order) **Blossom's Gate** remains, on the Charleville road; and, on the northern approach, **King's Castle** survives in Sarsfield St. The collegiate church of **SS Peter and Paul** has a ruined nave and transepts. **Kilmallock Historical Society** at the Hill have an audio-visual display on the history of town as well as a local folk-life exhibition (13.30–17.00 daily).

On the banks of the Loobagh rivulet, northeast of the centre, is the beautiful **Dominican Abbey**, founded in the late 13C by Gilbert Fitzgerald of Offaly. The finest part of the ruins is the church choir, with a well-restored east window. Here also are several interesting **tombs**, including that of Edmund Fitzgibbon. There is another good window in the transept; over the crossing is a tower, supported by unusually narrow arches.

Ash Hill Towers (1km west) is a mansion of 1781 with one façade rebuilt in the Gothick-Revival style in 1833; it contains Wyatt-type plasterwork (adm. by appointment).

8km southeast of Kilmallock is Kilfinnane, with a trivallate rath 9m high. At Ardpatrick, 6.5km south of Kilmallock are the remains of a Round Tower, and traces of a monastery founded by St. Patrick (?). Southwest of it, overlooked by Seefin (528m), is the demesne of **Castle-Oliver**, birthplace of Lola Montez, Marie Dolores Gilbert (1818–61), the dancer and adventuress made Comtesse of Lansfield by Ludwig of Bavaria.

Leaving Kilmallock through Blossom's Gate, bear southeast to (9.6km) Charleville (Rath Luirc).

If you want to explore the region to the **south of Limerick**, leave the town, passing Patrickswell, before forking left (N20). After passing the tower of Fanningstown, you enter **Croom**, an ancient fortress of the Fitzgeralds. Their castle (late 12C) was modernised by the Croker family early in the 19C.

The ruins of a Cistercian monastery can be visited at **Monasteranenagh** or **Monaster** (4km) on the Camoge. The monastery was founded in 1148 by Turlough O'Brien, King of Thomond, in thanksgiving for his defeat of the Vikings at Rathmore Castle (further east). Beside the ruins of the church (c 1170–1220) which shows some good carving, are remains of the abbey mill and an old bridge.

Bruree, to the south of Croom is important for its connection with **Eamon de Valéra**, founder of the *Fianna Fáil* party (1926). This was his mother's home and he spent much of his childhood here.

> **Eamon de Valéra** (1882–1975) was born in New York of Irish and Spanish parents. He returned to Ireland aged 2, and grew up in Bruree. He was one of the few leaders of the 1916 rebellion not to be executed. Elected president of the first Dail in 1919, he founded *Fianna Fáil*, now the largest Irish political party, and spent sixty-three years in public life, as Taoiseach on a number of occasions and serving two terms as President of Ireland. He was instrumental in maintaining Irish neutrality during World War II. The **de Valera Museum** (10.00–16.00 daily, June–Sept; £) is in the old schoolhouse.

The Craggaunowen Project, Bunratty Castle, Ennis, Milltown Malbay

Leaving Limerick on the N18 from the Sarsfield Bridge, pass **Cratloe Wood House**, a red-painted 17C longhouse, now open to the public. It remained in the ownership of the O'Brien's (who built it) for almost 300 years. **Cratloekeel Castle** and **Castle Donnell** are on the left before a right-hand turn leads onto the R462 at Cratloe.

Just east of **Sixmilebridge** is the Georgian mansion of **Mount Ievers Court** (Isaac and John Rothery, c 1736–37). The entrance front is of ashlar stone, and the garden front of brick. For the **Craggaunowen Project**, continue (4km) north across a plain studded with small lakes and dotted with the ruined castles of the MacNamaras and the Fannings, and fork left onto the R369.

The Craggaunowen Project

The project (second turning to the right) is centred around the castle (c 1550) which was restored in the 19C, and acquired in 1965 by John Hunt (see Hunt Museum, Limerick). Since then a number of authentic replicas of ancient dwellings have been constructed in the grounds, among them a **Late Bronze Age crannóg**, and a **ring-fort**. They dramatically bring to life the architecture and living conditions of the periods.

The **entrance lodge** contains early 19C cottage furniture and utensils and the **castle** contains a good representative collection of (14C–17C) Irish, English and continental furniture and sculpture. There are also examples of metalware, pottery, and reliquaries.

The Brendan, a leather replica of the boat used by St. Brendan on his legendary voyage to America is also kept here. Tim Severin sailed it on the same voyage from the west coast of Ireland to Newfoundland in 1976.

Regaining the main road, turn right, and shortly pass the over-restored **Knappogue Castle** (1467) (09.30–17.00 daily; Apr–Oct) which vies with Bunratty Castle in providing pseudo-medieval banquets. There are remains of an early monastic foundation at **Finlough** or **Fenoe**, to the south.

The village of **Quin** (*Cuinche*, arbutus), contains one of the best preserved abbeys in Ireland. This is the country of the MacNamaras, whose fortresses abound in the vicinity. The **Franciscan abbey** here was founded by Sioda MacNamara in 1402 within the four towers of the Norman castle (destroyed 1286), three of which still partly exist. The abbey church consists of a nave and chancel with a tower between them, and contains tombs of the MacNamaras, including that of the notorious duellist John 'Fireball' MacNamara (d. 1836). The **cloister** has coupled columns and later buttresses. Quin Abbey was suppressed in 1541. In 1584 Donough Beag O'Brien was brutally executed here by Sir John Perrot, Lord Deputy. The Franciscans returned however, and although their community was officially disbanded in 1651 the last monk, Fr John Hogan, died only in 1820 (he is buried in the north-east corner of the cloister).

Nearby is the early 13C church of **St. Finghin**. About 3km northeast is the mound of **Magh Adhair**, the ancient inauguration-place of the **Kings of Thomond**. The road continues to Ennis.

Bunratty Castle

The Castle of Bunratty (c 1425) with its four square angle-towers, is on the N18, from Limerick, beyond **Cratloe** (09.00–17.30 daily, all year; £). It is now a popular venue for candlelit 'medieval' banquets, adjoining **Bunratty Folk Park** (09.00–18.30, June–Aug), where traditional dwellings have been erected and furnished.

In 1276 Brian O'Brien, King of Thomond, was expelled from his dominions, which were granted to Sir Thomas de Clare (who built the first stone castle here).

However, in the next year De Clare was forced to ally with Brian O'Brian (the Normans were always numerically at a disadvantage) against the rebellious Turlough O'Brien. But the alliance was unsuccessful and De Clare, in mortification at his defeat, arrested O'Brian in the castle and had him dragged to death by horses. Bunratty reverted to the O'Briens however, and was restored by Donough O'Brien, Earl of Thomond (d. 1624).

In 1646 it was taken by the Irish Confederates inspired by the presence of Cardinal Rinuccini, the Papal Legate, who Cardinal rallied the Old English (ie. Catholic Anglo-Normans) and Catholic Irish against the Protestant New English (Elizabethan Planters). The castle was continuously inhabited until the 19C when it was for a time used as police barracks. It was acquired by Viscount Gort in 1956, and has been restored to its 15C–16C condition. It contains an important collection of 14C–17C furniture and tapestries in the re-roofed banqueting hall above the stone-roofed guard-room and some early 17C stuccowork is preserved in the adjoining chapel.

Shortly beyond Bunratty, the road to **Shannon International Airport** bears left, passing Shannon town, one of the few entirely new 20C urban settlements in Ireland. Opened in 1945, the airport has the distinction of being the most westerly air-base in Europe; it was also the first duty-free airport in the world.

Urlanmore Castle, on the way to Newmarket, contains medieval outline paintings of animals in the main tower-room. Before reaching Newmarket-on-Fergus there is an important Baroque monument (c 1717) by William Kidwell

(1662–1736) in the church of **Kilnasoolagh**. It portrays the obese and indolent recumbent figure of Sir Donough O'Brien (1642–1717) son of the extraordinary '**Máire Ruadh**' or 'Red Mary' (see Leamaneh, Ch. 10) and ancestor of Lord Inchiquin (for whom **Dromoland Castle**, to the northeast of Newmarket, was built). The castle (by the Pain brothers, 1826) is set in elaborate formal gardens designed by John Aheron. Now an hotel, it was the birthplace of William Smith O'Brien (1803–64) a leader of the 'Young Ireland' party. Near the south-east entrance of the demesne is a large **stone fort**, where in 1854 the great Clare Gold Hoard was discovered.

Passing **Carnelly House** (c 1740; probably designed by Francis Bindon), cross the river Fergus at **Clarecastle** (named after a fortress of the O'Briens that stood on an island in the river). Beyond, to the right, are the ruins of **Clare Abbey**, an Augustinian priory, founded by Donal O'Brien (1195) the last King of Munster. The lofty central tower, a later addition, is its most conspicuous feature; there are fragments of a cloister and other dependencies on the south side.

Ennis

Ennis (Tourist Information, Clare Rd, ☎ 065-28366) the rapidly growing county town of Co. Clare, is an attractive and historic town of considerable interest.

North of the narrow streets of the old town stands the **Court House**, a Classical building of 1850–52 (J.B. Keane) with original interior finishes. The ruined **friary** (09.30–18.30 daily, May–Sept; OPW; £) nearer the centre by the river, was founded by Donough Cairbreach O'Brien in 1242, and suppressed in 1543. An incongruous top storey with ugly spirelets has been added to the slender tower. The **south transept**, with its stepped gable and graceful window tracery, and the row of twin and triplet windows in the choir, are fine. The choir shelters (north side) the MacMahon monument (c 1470), altered in 1843 and restored in 1953; the Inchiquin tomb on the south side, and other good sculpture. There is a **vaulted sacristy** or chapter room (north side) but only fragments survive of other buildings. The Cathedral (RC) dates from 1831–43, the interior was reordered in 1975.

Monuments in the town commemorate Daniel O'Connell, MP for Clare, (1828–31) who is poised on a tall classical column (John Neville, 1850), and the 'Manchester Martyrs' (Allen, Larkin and O'Brien), executed in 1867 for their violent rescue of Fenian prisoners in Manchester gaol.

Among Ennis' citizens were the artist William Mulready (1786–1863), the precocious poet Thomas Dermody (1775–1802) and the actress Harriet Smithson (1800–54) who married Hector Berlioz in 1833. Eamon de Valéra (see above) represented the county from 1917–59.

From Ennis, turn back along the Limerick road for c 2km before forking right. The road passes between two lakes in the grounds of **New Hall** (c 1764; probably by Francis Bindon) to the ruins of **Killone Abbey** (founded by Donal O'Brien in 1190). The founder's grand-daughter, Slaney (d. 1260) was possibly abbess. It has several unusual features, including a passage through the central pier, a curious corbel at the southeast angle, and a crypt (the burial-place of the MacDonnells).

The road hugs the shallow estuary of the Fergus, studded with low islands, passing the ruined **Dangan Castle**; on offshore **Canon's Island** are the ruins of another abbey (early 13C) surrounded by a circular wall. Skirt the demesne of **Cahiracon**, and then follow the Shannon shore, with views across the estuary towards Glin, eventually reaching the head of **Clonderlaw Bay**.

Killimer is the north terminus of the **car-ferry** to Tarbert and the Kerry bank of the Shannon. In the churchyard of Killimer the '**Colleen Bawn**', Eily or Ellen Hanley is buried. Her beauty led to her tragic end at the hands of her secretly married husband, who drowned her in the Shannon in a fit of jealousy (1819). She was 16 years old (see Limerick, above).

The road leads along a ridge to approach **Kilrush**, a small market town of some character, with a harbour. At **Cappagh Pier**, to the southwest, boats may be hired for visiting the low-lying offshore island of Scattery. At Merchant's Quay is the **Scattery Island Centre** (09.30–18.30 daily; June–Sept) which acts as an information centre for the antiquities and wildlife of Scattery.

St. Senan (d.554) used **Scattery Island** (Inis Cathaigh) as a retreat and like St. Kevin at Glendalough, he excluded all women. Legend states that St. Cannera, a sociable female saint, wished to share the island with him; but, more tractable than St. Kevin's admirer, she returned to the mainland at his express command. (St. Cannera was born at Moylougha, 7km east of Kilrush, where a lake and a ruined church mark the site).

Remains of **five churches** survive, among them the 9C–10C cathedral with a good west door and later windows. Near it are the **oratory** (11C; rebuilt) and **Round Tower**, 38m high, the tallest and perhaps the oldest surviving in Ireland, unique in having its entrance at ground level. **Temple Senan**, to the northwest, with the alleged site of the saint's grave, has been much rebuilt. To the west of it is the early Christian memorial slab to **Moenach**; an inscribed stone. Near the east shore at **Templenamarve** (14C–15C) are the vaults of a castle, probably erected by the burghers of Limerick, to whom the island was assigned by Elizabeth I in 1582 (to the southwest is Knocknanangel, with fragments of a primitive church).

Returning to the mainland, there is splendid coastal scenery in the neighbourhood of **Kilkee** (13km northwest of Kilrush) a resort with good bathing. The inlet, **Moore Bay**, is protected from the full fury of the Atlantic by a reef known as Duggerna Rocks. On the south shore is a natural ampitheatre of terraced limestone, and the **Puffing Hole**, a blow-hole through which the spray bursts in stormy weather.

Following the coast road, you pass **Bishop's Island**—with a beehive oratory and house ascribed to St. Senan—beyond which is the rock stack of **Green Rock**, Castle Point and the ruins of **Doonlicky Castle**. You eventually reach Kilbaha, the last village on the peninsula where the Shannon meets the sea. The lighthouse (84m high) at **Loop Head** lies further west.

The view from here is superb, extending from MacGillycuddy's Reeks, rising behind the Slieve Mish Mountains to the south, and Brandon Head and Mt Brandon to the southwest. To the north, beyond the Aran Islands, is the coast of Connemara, with the Twelve Bens, and Slyne Head to the northwest.

An alternative road back to Ennis follows the south shore of the peninsula through Carrigaholt, with a castle of the O'Briens, and Doonaha, birthplace of Eugene O'Curry (1796–1862), scholar and topographer.

Driving northeast from Kilkee you pass near cliffs increasing in height as far as **Ballard Bay** and **Doonbeg Castle** (an O'Brien stronghold) beyond. Bear left near **Lough Donnell**, cut off from the sea by a shingle bar. **Mutton Island** lies off Lurga Point (on the headland of which is **Tromra Castle**, another O'Brien seat) and may be visited by *currach* (a tradional open fishing boat) from the fishing village of **Quilty**. The island, said to have been torn off the mainland by a storm in c 800, retains an oratory of St. Senan. A ship from the Spanish Armada was wrecked on the landward reef.

At **Spanish Point**, in the centre of Mal Bay (just north of Quilty) numerous bodies were washed ashore from the Armada, and buried here. Several vessels were wrecked off the Clare coast in September 1588. Its cliffs were manned by followers of Sir Turlough O'Brien of Liscannor (who favoured the Protestant party) to prevent any survivors actually landing.

The main road continues northeast to the village of **Milltown Malbay**, venue of the **Willie Clancy Summer School** (July), which celebrates the memory of Clancy (1921–1973), a celebrated Uilleann piper, traditional musician and folklorist. The whole area is famous for its strong musical tradition. To the east rises **Slievecallan** (390m) on the south side of which is a huge dolmen.

Killaloe, Lough Derg, Holy Island

Leave Limerick via Athlunkard St. After crossing the Shannon you pass the largest hydro-electric installation in Ireland at **Parteen** (or **Ardnacrushna**). The first of its kind, it was built in 1925 by the Siemens-Schuckert company who undertook the regulation of the tremendous supply of water-power provided by the 30m fall in the river Shannon between Lough Derg and Limerick. Apart from the hydro-electric power station, this project included the construction of a dam near the foot of the lough, a 12km-long Power Headrace Canal and navigation locks at Ardnacrushna. Sean Keating, (1889–1977), a student of Sir William Orpen, was commissioned by the Electricity Supply Board (ESB) to commemorate the construction project and his paintings (Limerick Art Gallery) are of considerable interest.

For **Killaloe**, turn right through Cloonlara and O'Briensbridge, the only bridge between Limerick and Killaloe. Above the bridge the dam has so widened the river as to make it an extension of Lough Derg.

Killaloe

Killaloe (Tourist Information, The Bridge, ☎ 061-376866; seasonal) is a riverside town beautifully situated at the southern end of Lough Derg and surrounded by the **Arra Mountains**, **Slieve Bernagh** and **Glenmagalliagh**. It is also the terminus of the **Shannon cruiser** which runs from Carrick-on-Shannon. A long narrow bridge of 13 arches spans the lough to the village of Ballina in Co.. Tipperary. There is glass work by Harry Clarke (1927) in the Catholic church.

The town has grown up around the site of a church founded by St. Dalua or Molua (*Cill Dalua*, known also as Luanus, died c 622) who was succeeded by St. Flannan. The church was replaced by the **Cathedral of St. Flannan** in 1182 (probably built by Donal O'Brien). The cruciform building was restored in 1887 and the upper part of the tower is modern. The **chevron moulding** above the east window and the corbels on the north side of the choir should be noted, while the east window of the south transept is unusual. The most notable feature of the church is the interior of the blocked **south doorway**, of earlier date, adorned with richly carved ornamentation and grotesque heads, and said to be the entrance to the **tomb of Murtogh O'Brien, King of Munster** (d. 1120). Beside it is the **Thorgrim's Stone**, the granite shaft of a cross, with an inscription (c 1000) in both runes and Ogham, was found built into the church-yard wall in 1916 and is the only bilingual one known. The inscription asks for 'a prayer for Thorgrim who made the stone'. Against the west wall is a Celtic cross. The adjoining font has floreated decoration, the other font in the choir dates from 1752.

In the churchyard are the well-preserved nave and chancel of a **church** or oratory, said to have been erected by St. Flannan. Its steeply pitched stone roof is similar to those at Glendalough and Kells; the doorway has two curious but worn capitals, one like a rough Ionic scroll, the other with two lambs. **Killaloe Heritage Centre** (09.30–17.00 daily, Apr–Sept) has a local history audio-visual programme.

Next to the Catholic church stands **St. Molua's Oratory**, reconstructed here after its removal from Friar's Island when the level of the lough was raised by the Shannon hydro-electric scheme.

Lough Derg

Lough Derg, the largest of the Shannon lakes (40km long and 3–5km wide) is studded with islands like Lough Ree further up the river. Its very irregular shore is probably due to the slow decomposition of its limestone bed. The water level rises rapidly rise after rain, sometimes as much as 30cm in 24 hours, so it provides a natural reservoir for the Ardnacrushna hydro-electric station. Dromineer is the home of the Lough Derg Yacht Club with good fish and other restaurants. Killaloe, Terryglass and Kilgarvan are also good points from which to fish.

The beautiful road on the **Clare bank** of Lough Derg commands an even better view than that from the lake itself. Bear northeast from Killaloe, passing on the right a large fort, **Beal Ború**, which may represent the palace of Kinora, the headquarters of Brian Ború (926–1014). When excavated, it revealed remains of a rectangular timber house of the 11C. A lower road follows the lough-side before ascending, with a view of the fortress of Castlelough on the far bank; the newer road diverges left, with a wider view on its descent towards Tuamgraney (birthplace in 1932 of novelist and playwright Edna O'Brien), with a ruined castle and 10C church.

Scarriff is charmingly situated above the lough and the demesne of Woodpark. A few kilometres north, the village of **Mountshannon** nestles on the shore beneath the Slieve Aughty mountain range. It is a popular place for both fly (trout) and coarse fishing (pike).

Two minor roads lead from Scarriff towards Gort, skirting **Lough Graney** One passes near **Feakle**, where Brian Merriman (1757–1805) is buried. He is the author of *Cúirt an Mheán-Oíche* (**The Midnight Court** c 1780) a lengthy humorous and satirical poem dealing with sex, clerical celibacy and male inadequacy (perennial themes for Irish writers) and is commemorated by the Merriman Summer School; excellent translations by Frank O'Connor, among others, are available.

Offshore to the southwest lies **Inishcaltra** (*Inis Cealtra*) or **Holy Island**, the seat of a monastic establishment founded by St. Caimin in the 7C, destroyed by the Vikings in the 9C, and rebuilt by Brian Ború (10C). There are remains of four churches and a capless Round Tower: **St. Caimin's**, an early rectangular building with a Romanesque chancel added and an inserted west door; **St. Brigid's** (the smallest), with an elaborate Romanesque doorway; **St. Mary's**, much altered in the 16C, containing a monument to Turlough O'Brien and his wife (d. 1626 and 1625), and **St. Michael's**, almost totally ruined. In St. Caimin's are the Cross of Cathasach, with inscriptions on its edges (c 1094), and another remarkable cross with nearly straight sides to its 'wheel'. To the north-east, beyond the 'Saint's Graveyard', in an enclosure containing a well-preserved collection of early grave-slabs and the so-called 'Temple of the Wounded Men'. The 'Anchorite's Cell' was possibly a tomb-shrine.

Beyond Mountshannon bear northeast for some 23km before turning east at a T-junction for Portumna. 4km northwest of this point stands the well-preserved tower-house of Pallas; at Abbey, 5km west, are ruins of a 14C **Carthusian monastery**, later Franciscan.

10 · The Burren

The landscape of the Burren is one of the most remarkable geological formations in Ireland. The springs and curious scenery of this wild karstic limestone plateau are due to its position; porous carboniferous limestone and shale systems meet here. The conditions of the Burren are typical of a karstic terrain—shortage of soil and water as a result of glacial and later erosion. The rock is honeycombed with underground water-courses and cave-systems. Along with the Giant's Causeway (see Ch. 17) it is an area of unique geological significance. The flora of the area includes many rare species not found elsewhere in Ireland and the whole area is a haunt of geologists and botanists, who will find a remarkable number of calcium-loving plants, including blue spring gentians, mountain avens, bloody cranesbill, white anemones, and yellow primroses, thriving in the crevices of this natural rock-garden.

Among the more dramatic features of the region are **Ailwee Caves** and the **Cliffs of Moher**, some of the most impressive natural sights in the country, while off the coast are the **Aran Islands**.

Caves and potholes (many dangerous, and only to be entered with a guide, or by experienced cavers) are numerous. **Pollnagollum**, 5.5km to the north, is the longest cave known in Ireland (over 11km). This area of the north Clare coast-line is, at close quarters a location of singular beauty, although agriculturally it appears quite desolate. **The Burren Way** (from Ballyvaughan to the Cliffs of Moher; 35km) includes the finest terrain of this rugged area.

The entire area of the Burren is rich in archaeological remains, the Megalithic tombs at **Gleninsheen**, a portal tomb at **Poulnabrone** and medieval monas-teries at **Dysert O'Dea** and **Corcomroe**. Other places of interest include **Thoor Ballylee**, the tower-house restored as a home by W.B.Yeats, and **Coole Park**, the estate of Lady Gregory.

Doolin, **Ennistymon** and **Lahinch** are noted for some of the best traditional music in the country and the bars of the area have become a mecca for music enthusiasts from all over Europe and North America.

How to get there
■ **Train**. Limerick and Galway the nearest main-line stations.
■ **Air**. Shannon International Airport.
■ **Sea**. Aran Islands.

Listings
Accommodation
Corofin. Caherbolane Farmhouse, B&B, with the sort of view few B&Bs offer (☎ 065-37638); **Clifden House**, B&B, restaurant, self-catering (☎ 065-37692); **Corofin Village Hostel** (☎ 065-37683); *Croide Na Boirne*, engaging pub-restau-rant (☎ 065-89109).
Kilfenora. **Vaughan's**, pub-restaurant (☎ 065-88004).
Lahinch. **Atlantic Hotel**, family run, sea-food restaurant (☎ 065-81049); **Barrtra Seafood Restaurant**, small, excellent, unpretentious (☎ 065-81280); **Lahinch Hostel** (☎ 065-81040).

Irish Traditional Music in Clare
Ennistymon. Phil's Bar & Nogles, Main St.

Ennis. *The Fleadh Nua*—a music festival on the last weekend in May; **Farrell's**, O'Connell Square; **P.J. Kelly's**, Carmody St.
Miltown Malbay. **Willy Clancy Summer School** (second week of July); **The Flowing Tide**, traditional music summer school.
Lahinch. O'Looney's, Main St.
Doolin. O'Connor's Pub, McGann's, McDermotts.

Lahinch, Cliffs of Moher, the Burren, Ailwee Caves.

The N67 from Milltown Malbay skirts the coast north of the town, passing the ruin of **Freagh Castle** (near a curious blow-hole), before entering **Lahinch**, a small resort on Liscannor Bay, Hag's Head and the ruins of **Dough Castle**. **The Burren Way**, which begins at Liscannor, follows the coastline, with excellent views towards the Aran Islands. The road now climbs the landward ridge of hills which form the Cliffs of Moher.

The Cliffs of Moher

The cliffs (Tourist Information, ☎ 065-9681171), form a sheer precipice, 8km long; one of the most impressive stretches of the coast in the west of Ireland. During the nesting season a remarkable variety of seabirds nest here, among them guillemots, razor-bills, puffins, kittiwakes and shags. The best view is enjoyed from **O'Brien's Folly**, approached by a track (parking) leading left from the main road. Steps climb to the right to a walled path running parallel to the cliff edge (beware of gusts of wind). From the path and tower (restored) the junction of the lime-stone flags with the black shale above them in the stratified cliff is well seen, in between which is a calcareous band, rich in fossils. Just below the tower is the spire-like stack of **Goat's Island**; out to sea are the **Aran Islands** (Inisheer, Inishmaan, and Inishmore), with the Galway coast on the right. On a clear day, the mountain of Croaghaun, on Achill, over 100km north-west, is visible.

The road descends past **Doolin**, noted as a centre for traditional music. A ferry service to the Aran Islands operates from mid-March to October). **Lisdoonvarna**, has a spa with sulphur and chalybeate springs rich in iodine and radioactive properties. In September the **Match-making Festival** is held here, during which elderly farmers in possession of a bungalow and EU milk-quota are seen in avid search of nubile young wives.

The road (R477) leaves the coast after Ballyvaughan, passing (right) **Ballynalackan Castle** on a crag, and turns inland. Passing several ruined churches and stone forts, you reach **Black Head**, a bleak and barren headland commanding a good view of Galway Bay, and turn along the north side of the terraced limestone cliffs, the 16C tower of **Gleninagh Castle** visible.

Ballyvaughan, 16km northeast, an old seaside village can be approached direct from Lisdoonvarna by the N67, crossing the **Burren plateau** and passing **Cahermacnaghten**, a stone fort known as O'Davoren's House (1675), where the old Irish pre-Christian Brehon laws continued to be studied although previously abolished. Descending Corkscrew Hill, you pass the prominent five-storey cylindrical tower of **Newtown Castle** (16C). Some 3km south of Ballyvaughan is the entrance to **Ailwee Caves** (10.00–18.30, Mar–Nov; 10.00–19.30, July–Aug; £), among the more accessible in the region. South of Ailwee are the

Gleninsheen megalithic wedge-tombs, and at **Poulnabrone** is a fine dramatically formed portal tomb; excavations in 1986 revealed the bones of 14 adults and six children.

Bearing northeast, you round a spur of the plateau, passing ruined Drumcreehy church, with its lancet window and 16C north door, and the castle of **Muckinish**. At this junction, turn left down a lane off the right-hand fork, for the Cistercian **Corcomroe Abbey** (founded 1194). The church dates from 1210–25 and the mouldings (recalling Killaloe) and capitals in the choir and the sedilia (seating used by the clergy) are all worth noting. There are also traces of incised drawings on the north wall, below which is the tomb of Conor O'Brien, King of Thomond (d. 1267) and grandson of the founder, Donal Mor O'Brien.

Returning to the road and turning left and left again, you pass near Oughtmama, where three churches from an early monastic settlement remain. The westernmost church has a pre-Romanesque nave and Romanesque chancel; note the interlaced antlers of two stags on the font. Continuing on this minor road you shortly descend to regain the N67 to Kinvara, a small port, with the well-restored 16C tower and bawn of Dunguaire (which serves medieval banquets).

The road bears northeast to Kilcolgan and **Kilcolgan Castle** (c 1801), just short of which you pass (left) the ruined church of **Drumacoo** (13C), with a finely carved south door and **Tyrone House** (1779). This was the model for the 'Big House of Inver', described by Somerville and Ross in their eponymous novel (1925). It was abandoned in 1905 and burned in 1920.

Dysert O'Dea, Leamaneh Castle, Kilfenora

At Fountain Cross, 4km northwest of Ennis, the right fork onto the R476, passes the ruins of **Ballygriffy Castle** while the N85 descends the Cullenagh valley through Ennistymon. Keep on the R476 for the ruins of **Dysert O'Dea** (next turning on the left) which consists of a church, 32m long, with 13C–14C windows and a 12C doorway with a semi-circle of sculptured heads. In the adjacent field there is a High Cross with interlaced and zoomorphic patterns and a Crucifixion (east side) above a figure said to represent St. Tola, founder of the church (the penultimate stone of the cross appears to be missing).

Inscriptions record its repair in 1683 by Michael O'Dea, a member of the family that owned the adjoining (15C) castle, re-erected in 1871. The castle is now the **Dysert O'Dea Archaeology Centre** (10.00–18.00, May–Sept; £), with a good antiquities exhibition, audio-visual show and café. Dysert was the scene of a battle in 1318, when Sir Richard de Clare and his son were killed and Anglo-Norman control of Thomond brought to an end. Romanesque remains and other features of interest, including a Sheila-na-gig may be seen in the church at Rath, nearby.

You can regain the road just south of

Romanesque carved heads on west door of church, Dysert O'Dea

Corrofin, a village lying between Lough Atedaun (right) and **Lough Inchiquin**, backed by wooded hills. The artist Sir Frederick William Burton (1816–1900) was born at Corrofin House. Skirt the east shore of the lough, passing Inchiquin castle.

The low hills that rise to the north between this point and the coast abound in ruined churches and cahers; the finest of these Iron Age rock-forts is at **Ballykinvarga**, 3km northeast of Kilfenora, which has a limestone *chevaux de frise*. The rock-fort at **Cahercommaun**, north of Killinaboy, has been excavated to reveal the interior chambers.

You pass the ruined 17C mansion of **Leamaneh** (right), incorporating an earlier tower (c 1420). Here, in 1651 '**Máire Ruadh**' ('Red Mary' O'Brien) married a Cromwellian officer after the death of her husband in a skirmish (at the hands of the Cromwellians). She married in order to preserve her estate for her son who was brought up a Protestant and is buried in the C of I church at Kilnasoolagh (see Ch. 9)—but is reputed to have subsequently murdered the officer by pushing him out a window.

Shortly beyond you reach **Kilfenora**, a place of ancient importance. The **cathedral** of St. Fachan is a small 12C building with a stepped square tower; the nave has been tastelessly fitted up as a parish church, but the roofless choir has a fine east window and a monument, believed to be of St. Fachan. An imposing 12C High Cross, with a Crucifixion on one side and a bishop and two other clerics on the other stands in the graveyard.

The small **Burren Display Centre** at Kilfenora (open mid-April to mid-September) provides an audio-visual description of the area, and its varied botany and wildlife.

Kilmacduagh, Thoor Ballylee, Coole Park, Clarinbridge, Kinara

A very interesting group of ecclesiastical ruins can be seen at **Kilmacduagh** (R460 from Corofin), southwest of Gort. It was here that St. Colman MacDuagh founded an episcopal see in c 610 and the original church was built for him by his kinsman Guaire Aidhne, King of Connacht. The present **cathedral**, rebuilt in the 14C–15C style, incorporates the 10C west doorway with a massive lintel.

The north chapel contains 16C–18C O'Shaughnessy tombs (Fiddaun Castle, 4km south of Gort, is a well-preserved stronghold of the O'Shaughnessys) and a figure of St. Colman.

O'Hyne's Abbey, to the northwest, a 13C foundation with evidence of earlier occupation (c 10C) is more interesting. The piers of the chancel arch and the two-light east window are in the mature Irish Romanesque style (c 1266) and the vaulted sacristy and chapter house can still be seen on the south side. The **Oratory of St. John**, north of the cathedral may date from St. Colman's time. Beyond it is the 14C

Incised slab with portrait of a head with pigtails, Kilmacduagh

Bishop's Castle and restored Round Tower, leaning 60cm out of the perpendicular. Teampull Muire, on the far side of the road, retains two round-headed
windows and a doorway.

Thoor Ballylee and W. B. Yeats

Turn left and left again off the N66 to Loughrea for Thoor Ballylee, known as
Islandmore Castle in the 17C. This was intermittently the residence of W.B. Yeats
(1865–1939) between 1921–29. In 1896, Yeats and Arthur Symonds, were
staying at nearby Tullira Castle as guests of Edward Martyn when they were
introduced to Lady Gregory who profoundly influenced Yeats' development as a
poet. With Yeats, she later founded the Abbey Theatre in Dublin (1904).

Yeats bought Thoor Ballylee for £35 in 1916 from the Congested Districts
Board and started to convert it the following year. In 1948 a stone was set up
here, inscribed with his words:

> I, the poet William Yeats
> With old millboards and sea-green slates
> And smithy work from the Gort forge
> Restored this tower for my wife George.
> And may these characters remain
> When all is ruin once again.

By then the tower—depicted on the cover of Yeats' volume of poems called *The
Tower* (1928)—was already in a sorry state of dilapidation, as he had predicted.
It was saved and restored by the Kiltartan Society and can be seen from across
the mill-stream, or the small walled garden.

The interior, now restored, (open March to late October; £) retains much of
the original china and oak furniture—the latter made on the spot and designed
by W.A. Scott (note the bookshelf over the bed-head). There is also a complete set
of broadsheets illustrated by Jack Yeats, and a collection of first editions of W.B.
Yeats. You can still see the 'narrow winding stair, a chamber arched with stone,
a grey stone fireplace with an open hearth' (referring to the principal apartment). The walls have been repainted in their original colours and a stair
ascends to the flat roof.

Coole Park

Coole Park, further along the N18, north of Gort (10.00–17.00, Tue–Sun;
09.30–18.30 daily, June–Aug; 10.00–17.00 daily, Sept; OPW; £) was the home
of Augusta, Lady Gregory (1859–1932) and from 1880 was a centre of the
Irish literary revival. Yeats, who first visited it in 1897, wrote of it in 'Coole
Park', (1929)

> Here, traveller, scholar, poet, take your stand
> When all those rooms and passages are gone,
> When nettles wave upon a shapeless mound
> And saplings root among the broken stone...

Lady Gregory is a pivotal figure in the Irish cultural revival of the late
19C–early 20C. Her work as folklorist, translator, playwright, theatre

producer and host to the principal intellectual figures of her day at Coole Park gave her widespread influence in the shaping of the culture of the time. Her principal contributions to Irish writing lie in her realisation that the Hiberno-English folk speech of country people which combined English language vocabulary with language structures and imagery from Gaelic, was a rich source of poetic expression, and an appropriate medum for a new Irish literature. Yeats, Synge, O'Casey and just about every other Irish writer of the period were influenced by her ideas and knowledge (she spoke Irish fluently which W.B. Yeats did not).

The demesne is now part of the **Coole-Garryland Nature Reserve**. The house, bought by the Free State government in 1937 after the death of Lady Gregory, (whose only son was killed in World War I) became progressively more derelict, and was pulled down by a building contractor in 1941 for the value of the stone. Only the stable-block remains, housing an audio-visual show and tearooms. In the grounds is the **Autograph Tree**, a copper beech inscribed with the initials of W.B. and J.B. Yeats, G.B. Shaw, J.M. Synge, Seán O'Casey, John Masefield, Violet Martin (real name of 'Ross', from the Somerville and Ross partnership), Augustus John, Katherine Tynan, and others.

Continue to **Kiltartan**, with a ruined 13C castle and church, and shortly pass (right) **Tullira Castle**, a 17C tower-house encased by a mock-Tudor rebuilding of 1882, and the home of Edward Martyn (1859–1923), the dramatist and eccentric patron of the arts, stained glass in particular. The Palestrina choir which he founded to sing sacred music still performs at the RC Pro Cathedral in Dublin.

The road then veers northwest through the villages of Ardrahan, Kiltiernan and Kilcolgan, passing a number of ruined castles and churches. At the head of the creek of **Dunbulcaun Bay** lies **Clarinbridge** where an Oyster Festival is held for a week in September. **Kilcorman House** incorporates the tower of a 15C–16C castle. Bear round the head of Galway Bay, meeting the N6 east of Oranmore (by-passed) and veer west for Galway. **Dunghaire Castle** (09.30–17.30 daily, May–Oct; £) at **Kinvara**, to the southeast on the N67, is named after a 7C king of Connaught. The 16C tower-house with complete six-sided bawn wall, hosts medieval banquets.

Gort, Tuamgraney

Beyond Ennis the N18 runs through a wide lough-studded valley to Crusheen. Pass (right) **Lough Inchicronan** with its ruined 12C–15C abbey standing on a peninsula. Not far north of Crusheen you enter Co. Galway, at a bridge between two small lakes. A bit further on is the demesne of **Lough Cutra Castle** (£) a handsome Regency residence designed by Nash and built by the Pain brothers (c 1816).Having stood empty for 40 years it was restored in the early 1970s and the Victorian additions were removed. It is well sited with views of the lough through the trees.

Further along on the right is the 'Punchbowl', a deep wooded chasm. The stream at the bottom of it flows underground from Lough Cutra to Gort (a former garrison town with a triangular market-place).

Feakle, (east of the N18) is noted for its traditional music. The **East Clare**

Heritage Centre (10.00–18.00 daily, Apr–Sept; OPW; £), further east at Tuamgraney, is actually in St. Cronan's Church (c 969), the earliest church in the British Isles still in use. It has an audio-visual programme on the antiquities of Holy Island, in Lough Derg. Boat trips to Holy Island are available from here.

Gort (*Gort Inse Guaire*) takes its name from a Guaire, a 6C king of Connacht. The town was laid out by the Vekers, ancestors of Lord Gort who restored Bunratty Castle. They lived at Lough Cultra Castle. The charming Kiltartan School in the town was commissioned in 1900 by Sir William Gregory, husband of Lady Gregory, and designed by her brother F.H. Persse in an Arts & Crafts manner. It is being developed as a museum to the Gregory's.

11 · The West: Galway and Connemara

Lough Corrib and **Lough Mask** almost cut County Galway in half. Between the lakes and the Atlantic coast is Connemara, much of which is included in the **Connemara National Park**. This is wild and beautiful countryside, comprising 2000 hectares of mountain, bogs and heathland, with the **Twelve Pins**, **Partry** and **Maumturk Mountains** at its northern border; all excellent hill-walking territory. North of the mountains is **Killary Harbour**, the only true fjord in Ireland. Part of the **Western Way** walking route (from Maam to Leenaun, 28km and from Lough Corrib to Killary Harbour, 50km) runs through this region, and there are **Aran Ways** on each of the Aran Islands (Inishmore Way, 34km; Inishmaan Way, 8km; Inisheer Way, 10.5km).

The impressive antiquities and windswept landscape of the **Aran Islands** are easily accessible from Galway by plane or boat. **Dun Aengus**, on Inishmore, is one of the best-preserved stone forts in Ireland, and among the most dramatically sited Iron Age monuments in Europe. The **Turoe Stone**, **Knockmoy Abbey**, and **St. Nicholas' Church**, Galway, are also important. **Pearse's Cottage** in Rosmuc commemorates the 1916 leader. **Tuam**, with two fine churches, is the principal town east of the lakes.

Irish music and the Irish language are strong in the area; **Galway City** has the largest concentration of urban Irish speakers in the country. An important late-medieval walled town, it still retains much of its original character. The **Galway Arts Festival**, held in the last two weeks of July, offering theatre, film, literature, readings, street theatre, music and the visual arts is the most dynamic and popular event of its kind in Ireland. The Macnas street parade rivals the St. Patrick's Day parade in Dublin. These, combined with the **Galway Races** and **Oyster Festival** guarantees various forms of stimulating, exciting and good-humoured activities.

How to get there
■ **Rail**. Direct from Dublin, connections from Cork, Belfast and Rosslare.
■ **Air**. Shannon International; Knock, Co. Mayo; Connemara for Aran Islands.
■ **Sea**. Ferry to Aran Islands.

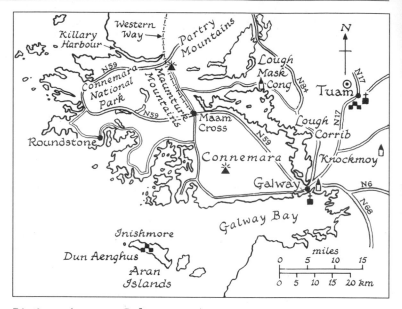

Listings (except Galway city)

Clifden. **Destry's**, restaurant taking its theme (and title) from the classic Marlene Dietrich movie *Destry Rides Again* (1939). Could one go wrong? They haven't (☎ 095-21722); **The Quay House**, waterside restaurant for exciting innovative eating (☎ 095-21369).

Cashel Bay. **Cashel House**, one of the most noted hotels in Ireland, set in gorgeous gardens and landscape (☎ 095-31001).

Letterfrack. **Rosleague Manor**, in wooded coastal setting, small hotel in 18C building (☎ 095-41101).

Oughterard. **Currarevagh House**, hotel on the shores of Lough Corrib, 19C mansion, informal ambience, fine food (☎ 091-82312).

Recess. **Ballynahinch Castle Hotel**, romantic Gothic extravaganza, once home of the great cricketer, HRH Ranjitsinhji, Maharaja of Nawangar; effortless old-world grandeur (☎ 095-31006).

Tuam. **Imperial Hotel**. Popular country-town hotel with weekend dancing (☎ 093-24188).

Galway City

Galway (*Gaillimh*, the place of the foreigners) a cathedral and university city, is the largest and fastest growing town in Connacht. The only coastal population centre of major significance between Limerick and Derry, it has a strong Irish language tradition; its hinterland has the most extensive Irish-speaking areas (*Gaeltacht*) of the country.

Situated at the head of Galway Bay and below Lough Corrib, it spans the Corrib river and its islands. Oysters thrive in the clear waters of the bay, warmed by the North Atlantic Drift, while during the spring run the river between neighbouring Lough Corrib and the sea is often packed with salmon.

Galway is the home of **Taibhdhearc na Gaillimhe**, an important Irish-language theatre company (1928). The **Druid Theatre** (1975) presents the work of present-day English language playwrights and **Macnas** (1990) is an innovative street theatre company.

The first authentic account of Galway occurs in the *Annals of the Four Masters*, who record a fort built here by the men of Connacht in 1124. In 1232 Richard de Burgh took this from the O'Flaherty's, and colonised the district. In 1396 it became a Royal Borough, and in 1484 it acquired Mayoral status, from which point the 14 families (Athy, Blake, Bodkin, Browne, Darcy, Deane, Ffrench, Ffont, Joyce, Kirwan, Lynch, Martin, Morris and Skerrett), later known as 'The Tribes of Galway', became powerful. This opprobrious name was given to them by the Cromwellians, mainly because of their clannishness, which has since been regarded as a mark of distinction. Among the more prominent of this oligarchy were the Lynch family, who are said to have provided the town with 84 mayors between 1485 and 1654.

Between the 14C and 16C Galway city developed a character unique among Irish towns as a wealthy independent mercantile city-state, trading extensively with continental ports. Geographically far removed from the direct influence of Dublin and London, it remained nonetheless a firm bulwark of English power, language and culture, and in 1518 the Corporation resolved 'that neither O nor Mac shall strut nor swagger through the streets of Galway', so great was their antipathy towards their Gaelic neighbours. During the 15C–16C the domestic architecture of the town reached a high level of sophistication, with fine stone houses, richly decorated with sculptural and armorial bearings, and covering over 12 hectares within extensive fortifications.

In 1652 Galway was taken by the English General, Edmund Ludlow, and barbarously treated by the Parliamentary army. Its once-flourishing seaborne trade with France and Spain declined and the town decayed, in 1691 surrendering on honourable terms to the Dutch General of William III's forces, Godert de Ginkel after his victory at Aughrim. Galway was the base of the old 88th Regiment, the Connaught Rangers, from the domestic annals of which Charles Lever drew numerous stories for his novel, *Charles O'Mally* (1841).

Among Galway natives were Frank Harris (1856–1931) author of salacious memoirs, Padraic O'Conaire (1883–1928), Gaelic writer and Nora Barnacle (1884–1951), the wife of James Joyce. Mairtin O'Direain (1910–88), Irish language poet from Aran, worked in Galway. Lady Gregory (1852–1932) was buried here.

Stephen Gwynn (1864–1950) whose *Masters of English Literature* (1904) became a best-seller, was MP for Galway City 1906–1918. William Joyce, better known as 'Lord Haw-Haw' (1906–46), was educated here. He was hanged for treason for his Nazi propaganda broadcasts from Germany in World War II and reburied in Galway in 1976.

How to get there

■ **Air**. Carnmore (internal flights) (☎ 091-52874); Inveran for the Aran Islands (☎ 091-93238).
■ **Bus**. Bus Station, Eyre Square (☎ 091-63555).
■ **Train**. Railway Station, Eyre Square (☎ 091-64222).
■ **Sea**. Ferryport. (for Aran Islands), Dock Road (☎ 091-68903).

■ **Tourist Information**. Victoria Place, off Eyre Square (☎ 091-63081).
■ **Post Office**. Erlington St (☎ 091-62052).
■ **Festivals**. April. *Cuirt*, an International Poetry Festival; July: Galway Arts Festival, the principal arts festival in the Republic; August (Bank Holiday weekend): Galway Races; September: Oyster Festival.

Listings

Galway. **Brennan's Yard Hotel**, good city-centre hotel with Oyster Bar (☎ 091 - 568166); **Jury's Galway Inn**, well sited budget hotel (☎ 091-66444); **Kinlay House**, hostel (☎ 091-565244); **The Snug**, 16C hostelry, dark and moody, (☎ 091-62831); *Tigh Neachtain*, good food and music pub, former town house of 'Humanity Dick', founder of the RSPCA (☎ 091-66172).

The City. There are two separate zones of interest, the harbour area, river and canals—with over a dozen bridges it has an attractive waterside environment—and the narrow medieval streets. Much of the character of the 16C town is preserved, the fabric and interiors of the medieval houses often concealed behind later façades. Galway is unquestionably one of the most distinctive towns in Ireland.

Old Town

The centre of **Eyre Square** (re-named **John Fitzgerald Kennedy Park**) has a number of monuments. The **Browne Doorway** is an orphaned fragment of a 17C merchant's house (1627); there is a diminutive statue of the writer **Padraic O'Conaire**, author of *M'asal Beag Dubh* (My Little Black Donkey) by Albert Power (1936); one of the revolutionary, **Liam Mellows** (Domnall O'Murchada, 1957), and a portrait plaque of J.F. Kennedy by Albert O'Toole. Dominating the square is the **Quincentennial Fountain** suggesting the sails of 'Galway Hookers', a local type of fishing boat (Eammon O'Doherty, 1984). Both the railway station and bus terminus are on the south side of the square, behind the Great Southern Hotel. Both station and hotel are by the railway pioneer J.S. Mulvany (1850), but only the hotel retains any distinction and it is the sole building of note in the square. The park in the square continues to be a popular meeting place.

The silver **Sword of Galway** (1610) and the **Great Mace** (1710) are

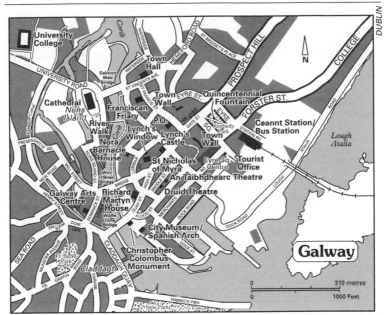

displayed in the Bank of Ireland. They were acquired by William Randolph Hearst in 1938 and generously returned to Galway in 1960 by the Hearst Foundation. Remains of sections of the town fortifications with the restored medieval Penrice and Shoemaker's Towers of the city wall can be seen in Eyre Square Shopping Centre.

William St (prolonged south into Shop, High and Quay Streets), is at the heart of the historic and shopping district, with many fragmentary late medieval buildings along its twisted length. 'The Snug' pub (right) has medieval features in its sepulchral interior. The deconsecrated former Catholic cathedral (1816, closed 1966) is now full of shops.

On the right of Shop St is **Lynch's Castle** (c 1600, open bank hours), the best preserved of the mansions erected by the prosperous merchants of Galway (now a bank). Although the façades have been drastically altered, the window hood-mouldings are finely decorated; one upper window retains its foliated spandrels and mullions. The arms of Henry II and the lynx of the Lynch family are still visible on the Shop St façade, as are those of the Fitzgerald's on Abbeygate St. The ground floor has been completely altered by a new street façade; the carved entrance is by Laurence Campbell (1933). There is a good display documenting the history of the building in the foyer.

Further south, in a turning to the right off Shop St, stands the church of **St. Nicholas of Myra** (C of I), founded in 1320. Its nave and chancel form has been disguised by widening the aisles (16C) to make the nave area rectangular. The central tower of c 1500 is crowned by a 17C pyramidal steeple. The finials of the 15C west door have been shortened to accommodate the 17C west window. A fine 15C cut stone readers' desk has been set up in the north aisle outside the Blessed Sacrament Chapel, a rare early 16C holy water stoup stands nearby, and in the southwest corner is a decorated baptismal font.

Decorated 16C window fragment in Flood Street, with amphisbena (two-headed dragon), hound and arms of the Martin Family

In the disproportionately long south transept among the many **Lynch tombs** is the flamboyant late 15C tomb on the east wall, with elaborate carving. Against the south wall a large tomb covers the remains of James Lynch FitzStephen, mayor of Galway in 1493. He is commemorated by the **Lynch Window**—a fanciful Victorian pastiche of unrelated fragments embedded in a wall, west of the churchyard—said to record his summary act of justice in condemning his own son to death for murder and then personally hanging him when none of the citizens would serve as executioner (the story and its association with 'Lynch Law' are apocryphal).

In Bowling Green, west of the Lynch Window, is the cottage home of Nora Barnacle (1884– 1951), wife of James Joyce, now preserved as a **museum**.

Continuing south on High St (left) is **Kenny's Bookshop**, one of the leading antiquarian and general bookshops in Ireland with an art gallery and print department. Features of the 17C interior are visible. There are fine 15C–16C architectural fragments throughout the High Street, either in situ or replaced in later buildings. Behind it, in Middle St (left) are the *An Taibhdhearc* (☎ 091-562024) and Druid Theatres (☎ 091-568617). At the Quay St-Cross St corner is the 17C and earlier town house (now a pub/restaurant) of Richard Martin (1754–1834) otherwise known as 'Humanity Dick', the greatest landholder in Connacht, and one of the founders of the RSPCA.

The Waterside

Quay St reaches the river at **Wolfe Tone Bridge**, which used to lead towards a picturesque settlement of thatched cottages known as **The Claddagh** (the beach), but were replaced by modern local authority housing in 1937. The **Claddagh ring**, a small amulet shaped by two hands holding a crowned heart symbolising trust, used both as a betrothal and wedding ring, is still commonly worn by both sexes in the west of Ireland. It was originally a man's ring and the style (peculiar to the region), derives from rings recovered from the wrecked ships of the Armada, which sank around the west coast in 1588.

To the left of the bridge is **Spanish Parade** with (left) Blake's Tower (16C), now incorporated into Jury's Inn and opposite a late medieval corner house. On the quayside is a fragmentary bastion romantically called the **Spanish Arch** (actually the remnant of an English fort but popularly believed to have protected Spanish ships trading in wine with Galway before 1584, when their privileges were removed by the English), and a fine external section of the city wall.

The Galway City Museum (10.00–17.00 daily, June–Sept; £) in an adjacent building has a good local history collection, if amateurishly displayed. A reproduction of the 2m-wide 1651 pictorial map of Galway, the finest 17C map of any Irish city, is on display (only two copies of the engraving survive, at Trinity College, Dublin and University College, Galway). It gives a bird's-eye-view of the walled city at the peak of its pre-Cromwellian prosperity in fascinatingly accurate detail. There is also a reconstructed façade of a 16C town house (1577) on the roof terrace.

From Spanish Parade the riverside walkway leads to **William O'Brien Bridge** (a portion of which dates from 1342) where there are fine restored 19C mills. Cross the bridge, which leads (left) into **Lower Dominick St**, a terrace of the characteristic Galway type of late 18C stone-built town houses. No. 47, now the **Galway Arts Centre** was Lady Gregory's town house.

Further along the riverside walk, at **Salmon Weir Bridge** (1818) there is a salmon trap where the fish can be seen swimming upstream to their spawning grounds during the spring run. East of Salmon Weir Bridge in St. Vincent's Ave is the **Court House** by Sir Richard Morrison (1812), which faces the 18C **Town Hall Theatre** (☎ 091-569777) across a small square. To the right is the Franciscan **friary**, a Greek Revival building (1836) with a Doric portico and nave arcade.

Salmon Weir Bridge leads to **Nun's Island**, through which run branches of the Corrib, directly to the **Cathedral** (RC)—by John J. Robinson (1957), although Bishop Michael Brown is now credited with its inspiration—one of the last cruciform churches to be built in Ireland. Its concept harks back to the scale and glories of 19C cathedral building, without the sense of discipline exercised by working in a well-understood style. Externally it a large plain limestone building (91m long) with Romanesque windows, bizarre Tudor rose-shaped rose windows, a Renaissance dome and Mexican Baroque cupolas! The stations of the cross are by Gabriel Hayes, the mosaics by Patrick Pollen and in the east transept are 17C panels of the Trinity. It remains one of the great lost opportunities of 20C Irish church building, being 'neither fish, fowl, nor good red herring' and the surrounding acres of car parking do not contribute to its dignity.

On the far bank of the Corrib is the severe Tudor-Gothic **University College** (1846–50) by Joseph B. Keane, the only one of what John MacHale, Archbishop of Tuam (1845) called the 'Godless Colleges' (Belfast, Cork and Galway) to have a completely enclosed quadrangle. The college was founded in 1849 as Queen's College, and inherited a tradition of 16C scholarship which briefly earned for Galway the reputation of being the intellectual capital of Ireland. It is the only one of the Universities to offer bilingual courses.

Galway harbour, which opens out into Galway Bay, is well protected by Rinmore Point on the far side of Lough Atalia, and Nimmo's Pier, built by the famous Victorian engineer, Alexander Nimmo. There is a coastal public park south of the pier.

Beyond the eastern suburbs of Galway (N6) is **Oranmore Castle**, its massive keep dating from the 14C–15C. It surrendered to Sir Charles Coote, president of Connaught and general of Cromwell's troops in 1651. The later residence was dismantled and the restored castle remained unroofed until 1947.

The Aran Islands

The Aran Islands lie c 45km (28 miles) southwest of Galway. The landscape of the Islands has changed less than that of the mainland due to its unsuitability for modern agricultural practice. Fields of stony soil are enclosed by dry-stone walls, cast over the land like the web of a fishing net. The fields are genuinely tiny and the hills marked by great swathes of barren rock-faces. The flora and fauna of the Burren are also found on the Arans, which are a continuation of the mainland terrain. The principal industries are fishing and tourism and regular ferries operate during the summer with a reduced service in winter.

How to get there

■ **Air**. Minna, Connemara to the three islands. Flying time 6/10 mins. Three flights daily, Mar–Oct; two flights daily, Oct–Feb.
  The air terminus in Galway city is in Dominick St (to the west of Shop St, ☎ 091-93034). Further details from the Tourist Office, immediately southwest of Eyre Sq.

■ **Sea**. Galway City to Kilronan, Inishmore. Sailing time 90 mins. June & Sept, one sailing; July & Aug, two sailings.
  Rossaveel (near Costelloe, 36km west of Galway) to Inishmore. Sailing time 20 mins. June–Sept three sailings; Oct–May, one sailing.
  Inishmaan and Inisheer. One sailing daily.

Listings

Inishmore. **Mainistir House Hostel**, the Savoy of hostels, good ambience, greater food (☎ 099-61169); **Joe Watty's Pub**, Kilronan, drink & pub-grub, excellent value (☎ 099-6155).
Inisheer. *Baile an Caislean*, B&B and restaurant. Good value (☎ 099-75019); **The Fisherman's Cottage**. Restaurant (☎ 091-75073).

The three islands of Inishmore, Inisheer and Inishmaan (Tourist Office ☎ 099-61263; May–Sept) are formed by a ridge of carboniferous limestone, like the Burren region. In general they are barren and stony, most of the soil being man made, produced by a compost of sand and seaweed. A striking feature of the landscape is the maze of dry-stone walls separating the small-holdings. The vegetation is peculiar, trees being absent except in the most sheltered spots, while maidenhair and other rare ferns and rock-plants proliferate in the lime-stone crevices.

Until the 1950s the islanders, mostly Irish-speaking, used to wear a charac-teristic local dress of shawls, 'Aran' knitted sweaters of oiled wool and heel-less rawhide shoes or *Broga Urleathair*, commercially known as 'pampooties'. The different patterns were knitted as a way of identifying fisherman if lost at sea. Their fishing boats or *currachs* are made of tarred canvas, an adaptation of the ancient coracles of stretched skin.

The past life of the community has been portrayed in J.M. Synge's *The Aran Islands* (1907) and in the film *Man of Aran* (Robert Flaherty 1934). The author, Liam O'Flaherty (1896–1984) was born on Inishmore.

Perhaps the most remarkable feature of the islands is the quantity of pre-Christian and early Christian remains. *Ara Naoinch*, 'Ara of the Saints', owes its name to **St. Enda**, who obtained a grant of the islands from Aengus, King of Munster in c 490, and evangelised the inhabitants (legendary early settlers in Ireland, known as the Firbolgs). He founded ten convents, which flourished until 1587—whilst the O'Briens and O'Flaherties fought over the islands—when the English defeated the O'Flaherties and the monks

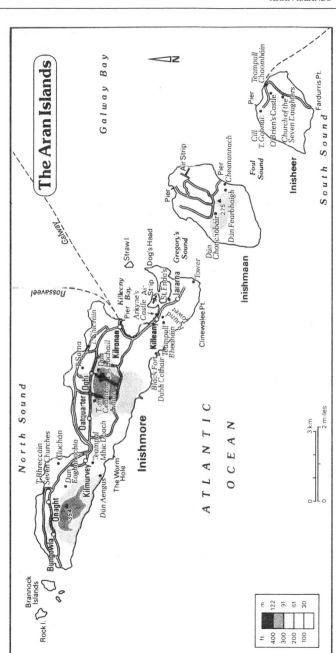

The Aran Islands

Galway Bay

North Sound

South Sound

Atlantic Ocean

Brannock Islands
Rock I.

Bungowla
Onaght
354
Dún Aengus
The Worm Hole
Kilmurvey
Dún Eoghanachta
T-Bhreacáin
Seven Churches
Clochán
Teampull
Mhic Duach
Oatquarter
Oghil
T. Sorna
Dún Eochla
Dún Ceathair
Dubh Cathair
Black Fort
Dubh Cathair
Teampull Bheanáin
Killeany
Inishmore

T. Chiaráin
Kilronan
Killeany
Pier Bay
Killeeny
Arkyne's Castle
Air-Strip
St Enda's
Iararna
Tower
Clinewalee Pt.
Strawl
Dog's Head
Gregory's Sound

Galway
Rossaveel

Inishmaan
Pier
Air-Strip
Pier
Cheanannach
275
Dún Fearbhaigh
Dún Chonchúir
Foul Sound

Inisheer
Cill
T. Gobhrái
O'Brien's Castle
Church of the Seven Loughers
Pier
Teampull Chaomháin
Fardurris Pt.

N

0   3 km
0   2 miles

ft   m
400   122
300   91
200   61
100   30

dispersed. In 1651 the castle of Arkyne on Inishmore, held out against Cromwell for a year after Galway had surrendered. When it finally fell, the church of St. Enda was demolished by Cromwell's men in order to construct a fort.

Inishmore

Inishmore (Great Island, or Aranmore) which lies some 11km south of the Galway coast is by far the largest (14.5km by 4km). **Kilronan**, the principal village on Inishmore (where the ferry docks) lies on the north side of Killeany Bay, while on the south side is the hamlet of **Killeany**, once the headquarters of St. Enda. The remains of Cromwellian **Arkyne Castle** are on a headland. The **Aran Centre** or *Ionad Arann* at Kilronan (10.00–17.00, April–May; 10.00–19.00, June–Aug; 11.00–17.00, Sept–Oct) covers the history and archaeology of the Aran Islands and there are daily screenings of the film *Man of Aran*.

Passing the remains of a round tower south of Killeany, you can climb to the diminutive but well-preserved 6C hilltop church of **St. Benignus** (*Teampull Benen* or *Bheanáin*; 6C) with gables 4.5m high. The neighbouring cashel encloses some *clocháns*, probably monks' cells. Further south, near Iararna, are the ruins of **St. Enda's** church. The **grave of St. Gregory** is said to be marked by the dry-stone Round Tower at the extreme southeast point. You can return to Kilronan on foot by a track along the southwest coast (a circular walk of c 13km) passing **Black Fort** (*Dubh Cathair* or *Doocaher*), a restored promontory fort somewhat difficult to reach.

The important remaining antiquities of the island can be visited from the road leading northwest from Kilronan. After 1.5km you pass *Teampull Chiaráin* (St. Kieran's church) on the right, and a little further on (left) *Teampull Sorna* (St. Sorney's church). On the hill to the left above Oghil is *Dún Eochaill*, a fine circular fort (restored). Further west is *Teampull an Ceathrar Alainn* (the Church of the four Beautiful Saints), also restored. Beyond, to the left, is Kilmurvey, with the well-preserved *Teampull MacDuach*, dedicated to Colman MacDuagh, founder of Kilmacduagh. The original windows have sloping lintels; the round-headed east window is a later addition.

On the coast, 1.5km south, is *Dún Aengus*, a huge Iron Age or earlier fort, built on the edge of the cliffs. It has three concentric lines of ramparts, of which the inner and middle are well preserved. Beyond the outer line is a ring of pointed stone stakes stuck in rock fissures serving as an antique *chevaux de frise* (see Kinvara, Ch. 10).

South of Onaght (9.5km from Kilronan), is another circular fort, *Dún Eoghanachta*, and on the north side of the road a perfect *clochán*. Near the shore are the mis-named 'Seven Churches'; one of which—*Teampull Bhreacáin* (St. Brecan's church)—has been rebuilt and restored. The saint's grave, to the west, is marked by a richly carved cross-shaft.

Inishmaan

Inishmaan (Middle Island) at 5km long by 2km broad is slightly larger than Inisheer. It is divided from Inishmore by Gregory's Sound, a strait 1.5km wide. Three sights to see are the well-restored oval fort of *Dún Chonchobáir* (Dún Conor or Chonchúir), *Teampull Cheanannach*, an oratory built of cyclopean blocks and to the west of the Teampull, **Dún Fearbhaigh**, a well preserved fort. The island was visited by J. M. Synge sporadically between 1898 and 1902, and is portrayed in a scene of his play, *Riders to the Sea* (1905), a one-act tragedy about an islander's loss of all her sons to the sea. It ends with the woman's acceptance of death 'No man at all can be living for ever and we must be satisfied.'

Inisheer

Inisheer (Eastern Island), the smallest island at just over 5km across, lies 8km from the Clare coast and is separated from Inishmaan by Foul Sound. Several sites are worth visiting; **St. Cavan's Church** (*Teampull Caomháin*), the **Church of the Seven Daughters**, **Dún Firmina**, a medieval stronghold belonging to the O'Briens, and the ruins of **Kilgobnet church** (*Teamphull Gobnait*).

Connemara: Spiddal, Carna, Roundstone

Connemara (from *Cuain na Mara*, harbours of the sea, or named after Conmac, the son of Fergus and Maeve) is the name loosely given to the beautiful but barren mountainous region bound by Galway Bay on the south, **Lough Corrib** and **Lough Mask** to the east and Clew Bay to the north. Connemara proper is almost identical with the Barony of Ballynahinch, and runs west of a line from Killary Harbour along the **Maumturk mountain range** to Gortmore, encompassing the **Twelve Bens** and a wilderness of tiny lakes to the south.

Iar Connacht (West Connacht) near Galway, known as **Joyce Country** (named after a family of Welsh extraction that settled here after the Anglo-Norman invasion) is a wilderness of granite. In Co. Mayo, north of Killary Harbour, there is an equally mountainous district known as **The Murrisk**. The scenery of the whole area is austerely beautiful, with some spectacular peaks and glens. Its rivers team with fish and it is also the country of the hardy Connemara ponies. The long established tweed industry is also world famous.

Galway Bay

A submerged peat-bog, c 3m below high-water mark, lends probability to the legend that Galway Bay was once a freshwater lake invaded by the Atlantic. Beyond Furbogh the country grows more desolate, but with good views across to the Clare coast. **Spiddal**, at the mouth of the Owenboliska, has a few fragments of the hospice after which it is named. Continue due north through what was once part of the notorious 'Congested Districts', where crofters subsisted on the harvest of the sea; fish and seaweed to fertilise their pocket handkerchief-sized fields. The average farm size was rarely more than a few acres and large sections of the population were moved elsewhere by the Congested Districts Board. Some 13km beyond, the road (R336) veers northwest, leaving the rock-bound peninsula of Carraroe to the left.

At (8km) Costelloe a lane forks left to **Bealadangan** from which bridges—often built as famine relief schemes during the mid 19C—cross to the Islands of **Annaghvane**, **Lettermore**, and **Gorumna**, the last only 11km north of the Aran Island of Inishmore (also approached by boat from Rossaveel, just south of Costelloe).

From Costelloe (headquarters of the radio service for the Gaeltacht), drive north to (10km) Screeb (9km beyond which you can regain the main road at

Maam Cross to the south of which, at **Rosmuc**, is *Teach an Phiarsaigh*, **Patrick Pearse's Cottage** (09.30–18.30, June–Sept; OPW; £), built and used as a summer retreat by the poet and leader of the 1916 rebellion, Patrick Pearse (1879–1916). Important as an educationalist, his poetry concerns the need for blood-sacrifice and is imbued with Christian imagery. Beyond Gortmore, the road circles the hilly peninsula to the remote fishing village of **Carna** (24km), an angling resort at the head of land-locked Bertraghboy Bay. **Lough Skannive**, with its two crannóg-like islands lies to the east. Offshore is **St. MacDara's Island**, with an ancient oratory (recently restored). The lonely tower of **Ard Castle** can be seen to the west. The road from Carna to Cashel (R342) offers a good view of the Twelve Bens.

A second circle seawards (R341) via Toombeola, leads to **Roundstone**, a lobster-fishing village, laid out by Alexander Nimmo (1783–1832) in the 1820s. The other local industry is the production of traditional musical instruments. At the **IDA Craft Centre** in Roundstone (09.00–19.00, Mar–Oct; 09.00–21.00, July–Sept; for winter opening times, except Sun, ☎ 095-35808), Malachy Kearns manufactures a unique traditional instrument, the *Bodhrán* (*Bodhar*, haunting) goatskin drum, which creates the pulse in Irish music. The shallow hand-held *Bodhrán* is a one-sided drum, stretched on a beech frame and played with a timber twin-headed stick or 'tipper'. Special *Bodhráns* were commissioned from Kearns for *Riverdance*, the internationally successful Irish traditional music and dance show.

The exhilarating quality of the air between Roundstone and Clifden has earned this route the name of the 'brandy and soda' road. It passes the white, shelly strand of Dog's Bay formed by microscopic foraminifera (seashells) and circles the isolated hill of **Errisbeg** (300m). The Mediterranean heath on the west slope flourishes, commanding a curious view over the numerous small lakes of this flat waterlogged district. You reach **Ballyconneely**, also known as 'Coral Strand' because of the texture of its sand, (produced by a calcareous seaweed known as lithothamnion), pass Bunowen Castle, beyond which are the rocks of Slyne Head, and skirt Mannin Bay. It was near here that the first aeroplane to cross the Atlantic landed in 1919. Piloted by Sir John Alcock and navigated by Sir Arthur Whitten-Brown the non-stop flight took 16½ hours.

At Ballinaboy cross the head of Arbear Bay and, passing a monastery, enter Clifden.

Clifden, Letterfrack, Renvyle

Clifden, standing high above the bay, is the capital of Connemara (Tourist Information, Market St, ☎ 095-21163; Apr–Sept) and a good centre from which to explore the area. It was founded as late as 1812 by John D'Arcy of Killtullagh. and is distinguished by the fine spires of its Protestant (1850) and Catholic (1875) churches, against a backdrop of rolling hills. The principal streets are arranged in an oval, and the view over the town from the 'Sky Road' is extremely picturesque. There is a flourishing lobster fishery here and an excellent selection of fish restaurants. The town is also well-known for its Connemara tweeds. The **Connemara Pony Show**, held in August, promotes the survival of this unique miniature local breed. At Letterslea, outside Clifden, is the **Dan O'Hara's Heritage Centre** (10.00–18.00 daily, Apr–Sept; £), the pre-1840 home of O'Hara, a local hero.

The derelict ruin of the castle (1815), built by John D'Arcy, is on the shore. **Gortrummagh Hill**, north west of the castle, offers panoramic views of the neighbourhood, including the Twelve Bens and the lakes to the southeast towards Roundstone.

Climbing north from Clifden you have a brief view of the narrow inlet of Streamstown Bay on your descent and Doon Castle, a ruined O'Flahertie stronghold. The next left-hand turning leads to (5km) **Cleggan**, a small fishing village, where boats may be hired to the offshore islands of Inishbofin and Inishark, offering fine coastal scenery. (There are three sailings daily, May–Sept. Journey time: 45 mins). On **High Island** (*Ard Oilean*) are the considerable remains of a 7C **monastery** established by St. Fechin, but inaccessible except in fine weather Inishbofin has a good harbour guarded by a 17C castle, and traces of a monastery founded by St. Colman (c 660).

The N59 bears northeast and descends towards the broad hill-girt fjord of Ballynakill Harbour, with Tully Mountain (355m) rising boldly behind it. At the head of the bay is the village of **Letterfrack**, originally a Quaker colony (**Letterfrack Visitor Centre**, 09.00–17.00 daily, May–Sept). Diamond Hill, to the south in Connemara National Park (see below), commands a fine view of the coast and of the Twelve Bens to the southeast.

A small road leads north to **Rinvyle** which has several sandy beaches. It was a favourite spot for various artists in the 19C. and what is now the **Rinvyle House Hotel** was once the residence of Oliver St. John Gogarty, who entertained Shaw, Yeats and Augustus John here. The philosopher Ludwig Wittgenstein, who lived in Ireland 1947–49, spent the summer of 1948 at Rosro Cottage, in the neighbourhood. Crump Island (offshore to the northwest) is a ruined church. On twin-peaked **Inishturk**, some 11km out to sea, are remains of a church built by St. Columba.

Lough Corrib, Cong, Lough Mask, Ballinrobe, Tuam

Lough Corrib ~ *east bank*
Lough Corrib to the north of Galway covers 17 hectares and at over 43km long, is one of the largest lakes in Ireland. Irregular in outline, for the most part it is very shallow and studded with drumlin islets and shoals, although towards its northern end a depth of 45m has been recorded.

To explore the sites on the **northeast side** of the Lough, take the N84, passing **Ballindooly Castle**.

Annaghdown (*Eanach Dúin*, the marsh of the fort), on the shore of Lough Corrib, was once the seat of the oldest bishopric in Co. Galway. A monastery and nunnery were founded here by St. Brendan, who died here in 577 (after appointing his sister Brigid head of the nunnery). The extant ruins are those of a Franciscan church and priory, a Norman castle and the bishop's house. In the graveyard are the ruins of a later church, with a fine east window transferred from the priory church. You regain the main road by a lane leading north from the abbey.

Headford, a village sheltered by the woods of Headford Castle, lies just south of the Black River, which separates Galway from Mayo. From here the main road (N84) to Ballinrobe passes through Shrule, with its ruined abbey and castle tower.

The bridge here was the scene of a treacherous ambush in which a party of Parliamentarian troops and others, under Sir Henry Bingham, were set upon and massacred by one Edmund Bourke, a clansman of the Earl of Mayo.

Killursa church, some 3km west of Headford, marks the site of a 7C monastery, later enlarged, founded by St. Fursa, a disciple of St. Brendan.

Rosserrily Abbey, or **Ross Abbey**, northwest of Headford (R334), was founded in 1351 and refounded by Franciscans in 1498, but not finally abandoned until 1765. The church is of the usual aisled cruciform plan with a central tower, but has round-headed arches in the south aisle and the transepts, an uncommon feature at so late a date. On the north side of the church are small but nearly perfect cloisters, and its dependencies, among them the kitchen and guest-house, are particularly well preserved.

After crossing the Black River, pass between the ruins of **Moyne Castle**, with a church site enclosed by a cashel, and (right) the ruins of 16C Kinlough Castle (right) and a 13C church. To the west there is a view of **Benlevy**, and the mountains of Joyce's Country beyond. Further northwest, on the far side of Lough Mask, are the Partry Mountains.

At Cross, fork left for the village of Cong (R346) passing near **Moytura House**, built in 1865 by Sir William Wilde, father of the playwright Oscar Wilde. **Cong** (*cunga*, a neck) derives its name from its position on an isthmus between Lough Corrib and Lough Mask. It was one of the locations for the film *The Quiet Man* (John Ford, 1952) a classic black and white film on Ireland, based on a story in *Green Rushes* (1935) by the novelist Maurice Walsh (1879–1964), which is commemorated by a festival with talks and screenings. A 14C cross in the village bears an inscription to Nicol and Gilbert O'Duffy, abbots of Cong. Below the village is **Ashford Castle** (now one of the most majestic hotels in the country), an ostentatious baronial pile built by James Franklin Fuller (c 1870) for Sir Arthur Guinness the Dublin brewer, who by 1915 had spent £1 million on the castle.

Near the entrance to Ashford Castle is **Cong Abbey**. This was founded for Augustinians in 1128 by Turlough O'Connor, King of Ireland (probably on the site of a 7C establishment of St. Fechin) and was further endowed by Roderick O'Connor, his son. He was the last native king, and spent the last 15 years of his life in the abbey, dying here in 1198. The ruins retain several fine doorways of a type transitional between Romanesque and Gothic and showing French influence, and a tall early Gothic east window. The cloisters were partly rebuilt in 1860, displaying the work of Peter Foy, a local mason.

A curiosity in the region is the **Dry Canal** between the two lakes, dug in the 1840s as famine relief work with the idea of extending navigation from Galway to Upper Lough Mark. When completed, it was found to be quite incapable of holding water, owing to the porous nature of the rock.

The R345 leads west from Cong across the isthmus between the loughs to **Clonbur**, then skirts the northern end of Lough Corrib below flat-topped Benlevy (416m; views) to Cornamona.

Between Cong and the Westport road, continuing north from Cross, there are remains of several **stone circles** and **cairns**. The antiquarian, Sir William Wilde assumed that the battlefield of Moytura was near here, the scene of the first great defeat of the Firbolgs (mythological peoples of Celtic Ireland) by Tuatha de Danaan, seven years before they were finally crushed at Northern Moytura, but Co. Sligo is now considered the correct location (see Kilmactranny, Ch. 13).

Lough Mask ~ east bank

A minor road nearer Lough Mask passes **Loughmask House**, on the shore beside a ruined castle. This was the residence of Captain Charles Boycott (1832–97), land agent for Lord Erne, and notorious for his inconsiderate treatment of the local tenantry during the Land League agitation in 1880 (and responsible for the addition of a new word to the English language). On the nearby island of **Inishmaine** are the remains of a monastery (burned in 1227), and church, with a late Romanesque chancel arch, a good east window, and an archaic early Christian square-headed doorway.

Ballinrobe is a convenient village from which to explore the east bank of Lough Mask. The village church contains nine windows by Harry Clarke (1925).

Tuam

Tuam lies south of Ballinrobe N84 then R332). To reach Tuam from Galway city take the N17 via Prospect Hill passing a massive square castle at **Claregalway** (11km), on the Clare river—the scene of so much fighting in the Cromwellian wars—and a Franciscan friary, founded in 1290. Ostensibly suppressed at the Reformation, it was, according to Bishop Pococke still used as a 'Romish masshouse' in 1765. The most attractive feature of the ruins is the graceful tower; the choir contains a De Burgh tomb.

Tuam (pronounced Chew-am) is the ecclesiastical capital of Connacht and the seat of both a Catholic archbishop and a Protestant bishop. The see was founded by St. Jarlath (d 540), the teacher of St. Brendan and St. Colman of Cloyne. In 1049 Aedh O'Connor, King of Connacht, established his residence here and it became the seat of the Kings of Connaught in the 12C.

The most interesting building in the town is the spired Protestant cathedral (St.Mary's), west of the centre, founded c1130 (probably by Turlough O'Connor) and largely rebuilt in 1861–63 in an attempt to reproduce the original style (key held at the drapers, east of Tuam Cross). The only part of the earlier structure which has survived, the chancel, is unexpectedly of red sandstone. The main chancel arch, long used as a doorway, is the widest as well as one of the finest examples of 12C Romanesque work in Ireland, with its six recessed orders, elaborate mouldings and richly sculptured capitals. There is a fine three-light east window with round-headed arches, and beyond that a 14C Gothic church, erected when the nave was demolished. Now restored, it is used as a synod hall. The 1863 restoration by Thomas Newenham Deane has cleverly merged the Romanesque, Gothic and Victorian elements of the building.

The **Catholic cathedral**, to the east of Market Square, is one of the finest examples of early Gothic Revival (c1830). It has an impressive spire and windows by Harry Clarke. The **Cross of Tuam** in the Market Square, bears inscriptions in honour of Turlough O'Connor and Abbot O hOisin, archbishop in 1152.

A small museum (10.00–18.00, Mon–Sat, June–Sept; £) has been installed in **Farrell's Gate Mill** (17C) (09.00–17.00, Mon–Sat, June–Sept), describing the process of milling. **Bermingham House** (1730), 3km east of Tuam, is open to the public.

Oughterard, Maam Cross, Recess

Lough Corrib ~ west bank

The main road from Galway (N59) turns inland after crossing to the west bank of the Corrib, briefly running parallel to the river and **Lough Corrib** before passing the bleak moors beneath **Knockalee Hill** (290m) (OPW). The **Iar Connacht** area is the ancestral home of the O'Flaherties; the mountains of Joyce Country in the distance. Beyond Ballycuirke Lough (right) is the lonely tower of *Caisleán na Caillighe* (or Hag's Castle). Beyond Moycullen, on the other side of the main road, is **Ross House**, birthplace of Violet Martin (1862–1915), the 'Ross' half of the Somerville and Ross partnership (the family were known as 'Martins of Ross', see Castletownshend, Ch. 7). The partly restored ruins of **Aughnanure Castle** (09.30–18.30, June–Sept; OPW: £) are on the banks of the Drimneen. This was the main O'Flahertie fortress (16C).

Inish an Ghoill Craibhthigh, or **Inchagoill** (Isle of the devout foreigner), in Lough Corrib, can be reached by boat from **Oughterard**, an angling village on the Owenriff. The ruins of two churches, the earlier of which, **Templepatrick**, contains an early inscribed stone; *Teampull na Naoimh* is a good example of Irish Romanesque (restored). Beyond Oughterard the road crosses a desolate waterlogged region, skirting Lough Bofin, to Maam Cross.

Those driving direct to Westport may turn north here, climbing through a pass between Leckavrea Mountain (left; 612m) and the lower Lackavra before reaching Maam Bridge, and turning left.

Hen's Castle

Hen's Castle (*Caisleán na Circe*), another O'Flahertie island stronghold, stands in the western arm of **Lough Corrib**. The present ruins date from the 13C rebuilding.

The name is said to derive from a wonderful hen, a witch's gift to the O'Flahertie, that would lay enough eggs during a siege to feed a garrison. Perhaps a more likely story is that the castle was saved from the Joyces by the prowess of Grace O'Malley, O'Flahertie's wife, described by Sir Philip Sidney as 'a most famous feminine sea captain'.

Ascend Joyce's River, a salmon and trout stream, north of Maum, with Lugnabricka rising on your right, away from Lough Corrib into the heart of the **Joyce Country**. Beyond Kilmeelicken church, a track diverges right, climbing up to **Lough Nafooey** (dangerous descent) and **Lough Mask**. The road then passes the isolated **Joyce's graveyard**, descending the Devil's Mother (right; 648m) to Leenane.

The area to the west of **Maam Cross** skirts the south bank of **Lough Shindilla**, with rugged Leckavrea (or Corcogemore; 612m) rearing up to the right. The valley soon opens out, flanked by the Maumturk range (701m). This marks the boundary between Connemara and Joyce Country. The hamlet of **Recess** is an angling resort between Glendollagh and **Derryclare Lough** beside which the finest green Connemara 'marble' is quarried (black marble is also quarried at **Anglihan** on the southern shore of Lough Corrib).

Immediately north of Recess rises **Lissoughter**, commanding a fine view of the Maumturk Mountains (northeast), the most conspicuous peak of which is **Letterbreckaun** (667m) and the group of mountains (to the west) known as **Twelve Bens** (Benna Beola) sometimes corrupted to the 'Twelve Pins'.

From the central peak, **Benbaun** (728m), a series of ridges radiates in a roughly star-shaped formation, each rising in a number of quartzite peaks (all over 520m). Much of their beauty lies in their symmetrical cone-like forms, the colour of the heaths and lichens covering them, and the glint of the quartz on a sunny day, which adds much to the enchantment of the scene.

On the southeast ridge (extending towards Derryclare Lough) are **Bencollaghduff**, **Bencorr** and **Derryclare**, with **Bencorrbeg** an irregular offshoot towards Lough Inagh. On the south ridge are Benbreen, Bengower and Benlettery, with Benglenisky a little to the west. The western ridge has as its summits Muckanaght and Bencullagh; and on the northern ridge is Benbrack.

Benlettery (580m), immediately above the road, offers the most rewarding ascent, owing to its more isolated position. From the summit you can see **Bertraghboy Bay** to the south, with Errisbeg on the right and Cahel Hill on the left. To the southwest is the labyrinth of lakes towards Clifden; to the northwest Inishark and Inishbofin can be seen out to sea; and to the east is the long ridge of the Maumturk Mountains, with the melancholy Pass of Maumeen.

On the south bank of the lough stands Ballynahinch Castle (now a hotel), once the residence of Richard Martin, 'Humanity Dick' (1754–1834) (see Galway, *Teach Neachtain*) (1754–1834), and later that of Maharaja Ranjitsinhji (1872–1933).

Connemara National Park

From **Letterfrack** the main road (N59) runs inland skirting an area of c 2000 hectares designated the **Connemara National Park** (10.00–17.30 daily, Easter, April, May & Sept; 10.00–18.30, June; 09.30–18.30, July & Aug; OPW; £), and crosses the **Pass of Kylemore**.

On the north side of Lough Poolacappul (also called Lough Kylemore), amid a forest of rhododendrons, is **Kylemore Abbey** (1864), (grounds, restaurant and farm shop open all year) the mock-Tudor residence of the Manchester merchant and Irish politician Mitchell Henry (1826–1910). It has been a convent and girl's school of the Benedictine Dames Irlandaises from Ypres since 1920. The house is spectacularly sited above the waters of Lake Pollacappul. A chapel in 14C English style, with stone vaulting has recently been restored (open to public).

Below **Garruan** (600m) skirt the north side of **Kylemore Lough** for a fine close view of the Twelve Bens. A 'famine road' to the right, beyond the lake, built in the 1840s, ascends up the glacier-scored valley, to **Lough Inagh** and Recess.

The main road skirts the southern end of **Lough Fee** offering fine views, before descending towards the shore of **Killary Harbour**. At 16km long, this is one of the most impressive of the Connemara inlets, a true fjord with deep water between steep mountains.

At the far end of the estuary lies **Leenane**, a centre for fishing and for the exploration of this wild mountain region. There is also a Wool Museum at the **Leenane Cultural Centre** (09.30–18.30, Apr–Oct or by appointment; £), with audio-visual and live demonstrations of local weaving.

The main road from Leenane ascends the Erriff valley under the lee of the **Partry Mountains**, rising to Benwee and Maumtrasna. Beyond Erriff Bridge the country opens out towards Westport, passing **Lough Moher** and descending the wooded Owenwee valley towards Westport.

12 · Mayo, Achill and Clew Bay

The north and west coasts of Mayo are deeply indented by **Killala**, **Blacksod** and **Clew Bays**, and the **Nephin Beg** and **Ox Mountains** run across the centre of the county. A superb long distance walking route in the region is the **Foxford Way** (from Foxford to Derrybrick, 86km). **Achill Island**, reached by a road-bridge, is the largest of the many islands off the coast. Overlooking Clew Bay on its southern shore is **Croagh Patrick**, the mountain where according to legend, St. Patrick banished snakes from Ireland, and for centuries the site of popular pilgrimage in August when vast crowds climb 'the Reek'. Inland from Croagh Patrick is **Knock**, a strange combination of contemporary place of spiritual pilgrimage, and fairground.

The remarkable Neolithic farming landscape of **Ceide Fields** on the north Mayo coastline is not only of unique archaeological significance, its location overlooking precipitous cliffs is spectacularly beautiful. **Ballintober**, **Boyle** and **Roscommon Abbeys**, and **Strade Friary** are important medieval remains. **Killala** was the scene of the French Invasion in 1798. **Westport** is an 18C planned town on Clew Bay, and **Westport House**, seat of Lord Altamont, is one of the great houses of the West of Ireland.

How to get there
- **Train**. Services to Ballina and Westport via Athlone.
- **Air**. Knock Airport.
- **Sea**. Clare Island.

Listings
Achill Island. Slievemore Hotel, Dugort, small family hotel (☎ 098-43224); The Wayfarer Hostel, Keel (☎ 098-43266). Also a wide choice of B&B's.
Ballina. Mount Falcon Hotel, Victorian Gothic country house, popular with anglers (☎ 096-70811); Belleek Castle, historic mansion, gourmet organic food (☎ 096-22400).
Cong. Ashford Castle, 5-star Gothic delirium on a very grand scale, lakes, wood-lands and any facility you could possibly imagine (☎ 092-46003); Echoes, restaurant serving a cornucopia of fresh and lavish foods (☎ 092-46059).
Castlebar. Hughes House Holiday Hostel (☎ 094-23877).
Claremorris. Lough Mask Hostel, Tourmakeady (☎ 092-44028).
Crossmolina. Enniscoe House, archetypal Irish Georgian mansion offering elegant B&B facilities (☎ 096-31112).
Knock. Knock International Hotel, catering for pilgrims to the shrine, motel style, meat and two rosaries (☎ 094-88466).
Newport. Newport House, angler's hotel specialising in seafood (☎ 098-41222).
Westport. Bernie's High St Café, local and exotic food (☎ 098-27797).

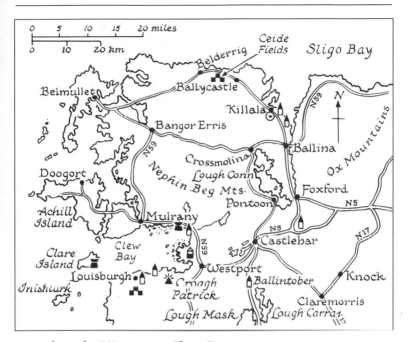

Louisburgh, Westport, Clew Bay

From Leenaun, the N59 leads to Louisburgh. The longer but more interesting road (R335) which turns left at Aasleagh church, and bears round the head of Killary Harbour, skirting Ben Gorm. **Aasleagh** is the centre of the Erriff salmon-fishery. At Bundorragha turn due north up the narrow valley dominated to the west by Muilrea, best ascended from the shore of Killary Harbour further west.

The easiest route is by following a cut in the face of the hill and bearing over a saddle onto the main ridge. The **view** of the coast extends from Slyne Head to Achill, while immediately northeast is the ridge overhanging the Delphi valley.

An alternative route to Westport is to cross the depression on the north between Benbury, connected to a third peak (Benlugmore) by a finely scarped ridge. From the summit of the former strike north to avoid the precipitous northeast face, to regain the road north of Glencullin Lough, a heavy and boggy route not to be attempted after wet weather.

Passing (left) Lough Fin, you reach **Delphi**, a fishing lodge near the southern end of sombre Doo Lough, well-deserving its name of 'Black Lake' in stormy weather. Skirting its northern side, flanked by the Sheeffry Hills (761m), climb out of the valley and descend past **Cregganbaum**, with a megalithic tomb, and across a desolate moor to the village of **Louisburgh**, taking its name from Louisburgh, Nova Scotia, at the capture of which in 1758, Henry Browne (uncle of the 1st Marquess of Sligo) was present as a young officer. The **Granuaile Centre** (11.00–17.00, Mon–Sat; 10.00–17.00, Sun, June; 10.00–18.00, July & Aug; 10.00–17.00, Mon–Fri, May, Sept & Oct; £) deals with local history and legend, including the full story of the local 16C Pirate Queen, Grace O'Malley (see Clare Island, below). There are some good beaches in the neighbourhood, at Cloghmoyle to the north, and at Old Head (northeast). To the southwest (also reached direct from Cregganbaum), are the extensive sands of **Carrowniskey Strand**, to the west of which is Caher Island, the haunt of wild geese, and Inishturk Island.

Clare Island

Clare Island lies northwest of Louisburgh, offshore from Roonah Quay. (**Ferry sailings**: Roonagh–Clare Island, Apr–May, one sailing; Jun–Sept, three sailings. Additional sailings on demand). It is a mountainous but fertile island and the local mountain of Knockmore (461m) on the north-west side, commands a good view of the south coast of Achill. In the centre of the island are the ruins of a small **Cistercian church**, possibly founded or rebuilt in 1460. The murals in the chancel indicate that the church was richly decorated. On the north side is a traceried tomb-canopy.

Grace O'Mally the Pirate Queen

The **castle**, at the eastern end of the island, was the stronghold of Grace O'Malley (*Grainne ni Mháille*; c 1530–c 1600), the Amazonian queen of the island, as famous for her piratical forays as for her modern way of treating her husbands, the first of whom was the O'Flahertie of Connemara. It is said that his castle in Lough Corrib was saved from the Joyces by her bravery. On O'Flahertie's death she married Sir Richard Burke of Mayo (called MacWilliam Oughter), on condition that at the end of a year either party might end the union by merely dismissing the other. In due time she closed the doors of Carrigahowley Castle against MacWilliam having first astutely garrisoned all of his castles with her partisans.

Also well known is the story of her interview with Elizabeth I in London, from whom she refused all favours, proudly regarding the English queen as her equal (for her alleged exploit at Howth, see Ch. 1). Remains of late 15C Kilgeever Abbey may be seen on the right.

Returning to the mainland drive east from Louisburgh, to reach **Croagh Patrick** (*Cruach Phádraig*; 763m) on the right. The ascent of the 'Reek' of St. Patrick may be made from the church of Leckanvy or (better) from **Murrisk Abbey**, further east. The abbey of Augustinian friars was founded by the O'Malleys in 1457, its aisleless church retaining a fine east window.

The Legend of Croagh Patrick

The summit of Croagh Patrick, which appears to be conical from a distance, is in fact a small plateau crowned by a chapel. Here, it is said, St. Patrick banished with the ringing of his bell all the noisome reptiles of Ireland. Each time he rang the bell, he hurled it down the precipice of Lugnanarrib (to the south), and was followed by an avalanche of toads, serpents and other repellent beasts. The bell was conveniently returned to him by fielding spirits. The event is annually celebrated on 'Reek Sunday' (first Sunday in August), when many thousands climb to the summit.

The **view** from the summit extends south to the Twelve Bens, and to the north across Clew Bay to the mountains of Achill; to Nephin (northeast), and beyond to Slieve League in Donegal. Clare Island is prominent out to sea.

Westport

Westport (Tourist Information, North Mall, ☎ 098-25711) is situated at the head of Westport Bay and is bisected by the Carrowbeg river. Its attractive 18C design was laid out by James Wyatt, in 1780 for Peter Browne, 2nd Earl of Altamont and still retains some of its elegance. The first John Browne established himself in Westport during the 17C, and his successors gradually acquired wealth and influence. John Dennis Browne became 1st Marquess at the Act of Union in 1800. In the 19C Westport was the scene of the influential meeting at which Michael Davitt organised the local Land League (August 1879) later to become a national organisation, led by Charles Stewart Parnell for the defence of tenant farmers against exploitation by landlords.

The canalised river Carrowbeg, flanked by the tree-lined malls, and crossed by attractive old bridges is the most pleasing survival of the 18C layout. The Arts and Crafts movement Post Office (J.H. Pentland, 1899) on the North Mall has a triple arched façade with broad eaves and St. Mary's church (R.M. Butler, 1932; RC), on the South Mall has a fine Art Deco baldacchino, and opus-sectile Stations of the Cross by Hubert McGoldrick; the façade dates from 1961. Opposite is a bust of Major John MacBride (1865–1916), one of the executed 1916 leaders, (see history) born in Westport (Peter Grant, 1982).

Uphill to the south is the Octagon, in the centre of which is a classical column with a figure of St. Patrick and bas-relief panels at the base by Ken Thompson (1991), replacing a statue of a benefactor of the town, the banker George Glendenning, removed and its inscription obliterated in 1922.

Holy Trinity church (C of I) by T.N. Deane, 1872, built by the 3rd Marquess, contains memorials to the Browne family. It has a lavishly ornamented interior with stone carving by Charles Harrison; the nave walls are unusually decorated with a frieze of black and white *intaglio* marble panels representing Italian Renaissance and other paintings (including da Vinci's 'Last Supper' and Holman Hunt's 'Light of the World'). Canon James Owen Hannay (1865–1950; the novelist 'George A. Birmingham' was rector here between 1892 and 1913.

Westport House

To the west of the town, reached by a turning to the right of the main road climbing south from the Octagon, is the entrance to the demesne of Westport House (14.00–18.00, Tue–Fri; 14.00–18.00, Sat & Sun, June; 10.00–18.00 daily, July & Aug; 14.00–17.00, Sept; £). It is still the home of the Brownes but the demesne now contains a zoo and other tourist facilities. The house was built by Richard Castle in 1730 around an earlier house (c 1650). Further additions were made c 1778 by Thomas Ivory and James Wyatt. Thomas de Quincey, the 19C celebrated English writer was a guest here in 1800.

From the imposing entrance hall, to the left of which is the library, you enter a series of rooms including the long gallery, containing family portraits by Opie, Beechey, and Reynolds; the dining-room, with good plasterwork and a fine set of four sideboards; a smaller dining-room decorated with equestrian paintings, and a further gallery. A white Sicilian marble staircase ascends to the first floor.

One of the bedrooms is decorated with 18C Chinese hand-painted wallpaper and on the bedroom walls there are an interesting series of paintings depicting local views by George Moore and James Arthur O'Connor (1792–1841). Two landscapes in the hall are also by O'Connor. A *Holy Family* attributed to Rubens and a collection of naval prints also hang in the bedroom. Among the many objects of interest held in the house is the 'Mayo Legion' banner, depicting Hibernia wearing the Cap of Liberty which was carried by the invading French troops who supported the 1798 rebellion (small dining room).

In 1812, while on the Grand Tour, the alabaster ornamental columns flanking the entrance to the 'Treasury of Atreus' at Mycenae (c 1300 BC)—one of the primary works of world architecture—were removed by Howe Peter Browne. 2nd Marquess, in an act of high-handed pillage as souvenirs. Until 1910 they flanked a side door to the house (they are now in the British Museum) replaced by replicas at Westport (south front), but not at Mycenae. Howe Peter's reputation is somewhat redeemed by his behaviour as an abolitionist when Governor of Jamaica (1834–37).

Further west is Westport Quay, where there are some late 18C warehouses. Westport Bay leads into the much larger **Clew Bay**. Its islands look like stranded whales, formed by submerged drumlins, which make navigation hazardous.

Mulrany, Achill Island

Between Westport and Newport you cross a broken drumlin district, without obtaining much of a view of Clew Bay to the west. Newport is a small angling resort, both for sea-fishing in Clew Bay and for sea-trout in **Loughs Beltra** (northeast), **Furnace** and **Feeagh**, is dominated by an old railway viaduct and the highly individual interpretation of the Hiberno Romanesque style of R.M. Butler's Catholic church (1910).

West of the village is Burrishoole. On the east bank of the river (left) are the remains of **Burrishoole Abbey**, founded for the Dominicans in 1486. The church has a solid central tower, the vault of which survives, supported by Romanesque arches leading into the south transept. The four-light east window remains, and there are traces of stone stalls; remains of dependencies lie to the north.

Continuing west, Cushcamcarragh (712m), dominates the southwestern part of the **Nephin Beg range** to the right. The square tower of Grace O'Malley's castle of **Rockfleet** (15C–16C; formerly known as Carrigahowley castle) is visible on the left and Rosturk Castle (19C) is 6.5km further west. The next village, Mulrany (or Mallaranny), is on the narrow isthmus that joins the Corraun peninsula to the mainland and enjoys a mild climate; fuchsias, rhododendrons, and Mediterranean heath abound. Behind the village the hill of Claggan (382m) dominates the skyline. The main road turns due north here, but the circuit of the Corraun (rising to 521m) and the excursion to Achill are recommended.

Achill Island

Achill Island (Tourist Office, The Courthouse, Achill, ☎ 098–45384; July–Aug) can be reached from Mallaranny across the isthmus, crossing to the island by a swivel bridge. The village of **Achill Sound** lies on the far bank of a narrow strait between Achill Island and the Corraun peninsula, its entrance guarded by Achillbeg Island.

Achill is the largest island off the Irish coast and is largely covered with wild heather or bog. Its Irish-speaking inhabitants barely subsisted, until comparatively recently, when they prospered from tourism and the development of cottage industries. Shark-fishing is quite common here (April–July); the sharks are of the harmless basking variety.

The main road runs northwest across the island through rhododendron plantations to the village of **Cashel** where there are good views of the other hills on the island (Slievemore, Croaghaun and Minaun). **Dugort** on the north coast, is known as 'The Settlement'. Founded in 1834 by a philanthropic Protestant clergyman, the Rev. E. Nangle, who built schools and published the *Achill Herald* newspaper on his own. This aroused the rancour of the Catholic clergy with whom he waged a bitter war in the columns of the newspaper. His efforts to proselytise the poverty-stricken islanders were unsuccessful (as a result of opposition from both RC and Protestant clergy), although he eventually purchased three-fifths of the island. Dugort is now a small tourist resort. The deserted village at the foot of Slievemore is occupied only during summer cattle-pasturing.

Heinrich Böll (1917–85), the German novelist and Nobel Laureate came to live at Dugort, in the 1950s, and in his will left his house for the use of writers as a retreat. His *Irish Journal* (1957), is an acutely perceptive outsider's view of post-World War II Ireland (not unlike post-1922 Ireland in many respects).

Slievemore, a 670m peak of quartzosc and mica, dwarfs the village on all sides, especially towards the sea. The **Seal Caves** below (frequented by seals) can be visited by boat from Dugort in calm weather. On its southern slope is a dolmen with a circle at each end and several primitive cabins occasionally used during summer cattle-pasturing. The main road towards the end of the island descends past a lough to **Keel**, at the far end of a 3km-long beach. At its eastern end rise the **Cathedral Rocks**, where the cliffs have been fretted into a series of caverns and columns, forming part of the Minaun. The mountain can be climbed from the hamlet of Dookinelly and there is a fine view of Clare Island from from the top.

West of Keel is the village of **Dooagh** and the workshops of the St. Colman knitting industry. Beyond Dooagh, at the end of the island, is Croaghaun. Corrymore Lodge, once occupied by the unfortunate Captain Boycott (see Ch. 11) stands on its eastern side. Amethysts are found on the south side of the mountain; on the northwest, sheer and overhanging cliffs rise almost 600m above the sea. To the west the mountain ends in the razor-like ridge of Achill Head; to the north is Saddle Head, on the shoulder of which is a tarn known as the 'Mermaid's Looking Glass'.

The **summit** of Croaghaun is best reached from Lough Acorrymore, above Boycott's lodge, bearing to the left beyond the lake. From Dugort (or Keel) you can follow a ridge rising northwest of Slievemore from a signal tower. It soon overlooks **Lough Nakeeroge** (right) on a curious rock shelf raised slightly above the sea. The **view** here is superb: to the north arc the islands of Duvillaun and Inishkea, and the Mullet; to the south lie Clare Island, with Inishturk, Inishbofin and Inishark in the distance. From south to southeast rise the Twelve Bens, Muilrea and Croagh Patrick; to the east is the Nephin Beg range, while to the west extends the boundless Atlantic.

On returning to Cashel, the southeast of the island may be explored by taking the second turning to the right for Dooagh, there bearing left and following the 'Atlantic Drive'. This circles the southern point of Achill, returning along the Sound and passing the old graveyard and 15C Tower of Kildownet (or Carrick Kildavnet), the latter once a stronghold of Grace O'Malley.

Ceide Fields, Killala, Ballina

From Mulrany the road leads due north along the shores of Bellacragher Bay, an extension of Blacksod Bay, with mountain views after a few kilometres. Beyond Ballycroy, a lane leads seaward to Doona Castle, another of Grace O'Malley's possessions. The road shortly veers northeast across the extensive bog to Bangor.

Bangor to Ballina ~ the short cut

The N59 ascends the bleak Owenmore valley to the east to Bellacorrick, with a power station. Beyond, you cross the desolate barony of Tyrawley before descending to Crossmolina, with another power station, and a good centre for pike and perch fishing in **Lough Conn**.

On a promontory in the lough (some 8km south) are the remains of **Errew Abbey** (founded 1413), with a 13C church, while nearby is the oratory of Templenagalliaghdoo (the 'Church of the Black Nun'), probably the site of a 6C monastery founded by St. Tighernan.

The N59 continues east from Crossmolina past the demesne of Castle Gore, in which is the well-preserved ruin of Deel Castle, to enter Ballina.

Bangor to Ballina ~ the scenic route

The R313 leads northwest from Bangor, briefly passing along the south bank of **Carrowmore Lough** to Belmullet (19km), at the narrowest part of the isthmus joining the Mullet peninsula to the mainland, here crossed by a canal. Belmullet lies at the northern extremity of Blacksod Bay, where in 1588 the flagship of the Armada, commanded by Don Alfonso de Leyva was stranded. He was rescued by the O'Rourke and entertained at Dromahair castle (see Ch. 13), only to lose his ships and his life at Port-na-Spania, Co. Antrim.

The Mullet is a curious mattock-shaped peninsula, its wild coastline sheltering the northern reaches of Blacksod Bay from the Atlantic. At **Doonamo Point**, 8km northwest, is a fine promontory Iron Age fort with a wall 5.5m high in places, built across the neck of its headland, and enclosing three clochans and a ring fort. The main road leading south from Belmullet passes through the hamlet of Binghamstown (*An Geata Mór*), Bingham Castle and (16km) Aghleam, beyond which is Blacksod Point. Off the west coast opposite Binghamstown is the island of **Inishglora** which has ruins of a chapel built by St. Brendan (66AD). The few inhabitants of the Inishkea islands, further south, were transferred to the mainland in 1927 after a storm had sunk the fishing-fleet. Engraved pillar-stones of the 7C style are on both islands.

Leaving Belmullet take the R314, at first skirting the south shore of Broad Haven then the north side of Carrowmore Lough. Before Glenamoy Bridge a road leads to the south side of Sruwaddacon Bay and Dooncarton cliff fort where there are fine views; also a stone circle and megalithic tomb. At Glenamoy Bridge (22.5km) there is a bog reclamation station.

A road to the left here leads to (14km) Portacloy, a tiny harbour shut in by high cliffs, to the west of which, past the detached headland of Doonvinallagh and a cave, is **Benwee Head** (250m), a stupendous cliff buttressing the north-west corner of Mayo, with views southwest towards Achill and northeast to the Donegal coast. Offshore are a group of seven **rock-stacks** 90m high, known as the Stags of Broadhaven. Some 5km east, at Porturlin, is another little harbour near some curious rock-formations. There is also a **megalithic tomb** southwest of Portacloy at Ross Port.

The main road bears northeast to **Belderrig**. The wild cliffs here, dominated by Glinsk (305m), can be visited on foot or by boat. Beyond Belderrig the road follows the coast, where dark rocks are pierced by a number of blow-holes. The desolate moors of the Barony of Erriswhile rise inland. There is a megalithic tomb on the hillside to the right of the road here, near the bog of Behy (or Glenulra).

Ceide Fields

Perched on the edge of the precipitous cliffs and encompassing two hills, Ceide Fields (OPW) is the largest identified Neolithic farm settlement in the world (over 1000 hectares). Sealed beneath the blanket bog, a network of stone-walled fields has been discovered. Although planned as a single enterprise and carried out in an organised building project, with dwellings and megalithic tombs, there is no evidence of a defensive wall. Sections of the settlement have been excavated and these are all explained at the **Ceide Fields Visitor Centre** (by Mary MacKenna, 1993) (10.00–17.00 daily, Mar–May; 09.30–18.30 daily, June–Sept; 10.00–17.00 daily, Oct; 10.00–16.30 daily, Nov; OPW; £) . This is an imaginatively designed complex which takes the form of a subterranean display dealing with the archaeology, botany, geology and landscape of the area. With its pyramidal roof rising above the barren bogland, it is certainly one of the best contributions to the recent phenomenon of interpretative, heritage, and visitor centres, in this case informing rather than interfering with the antiquities and landscape.

Two more megalithic tombs can be seen immediately to the west of the next village, **Ballycastle**, near the mouth of the Ballinglen river.

From here the R315 leads almost due south to (10km) Crossmolina. To the northeast of Ballycastle is **Downpatrick Head**, off which is seen the detached fort of Doonbristy. Crossing a low pass, the road descends to Palmerstown, where you turn left for Rathfran Abbey (1274), a ruined Dominican house. The road leads north, through a district rich in ancient remains, to Kilcummin (9.5km). Here there is a ruined church dedicated to St. Cuimin, with his well and gravestone marked with an incised cross. You shortly enter Killala, situated at the head of a deep bay and surrounded by fine coastal scenery.

Killala Bay was the scene on 22 August, 1798, of the landing of 1100 French troops under General Humbert (1755–1822), who invaded Ireland with the intention of assisting the rebellion of the United Irishmen. They were initially successful, but were forced to surrender on 8 September to Cornwallis (who represented the English government) at Ballinamuck.

The **cathedral**, with a fine steeple, dates from a rebuilding of c 1670, except for a Gothic doorway (blocked) on the south side. The bishopric is claimed to have been founded by St. Patrick himself. A Round Tower (25.5m high), repaired since struck by lightning in 1800 is near the cathedral. An underground passage in the churchyard is the only other relic of antiquity.

The main road on to (12km) Ballina is not particularly interesting, but a minor road forking left immediately south of the town and running parallel to the Moy estuary passes **Moyne Abbey**. The abbey stands in a field (entrance by farm) overlooking the sandhills of Bartragh Island. It was founded by MacWilliam Burke in 1460. The entrance is by steps to the upper chambers of the ruined monastic buildings, of which several lower rooms still have vaults. The church has a lofty tower and good tracery in its windows, while the cloisters are almost perfect.

4km further south on the R314 (left) lies **Rosserk Abbey**, founded for Franciscans by the Joyce family c 1400, with an imposing tall tower and also with well-preserved cloisters. On the piscina there is a miniature carving of a Round Tower in relief. Regain the main road at the demesne of Belleek, immediately to the north of Ballina.

Ballina

Ballina is one of the more important towns in the area, and a centre for anglers who fish on the Moy and its tributaries. The town was established by Lord Tyrawley in the early 18C, and was the first town to be captured by the French after landing at Killala in August 1798 (see above).

The **Cathedral of St. Muredach** (RC), an externally severe building, is by Dominic Madden (1829–92), who also designed the cathedral at Tuam (which it resembles). It took so long to build because work was interrupted by the Great Famine (*An Gorta Mor*, 1845–47); Queen Victoria was known as 'the Famine Queen'. The spire by Sir John Benson was added to Madden's Perpendicular Gothic building in 1853, the glass is by Meyer of Munich. It is adjoined by remains of an Augustinian friary of 1427, with a fine west door.

About 1.5km southwest of the town on the road to Lough Conn is the Neolithic **Dolmen of the Four Maols** (c 3000 BC). According to legend it marks the grave of four foster-brothers (whose names all began with 'Maol') who murdered their master Ceallach, Bishop of Kilmoremoy. They were hanged by the bishop's brother at Ardnaree (*Ard na Riaghadh*, 'hill of the executions').

Towards Sligo

The direct road to Sligo crosses the Moy northeast of Ballina and runs parallel to Slieve Gamph or the **Ox Mountains** to meet Sligo Bay at Dromore West, a pleasant village by a stream. To the east are the ruins of the medieval church of Kilmacshalgan.

Alternatively, the R297 keeps closer to the sea, running through **Enniscrone** (or Inishcrone), a resort between dunes and low cliffs. The **Family History and Heritage Centre** (10.00–16.00, Mon–Fri, Oct–June; 09.00–18.00, Mon–Fri, 14.00–18.00, Sat & Sun, June–Sept; £) is a folk museum and genealogy centre. Duald MacFirbis (1585–1670) was the last of the hereditary genealogists or 'Sennachies' of Ireland. He came from a family of poets and annalists and lived some 3km north at Castle Firbis (left).

The fishing village of Easky is east of Enniscrone, near which are several ruined castles of the O'Dowds. At Dromore West is the purpose-built **Culkin's Emigration Museum** (10.00–17.00, Mon–Sat; 13.00–17.00, Sun, June–Sept; £) on the site of Daniel Culkin's Shipping & Emigration Agency, incorporating the original 19C shop. The displays deal with Irish emigration from the early 19C to the 1930s.

The road takes you past the north side of Knockalongy and Skreen (right) where there is a large ring-fort. Between Red Hill and Knockachree to the south is **Lough Achree**, known as 'the youngest lake in Ireland', having been formed by an earthquake in 1490. There is a good view of the Dartry Mountains to the northeast across Sligo Bay. Woods lead down to the shore of Ballysadare Bay. At Ballysadare, turn left for Sligo (8km).

Castlebar, Ballintubber Abbey, Claremorris, Knock

Circling the hills to the southwest of Westport on the R330, you pass (19km due south) the church of Aille and the remains of MacPhilbin's Castle crowning a mound. About 2.5km south west of the next crossroads is Aghagower (*Achadh-fhobhair*, field of the spring), where there is a Round Tower of rude workmanship and missing its conical cap, a ruined church and oratory. 4km beyond this turning you enter Westport.

Climbing east on the N60 from Westport, passing (left) a series of small loughs, you come to **Castlebar** (18km), the county town of Mayo.

The town was founded by Sir John Bingham and incorporated in 1613. In 1641 Sir Henry Bingham was forced to surrender to the Irish Confederates under the Earl of Mayo, and although he marched out with a safe-conduct his party was massacred at Shrule Bridge. In 1798 General Humbert's invading French army, which had landed at Killala on 22 August, put to flight a stronger force under General Lake at the engagement known as the '**Castlebar Races**', and entered the town in triumph (see also Ballinamuck). Continuing east from Bellavary, after 11km passing (left) at Meelick a Round Tower, you reach the agricultural town of Swinford 5km beyond.

Take the N60 from Claremorris for Castlebar and the N84 south of Castlebar for Ballintubber Abbey.

Ballintubber Abbey

Founded by Cathal O'Connor, King of Connacht, for Augustinian canons in 1216, it was largely rebuilt in 1270 after a fire. The remains are substantial, and following restorations in 1846, 1889 (Ashlin) and 1966 (09.00–20.00 daily; OPW), the entire church has been re-roofed and sensitively restored with the internal walls limewashed and a refreshing absence of intrusive devotional objects. The claustral complex, which includes a calefactory, remains in ruins. The nave, chancel and transepts are interesting for their transitional Late Romanesque-Early Gothic detailing. The west door is 15C and in the sacristy, south of the choir, is a 16C altar-tomb of *Tiobod na Long-a* (Theobald of the Ships), son of the pirate Queen Grace O'Malley (see above), with remains of a row of weepers incorporated. The naïve polychrome *Stations of the Cross* are by Imogen Stuart (1972), the Virgin in the Lady Chapel by Oisin Kelly, and windows in the north transept by Gabriel Loire. In the grounds is a 'Way of the Cross' which incorporates spurious megaliths and a portal-tomb into a religious context with doubtful appropriateness.

Cecil Day-Lewis (1904–72), Poet Laureate and critic (and as Nicholas Blake, detective story writer), was born at Ballintubber. At Clogher, to the east is **Doon Promontory Fort** (12.00–15.00 daily, June–Sept; self-guided tours; OPW; £), the largest lakeside fortified site in Ireland, a site rich in antiquities of other periods, including a Bronze Age burial mound and Famine Grave. The Interpretative Centre has received major awards for the quality of its displays.

The same road (south) bears around the northern end of Lough Carra to the shell of **Moore Hall** (1795), birthplace of George Moore (1852–1933), described in his novel *The Lake* (1905).

Only traces of Mayo abbey survive, where in the 7C St. Colman founded a once famous school (leaving his cell at Lindisfarne for the purpose).

From Tuam, (south of Claremorris on the N17) the N83 to Charlestown (55km north) passes through Dunmore, with a ruined abbey (1428) founded on the site of an alleged monastery of St. Patrick.

Apparitions at Knock

Northeast of Claremorris is Knock. The village was brought into the limelight after apparitions were reputedly sighted in 1879–80 on the external gable end of the Catholic church, followed by miraculous cures. Both the village and shrine have grown rapidly in recent years, to provide facilities for the pilgrims (including a modern basilica). Knock Airport (1986), was inaugurated to accommodate the increasing numbers of pilgrims to the shrine. The **Folk Museum** (10.00–18.00, May–June, Sept–Oct; 10.00–19.00, July & Aug; £) is concerned with life in 19C Ireland, and documentation of the 1879 apparition.

Lough Conn, Crossmolina

From Castlebar a minor road (R310) bears northeast to (15km) Pontoon, passing by the long slopes of Croaghmoyle which rise to the left (429m). This small angling resort takes its name from the Pontoon Bridge (near a perched block of granite, one of many in the vicinity) crossing the stream between **Lough Conn**, to the north and **Lough Cullin**, both known for their 'gillaroo' or white trout, as well as the common brown trout. Their waters rise and fall at different times and consequently the stream connecting them flows in either direction alternately.

The west bank of the lough leads to **Crossmolina** (20km), passing (left) Nephin (804m; easily ascended), and fragmentary Errew abbey on the lough shore to the right.

Alternatively, the main road from Castlebar to Crossmolina bears northeast through Turlough with a well preserved Round Tower and on to Bellavary (4km).

Take the N58 soon after Bellavary to Strade. The influential Fenian leader Michael Davitt (1846–1906) was born here and there is a museum of mementoes. The interesting remains of **Strade Abbey** are nearby. It was founded originally for Franciscans, but transferred to the Dominicans in 1252 and much of the building is 15C. There is a fine **sculptured tomb** on the north wall of the chancel.

Foxford has a flourishing wool industry. The Visitor Centre at **Foxford Woolen Mills** (10.00–18.00, Mon–Sat; 14.00–18.00, Sun; 12.00–18.00, Sun; July & Aug) is devoted to the tradition of weaving in the area and the manufacture of Foxford blankets, which continue to be produced by expert craftsmen. The weaving process can also be seen. It was also the birthplace of William Brown (1777–1857), an admiral in the Argentine service. Continuing north on the N57, follow the west bank of the Moy. Some 5km east, beyond the Moy, is the 12C church of Kildermot, on the shore of Lough Ballymore. The road continues to Ballina.

At Swinford, southeast on the N26, **Hennigans Heritage** relates the story of a local family's experiences over a 200-year period on a ten acre farm. Southwest, at the monastic site of Meelick is a well-preserved Round Tower and early Christian memorial slab with the inscription 'Or Do Gricour' ('a prayer for Gricour').

13 · Sligo ~ Yeats Country

Although W. B.Yeats was born in Dublin, his poetry was inspired by the beautiful and dramatic countryside around Sligo. He is buried at **Drumcliff**, a few miles northwest of the town. The distinctive flat topped contours of **Ben Bulben** and **Knocknarea**, (Benbulbin and Knocknarra on the Ordnance maps), are north and south of the town. **Innisfree** is in Lough Gill to the east, and **Lissadell**, home of the Gore-Booth family, is north on Drumcliff Bay. As a boy, Yeats spent many holidays here with his maternal grandparents, the Pollexfens. He and his brother, the artist Jack B. Yeats, are both commemorated in the important **Sligo County Museum** and **Art Gallery**. Anybody familiar with his poetry will find an abundance of resonances and references in the area. The distinctive form of **Knocknarea** with its cairn on the summit would excite the attention of any traveller, and there is little difficulty in understanding why it is associated with the Celtic myths and legends which fired Yeats' imagination. **The Yeats International Summer School** has been held in Sligo for over thirty years (August).

The **Carrowmore Megalithic Cemetry** and **Creevykeel Court-tomb** are among the most impressive Neolithic monuments in the country. **Inishmurray**, off the Sligo coast has a remarkable collection of early Christian antiquities.

How to get there
■ **Train**. From Dublin direct via Mullingar.
■ **Air**. Sligo, and Knock International Airport.
■ **Sea**. To Inishmurray.

Listings
Collooney. **Markree Castle**, distended Gothickry, family home since 1640, B&B (☎ 071-67800).

Riverstown. **Coopershill House**, a family home since 1774, atmosphere and comfort within the seclusion of a 500-acre demesne, B&B (☎ 071-65108_.

Sligo. **Clarence Hotel**, town centre, comfortable, good restaurant (☎ 071-42211); **Truffles**, restaurant, fine food, relaxed atmosphere (☎ 071-44226); **Eden Hill Holiday Hostel** (☎ 071-43204).

Strandhill. **Glen Lodge**, small country house and restaurant below Knocknarea (☎ 071-68387).

Sligo Town
Sligo (Tourist Information, Temple St, ☎ 071-61201), attractively situated in the centre of a wooded plain, lies mainly on the south bank of the Garavogue, connecting Lough Gill to the sea. Its Irish name is Sligeach, 'the shelly river'.

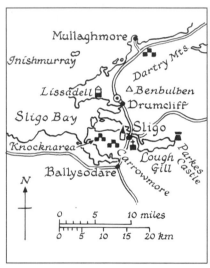

Sligo was first recorded in 537 as the scene of a battle between the men of Connacht and those of the North. It was plundered by the Viking pirates in 807, and four hundred years later (in 1245) became the residence of Maurice Fitzgerald, Earl of Kildare. His castle later became a bone of contention among the local septs, in particular the O'Connors and O'Donnells. In 1641 the town was sacked by Sir Frederick Hamilton (a Government General), and the abbey burned. A few years later (in 1645) it fell to Sir Charles Coote (a Cromwellian, later Royalist) after a battle in which Malachy O'Kelly, the martial archbishop of Tuam, was killed.

The Yeats Connection
The Yeats associations now dominate the town, particularly around Hyde Bridge (Sir John Benson, 1846), on the west side of which is the **Yeats Memorial Building** (a former bank, 1895), centre of the Summer School, with a vigourous bust of the poet on the ground floor (Frederick Herkner, c 1930). Across the bridge, in Bridge St, is a stylised figure of Yeats as a young aesthete, inscribed with lines from his poems (Rowan Gillespie, 1990).

In adjacent Stephen St, and next to each other are the **Sligo County Museum** (14.00–16.50, Tue–Sat, Apr & May, Oct–Dec; 10.00–12.00, 14.00–16.50, Mon–Sat, June–Sept; £) and **Art Gallery**. The gallery is housed in a rather grim 19C congregational church (now a library; 10.00–12.00; 14.00–18.00 daily; Mon–Sat) and the museum in its manse (1851). Above the **County Library** is the Art Gallery. one of the finest small collections of early

20C art in Ireland, including a large collection of paintings and drawings by Jack B. Yeats (1872–1957) and his family; John Butler Yeats (1839–1922), his father; his sisters Susan Mary (Lily) Yeats (1866–1949) and Elizabeth Corbet (Lolly) Yeats (1868–1940), and his niece Anne Yeats (1919). The Yeats sisters ran the Dun Emer and Cuala presses which published small editions of contemporary poetry and illustrated broadsheets. Among the portraits are those of *Susan and Jennie Mitchell*, W.B. Yeats, a *Self-portrait*, and *John O'Leary*; also portraits of Jack B. Yeats by Estella F. Solomons (1882–1968), and her husband Sean O'Sullivan; *W.B. Yeats* by George William Russell 'AE', and *Sean O'Sullivan*. There are other works by Paul Henry, 'AE', Orpen, Evie Hone, W.J. Leech, Sean Keating, Gerard Dillon and Le Brocquy.

The museum part of the complex has an extensive collection of first editions of W.B. Yeats and other Yeatsiana, including autographed letters, rare first editions, joint publications by W.B. Yeats and Jack B. Yeats, and the Irish tricolour which draped his coffin at Drumcliff. There are also works by Jack B. Yeats, his photographs and diaries and examples of the publications of the Dun Emer Press and the Cuala Press for whom he illustrated broadsheets.

In another room are local collections, including the violin of the celebrated traditional musician, Michael Coleman (1887–1945).

Stephen St is prolonged uphill by the tree-lined Mall, with the fine spire of Calary church (C of I) visible. The **Model Arts Centre** is on the left. The banks of the river, both up and downstream have pleasant riverside walkways. Rockwood Parade leads south along the river to Thomas and Abbey St, in which is Sligo Abbey.

Sligo Abbey

The only ancient building in the town (09.30–18.30 daily, June–Sept, £), founded for Dominicans by Maurice Fitzgerald in 1252, and destroyed by fire in 1414. The ruins now standing date mainly from the subsequent rebuilding, although the deeply splayed windows on the south side of the choir are evidently of 13C workmanship. The Abbey was destroyed during the sack of 1641.

Little remains of the nave except three arches on the south side and the north wall, in which is the elaborate tomb of a local worthy, Cormac O'Crean (1506). The triple-arched stone rood screen is unusual for an Irish church. The tower is supported by lofty arches and fragments of its vault.

Beneath the fine 15C east window is a **carved altar** of nine panels, the only sculptural altar to survive in an Irish monastic church, its table retains a fragmentary dedicatory inscription (*Johan—Me Fieri Fecit*, 'Jonathan—had me made') and on the south wall is the monument to O'Conor Sligo (d. 1609) and his wife Lady Eleanor Butler (d. 1623). The **cloisters** are perfect on three sides, and retain some ornamented coupled pillars; on the north side is a reader's pulpit on a projecting oriel, approached by a flight of steps above the cloister. The dormitory wall extends to the north; on the east side is the dark little chapter house.

Walk along Castle St and turn left into Teeling St to see the impressive scots baronial tower of the **Court House** (1878), the most distinctive feature of the Sligo skyline. At Market St the Maid of Erin (c 1898), commemorates 1798, in this case looking appropriately more like a militant French Marianne than the conventional bucolic Hibernia (almost every Irish country town has a Maid or Erin/Hibernia monument, erected in 1898 to commemorate 1798. The woman depicted is generally a plump Victorian maiden, not a French 'Liberty on the Barricades' type. The street continues as High St and has a modern **Dominican church** (Pearse McKenna, 1973), with an excellent interior, preserving a window by Michael Healy (1911) from the earlier church the roofless apse of which (still glazed), stands to the rear of the church.

Castle St extends into Grattan St from which we reach (left) **St. John's Cathedral** (C of I). This is the cathedral church of the dioceses of Elphin and Ardagh, elevated to that rank in 1961, following the destruction of Elphin Cathedral by a storm in 1955. It was founded in the 17C, rebuilt to a design by Castle in the 18C, and remodelled in 1812, and 1883. The exterior has been unhappily battlemented and a Gothic Revival chancel and transepts added. It has a massive west tower, and contains the mutilated double tomb of its founder Sir Roger Jones (1637) and his wife. The Symbolist reredos painting of the creation (1912), is by Percy Gethin (1874–1916). It commemorates his brother, Reginald, killed in the Boer War. In the north transept are memorial brasses to Susan Mary Yeats (mother of all the Yeats's, d. 1900) and wife of John B. Yeats, the Pollexfens (Yeats' maternal ancestors) and the Gethins.

Nearby is the **Cathedral of the Immaculate Conception** (RC), by George Goldie which dates from 1869–74, and which, unusually for the period, is in the Romanesque Revival style. The windows, a complete set of 67 pseudo-medieval roundels, also unusual for the time, are French (by Loglin of Tours), rather than the conventional Meyer of Munich glass. A superb oak medieval statue of St. Assicus or Molaise is displayed at the west end of the nave. Despite the reordering of the sanctuary in accordance with the new liturgy, the essentials of the original have been maintained, and it has one of the finest 19C church interiors in the country.

In Temple St, adjoining the Tourist Office, is the **Hawk's Well Theatre** (282 seats), named after a Yeats play. It presents a programme of contemporary and classic Irish plays, music and poetry throughout the year and is one of the few purpose-built theatres outside the major cities.

Returning to Hyde Bridge, in Quay St is the Italianate **Court House** (Hague, 1865), in front of which stands a white marble figure of a former mayor, P.A. McHugh (1916) resembling a singing barber. At the corner of Wine St and Adelaide St is the fine warehouse of the Pollexfens family. You can still see a viewing platform on the roof, from which the family's shipping fleet could be observed.

Knocknarea, Carrowmore

8km west of Sligo R292, on the south side of the estuary, is the resort of Strandhill. On the shore to the north is the church of Killespugbrone (church of Bishop Bronus), named after a disciple of St. Patrick. A curious feature of this little ruin is that the round-headed doorway normally at the west end, is on the south side instead. Long-preserved here, and a place of pilgrimage in the 17C, was the Shrine of St. Patrick's Tooth, now in the National Museum, Dublin.

To the south of Strandhill, but clearly visible from Sligo, rises Yeats's 'cairn-heaped grassy hill' of **Knocknarea**. An enormous un-excavated cairn (180m round) is conspicuous on its summit; it probably covers a passage-grave (see introductory essay). Called *Misgaun Meaghbh* or **Miosgán Meva** (Queen Maeve's grave) it is a monument to Maeve, Queen of Connacht (the 'Queen Mab' of English folklore), who reigned in the 1C AD, and is probably buried at Rathcroghan in Co. Roscommon. A passage from Yeats' 'The Hosting of the Sidhe' (1899) records the grave-site,

> The host is riding from Knocknarea
> And over the grave of Clooth-na-Bare;
> Caoilte tossing her burning hair,
> And Niamh calling 'Away, come away'.

The **view** of the surrounding mountains from the summit is extensive. On the southwest side is the Glen of Knocknarea, a chasm in the limestone bounded by steep cliffs.

You can return to Sligo by a minor road passing (right) **Carrowmore Megalithic Cemetery** (09.30–18.30, May–Sept; OPW; £), a low hill possessing the largest group of megalithic tombs in Ireland. There are over 60 partially complete passage and portal tombs, and many more have been destroyed by gravel quarrying; the oldest predate Newgrange by 700 years. Many are within easy reach of the road; there is a small on-site exhibition.

South of Sligo the N4 leads to **Ballysadare** (*Baile Easa Dara*, the town of the cataract of the oak). It is sited on the Owenmore river, and noted for its salmon fisheries. On the river bank are the ruins of an abbey founded by St. Fechin (c 645).

Further south is Collooney . Here in 1798 a skirmish between a detachment of Limerick militia and General Humbert's troops ended in the retreat of the former to Sligo; a monument commemorates the gallantry of Humbert's aide-de-campe.

Circuit of Lough Gill

Lough Gill, only 3km southeast of Sligo, rivals Killarney for sheer natural beauty, and is much less touristy. The lake abounds in trout, salmon and pike, and is connected with the sea by the Garavogue.

Driving northeast from Sligo shortly turn off the N16 onto the R286, passing the wooded, derelict demesne of Hazelwood. The house (c 1731) on the north bank of the lough is one of the earliest Palladian buildings designed by Castle (now offices). You shortly pass (left) charming **Lough Colgagh**. Above is the Deerpark Monument (3000 BC), a group of stones in a rough oblong. This is a double tomb of a type related to the 'horned cairns', and is still partly roofed, although the large central chamber was probably always open to the sky. The enclosures at either end are undoubtedly burial chambers. To the south are a fine cashel and remains of other stone monuments.

The road descends to the shore and passes 17C **Parke's Castle** (10.00–17.00, Tue–Sun, March–May; 09.30–18.30 daily, June–Sept; 10.00–17.00 daily, Oct; OPW; £), a well preserved fortified Plantation Manor House. It was built c 1620 by Captain Robert Parke who received lands confiscated from Sir Brian O'Rorke, indicted and hanged for sheltering Francisco de Cuellar, an officer of the shipwrecked Armada in 1588. The castle incorporates the bawn wall of an O'Rorke tower house, the foundations of which were revealed in recent excavations. De Cuellar, in an account of his adventures, described O'Rorke in less than complimentary terms, considering that the chieftain subsequently lost his life for offering hospitality, 'although this chief is a savage, he is a good Christian and an enemy of the heretics and always at war with them'.

At the east end of Lough Gill is **Doonie** (or Dooney) **Rock**, a view that inspired Yeats' poem, 'The Fiddler of Dooney' (1892), as did the tiny island of Innisfree, near the southeast bank.

> For the good are always merry,
> Save by an evil chance.
> And the merry love the fiddle
> And the merry love to dance.
>
> And when the folk there spy me,
> They will all come up to me,
> With 'Here is the fiddler of Dooney!'
> And dance like a wave of the sea.

From here, skirt the bank of the river Bonet to **Dromahair**, a pleasant village 21km from Sligo.

The King of Leinster seeks help from Henry II
The **Old Hall**, on the riverbank (Sir William Villiers, 1626) occupies the site of Breffni Castle, once inhabited by Devorguilla, wife of Tiernan O'Rourke. She either eloped with or was kidnapped by Dermot MacMurrough, King of Leinster, in 1152. The subsequent combination of chieftains against MacMurrough led him to seek help from Henry II in return for vassalage (1166). Henry refused direct intervention, but allowed Strongbow to go to his assistance (which turned out to be the initial step in the Anglo-Norman invasion of Ireland).

After the Norman barons had established themselves in Ireland in 1169, Henry II became concerned that they might create a separate (and rival) kingdom there. The King arrived in Ireland with a large army in 1171, to quell this possibility.

On the opposite bank are the imposing ruins of **Creevelea Abbey**, founded for Franciscans by a later Tiernan O'Rourke and his wife in 1508 (restored after an accidental fire in 1536) It is notable for its large south transept, east window, and tiny cloister.

Return to Sligo by turning right onto the R287, after 6.5km bearing right between Slish Mountain (right) and Slieve Daeane to the south bank of Lough Gill. Offshore lies Cottage Island, and to the northeast, Church Island. Bearing away from the lough pass (right) Cairns Hill, an eminence crowned by two cairns, two cashels, and a stone circle, before meeting the N4, where turn right for Sligo.

Drumcliff, Ben Bulben, Inishmurray, Mullaghmore
The Glencar valley runs northwest of Sligo N16, dominated to the north by Truskmore (644m), the highest peak of the Dartry Mountains. Glencar Lough, with its three waterfalls, either bank of which may be followed, is exceptionally pretty.

Driving north from Sligo, pass the turning for Rosses Point (R291) and continue to **Drumcliff** (also Drumcliffe; *Droim Chliahb*, ridge of baskets) with a fine view ahead of Ben Bulben. A fine but weathered **High Cross** (c 1000) with elaborate sculptures of figures and animals, and scroll-work, marks the site of a monastery traditionally founded c 575 by St. Colmcille (or Columba). William Butler Yeats (1865–1939) was buried in the graveyard of the Protestant church (where his grandfather had been rector) in 1948. His tombstone, bearing his own epitaph, is just north of the porch:

> Cast a cold eye
> On life, on death.
> Horseman, pass by !
> from 'Uncle Ben Bulben' (1938)

Yeats died at Roquebrune in the South of France. In accordance with the poet's wishes his body was returned to Ireland by a gunboat, sent to France by the Irish Government.

The Battle of the Books
This 'battle' was fought at **Cooladrummon**, near Drumcliff, between the followers of St. Columba and those of St. Finian of Movilla. St Finian claimed that the copy of his psalter which St. Columba had made was his property. The case was brought before Dermot, King of Meath, who (allegedly according to Brehon Law, a pre-Chrisitan native legal system) decided that 'as to every cow belongs its calf, so to every book belongs its copy'. St Columba appealed to his tribe against this decision. They won the ensuing skirmish, in which 3000 of their rivals (it is said) were slain. It was in penance for this that Columba was sent to Iona by St. Molaise to convert the heathen in Scotland.

To the north rises 'bare Ben Bulben's head' (526m; **view** from its table-topped limestone summit), the scarped side of which has been defaced by prominent graffiti. Ben Bulben is the most westerly of the Dartry Mountains, which run inland to Truskmore (644m), and retains some unusual flora. It was here that the final scene of the pursuit of Diarmuid and Grainne took place, when the hero was killed by the followers of Finn MacCoul.

A lane leads west from Drumcliff to (left) **Lissadell House** (10.30–12.15, 14.00–16.15, Mon–Sat, June–Sept; £), the demesne of the Gore-Booth family. The house was built in 1834 by Francis Goodwin for Sir Robert Gore-Booth, grandfather of the militant Countess Constance Markievicz (1884–1927). She was the first woman elected to the British House of Commons, but preferred to take her seat in the Dáil instead. Her poet sister Eva Gore-Booth (1870–1926) also lived here; both were friends of W.B. Yeats. An extract from his poem 'In Memory of Eva Gore-Booth and Con Markiewicz' (1933) conveys a rather exotic picture of the two women:

> The light of evening, Lissadell,
> Great windows open to the south,
> Two girls in silk kimonos, both
> Beautiful, one a gazelle

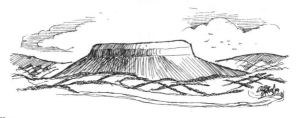

Ben Bulben

The dining-room contains a series of full-length portraits of family and retainers by Count Casimir Markievicz on the pilasters.

On the shore here are the scanty ruins of Dunfore Castle and, further on, the remains of a cashel with souterrains, a dolmen, and a stone circle. Beyond is the fishing village of **Raghly**, on the north point of Sligo Bay, with 17C **Ardtermon Castle**, (partly restored), once the seat of the Gore family.

From here regain the main road to the northeast near Grange (8km). A lane descends a few kilometers west to the slight ruins of **Staad Abbey**, built (perhaps by St. Molaise) on Streedagh Strand. Three vessels of the Armada were wrecked here, leaving 'eleven hundred dead corpses' on the shore. It was here that their captain, de Cuellar, first sought refuge, but he found it already in ruins. Boats may be hired here to visit **Inishmurray**, a small island to the north-west (inhabited until 1948). It is named probably after St. Muiredach, a follower of St. Patrick, and is remarkable for its extraordinary number of antiquities. The most important one is a large cashel (53m by 41m), a pre-Christian fort converted by St. Molaise into a small monastery in the 6C. It contains a beehive hut and three oratories: Teach Molaise, with thick walls of very large stones (c 9C); Teampull Molaise, much larger; and *Teampull-na-Teinidh* (Church of Fire; 14C). The whole was amateurishly restored in 1880. Other remains include inscribed gravestones, three pillar-stones, two bullauns, and two wells.

Creevykeel Court cairn, to the east of Creevykeel crossroads (8km beyond Grange), is one of the finest in Ireland. Excavations in 1935 revealed artefacts dating back to the Neolithic (c 2500 BC; in National Museum, Dublin. Not on display). A lane leads 5km northwest to **Mullaghmore**, with its harbour built by Lord Palmerston in 1842. **Classiebawn Castle** (1842–72), designed by Rawson Carroll, and likewise built for Palmerston, lies to the southwest. It was inherited by the late Countess Mountbatten, and it was offshore here that Earl Mountbatten of Burma and members of his family (1900–79) were blown up by members of the IRA.

14 · The Border Counties

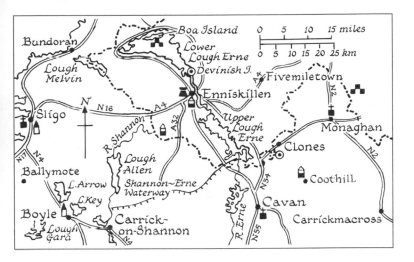

The **Drumlin Belt** forms a separate geographic region, composed of small, glacially contoured hills interspersed with reed-fringed lakes, which straddles the border counties from the Irish Sea to the Atlantic. This region includes parts of Counties **Leitrim**, **Cavan** and **Monaghan** in the Republic; **Fermanagh**, **Tyrone** and **Armagh** in Northern Ireland. Cavan and Monaghan are in the Province of Ulster, as are the six counties of Northern Ireland. Because the region spans both sides of the Border, currency, road distance measurements, telephone codes and public holidays differ, depending on which jurisdiction you are in. £ Sterling and miles are used north of the border, the Irish Punt and kilometres to the south. As the landscape, people, towns and villages are in most respects identical, it is often difficult when travelling (unless a customs post has been passed) to determine on which side of the border you are (mostly it does not matter). People are invariably hospitable and friendly and in Northern Ireland, reserve their invective for their neighbours.

The award-winning **Monaghan County Museum** (at Monaghan town) is among the best small regional museums in Ireland and **Enniskillen Castle** has both a fine local museum and the **Inniskillings Regimental Museum**.

The lake system of the upper Shannon at Lough Allen is connected by the **Shannon/Erne Waterway** to the lakelands area of Upper and Lower Lough Erne, with first-class fishing and boating. **Belleek**, in the west of the Region, has been producing fine Parian China since the 18C. **Carrowkeel** is an impressive Neolithic site and both **Florence Court** and **Castle Coole** are important 18C mansions. Portions of the Ulster Way, Cavan Way and Leitrim Ways cross the region, providing walking routes through its loveliest countryside.

The **Ulster Way** is the longest and finest waymarked walking route in Ireland— its 14 sections cover 168km (the longest is 21km, the shortest a mere 3km).

Areas vary from the St. Patrick's Country of Down to the Lagan Valley Towpath in Antrim, the extraordinary Causeway Coast and the Cuilcagh Mountains. Accommodation is available all along the route (the Northern Ireland Tourist Board leaflet *Where to stay on the Ulster Way* is informative; see *listings* for details on two excellent places to stay).

How to get there

- **Train**. This is the worst served region of the country. The Dublin-Sligo line in the southwest serves Boyle and Ballymote.
- **Air**. As above. The nearest airports are at Belfast, Sligo, Knock.
- **Water**. Boating on Lough Allen and Lough Erne. The Erne lakes above and below Enniskillen are particularly well-suited to cruising. The lower lake has four marinas and cabin cruisers can be hired.
- **Bus**. Ulsterbus service from Northern Ireland and Bus Éireann from the Republic serve the area.

Listings

Ballymote. Temple House, one of those legendary eateries which live up to their reputation for superlative food (☎ 071-83329).

Ballyshannon. Creevy Pier Hotel, a small family-run modern hotel overlooking Donegal Bay (072-51236).

Boyle. Royal Hotel, small traditional riverside hotel (079-62016).

Bundoran. Conroy's German Irish Club, where the 'fish' in fish-and-chips means salmon! (☎ 072-41280).

Carrick-on-Shannon. Canal View Restaurant, small; pleasant food (☎ 078-42056); Town Clock Hostel (☎ 078-20068).

Cavan. Lifeforce Mill, wonderful working mid-19C grain mill, café with the smell of fresh bread; bake your own, Oh! intoxicating (☎ 049-62722); The Old Priory, restaurant serving pizzas (☎ 049-61898).

Clones. Hilton Park, here everything is just large; the house, rooms and hospitality, B&B (☎ 047-56007).

Enniskillen. Blakes of The Hollow, one of the finest old, 'unimproved' pubs in the North (☎ 01365-322143).

Florencecout. Tullyhona Guesthouse (especially if walking the Ulster Way), 59 Marble Arch Rd (☎ 0365-348452).

Kingscourt. Cabra Castle Hotel, equestrian and golfing centre in pseudo-baronial castle (☎ 042-87030).

Monaghan. Castle Leslie, Glaslough, family home of the eccentric Leslies, B&B an inadequate description for so much comfort, atmosphere and history (☎ 047-88109); Westenra Arms Hotel, blushing Edwardian red brick in the town centre, cheerful and convenient (☎ 047-82588).

Newcastle. The Briers (especially if walking the Ulster Way), 39 Middle Tollymore Rd (☎ 03967-24347).

Enniskillen

Inis Ceithleann, the county town of Fermanagh (Tourist Information, Wellington Road, ☎ 0365-323110/325050) is partly situated on an island in the river Erne, between Upper and Lower Lough Erne.

Long known for its cattle market, and as an angling centre, it has given its name (with a variant spelling) to two famous regiments, the **Inniskilling Dragoons** and the **Royal Inniskilling Fusiliers**. Originally a stronghold of the Maguires, lords of Fermanagh, Enniskillen was awarded to Sir William Cole (d. 1653), a Planter of Cornish origin and ancestor of the earls of Enniskillen, following the confiscation of land after Tyrone's rebellion against the Crown forces. He settled it with 20 English families, and defended the place in 1641, when the castle—built on the site of Lisgoole Abbey—southwest of the town off the A509, was burned. In 1689 the men of Enniskillen beat off the troops of Tyrconnel, and pursued them as far as Cavan. The town was swept by fire in 1695, destroying all the buildings. It was visited by John Wesley in 1762 and 1769.

Boats may be hired at a jetty near West Bridge; a water-bus makes excursions down Lower Lough Erne.

The High St (extending under various names) leads from East Bridge to West Bridge. Of interest are *Blake's of the Hollow* (1887), a fine Victorian bar, and the plain Protestant **cathedral of St. Macartan** (c 1627; rebuilt 1840). The tower (1637) and font (1666) are of interest, while at the west end of the nave is the Pokrich Stone (1628), a memorial slab with a partly inverted inscription. A turning to the left before you reach West Bridge leads down to the **Castle** containing the **Fermanagh County Museum** and **Royal Inniskilling Fusiliers Museum** (10.00–17.00, Tue–Fri; 14.00–17.00, Sat–Mon, May–Sept; 14.00–17.00, Sun & BH, July–Aug). The attractive late 16C water-gate and foundations of a 15C keep, best seen from across the river, are all that remains of the castle. The museum collection of militaria is extensive and includes the bugle used to sound the charge at the Battle of the Somme on July 1st, 1916. There is also a good audio-visual introduction to the natural history and archaeology of the region. North of High Street is the **Butter Market**, housing the Enniskillen Craft and Design Centre.

In the attractive (but steep) park on Fort Hill, above East Bridge, a column commemorates Sir Galbraith Lowry Cole (1772–1842), a Peninsular War General and later Governor of Cape Colony (in 1828–33). The excellent **Ardhowen Theatre** (01365-325440) is on the outskirts, opposite the entrance to Castle Coole.

Castle Coole

Castle Coole (NT; recently restored), approached by a long drive, is the fourth house on this site, an imposing mansion built in 1790–98 for the Earl of Belmore by James Wyatt (who modified the plans of Richard Johnston). The portraits of George II and Queen Charlotte by Ramsay hang in the Hall (which leads to the library). Highlights include some notable plasterwork by Joseph Rose, an Italian marble-topped table and clock in the drawing-room; distinctively shaped doors by George Binns of Dublin and two impressive cast-iron stoves in the oval saloon; and furniture, including magnificent sideboards designed by Wyatt, and a wine-cooler in the dining room. A bow-fronted room on the first floor displays Wyatt's drawings for the house. The lake in the grounds is the habitat of the oldest non-migratory flock of greylag geese in the British Isles.

Some distance to the west, on the edge of town beyond the bridge, stands the **Portora Royal School** (present building, 1777) founded at Lisnaskea in 1608 by James I. Henry Francis Lyte (the hymn-writer), Oscar Wilde, and Samuel Beckett were all pupils here. The poet William Dunkin (1709?–65) was master from 1746 until his death. Just beyond, on the lough bank, are the ruins of Portora Castle (1615, built by Sir William Cole).

Lower Lough Erne to Belleek

The A46 runs roughly parallel to the west bank of **Lower Lough Erne**. For cruising the Upper and Lower Loughs of the Erne contact the **Lakeland Visitor Centre**, Shore Rd, Enniskillen, ☎ 01365-323110 (it also has information on fishing permits). Cabin cruisers, launches, rowing boats are for hire, and cabin cruiser tours of the lakelands are available. Island cruises from Round O Quay, Enniskillen are available July–Sept, ☎ 01365-322882).

After 6.5km passing the former demesne of Ely Lodge. This was formerly the site of Castle Hume, Richard Castle's first architectural design in Ireland (invited by Sir Gustavus Hume). It was demolished in 1812 and the stone recycled to build Ely Lodge. Near **Monea**, to the west on the far side of a ridge, is a ruined castle of 1618 in the Scottish Baronial style. The east window (1449) in the church beyond comes from Devenish Abbey and was transferred here in 1630 (a replica has been returned to Devenish). Further north, you can see from the lough-side the offshore island of **Inishmacsaint** (*Inismuighe samh*, the isle of the plain of sorrel), with an early cross and ruined church. Beyond, a track (right) leads to the ruins of **Tully Castle** (1610), built by the Humes (10.00–19.00, Tue–Sat, 14.00–19.00, Sun, Apr–Sept; £). It was the scene of a massacre in 1641 when Roderick Maguire induced the garrison to surrender under promise of safe-conduct to Enniskillen, and then burned the place down. Beyond this point the road runs along the lough, overlooked by the Cliffs of Magho, to **Belleek**.

Alternative route to Belleek via the Blackslee Forest

Fork left almost opposite Inishmacsaint, and after 2.5km bear left again, shortly passing between two small lakes. Beyond these a forest track climbs to the right through the **Blackslee** and **Lough Navar Forests**, to some 300m above Lower Lough Erne, providing both a plunging and panoramic view. To the west beyond Donegal Bay is Slieve League; the Blue Stack Mountains rising to the north; and to the northeast, Mullaghcarn, with the Sperrin Mountains beyond. Regaining the main road (B52), turn right and keep right for Belleek.

Belleek (*Beal Leice*, the ford of the flagstones) is a border village, famous for its pottery factory. It produces a fragile form of woven lustreware, the delicate glaze of which was based on a French invention. The original porcelain was made from clay and feldspar dug at Castlecaldwell, some 6.5km east between 1857–84 (the year in which its first art director, Robert Williams Armstrong died). **Belleek Pottery Visitor Centre** (10.00–18.00, Mon–Sat, 14.00–18.00 Sun, March–June & Sept; 09.00–20.00, Mon–Sat, 11.00–20.00 Sun, July–Aug; 09.30–17.30, Mon–Fri, Nov–Feb) provides tours of the works where the manufacturing process can be seen and there is also an important collection of early Belleek is on display.

The **Lakeside Centre**, (Belleek Rd, Assaroe Lough, ☎ 672-525555) a water-sports centre, also has details on waterbus tours. **'ExplorErne'** (10.00–18.00 daily, Mar–Nov; £) at nearby Corry, is an interpretative centre dealing with the flora, fauna, geology and history of the Erne basin.

Lower Lough Erne ~ east bank

The road north of Enniskillen (A32) skirts the east bank of Lower Lough Erne, its southern arm full of wooded islets. One of them, some 3km north of the town and reached by a ferry (10.00–19.00, Tue–Sat, 14.00–19.00, Sun, Apr–Sept; £; DOE; ☎ 013657-322122) is **Devenish** (*Daimh Inish*, the island of oxen). Its group of ruins are associated with St. Molaise of Devenish (6C). The principal building surviving is the particularly fine Round Tower, almost 25m high, notable for its masonry, its variously shaped windows, and its unique cornice of scroll-work with four sculptured heads beneath the conical cap. The tower has been fitted with floors and ladders so the visitor can now ascend to the top. The House of St. Molaise and the Teampull Mór have only one round-headed door each; higher up is the tower of the abbey church (1449) and part of the choir and to the south is a cross of unknown date and unusual design.

The road (A32) shortly veers away from the lough to regain it (via Irvinestown) at Kesh. **Necarne Castle** (or Castle Irvine; c 1831, by John B. Keane, built around its 17C predecessor) is 2km south of Irvinestown.

Lough-side route via Killadeas

Alternatively, a more interesting and slightly shorter route hugs the lough-side via Killadeas, a little angling and yachting resort. In the churchyard, near the Irish yews, are three **carved stones**, the most important of which (7C–9C) has a crude figure of an abbot in profile on one side; on another is a face similar to that on Boa Island (see below). Further up the lough is the demesne of **Castle Archdale**, where a stable block, displaying agricultural machinery is all that remains of a Palladian mansion (1773). The offshore islands are now a nature reserve.

Beyond the castle a lane forks left along the shore. **White Island**, in the bay opposite (the caretaker-boatman will ferry visitors from Castle Archdale) has a small ruined church with restored Romanesque south doorway and two windows of a similar style. The building protects seven curious Early Christian figures (repaired 1928), probably carved between the 7C–9C. At one time they were built haphazard into the wall for preservation.

The lane shortly passes the early 17C ruins of **Crevenish Castle** before entering **Kesh**, a lough-side village where the traditional broad-beamed eel boats were constructed (eels are still fished here). **Drumskinny Stone Circle** stands some 7km northeast.

The road now circles the northern end of Lough Erne, where you can either follow the next right-hand fork, to Pettigo (9km, see below) or take the left-hand fork (A47) to Belleek

Early-Christian figure of a bishop with crosier and bell, White Island

and Ballyshannon (36km) which threads along narrow **Boa Island**. The overgrown lakeside cemetery of **Caldragh** at its west end is well worth a visit. It is signposted left, but beyond the turning marked Lusty Beg Island. About 5 minutes' walk from the road is a squat Janus-formed statue known as the 'Lusty Man' beside a larger one. Both are earlier (possibly 5C–6C) than those on White Island (see above) and pagan. The road regains the mainland, passing on the next peninsula the ruins of Castlecaldwell (1610–19). At Belleek you cross into Donegal.

Pre-Christian Janus figure in graveyard, Caldragh, Boa Island

Pettigo, a village straddling the border with Donegal, is the starting-point for the excursion to Lough Derg, 7km north among the mountains. The lough is of no great interest in itself, but towards the southern bank, **Station Island** (information office on the shore) is said to be the scene of St. Patrick's vision of Purgatory. The island (on which penitential exercises are severe) is intensely built-over. The green pyramidal roof of the octagonal Basilica (William Scott 1921), rises from among the huddle of residential buildings, crammed on every available rock of the island; the result is impressive yet uninviting, like a Victorian prison. Pilgrimage to the island, which dates from c 1150, has persisted throughout the ages despite several attempts to suppress it (Popes Alexander VI and Pius III as well as Cromwellian troops attempted to prevent pilgrimage there) due to excessive religious practices. On **Saint's Island**, to the northwest, are the remains of a monastery founded by St. Daveog, a disciple of St. Patrick (destroyed in 1632).

From Pettigo, the R232 shortly bears northwest away from Lough Erne. Cross the **Black Gap** and **The Pullans**, a drumlin region of little lakes and hills, with extensive views over Donegal Bay and the mountains beyond, before descending to meet the N15, turning right for Donegal itself.

West of Enniskillen

The area west of Enniskillen to the border village of **Belcoo** is hilly and dotted with lochs. Limestone hills on both sides of the main road are riddled with caverns and underground streams. Follow the A4 to the west skirting **Belmore Mountain** (400m) and (left) Lough Macnean Lower. Belcoo may also be reached by two other minor roads: one circles north of Belmore via Boho, with a late 9C High Cross (imperfect); the other runs off the A32 past **Florence Court**, one of the most important 18C houses in the country (see below). The summit of Cuilcagh (665m) to the southwest marks the border.

From Belcoo, the B52 leads northwest along the bank of Lough Macnean Upper, to Garrison, a small angling resort on **Lough Melvin**, five miles south of Belleek. From here it is a short journey (R282) to Manorhamilton.

The main road from Belcoo (N16) crosses the border south of Lough Macnean Upper. The R207 leads southwest to Lough Allen, climbing the Glenfarne valley between the Thur (433m) and Dough Mountains (461m) to the right, and another range to the south, where there are numerous small tarns. **Manorhamilton** takes its name from Sir Frederick Hamilton (d. 1647), to whom the manor was granted by Charles I. The ivy-clad ruined mansion (1641) is a good example of 17C building. At Tullyskeherny, to the southeast, are two court-tombs, one with at least six subsidiary chambers.

The main road from Manorhamilton (R280) leads northwest up the narrow valley past Glenade Lough, between the precipitous **Dartry mountains** (Truskmore is the highest at 644m) and another range rising to 523m.

The village of Kinlough is at the western end of Lough Melvin. The road then heads towards the coast and village of **Tullaghan**, with an Early Medieval cross, before entering Bundoran.

Bundoran (Tourist Information, Main St, ☎ 072-41350) is a popular seaside resort 4km northwest of Lough Melvin. There is a good view north towards the Donegal coast, terminating with Slieve League to the west, and also fine retrospective views of Ben Bulben. The cliffs (to the north of the town) are rich in fossils and have been worn into curious shapes, among which is the natural arch known as the Fairy Bridge.

Ballyshannon, just north of Bundoran (N15), or Ballyshannagh (*Bal Atha Seanaigh*, mouth of Shannagh's ford), stands on the steep banks of the river Erne. Its castle has almost disappeared. Its proximity to the sea meant that it was besieged by English forces under Sir Conyers Clifford in 1597, but the inhabitants, led by Hugh Roe O'Donnell, drove them off, slaughtering many. Among its natives were Speaker William Conolly (c 1660–1729) and the poet William Allingham (1824–89). The 'traditional music' festival held in August is followed by an annual literary festival in October, which also includes traditional music, song and dance and commemorates the literary work of William Allingham, who is buried in St. Ann's graveyard on Mullaghnashee.

> Up the airy mountain,
>   Down the rushy glen,
> We darent go a-hunting
>   For fear of little men;
> Wee folk, good folk,
>   Trouping all together;
> Green jacket, red cap,
>   And white owl's feather.

'The Fairies'. William Allingham 1850.

Northwest of Ballyshannon, on the Kilbarron road, a house called The Abbey marks the site of the **Cistercian Abbey of Assaroe** (founded in 1178). *Eas Aedha Ruadh*, or the falls of Red Hugh—so-called after an early king who drowned there—has almost vanished and only the graveyard and some fragmentary walls remain.

Some 3km beyond, on the shore, are the ruins of **Kilbarron Castle**, an O'Clery fortress. Michael O'Clery (1575–1643) was chief of the Four Masters of

Donegal, ecclesiastical scribes who collated existing manuscript sources in the 17C in order to create a chronology of Irish history from Adam to their own time (see Donegal town).

The R230 leads east, crossing into Co. Fermanagh at (6km) Belleek and skirting the **Assaroe Lake** (created in 1948–52 when the Erne was dammed to make a reservoir). A good wide road now undulates through a belt of drumlins, an area called **The Pullans**. The N15 leads to Ballintra.

The demesne of Brownhall (about 9km east of Ballintra), is a curious limestone ravine through which the Ballintra river flows, intermittently penetrating a subterranean cavern.

Manorhamilton to Lough Melvin via the Black Pig's Dyke

This is a slightly quicker route to Bundoran and the coast, via Lough Melvin. Take the R282 from Manorhamilton which leads northeast, over Saddle Hill and down to the ruins of Rossinver church (11km). Beyond this turn left to skirt the south bank of Lough Melvin. A minor road to the right leads to the Black Pig's Dyke earthworks, a border dyke built by Ulstermen in the 3C AD. Lough Melvin, partly forming the border between Fermanagh and Leitrim, abounds in salmon, trout and gillaroo, and contains a number of small islands. Towards its western end, below Aghabohad (410m) on an artificial island near the shore, are the ruins of **Rossclogher Castle** (15C) the stronghold of the MacClancy, where De Cuellar (see Staad Abbey and Parke's Castle) eventually found refuge, and from which he made his way to Dunluce and back to Spain. **Rossclogher Abbey** is on the mainland.

Southwest of Enniskillen

The A4 descends southwest from Enniskillen through a wide valley reaching **Fivemiletown** (seven miles), founded in the reign of James I. The red sandstone building of **Colebrooke Park** (private) (1825, William Farrell) was once the home of 1st Viscount Brookeborough (1888–1973), Prime Minister of Northern Ireland 1943–63. The charming 18C church of Aghalurcher nearby has a fine spire.

To make a circle back to Enniskillen via Castle Coole pass through Brookeborough to Maguiresbridge, following signs for Lisbellaw (A4). Just beyond Tamlaght, on the outskirts of Enniskillen, is the main entrance to the demesne of Castle Coole.

Carrickmacross to Lough Muckno

Carrickmacross, a broad and pleasant typically 19C market town on the extreme east of the region in Co. Monaghan, was famous for its lace during the mid-19C and is still practiced by local nuns. A grant of land in the neighbourhood was made by Elizabeth I to the Earl of Essex, but little remains of his castle (the site is now occupied by the Convent of St. Louis). Southwest of the town is the wooded parkland and house of **Lough Fea**. The house (private) looks like an Oxford college in miniature (Thomas Rickman, 1827). The slender-spired Catholic church (J. J. McCarthy) has windows by Harry Clarke.

Shercock, 14km west, overlooks **Lough Sillan**, in which some of the largest specimens of horns from the extinct Irish elk have been discovered.

The road from Carrickmacross to Lough Muckno (N2) continues north for 18km, passing the great motte of Donaghmoyne. The market town of **Castleblayney** takes its name from Sir Edward Blaney, governor of Monaghan under James I. He received a grant of land on condition that he erected a fort between Monaghan and Newry. It stands on the shore of Lough Muckno, the largest and most beautiful of the many lakes in the district (240 hectares). Hope (or Blaney) Castle, adjoining the town, with fine grounds, is now a convent.

The R181 leads 7km north to the border, and skirts (right) **Clay Lake**, veering northeast through Keady, a market-town and nationalist stronghold, once a linen-manufacturing centre, for Armagh, 12km beyond.

From Castleblayney the main road (N2) continues northwest through Clontibret. A little to the east was the scene of a battle in May 1595 in which Hugh O'Neill, second Earl of Tyrone, humiliated the Government forces of Sir Henry Bagenal, repeated three years later at the Yellow Ford. Clontibret was also attacked by a mob of Loyalists, in August 1986. The road then bears west to Monaghan.

Monaghan

Monaghan (Tourist Information, the Market House, ☎ 047-81122), incorporated by James I in 1614, is a busy county town with many good examples of stone-fronted provincial Georgian houses. The pedimented Market-house (now the Tourist Office) in the centre dates from 1791–92 and was designed by Samuel Hayes for the first Lord Rossmore.

A crannóg in the grounds of a former convent, to the southwest of town, was the original headquarters of the MacMahons, lords of Oriel; otherwise, the town shows little trace of antiquity. The convent is now a **Heritage Centre**, commemorating the St. Louis teaching order, and Catholic education in 19C Ireland.

Monaghan was the birthplace of the prominent 'Young Irelander' Sir Charles Gavan Duffy (1816–1903), founder of the *Nation*, newspaper of the Young Ireland movement. Despairing of Irish politics after the failure of the 1848 rebellion, he emigrated to Australia in 1855 and became Prime Minister of Victoria in 1871. The historian of the Roman Empire, J.B. Bury (1861–1927) was also born here and John Wesley was arrested here in 1762.

Monaghan County Museum has fine displays covering archaeology, history politics and folklore. One of the most important exhibits is the 13C bronze **Cross of Clogher**. The museum also houses an art gallery. The Market Cross in Old Cross Square is an enigmatic monument, possibly a 17C sundial.

On a hill to the east is the imposing but plain Gothic-Revival **cathedral** of the RC diocese of Clogher (J.J. McCarthy, built in 1861–92). Its sanctuary has recently been successfully modernised. Rossmore Forest Park is on the western edge of the town.

Tedavnet 6.5km northwest of Monaghan (R186), takes its name from St. Damhnait, daughter of a 6C King of Oriel, who has been incorrectly identified with St. Dimpna of Geel in Flanders. A gold '**sun-disc**' has been unearthed here.

10.5km northeast of Monaghan, at **Glaslough**, is the tomb of John Leslie (1571–1671), known as the 'fighting bishop' of Clogher (he was a leader in the 1641 rebellion). **Glaslough House**, now open to the public and also known as Castle Leslie, (B&B; ☎ 047-88109, see listings), is a mid-19C building by Lanyon and Lynn, with an earlier lodge by Nash. Sir Shane Leslie (1885–1971) also lived here. A religious and nationalist writer, he became a friend of Tolstoy and was influenced by him. He was also a biographer of Jonathan Swift and George IV.

The Tynan Crosses

Four ancient crosses, probably dating from the 8C, stand near Tynan, northeast of Glaslough (A28). Of these, the most important are the **Village Cross** (4m high) and the **Terrace Cross**, with interlaced and spiral ornament, both removed from Eglish churchyard (south of Benburb, Co. Armagh) c 1844. Terrace cross, Island Cross and the Well Cross (with its wheel countersunk but not pierced) are all in the grounds of Tynan Abbey; the last two were removed from Glenarb c 1844.

Turning north you enter **Caledon**, a 'model' landlord inspired village, taking its name from the earls of Caledon, whose extensive park is adjacent. At the end of the 19C the park (noted for its avenue of monkey-puzzle trees) was inhabited by wapiti and black bears brought back by the 4th Earl of Caledon from America. In 1968 it gained notoriety for the discrimination shown against Catholic families in the allocation of council houses, which provoked the subsequent Civil Rights agitation. A monument to the 2nd Earl was blown up here in 1973.

The castle, built by Cooley in 1779, was enlarged in 1812 from designs by Nash, when the portico was added. It was the birthplace of Field Marshal Earl Alexander (1891–1969) who fought in both World War I and II becoming Supreme Allied Commander in the Mediterranean in 1944 and later, Governor General of Canada. The interior contains some good plasterwork; the gardens retain the ruins of a 'Bone House' folly (1747).

The road (A28) now bears northwest to Aughnacloy, the junction for the road between Monaghan and Derry, and shortly turns left for Augher, passing (left) the bawn of Favour Royal (1611).

Clones, Coothill, Cavan, Upper Lough Erne

From Monaghan the N54 continues southwest to **Clones**, an agricultural centre retaining a few 18C houses. An ancient episcopal town (*Cluain Eois*, the meadow of Eos), its first bishop was St. Tigernach (d. 548). All that remains of its abbey are a Round Tower (almost 23m high) of exceptionally rough masonry, a 10C sculptured High Cross, reconstructed, and placed in the central Diamond —an Ulster name for the main public square—and the nave of its church (c 1095). In the graveyard near the tower is a curious tomb, shaped like a house-reliquary. Clones Fort is a Norman motte and bailey in the town.

South of Clones, (R212), is the demesne of Hilton Park, a late Georgian mansion rebuilt after a fire in 1804. George Canning (1770–1827) a Pitt supporter and a strong advocate against slavery lived here. **Ballyhaise House** (c 1733, designed by Richard Castle) was brick-built with vaulted ceilings. It is now an agricultural college.

From Clones the R183 leads to Newbliss, outside which, at Annaghmakerrig, is the **Tyrone Guthrie Centre** (☎ 047-54003), a residence for the creative arts. It was once the family home of theatre director, Sir Tyrone Guthrie. The R189 continues to **Cootehill**, a pleasant little town taking its name from the Coote family, the owners of nearby **Bellamont Forest**. An imposing red brick Palladian villa (designed by Sir Edward Lovett Pearce in 1729–30) is on **Dromore Lough**, just to the north. It has a Doric portico and a central lantern with coffered plastcrwork ceilings.

To the right of the Monaghan road (R189), overlooking the inner lough, is the demesne of Dawson's Grove (house demolished), with a vandalised monument (1774; Joseph Wilton) to Anne, Lady Dartrey (1733–69), in a domed mausoleum by Wyatt.

Newtownbutler (west of Clones on the A34) was the scene of a rout and massacre of a larger attacking Jacobite force by the Protestants of Enniskillen on 31 July 1689. **Upper Lough Erne**, a curious maze of straits and islands, now comes into view on the left. On the island of **Galloon**, some 8km southwest of Newtownbutler, are the remains of three High Crosses, two of them elaborately carved. Crom Castle (about 5km to the west) is seat of the Earls of Erne, a Tudor-Revival pile (1829).

Turning north west, after 6.5km you leave on your left the ruins of the old church of Aghalurcher (15C) its graveyard containing some tombstones decorated with high relief carvings.

The road continues northwest, more or less parallel with the course of the meandering Erne, connecting the upper and lower loughs, itself more of a lake than a river, to meet the A4 three miles from Enniskillen, passing (right) the entrance to the demesne of Castle Coole (see above).

Cavan

The county town of **Cavan** (Tourist Information, Farnham St, ☎ 049-31942) was the scene of the final defeat of the Duke of Berwick by the men of Enniskillen under General William Wolseley (supporters of William III) in 1690, who then burned the place. Only the tower remains of the Franciscan church (originally Dominican) in which Owen O'Neill, Ulster leader and supporter of the Confederation of Kilkenny (1590–1649) was buried.

William Scott's **Town Hall** (1908), built of local sandstone, is an eccentric interpretation of Art Nouveau. John Bowden was responsible for designing a number of buildings in Cavan, including the pedimented **Court House**, the Parish church (1810) and the Protestant church (1820, with a fine monument to the Earl of Farnham, a local landowner, by Chantrey 1826), opposite the **Catholic Cathedral** (1942). The cathedral is built in the grandiose neo-Georgian style and replaces an earlier building re-erected at Ballyhaise (7km northeast). **Cavan County Museum** (10.00–17.00, Tue–Sat; 14.00–18.00 Sun, June–Sept; closed Mon; £) housed in a 19C convent, has a collection of archaeological, historical and folklore material. 8km southwest on the south-east bank of the lake rise the hill-top ruins of Ross Castle, an O'Reilly stronghold.

The **Lifeforce Mill** (1846) at Mill Rock on the Kennypottle River (in Cavan town) has been restored and is still milling (09.00–17.00, Tue–Sat; 14.00–18.00 Sun; £). The McAdam water turbine (c 1846) is virtually unique; backup is supplied by a Honsby-Royson engine of 1907. It also has a wonderful café (see Listings). Farnham demesne (3km northwest of Cavan), has a house of 1700. It was enlarged in 1801 by Francis Johnston.

Lough Oughter and surrounds

Labyrinthine Lough Oughter is broken up by numerous islands and penin-sulas—a feature of the landscape as far north as Enniskillen—and connected to **Upper Lough Erne**. The extraordinary contours are largely formed by the gradual decomposition of the limestone caused by the carbonic acid in the water. On an island in the Lough (possibly the site of a crannóg) is the recently conserved circular 13–14C tower of Clogh Oughter, built by the O'Reillys.

Kilmore, 5km west of Cavan, has been the seat of a bishop since 1454. It has a Protestant cathedral (1858–60) which incorporates a Romanesque doorway from the abbey of Trinity Island in Lough Oughter. In the graveyard is the tomb of Bishop William Bedell (1571–1642), translator of the Bible into Irish, who had spent his last two years imprisoned in Clogh Oughter (scene also of the death of Owen Roe O'Neill in 1649).

Diverge left on crossing the Annalee at (6.5km) Butler's Bridge for (10.5km) **Belturbet**, a village on the Erne, which lazily threads its way through this apparently disintegrated region. It was described some 200 years ago by John Wesley as having 'Sabbath-breakers, drunkards, and common swearers in abundance'.

Continue west on the R200 from Belturbet to (12km) **Ballyconnell** (early 17C church). Bronze Age skeletons have been excavated to the southwest and there are a number of slight megalithic remains in the area. The road (N87) circles to the south of Slieve Rushen (405) which marks the border with Brackley Lough on the left, to meet the R202 at (12km) Derrynacreeve.

The R201 leads southwest via **Milltown** on a detached tarn (5.5km). The ruined church and 12C Round Tower of Drumlane (probably an Augustinian friary) are just south of Milltown. Some 6.5km west of Milltown is Kildallon, the home of the ancestors of Edgar Allan Poe, beneath the Hill of Carn, with its rath. The road enters (8km) Killeshandra, frequented by anglers on Lough Oughter, and continues southwest across country via Mohill joining the N4 near Drumsna, 8km east of Carrick-on-Shannon.

Carrick-on-Shannon

Carrick-on-Shannon (Tourist Information, the Marina, ☎ 078-20170) is the county town of Leitrim, and an angling centre for the Shannon and neigh-bouring lakes and streams. Carrick was given its charter by James I, but has few remains of interest except the old gaol and a Court House (c 1825). As the upper limit of navigation on the river, it has in recent years grown into an important base for the hiring of boats for excursions down the Shannon. There are now 90 cruisers on the river.

The old Ballinamore and Ballyconnell Canal, between the Shannon and Upper Lough Erne, has been restored as the **Shannon-Erne Waterway** to provide a very considerable extension of the navigable waterway (the length of the navi-gable river from here to Killaloe is c 225km). You can spend up to nine leisurely days on its waters, passing through sixteen locks, although the journey can be made in 36 hours. The most pleasant months to do it are from June to early September. For further details—types of boat (from 2–8 berth) which may be hired, tariffs, etc.—apply to Tourist Offices.

Just south of Carrick-on-Shannon (N4) is Jamestown (founded by Sir Charles Coote in 1625), with its defensive town gate. Cross a loop of the Shannon at Drumsna. The so-called **Dun of Drumsna** is an extensive range of earthworks and ramparts. The N4 continues southeast to **Dromod**, shortly passing Derrycarne on the lough shore.

Lough Allen

The area to the north of Carrick-on-Shannon is dominated by two loughs, Lough Allen and Lough Arrow. The village of **Leitrim**, about 6km along the R280, which gives its name to the county, was formerly the residence of the bishops of Liathdroma. It is also the site of a castle a local clan chieftain, O'Rourke, Prince of Breffni, a few ruins of which still remain. **Drumshanbo** (7km) is an angling resort at the south end of Lough Allen, the third largest of the lakes formed by the Shannon. **Sliabh an Iarainn Visitor Centre** at Drumshanbo (10.00–18.00, Mon–Sat, 14.00–18.00, Sun, Easter–Sept; £), concentrates on the mining tradition of the area, and local folklore. The **Leitrim Way** (48km) from Drumshanbo to Manorhamilton, follows the east shore of Lough Allen up to its highest point of Doo Lough. The walk is most attractive when begun from Drumshanbo.

A minor road (R207) skirts the **east bank** of Lough Allen, below Slieve Anierin (586m) and Slievenakilla (543m), and, further north, part of the **Iron Mountains**, to Dowra. From here you can either circle the lough by turning west, or continue northeast, passing near the source of the Shannon, to meet the N16 from Sligo (immediately west of the border crossing of Blacklion-Belcoo, on Lough Macnean).

The R280 skirts the **west bank** of Lough Allen, off which a left-hand turn leads shortly to Keadew, the final home of the composer, writer and harpist, Turlogh O'Carolan (1670–1738), the 'last of the Irish bards'. He is buried in Kilronan church (to the northwest), which has a 12C–13C doorway.

The next left-hand lane leads to Arigina, with its former iron-mines and collieries. Further north, you pass the ruins of St. Patrick's church at Corglass (or Tarmon) and veer northwest and away from the lough to Drumkeeran, between mountain ranges rising to the west and to the northeast. The road skirts Belhavel Lough and bears north, ascending the Bonet valley to the mountain-girt village of Manorhamilton, on the Enniskillen–Sligo road.

Mohill to Enniskillen via Swanlinbar

The (N4) bears northwest away from Carrick-on-Shannon and keeps above the south bank of the Boyle river—in fact a chain of lakes—passing (right) the late Classical style **Woodbrook House**. David Thomson described it in *Woodbrook*, his autobiographical, nostalgic evocation of a declining Ango-Irish family in the 1930s. The demesne of Rockingham House is just beyond (right). The house was remodelled by Nash in 1810, but after several fires was demolished. The demesne, somewhat mutilated with conifer plantations, is now known as the **Lough Key Forest Park**.

Putto on the 17C Peyton-Reynolds monument in the 14C Fenagh church

If you plan to visit Enniskillen, the R201 runs northeast via Mohill (southeast of Carrick-on-Shannon) at the head of Lough Rinn. **Fenagh**, 12km north of Mohill, has two old churches remaining from an earlier monastery, and a megalithic tomb. Beyond Fenagh pass through Ballinamore and **Swalinbar** (25km). Cross the border into Co. Fermanagh and after 6.5km (A32) turn left for Florence Court.

Florence Court

Florence Court (13.00–18.00 daily except Tues, May–Aug; 13.00–18.00 Sat, Sun & BH, Apr–Sept; NT) is one of the most important neo-classical 18C houses in the country. It was named after Florence Bourchier-Wrey, who married John Cole in 1707. The property was inherited by their son, who was elevated to the Irish peerage as Baron Mountflorence in 1760. The present mansion dates from 1751–64, with wings added some years later by Davis Ducart. The finely proportioned central block is flanked by arcades with end pavillions and the interior contains a set of state rooms prepared for a visit of George IV in 1821. These are decorated with Rococo plasterwork by John West. The house has been opened to the public since its restoration after a fire in 1955, when the ceiling of the sitting-room collapsed. The fireplace in that room is exceptionally fine. The library, to the right of the entrance, contains prints of local views, and a portrait of the 2nd Earl of Enniskillen, by Lawrence. The collection of Meissen ware, and the Venetian Room (named after its Venetian window) on the first floor (ceiling restored) are of interest. The extensive gardens (700 acres) contain numerous fine trees including the parent tree from which the Florence Court Yew has been propagated.

5km west is the Cladagh Glen, with a footpath ascending to the **Marble Arch Caves**, where the stream flows out from an underground channel, beneath a detached archway. The caves may now be seen on a conducted tour in March–October (details from the NITB Enniskillen). The terrain is easy but wear warm clothes.

West of Carrick-on-Shannon—Boyle to Carrowkeel

Boyle (Tourist Information, ☎ 079-62145, May–Sept), to the west of Carrick-on-Sharron, was the home of the King family. Edward King (1612–37), whose death by drowning inspired Milton's poem, *Lycidas* was born here. **King House** (1730), (10.00–18.00 daily, May–Sept; 10.00–18.00 Sat & Sun, Apr–Oct; £; OPW) with its heavily pedimented front facing the river, was designed by Sir Edward Lovett Pearce and built by William Halfpenny, and has recently been restored. The King family burial-place was the Cistercian **Boyle Abbey**

(09.30–18.30, June–Sept; £; OPW), founded in 1161 and completed in 1220 is one of the earliest in Ireland. Monks were sent by St Bernard of Clairvaux, who established Mellifont then Boyle. It was plundered by Anglo-Normans in 1202 and 1235, and despoiled by Cromwell's troops in 1659. Its extensive and well-preserved ruins lie near the river. The long nave is notable for its early Gothic arches on the north side and Romanesque arches on the south; the details of the windows, pillars, capitals and corbels are also worth looking at.

Decorated 13C capital in the nave of Boyle Abbey

Lough Key, to the northeast of Boyle, is studded with wooded islands backed by distant mountains. On one of the islands are the remains of the Abbey of the Trinity, where the *Annals of Lough Ce* (a document compiled during the late 15C on the history of Connaught 1014–1590; now in Trinity College Library) were written. On the river bank near the lough is the ruined church of Asselyn.

Some 8km west of Boyle is **Lough Gara** with the ruined Moygara Castle on its west bank. Several crannógs have been excavated here, next to the lake, while on the right of the road to it is a very large dolmen.

From Boyle, the Sligo road climbs northwest across the Curlew Mountains, a striking feature of the landscape. **Ballinafad** (7km) is charming village at the southern end of Lough Arrow. Its **castle** has three cylindrical towers, and around it was fought a bloody battle (1599) between Hugh Roe O'Donnell and the Irish separatist forces and the English forces under Sir Conyers Clifford. Inland from the west bank of Lough Arrow, on the slope of Bricklieve Mountain (321m) and about 1.5km southwest of Tower Hill House, is the **Carrowkeel Passage-tomb Cemetery**. This group of passage-graves, dates from 2100–2000 BC, but, unlike the tombs of the Boyne Valley, is devoid of passage-grave art. 5km from Ballymote, on the western slope of **Keshcorran Hill** are some prehistoric caves to which many obscure legends are attached. One relates the birth here of Cormac MacArt and of the she-wolf that suckled him; another that it was a refuge of Diarmuid during his flight (having eloped with Grainne, the betrothed wife of Finn MacCoul, see p.224).

On the east bank of Lough Arrow are the ruins of the **Dominican abbey** of Ballindoon (1507), and further southeast, above **Kilmactranny** (on the Ballyfarnan road) are a number of cairns that are said to mark the site of the legendary battle of Northern Moytura, where the Firbolgs were defeated by the Tuathdé Danaan (see Cong).

Lough Nasool, c 2km north of Ballindoon Abbey, went suddenly dry for about a month in 1933, and local tradition states that this phenomenon occurs every 100 years, in memory of Balor 'of the Evil Eye'—a cyclops-eyed character in Irish mythology who lived on Tory Island—slain at Moytura.

Ballymote to Tubbercurry

From Castlebaldwin, just northwest of the lough (on the N4), a minor road leads 9km west to **Ballymote**, famous for its strong **castle**, flanked by six corner towers. Built in 1300 by Richard de Burgh, the 'Red Earl' of Ulster it became a bone of contention in the Civil War, when it was occupied and defended by Irish forces in 1641, only falling into English hands in 1645, after the united attack of Ireton and Coote. The remains of a Franciscan friary are also here. The late-14C *Book of Ballymote*, containing a genealogy, classical literature and local history was compiled here (it has been kept in the Royal Academy since 1785).

Tubbercurry (11km south-west) is a small market town with one long street. The 8C **Moylough Belt** (a belt-shrine, now in the National Museum, Dublin) was found near the castle and church at Bunnanaddan.

Achonry, just north of Tubbercurry (N17) is the seat of a bishopric founded in the 7C by St. Nathy. On the opposite side of the main road, at the foot of Knocknashee, with its hillfort, is the ruined Franciscan Court Abbey, with a square tower.

Descend into the valley of the Owenmore, with **Templehouse Lough** on the right. The ruins of a castle, said to have belonged to the Knights Templar, are in the Templehouse estate. Beyond the bridge a minor road leads left to Coolaney, where a curious bridge spans the Owenbeg. **Moymlough Castle**, nearby, is a ruined O'Hara stronghold (their more recent seat is at Annaghmore), an attractive demesne on the Owenmore, left of the main road.

15· The North West: Donegal

It is not surprising that the north-west corner of Ireland should have been the last to be brought under English rule, its remoteness and inaccessibility preserved it from easy conquest. The exclusion in 1922 of Donegal from its natural hinterland by the border with Northern Ireland and its tenuous land-link with the Republic, further contributed to its isolation in the 20C. Today, its western fringes are the last area of the country to remain significantly Irish-speaking, although the population are now bilingual rather than purely native speakers.

Lough Swilly, in the far north, which divides the **Inishowen Peninsula** from northwest Donegal, and **Donegal Bay** in the south of the county both help to preserve the separateness of the area. The region is one of the least developed and most scenic in Ireland, partly due to its natural combination of sea-coast, distinctive mountain-ranges and treeless landscape.

The entire centre of the county is mountainous, the **Derryveagh** and **Blue Stack Mountains** isolating the western seaboard from the rest of the County. **Errigal**, in the Derryveagh is strikingly volcanic in appearance.

From **Bloody Foreland** to **Rossan Point**, the coastline is indented with coves and bays, and the small picturesque villages of **Gortahork**, **Glenties** and **Glencolumbkille**. **Glenveagh National Park** is vast: over nine and a half thousand hectares of lake, mountain and forest offer some splendid scenery, and the smaller **Ards Forest Park** on Sheep Haven in the north of Donegal, is another attractive area of wilderness.

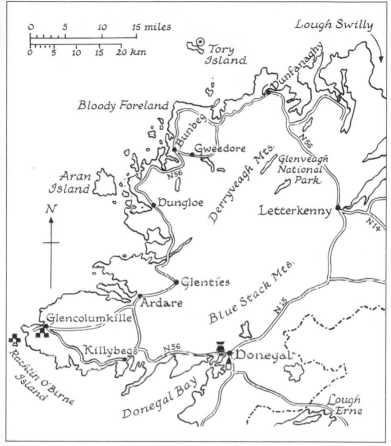

The coastal islands of **Tory** and **Aran** are still inhabited. **Letterkenny**, the county town, has an excellent museum, Donegal County Museum, and to the north, on the edge of Lough Gartan, is **Glebe House**, which has an important private collection of 19C and 20C fine and applied arts.

How to get there

- **Rail**. The region is poorly served; Sligo to the south; Derry to the east.
- **Air**. Carrick Finn Airport on the north coast; Derry Airport.
- **Sea**. Sailings to Aran Island from Burtonport and Tory Island from Meenlaragh.

Listings

Arranmore. Glen Hotel, relaxed family hotel (☎ 075-20505).
Ardara. Nesbitt Arms Hotel, traditional small town hotel (☎ 075-41103).
Donegal. Donegal Town Independent Hostel (☎ 073-22805); St. Ernans House Hotel, on an island, old fashioned charm (☎ 073-21065).
Dunfanaghy. Corcreggan Mill, hostel (☎ 074-36409).

Dunglow. Green's Hostel, Carnmore Rd (☎ 075-21021).
Glencolumbkille. Folk Village Tearoom, simple fare (☎ 073-30017); **Glencolumbkille Hotel**, efficient modern hotel (☎ 073-30003).
Kincasslagh. Viking House Hotel, country n'Irish music hotel (☎ 075-43295).
Letterkenny. Carolina House, Loughnagin, excellent restaurant (☎ 074-22480); **The Manse Hostel** (☎ 074-25238).
Lough Eske. Ardnamona House, celebrated cooking, celebrated gardens (☎ 073-22650); **Harvey's Point**, ultra-modern country house hotel, excellent facilities (☎ 073-22208).
Maghera. Ardtara Country House, 8 Gorteade Rd, Upperlands, Victorian manor house with luxurious interiors (☎ 01648-44490).
Rathmullan. Pier Hotel, old-fashioned coaching inn, good bar (☎ 074-58115); **Rathmullan House**, on the shores of Lough Swilly, country house hotel (☎ 074-58188).
Rossbeigh. Tirnarossa, *An Oige* hostel in building designed by Sir Edwin Lutyens.
Tory Island. Ostan Thoraighe, new hotel, sparse and cheerful (☎ 074-35920).

Donegal

The town stands at the head of Donegal Bay, and at the mouth of the river Eske, with the Blue Stack mountains rising beyond. Donegal (*Dún na nGall*, the fort of the foreigners, ie. the Vikings) is an ancient and historic town (Tourist Information, The Quay, ☎ 073-21148). It was the headquarters of the O'Donnell clan, *Cinel Conail*, and capital of their territory, Tirchonaill (or Tyrconnel; Tir, land). The town was laid out by Sir Basil Brooke (c 1610) as a Plantation town, with streets meeting at a central triangular Diamond.

Donegal Castle

Immediately north of the Diamond, on the banks of the River Eske, is an early 16C keep (09.30–18.30 daily, June–Oct; £; OPW), built by Red Hugh O'Donnell prior to the battle of Kinsale in 1607 (see Chapter 6). It was altered and rebuilt by Sir Basil Brooke (c 1623), after he had been granted the O'Donnell lands by James I. The monumental chimney-piece with the arms of Brooke (right) on the overmantle, flanking Brooke impaling Leicester, on the second floor of the castle, is particularly impressive. Brooke added a fine Jacobean five-bay, three storey, gabled manor house, and also replaced the upper slit windows of the keep with

stone mullioned windows and roof gables. The two 15C doorways on the ground floor of the manor house may have been re-used from the nearby friary.

The historical compilation, known as the *Annals of the Four Masters* (1632–36), was written by monks from **Donegal Abbey**, at Bundrowes near Bundoran. It covers the history of the world up to 1616 and is an important source of early Irish history. The four masters were Michael O'Clery and his assistants Fearfeasa O'Maolconry, Peregrine O'Duigenan and Peregrine O'Clery.

Arms of Sir Basil Brooke impaling Leicester, surrounded by the Tudor rose (17C), Donegal Castle

The obelisk (1937) is actually a monument to the four monks. It stands in the Diamond, which has recently been surrounded by a vaguely Shamrock-shaped enclosure, the stem of the composition being the obelisk.

East of the town is **St. Patrick's church** by Ralph Byrne (RC, 1931), known as the 'Church of the Four Masters'. Architecturally, it is almost the last fling of the Celtic Revival movement and incorporates the statutory Round Tower and a lightly chevroned west doorway. The Protestant church (1828) stands opposite the castle.

The ruins of a Franciscan friary stand on the shore, protected by a sea-wall. It was founded in 1474 by Hugh O'Donnell and his wife Fingalla O'Brien (both the founders and their son Hugh Og were buried in the precincts). The principal ruins are those of the choir, the south transept, and two walls of the cloister. The nave was used for Anglican worship up to the building of the current Protestant church. The rest was destroyed in 1601 by the explosion of several barrels of gunpowder, when Hugh Roe O'Donnell was besieging his cousin Niall Garbh, and an English garrison. Niall gained little by his desertion; having lost the confidence of the English, he was imprisoned in the Tower of London for seventeen years, until his death in 1626. His cousin Hugh died in Spain in 1602 on a mission to seek further assistance for Ireland.

West of Donegal

The largest place on the peninsula west of Donegal is Killybegs. From Donegal the road (N56) runs roughly parallel to Donegal Bay, with occasional views south towards the Sligo mountains and Ben Bulben, passing through **Mountcharles**, a hillside quarrying village, to the base of the Doorin peninsula. The Blue Stack (672m) and Binbane mountains are to the right. You can take a hill-road to the right (R262) climbing northwest across country to the village of Glenties (21km). Dunkineel stands at the base of St. John's Point, a narrow tongue of land, to the west of which lies MacSwyne's Bay. This inlet bears the name of a once powerful sept who controlled the Barony of Banagh (their castle lies on the shore to the south). Killybegs is a few kilometres northwest over the Oily river, in the next valley.

Killybegs, the major fishing-port of the northwest, resounding to the keening of gulls, is on one of the more attractive of the landlocked bays of Donegal. It is also well known for the manufacture of Donegal carpets. William Allingham, the poet, was a customs' officer here c 1849. In the forecourt of St. Mary's church (RC, J.B. Papworth, 1840), is the decorated tombstone of Neall Mor McSwyne (c 1524), a member of the powerful local clan. The stone is decorated with the figure of a gallowglass (mercenary soldier) and interlace patterns.

The South-west peninsula

From the T-junction north of Killybegs, the N56 climbs north up the Stragar valley to the 'Neck' of the Ballagh Pass, then descends to Ardara. From here you can continue west to make the circuit of part of the wild mountainous southwest peninsula of Donegal. The R263 skirts Fintragh Bay, overlooked by Crownarad (493m) to **Kilcar**, a charming hamlet at the confluence of two streams. The Slieve League, to the west of **Carrick**, provides some of the most imposing cliff-scenery in Ireland. Slieve League (601m) is easily climbed by those with suitable footwear and a head for heights. Just south of Carrick (1.5km), which stands on the Glen river in the fjord of Teelin Bay, a lane to the right leads to the mountain but it is not recommended to motorists—it later peters out—and is best reserved for the descent on foot. For the finest approach take the next turning at Teelin. The narrow and humpy lane takes you to **Carrigan Head** and then bears round, following a new track to a viewpoint on Bunglass Point. From here the whole curving seaward face of Slieve League is displayed, a precipice not only remarkable for its immense height—it falls practically sheer from the summit—but also for its colouring, caused by the stains of metallic salts. In fair weather you can take a closer look by boat from Teelin.

At **Eagle's Nest** (534m) the cliffs are at their steepest. Between this point and the summit **One Man's Path**, a narrow ledge 60cm wide between the steeply scarped landward side and the cliff, provides splendid views. In blustery or misty weather walkers should take the 'Old Man's Path' a little below the crest on the landward side.

From Carrick, turn left across moorland. After 3km a rough road descends west to **Malin More**. To reach the tip of the headland, leave the village, crossing a ridge to Malin More, and Malin Beg at the south end of the bay. The little bay of Trabane lies beyond, and to the west, the island of **Rathlin O'Birne**, where there is a hermitage with a collection of cross-slabs.

1.5km along the direct Carrick road from Malin More (R263), to the right, is the oval cashel (restored) of Cloghanmore, with two flag-roofed chambers. On the other side of the road are two standing stones and a dolmen.

Returning to Malin More, continue for 4km before descending into the Glen valley and Glencolumbkille.

Glencolumbkille

Glencolumbkille (the glen of St. Columba), is said to have been a favourite retreat of the saint and his disciples. On the hillside ascending north to **Glen Head**—a sheer precipice 227m high, with a Napoleonic signal tower above it—are the House, Well, 'Chair' and 'Bed' of St. Columba.

In the area surrounding the village, which is an important centre of the *Gaeltacht*, are a superb collection of early **cross-slabs** arranged in the form of a *turas* or 'stations'. On 9 June, the saint's feast day, a 5km barefoot journey, which begins at the 19C Protestant church, (the site probably representing an early ecclesiastical enclosure) visits 15 early Christian and pre-Christian monuments.

A **Folk Village** (10.00–18.00, Mon–Sat, Easter, June & Sept; 10.00–18.00, Mon–Sat, 12.00–18.00 Sun, July & Aug; £) which includes furnished examples of 18C, 19C and early 20C cottages, is west of the centre. There is an archaeological exhibition at the **Ulster Cultural Institute** (10.00–18.00 daily, all year) which also provides a wide range of courses in traditional music, dance and Irish culture.

The village is noted for the co-operative set up by the enterprising parish priest, Fr. James McDyer (d. 1987). His effort to halt the inexorable tide of emigration was successful and the Folk Village and much local industry are a result of his initiatives.

Sturrall, the next promontory, is approached by a dangerous knife-edge ridge. The tiny harbour of Port lies just beyond.

From Glencolumbkille follow the Ardara road, passing a well preserved cross, and climb due east. This road and that ascending the Glen valley from Carrick converge at Meenaneary, from where you continue east up the desolate Crow valley towards Crocknapeast (502m) before bearing northeast to the Pass of Glengesh. Descend towards Ardara, meeting the Killybegs road just south of the village. Intrepid walkers may follow a rough track along the north coast of the peninsula from Glen Head over the cliffs of Port Hill (248m) and Slievetooey (443m) to the primitive hamlet of **Maghera** (15km), with its waterfall, cliffs, caves and dunes. A coast road leads due east from here to Ardara.

Northwest Donegal

Portal dolmen, Kilclooney

Ardara (pronounced with the last syllable accented) is an important centre of the Donegal homespun and knitting industry, standing at the head of Loughros More Bay. **Ardara Heritage Centre** (10.00–18.00 daily, Easter–Sept; £) tells the story of local tweed weaving. There is a rose window by Evie Hone (1954) in the Church (RC).

Alternatively, the R261 takes you across the next peninsula to Maas. The first place of interest is **Kilclooney** where there is a huge dolmen (5 minutes' walk behind the church). The remains of a huge oval fort, known as **The Bawn**, lie further to the west in Lough Doon. Beyond the village is the road to Maas (right). If you have time, turn left, for **Narin** (or Naran) and adjacent **Portnoo**, two fishing villages facing the tidal islet of Inishkeel, with its ruined chapel. The views and walks in every direction are delightful. The road continues, passing (right) Dunmore Head, and several small loughs with remains of island fortresses, to Rossbeg on Dawros Bay. From Dawros Head, beyond, there are fine views of the cliffs of Slievetooey (south) and Aran Island to the north.

The main road (N56) turns right along the Owentocker river from Ardara to (9.5km) **Glenties**, another pleasantly sited angling resort where the Stracashel and Owenea rivers meet and more knitting takes place. The modern Church of St. Conall (RC, Liam McCormack, 1976) is attractive. The main road (N56) leads northwest of Glenties to (7km) Maas.

Alternatively, turn abruptly east out of Glenties (R250) and cross the Gweebarra estuary by a long bridge (5km), with a fine view up the valley towards Slieve Snaght (683m) in the distance. **Fintown**, 16km northeast of Glenties is beautifully situated at the far end of narrow Lough Finn and below Aghla (596m). Just before Fintown you can take the R252 to Doochay. The area north of Doochay is dotted with loughs; the road passes **Lough Barra** (with retrospective views), circling behind Moylenany (538m) to **Gartan Lough** on the R251. Gartan Lough is next to **Lough Akibbon**. A ruined chapel above its west side is said to have been built on the spot where St. Columba was born in 521. The saint is said to have been baptised at the ruined church at Temple Douglas, southwest on the Letterkenny road.

Columba was a descendant of Niall of the Nine Hostages, and on his mother's side, the Kings of Leinster. Although the saint's name ending 'cille' (a church) might confirm his devoutness, his character is better described by his other baptismal name, 'Crimthan' (a wolf; seeking souls for Christ); but his relentless energy was tempered by his missionary visit to Scotland after the 'Battle of the Books' (see Cooladrummon, p.341).

From Doochay, the main road turns north across moorlands to (13km) **Dunglow**, an angling centre. The best sport to be found is in **Lough Meela**, to the northwest. Maghery Bay (7km southwest) has a fine sandy strand, and the strange rocky coast here is worth exploring. The church of St. Crona, (RC, 1980) has a good interior.

Burtonport, a little further along the coast, is an 18C herring-fishing village with granite quarries and owes its name and origin to the 4th Marquess Conyingham (William Burton). About 3km northwest is the lonely ruin of Castle Port while close inshore is **Inishmacduirn** or **Rutland Island**. You can still see the sand-strewn remains of a futile attempt to establish a port here (1785) under the Lord-Lieutenancy of the Duke of Rutland. Napper Tandy (1740–1803) a United Irishman, landed here for a few hours on 16 September 1798, together with a body of French soldiers, before being carried back aboard the *Anacreon* in a state of inebriation.

Aran Island

Aran Island, also known as **Aranmore** (*Arainn Mhór*) with its lighthouse (originally of 1798, but replaced in 1865) on its north-west point, is visible for 25 miles. There is a regular ferry between Burtonport and Leabgarrow on the island (journey time 20–30 minutes; June–Sept daily), which, like the smaller islets of Inishcoo and Eighter, has good sandy beaches. There are fine views from the highlands of Aranmore back over the low-level coastline. The land is open and boggy with the villages (and the pubs) on the south and east of the island.

From Burtonport the coast road bears north across an area known as The Rosses, well described by the naturalist Lloyd Praeger (1865–1953) as 'a land of innumerable lakelets, a windswept heathery region, with small peaty fields grudgingly yielding difficult crops of potatoes and oats and turnips, and roads meandering through granite hillocks'. The road passes the offshore island of Cruit, and beyond, Inishfree Bay, before turning inland through Annagary to regain the main road at Crolly.

Bunbeg is a little port, further north along the coast. Beyond, **Derrybeg**, on the coastal slopes, are numerous houses and cottages, typical of the 'Congested Districts'. You shortly round the hill known as Bloody Foreland (so-called from its red hue when lit up by the setting sun) the most northwestly point of Donegal mainland.

Tory Island

The treeless and windswept landscape of Tory Island (ferries from Bunbeg and Meenlaragh) is 11km north of Bloody Foreland. The island is still inhabited but nothing much has changed since the 19C and the majority of the population are lobster fishermen and Irish-speaking.

According to legend, it was once the stronghold of the Fomorians, a legendary race of gigantic pirates, whose chieftain was the one-eyed Balor (the Celtic god of darkness) of the Mighty Blows (or Evil Eye). In 1884, a gunboat endeavouring to land rate-collectors was mysteriously wrecked, with much loss of life in calm weather. Their misfortune was attributed to the successful use of 'Cursing Stones' by the islanders (the stones were considered to grant special powers to a person who held them while casting a curse).

There are two separate villages, East and West Towns. Most of the antiquities are in West Town, where you can see the remains of two oratories, a round tower and **tau cross** ('T'-shaped), remains of a monastery established by Columba in the 6C. **St. Columcille's church** (RC, E.W. Godwin, 1857) has a window by Beatrice Elvery (1910) and Patrick Pollen. At the east end of the island is Dun Balor, a virtually impregnable promontory fort, with remains of hut sites.

Under the influence of Derek Hill a group of naïf painters emerged on Tory during the 1950s. Their work, reminiscent of the painters of St. Ives School in Cornwall (such as Alfred Wallis), depicts the harshness of island life. Jimi Dixon is the most well-known (see Glebe Gallery, below).

Nearer the coast are the smaller islands of **Inishbofin, Inishdooey** and **Inishbeg**, each with its melancholy cluster of abandoned houses, attached like barnacles to a rock (ferry trips in summer, from Falcarragh).

As you round the head of Ballyness Bay (east of Bloody Foreland), you leave the district known as Gweedore and enter that of Cloghaneely, regaining the main road (N56) at Gortahork and Falcarragh.

Alternatively, from Crolly the main road veers inland past the village of **Gweedore**. It was once an overpopulated district in the wilds, which owed its existence to an hotel (now closed) built by Lord George Hill (1801–79) in an attempt to improve the lot of the poor inhabitants. Lough Nacung is beyond. To the left rises Tievealehid (431m), while to the east is the splendid conical quartzite peak of Errigal Mountain (752m), the highest in Donegal. The **ascent of Errigal** is usually made from Dunlewy, and is laborious but not difficult (allow a day). The grass and heather slopes are succeeded by a stretch of awkward loose stones, from where a steep incline leads to the first pinnacle of the crest. This is connected with the main peak by the One Man Path—a narrow path, 27m long and 60cm wide—the only dizzy part of the ascent. The north side towards Lough Altan should be avoided, as it is covered by loose and dangerous scree. The immense panorama extends from Knocklayd, in Antrim, to Ben Bulben above Sligo, and a fine view of coast.

The Derryveagh and Glenveagh Mountains

The R251 skirts the base of Errigal, leading into Glenveagh National Park. At **Dunlewy**, the Church of the Sacred Heart (RC; Timothy Hevey, 1877), over-looking the lake, against a backdrop of mountains, is a surreal sight, appearing as though it had been superimposed on the landscape. It was built by the land-lord William Ross for the people of the valleys (his portrait in silk topper and hunting pink is displayed left of the altar). Below the church is the **Dunlewy Lakeside Centre** where the 19C cottage of the renowned weaver Manus Ferry has been reconstructed. The weaving and *poitín* (illicit alcohol) brewing skills of the area are demonstrated.

To the southeast of Dunlewy there is a steep rift in the Derryveagh Mountains, called the **Poisoned Glen**. In fact the water here was long unfit to drink, owing to the poisonous spurge that grew on its banks. Mountains to the south of the glen are Slieve Snaght (683m), and to the northeast, Dooish (633m). The road climbs northeast, offering striking views of mountains Aghla More (582m), Aghla Beg and wild **Lough Altan**. From Calabber Bridge the road bears round the northern spur of the Derryveagh range and passes the northern end of mountain-girt Lough Beagh (6.5m long), with a deer forest in the glen to the southwest. This is approached from the Lakeside Centre by a private road on the south bank, passing **Glenveagh Castle** (1870), beautifully sited on a rock promontory, with attractive gardens and splendid rhododendrons. The area (nearly 10000 hectares) is now designated the **Glenveagh National Park** (OPW).

Glebe House

Continuing east bear left onto the R255 to regain the N56 just south of Termon; the right-hand turning leads to Lough Akibbon (4km south; see above). Between this and Gartan Lough, is the colourful **Glebe House and Gallery** (11.00–18.30, Mar–April; 11.00–18.00, Sat–Thurs, May–Sept; £; OPW), long the home of the artist Derek Hill, and donated to the State in 1981. The work on display includes William Morris textiles and wallpaper, Wemyss Ware and Japanese prints, Tory Island naif paintings (see above), contemporary Irish and international art (such as Picasso, Kokoshka, Morandi, Sidney Noland and John Bratby), and an extensive collection of Victoriana.

Continue due north on the R251/255 to Creeslough. The N56 leads southeast, soon crossing the Owencarrow at New Bridge, with a fine view southwest up Glenveagh, and ascends to Barnes Gap between Stragaddy and Crockmore, with Loughsalt Mountain (470m) further east. It descends into the Lurgy valley at Termon and, 3km beyond, enters Kilmacrenan, in the Lenan valley. Slight remains of a 15C Franciscan friary and a later church tower survive, succeeding a church said to have been founded by St. Columba.

The **Stone of Cloghaneely** (which gives its name to the district) at **Falcarragh**, in the grounds of Ballyconnell House, is steeped in legend. It is said that the ubiquitous pirate Balor carried off a celebrated cow belonging to MacKineely, the local chief, to Tory Island. Hearing that the owner was plotting retaliation, he decapitated MacKineely on this stone, its red veining recalling the bloody deed. In another version, MacKineely seduces Balor's only daughter; the resultant child, who becomes a blacksmith, runs a red-hot iron through Balor's Cyclopean eye, in revenge for his father's death.

After 5km pass in **Myrath** old churchyard (left) a monolithic cross. It is said to have been cut by St. Columba out of the rocks of Muckish (or the 'Pig's Back'), a huge truncated cone to the south east, usually ascended from Creeslough.

Dunfanaghy, 16km from Gortahork, overlooks Sheep Haven and is dominated by Horn Head, a precipitous cliff 190m high, commanding splendid views.

The arcaded **Market House** in the square was erected in 1845 by Robert Stewart, the local landlord, in front of which stands a blunt pedestal commemorating Edmund Murphy (d. 1898), his land agent for 44 years. Such a monument (the only one in the village), is an anomaly among the generality of nationalist, religious or Imperial memorials. Holy Trinity (C of I) and the miniature Methodist church (Robert Young, 1875) are both of interest. **The Workhouse** (1845), has a display of living conditions in the institution during the Famine.

By the shore to the west of the village is a colossal blow-hole known as **McSwyne's** (or MacSweeney's) **Gun**, into which the tide rushes with a deafening sound in stormy weather. From here cliff paths circle the cape, with its curious rock formations and rare types of seabirds.

Beyond Dunfanaghy the road turns southeast, passing (left) **Portnablagh**, on a charming little bay opposite the Rosguill peninsula, while on promontories further south are the wooded demesne of the Capuchin friary of **Ard Mhuire** (Ards), and at Sheep Haven, the tall but battered keep of **Doe Castle**, an ancient stronghold of the MacSweeneys, still surrounded by its bawn. It was the headquarters of Sir Cahir O'Doherty's ill-starred raid on Derry in 1608; although at first successful, he was forced to retreat and met his death within a year at Kilmacrenan (see Derry, below).

The modern **church of St. Michael** at Creeslough, (RC, 1971; by Liam McCormick, also architect of the fine modern churches in Burt, Creeslough and Glenties), is one of the finest late-20C churches in the country. The contour of its roof reflects that of the mountain range behind, and the interior glows with light. There are also some excellent small windows in the lady chapel.

The R245 turns sharply northeast. A minor road shortly forks right for Glen, at the head of **Lough Glen**. From here a track leads 5km south towards precipitous Loughsalt Mountain (470m), at the foot of which is a wild tarn of great depth (73m), reputed never to freeze.

You regain the main road north of Glen not far short of **Carrickart**, a tweed-weaving village, to the northwest of which lies Rosapenna, on the narrow neck of the Rosguill peninsula. Further north is Downies, with a fine beach and good views across Sheep Haven towards Muckish. From here the 'Atlantic Drive' circles the peninsula except for its northeastern promontory of Melmore Head. On the return, at the eastern foot of Ganiamore, you pass **Mevagh**, with a ruined church and early stone-cross inscribed stones.

From Carrickart, the road skirts the west side of the 19km-long estuary of Mulroy Bay, almost landlocked, passing (left) near **Mulroy House**, the demesne of the earls of Leitrim, and Cratlagh Woods, where in 1878 the 3rd Earl was murdered for his callous policy of evicting any tenant who disobeyed him. You later cross a bridge over the Bunlin river, near which is a dolmen and a waterfall called Goland Loop, to enter Millford (or Milford), charmingly placed a few kilometres north of Lough Fern.

For a detour to Portsalon on the Fanad peninsula, turn north onto the R246, skirting the east bank of Mulroy Bay below Crockmore Hill, further east, with a fine dolmen, via Carrowkeel. A right fork brings you almost parallel to the ridge of Knockalla Mountain (364m), known as 'The Devil's Backbone'.

Portsalon, facing southeast up Lough Swilly, is finely situated opposite Dunree Head and the Urris Hills. Its church bell was the ship's bell of the *Laurentic*, sunk by a U-boat in 1917, the cargo of which was salvaged by divers in 1924. The far end of the peninsula can be circled on minor roads, but it is not spectacular.

At the north end of Knockalla, a road skirts the banks of **Lough Swilly** (the Lake of the Shadows), in fact an estuary 48km long, with some impressive scenery at its seaward end. The next place of any size is **Rathmullen**, reached via Killygarvan, with its ruined church and the dolmen and cross-slab of Drumhallagh. To the west rises Croaghan Hill, and further west is Crockanaffrin (347m), with a view of the fjord-like arms of Lough Swilly and Mulroy Bay.

Rathmullen

Rathmullen, a pleasant village overlooking Lough Swilly, was the scene of the 'Flight of the Earls' (14 September 1607), when the Earls of Tyrone and Tyrconnel set sail for Spain with about 100 minor nobility and followers (the final episode of the Elizabethan wars in Ireland). They failed to land in Spain and went to Louvain, reaching Rome six months later, where they unsuccessfully agitated for Spanish aid for their cause. Both died there, without ever returning to Ireland. The ensuing confiscation of the earls' extensive estates led to the Plantation of Ulster and all the subsequent events. The **Flight of the Earls Heritage Centre** (10.00–18.00, Mon–Sat; 15.00–18.00, Sun; £) is in one of the six Napoleonic batteries (1810) which guard the mouth of the lough. The events leading up to the Plantation of Ulster are shown in documentary style, providing a useful background to the contemporary conflict.

The ruins of a Carmelite priory can be seen in the town. The tower and chancel were erected by the MacSweeneys in the 15C, while the west portions were rebuilt in 1618 by Bishop Knox of Raphoe (to whom the lands of Turlough Og MacSweeney were awarded after the confiscations).

On 12 October 1798 the French frigate *Hoche*, with Wolfe Tone on board (see Ch. 7), was intercepted by Sir John Warren's squadron, and its crew landed at Rathmullen. Tone was identified in Letterkenny, and transferred to Dublin Castle, where he committed suicide.

Rathmelton (pronounced Ramelton), is on a creek of Lough Swilly, its harbour retaining some imposing old warehouses on the water's edge. It was the birthplace of the Rev. Francis Makemie (1658–1708), the founder of the Presbyterian church in America. The curious east window of the church here may be as late as the 17C. Some 5km southeast, on the road to Letterkenny, lies the 17C ruin of Fort Stewart. Just before you reach Letterkenny you pass the ruins of Killydonnell Abbey, a small Franciscan house founded in the 16C by an O'Donnell.

From Donegal to Derry

For a quick route to Letterkenny from Donegal, drive northeast towards Derry, after 6.5km passing (left) Lough Eske, fringed with the groves of partly gutted **Lough Eske Castle** (1866). The lough is backed to the north by the Blue Stack or Croaghgorm range (672m), to the east of which rise three 500m mountains. The ruined O'Donnel Tower on an island in the lough was once used as a prison by that powerful clan.

The road climbs the Lowerymore valley (once infested by highwaymen), with a fine backward view, and winds up through the narrow Barnesmore Gap, descending past (right) the desolate tarn of **Lough Mourne** to **Ballybofey**. The founder of the Irish Home Rule Party, Isaac Butt (1813–79) was born at neighbouring **Glenfinn** and is buried in the Protestant churchyard. A detour may be made by crossing the Finn at Stranorlar, and driving down the valley via (12km) Castlefin, formerly a fief of the O'Donnells, just short of Clady (in Tyrone). Otherwise, continue on the N56, branching left on to the N14 for Letterkenny.

Letterkenny

The city (Tourist Information, Derry Rd, ☎ 074-21160) formerly consisted mainly of one long street on the slope of a hill (*Leitir Ceanainn*, the hillside of the O'Cannons), over which it now sprawls. The **Cathedral of St. Eunan** (Hague and McNamara 1891) was the last Gothic Revival cathedral to be built in Ireland. It is extensively decorated internally by all of the available applied arts, and contains glass by Child, Clarke, Elvery, Healy and Rhind.

Donegal County Museum (open all year 10.00–16.30, Mon–Fri, 13.00–16.30, Sat; closed daily 12.30–13.00) in High Road, occupies a portion of the old Letterkenny workhouse (1843); it has archaeological, historical, and folklife sections in the permanent collection, and facilities for temporary exhibits. The Corn and Flax Mills at **New Mills** (OPW), the earlier dating from the 16C, have an exhibition on the development of milling technology.

A battle took place at **Farsetmore**, northeast of the town, in May 1567. Shane O'Neill 'the Proud' (who was brought up in England, returned to Ireland and changed loyalties from Elizabeth to the Irish cause) was vanquished by Hugh O'Donnell and many of his cavalry drowned while recrossing the Swilly estuary; a sandbank is still named 'the Marcaghs' (or horsemen's bed'). Another battle took place at **Scarriffhollis**, below the hamlet of New Mills, 5km south-west of Letterkenny. Sir Charles Coote's army destroyed the Bishop of Clogher's forces in June 1650, the bishop-general later being captured; he was hanged at Enniskillen six months afterwards.

6.5km east of Letterkenny (N14) you pass through the villages of Manor Cunningham and Newtown Cunningham, 3km north of which stands the 16C tower-house of **Burt** (showing Scottish Baronial influence), with Dooish Mountain prominent to the right.

If you want to avoid Letterkenny and take a cross-country route to Derry, follow the N13 from Stranorlar and shortly bear right onto the R236 for the village of **Convoy** on the Deela, a stream rising on the flank of the Cark Mountain (366m) to the west. There is a fine **stone circle** on a hilltop at Beltany, some 4km downstream.

The next village, **Raphoe**, was once the seat of a bishopric joined to the see of Londonderry in 1835. It is said that a monastery, founded here by St. Columba, was converted into a cathedral by St. Eunan in the 9C. The present cathedral is a plain Gothic building with transepts of 1702 and a tower of 1738, with some curious carvings of an earlier date. The neighbouring Bishop's Palace or Castle (1636), with four bastion-like towers, still occupied in the 1830s, is now a ruin.

Shortly cross the Strabane-Letterkenny road and descend into the Foyle valley past **St. Johnstown**. The square tower of **Montgevlin**, 3km south of St Johnstown is all that remains of a castle where James II held court during the siege of Derry. You soon fork right towards the border-post at Carrigans and Derry.

16 · Derry and Tyrone

Derry, or **Londonderry** is the second city of Northern Ireland, and historically the most important settlement both in the Plantation of Ulster, and of Plantation throughout Ireland. Its 17C walls are still intact and it remains one of the most impressive and interesting urban centres in the country. The region covered in this chapter includes most of counties Londonderry and Tyrone.

North of the city, the **Inishowen Peninsula** is separated from the mainland on both sides by the waters of **Lough Swilly** to the west and **Lough Foyle** to the east. One of the major antiquities of the north of Ireland is on the peninsula; the **Grianán of Aileach**, a dramatically sited Iron Age fortress, overlooking the mountains of Donegal.

Southeast of Derry are the **Sperrin Mountains**, with the principal towns of the region, **Strabane**, **Omagh**, **Dungannon** and **Coleraine** lying in a circuit around them. **Gortin Glen**, **Parkanur**, **Drum Manor**, and **Davagh Forest Parks** are all south of the Sperrins.

The Ulster Way (560m/890km), the foremost long-distance walking route in Ireland, crosses attractive and unspoiled countryside. Its fourteen sections include landscapes as different as the Mourne Mountains, Fair Head and the Causeway Coast. Two sections of the Way (through Fermanagh and Tyrone) run southwest through the Sperrins to Lough Erne.

North American associations are to be found in every part of Ireland; in Northern Ireland they are particularly strong, with an impressive number of prominent early American presidents, statesmen and civic leaders having Ulster ancestry. The **Ulster-American Folk Park** at Omagh celebrates this connection, as do **Gray's Printing Shop**, Strabane, and **Cavancor House**, Lifford.

Museums, heritage centres and historic houses of the Region include the excellent **Tower Museum** in Derry, the **Ulster History Park**, **Wellbrook Beetling Mill**, and the **Amelia Earhart Cottage**.

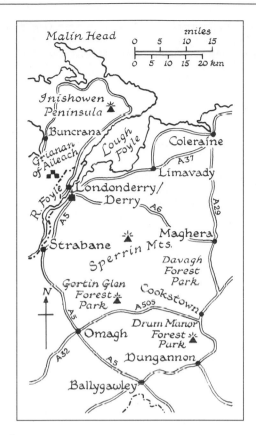

How to get there
- **Train**. Belfast-Derry line.
- **Air**. Belfast International or Derry Airports.
- **Sea**. Boating on Loughs Swilly and Foyle.

Listings

Aughnacloy. Garvey Lodge, 62 Favour Royal Rd, B&B (☎ 0166-252239).

Coleraine. Blackheath House, 112 Killeague Rd, Blackhill, 18C Rectory built by the eccentric Earl-Bishop of Derry; B&B, noted restaurant (☎ 01265-868433); Macduff's, also in Blackheath House (same ☎ no).

Cookstown. Royal Hotel, 64 Coagh St (☎ 06487-622240).

Derry. 36 Great James St, excellent B&B in Georgian town house, convenient and welcoming (☎ 01504-269691); Austin's Department Store café, overlooking the Diamond (☎ 01504-261817).

Dungannon. Inn On The Park Hotel, Moy Rd, extensive grounds, fine restaurant (☎ 018687-25151).

Inishowen Peninsula. Moville Holiday Hostel, Malin Road, Moville, (☎ 077-82378).

Limavady. **Drenagh**, 17 Dowland Rd, early-19C mansion, fine interiors, in extensive grounds, B&B (☎ 015047-22649); **Streeve House**, important country-house restaurant, accommodation (☎ 015047-66563).

Omagh. **Royal Arms Hotel**, 18C inn, labyrinthine interior, comfortable (☎ 01662-243262); **Omagh Independent Hostel**, 9A Waterworks Rd (☎ 01662-241973).

Strabane. **Mulvin Lodge**, 117 Mulvin Rd, B&B (☎ 01662-658269).

Derry/Londonderry

■ **Railway Station**. Waterside (☎ 01504-42228).
■ **Bus Station**. Foyle St (☎ 01504-262261).
■ **Airport**. For flights to Britain and the Republic (☎ 01504-810784).
■ **Tourist Information**. 8 Bishop St (☎ 01504-267284).
■ **Post Office**. 3 Custom House Quay (☎ 01504-362274).
■ **Festivals**. Two Cathedrals Music Festival, Autumn; Foyle Film Festival, October.

Derry City Council officially changed its name from 'Londonderry' to 'Derry' in 1983. Colloquially Derry is widely used by all sectors of the population although Unionists prefer (but frequently do not use) Londonderry as an expression of British loyalty and identity; the name of the county is similarly interchangeable. With a population of 94,721, it is the second city of Northern Ireland.

Historically and architecturally, Derry is one of the most interesting cities in Ireland, it has the only complete town walls in the country and was not only the first planned town in Ireland (1613) but also an important influence on the planning of early American colonial settlements such as Philadelphia. The defensive layout and internal organisation of Derry is probably based on that of Vitry le François (1560), designed for Francis I by Hieronimo Marino. Its historically transitional status is emphasised by the fact that it was the last fortified town built in the British Isles, and contains the first post-Reformation cathedral.

Derry occupies a unique place in Irish political mythology as a symbol of the Plantation of Ulster and as a Unionist holy place. Of the two 18C tapestries which hang in the Dublin House of Lords, one depicts the Battle of the Boyne, the other, the Siege of Derry; twin generative events in the emergence of a separate cultural entity in Ulster.

The highly visible military presence in the city forms a spectacle which to anyone familiar with mainland Britain or the Republic, will appear both extraordinary and shocking. The resemblance which it bears to military activity in non-democratic states is hard to avoid. Naturally the terrorist presence, its converse, is not so readily apparent.

The modern industrial town, noted for the manufacture of clothing, particularly shirts, surrounds the old centre.

Derry has its origins in a monastery founded by St. Columba (Columcille or Columb) (521–597) in c 546. The monastery was probably on the site of the present St. Augustine's (C of I) chapel-of-ease in the south-west corner, which was then covered with an oak forest—hence the placename *Daire*, an oak grove—and is now the walled area. Oak groves were sacred places among the pre-Christian, Celtic population of Europe, and something of this respect was retained up to the Reformation. In the late 10C the monastery was burned by the Vikings, the only occasion on which they raided it. In 1164 Abbot Flahertagh O'Brolchain built the great church of Templemore where St. Columba's **Long Tower Church** (RC) now stands. In 1311 the town was granted to Richard de Burgh, Earl of Ulster.

There were several attempts by Irish leaders to reject the English from Derry in the 16C-early17C. In the autumn of 1566, Shane O'Neill, Earl of Tyrone, incited a rebellion against English authority. The town resisted O'Neill's attack, although the English commander, Edward Randolph, was killed. Templemore church was largely destroyed, and only the round tower remained by the time Sir Henry Docwra had firmly established English dominance in 1570–1603. In May 1608, Sir Cahir O'Doherty ransacked the town but was killed two months later, and his lands, together with those of Tyrone and Tyrconnel, were confiscated (1613). Derry was handed over to the Corporation of London, its name was changed to Londonderry, and a large colony of Protestants from England 'planted' by James I. In 1649 Royalist forces under General Robert Stewart and Lord Montgomery of the Ards besieged the place for 20 weeks, but the defender, Sir Charles Coote, hired Owen Roe O'Neill to support him.

The **great siege**, lasted from 7 December 1688 to 12 August 1689 (and is commemorated by stained glass windows in both Guildhall and Cathedral). It was conducted against the planter supporters of William III and the Protestant interest by James II's army under three French generals; Maumont, Pusignan and Rosen and 20,000 troops, who besieged the city, completely blockading it for 105 days by throwing a boom across the Foyle to bar the approach of provision ships. Fired by the apostolic fervour of the Rev. George Walker, the starving citizens, among whom the death toll was very high, stubbornly held out (in spite of attempts by Robert Lundy, the governor, to seek a compromise) until the boom was forced by the *Mountjoy* on 28 July, and the city liberated.

During the 18C Derry went through a period of religious liberalism, reflected in the enthusiasm expressed by Protestants for the building of the first Catholic church. 19C developments are mainly concerned with trade and the establishment of the milling and manufacturing industry.

The Boundary Commission of 1924 included Derry in Northern Ireland despite the predominantly Catholic and Nationalist population west of the Foyle. Political gerrymandering has been a characteristic of municipal government in the city. Recent population trends have led to Protestants moving to the Waterside area on the east bank of the Foyle.

Its recent history has been less edifying. On 5 October 1968 the first major confrontation took place between Civil Rights demonstrators and the police, repeated on 4 January 1969, the Royal Ulster Constabulary justifying their reputation for sectarian bias. On 12 August the Bogside was in a state of siege, which has more-or-less continued ever since. 'Free Derry Corner' is painted on the gable-end of a demolished house in the Bogside, below the Derry city walls and commemorates the events. This nationalist quarter became a 'no-go' area to the RUC during the civil rights disturbances of the late 1960's and 70s. On 30 January 1972 the 1st Battalion Parachute Regiment killed 13 people, bringing home to the world at large the seriousness of the situation in Northern Ireland. The 1994 and 1997 cease-fires have contributed to the relaxation of tension in the area.

Among Derrymen were the dramatist George Farquhar (1678–1707), the novelist Joyce Cary (1888–1957); Sir Robert Montgomery (1809–87), who brutally suppressed the Indian Mutiny at Lahore, and was later Lt-Governor of the Punjab. George Berkeley, Anglican bishop and philosopher, was Dean here in 1724–33. Frederick Hervey (1730–1803) the celebrated Earl-Bishop of Derry occupied the see for thirty five years.

Amelia Earhart, the aviator, landed outside Derry at Ballyarnett in 1932 and is commemorated there.

The music of the *Derry Air* is said to have been first noted down in Limavady in 1851 by Jane Ross, on hearing an itinerant fiddler play the tune.

The Town. The historic town is on the west bank of the river Foyle. The original bridge (1791, Lemuel Cox and Jonathon Thompson) was made of timber. It is now crossed by the double-decker Craigavon Bridge (1933), built to carry road and rail traffic.

The walled enclosure of the 17C city surrounds an oval hill rising steeply from the river. It is separated from its hinterland by a valley, now known as the Bogside, which was a rivercourse in the 17C, making the site of the settlement virtually an island. However, the city is overlooked by land further west; its weakest defensive point. In its subsequent development in the 18C and 19C, the city failed to exploit its river frontage and as a result it lacks any waterfront identity.

Carlisle Rd ascends half-right from the bridge to **Ferryquay Gate**, one of the four gates in the old City Walls (which was shut in the face of Lord Antrim's troops in 1689 by the apprentice boys of Derry). Alternatively, Abercorn Rd ascends half-left, passing (left) a sculpture called 'Friendship' by Maurice Harron), to **Bishop Gate** (Henry Aaron Baker, 1798); a triumphal arch and the finest of the four gates with sculptural decoration by Edward Smyth. A military observation post sits on top of the gate and the whole area is festooned in anti-rocket screens.

Derry City Walls

The walls are of great interest. They have a circuit of 5,124 feet and were built 1613–18 at the expense of the City of London (designed by Captain Edward Doddington); they still belong to 'the Honourable, the Irish Society' (a group of London City Guilds from which the city name derives and originally an instrument of plantation, they are now a philanthropic society). Four additional gates were introduced in the 19C. The defences consist of an earth rampart, faced with a stone wall with battlemented parapet and with a broad walkway on top to facilitate movements of troops and artillery. Angle bastions punctuate the wall at regular intervals, although three of these are now missing. A tour of the walls may begin, right or left, from Shipquay Gate.

On the Double Bastion (left) is 'Roaring Meg', a brass cannon of 1642, which was famous during the siege. The adjacent Royal Bastion bears the rebuilt stump of the **Walker Monument**, commemorating the man who inspired the citizens to hold out during the great siege. A classical column, which once had a statue

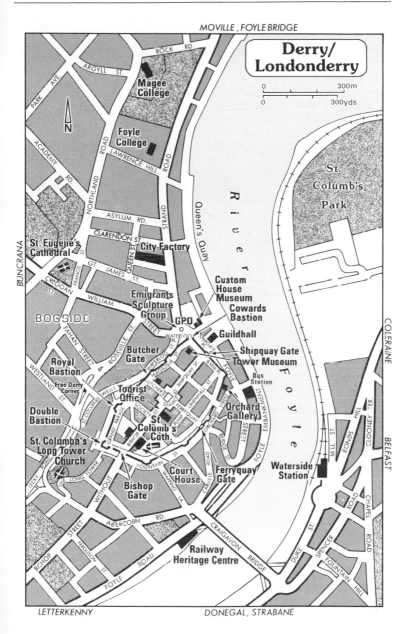

MOVILLE , FOYLE BRIDGE

Derry/ Londonderry

0   300m

0   300yds

ROCK RD

ARGYLL ST.

PARK AVE

Magee College

ACADEMY RD.

NORTHLAND ROAD

Foyle College

LAWRENCE HILL

STRAND ROAD

River

St. Columb's Park

ASYLUM RD.

CLARENDON ST.

St. Eugene's Cathedral

Queen's Quay

GT. JAMES ST.

QUEEN ST.

FRANCIS ST.

CREGGAN ST.

City Factory

WILLIAM STREET

BOGSIDE

FAHAN STREET

Custom House Museum

Emigrants Sculpture Group

ROSSVILLE ST.

GPO

WATERLOO PL.

Cowards Bastion

Guildhall

Butcher Gate

WATERLOO ST.

MAGAZINE ST.

SHIPQUAY ST.

Royal Bastion

WESTLAND ST.

WELLS ST.

Free Derry Corner

Shipquay Gate Tower Museum

BANK ST.

FOYLE STREET

Bus Station

Tourist Office

ST. COLUMB'S WELLS

BUTCHER ST.

DIAMOND

LINENHALL ST.

Double Bastion

GRAND PARADE

SOCIETY ST.

SHIPQUAY ST.

St. Columb's Cath.

Orchard Gallery

ORCHARD STREET

FOYLE STREET

EMBANKMENT

BISHOP ST.

FOYLE ST.

St. Columba's Long Tower Church

THE LONG TOWER

WITHOUT

FOUNTAIN ST.

WATLING LA.

Court House

Ferryquay Gate

BRIDGE ST.

Waterside Station

MILL ST.

BONDS HILL

CLOONEY TER.

LECKY ROAD

Bishop Gate

CARLISLE RD.

COLERAINE

BELFAST

BUNCRANA

ABERCORN RD.

BISHOP STREET

TENSION ST.

FOYLE ROAD

Railway Heritage Centre

CRAIGAVON BRIDGE

DUKE ST.

SPENCER ROAD

CHAPEL ROAD

FOUNTAIN HILL

LETTERKENNY

DONEGAL, STRABANE

of the Governor, was blown up in 1973. The mutilated statue of Walker (by John Smyth) is now in a Garden of Remembrance beside the Apprentice Boys Hall in Society St.

At the end of each street the wall is visible although a complete circumlocution is not possible for security reasons. Passing through the gates into the old city, you approach the Diamond, the central square of the town and site of earlier town halls. The 1914–18 war memorial in the square is by Vernon March (1927). From here the quadrant plan is obvious, with streets radiating at right angles to the four original city gates, Bishop, Butcher, Shipquay and Ferryquay.

From the Diamond, turning left up Bishop St, you soon reach (left) the Ionic-porticoed Greek-revival **Court House** (1813–17, John Bowden), opposite which is the former Bishop's Palace. Turn down St. Columb's Court (adjacent to the Court House), in which No. 1 is the home of the Hon. Irish Society (1740), for St. Columb's Cathedral.

St. Columb's Cathedral

The cathedral (C of I, 8.00–17.00) was founded by the Corporation of London in the early 17C. It is a long narrow aisled building without apses, with a west tower. The nave dates from 1628–33 but the chancel was only built in 1885–87, when the original plaster ceiling was replaced with a wooden one. The rather archaic style of the building is known as 'Planters' Gothic'.

In the entrance hall is the alleged bombshell thrown into the city, which contained General Richard Hamilton's proposed terms of surrender. The historic and uncompromising answer to which was 'No Surrender', a phrase which has become a Loyalist mantra. A plaque dated 1633, carries the eloquent dedicatory inscription,

If stones could speake
Then Londons prayse should sounde,
Who built this church and cittie
From the grounde.

The cathedral has numerous **monuments** of interest; on the north wall is a quaint 17C monument to mayor John Elvin (d. 1676, aged 102), and one to Captain Boyd of *HMS Ajax* (see St Patrick's Cathedral, Dublin, and the East Pier, Dun Laoghaire), by Thomas Farrell (c 1861); Bishop Knox by William Behnes, 1834; Bishop Ponsonby (T. Gough) and Francis Rogan (c 1854, J.R. Kirk). In the west gallery is a mahogany organ-case (1747).

The **Chapter House** contains more souvenirs of the siege. Cecil Frances Alexander (1818–95) hymnist and author of such favourites as *All Things Bright and Beautiful, There is a Green Hill Far Away* and *Once in Royal David's City*, is commemorated by a window in the Baptistry.

Return to the Diamond for Butcher St which leads to Butcher Gate, overlooking the Catholic district of **Bogside**. The 'Free Derry Corner' is visible with Creggan beyond. Shipquay St (with several 18C houses) slopes steeply away from the Diamond, to Shipquay Gate. To its left is a rampart lined with cannons, and beyond, the site of Coward's Bastion, the safest sector during the great siege. In Union Hall Place (inside Magazine Gate) the O'Doherty Tower (1989), a spurious though convincing tower house, forms part of the **Tower Museum** exhibition centre (10.00–17.00, Tue–Sat, Jan–June & Sept–Dec; 10.00–17.00, Mon–Sat; 14.00–17.00, Sun; 10.00–17.00 BH, July–Aug) which combines a display of important antiquities with tableaux relating the history of settlement in the area from the Neolithic to World War II. The museum ultimately intends to display the finds from the Armada ship *Trinidad Valencera*, now in the Ulster Museum.

Long Tower Church

A short walk downhill from Bishop's Gate, via Long Tower St, brings you to the St. Columba's Long Tower Church (RC), built on the site of Templemore. The Early Christian Round Tower survived from St. Columba's monastery until 1688 when it was destroyed during the great siege. Sir Henry Docwra (1563–1631) Governor of Derry, had spared it during the destruction of Templemore, the surrounding monastery.

The first post-Reformation Catholic church on the site was built in 1783, with support from the liberal Protestant Earl-Bishop who also presented the Corinthian capitals of the baldacchino. The church was enlarged and rebuilt progressively between 1818 and 1909. The **interior** is decorated in a manner reminiscent of the German 'Nazarene' movement (who aimed to restore the quality of religious art), and the assemblage of stained glass, mosaic, painting and metalwork make it one of the most elaborately decorated 19C churches in the country, a survival which has ignored successive fashions and papal decrees.

A Calvary in the forecourt of the church has a figure of St. Columba and a double bullaun set into the scene with total incongruity; the bullaun, placed here in 1907 is known as 'St. Columb's or Columba's Stone', and is the only remnant of the original monastic foundation now visible.

The **Guildhall** (Mon–Fri, 10.00–17.00) and Clocktower flank Shipquay Place. Originally built in 1890, it was rebuilt in 1912 after a fire and again in 1972 after bomb damage. Its interiors are richly ornamented and the upstairs Assembly Hall has good windows and Gothic hammer-beam roof. The **Harbour Museum** (Mon–Fri, 10.00–17.00) in Harbour Square is concerned with the city's maritime history. In Waterloo Place, just west of the Guildhall, is a bronze sculpture group '**Emigrants**' by Eammon O'Doherty. Derry was a major port of embarkation for emigrants to America throughout the 19C.

At the south-west corner of the walls in Orchard St is the **Orchard Gallery** (Mon–Sat 10.00–17.00), one of the most innovative arts centres in the country, which promotes exhibitions of contemporary work.

William St leads towards the **St. Eugene's Cathedral** (8.00–18.00) (RC), a plain Gothic-Revival building (1853–73) by J.J. McCarthy, with a nave arcade based closely on that in St. Columb's cathedral. Its tall and distinctive spire was added in 1903.

From St. Eugene's, turn east into Great James Street. In parallel Clarendon St and Asylum Rd are a group of streets with good examples of early 19C Georgian houses, the closest Derry gets to an 18C grid plan. In Queen St is the **City Factory** (Young and MacKenzie, 1863), an impressive L-shaped brick building decorated with sculpted heads and is one of the few Victorian shirt factories in the city still in production.

On the corner of Clarendon St is an eccentric Gothic Revival former Presbyterian church c1860, and at the southern end of Queen St is the fine classical portico of Great James St Presbyterian church (1837).

Foyle College (1814), off Lawrence St, is the successor of the Free Grammar School (1617) where George Farquhar was educated. Among its pupils was the historian J.B. Bury, and Sir Robert Montogomery, who achieved prominence for service in India. It is now the **Foyle Arts Centre** (Mon–Sat, 10.00–18.00), with a good figure by F.E. McWilliam in the forecourt. Further north is the University of Ulster at **Magee College** (A.P. Gribbon, 1865), for students training for the Presbyterian ministry. At Altnagelvin Hospital 'Princess Macha' is another excellent figure-sculpture by F.E. McWilliam (1909–92), the most significant Northern Irish sculptor of the 20C. Continuing north you shortly pass (right) **Boom Hall** (c 1770), marking the site where the boom was thrown across the Foyle during the siege of Derry (1688–89).

At Ballyarnet on the north edge of the city, on 20 May 1932, Amelia Earhart (1898-1937), the first woman to make a solo crossing of the Atlantic (from Newfoundland), completed her flight in 15 hours, 35 minutes. She is commemorated at the **Amelia Earhart Cottage** (seasonal opening times; enquire at NITB local office). The 'Wind Sculpture' is by Eilish O'Connell.

On the other side of town, southwest of the Craigavon Bridge in Foyle Road is the **Railway Heritage Centre** (Tue–Sat 10.00–17.00; Sun, 14.00–18.00) a small railway museum with antique engines, carriages, rolling stock and train memorabilia from the various defunct railway systems of the northwest of Ireland. Among the fine warehouses at the west end of the bridge is the Tillie and Henderson shirt factory (John Guy Ferguson, 1857), an intimidating five-storey cliff of brickwork which expresses both the industrial power and human misery of the Industrial Revolution in Ulster. Across the river is the original Waterside railway station (John Lanyon, 1873).

Circuit of the Inishowen Peninsula, Grianán of Aileach

A circular tour of this peninsula, the northernmost part of Ireland, may be made with ease from Derry. The **Grianán of Aileách**, the most impressive antiquity on the vicinity, lies 11km northwest of the city (off the N13), via Bridge End.

The mountains of Eskaheen (419m) and, further north, Crockglass (398m) rise as you skirt the broad waters of Lough Foyle (R238). The direct road to (14.5km) Cardonagh branches left at Carrowkeel, but continues along the lough side (13km) to enter the resort of Moville (pronounced with the accent on the second syllable). Greencastle, with a disfigured fort of 1812 and the ruined castle of Richard de Burgh (1305), lies some 4km beyond opposite Magilligan Point, the narrowest part of the estuary. Two parallel roads—the upper provides the better views—peter out at Inishowen Head (90m high), commanding a view of the coast to the east as far as the Giant's Causeway, and dominated by Crocknasmug (327m). In 1971, the *Trinidad Valencera*, a wreck from the Spanish Armada, was discovered in Kinnagoe Bay, to the northwest. Objects from the wreck are in the Ulster Museum, Belfast.

Just west of Moville a lane climbs inland to Cooley. There is not much to see apart from some scanty remains of a church, beside which is an ancient cross. There are several minor megalithic sites in the neighbourhood.

The main road from Moville (R238) ascends Bredagh Glen between Crockavishane (left) and Crockaulin to approach (9km) Gleneely. 3km beyond Gleneely, a lane to the left leads shortly (1km) to the ruined church and partly restored weather-beaten Cross of Clonca (or St. Bodan's Cross), with good ornamentation (depicting the Miracle of the loaves and fishes, Sts Paul and Anthony and geometric designs). Further on (right) is Culdaff House (1779), rebuilt since it was burnt in the early 1920s. A narrow road leads north to Glengad Head, where cliffs rise to over 150m, commanding a view of the Scottish islands of Islay and Jura, and the Kintyre peninsula. **Malin Head** (with its meteorological station) is the most northerly point in Ireland. Although only 70m high, it has a fine sea view and is within easy reach of some splendid cliff and rock scenery. To the west is **Hell's Hole**, where the tide surges through a narrow rock-cleft and the prospect southwest of the Clonmany hills opens out. The reef-girt island of Inishtrahull had a population of about 50 until 1930 and now has only a lighthouse.

Regain the R238 south of the village of Malin. An 18C mansion overlooks the sandy expanse of Trawbreagha Bay. **Cardonagh**, 7km southwest of Culdaff, is the agricultural centre (dairy farming and grain crops) of the peninsula. By the church below the village (not the modern domed hill-top church) stands an **8C cross**, with an interlaced ribbon design and two stumpy 9C guardstones, carved with naïve figures possibly representing King David and Goliath. 9km west is Ballyliffin, at the southwest end of Doagh Isle, a peninsula of dunes bound to the west by the beach at Pollan Bay. The ruined tower of Carrickabraghy Castle, an O'Doherty stronghold is at the north end.

Continue south through Clonmany, with a view of Raghtin More (505m), with its glittering mica schists (commonly found in granite), to the west, beyond which rises Dunaff Head (189m) at the east point of the entrance to Lough Swilly.

From Clonmany an alternative, less direct route to Buncrana (30km) skirts the base of Raghtin More and climbs steeply to the **Gap of Mamore** (262m; finest view in retrospect). Mamore Hill, the wild rocky peak north of the pass, is worth climbing for the view. The road descends southwest towards Dunree Head, where a fort of 1812 guards Lough Swilly. **Fort Dunree Military Museum** (10.00–18.00, Mon–Sat; 12.00–18.00 Sun; June–Sept; £) has a good collection of original artillery pieces and militaria. The **Urris Hills** (420m), immediately above Dunree Head, are continued on the other side of Lough Swilly by the Knockalla Mountain.

The main road to Buncrana from Clonmany turns south, ascending the valley past Mintiagh's Lough, a small tarn, passing near (left) Slieve Snaght (615m), the highest point on Inishowen. At Buncrana—a seaside resort for Derry—there is a veteran car collection, including a Rolls Royce Landaulette, and a textile museum at **Tullyarvan Mill** (10.00–20.00, summer; by appointment off-season (☎ 077 61130) which records three centuries of weaving in the area.

Skirting the lough-side and circling Mouldy Hill, you enter Fahan, Co. Donegal. A monastery was founded here by St. Columba, now represented only by an **8C cross-slab** of St. Mura, a 7C abbot, with interlaced ribbon carving. The cross-slab is unique, in that in addition to the figures and geometric decoration it has the only Greek inscription from the Early Christian period in Ireland. It reads 'Glory and honour to the Father, Son and Holy Spirit'. The castle (now ruined) on the south tip of the Inch peninsula, was awarded to Sir Arthur Chichester by James I (as were most of the O'Docherty lands), after the 'Flight of the Earls'.

Bearing inland, turn right along a minor road and then left to meet the N13. Opposite the junction is the interesting church of St. Aengus, a circular spired structure (1967, Liam MacCormick), inspired perhaps by the ring-fort overlooking it to the south. This is approached by crossing the main road and taking the first turning on the right, later climbing left.

The Grianán of Aileach
The principal antiquity in the neighbourhood of Derry, dating from the late Bronze-Early Iron Age, crowns a hill (244m), and commands extensive panoramic views. Although over-restored and 'tidied up' unnecessarily in 1874–78, it is nonetheless one of the most remarkable concentric forts in Ireland. It was the residence of the O'Neills, Kings of Ulster, and was despoiled by Murtogh O'Brien, King of Munster, in 1101 in revenge for the destruction of Kincora, Co. Clare, his royal fortress. Remains of three rough stone ramparts enclose the central cashel, a circular wall over 5m high and 4m thick at the base and 73m round. In the thickness of the walls are galleries; there are impressive views from the ramparts overlooking the Donegal mountains. Housed in a mid-19C church, 2km below, at the base of the hill, the **Grianán of Aileach Visitor Centre** (10.00–20.00 daily, all year, except Christmas; £), interprets the mythology, history, flora and fauna of this remarkable site.

East of Derry/Londonderry
Coleraine (*Cuil Rathain*, Fern Recess) is an irregularly built river-port at the head of the navigable reach of the Bann (Tourist Information, Railway Rd (☎ 01265-44723).

Its prosperity dates from 1613 when the land was given by James I to the City Companies of London; but it claims a history going back to the 5C. Linen factories once flourished here. Since 1968 it has been the site of the University of Ulster.

Its parish church, on an ancient foundation, was rebuilt in 1883. No trace remains of the castle and priory except the rath at Mountsandel. This stands in a wood a mile southeast of the town and is supposed to mark the site of the fort of Fintan, King of Ulster, and of the later stronghold of De Courcy, Norman baron and conqueror of Ulster. It has also yielded flint implements of c 6650 BC, the earliest record of man in Ireland.

In the town centre, a stone bridge of 1844 spans the river Bann, the 'fishy fruitful Bann' of Edmund Spenser ('Faerie Queene', 1596), on which there is a commercial salmon fishery; upstream is the semicircular Salmon Leap. Coleraine was the birthplace of the artist and book illustrator Hugh Thomson (1860–1920).

The A29 swings south around the foot of Binevenagh (385m), its wooded escarpments furrowed by waterfalls, passing (right) at Bellareena, a 19C house, parts of which date back to 1690, and Folly Tower.

Southwest of Coleraine, on the A37, you pass (right) Sconce Hill, crowned by the Cyclopean fortress of **Dún Ceithern**. These were the legendary headquarters of the Red Branch Knights (pre-Christian Celtic warriors). In 1854, a large hoard of Roman coins and silver dating from c AD 210 was discovered on the eastern side of Sconce Hill, near Ballinrees, probably the loot of Irish pirates taken on English shores (now in the British Museum).

Descending between Keady Mountain (337m; left) and Binevenagh Forest, you pass (right) the estate of Drenagh. The house (c 1837) is an early work of Sir Charles Lanyon.

Limavady (Tourist Information, Council Offices, 7 Connell St, ☎ 015047-22226) is a very ancient town taking its name, *Leim an Madra* (the dog's leap), from the site of a castle. It overhangs a deep glen two miles south, up the valley of the river Roe; the original settlement. The town was re-established in the early 17C under the name of Newtown Limavady by Sir Thomas Phillips.

The sheet-gold boat from the Broighter hoard (now in National Museum, Dublin)

The parish church in Main St dates from 1750; the six-arched bridge over the Roe was built in 1700. James Monroe, 5th President of the United States, was descended from a family who took their name from nearby Mount Roe. William Massey (1856–1925), Prime Minister of New Zealand 1912–25, was born here. Thackeray's 'Sweet Peg of Limavady' (a local woman mentioned in his *Irish Journal*, 1843) lived at an inn in Ballyclose St.

In the neighbouring demesne of Roe Valley Park is a ridge, now called The Mullagh. This is believed to represent Drumceat, the site of an ecclesiastical assembly in 574, attended by St. Columba, who sailed over from Iona for the occasion. A road leads south along the attractive valley of the Roe, offering good views ahead of the Sperrin Mountains.

At Broighter, c two miles northwest of Limavady, the Broighter Hoard, a collection of gold objects, was discovered in the 1890s (now in the National Museum, Dublin). The road to Derry—after passing (left) a fortified mansion (1619) erected by the London Fishmongers' Company, at Ballykelly—keeps fairly close to the southern shore of Lough Foyle. Walworth House (18C, with 17C flankers), stands north of Ballykelly Bridge.

The Derry suburb of Waterside is near Culmore Fort on the Foyle estuary. It was built in 1824 within an old castle belonging to the O'Docherty. Cross the Foyle by the two-decker Craigavon Bridge (1933) into central Derry. The Foyle Bridge (1985) spans the estuary to the north, providing a bypass for those driving into Donegal and the Inishowen Peninsula.

The Sperrin Mountains

The scenery improves south of Limavady towards Dungiven. The B68 climbs the Pass of Glenshane through the Sperrin Mountains between Carntogher (462m; right) and Mullaghmore (555m; to the southwest). A minor but scenically finer road (B40) may be reached by turning left not far west of the Maghera junction, which regains the main road at Killaloo, 11 miles west of Dungiven.

Descend the Roe valley to **Dungiven**, retaining the ruins of a fortified mansion of the Skinners' Company (1618), and of an abbey, approached by turning left on entering the town. The **Abbey**, founded c 1100 by the O'Cahans and restored in 1397 by the Archbishop of Armagh, contains the elaborately

14C figure of Cooey-na-nGall O'Cahan incorporated into 15C altar tomb with row of Gallowglass in arcaded front, Dungiven Priory

carved **tomb of Cooey-na-nGall** (d. 1385). In 1971, during the civil rights agitation which led to loyalist and nationalist rioting, Dungiven Castle (1839) was the scene of an attempt to set up an independent loyalist Ulster parliament.

At **Banagher**, to the southwest, there is a ruined church with some interesting features. The west door is small and square-headed outside and large and semicircular within (as at Maghera, Ch. 19), and the two south windows are loopholed. The **tomb of St. Muiredach O'Heney**, in the churchyard is a gabled house-shrine, with a figure of the founder in relief on the west gable (11C). There is another similar but later tomb at **Bovevagh church**, two miles north of Dungiven.

The A6 continues west, with views south towards the Sperrin Mountains, after nine miles passing (left) Claudy. Beyond Claudy descend the charming wooded valley of the Faughan, which leads towards the banks of the Foyle, and Derry. It was near the bridge of **Burntollet**, about seven miles from Derry, that a Civil Rights march was ambushed by Unionists in January 1969; an action with far-reaching repercussions.

Maghera, Cookstown, Dungannon, Clogher

The A29 leads south from Coleraine to Garvagh, situated on a hill. Garvagh House (early 17C; twice enlarged since) was the seat of the Canning family and the birthplace of George Canning (d. 1771), father of the more famous statesman (see p352). Foothills of the Sperrin range rise to the west, among them Carntogher (462m) and further southwest, Mallaghmore (555m).

Maghera (10 miles southwest) has an 11C ruined church with a square-headed doorway, its sloping sides enclosed by a square band of carving and surmounted by an elaborate Crucifixion panel. Upperlands, three miles northeast, was the birthplace of Charles Thomson (1729–1824), secretary of the first United States Congress, known as the Continental Congress from its inception in 1774 until 1789. He designed the Great Seal of the United States in 1782 and was the final writer of the Declaration of Independence (which he read to the Congress in 1776). To the south of Marghera cross the A6 from Belfast to Derry, and shortly enter Tobermore, with an old church rebuilt in 1816, and Presbyterian meeting-house of 1728.

A wild mountain road (B47) leads southwest from here via **Draperstown**, founded by the Drapers' Company of London. Beyond, it bears west over a southern spur of the Sperrin Mountains, which is crossed between Oughtmore (right) and Carnanelly. The road then descends the Glenelly valley below Sawell, (678m; right), the highest peak of the range. At Cranagh the **Sperrin Heritage Centre** (11.00–18.00, Mon–Fri; 14.00–19.00, Sun; Mar–Oct; £) recounts the history and folklore of the Sperrins.

The main road (A29) passes the village of Desertmartin, to the southwest of which is Slieve Gallion (527m), where a track climbs to Windy Gap and the Ballybriest horned cairn, a megalithic burial site. **Springhill** (NT) (14.00–18.00, Sat, Sun & BH; Apr, May & Sept; 14.00–18.00 daily, except Thurs, June–Aug), just to the southeast of Moneymore (B18), is a good example of a fortified Planter manor house. It contains collections of 18C and 19C costumes and furniture.

Walking in the Sperrins
Information, maps and booklets on walks are available from NITB offices. The Ulster Way runs southwest through the Sperrins from Dungiven to Gortin Glen Forest Park.

The A29 bears southwest. At Lissan, (to the right) the Rev. George Walker was rector in 1669–74 (see Derry, above). The rectory was later redesigned by Nash. Nearby Lissan House is by Davis Ducart.

Cookstown (Tourist Information, Council Offices, 12 Burn Rd, ☎ 06487-62205), the dairying centre of the district, has a wide main street almost 1.5 miles long, and is named after its founder Allan Cook, who designed the layout in 1609. The Catholic church was erected by J.J. McCarthy (1860).

Southeast of the town is **Killymoon Castle** (1803), a huge castellated edifice designed by Nash for Col. William Stewart, MP. (now a golf club). The Ballinderry river, a good trout stream, flows through its grounds and later enters Lough Neagh just south of the remains of Salters Castle (the Salters' Company planned to build a town here).

Follow the A505 2.5 miles due west to Drum Manor, with the remains of a small Scots-Baronial mansion surrounded by its Forest Park, in which a Lepidoptera Reserve (mainly butterflies and moths) has been established. A short distance beyond, to the right, is the 18C **Wellbrook Beetling Mill** (NT) (09.30–18.30 daily, Apr, June & Sept; 14.00–18.00 Sat, Sun & BH; 14.00–18.00 daily, except Tues; Mar–Apr), water-powered, restored, and in working order.

After another 1.5 miles along the A505 a lane (right) leads to the hamlet of **Dunnamore**. Just beyond there is an extensive complex of **seven stone circles** (including three 'pairs'), nine alignments, and twelve **cairns**, at **Beaghmore**, uncovered since 1945 by the removal of peat. The main road continues west across country towards Mullaghcarn (542m).

Off the A29 (left), the B520 leads to **Coalisland**, at the centre of the Tyrone coalfield, which has never been profitably worked; some buildings of industrial archaeological interest may be seen in the neighbourhood. To the left of the A29 you pass the demesne of Loughry (now an agricultural college), the home of the Lindesays, where Swift was an occasional visitor. Thomas Lindesay (1656–1724) archbishop of Armagh in 1714, had briefly been dean of St. Patrick's, Dublin, in 1693. (Swift became dean in 1713).

Dungannon (Tourist Information, Council Offices, Circular Rd, ☎ 08687-25311), a textile-manufacturing town, was once the headquarters of the O'Neills, earls of Tyrone, but all trace of their castle has vanished; the Towers on Castle Hill were built in 1790. The Royal School (1628), founded by James I, occupies a building erected by the energetic Archbishop Robinson of Armagh in 1786–9. Among its pupils was General John Nicholson (1821–57), the hero of the siege of Delhi (where he was killed). His bronze statue (by Brock) once stood by the Kashmir Gate in Delhi, but was retrieved and erected at the school in 1960.

Donaghmore, two miles northwest, once the site of an abbey, preserves an imperfect sculptured High Cross—perhaps a combination of two—set up here in 1776, having been thrown down during the 17C troubles. Six miles further north, near **Lough Bracken**, are the seven **stone circles of Moymore**, among other archaeological sites in the area.

West of Dungannon

Travelling west from Dungannon on the A4, you shortly pass a right-hand turning to adjacent **Castlecaulfield**, with the picturesque ruins of a Jacobean mansion (1612). Sir Toby Caulfield (1565–1627) was an ancestor of the earls of Charlemont. Wesley preached by its gate in 1767. The church (of the parish of Donaghmore) has a gabled porch of 1685; the south nave window and some figures on the north side of the tower were brought from the vanished church at Donaghmore. The Rev. George Walker (1616–90) was rector here from 1674 before going to the defence of Derry (see above) and was buried here after his death at the Boyne. Charles Wolfe, the poet, served here as curate in 1818–21. His famous lines on the burial of Sir John Moore were first published in the *Newry Telegraph* in 1817:

> Not a drum was heard, not a funeral note,
> As his corse to the rampart we hurried;
> Not a soldier discharge his farewell shot
> O're the grave where our hero we buried.
>
> 'The Burial of Sir John Moore after Corunna' 1817.

Thirteen miles west of Dungannon you cross the A5 just beyond Ballygawley. The mother of Ulysses S. Grant, President of the USA in 1869–77 lived nearby at Dergenagh. Cross the Blackwater at Augher, with the Plantation castle of **Spur Royal** (c 1615, on the site of an earlier fortress), restored and enlarged in 1832 by William Warren, the Sligo architect. Some three miles north is the imperfect **passage-grave of Knockmany**, with remarkable inscribed designs of the Early Bronze Age (key at Clogher police-station).

Clogher, now a mere village, claims to be the seat of the most ancient bishopric in Ireland (5C). The little cathedral on the hill-top, rebuilt in the 18C, altered in 1818, and restored in 1956, is dedicated to St. Macartin (d. 506), a disciple of St. Patrick. After a period of amalgamation with Armagh (1850–86), the see was again made independent. The *Clogh-oir* ('Golden Stone') in the porch is most likely part of the 9C church; in the churchyard are two re-erected High Crosses (9C–10C). The first Protestant bishop was Myler Magrath, the pluralist, who became Archbishop of Cashel. In the same year (1570) John Stearne (1660–1745), the scholar was bishop here from 1717, while Thomas Parnell (1679–1718), the poet and scholar, and friend of Swift and Pope, was archdeacon from 1706–16. William Carleton (1794–1869), folklorist and author of *Traits and Stories of the Irish Peasantry*, was born in the neighbouring hamlet of Prolusk, where the **Carleton Ancestral Home** (12.00–17.00 daily; June–Sept) is preserved, a tiny and charming thatched cottage in the midst of rolling hills. The A4 continues southwest to Enniskillen.

South of Dungannon

Beyond Dungannon bear southeast to **Moy**, on the river Blackwater, with its tree-planted square. It owes its exotic air to its founder, James Caulfield, Earl of Charlemont (1728–99), who built it on the plan of the Lombard town of Marengo. 18C Roxborough Castle nearby, remodelled from 1842, was burned in 1922. On the opposite bank of the river is Charlemont, where Mountjoy erected a fort in 1602 as a counter to the activities of Hugh O'Neill (largely burnt down in 1922). It was held from 1642–50 by Phelim O'Neill, who killed the governor, Lord Charlemont, but was eventually driven out by Sir Charles Coote.

Some three miles northeast of Charlemont is **The Argory** (NT) (14.00–18.00, Sat, Sun & BH, Apr, May & Sept; 14.00–18.00 daily (except Tue), June–Aug; £), a Classical mansion of 1820. It contains an unusual cabinet barrel-organ. The house is still lit by acetylene gas, installed in 1906 by the Sunbeam Acetylene Gas Company of Belfast and said to be the only such surviving in the British Isles. **Ardress House**, (NT) (14.00–18.00 Sat, Sun & BH, Apr, May & Sept; 14.00–18.00 daily (except Tue) June–Aug; £) four miles southeast on the B28, is a mansion of c 1664, enlarged by the architect George Ensor (brother of the better-known John Ensor) for his own use in c 1770. It contains some very good plasterwork by Michael Stapleton and a working 18C farmyard.

It was after a sectarian skirmish between a party of Catholic 'Defenders' and Protestant 'Peep O'Day Boys' (ie. 'alert'; an 18C English expression, meaning early morning) at the hamlet called **The Diamond** (two miles south east), that the Orange Order was established, in September 1795. Two miles south at **Loughgall**, surrounded by orchards, are two Planters' bawns. The poet W.R. Rodgers was Presbyterian minister here, 1934–1946.

The Battles of Benburb and Yellowford

Benburb is four miles southwest of Moy (B106). A ruined castle, finely situated above the Blackwater, was erected in 1615 by Sir Richard Wingfield, who also built the parish church. When Owen Roe O'Neill inflicted a crushing defeat here on General Monro and the Parliamentary army in June 1646, the beaten troops are said to have fled dryshod across the river on the bodies of the slain. The estate contains a mansion of 1887, a Servite Priory since 1949. **Benburb Valley Heritage Centre** (10.00–17.00, Tue–Sat, 14.00–19.00, Sun, closed Mon; Easter–Sept; £) at Milltown, is in a former linen mill with weaving equipment; it has a section on the Battle of Benburb, with scale model of the action.

At **Blackwatertown**, 1.5 miles east, stood the Earl of Sussex's **Portmore Fort** (1575). It was razed by O'Neill in 1595, and rebuilt in 1598. At the Battle of the Yellow Ford on 14 August that year Sir Henry Bagenal's army, marching north to relieve the fort, were forced into a bog by O'Neill and slaughtered.

Aughnacloy, Omagh, Strabane

The wide main street of **Aughnacloy** straddles a ridge, with views to the west towards Slieve Beagh (371m). The shell of **Garvey House** (1815, by Francis Johnston) is 2km west of Aughnacloy. Two miles beyond, you enter **Sess Kilgreen**, where there is a standing-stone inscribed with a rude cross, and remains of various cairns and passage-graves in the vicinity.

Omagh (13 miles) is the county town of Tyrone (Tourist Information, 1 Market St, ☎ 01662-247831/2). It is a market-town, attractively situated at the confluence of the Drumagh and the Camowen rivers, which unite to form the Strule. The castle played too important a part in the wars of the 16C–17C to have survived and was finally demolished by Sir Phelim O'Neill in 1641, while almost exactly a century later the whole town was virtually destroyed by a ravaging accidental fire. Apart from its **Classical Court House** (1820; by John Hargrave), the chief attraction of Omagh is its hillside setting; the Catholic church (1899), with two unequal steeples, dominates the town. **Jimmy Kennedy** (1902-84), the songwriter, was born in Omagh; among his most popular songs are *The Teddy Bears' Picnic* (1932), *The Siegfried Line, The Hokey Cokey, South of the Border* and *Red Sails in the Sunset.* Brian Friel (1929) playwright and author of *Philadelphia, Here I Come!* (1964) and *Dancing at Lughnasa* (1990) was also born in Omagh.

Dromore (southwest on the A32) is a village where St. Patrick is said to have founded an abbey for the first woman who took the veil from his hands. A Cistercian abbey grew up on the site and burnt down in 1690; there are ruins of a 17C church (1694) nearby.

From Omagh, the B48 is an attractive alternative to the more direct A5 road to Derry, which climbs due north through the Gortin Glen Forest Park. This incorporates the **Ulster History Park** (10.30–18.30, Mon–Sat, 11.00–19.00, Sun, Apr–Sept; 10.30–17.00, Mon–Fri, Oct–March; £) containing replicas of buildings from the Neolithic period to the 17C in an appropriate landscape setting. The road then passes (right) Slieveard (422m) and Mullaghcarn (542m) to (10 miles) **Gortin**, a one-street village adjoining the demesne of Beltrim Castle. Beyond this the road continues via Plumbridge, crossing the western spurs of the Sperrin Mountains through the Butterlope Pass to Dunnamanagh to rejoin the A5 three miles from Derry.

The 'Ulster-American' Folk Park

The A5 continues northwest, after three miles passing (left), the **'Ulster-American' Folk Park** (11.00–18.30, Mon–Sat, Easter–Sept; 11.30–19.00, Sun & BH; 10.30–17.00, Mon–Fri, Oct–Easter) established in 1976 at Camphill to demonstrate points of contact between the Old World and the New. At the core of the Park is the farmhouse where Thomas Mellon (1813–1908), founder of the American banking empire, was born. His family emigrated in 1818. Buildings include a forge and weaver's cottage (replicas); a schoolhouse (re-erected); the cottage of John Joseph Hughes, first RC Archbishop of New York. He emigrated from Augher in 1817, and initiated the building of St. Patrick's Cathedral, New York, in 1858. In another section in the park a Pennsylvania farmstead, largely constructed of logs, has been erected. Amongst other projects is a computer-bank for genealogical information.

To the north of the park the Strule valley runs between two hills named Bessy Bell (left) and Mary Gray after the heroines of an 18C Scots ballad:

Oh Bessy Bell and Mary Grey,
   They are twa Bonny lasses;
They bigged a bower on yon Burn-brae,
And theeked it ore wi rashes.

Allan Ramsay, *Poems* (1721)

Delightfully situated on the Mourne, a stream formed by the merging of the Strule with the Glenelly, **Newtownstewart** is named after William Stewart, ancestor of the Lords Mountjoy, to whom the barony was granted by Charles I. James II spent a night here after the siege of Derry, ordering the castle of c 1618 to be dismantled and the bridge destroyed after his retreat. The present six-arched bridge was built in 1727.

Only the twin hill-top towers of Harry Avery's Castle survive (to the south-west). It is ascribed to Aimhreidh O'Neill (d. 1392), but is probably of later date, and was destroyed in 1609. It is said that this O'Neill had a sister with a pig's head. He offered a handsome dowry in compensation in order to marry her off, but any suitor who declined to carry out the bargain after seeing her would be hanged; 19 considered this the lesser evil.

Barons Court, three miles southwest, is the seat of the Dukes of Abercorn (not open to the public). An early 18C house altered in 1791–92 by Sir John Soane, it burnt out in 1796, and was later transformed by William Vitruvius Morrison. The Palladian Agent's House (1741) is also of interest.

From Newtownstewart follow the road skirting the west bank of the Mourne via Sion Mills, with linen works, to Strabane.

Strabane

Strabane (Tourist Information, Abercorn Square, ☎ 01504-883735, May–Oct) is an important agricultural centre. The town lies just above the junction of the rivers Mourne and Finn, their united course being known as the Foyle; all three are noted salmon streams. The town was never of great architectural interest, and it has suffered in the recent 'troubles'.

The main building of interest—now that the courthouse has been demolished—is **Gray's Printing Shop** (NT) (14.00–17.30 daily, except Thurs, Sun & BH; £) at 49 Main St, with several 19C presses in operation and an excellent Audio-Visual program. It is probable that John Dunlap (1746/7–1812), a native of Strabane, was an apprentice here before emigrating to America, where he issued the *Pennsylvania Packet* in 1771. From 1784 this became the first American daily paper. Dunlap was also the first to print the Declaration of Independence (1776). Another apprentice was James Wilson, employed here until 1807, when he also emigrated; he was the grandfather of President Woodrow Wilson, and was born at **Dergalt**, 3km to the east, where his farmhouse home is preserved (NT).

Another native of Strabane was Guy Carleton, Lord Dorchester (1724–1808), governor of Quebec for most of the period 1766–96. He defended Quebec and defeated the Americans on Lake Champlain in 1775–76, and was commander-in-chief in America in 1782–83. George Sigerson (1838–1925), Fenian, poet, and physician; and Brian O'Nolan (1911–66; better known as 'Flann O'Brien'), the author, were also born in Strabane.

Lifford (northeast, across the border) was the scene of a battle in 1600 between Hugh Roe O'Donnell and his cousin Niall Garbh O'Donnell who led the English garrison of Derry. Niall had deserted to the English side in resentment at Hugh's appointment as Earl of Tyrconnel.

Port Hall (1746) and the courthouse, were designed by Michael Priestley. At the **Old Courthouse** (1746) the Visitor Centre (14.00–18.00, Sat, Sun & BH,

Mar–Easter; 10.00–18.00, Mon–Sat; 14.00–18.00 Sun; Easter–Sept; £) has an audio-visual presentation dealing with the O'Donnell Princes in the 16C, and 18C prison conditions. The Clouleigh Parish church (1622, and late 18C) contains part of a monument to Sir Richard Hansard and his wife, kneeling figures in Jacobean costume.

At Ballindrait, northwest of Lifford, off the N1 is **Cavancor Historic House** (12.00–18.00, Tue–Sat; 14.00–18.00 Sun, Easter & summer season; closed Mon except BH Mondays; £), the ancestral home of James Knox Polk (1795–1849), elected 11th President of the United States in 1844. There is a small museum with information on his life. James II dined in the house in 1689.

The A5 continues north of Lifford, following the course of the Foyle, to Derry.

17 · The Causeway Coast

The beautiful north Antrim coast is the location of the Giant's Causeway, one of the wonders of the natural world. No photograph can do justice to the perfection and mystery of its actual forms. Off the coast is **Rathlin Island**, associated in legend with Robert the Bruce, and on the Ballycastle coast, the **Carrick-a-rede Rope Bridge**. Further west are **Dunluce Castle**, the most preposterously sited fortification in Ireland, and **Downhill**, the ruined palace of the eccentric Earl-Bishop of Derry, after which a visit to the whiskey distillery at **Bushmills** is recommended.

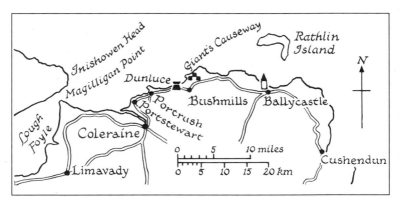

Getting to the area
■ **Train**. Coleraine on the Belfast-Derry line.
■ **Air**. Belfast International Airport.
■ **Sea**. To Rathlin Island from Ballycastle.

Listings
Ballycastle. Castle Hostel, 62 Quay Road (☎ 01265-762337); **Marine Hotel**, modern waterfront hotel (☎ 01265-762222).
Bushmills. Old Bushmills Inn, 25 Main St, atmospheric, popular hotel-restaurant (☎ 01265-731521).

Cushendun. The Cushendun, 10 Strandview Park, B&B (0126-674266); **Mary McBrides**, tiny National Trust pub, (and tearoom) (☎ 0126-506).
Giant's Causeway. Causeway Centre, National Trust Tearooms (☎ 01265-731582).
Portrush. Causeway Coast Hotel, 36 Ballyreagh Rd, modern, good facilities (☎ 01265-822435); **The Harbour Bar**, early 19C pub (☎ 01265-822430).
Portstewart. Causeway Coast Hostel, 4 Victoria Terrace, Atlantic Circle (☎ 01265-833789); **O'Malley's**, the bar of the Edgewater Hotel, 88 Strand Road, (☎ 01265-833314).
Rathlin Island. Rathlin Guest House, The Quay, B&B (☎ 012657-63917); Rathlin Restaurant, The Harbour (☎ 012657-63939).

Cushendun, Ballycastle, Rathlin Island

From Cushendall the A2 leaves the Antrim coast, circles inland and soon bears uphill to the left, and crosses the Glendun viaduct, zigzags up through woods. Bear right for the coast and **Cushendun**, a well-sited little village on the outflow of the Glendun (*Cois abhann Duine*, the mouth of the brown river). The village was largely rebuilt in an Arts and Crafts style (1912) by Clough Williams-Ellis (who also designed Port Merrion in Wales), for Lord Cushendun. Nearby are the scanty ruins of a castle (north) and some caves in the sandstone (south). Shane O'Neill (1530–1569), chieftain of the O'Neills, attacked the MacDonnell's (Scots-Irish) settlements in Co. Antrim, and was then defeated by them at Ballycastle. Later, he was defeated by the O'Donnells (Gaelic-Irish) at **Lough Swilly** and sought refuge with the MacDonnells who (not surprisingly) murdered him at Cushendun in 1567. His grave is marked by a cairn on the shore of the lough.

A narrow and winding minor road hugs the coast, here only 13 miles from the Mull of Kintyre. At Ballyvoy, the main road crosses a wide expanse of moorland, with Ballypatrick Forest to the left, and leads along a causeway through the tarn of Loughareema, descending towards Ballycastle.

Ballycastle (Tourist Information, 7 Mary St, ☎ 02657-62024), a well-situated resort at the junction of two valleys, with a view of Rathlin Island, has a church of 1756, and a few early 19C houses, but its old stone harbour is now silted up. In August, the **Ould Lammas Fair** (Candle Mass), for sheep, cattle and general goods is held here, attracting enormous crowds, both from the locality and from Scotland.

> 'At the Ould Lammas Fair
> Now were you ever there?
> Were you ever at the fair in Ballycastle-O ?
> Did you treat your Mary-Ann
> To Dulse and Yella Man
> At the Ould Lammas Fair in Ballycastle-O ?'

Dulse, an edible seaweed and Yellow Man, a sweetmeat, are still sold at the fair.

On the seafront at Ballycastle (left) are the ruins of Bonamargy friary, founded in 1500 by Rory MacQuillan, and burned in 1584 by the MacDonnells and the Scots. It was probably repaired and in use until 1642. Beside the church, refectory, and another stone-roofed room, the main interest is the **MacDonnell**

vault, the burial-place of the earls of Antrim (c 1666). Here lie Sorley Boy MacDonnell (1505–1590) and his son, the 1st earl (d. 1636), and Randall, the 2nd earl (d. 1682), on whose tomb is an inscription in English, Latin and Irish (the use of three languages is highly unusual):

> Every seventh year a calamity befalls the Irish.
> Now that the Marquis has departed, it will
> occur every year.

On the left rises conical Knocklayd (514m), crowned by a large cairn.

The cliffs to the east and west show the beginning of the dykes or intrusive masses of basalt which culminate in the Giant's Causeway further west. To the west is the small ruin of Dunaneanie Castle, the probable birthplace of Sorley Boy MacDonnell, and the scene of his death. In 1898 Guglielmo Marconi's first wireless installations for communication between a lighthouse and the mainland were set up at Rathlin and Ballycastle, assisted by George Kemp.

Fair Head and the cliffs of Murlough Bay

Fair Head, or Benmore, (five miles to the east) is approached by a lane which leads to the hamlet of Cross, a scarped headland rising to 194m above the sea. Half this height consists of a sheer cliff of basalt split into enormous columns from the base of which a mass of debris slopes down to the water. A fine close view is obtained from the rough and somewhat dangerous Grey Man's Path, descending to the foot of the cliff. Its summit commands an extensive view towards Rathlin and, off the Scottish coast, Islay, with the Paps of Jura behind it, and the Mull of Kintyre, 13 miles northeast. Just behind the summit are three small loughs, one with a well-preserved crannóg. The cliffs of **Murlough Bay**, to the east, contain a coal seam worked from a remote period, the beach of which is now approached by a road.

Beneath the headland are rocks known as 'Carrig Uisneach', the legendary landing-place of Deirdre and the sons of Uisneach. A story of Celtic mythology from the Ulster Cycle of tales tells how Deirdre (under a curse since birth) flees to Scotland with Noisi, her lover. The sons of Uisneach come to escort her to Navan Fort (Eamain Mach, Armagh, Ch.19) where they are treacherously slaughtered. Deirdre smashes her head on a rock when she is sent by the king as a wife to one of the murderers. Off the coast are the turbulent Waters of Moyle where, legend has it, the Children of Lir, were turned into swans by the jealous Boife and forced to remain for 300 years.

Rathlin Island

Five miles north of Ballycastle lies **Rathlin Island**, reached daily from Ballycastle, weather permitting, by mailboat and tourist boats, in summer. At other times the intervening race of Sloch-na-Marra (Valley of the Sea) can be unpleasant if not dangerous. Brecain, son of Niall of the Nine Hostages, was lost here with a fleet of 50 corraghs. Rathlin is c six miles long and its shape has been compared to 'an Irish stocking, the toe of which pointeth to the main lande'. It is associated with St. Columba and St. Comhgall, and because of its exposed position, was among the first places in Ireland to suffer from Viking raids. Its main historical interest is that it contains **Bruce's Cave**, a cavern in the basalt near the north-east corner of the island, which is said to have harboured Robert Bruce who fled Scotland in 1306, following Edward I's invasion, and his spider companion, whose perseverance inspired him. It is difficult to approach except in calm weather. Near the landing-place in Church Bay is the Manor House, where the viscounts Gage formerly held patriarchal sway. To the east, Bruce's Castle stands on an isolated crag. Almost all the coast is cliff-bound, the highest, on the northwest side, rising to over 120m, the haunt of innumerable seabirds, particularly guillemots.

Southeast of Ballycastle is the valley of **Glenshesk**. Above the road on the west side are the ruins of Gobhan Saor's castle, in fact the remains of an old chapel said to have been founded by St. Patrick.

Carrick-a-rede Rope Bridge and the Giant's Causeway

To reach the bridge follow the B15 along the coast. The road passes near a narrow headland on which are perched the ruins of **Kilbane Castle**, beyond which the cliffs become higher. On the right a path descends to the **Carrick-a-rede Rope Bridge** (NT; in position from mid-May to mid-September) connecting a basalt stack with salmon-fishery to the mainland. The swinging bridge with its board floor looks more perilous than it is.

At **White Park Bay**, a turning (right) leads to Dunseverick Castle. From this point a cliff path 4.5 miles long has been constructed by the NT, bearing around Benbane Head to the Giant's Causeway (also reached by road two miles west).

The Giant's Causeway

The remarkable basaltic formation known as the Giant's Causeway was brought to a wider public notice by Dr William Hamilton (1755–97) in his *Letters Concerning the Northern Coast of Antrim* (1786). Since then it has ranked among the natural wonders of the world. It had of course been visited previously by—among other commentators—Mrs Delany in 1758 and the Earl-Bishop of Derry, who built a footpath there for travellers interested in natural curiosities (two early paintings of it by Susanna Drury (1739) are in the Ulster Museum.

The **Causeway Visitor Centre** (NT) (11.00–17.00, Mar–May; 11.00 17.30, June; 10.00–19.00, July–Aug; 11.00–17.00 Sept–Oct; £; ☎ 0265-731855), is devoted to the geology, flora and fauna of the area, with audio-visual displays and restaurant. A bus shuttle-service is available to the base of the causeway but it is much more interesting to walk. Boats may be hired to visit those caves not accessible at low tide. Visitors are warned that the surface of the basalt is often very slippery. A road descends past the first headland, beyond which in the cliff to the right are seen some columns twisted into a horizontal position.

The cliff walk is first described, from east to west.

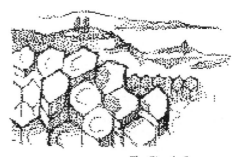

The Giant's Causeway

You first pass Bengore Head and then Benbane Head (112m), to the west of which is Hamilton's Seat, a favourite spot of William Hamilton, 'discoverer' of the Causeway and Pleaskin Head (122m). Between this point and Chimney Point (whose castellated appearance led vessels of the Spanish Armada to fire on it under the impression that they were attacking Dunluce Castle, further west) is Port-na-Spania, where the *Girona*, a vessel of the same Armada, ran ashore with the loss of 260 lives including Don Alfonso de Leyva, a Spanish nobleman and one of the leaders of the invasion force. The ship also happened to be carrying a large amount of treasure, much of it recovered in 1967–68 by a team of Belgian divers, and several of the more valuable items have since been displayed at the Ulster Museum, Belfast. The path next passes the Amphitheatre, with columns broken up into terraces, before reaching the Causeway proper.

It has been estimated that there are c 37,000 basalt columns altogether, caused by a series of violent, volcanic underground explosions some 60,000,000 years ago. These explosions found a vent along a fault line from the Antrim coast to Skye, the effects of which may be traced through Rathlin, Islay, Staffa (Fingal's Cave) and Mull. A great quantity of molten basalt was ejected to the surface, which, when cooling, formed numerous nuclei equidistant from each other. These gradually absorbed the intervening mass, and, eventually intercolumnar pressure caused the nuclei to assume a prismatic shape, hexagonal where the pressure has been regular, less often pentagonal, and on rare occasions with irregular numbers of sides, some even ten-sided. The cliffs of the causeway consists of two beds of columnar basalt separated by an 'ochre bed' between 9m and 12m thick, formed by the weathering of the lava flow during a period of quiescence. A panoramic view may be obtained from Aird Snout, a promontory east of the Visitor Centre.

On the next promontory are the Little and Middle Causeway, beyond which is the Grand Causeway, with several impressively regular formations. On the far side of the next bay is the so-called **Giant's Organ**, a perfect example of the columnar structure. The nearby Shepherd's Path ascends to the cliff top, from which the car park can be reached. The principal caves are mostly to the west of the Causeway proper. Among them are Portcoon (with a landward entrance northwest of the hotel) and **Runkerry Cave** (over 200m long).

The **Causeway School Museum** (11.00–17.00 daily; July–Aug) at 60 Causeway Rd, adjacent to the car park, is in an Arts and Crafts style National School. It was designed by Clough Williams-Ellis (c 1920) and is furnished in the manner of a school of the 1920s.

There are plans to restore part of the hydro-electric tramway which once ran from here to Portrush. It was the first to be constructed on this principle (1883), and was closed in 1949.

Bushmills Distillery and Dunluce Castle

Leaving the Causeway, turn inland to **Bushmills**, noted for the 'Old Bushmills' Whiskey Distillery (Tours: Mon–Thurs AM & PM; Fri AM only; £; for details ☎ 02657-31521). This had a licence to distil whiskey dated 1608, although it was distilled for some centuries earlier. The town also has a salmon research station. From here the B17 leads directly southwest to Coleraine.

The A2 shortly regains the coast before passing **Dunluce Castle** (10.00–19.00, Mon–Sat; 14.00–19.00, Sun; 10.00–19.00, Mon–Sat; 11.00–19.00, Sun; July–Sept; 10.00–16.00, Mon–Sat; 14.00–16.00, Sun; Oct–Mar; £). With its picturesque towers and gables it stands spectacularly on a projecting rock, separated from the mainland by a deep chasm, spanned by a bridge which replaces a drawbridge. Probably begun c 1300 by Richard de Burgh, Earl of Ulster, it was reconstructed c 1590 by James MacDonnell. It consists of a barbican, two main towers, and the remains of the great hall. The buildings on the mainland were erected after 1639, when part of the kitchen and eight servants subsided into a cave below during a storm.

Dunluce was taken by the MacDonnells (a sept of the McDonalds of the Isles) in the 16C, and Sorely Boy (*Somhairle Buidhe*, Yellow Charles) MacDonnell was a prominent figure in the struggle against Shane O'Neill and the English. Sir John Perrot entered the place after a nine-month siege in 1584, but Sorely Boy recaptured it and made peace with the English, although his son James assisted Cuellar and other Spaniards to escape to Scotland in 1588, avoiding death at the hands of the English and their allies. Randal, James's brother, was made Viscount Dunluce and Earl of Antrim by James I. The castle fell into decay during the 17C wars. There is a shop and video-show on the history and geology of the Causeway coast.

To the west are the curious limestone formations known as the White Rocks (with numerous caves accessible by boat in calm weather), and offshore lie a line of reefs known as The Skerries. Beyond is the promontory of Ramore Head, on which stands the resort of **Portrush**. Coleraine lies 4.5 miles southwest, but the main road continues to the adjacent resort of **Portstewart**, extending from the harbour on the east to Back Castle, beyond which the cliffs die away into a sandy beach. Charles Lever (1806–1872), who wrote the novels of comic military adventures, *Harry Lorrequer* (1839) and *Charles O'Malley* (1841), worked as a dispensary doctor here in 1832–7.

Portstewart

The A2 drives northeast, passing **Hezlett House**, 103 Sea Road, Castlerock (1691) (12.00–17.00 daily, Mar–Apr; 12.00–17.00, Sat, Sun & BH, Apr, May & Sept; 12.00–17.00 daily, Jun–Aug; closed Oct–Mar; £). It is a thatched 17C single-storey cottage with interesting cruck-truss roof construction. The furnishings are late 19C and there is also a display of period farm implements

Downhill, Mussenden Temple, Magilligan Peninsula

Beyond Portstewart are the sad remains of **Downhill Castle** (1780–87); twice damaged by fire in the 19C but unroofed only in 1950. It was begun by Frederick Hervey, the urbane and eccentric Bishop of Derry (1730–1803), later 4th Earl of Bristol (known as the Earl-Bishop) an inveterate 'Grand Tourist', after whom innumerable 'Bristol' hotels in Europe are named. A statue of his brother, the 3rd Earl (by Van Nost), was blown down by a gale in 1839 from the summit of his mausoleum (by Michael Shanahan, modelled on the Roman mausoleum at

St. Rémy-de-Provence) and now stands headless by the Bishop's Gate. A path leads past the castle to the **Mussenden Temple** (1783–85), an elegant Classical rotunda on the cliff edge, erected by the earl as a compliment and memorial to his cousin Mrs Mussenden, who died aged 22 (NT); the view is impressive. Less prejudiced than many of his contemporaries, the Anglican bishop allowed a Catholic priest to celebrate mass here once a week, as there was no local Catholic parish church; and both the priest and his horse were provided for in his will.

Beyond Downhill, the road descends to the coast before veering southwest across the flat expanse of the **Magilligan Peninsula**, with a six-mile-long beach. A Martello tower stands on the promontory at the narrow entrance of Lough Foyle, opposite Greencastle, backed by the hills of the Inishowen Peninsula (Co. Donegal).

18 · Belfast and the Glens of Antrim

Belfast, at the head of Belfast Lough, lies at the centre of a region which contains landscapes and seacoast of remarkable variety. To the north is the windswept Antrim coast from which deep green valleys, known as the celebrated **Nine Glens of Antrim**, extend inland. Directly west of the city is the inland sea of **Lough Neagh** (400 sq km/153 sq miles), an important wildlife and angling reserve, and the largest stretch of open water in Ireland or Britain. To the southeast is the Ards Peninsula, enclosing **Strangford Lough**, which opens to the Irish Sea at a narrow channel between **Strangford** and **Portaferry**, a marine reserve and popular sailing resort. The region covers most of Co. Antrim and north Co. Down.

Since the 19C shipbuilding has been a major industry in Belfast and the vast cranes of the shipyard are a permanent reminder of the area's industrial history; Belfast is also the cultural and political centre of Northern Ireland.

The **Ulster Museum** has major holdings of antiquities from the Mesolithic to the Industrial Revolution, as well as significant collections of fine art, ethnographic and folklore material, while the **Belfast Festival** (November) is the largest arts festival in Ireland.

On Cave Hill, north of the city, is **Belfast Zoo**, and to the east at Cultra, the **Ulster Folk and Transport Museum**, one of the finest collections of vernacular architecture and historic transport in the world; the **Battle of the Somme Heritage Centre** is at Newtownards.

Getting to the area
■ **Train**. Main line from Dublin and Derry to Belfast.
■ **Air**. Belfast International Airport; Belfast City Airport.
■ **Sea**. Belfast from Stranraer in Scotland, Douglas in the Isle of Man, and Liverpool. To Larne from Stranraer and Cairnryan. Cruises on Belfast Lough; Lough Neagh from Antrim town.

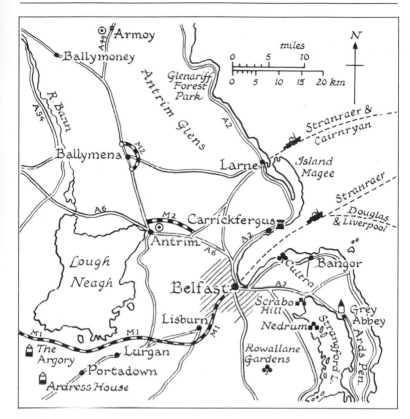

Listings

Antrim. The Dunadry, 2 Islandreagh Drive, Dunadry, 4-star, great character and comfort (☎ 01849-432474).

Ballymena. Adair Arms Hotel, Ballymoney Rd, mid-19C old-world hospitality (☎ 01266-653674); Country House Hotel, 20 Doagh Road, attractive, modern, good restaurant (☎ 01266-891663).

Ballymoney. Drumaheglis Marina Caravan Park, Glenstall Rd (☎ 012656-65150); Moore Lodge, 18C country-house, fishing (☎ 012665-41043).

Bangor. Tedworth Hotel, Princetown Road, well-sited waterfront hotel (☎ 01247-463289).

Carrigfergus. Langsgarden, 70 Scotch Quarter, B&B (☎ 019603-66369).

Hillsborough. Sylvan Hill House, 79 Kilntown Rd, Dromore, 18C, charming B&B (☎ 01846-692321).

Larne. Maghermore House Hotel, 59 Shore Rd, Victorian house and grounds (☎ 01574-279444).

Lurgan. Ashburn Hotel, 81 William St (☎ 01762-325711).

Portaferry. The Narrows, attractive guesthouse/restaurant on the waterfront, friendly and comfortable, fascinating programme of workshops; arts, crafts and stonemasonry (☎ 012477-28148).

Belfast Listings
Accommodation
Arnie's Backpackers, 63 Fitzwilliam St, hostel (☎ 01232-242867); **Europa Hotel**, Great Victoria St, 5-star, international high-rise (☎ 01232-327000); **Malone Guest House**, 79 Malone Rd, B&B (01232-669565); **Stranmillis Lodge**, 14 Chlorine Gardens, B&B (☎ 01232-682009).

Food and Drink
Bookfinders, bookshop-café, 47 University Road, combines hearty meals, at the rear of the premises, with its advertised trade (☎ 01232-328269); **Crown Liquor Saloon (NT)** 56 Great Victoria St, extravagant 19C gin palace (☎ 01232-249476); **Morning Star**, 17 Pottinger's Entry, traditional Belfast drinker's pub (☎ 01232-323976); **Roscoff**, 7 Lesley House, Shaftesbury Sq, superb and imaginative cooking (☎ 01232-331532). **Saints and Scholars**, 3 University St, excellent café (☎ 01232-325137) and **La Belle Epoque**, 103 Great Victoria St, French cuisine (☎ 01232-323244) represent the cheap and the expensive ends of dining well in the area.

- **Tourist Information**. The **Northern Ireland Tourist Board**, St. Anne's Court, 59 North St, Belfast BT1 1ND (☎ 01232-246609). **Bord Fáilte**, 53 Castle St, (☎ 0232-327888). Tourist information is widely available throughout the province, in the local library and post office of most towns and villages.
- **Post Offices**. Donegall Square (☎ 0232-321532). Head Post Office. 25 Castle Place; with a Philatelic section.
- **Festivals**. November: **The Belfast Festival** at Queens is the largest arts festival in Ireland, with an emphasis on music and dance; offices at 25 College Gardens, University Rd (☎ 0232-667687). September: **Belfast Folk Festival**.
- **Airports**. **Belfast International Airport** (all international flights), 16 miles west of Belfast, the air terminal is at Great Victoria St (☎ 0849-422888). **Belfast City Airport** (to British provincial airports), four miles northeast of the city (☎ 0232-457745). **Airline Offices. Aer Lingus**, 46 Castle St (☎ 0849-245151); **British Airways**, Fountain Centre, College St (☎ 0849-422888).
- **Shipping Offices**. Sealink (Larne–Stranraer ferry), 33 Castle Lane (☎ 0232-327525); **P&O European Ferries** (Larne–Cairnryan), Larne Harbour (☎ 0574-74321); **Sea Cat** (Belfast–Stranraer), at Belfast Harbour (☎ 0232-312003).
- **Railway Stations**. Belfast Central (East Bridge St) for Dublin and the south (☎ 0232-230301); York St for the Larne line, and Derry (☎ 0232-235282).
- **Bus and Coach Stations**. Gt Victoria St (☎ 0232-320574) and Oxford St (☎ 0232-246485). The main coach offices of **Ulsterbus** are at Milewater Road.
- **Automobile Clubs**. AA, Gt Victoria St; RAC, 79 Chichester St; **Ulster AC**, 3 Botanic Ave.
- The **Port of Belfast** is, for reasons of security, closed to the casual visitor, but visits may be arranged on application to the PRO at the Harbour Office, Corporation St.
- **Other useful addresses**. **Arts Council for Northern Ireland**, Bedford House, Bedford St; **Central Public Library**, Royal Ave; **Linenhall Library**, 17 Donegall Sq. North; **HMSO Bookshop**, Chichester St; **Public Record Office** (and Ulster Historical Foundation), 66 Balmoral Ave; **Ordnance Survey**, Stranmillis Court; **Presbyterian Historical Society**, Church House, Fisherwick Place; **The**

Archaeological Survey of Northern Ireland, 66 Balmoral Ave; The **National Trust** is at Rowallane House, Saintfield, Ballynahinch, Co. Down BT24 7LH. **Ulster Architectural Heritage Society**, 181A Stranmillis Rd; **Ulster Archaeological Society**, Dept. of Archaeology, Elmwood Ave; **Ulster Arts Club**, 56 Elmwood Ave; **Ulster Folklife Society**, Ulster Folk Museum, Cultra Manor, Holywood.

Central Belfast

Belfast (*Beal Feirste*, the ford of the sand bank), is the second city in Ireland (303,000 inhabitants) and the political and industrial capital of Northern Ireland. Architecturally, Belfast today appears as a late Victorian city displaying little evidence of its earlier history. It experienced the most phenomenal growth of any population centre in the British Isles throughout the 19C; from being the 22nd largest town in 1800 it became the 9th largest in 1911. The rapidity of this growth began to decelerate after 1918 and the German bombing of 1941 hastened a dismembering of the city which in more recent years has been continued with equal enthusiasm by developers, town planners and terrorist bombers. Between 1969 and 1976 over 25,000 buildings were damaged by explosions, a circumstance which would have daunted a city of less determination and civic fortitude. Despite such havoc, Belfast still contains a wealth of Victorian and Edwardian buildings and its character is strongly commercial, lacking any suggestion of the market-town antecedents of most Irish urban centres. The lack of good building stone and the abundance of clay has produced a largely red-brick metropolis, often concealed behind stucco, although many of the larger buildings are of sandstone, Mourne granite or Portland stone.

Although situated at the head of Belfast Lough, this is not apparent because of the flatness of the land in the city centre, and it is the dominant form of Cave Hill, overlooking Belfast on the northwest, which provides the dramatic backdrop to the city. Cave Hill rises abruptly behind the buildings and on a clear day its presence invades the city streets with a breath of rusticity; there are also a number of attractive public parks on the banks of the River Lagan. With the exception of the famous dockyards, all historic development has been on the west bank of the Lagan and everything of interest in the city is easily accessible.

As well as being a university city, in the Belfast environs are two cultural institutions of major importance, the **Ulster Museum** and at Cultra, to the east of the city and the **Ulster Folk and Transport Museum** which concentrates on rural architecture and historic transport, with particular reference to Ulster.

The site of Belfast was in occupation during both the Neolithic and Bronze Ages, while more than two dozen ringforts of the Iron Age (500 BC–AD 500) can be traced on the hill slopes within a few miles of the city centre.

John de Courcy, on invading Ulster in 1177, erected a castle. This, with the town which grew up around it, was destroyed by Edward Bruce in 1315. The place then came into the possession of the O'Neills, Earls of Tyrone, and when their lands were confiscated in 1603, Belfast was granted to Sir Arthur Chichester, who colonised it with Devon men. In 1613 it was incorporated by Charter of James I, with the right of sending two members to Parliament in Dublin, and authorised to construct a wharf or quay. This Charter was annulled by James II and a new one issued in 1688, but the original was restored by George II.

During the 17C progress was hampered by the unsettled state of the country. A protest by the citizens against the execution of Charles I was met with a bitter response from Milton, levelled at the 'blockish presbyters of Clandeboye' (the barony in which Belfast stood).

The trade of Belfast, encouraged by Sir Thomas Strafford (who purchased from Carrickfergus, on the lough-side to the northeast, the monopoly of imported goods), was materially benefited by the influx of French Huguenots after the revocation of the Edict of Nantes (1685) which had guaranteed freedom of worship to French Protestants. They improved the methods of the already-established linen trade, which increased steadily during the 18th and 19C. The *Belfast News Letter* which is still in print, was first published in 1737. In 1784 a Corporation for 'Preserving and Improving the Port and Harbour of Belfast' was set up, and at about the same time the architect Roger Mulholland planned a grid of streets as a framework for the future growth of the town.

Cotton-spinning was introduced in 1777 and by 1810 employed 2000 people, while the revival of shipbuilding (initiated by William Ritchie in 1791) added a further impetus to growth (the dredging of the Victoria Channel, from the port to the centre of Belfast Lough, was completed in 1849). On 18 October 1791 the first open meeting took place of the Society of United Irishmen (three weeks prior to that in Dublin, founded by Napper Tandy). It was inaugurated primarily by Wolfe Tone and Samuel Neilson (1761–1803).

By 1800, Belfast's population (8550 in 1757) had more than doubled and during the 19C there was a population explosion; by 1821 it had grown to 37,000; in 1841, 70,000; in 1861, 121,000; in 1881, 208,000, rising to 400,000 by 1925. In 1888 Belfast, which had been incorporated as a borough in 1842 (and visited by Queen Victoria in 1849), was raised to the rank of a city, and its chief magistrate granted the title of Lord Mayor in 1892. By the Government of Ireland Act, 1920, it became the seat of government of Northern Ireland overnight.

The Twentieth Century

The scene of sectarian riots in 1935 (similar scenes had occurred in 1857, 1864, 1876, 1878, 1886, 1898 and 1912), apart from being a hotbed of trouble in 1920–22. (C.E.B. Brett has pointed out that the dividing line recorded by the Commission of Inquiry after the riots of 1886 follows almost exactly the same barrier between the Falls and Shankill Road).

In 1942 the first contingent of the United States army to set foot in Europe landed here.

In 1964 what became known as the 'tricolour riots' took place, in which the Rev. Ian Paisley became involved, and from 1968 the city again became a sectarian battlefield. In certain respects little has changed since Giraldus Cambrensis wrote of the Irish that they 'hurl stones against the enemy in battle with such quickness and dexterity that they do more execution than the slingers of any other nation'; the 'enemy' now generally live a few streets away.

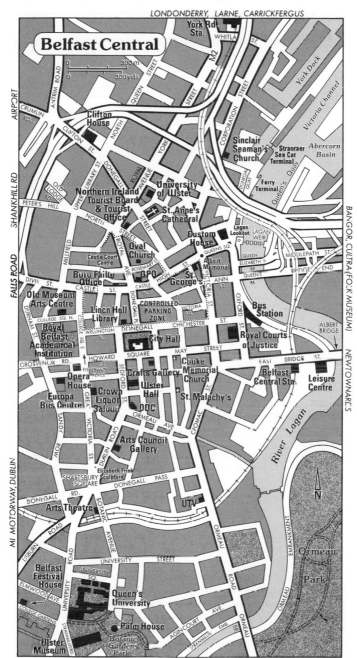

LONDONDERRY, LARNE, CARRICKFERGUS

Belfast Central

300 m
300 yds

AIRPORT

SHANKHILL RD

FALLS ROAD

MI MOTORWAY, DUBLIN

York Rd. Sta.
WHITLA ST.
M2

York Dock

Victoria Channel

CRUMLIN RD.

ANTRIM ROAD

Clifton House

CLIFTON ST.

NORTH ST.

QUEEN STREET

YORK STREET

CORPORATION STREET

Sinclair Seaman's Church

Stranraer Sea Cat Terminal

Abercorn Basin

OLD LODGE RD

PETER'S HILL

MILLFIELD

UPPER LIBRARY ST.

DONEGALL ST.

ROYAL AVENUE

University of Ulster

St. Anne's Cathedral

Ferry Terminal

Custom House

Lagan Lookout

LAGAN WEIR

DONEGALL QUAY

QUEEN'S QUAY

Northern Ireland Tourist Board & Tourist Office

NORTH ST.

Oval Church

GPO

Castle Court Centre

ROSEMARY ST.

Bulu Faille Office

DIVIS ST.

Old Museum Arts Centre

CASTLE ST.

HIGH ST.

Albert Memorial

St. George's

Queens Sq.

QUEEN ELIZABETH II BRIDGE

MIDDLEPATH ST.

BANGOR, CULTRA (FOLK MUSEUM)

BRIDGE END

DURHAM ST.

COLLEGE SQ. N.

Lincn Hall Library

CONTROLLED PARKING ZONE

ANN ST.

Bus Station

OXFORD ST.

ALBERT BRIDGE

Royal Belfast Academical Institution

COLLEGE SQ. E.

WELLINGTON

DONEGALL PL.

City Hall

VICTORIA ST.

CHICHESTER ST.

Royal Courts of Justice

NEWTOWNARDS

GROSVENOR RD.

HOWARD ST.

DONEGALL SQUARE

MAY STREET

EAST BRIDGE ST.

Opera House

FISHERWICK PLACE

BEDFORD ST.

Crafts Gallery

GREAT VICTORIA ST.

Clonke Memorial Church

Ulster Hall

St. Malachy's

CROMAC ST.

Belfast Central Sta.

Leisure Centre

Europa Bus Centre

Crown Liquor Saloon

DDC

ORMEAU AVE.

SANDY ROW

VICTORIA ST.

DUBLIN RD.

Arts Council Gallery

River Lagan

SHAFTSBURY SQUARE

Elizabeth Frink Sculpture

DONEGALL PASS

EMBANKMENT

Arts Theatre

DONEGALL RD.

BOTANIC AVENUE

UTV

ORMEAU ROAD

Ormeau Park

LISBURN ROAD

UNIVERSITY ROAD

UNIVERSITY STREET

AGIN COURT

ORMEAU AVE.

FITZWILLIAM ST.

Belfast Festival House

ELMWOOD AVE.

UNIVERSITY SQ.

Queen's University

LODGE GARDENS

OBSERVATORY ST.

Palm House

AGIN COURT

ORMEAU EMB.

Ulster Museum

Botanic Gardens Park

N

NEWCASTLE

Among natives of Belfast were William Drennan (1754–1820), the poet, known for his apt but now cliché-ridden phrase for Ireland, 'the emerald isle', and first president of the United Irishmen; Peter Turnerelli (1774–1839), sculptor; Sir Samuel Ferguson (1810–86), poet and antiquarian; the scientist, William Thomson, later Lord Kelvin (1824–1907); Sir John Lavery (1856–1941), the artist; Lord Craigavon (1871–1940), first Prime Minister of Northern Ireland, and his contemporary Joseph Devlin (1871–1934), the Nationalist leader; St. John Ervine (1883–1971), dramatist; Clive Staples Lewis (1898–1963), scholar; poets Louis MacNeice (1907–63) and W.R. Rodgers (1909–69); and John Boyd Dunlop (1840–1922) a veterinary surgeon in Belfast from 1867 who invented the pneumatic rubber tyre in 1887. Anthony Trollope lived in Belfast for 18 months and adjacent Whiteabbey from 1853, where he completed *The Warden*.

Central Belfast has two distinct hubs of activity, neatly divided into the spheres of 'town and gown'. The 'town' end is the area around Donegall Square, the political, commercial and shopping heart of the city; the 'gown' area is to the south in the streets of the Queen's University quarter, incorporating the 'Golden Mile' where most of the city's art galleries, restaurants and cultural institutions are to be found.

Donegall Square

■ Vehicle access to a large central area of the city may be restricted, as shown on the map.

The square exudes a consciousness of Empire, the great bulk of the **City Hall** (Wed 10.30; conducted tours) an inescapable statement of civic pride and commercial probity. It is the sort of late classical architecture which more than anything else spelled the end of the classical movement, not because it is architecturally inferior but rather, that the Imperial dream—which it so ably expresses—had evaporated. Designed by Brumwell Thomas in 1896 (Belfast only became a city in 1888), and built of Portland stone, it occupies the site of the old White Linen Hall of 1784. The central copper dome rises to a height of 53m, and the pile accommodates a number of sumptuous marble-decorated reception rooms. The main entrance on the north side is through a small foyer which acts as a memorial chapel to Frederick Chichester, Earl of Belfast (d. 1853), with a startlingly pallid marble pietà of the dying Earl embraced by his mother (Patrick MacDowell). On the main landing is a mural by John Luke, 1951 and another statue of the Earl, this time in rude good health (also by MacDowell). The Northern Ireland Parliament sat here 1922–32 prior to its move to Stormont (see below).

Monuments

The lawns which surround the City Hall on three sides have a number of monuments; the most interesting of which are, on the west side; the Marquess of Dufferin and Ava (F.W. Pomeroy, 1906), which incorporates figures of a North American trapper and a Hindu warrior, representing the territories where he had acted as Governor General and Viceroy; on the north side; Queen Victoria, with figures of shipbuilding and spinning (Thomas Brock, 1903); a stone column commemorating the 1942 US Expeditionary Force (T.F.O. Rippingham, 1946). On the east side, 'Fame', an allegorical figure in remembrance of those lost on the *Titanic* (Thomas Brock, 1920); Royal Irish Rifles (Sydney Marsh, 1905).

Buildings around the square

North-west corner. Nos 16–18 is the **Linenhall Library** (open Mon–Sat 10.00–20.00) (Lanyon & Lynn, 1864), a charming and informal institution, founded in 1788. This important library is housed in a building which is an essential stop for any visitor to the city. The first floor reading rooms (with café) are a mecca for the most interesting people. It also contains an important and rapidly growing collection of material, including ephemera, relevant to the recent 'troubles'. No.1 (now Marks and Spencer) is one of the great 19C linen warehouses, bombed during World War ll. Its steep roof has recently been restored (1985) but without the original tall chimneys and gables (erected in 1867 by W.H. Lynn).

East side. No 1. Pearl Assurance. A splendidly confident asymmetrical Gothic insurance office (Young and Mackenzie, 1899); Methodist Church, Isaac Farell (1846), the last classical church to be built in Belfast.

South side. No 10, Jaffe Brothers (1862), a linen warehouse, decorated with heads of such notables as Newton, Schiller, Columbus and Washington.

West side. Scottish Provident Institution (Young and Mackenzie, 1899), a Victorian Baroque palace of trade.

From the north front of the City Hall, and passing through the main shopping district of the city is the wide and pedestrianised Donegall Place continuing into Royal Avenue, on which are left in Chapel Lane, St. Mary's church (RC) John O'Neill, 1868, and right in Rosemary St, the elliptical **First Presbyterian Church** (Roger Mulholland, 1783) (only open during services). This has the most interesting church interior in Belfast because it retains its box pews and graceful galleries. On the left is the **Castlecourt Centre** (Building Design Partnership, 1985), a shopping complex with a successful high-tech stainless steel and glass façade, the best example of late 20C architecture in the city. At the northern end of the street is the excellent Art Deco **Bank of Ireland** (J.V. Downes, 1928), a finely detailed building with corner tower which visually closes both Royal Avenue and the adjacent North St in which are the offices of the **Northern Ireland Tourist Board** and **Tourist Office**. In the eastern continuation of Royal Avenue are (left) the offices of the *Belfast Telegraph*, and looking down Library St are the fine curved and turreted brick showrooms (W.J. Fennell, 1907), which like the 'Flat Iron Building', represent archetypal 19C solutions to making a building on an awkward site interesting.

Beyond the northern end of Donegall St stands Belfast's oldest public building, **Clifton House** (Robert Joy, 1771), with an attractive brick façade retaining its original external appearance. It was built as a poorhouse and is still in use as an old people's home. (It is worth walking further along the street to the Frederick St junction from which the axially planned building can be viewed as it was intended to be seen). The central two-storey block with pediment, tower and spire is flanked by single storey wings with gabled end pavilions. The first cotton looms in Ireland were set up in the north wing in order to provide employment for the children of the inmates, shortly after it opened in 1774.

St. Anne's Cathedral

North St Arcade leads east into Donegall St and at the far side of an open piazza is St. Anne's Cathedral (open 08.00–17.00) (C of I), a still-unfinished building in a Romanesque Revival style. It is a surprisingly harmonious result considering that it is the work of eight architects over a period of 80 years. Begun in 1899 from the designs of Sir Thomas Drew (d. 1910), it was continued by Sir Charles Nicholson (d. 1949) who built around the old parish church of St. Anne (demolished in 1903). Basilican in plan, with shallow transepts and an apsidal east end with ambulatory (completed 1959), the heavily ornate west front, with three portals, was dedicated as a war memorial in 1927 (carvings by Esmond Burton).

The nave (26m long) has a floor of maple and Irish marble, and at its west end is a maze. Here also is the tomb of the Unionist leader, Lord Carson (1854–1935), with an additional memorial on the south wall. At the southwest corner is a richly decorated baptistery, and opposite, the domed chapel of the Holy Spirit. The capitals of the nave arcade, by Rosamund Praeger and Morris Harding, represent the Occupations of Mankind, above which are corbels commemorating leaders of the Church of Ireland. There are stained glass windows by A.K. Nicholson and Patrick Pye.

The external massing of the building from the northeast is impressive and the gargantuan Celtic cross, which rises to the full height of north apse, can be seen from Academy St (John MacGeagh, 1964), an addition to the cathedral which has neither architectural precedent nor any convincing relationship to the building. A crossing tower, part of the original design, is still required to complete the building.

Proceed south to High St in which is **St. George's church** (C of I, John Bowden, 1811), with a Corinthian portico from the Earl-Bishop of Derry's unfinished palace at Ballyscullion (Michael Shanahan, 1788). Pottinger's Entry, a survival of a common type of Belfast alleyway is decorated by a wrought-iron arch at its opening. At the east end of High St rises the Albert Memorial (1865, by W.J. Barre), leaning a metre from the vertical due to subsidence.

In Waring St the Northern Bank was built in 1769 as the **Assembly Rooms**, and faced in stucco by Lanyon in 1845. In 1792 it was the scene of the famous Belfast Harp Festival, the last gathering of traditional musicians of the Gaelic tradition. At No.5 Waring St is the **Royal Ulster Rifles Regimental Museum** (☎ 0232-232086), reflecting the history of the regiment from 1793–1968, with a collection of militaria.

Beyond, on the north side of Queen's Square, stands the **Custom House** (1854–57; by Sir Charles Lanyon), with sculptures by S.F. Lynn, and containing a collection of paintings of maritime subjects. It overlooks Donegall Quay, the embarkation point for the Sea Cat Ferry Terminal and Isle of Man Ferry Terminal. The Liverpool Ferry Terminal is further north (at Dargan Road) on Belfast Lough.

Sinclair Seamen's church (open during services) in Corporation St, to the west of Donegall Quay (Lanyon and Lynn, 1856) is an L-shaped Lombardo-Romanesque building with a tall campanile at the street corner. It is part place of worship, part maritime museum—with the pulpit lectern in the form of a ship's prow, flanked by navigation lights from a Guinness barge, and the baptismal font a converted compass binnacle—no child baptised here should fear the sea. The maritime theme is sustained throughout the church with ships' models and other memorabilia in a remarkably indulgent exercise of pure whimsy, hardly expected in a Presbyterian church.

Return (right) to Donegall St and Donegall Square. Parallel to the north front of the City Hall is Chichester St. Immediately to the right there is a terrace of Georgian houses, of a type largely swept away since the 19C. This leads east, towards the river and the embattled Royal Courts of Justice (1929–33; by J.G. West), another massive pile of Portland stone.

At the junction with Victoria St look left, to the almost disappearing '**Flat Iron Building**' which looks like a slim wedge of cheese. Abercorn Buildings (Thomas Jackson, 1868) is the actual name of the building, but it is popularly called the 'flat Iron' building after the better-known Flat Iron Building in Chicago. This presently unloved brick warehouse is on a narrow triangular site and is among the curiosities of Victorian Belfast.

The Lagan river, to the northeast of Victoria St, is crossed by Queen's Bridge (opened in 1841 and widened in 1886), standing on the site of the 17C Long Bridge. Parallel to the north is Queen Elizabeth Bridge (1966).

Below the bridge is the Lagan Weir which can be crossed by a footbridge. It maintains upstream water levels as part of the Laganside urban renewal project, designed to develop the hitherto neglected riverbanks as amenity areas as far up the river as Stranmillis Weir. The circular **Lagan Lookout Building** at the west end of the weir is a visitor centre. North of the weir the river is crossed by the new motorway. South of the weir and bridges is the new **Waterfront Concert Hall**, the finest venue in Belfast for concert performances.

Beyond the southern end of the Courts, East Bridge St leads past Central Railway Station to Albert Bridge, immediately to the southwest of which is the Maysfield Sports and Leisure Centre (1977), with a riverbank marina.

Castle St leads west off Donegall Place towards Divis St, which in turn continues on through a predominantly Catholic area by the Falls Rd. The externally severe but impressive **Cathedral of St. Peter** (RC; Jeremiah McAuley, 1860), (open 07.00–18.00) with twin spires added in 1886 is in Derby Street. The nave is aisled but without transepts and the most interesting aspect of the interior is the hammer-beam roof and the decorated chancel. The nave columns have recently been painted powder-blue.

Royal Avenue is crossed by North St, extended to the west by Peter's Hill and the Shankill Rd (a Protestant enclave). Roughly parallel, but further north, is the Crumlin Rd, leading to the Catholic district of Ardoyne, all, sadly, names well-known as focuses of sectarian violence, but in themselves of more interest for the enormous number of gable-end political murals—all making statements about the political divide in Northern Ireland—which range from naïve folk-art to sophisticated professional commissions. Originally a purely Loyalist (i.e. working-class Protestant) activity, mural painting has, since the 1960s, also been embraced by Nationalists.

The **Port of Belfast** lies at the head of Belfast Lough, c 19km from the open sea. It is the largest port in Ireland, long famous as one of the world's great shipbuilding centres, with the yards of Harland and Wolff. There was a revival of shipbuilding in 1833 on the site of Queen's Island, which within a few years was virtually controlled by Edward James Harland, a Yorkshireman, who in 1858 recruited the marine draughtsman Gustav Wilhelm Wolff from Hamburg. Among numerous other liners constructed here was the *Titanic*. The ship collided with an iceberg on 14 April 1912. Out of 2201 passengers, 711 survived. The *Titanic* was the largest vessel afloat (45,000 tonnes); she sank within three hours of the impact. The tragedy is commemorated on the east side of the City Hall.

The port contains four dry docks, including the huge Belfast Dry Dock, 335m long, which have seen the repair of some of the largest liners, and more recently, tankers. There are c 13km of quays and some 500 hectares of water. Noticeable among a forest of cranes and gantries are the two cranes 'Samson' and 'Goliath', one of which is 106m high and 140m long, straddling the 556m-long Harland and Wolff Shipbuilding Dock. The *Canberra* (1960), was the last great liner to be launched in Belfast, although the 20,000 who cheered her down the slipway did not realise they were witnessing the end of an era.

On the west bank at the north end of Donegall Quay at the harbour offices is Clarendon Dock with two graving docks. No. 1 was built by William Ritchie (1795), who was responsible for establishing shipbuilding as an industry in Belfast.

West of Donegall Square, Wellington Place leads into College Square North, in which is the **Old Museum Arts Centre** (10.00–17.00) (Duff and Jackson, 1830). Established as the predecessor of the Ulster Museum by the Belfast Natural History and Philosophical Society, it was the first museum in Ireland founded by public subscription. The curator was actively involved in preparing displays, and was described in 1870 as both 'curator and bird stuffer'.

Behind the Technical College is the Royal Belfast Academical Institution, one of the small number of Georgian public buildings in the city (John McCutcheon and James Boyd, after a design by Sir John Soane, 1807). It is an important non-denominational day school (usually referred to as 'Inst') at which the dramatist James Sheridan Knowles (1784–1862) and the mathematician James Thomson (1786–1849; Lord Kelvin's father) were masters.

To the south, at the corner of College Square and Howard St, is the Presbyterian Assembly building with a fine openwork spire, now housing a small shopping centre.

The **Opera House** (1894) in Great Victoria Street combines an eclectic mixture of Oriental and Art Nouveau influences by the celebrated theatre designer, Frank Matcham (1854–1920). It has a lavishly gilt interior and elephant's heads and 'cod-Sanskrit' (imitation) inscriptions on the balconies. Sarah Bernhardt and Beerbohm Tree are among the many great names of the stage who trod its boards. In 1980 it re-opened, after a thorough restoration, but suffered from serious bomb damage in 1991 and 1993; it has now been restored (open during performances).

The ornate **Crown Liquor Saloon** (NT) (1885, E. & J. Byrne), stands almost opposite in this street. It is an excellent example of a Victorian gin palace at its most exuberant. The interior is well preserved and follows the 'horror-vacui' style of interior decoration, with no surface left un-embellished; bevelled mirrors, embossed ceiling, panelled snugs, tiling, brasswork, everything in fact which Victorian manufacturing skill could provide to impress the customer (the snugs have brass match-strikers and bells to summon fresh supplies of drink), it is hardly surprising that it is still a popular bar.

East of Donegall Square, in May St, is the May St Presbyterian church (William Smith, 1828), with an Ionic portico, built for the Rev. Henry Cooke (1788–1868), a demagogic preacher with a faultless ear for 'theological error' in his contemporaries' sermons (his influence is still felt in the religious temperature of Belfast). The portrait medallion of Cooke is by Foley.

In Alfred St, southeast of Donegall Square, is **St. Malachy's church** (RC; Thomas Jackson, 1840) (open 08.00–18.00), an early Gothic Revival building of great character. The brick façade has tall octagonal battlemented turrets flanking the entrance. The **interior** is unusually planned, the altar being in the middle of the long side of a rectangle, rather than at the end, surrounded on three sides by galleries with box-pews. The main feature of the interior is the superb and almost overpowering fan-vaulted ceiling which reaches down to the worshippers. In the 1860s one of the church bells had to be removed when it was thought to be interfering with the whisky maturation in a nearby distillery! The church was badly damaged by fire in 1996 (restoration work in progress).

Linenhall St, running south from the middle of Donegall Square—from which there are good views of the rear façade of City Hall—has some interesting 19C linen warehouses.

Belfast South

From the south-west corner of Donegall Square, Bedford St leads south past the Ulster Hall (1860, by W.J. Barre) into Dublin Road. The **Arts Council Gallery** on the left (Mon–Sat, 10.00–17.00) is the city's main venue for contemporary art. The **Ulster Bank**, at the apex of Shaftesbury Square and Great Victoria St faces south. High up on its gable end are a pair of bronze human torsos by Dame Elizabeth Frink (erected 1988) floating in the blank area of the wall; they are popularly known as 'Draft and Overdraft'.

From the end of Bedford St turn right into Ormeau Avenue and left into Ormeau Rd for the gasworks, one of the most interesting 19C industrial complexes in the city. The multi-gabled office block and octagonal tower (James Stelfox, 1888) form the street front of this now defunct works (city coal gas ceased production in 1978). The entrance and stair hall are entirely clad in many coloured glazed tiles and are as lavish in surface decoration as the interiors of the City Hall. The connection does not end there because the construction of the latter was largely financed from the profits of the former. The Klondyke House (1891) is a cathedral-size works-shed with classical gable-end and pediment, below which is a frieze relief depicting cherubs feeding a furnace. The dome of the Middle Section Meter House is at present under restoration. The **Ormeau Baths Arts Centre** is a venue for contemporary art exhibitions.

Ascending gently almost due south along University Rd you pass on the left the original buildings of **Queen's University** (8500 students), designed by Sir Charles Lanyon in a Tudor style. Founded as Queen's College in 1845, inaugurated in 1849, and formerly associated with the other 'Godless Colleges' at Cork and Galway, it was later known as the Royal University. The University of Belfast was incorporated separately in 1909. The intended quadrangle was never completed and the façade to the University conceals undistinguished modern extensions. Good restaurants abound in this area (see *Food & Drink* section, Belfast Listings).

In University Avenue is the First Church of Christ Scientist (Clough Williams-Ellis, 1923), a restrained Arts and Crafts alternative to the enthusiasm for all things Celtic which prevailed at the time. To the east is the conspicuous Assembly's College (1853; also by Lanyon), a Presbyterian training school occupying a Tuscan Doric edifice.

Opposite the University is Elmwood Hall (1859), with an attractive Romanesque Revival facade. The Agricultural College is in Elmwood Avenue.

To the left is the entrance to the attractive **Botanic Gardens** (open daily to dusk), with the glass-domed **Palm House** (1839–40) designed by Lanyon and constructed by the Dublin iron-master Richard Turner (1798–1881) who also designed the Palm Houses at Kew and Glasnevin. It is the earliest surviving example of curviliniar glasswork, now well-restored after years of neglect and it belongs to the pioneering period of cast iron and glass architecture which culminated in the erection of the Crystal Palace in 1841. Also in the gardens is the Tropical Ravine 1886, which re-creates a jungle environment.

The Ulster Museum

To the south is the Ulster Museum, with a re-erected Court Cairn from Ballintaggart, Co. Armagh in front of the entrance (open Mon–Fri 10.00–17.00; Sat 13.00–17.00; Sun 14.00–17.00). It fulfils the combined function for Northern Ireland of national gallery, antiquities museum, natural history and science museums, all under one roof. This impossibly ambitious programme puts a strain upon the capacity of a not-very-large building and only a selection from the very fine collection may be on display. The older part of the building facing Stranmillis Rd is a late classical structure of 1924 by J.C. Wynn, to which was added an extension reminiscent of London's South Bank development in 'New Brutalist' style by Francis Pym in 1971. The manner in which the Ionic façade of the older building elides into the windowless concrete cubes of the extension is a heroic attempt at reconciling the unreconcilable. There is a restaurant and bookshop.

■ The museum is divided into the divisions of Art (fine and applied), Human History (antiquities, local history and Armagh County Museum) and Natural History (geology, botany and zoology).

It is best to start from the top floor (lift) and descend on foot by a series of ramps.

Galleries 10, 9, 8. A comprehensive collection of 20C contemporary international painting and sculpture, including works by Dubuffet and Tapies.

Gallery 7. Displays from the permanent collections of fine and applied art.

Gallery 6. Watercolours, prints and drawings from a large collection of mostly British and Irish work, including works by Edward Lear, David Cox, David Roberts, Samuel Palmer, Francis Wheatley, Alexander Cozens, Thomas Shotter Boys, Paul Sandby, Thomas Rowlandson, Gerald Brockhurst, John Varley, J.F. Lewis, Percy Wyndham Lewis, Philip Wilson Steer, William Henry Hunt, John 'Warwick' Smith, Thomas Hearne, and Henry Fuseli. Outstanding among the watercolourists are Andrew Nicholl, James Moore, of which the museum has an extensive collection, George Petrie, William Miller (of Lurgan; d. 1779), Charles Ginner, John Percival Glich and James George Oben (fl. 1779–1819). There is also an important collection of paintings of over 180

Irish birds by Richard Dunscombe Parker (1805–81). Further works from the collection may be seen in the Print Room.

Gallery 5. Irish painting and sculpture 17C–20C contains works by Hector McDonnell, Anthony Green, *Woman in Bomb Blast* by F.E. McWilliam; *Self-portrait* by Nathaniel Hone the Younger, *Landscapes* by Joseph Peacock (1783–1837), *Festival at Glendalough* by James Glen Wilson (1827–63), *Emigrant Ship leaving Belfast* by W. Clarkson Stanfield, *Stack Rock, Antrim* by George Barret, senior, *The Waterfall at Powerscourt* by Nathaniel Grogan; *View of Kilkenny*; attrib. Philip Hussey, *The Bateson family* by Susanna Drury (fl. 1733–70), two *Views of the Giant's Causeway* (1740) by Susanna Drury; *Portrait of William Bogle* by Colin Harrison; *Portrait of Seamus Heaney* by Edward McGuire (b. 1932); *Girl in White* by Louis Le Brocquy (b. 1916); *Jaunting Car* by William Conor; *On through the Silent Lane* by Jack Butler Yeats; *Self-portrait*, Sir William Orpen; *Portrait of Harry Clarke* by Margaret Clarke (1881–1961); Portraits of James Moore O'Donnell, and Colonel Hugh O'Donnell by Hugh Douglas Hamilton; *Captain Charles Janvre de la Bouchetière* by James Latham.

Shrine of St. Patrick's hand, silver guilt reliquary, c 1400

Gallery 4. Major temporary exhibitions.

Gallery 3. Old Master and British paintings and sculpture. Arthur Devis, *Portrait of Viscount Boyle*; Pompeo Battoni, *Portrait of Wills Hill, Earl of Hillsborough* (1766); Richard Wilson, *Landscape with Bandits*; Anon. (English School, c 1600), *Portrait of the 2nd Earl of Essex*; Turner, *The Dawn of Christianity*; Gainsborough, *Portrait of the 1st Marquess of Donegal*; Lawrence, *Harriet Anne, Countess of Belfast*; Reynolds, *Theodosia Magill*, later Countess of Clanwilliam; Lucien Pissarro, *Vanessa Bell*, and among notable individual works Sickert, *Suspense*; Stanley Spencer, *Portrait of Daphne Spencer*, and *Betrayal*. Also notable are Henry Moore's sculptures entitled *Oval with Points*, and *Three-piece reclining figure draped*. J.M. Wright the elder, *Gentleman in armour*; and Stubbs, *James Hamilton*.

Gallery 2. Applied art, costume and textiles, silver, glass and ceramics. Works of art displayed here may include the Lennox Quilt (1712); jewellery; Irish glass, with examples of early Waterford, and the wheel engraved goblet of Archbishop Charles Cobbe (1743–5) of Newbridge House (see Ch.1B). Irish silver tankards and porringers (among them the Dopping and Freke porringer of 1685), including the Great Seal Cup of 1593 (made for Adam Loftus, Archbishop of Armagh and first provost of Trinity College, Dublin), and a fine epergne (branched ornamental centrepiece for the table) of 1790 are also on display.

Gallery 1. Small temporary exhibitions.

The **ground floor** is occupied by the **Local History** and **Engineering Gallery**. Some fine working machinery of the industrial revolution leads through to an interesting collection of engines, many in working order, explaining flax and linen technology; also spinning-wheels.

The **Natural History Galleries** on the ground floor contain the marvellous Mineralogy Gallery and Paleontological collection (including a skeleton of the extinct Irish giant deer; a Coelacanth dredged up off Madagascar in 1973 and a Giant Japanese spider-crab). In 1968, the University Herbarium, a collection of c 40,000 specimens of plants, largely formed by Charles Bailey (1838–1924), was donated to the museum. The Geology of Ireland is graphically displayed.

A flight of stairs on the west side of the ground floor leads to the **Antiquities Galleries** which display Irish archaeological material from local excavations, Mesolithic sites in the Glens of Antrim and medieval artefacts from Carrigfergus. An adjacent section is devoted to the *Girona* and the *Trinidad Valancera* (see Port-na-Spania, pxx). The material salvaged from the vessels off Lacada Point (near the Giant's Causeway) by Robert Sténuit in 1968–69 was acquired by the museum in 1972. It includes bronze cannon, breech blocks and other artefacts, also an invaluable hoard of jewellery, including a gold salamander set with rubies, gold chains, buttons, crosses, rings, cameos, and coins. Nearby is the ethnographic collection and Egyptian antiquities.

The **Numismatics Gallery** has a particularly strong collection of medieval and early Irish coinage. In the **Local History Galleries** the history of Belfast is related with material from the various strands of political opinion which have coloured the city's history. In adjoining rooms are some of the treasures of the museum, among them a gilt bronze cross from Altikeeragh (Co. Londonderry); a silver mace from the borough of Cavan (by John Hamilton, Dublin, 1724); a silver penannular brooch from near Ballymoney (late 9C), Irish made but Saxon inspired and an amber necklace from Kurin Moss (Co. Londonderry, c 800 BC.). The important finds from Nendrum (on the west shore of Strangford Lough, Co. Antrim, Ch. 18) may also be seen here.

In the **Archaeological Galleries** are a representative selection of Bronze Age gold ornaments; bronze cauldrons and other implements, including cordoned and collared urns (1750–1000 BC), two types of cast bronze horns (c 800 BC); and the Malone hoard of polished stone axes. In this area also are general ethnological exhibits, and a section on local history.

Also in Stranmillis Rd is (right) the Science Building of the University (by John McGeagh), while from the far side of the Botanic Gardens the Stranmillis Embankment skirts the Lagan to Ormeau Bridge and Ormeau Rd (continued as the A24 to Downpatrick). Beyond the bridge, on the south bank of the river, is Ormeau Park.

Belfast Environs

Crossing the Lagan by the Queen Elizabeth II Bridge, and driving due east, after 3.5 miles you pass (left) the avenue leading up to the Parliament building of Northern Ireland at **Stormont**. The severely plain classical building with a central portico (1928–32) is by A. Thornley. On the right of this, other government offices are housed in the Scots Baronial **Stormont Castle**. At the approach to the former is a statue of Sir Edward Carson (1854–1935), Unionist leader. A statue of the first prime minister of Northern Ireland (1921–1940), Lord Craigavon, stands in the main hall.

The M2 motorway, joined immediately north of the city centre (skirting the west bank of Belfast Lough) now extends some 23 miles northwest from Belfast, providing a rapid exit from the city and rejoining the A6 between Antrim and Castledawson.

Leaving Belfast by Donegall St and Carlisle Circus, the road steadily climbs, with Cave Hill (368m) on the left, the northernmost peak of a range of hills that overlooks the city to the west, the highest summit of which is Divis (478m). Cave Hill commands the best view, extending across Belfast Lough to Down and Strangford Lough, while on a clear day the Ayrshire coast and the Isle of Man can be seen. To the west, Lough Neagh is backed by the Sperrin and Carntogher ranges. The easiest approach to Cave Hill is from the Antrim Rd and Hazelwood Gardens, adjoining which is **Belfast Zoo** (10.00–17.00 in summer; –15.30 in winter (closed Christmas day); £).

On the hillside stands **Belfast Castle** (1867–70, restored) largely designed by W.H. Lynn in the Scots Baronial style. On the summit are the earthworks known as **MacArt's Fort** (named after Brian MacArt O'Neill, killed by Lord Mountjoy in 1601); its natural defences are a precipice on one side and a ditch on the other. It was here in 1794 that Wolfe Tone vowed to overthrow English Rule in Ireland.

East of Belfast

Cross the Lagan by Queen Elizabeth Bridge, driving east past Stormont. Shortly beyond, fork right onto the A22 for **Comber**, which may be by-passed. The church of 1840 stands on the site of a Cistercian abbey founded c 1200 on the site of an earlier monastery. The abbey buildings were burned in 1573 and the ruins served as a quarry.

The main road heads directly southeast to Killyleagh. At the next fork a by-road turns left to skirt the island-studded western shore of Strangford Lough, the foreshore of which is now a Nature Reserve.

A causeway crosses to **Mahee Island**, beside which is the ruin known as Captain Brown's Castle (1570). On rising ground on the island are the remains of the **monastery of Nendrum**, founded by St. Mochua (7C), but destroyed in 974 by Vikings. The site was discovered in 1844 and its remains were restored in 1922. The ruins, surrounded by a trivallate cashel, include part of a Round Tower (10C) and the church with its sundial (8C). Although the buildings are ruinous, this beautiful site overlooking Strangford Lough gives a strong impression of the isolation and appearance of Early Christian monastic settlements. The important finds from recent excavations may be seen in the Ulster Museum, Belfast, but the site museum is also of interest. On the promontories and other islets are the ruins of several tower-houses erected in the 15C–16Cs and early 17C by the Ulster landowners. From Ringneill Bridge, the road turns south via Ardmillan to rejoin the A22 five miles north of Killyleagh.

Killyleagh was the birthplace of Sir Hans Sloane (1660–1753), the founder of the British Museum. From the obscurity of this village, Edward Hinks (1792–1866), rector from 1826 until his death, gained the reputation of being one of Europe's foremost orientalists, having discovered the essential principles of Egyptian hieroglyphics and Persian cuneiform.

The castle was built by the planter Sir James Hamilton, first Viscount Clandeboye in 1610. Reconstructed by Lanyon in 1850, it incorporates two round towers, one dating from the 13C, the other of 1666. Originally erected by De Courcy, it was later held by the O'Neills, and rebuilt by the Hamiltons after its destruction by General Monk in 1648. 'It pricks castellated ears above the smoke of its own village and provides a curiously exotic landmark, towering like some château of the Loire above the gentle tides of Strangford Lough', wrote Sir Harold Nicolson of his mother (Lady Carnock)'s home.

To visit the Ulster Folk and Transport Museum, head for Holywood on the east bank of Belfast Lough. Crossing Queen Elizabeth II Bridge, bear northeast on the Sydenham bypass along the east bank. After passing (right) Palace Barracks, enter **Holywood**, birthplace of the author and revolutionary Bulmer Hobson (1883–1969). It was originally called Ballyderry (town of the wood), and then had its name changed to Sanctus Boscus (the Holy Wood) by the Normans. A church built here in the 7C by St. Laserain, was connected to Bangor Abbey. In the 16C a Franciscan monastery was established, which with others in the district was burned by Sir Brian O'Neill in 1572 to prevent Queen Elizabeth's English troops from garrisoning them; its ruins lie at the end of High St.

The Ulster Folk and Transport Museum

On leaving the town, you pass (right) the entrance to the demesne of Cultra Manor, now containing the combined Ulster Folk and Transport Museum (Mon–Sat 10.00–18.00; Sun 12.00–18.00; seasonal variations). It is one of the most interesting and important museums in Ireland, and deserves an extended visit; detailed descriptive leaflets are available. Unlike some other fabricated 'folk parks', almost all the buildings in the open air have been brought from their original sites and re-erected in similar surroundings. Many are furnished as they would have been around the turn of the century, admirably displaying agricultural and domestic equipment and other bygones, and the unenviable conditions of a rural life now past.

The **Folk Gallery**, with changing exhibitions, should be visited first. Notable are the early photographs (c 1890–1920), taken by W.A. Green (1870–1959), the paintings of William Conor (1881–1968), and the prints of William Hincks (1783), which may be on view.

Among some 20 different examples of traditional buildings to be seen are two cottiers' cabins, three types of farmhouse, a weaver's house, a rectory (1717), a spade mill from Coalisland (1840s), a flax scutching mill (1850s), and bleach-green watchman's hut; a forge (1830s), two schoolhouses (1836; 1865), a church (1790), a market and court house from Cushendall, and two urban terraces. Other types of building are planned.

A bridge spans the main road to the **Transport Museum** where, near the turntable, a railway gallery was inaugurated in 1993. The main exhibition halls are divided into various sections: Archaic Transport displaying examples of the

shoulder creel (for carrying peat or potatoes); panniers; sledges or slipes; slide-cars and wheel-cars; truttle cars, and side-cars or jaunting cars. Horse-drawn carriages include dog-carts and pony-traps; the Waggonette Brake, the Phaeton, the Victoria, the Brougham; a private omnibus; a stage coach; and the Marquess of Abercorn's Dress Chariot (mid-19C).

The Bicycle Collection of Thomas Edens Osborne (1885–1930) includes the Beeston Humber Ordinary, c 1885 (or Penny Farthing), the earlier Dandy Horse (c 1810–1865), the pedal Velocipede (c 1867), the Dublin

Bleachgreen watchman's hut (19C), Cultra

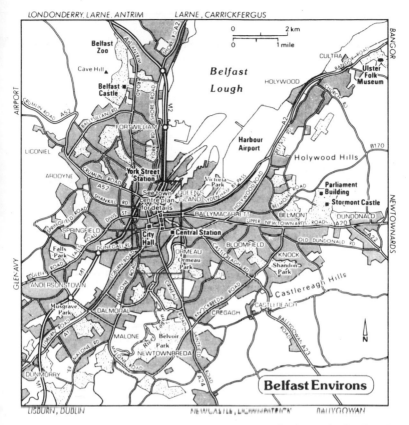

Tricycle (1876) and the Edlin Racing Safety (1889), the first to be fitted with pneumatic tyres (fixed by rubber solution directly to the wheel rims). A collection of motor bicycles is also to be seen, ranging from the Levis of 1921 to the Yamsel of 1971.

A third gallery displays a representative selection of veteran motor-cars, from the MMC of 1903 to the Rolls-Royce Limousine of 1937. Among them is the Chamber's Car (Belfast, 1906), a two-seater Peugeot of 1913, the only surviving prototype of the Fergus Car (1915), a Humber (1924) and Lancia (1924), a Bentley of 1926, and a Riley of 1936. There is also a gull-winged De Lorean, built in Northern Ireland (1982).

Among aircraft are examples of the Short Bros and Harland vertical take-off plane, the 'flying bedstead' (1953), and a full-scale model of a Ferguson monoplane of 1909.

A further section is devoted to the shipbuilding industry of Belfast, while among other individual exhibits are a Dublin-Kingstown railway carriage (1840), a horse tramcar from Fintona, a 'toast-rack' trailer car from the Giant's Causeway hydroelectric railway and an itinerant's caravan.

On the lough shore near here is the North of Ireland Yacht Club, and at Craigavad, to the northeast, the Royal Belfast Golf Club.

Shortly bear inland, passing (right) the demesne of **Clandeboye** (c 1820 by R.A. Woodgate and Sir Richard Morrison, with later additions), the seat of the Marquess of Dufferin and Ava. In the chapel is an 8C cross-shaft from Bangor Abbey; two miles southeast. At the far end of the estate, rises Helen's Tower (1858–62), erected in honour of Helen, Lady Dufferin (1807–67), granddaughter of Sheridan, and composer of the ballad, *The Irish Emigrant.*

Bangor (Tourist Information, Tower House, 34 Quay St, ☎ 01247-270069) is a flourishing resort and dormitory town.

The seat of a great missionary abbey Bangor (*Banchor*, the white choir) was founded by St. Comhgall in c 555. Among his pupils were St. Columbanus and St. Gall, who went to evangelise the Germanic tribes of central Europe. In Switzerland, St. Gallen, (named after St. Gall), became an influential foundation. The 'Bangor Antiphonary' dating from the 680s, is now in the Ambrosian Library, Milan. Its riches naturally attracted the Vikings, who destroyed the monastery, but the abbey was rebuilt in c 1140. The Normans gave it to the Augustinians, but in 1542 it was dissolved. James I granted the lands to Sir James Hamilton (1559–1643), who in 1622 became Lord Clandeboye.

Main St descends to Bangor Bay, to the east of which is the beach of Ballyholme Bay. Near the inner quay is a small tower, built by Lord Clandeboye as a custom house in 1637, and now housing a tourist office. On a low hill above the town is Bangor Castle (1859), now the Town Hall, with a public park in its wooded grounds. It contains a small museum of relics from the abbey including a 14C Sanctus bell. Abbey St, at the foot of Castle Park, leads to the abbey church (rebuilt 1960), where a spire of 1693 surmounts the original central tower of the Augustinian church. Several early 17C memorials are preserved, among them that of John Hamilton (d. 1693) and his wife, by Peter Scheemakers (1691–1769).

The road skirts Ballyholme Bay to Groomsport, where General Schomberg (1615–1690)—the German-born Commander of William III's forces in Ireland, killed at the Battle of the Boyne—landed in 1689, now spoilt by caravan sites. Beyond, three small islands come into view; the nearest and largest is Copeland Island, beyond which is Lighthouse Island (with no lighthouse) and Mew Island, with a lighthouse (1884), whose powerful beam guides shipping towards the entrance of Belfast Lough.

The Ards Peninsula

Donaghadee (Tourist Information, Town Hall, ☎ 01247-882087), a small resort, is the nearest Irish port to Great Britain. Until 1849 it was connected by a regular mail service with Portpatrick in Scotland, 21 miles northeast, but this was abandoned in favour of the Stranraer–Larne route owing to the unsuitability of Portpatrick harbour. In 1818 Keats and Charles Brown, intending to visit the Giant's Causeway, came over in a packet, but having briefly seen Belfast, they re-embarked without further delay for Scotland.

The lighthouse at the end of the large harbour was built by Sir John Rennie and David Logan. There are a few old houses surviving in the town, among them the Manor House in High St. A castle of 1818 crowns the motte, from the summit of which the coast of Galloway may be seen in clear weather.

The Ards Peninsula can be easily visited from Donaghadee. The barony of Ards occupies a tongue of land c 20 miles long and four miles broad which separates the Irish Sea from **Strangford Lough**. This arm of the sea is of much the same area as the peninsula, although from its entrance at the Narrows, and the number of islands around its shores, it has much more the appearance of a freshwater lough. Most of the islands are in fact the summits of submerged drumlins, as in Clew Bay. It is an important Nature Reserve, and the entire inner foreshore of the lough has been designated a wildlife and ornithological reserve.

Strangford Lough ~ East side

The A2 passes along the eastern side of the peninsula between sandy beaches and caravan sites to Millisle (2.5 miles). **Ballycopeland Windmill** (10.00–19.00, Tue–Sat, 14.00–19.00, Sun; closed Mon; June–Sept; £) stands to the west, dating from the last decade of the 18C (restored). The poet Louis MacNeice (1907–63) is buried at **Carrowdore**, further inland. In the cemetery at **Ballywalter** are the ruins of the 'White Church' of Templefinn, with three Anglo-Norman grave-slabs. Skirt Ballywalter Park, an Italianate palazzo (c 1846; by Lanyon), built for Andrew Mulholland, mayor of Belfast, to approach **Ballyhalbert**, where the road turns inland. The small offshore islet, known as Burial Island, is signed as being the most easterly part of Ireland. Follow the coast road to **Portavogie**, with its tiny fishing harbour, and skirt Cloghey Bay, passing **Kirkistown Castle**, one of the better examples of a bawn erected by the 17C settlers. **Kearney** (NT), is a restored complex of vernacular cottages on the coast.

   Portaferry has a pleasant waterfront and faces the narrow channel, five miles long and half a mile broad, connecting Strangford Lough to the open sea. Near relics of a castle is the **Exploris aquarium** complex. Two miles to the east is **Quintin Castle**, an early 19C castellated building incorporating a 17C tower house, on the site of the stronghold of Sir Thomas Smith (c 1580).

Strangford Lough ~ West side

Return along the western side of the Ards Peninsula, skirting the lough to Newtownards, or take the ferry across the estuary to Strangford, eight miles from Downpatrick and 22 miles from Belfast by the direct road.

   Driving north, you reach the lough-side at Ardkeen (also approached by a minor road hugging the shore) where in c 1180 a motte-and-bailey was founded by William le Savage, one of de Courcy's companions in the conquest of Ulster. 7.5 miles **Kircubbin** has a Penal Law Chapel of c 1780 (restored). Four miles beyond is **Greyabbey** (10.00–19.00, Tue–Sat, 14.00–19.00, Sun; Apr–Sept; £) a one-street village with the ruins of the Cistercian Monastery of Grey Abbey, founded in 1193 by Affreca, daughter of Godred, King of Man, and the wife of John de Courcy. Its chief features are the aisleless church, a good example of 13C Gothic style, with a beautiful west doorway and fine lancets at the east end. The south gable of the refectory is likewise pierced by lancets. It contains several tombs of the Montgomery family.

The road next skirts the wooded grounds of **Mount Stewart** (NT) (**House**: 13.00–18.00, weekends only, Apr–Oct; 13.00–18.00 daily (except Tue), May–Sept; **Gardens**: 10.30–18.00 daily, Apr–Sept; 10.30–18.00, Sun only, Mar; £). the seat of the Marquess of Londonderry and the birthplace of Viscount Castlereagh (1769–1822), who was nearly drowned in the lough in 1786. It is known for its **gardens**, designed by the wife of the 7th Marquess in 1921.

The west end of the mansion, completed by William Vitruvius Morrison in 1828, dates from 1803. There is a painting of the racehorse Hambletonian, by Stubbs. Empire chairs which were used by delegates to the Congress of Vienna in 1815—in which an attempt to settle peace in Europe was made; France agreed to reduce its borders to those of 1790, but Napoleon escaped from Elba before the Congress had ended—and presented to Castlereagh's half-brother, Lord Stewart, at its conclusion are in the dining-room. The octagonal **Temple of the Winds** (1785, by James 'Athenean' Stuart; restored) (opening hours as for house) is an adaptation of the Horologium of Andronikos (c 48 BC) in Athens. The stucco-work is by William Fitzgerald.

Newtownards (Tourist Information, Council Offices, 2 Church St, ☎.01247-812215), now a busy manufacturing centre in an old town, in spite of its name. It dates from 1244, when a Dominican priory (open by request; £) was founded here by Walter de Burgh, the church of which still stands in ruins in Court Square, off Castle St. Of the existing remains the nave is the only original part, the tower having been rebuilt under James I. The Londonderry family vault is in the south-east corner. At the junction of High St and Castle St stands the octagonal Old Cross, reconstituted in 1666 with as many fragments of the original as had survived destruction in the rebellion of 1653. Overlooking the extensive market-place (Conway Square) is the Town Hall (1765; by F. Stratford), revealing the Scottish tradition of stonemasonry. On Bangor Rd, the **Somme Heritage Centre** (10.00–17.00 daily; £) has an interactive exhibition and database on Irish regiments' involvement in World War l, with particular reference to Ulstermen at the Somme. It is among the best presented heritage centres in the country. About a mile east, on the south of the B172, are the 15C remains of the abbey church of Moyvilla (*Magh Bhile*), founded c 540 by St. Finian; several grave-slabs with foliated crosses of the 10C–13C have been built into the north wall.

The A20 leads west from Newtownards to approach the eastern suburbs of Belfast, first passing near **Scrabo Hill**, on which rises a 41m-high Scottish Baronial folly (by W.H. Lynn, 1858) erected as a memorial to the 3rd Marquess of Londonderry. To the right of the road is the dolmen known as **Kempe Stones**, passed before reaching industrial **Dundonald** (with a Rolls-Royce aero-engine factory). The old village centre surrounds a Norman motte.

East Coast ~ Carrickfergus to Glenarm

A direct road (A8) to Larne (20 miles) turns off the M2 motorway 6.5 miles northwest of Belfast, shortly by-passing Ballyclare, a busy market-town, once a centre of the linen industry and now with a synthetic fibre plant. Boneybefore, two miles west of Ballynure, was the birthplace of the grandfather of Andrew Jackson, 7th President of the United States, who emigrated c 1750. The **Andrew Jackson Centre** (10.00–13.00 & 14.00–16.00, Mon–Fri; 14.00–

16.00 Sat & Sun, Apr–May; 10.00–13.00 & 14.00–18.00, Mon–Fri; 14.00–18.00 Sat & Sun, June–Sept; £) examines Jackson's life and times, and traces Ulster-American connections, as does the **U.S. Rangers Centre** (10.00–14.00, Mon–Fri, 14.00–16.00, Sat & Sun, Apr–May; 10.00–13.00, Mon–Fri, 14.00–18.00, Sat & Sun, June–Sept; £), a part of the same complex which details U.S. military presence in Ulster during World War II. Larne lies seven miles northeast of Ballynure.

Larne (Tourist Information, Narrow Gauge Road, ☎ 01574-260088), is a flourishing but dull industrial town. The neighbourhood of Larne has yielded numerous Mesolithic artefacts, including 'Larnean flints'.

This is the terminus of passenger and freight services from Stranraer and Cairnryan (a new road now approaches the ferry terminus and harbour). At the end of a promontory (The Curran) is the stump of a tower, all that remains of the 16C Bisset stronghold of Olderfleet Castle. It was here that Edward Bruce landed in 1315. At the harbour entrance is a reproduction of a Round Tower. The neighbourhood has yielded numerous Mesolithic artefacts, including 'Larnean flints'.

Larne was the scene of the 'gun running' of 25 April 1914, largely organised by Carson for the Unionists, when 24,600 rifles and 3,000,000 rounds of ammunition acquired by Major Frederick Crawford from Hamburg entered Ulster. Between 1914–18 all the illegal arsenals held in Ireland by Unionists and Nationalists were brought in as secret shipments from Germany.

Earlier this century, the stationmaster's wife, 'Amanda McKittrick Ross' (her real name being Amanda Malvina Fitzalan Ann Margaret McLelland Ross, neé McKittrick) wrote those literary curiosities, *Irene Iddesleigh and Delina Delaney* here; intentionally comic romantic novels.

For Carrickfergus, follow the A2 north, skirting the west bank of Belfast Lough, and the suburban 'new town', known as Newtownabbey, beyond which Knockagh, with its conspicuous War Memorial, overlooks the road.

Carrickfergus

Carrickfergus (Tourist Information, Antrim St. ☎ 01960-366455), once a flourishing port, is now a yachting centre, with clothing factories and other small industries. The name 'the Rock of Fergus' recalls King Fergus MacErc, who was shipwrecked off the coast c 320. It was here that the first regular Irish presbytery was established in 1642. William Congreve, Laurence Sterne, and Louis MacNeice spent part of their childhood here. The ancestors of President Andrew Jackson (1767–1845) originated from here.

Carrickfergus Castle (10.00–18.00, Mon–Sat, 14.00–18.00 Sun, Apr–Sept; 10.00–16.00, 14.00–16.00, Sun; £), standing on a rocky spur above the harbour, is the largest Anglo-Norman castle in Northern Ireland. It was begun c 1180 by John de Courcy, who was defeated in 1204 by Hugh de Lacy, Earl of Ulster. In 1210 it was besieged by King John. Edward Bruce, aided by King Robert of Scotland, took it with difficulty in 1316, but it reverted to the English on his death at Dundalk. In 1688–89 it was held for James II by Lord Iveagh, but Schomberg later captured it. Robert Monroe landed the first of several contingents of Scots here in April 1642 to help

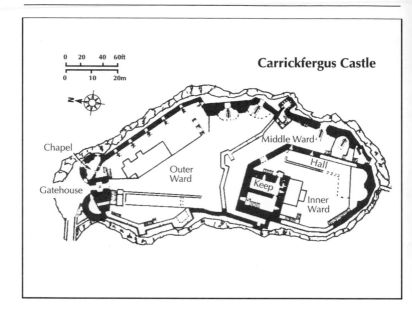

the planters, and William of Orange disembarked here on 14 June 1690. In 1760 it was surprised and occupied briefly by a French expedition under General Thurot, but his squadron was dispersed and he was killed in an engagement off the Isle of Man. John Paul Jones fought a successful battle with HMS *Drake* offshore in 1778. Garrisoned without a break until 1928, the castle now has historical tableaux on the battlements and in the rooms of the keep. The 13C gatehouse opens onto the outer ward; the storehouses on the left date from the 16C. From the inner ward enter the imposing square keep (before 1214), five storeys high (27.5m) with walls 2.5m thick.

The church of **St. Nicholas** (across the main road and left) is contemporary with the castle, with late 12C pillars in its nave. The chancel, which is not in line with the nave, was completed in 1305–6; the skew is thought to symbolise Christ's head on the cross. The church suffered many vicissitudes, notably in the 14C, when the Scots and Irish ravaged the English possessions in Ulster, and in 1513, when the town was again set on fire by the Scots. Considerable restoration took place in 1614; the west tower dates from 1778. The north transept contains the monument of Sir Arthur Chichester, first Earl of Belfast (1563–1625) and his wife and infant son; below is a smaller effigy of Sir John Chichester (d. 1597). Noteworthy in the nave (south side and west end) is the 16C stained glass, brought in 1800 from Dangan House, Co. Meath. The south porch (c 1614) is used as the baptistery.

In Irish Quarter West are the **Carrickfergus Gasworks** (14.00–17.00, Sun, July–Aug; £) which supplied coal-gas to the town 1855–1964. Mechanical exhibits include antique hair dryers and hot water geysers.

The **North Gate** (restored), is the only other ancient building in Carrickfergus, with remains of the town walls, together with Dobbins Inn (17C) in the High St. The blue-painted one-storeyed Town Hall (1797) stands at the north end. **Carrickfergus Knight Ride**, on Heritage Plaza (10.00–18.00 Mon–Sat, 12.00–18.00, Sun; Apr–Sept; 10.00–17.00, Mon–Sat; 12.00–17.00, Sun; Oct–Mar; £), is an audio-visual presentation of the town's history.

Sir Arthur Chichester, c 1625, from the family tomb in St. Nicholas' church

You shortly reach the village of Eden, opposite the demesne of Castle Dobbs (1730; with later additions), built for Arthur Dobbs (1689–1765), Surveyor-General of Ireland, and Governor of North Carolina. To the right lies the ruined church of Kilroot, where Swift worked for a year after his ordination in 1695; he found it uncongenial and abandoned it. His home, in which he wrote *A Tale of a Tub*, was burnt out in 1959 and demolished. It has been suggested that his later *Polite Conversation* was a satire on local provincial society.

1.5 miles north of Eden is the fortified Plantation farmhouse of **Dalway's Bawn** (c 1609), the best surviving example in Ulster.

Island Magee

Whitehead, with its small harbour and scanty remains of Castle Chichester, is near the road to Island Magee. The Whitehead Excursion Station is also the headquarters of the Railway Preservation Society of Ireland and on summer weekends their steam train shuttles to Portrush from Belfast.

The narrow peninsula (seven miles long by two miles broad) separates **Larne Lough** from the open sea. In the reign of Elizabeth I it was held by the Bissett family on the unusual tenure of an annual tribute of goshawks, which breed on the cliffs. The finest of these cliffs, on the east coast, are known as The Gobbins.

Portmuck (northeast side) has a small quay, while Brown's Bay at the northern end, with good beaches, can also be reached by ferry from Larne. The peninsula achieved notoriety for the massacre of 1642, when numbers of the Catholic community are said to have been hurled off the cliffs, presumably in reprisal for the massacre of Protestants in the previous year. It also had a reputation for witchcraft, and the last trial in Ireland for this took place in 1711, when a native of the district was pilloried at Carrickfergus.

Skirt the shore of Larne Lough past Ballycarry (left), the site of the first Presbyterian church in Ireland, founded in 1613. Beyond Magheramorne, with Portland Cement quarries, is the village of Glynn, at the foot of the Valley of Glenoe, with its four waterfalls.

The Coast Road via Black Cave

The finest section of the road, built by Lanyon in the 19C, begins beyond Larne. It skirts the shore below steeply rising basalt or limestone cliffs, passing through a tunnel known as Black Cave, and along Drains Bay (by no means as unattractive as its name might imply), before rounding the bold escarpment of Ballygalley Head. On the right an isolated rock bears the remains of Carncastle, a haunt of the outlawed O'Halloran. The road continues through the village of Ballygally, with a fortified Scottish baronial manor (now an hotel) built by James Shaw in 1625. Glenarm is an ancient village with a small harbour, but covered with a shroud of white dust from adjacent limestone quarries. It was the birth-place of Eóin MacNeill (1867–1945), co-founder of the Gaelic League (which promoted native culture and opposed 'foreign games'; also involved in the revival of the Irish language and Gaelic sports; gaelic football, hurling etc) in 1893. In the glen, approached through a 'medieval' entrance-gate of 1825, stands **Glenarm Castle** (seat of the Earl of Antrim), a quasi-feudal structure begun in 1603 and transformed several times since, notably in c 1825, when it received a Tudor-Revival mask. It was rebuilt after a fire in 1929. The founda-tions of a 15C Franciscan monastery are in the churchyard.

The Glens of Antrim

Carnlough, on the opposite side of the next bay, is a resort at the foot of Glencloy. The coastline becomes abrupt once more, the steep escarpment broken here and there by little dells. Just before you round Garron Point, a road winds up to the left to Garron Tower, a castellated black basalt mansion built by Lewis Vulliamy for Frances, Marchioness of Londonderry, in 1848 (now a school). Knockore, to the southwest, commands a fine distant view of Mull of Kintyre, on the Scottish coast. Just off Garron Point is the isolated chalk stack of Cloghastucan.

Red Bay is perhaps the most attractive part of the coast, carved from the cliffs of Triassic sandstone on the northwest (or Cushendall) side, while to the south the hills gradually recede from the road, their gullies marked by a succession of waterfalls. Waterfoot stands at the outflow of Glenariff river, beyond which the road penetrates a sandstone arch beneath the ridge of Lurigethan, with its promontory fort, passing Red Bay Castle, a ruined MacDonnell stronghold.

The Glens of Antrim is the name given to the series of valleys intersecting the range of hills between Larne and Ballycastle. There are nine: Glenshesk, Glencorp, Glendun, Glenaan, Glenballyemon, Glenariff, Glencloy, Glentaise and Glenarm. Among the more attractive is Glenariff, threaded by the road from Cushendall to Ballymena (18 miles southwest). The finest part of the glen, notable for its waterfalls is approached by a path crossing a bridge on the left (park on the roadside). The road (A43) may be followed to (6.5 miles) Parkmore Station (disused), where the B14 leads back to Cushendall down Glenballyemon, beneath the slope of Trostan (550m), the highest point in Antrim.

Another short trip which includes two of the glens may be made by turning left off the A2, 1.5 miles further north, ascending Glenaan (five miles) to Bryvore Water Bridge. By turning sharp right here, you descend wild Glendun to Cushendun.

Cushendall retains an ancient gaol-tower. The so-called **Ossian's Grave**— pagan poet and hero of the Ulster cycle, who lived in *Tir-na-Nog*, the 'land of youth' and returned 300 years later to be met by St. Patrick and a Christian Ireland—a two-chambered 'horned' cairn, lies two miles west. The ruins of Layde church (with tombs of the MacDonnells), is on the direct road (right) to Cushendun.

Antrim, Ballymena, Ballymoney

The M2 north of Belfast branches left for **Templepatrick**, said to derive its name from the Knights Templar. **Patterson's Spade Mill** (14.00–18.00, Sun & BH, Apr–May & Oct; 14.00–18.00 daily, except Tues, June–Aug; £) in Antrim Road is the last working water-powered spade mill in Ireland. It is a late product of Victorian engineering skills which ceased commercial operations in 1900. Displays explain the manufacture of one of agriculture's most basic tools. **Castle Upton** to the right, once the seat of the Upton family (Viscounts Templeton), was built in 1612 and remodelled in 1788–89 by Robert Adam, who also designed the Upton mausoleum in the churchyard (the mansion may be visited by prior arrangement). Further north, beyond the motorway, rises Donegore Hill, crowned by a prehistoric cairn. The poet and antiquary Sir Samuel Ferguson (1810–86) is buried in Donegore churchyard. The slight remains of Muckamore priory lie 6 miles (left) on the outskirts of Antrim (founded c 550 by St. Colman).

Antrim

Antrim, a linen-spinning town on the Six Mile Water (Tourist Information, Pogue's Entry, Church St, ☎ 018494-428331), is near the north-east corner of Lough Neagh, on which a steamer makes day cruises. The town was burnt in 1643 by General Monro during the Irish rebellion. In 1798 it put up a stout defence and beat off the insurgents who attempted to overthrow British rule, led by Henry Joy McCracken (soon after executed), although Lord O'Neill, their commander, was killed.

The Protestant church, dating from 1596, has a spire of 1816 and some Renaissance glass. Near the Court House (1726) is the Tudor gateway to **Antrim Castle** (enlarged 1662, and rebuilt by John Bowden in 1813), a seat of Viscount Massereene and Ferrard. It was burned down in 1922 (accidentally) but retains its Dutch-style garden, with a T-shaped canal. Railway St leads to the **Round Tower** (28m; with its conical cap restored). It is the only visible remains of the ancient monastery of Aentrebh; the door is almost 3m from the ground, and the rude masonry indicates an early date (c 900).

Belfast International Airport is only four miles south of Antrim, but is more directly approached from the city (14 miles east) by the A52.

Continue northwest on the M2, passing another **Kells**, the seat of a once wealthy priory of very ancient foundation, which has almost entirely disappeared.

Ballymena (Tourist Information, Council Offices, Ardeevin, 80 Galgorm Rd, ☎ 01266-44111), by-passed, now the county town of Antrim with a modern County Hall, owed its prosperity to the linen trade, but its reputation for parsimony, it is known as the 'Aberdeen of Ireland', is no better deserved that of Aberdeen. The old parish church (in Church St) retains a tower of 1721. The motte and bailey of Harryville is in the southern suburbs. 1.5 miles west of Ballymena lies the demesne of Galgorm Castle (17C). Beyond this is the charming village of **Gracehill**, a Moravian settlement of 1746, with a typical central square, and a church of 1765.

The A42 leads northeast of Ballymena, passing an ancient rath, to (three miles) **Broughshane**, a village of no pretensions, but the home of Alexander Brown, founder of America's first bank, at Baltimore. It was also the ancestral home of F.M. Sir George White (1835–1912) who defended the town of Ladysmith for 118 days during the Boer War. The Presbyterian church with an unusual roof, retains its 17C wall.

East of the village rises Slemish (437m), long assumed to be the mountain on which young St. Patrick meditated while tending his master's swine.

The A43 leads north from Ballymena towards the Glens of Antrim (see above) at first ascending a rather boggy upland, before approaching (left) Parkmore Forest, and descending Glenariff to the coast after 18 miles, just south of Cushendall.

The A26 leads almost due north, and is without interest except for its fine avenue of firs. After 11.5 miles, the A44 bears right for (15.5 miles) Ballycastle. To the left of this road, two miles from the turning, is the fine **motte** of Knockaholet, built within a ring-fort. Beyond are the ruins of **Lissanoure Castle** on Lough Guile, originally erected by Sir Philip Savage in the 14C, and rebuilt by Lord Macartney (1737–1806) in 1787 (dismantled in the mid-19C). The road continues towards the coast via Armoy, with a Round Tower 10.5m high.

Twelve miles southeast of Armoy is Kilrea, an angling resort on the Bann. Some 5.5 miles south of Kilrea, on the far bank, in a Georgian mansion at Portglenone, is a Cistercian monastery. Founded in 1951, it was the first in Northern Ireland since the Reformation and contains columns and fireplaces from Ballyscullion (see p421).

Ballymoney (Tourist Information, Council Offices, 14 Charles St, ☎ 012656-62280), a thriving agricultural centre, has a market-house of 1775. The 17C parish church has been superseded by St. Patrick's (1783). James McKinley, grandfather of the William McKinley, 25th President of the United States, was born 3.5 miles north at **Conagher** in 1783. In **Drumabest Bog**, to the east of Ballymoney, four Bronze Age trumpets were found in 1840, and can be seen in the Ulster Museum, Belfast.

Circuit of Lough Neagh

Immediately west of Antrim, the A6 runs beside Lough Neagh. A circuit of the Lake may be made from here; the roads close to the lakeside are uncluttered and there are numerous towns not far from its southern shore. It is by far the largest lake in the British Isles; indeed it is more like an inland sea, being 18 miles (29km) long, 11 miles (17.5km) broad, and 65 miles (104km) round, with an area of almost 400 sq km; it is bordered by every county of Northern Ireland except Fermanagh. Legend relates that the lough was created by the sudden overflow of a fountain which buried many cities, as quoted by Giraldus Cambrensis and alluded to in Thomas Moore's ballad 'Let Erin Remember' (1808):

> Let Erin remember the days of old,
> Ere her faithless sons betrayed her;
> When Malachi wore the collar of gold,
> Which he won from her proud invader;

When the kings with standard of green unfurled,
Led the Red Branch knights into danger;
Ere the emerald gem of the western world
Was set in the crown of a stranger.

On Lough Neagh's bank, as the fisherman strays
When the clear cold eve's declining,
He sees the round towers of other days
In the wave beneath him shining.

Its banks are low and the water level lower than in previous centuries. In many places it is marshy and it contains few islands, none of any size. Ten rivers flow into the lough, and its outflow is the Lower Bann. It contains char, pollan, the gillaroo trout (*giolla ruadh*) and, above all, eels, and is supposed to have petrifying properties. Hawkers used to walk the streets of Belfast with the cry 'Lough Neagh bones, put in sticks and taken out stones'. Also of interest is its marsh flora, ducks and waterfowl, including the great crested grebe.

The road shortly passes (right) a large nylon-making plant, and (left) the lakeside estate of Shane's Castle, with some ruins of the 16C stronghold of Shane O'Neill. John Nash rebuilt it in c 1812 but only the greenhouse survived the fire of 1816.

Randalstown is a linen-bleaching and market-town, known as Mainwater until its incorporation in 1683. The oval Presbyterian church of 1790, was built higher in 1929, when oculi were inserted; also of interest is the 18C former Market House. Randalstown Forest extends to the lakeshore.

At Toome Bridge you return to the Lough, at the mouth of the river Bann. There is a large eel fishery here and several hundred tonnes are caught each season. The next right-hand fork leads north towards the shores of tiny Lough Beg, an expansion of the Bann, and the preserve of pike. On **Church Island** are 12C–13C ruins adjoined by a spire erected by the Earl-Bishop of Derry in 1788. Further north on the lake shore is a fragment of his former palace at **Ballyscullion**, the portico of which now adorns the façade of St. George's church, Belfast. The B18 follows the western shore to Ballyronan.

After Toome Bridge, turn southwest to the market-town of **Magherafelt**, granted to the Salters' Company at the settlement of James I. It has a curious 19C court-house.

On the lakeshore, to the south of Ballyronan, at **Ardboe**, are the remains of an abbey, said to have been the home and burial-place of St. Colman of Dromore (d. 610). Beside the remains of the church is a **High Cross** (over 5.5m), with remarkable sculptures, but its upper part is damaged.

Again turning inland, northwest of Stewartstown is the rath of Tullaghoge, once the residence of the O'Hagans, Justiciars of Tyrone. Each O'Neill chief of Ulster was inaugurated here. The last ceremony was held in 1595, and the inauguration stone was destroyed in 1602 by Lord Mountjoy. The family kept up its connection with the law, however, for the first Lord O'Hagan (1812–85) was twice Lord Chancellor of Ireland.

To the east of Stewartstown a lane leads past the remains of Stuart Hall (c 1760), the seat of Earl Castle Stewart, bombed in 1974 and subsequently demolished, and then south to Mountjoy Castle, overlooking the lake, the ruins of a fortress (1601–5), with good Tudor brickwork.

Coney Island (3 hectares)—from which the American island may derive its name—lies off the southwest bank. Nearer the shore to the west lie the ruins of an O'Connor stronghold, at the mouth of the Blackwater. The B161 proceeds south through Coalisland to the southern shore to the hamlet of **The Birches**, birthplace of Thomas Jackson, the grandfather of General 'Stonewall' Jackson, who emigrated to America in 1765.

The 'new town' of **Craigavon** is less than 2 miles south of Coalisland. Built on a 'lineal' plan (or a 'neo-ribbon' development) it was established in an attempt to reduce the congestion of Belfast. It preserves the names—some say provocatively—of James Craig, first Viscount Craigavon (1871–1940), the first Prime Minister of Northern Ireland (from 1921–40).

Portadown, immediately southwest on the south reach of the river Bann, (Tourist Information, Library, Edward St, ☎ 01762-332499), is almost entirely a 19C development, with linen-weaving and handkerchief factories, and others manufacturing carpets and canning fruit from neighbouring orchards. The embroidered saddle-cloth used by William III at the Boyne, now in the possession of the Orange Lodge, was formerly kept in the Carnegie Library here.

Lurgan (Tourist Information, Library, Carnegie St, ☎ 01762-323912) dates its prosperity from the introduction of the manufacture of linen-damask at adjacent Waringstown (built by Samuel Waring in 1691). After 1607 the district was taken from the O'Neills and given to a planter, Sir William Brownlow, to 'colonise'; the grounds of the Brownlow's mansion, east of the town are now a public park. To the southeast is **Waringstown House** (1682), an early unfortified house (built for William Waring; 1667). Both house and church (with notable woodwork) are good examples of Carolean architecture.

James Logan (1674–1751), one of the founders of Pennsylvania, emigrated from Lurgan in 1699; George W. Russell 'AE' (1867–1935), poet, artist, and patriot (see Dublin) was born here. The first settled Quaker meeting of English Friends in Ireland was held here in 1654 by William Edmundson.

Moira was once famous for its gardens, laid out in the early 18C by Sir Arthur Rawdon. Congal, King of Ulster, was defeated here by Dromhnall, the Ard Rí, in 637.

Ballinderry Church was built in 1665 by Jeremy Taylor, and contains its original furniture. Beyond Ballinderry (north on the A26 towrads Glenavy), is Brookmount, the birth-place of the conductor Sir Herbert Hamilton Harty (1879-1941); he is buried at Hillsborough.

Offshore from Glenavy is **Rams Island**, the largest of Lough Neagh's few islands, with a Round Tower, 13m high, missing its cap.

Lisburn is an industrial town (east of Moira on the A3). The castle grounds have been laid out as a public park. With its conspicuous spire (added in 1804), the **cathedral** (1623, raised to its present rank in 1662) is the most interesting building, and a good example of 'Planters' Gothic', embodying Renaissance detail, but reconstructed in 1708, after the fire which ravaged the town the previous year. Many of the Huguenots who introduced improvements in the manufacture of linen in 1699, under the supervision of Samuel Louis Crommelin (1652–1727) are buried in the churchyard.

Bewley's Coffee shop —
Grafton Street —
(near Stephen's Green)
& Trinity

O'Connel St. - below Trinity
then top of wk

Fitzwilliam Dalkey
As Harbour Cottage

Uncle

Edward Delaney — Mum's brother

Sculptor

Galway Cathedral doors. outside

Thomas Davis' statue — officials + angels

Trinity College

Wolf Tone
St Stephen's Green   (PTO)

In the triangular market square, adjacent to the cathedral, are the 18C Assembly Rooms, now housing the **Lisburn Museum and Irish Linen Centre** (09.30–17.00, Mon–Sat; 14.00–17.30, Sun; Apr–Sept; £). This has a good local history collection and an extensive display devoted to the development of Northern Ireland's most characteristic industry since the 17C.

In Castle St is a mansion (now a Technical College) built on the plan of Hertford House (London) by Sir Richard Wallace (1818–90), who was MP for Lisburn 1873–1885. The only Quaker school in Northern Ireland, founded 1774, is on Prospect Hill.

Saintfield, Hillsborough, Dromore

Leaving Belfast by the A501, follow the Lagan valley, passing through residental suburbs, and the grounds of the Royal Ulster Agricultural Society, to (four miles) **Dunmurry**. There is a fine Presbyterian 'barn' church, above which rises Collin Mountain. To the east is Dixon Park, site of the Rose Show in July.

The A7 leading southeast from Belfast reaches the village of **Saintfield** after five miles, the scene of a sharp engagement on 12 June 1798 between the United Irishmen under Henry Monro, and the Yeomanry under Stapleton. Monro won a momentary success, but pressing on to Ballynahinch he was captured, and soon after hanged at Lisburn. Many of the United Irishmen lie in the graveyard of the Presbyterian church (1777). A mile south are the gardens of **Rowallane**, notable for its rhododendrons and azaleas, now the HQ of the National Trust of Northern Ireland. The philosopher Francis Hutcheson (1694–1746) was born at **Drumalig**, four miles northwest. Known as the 'father of the Scottish school of philosophy' he is best remembered for the much quoted 'That action is best, which procures the greatest happiness for the greatest numbers.' (1725).

Hillsborough

Continuing south of Lisburn (by-passed by the A1), you reach Hillsborough, which either takes its name from Moyses Hill, a settler from Devon, or Sir Arthur Hill (1601?–63), who built the well-preserved fort in the park here in c 1630. William III is said to have spent four nights here en route south during his 1690 campaign. The Gothick tower-house was added in 1758 and the church was rebuilt in 1773 by Wills Hill (1718–93). It contains remarkable Gothick woodwork, an organ of 1772 by John Snetzler, and a monument to Archdeacon Henry Leslie (1580–1661) by Nollekens. The 1st Marquis was largely responsible for the Georgian town. The Market-House, with its cupola, dating from 1790, is by James McBlain.

Hillsborough Castle (1797) formerly a seat of the Marquesses of Downshire, is now the official residence of visiting diplomats to Northern Ireland, and previously (1925–73) of the Governor. It was here, in November 1985, that Margaret Thatcher, former PM of Great Britain, and Garret Fitzgerald, Taoiseach of the Republic, signed the Anglo-Irish Agreement which established inter-governmental agencies, in an attempt to end sectarian and political friction between the two countries, and the two communities in Northern Ireland. The gates (1745; possibly by the Thornberry brothers), brought here in 1936 from Richhill, are amongst the finest in the country. **Hillsborough Fort** (10.00–19.00, Tue–Sat, 14.00–19.00, Sun, Apr–Sept;

10.00–16.00, Tue–Sat; 14.00–16.00, Sun; Oct–Mar) across the village green from the Castle, is a 17C artillery fort remodelled in the 18C.

Harry George Ferguson (1884–1960), inventor of the tractor, was born at Growell, near Hillsborough.

Dromore (also by-passed) on the Lagan, is the ancient ecclesiastical capital of Down, and believed to be the site of an abbey founded by St. Colman (c 510). In James I's reign the see was refounded and the cathedral rebuilt, but this was destroyed in 1641. The present church was erected in 1661 by Jeremy Taylor (bishop in 1661–67), who administered the see together with Down and Connor, which in 1842 were merged into one. Thomas Percy (of the 'Reliques'; bishop in 1782–1811) built the 'Percy Aisle' and rebuilt the tower; both he and Jeremy Taylor are buried here. The badly restored Cross of Dromore (8C–9C) abuts the road.

Above the right bank of the river is a good example of a motte and bailey (late 12C). Two miles west stands the reputedly haunted **Gill Hall** (partially designed by Castle) long in a sad state of decay and now burnt out—the ghost of Lord Tyrone appeared to Lady Beresford here in 1693, to confirm his death, and the existence of God. **Dromara**, six miles southeast, lies in the centre of a former flax-growing district, and from it may be explored a range of hills to the south, culminating in Slieve Croob (534m), on which the river Lagan rises. Craitlieve is to the southwest; south of its summit is the tripod-dolmen of Legananny.

Newtownbreda, on the A24 from Belfast has a parish church built by Richard Castle (1747). At six miles you reach a road junction. Castlereagh Hill, east of Newtownbreda, was the site of a residence of Con O'Neill (d. 1559), the last chieftain of his sept. Two miles to the southwest of Castlereagh (via the B205) is the **Giant's Ring**, a rampart enclosing a dolmen, and the site of several Bronze Age burials.

The right-hand fork (A24) leads due south to (nine miles) **Ballynahinch**, an agricultural town with chalybeate and sulphur springs. Early 19C Assembly Rooms with a Doric timber portico, a parish church of 1772, and a market-house of 1795 are of interest. To the southwest is the demesne of Montalto, with a mid-18C mansion.

On leaving the town, you pass the water-wheel of Harns's Mill. To the southwest rises Slieve Croob (534m) while the road south commands a fine view of the Mourne Mountains.

19 · Armagh and the Mournes

Armagh, in the northwest of the region, is at the heart of the countryside associated with St. Patrick, who according to legend is buried at **Downpatrick**. Saul, Struell and many other sites nearby also have connections with Patrick. Armagh has some of the most interesting Irish 18C architecture outside Dublin, and **St. Patrick's Trian** is devoted to the historic and cultural background of the region. **Armagh Planetarium** uses advanced technology in multi-media presentations of the solar system. **Navan Fort/Emain Macha**, east of Armagh, former seat of the Iron Age Kings of Ulster, is a major archaeological site and interpretative centre.

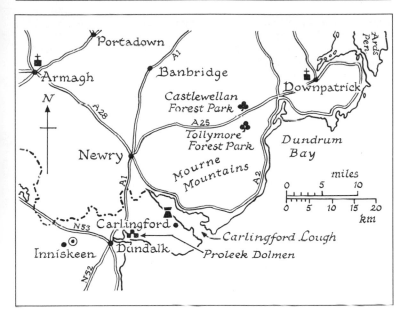

The **Mourne Mountains**, between Newry and the coast, are an attractive range of hills, with **Tollymore Forest Park** providing access to hill-walking and recreational areas in the foothills. Four sections of the **Ulster Way** (19km, 14km, 11km and 8 km) cross the coastal and mountain terrain of the area. The **Tain Way** (40 km) runs through the **Cooley Peninsula** which is associated with events in the great Bronze Age epic of the Ulster Cycle of sagas, the *Táin Bó Cuaiglne* (the cattle-raid of Cooley). The **Ring of Gullion** surrounding Slieve Gullion is an area of outstanding natural beauty, rich in historic remains.

Armagh and Downpatrick have good local museums, and **Ardress House, The Argory** and **Castle Ward** are important 17C–19C houses.

Getting to the area
■ **Train**. Dundalk on the Dublin–Belfast Line.
■ **Air**. Dublin or Belfast Airports.

Listings
Annalong. Glassdrumman Lodge, Mill Road, restaurant, the best of home-produced food, B&B (☎ 01396-768451).
Armagh. Charlemont Arms Hotel, 63 English St, country town hotel (☎ 01861-522028); Calvert's Tavern, 3 Scotch St, seafood (☎ 01861-524186); Dean's Hill, College Hill, fine secluded 18C family home, B&B (☎ 01861-524923).
Banbridge. Bella Vista, 107 Scarva Rd, B&B (☎ 018206-27066); Belmont Hotel, Rathfriland Rd (☎ 018206-62517).
Carlingford. Carlingford Adventure Centre, Tholsel St, hostel, (☎ 042-73100); Jordan's, Newry St, distinguished local restaurant, pub and B&B (☎ 042-73223).

Downpatrick. **Tyrella House**, Clanmaghery Rd, Tyrella, 18C house, private beach, riding, mountain trekking (☎ 01396-85422).
Dundalk. **Derryhale Hotel**, Carrick Road (☎ 024-35471); **The Hazel Tree Restaurant**, Roden Place, vegetarian, organic, excellent (☎ 024-32804).
Newcastle. **The Briars**, 39 Middle Tollymore Park Rd, pleasant B&B (☎ 013967-24347); **Burrendale Hotel and Country Club**, 51 Castlewellan Rd, ultra-modern leisure complex (☎ 013967-22599); **Slieve Donard Hotel**, Downs Rd, rambling red-brick, turreted, fine facilities (☎ 013967-23681).
Newry. **Heritage House**, 21 Derrybeg Lane, B&B (☎ 01693-65119); **Mourne Country Hotel**, 52 Belfast Rd (☎ 01693-67922).
Newtownards. **The Gaslamp**, 47 Court Street, just good food (☎ 01247-811225).
Warrenpoint. **Carlingford Bay Hotel**, 3 Osborne Promenade, family hotel (☎ 016937-73521).

Downpatrick to Rathfriland

Downpatrick

Downpatrick (Tourist Information, 74 Market St, ☎ 01396-612233 and Council Offices, 24 Strangford Rd, ☎ 0396-614331), the ancient county town of Down, overlooks the marshy vale of the Quoile, which flows into the southern end of Strangford Lough. It is an attractive, largely 19C town with fine architecture, set among hills and dominated by its cathedral. The trivallate Dun, 18m high, from which the town is named, lies immediately to the north. Either this, the cathedral hill, or the remains of ramparts to the southwest of the cathedral may be the Rath Celtchair, named after one of the Red Branch Knights. The Knights, a military order in the *Ulster Cycle*, derived their name from the assembly hall at *Emain Macha* (Navan Fort), whose residence it is believed to represent.

> Downpatrick, the referred to in Ptolemy's 'Geography' as 'Dunum', and the *Dun-da-lath-glas* (Fort of the two broken fetters) of Irish chroniclers, was a place of importance before the arrival of St. Patrick, who converted the local prince, Dichu, and founded a monastery on land granted to him. After a period of Viking pillage, the church was rebuilt by Bishop Malachy O'Morgair in 1137. In 1176 John de Courcy took possession of the baronies of Lecale (which included Downpatrick) and Ards, and enlarged the church. It is claimed that he brought the bones of both St. Brigid and St. Columba to lie beside those of St. Patrick.
>
> Having supported Arthur of Brittany against King John, De Courcy was seized while at prayer in the cathedral and his lands were awarded to Hugh de Lacy (1205). The cathedral was burned by Edward Bruce in 1315, and again in 1538 by Lord Leonard Grey, an act of sacrilege to which he largely owed his execution three years later.

From the town centre, English St ascends steeply to the cathedral, passing (right) the New Gaol Gatehouse (1824–30), housing the **Down County Museum** (10.00–18.00 Mon, 14.00–18.00, Sun; June–Aug) which is good on local history. Behind this is the restored **gaol**, dating from 1796. On the left, beyond, stands a mellow red-brick building known as the **Southwell Charity**, erected and founded in 1733 by Edward Southwell as an almshouse and school, and possibly designed by Sir Edward Lovett Pearce.

Downpatrick Cathedral
The cathedral was built in 1790–1827, but it retains some portions of the older building, notably part of the east end (possibly the work of de Courcy), with its recessed doorway and trefoil niches. Within, arcades survive from the 13C, 15C and 16Cs, and the font (retrieved in 1931 from a farmyard after being lost for centuries) is believed to be medieval (11C). The walls are embellished with coats of arms of county families, and several of the early 19C box-pews have semicircular fronts. The rebuilt organ dates from the late 18C. In the wall beside the vestry door is an unusual diminutive figure of a cleric of c 1150, and in the porch is the Cromwell Stone, commemorating Edward, third Baron Cromwell (d. 1607), governor of Lecale. There is a good view of the Mourne Mountains from a terrace behind the cathedral.

The monolith carved with the name *Patric*, purporting to represent the tombstone of the saint, is a bogus antiquity; it was placed there in 1900 by the Belfast antiquarian, Francis J. Bigger (his collection of antiquities is on display in Jordan's Castle, Ardglass). No trace remains of the Round Tower which once stood to the south, but a 10C High Cross, pieced together in 1897 stands near the east end of the cathedral.

The tower (1560) of the parish church (1735), in Church St, to the north of the town centre, may have been part of a castle erected by De Courcy. Thomas Russell (1767–1803), the United Irishman, was executed in Downpatrick and lies in the graveyard. To the southeast in Stream St. is the **Presbyterian church** (1710), with an interesting, largely intact interior.

The Wells of Struell
The Wells of Struell are 1.5 miles east of the town, beside which St. Patrick is said to have built a chapel. Adjacent are a stone-roofed bath-house and a number of smaller well-houses, including the 'eye well' (specifically for eye cures). The buildings, through all of which a stream runs, are believed to be 18C.

A mile to the north, on the direct road from Downpatrick to Strangford, are the scant remains of **Saul Abbey** (12C), where, it is claimed, St. Patrick landed on his first missionary journey, some time after 432. He also died there around 461. Beyond, at **Raholp**, is a primitive church in ruins.

Northwest of Downpatrick and overlooking the river Quoile, are the ruins of **Inch Abbey**, originally founded for Benedictines and refounded for Cistercians by De Courcy in 1187. The most striking feature of the ruins (late 12C) is the group of three pointed windows in the chancel; south of the church are the remains of a quadrangle surrounded by dependencies.

Castle Ward
Heading towards Strangford Lough and the village of Strangford, eight miles northeast, (on the A25) you pass (left) the entrance to the extensive demesne of **Castle Ward** (NT) (13.00–18.00, Sat & Sun, April, Sept & Oct; 13.00–18.00

daily, March–Apr; 13.00–18.00 daily (except Thurs), May–Aug; £). This fine but eccentric mansion was built by an unknown architect for the first Lord Bangor and his wife, Lady Anne, between c 1762–68. He preferred the Classical idiom so the south front was constructed of Bath stone, brought from Bristol in his own ships; she favoured the then-fashionable Gothick. There was no compromise, and the north front reflects the Strawberry Hill style (the couple later separated, understandably). Most of the original furnishings were dispersed before 1827, but the well-restored rooms have been refurnished with contemporary or early 19C pieces, family portraits, and early views of the building. The Laundry should also be visited.

In the grounds are the previous castle of 1610, a Palladian temple, and to the north, overlooking Strangford Lough, the ruined keep of Audley's Castle (c 1500), and a 'double horned' cairn nearby.

Strangford, an attractive little fishing village, lies on the narrow strait between Strangford Lough and the sea opposite Portaferry, with which it is connected by car-ferry (which runs on the half-hour). The castle is a late 16C tower-house, one of many in the neighbourhood.

Ferry sailings ~ Portaferry–Strangford

From Portaferry	Mon–Fri	07.45–22.45
	Sat	08.00–23.00
	Sun	09.30–22.00
From Strangford	Mon–Fri	07.30–22.00
	Sat	08.00–23.00
	Sun	09.30–22.30

The Lecale Peninsula

From Strangford, the circuit of the Lecale peninsula, the low-lying area to the southeast and south of Downpatrick, is easily made, passing through several villages to Clough (22 miles). Kilclief, to the south along the coast road (A2) retains a tower house (c 1430). 5.5 miles beyond pass the ruined medieval church at **Ardtole** and enter **Ardglass**, once the main port of Co. Down and still noted for its herrings. It was protected by seven 'castles' or fortifications, among them the New Works (probably fortified warehouses) erected by a trading company in the reign of Henry IV; and Jordan's Castle, where the planter, Simon Jordan, held out for three years against Tyrone before Mountjoy came to relieve him in 1601.

On **St. John's Point**, south of the next village of Killough, laid out in the 18C, are the remains of a 7C chapel. From here the road follows the coast via Minerstown, on a long beach, to Clough, with its ruined castle. 1.5 miles inland, beyond Minerstown, near **Lagamaddy**, there is a fine double stone circle, important as a link between the 'henge' monuments and the burial mounds.

Castlewellan (open daily, 10.00–sunset; £) south of Clough, a small market town with a wide main street and tree-shaded squares, was laid out by the Annesley family in the 1670s. Their demesne, to the northwest of the town (replaced by a Scots-Baronial style castle by William Burn, 1852; now offices) is open to the public, and contains an arboretum established in 1740. The estate is now owned by the Department of Agriculture, which has nurseries for reafforestation here.

From Castlewellan pass (right) Lough Island Reavy (A25). From Kilcoo, the B8 forks left for (4.5 miles) to **Hilltown**, an angling resort on the Upper Bann. The ruined church of **Clonduff** (the ancient burial-place of the Magennis clan, Lords of Iveagh) is a mile east. If you want to cross the Mourne Mountains, which rise to the southeast, two roads lead from Hilltown; the B27 climbs southeast through the Spelga Pass to the source of the river Bann, skirts a reservoir and turns south below Slieve Muck (670m) before descending to Kilkeel and the B180 runs northeast to Newcastle.

The A25 continues west from Kilcoo to **Rathfriland**, a well-placed Plantation town, beyond which you veer southwest to Newry or north to Banbridge (see below).

South of Clough (A2) is **Dundrum**, a former port. The medieval castle, begun by John de Courcy was dismantled by Cromwellians in 1652. It is partly surrounded by a dry moat cut in the rock, and retains a fine cylindrical keep of c 1230. North of Clough, on the A24 is Loughinisland where three ruined churches can be reached by a causeway.

A right-hand fork just beyond the village leads shortly to **Maghera**, with an old church and stump of a Round Tower. **Tollymore Forest Park** is to the south of Bryansford village. It was long the seat of the Jocelyns, earls of Roden, and has a number of pinnacled gates and a 'hermit's cell' folly overlooking a torrent in the grounds. The house is no longer there but the Bryansford Gate (1786) remains, and the estate is now a forest park noted for its conifers. **Park Field Museum** (no longer functioning) opened in 1965 and was the first environmental centre in the British Isles. It was burnt in 1972, and many valuable specimens associated with the Mourne area were destroyed.

The road continues southwest towards Hilltown (B180), with a fine view ahead of the Mourne Mountains. From east to west rise: Slieve Donard (850m), the highest in the range; Slieve Commedagh; Slieve Bearnagh, and Slieve Meelmore, with Slieve Meelbeg behind it.

Newcastle, the Mourne Mountains, Warrenpoint

The **Mulough Nature Reserve** is on the sand dunes, south of Dundrum, (NT); **Newcastle** is a somewhat characterless resort, but does have a sandy beach. It is dominated by Slieve Donard (852m), which can be climbed with ease. The 'New Castle' (1588), now almost vanished, was built by Felix Magennis at the mouth of the river Shimnagh, where the bridge now crosses it.

The Mourne Mountains

In view wherever you are in this area, although not an extensive range—c 15 miles in length by 8 miles in breadth—these mountains are generally considered to be the most beautiful in Northern Ireland.

The **ascent of Slieve Donard**, the highest peak (2796ft; 852m), may be made by following a path up the north side of the Glen river, behind Donard Lodge. The view from the summit is superb. In clear weather Snaefell, on the Isle of Man, is clearly visible out to sea; the coast of Scotland can be seen to the northeast; to the northwest the mountains of Donegal are sometimes distinguishable, while in the foreground lie the other peaks of the range.

The coast road towards Annalong now climbs, affording several mountain views, and after two miles crosses Bloody Bridge (where a massacre of Presbyterians took place in 1641). A stream descends between Slieve Donard and Chimney Rock.

The explorer Francis Rawdon Chesney (1789–1872), known as the 'father of the Suez Canal'—he travelled extensively in the Middle East and proposed the feasability of a canal route to the Red Sea and India—was born in the granite-quarrying centre of Annalong. Beyond, you approach the fishing-port of **Kilkeel**. Near the north-eastern outskirts is the dolmen of Crabstree Stone. The Kilkeel river descends from the Silent Valley Reservoir, providing water for Belfast and neighbouring towns.

Southwest of Kilkeel, a road passes a large rath adjoining an unroofed 'giant's grave', an *alle couverte* 12m long, and after four miles enters **Greencastle**, where a huge Norman keep (c 1260) guards the entrance to Carlingford Lough. It was once of some importance being the capital of the Kingdom of Mourne, and later one of the main English strongholds in the area. On the far bank of the lough stands Greenore. To its right is Carlingford, behind which rises Slieve Foye (587m). The A2 leads west from Kilkeel, after two miles passing **Mourne Park**, in which is a ruined court cairn and a good trout stream—White Water—which flows through the grounds. On the right bank of the Causeway Water, which you next cross, stands the Kilfeaghan dolmen, with a 35-tonne capstone. The mountains, here a good deal lower, once more approach the coast, with Carlingford Mountain visible on the opposite bank of the lough.

Slievemartin rises steeply above the village of **Rostrevor**. A singular erratic 40-tonne block of stone called Cloghmore stands on the east side of the mountain. An obelisk (William Vitruvius Morrison, 1826), commemorates the birth here of General Robert Ross of Bladensburg (1766–1814), who took Washington on 24 August 1814 during the American wars.

Warrenpoint, two miles west, is an attractive lough-side resort, also with dockyards. The **Burren Heritage Centre** (14.00–18.00, Sat & Sun, Apr–Sept; 09.00–13.00, Mon; 09.00–17.00, Tue–Fri, rest of the year; £) 15 Bridge St, housed in an 1839 National School, illustrates the history and archaeology of the Carlingford and Mourne regions. For Newry (7 miles) follow the dual-carriageway which climbs the bank of the Newry Canal, passing **Narrow Water Castle**, a square tower (restored) built soon after 1560, the bawn of which was altered in the 19C.

Banbridge and surrounds

Banbridge (Tourist Information, Leisure Centre, Downshire Rd, ☎ 018206-23322), by-passed on the Upper Bann, is a prosperous industrial and market-town, with a steep but wide main street, part of which is at a lower level and is bridged by a cross-road. A monument (by W.J. Barre) near the river commemorates Captain Francis Crozier (1796–1848), who was born here, and Sir John Franklin, the Arctic explorer's second-in-command on his last ill-fated voyage (during which the North-West Passage was discovered).

Helen Waddell (1889–1965) the medievalist, is buried at **Magherally**, two miles northeast of Banbridge. A Bronze Age cemetery was excavated to the east of Katesbridge at **Closkelt** in 1973. It is sited on the slope of Deehommed, with its cairn.

The village of **Loughbrickland** (three miles) dates from 1585–1600. At **Emdale** (five miles southeast off the Rathfriland road on the left) are the remains of the cottage in which the Rev. Patrick Brontë (1777–1861)—whose real name was Prunty—father of the more famous sisters, was born.

You pass (4.5 miles; left) **Donaghmore**, in the graveyard of which is a fine 9C–10C High Cross.

Newry

Newry (*An Iubhar*, the yew tree) is named from a yew planted by St. Patrick, according to legend. A Cistercian monastery once stood here. An ancient frontier town, with a small port (Tourist Information, Arts Centre, Bank Parade, ☎ 0693-66232), Newry appears not to have changed much since its condemnation in Swift's critical couplet 'High church, low steeple, Dirty streets, and proud people'. It is connected with the sea at Carlingford Lough by the Newry Canal, begun in 1729 and extending north to Lough Neagh. Richard Castle, the architect, who had come to Ireland in 1728, also worked on the Newry Canal, the first navigational canal built in the British isles. The town's strategic position at the gap in the mountains (known as 'the Gap of the North') that separate the plains of Louth from those of Ulster has brought with it much fighting and hard usage. The original castle was destroyed by Edward Bruce in 1315, and its successor by Shane O'Neill in 1566; the town was set alight by Berwick in 1689.

Among distinguished natives are Lord Charles Russell of Killowen (1832 1900), the lawyer who advocated Home Rule, and leading counsel for Parnell (in 1888–89). John Mitchel (1815–75), Irish patriot and author of *Jail Journal* (1854) is buried in the old Meeting House Cemetery. Samuel Neilson (1761–1803), a founder of the Society of United Irishmen in 1791, was born at Ballyroney, three miles northeast.

Little of old Newry has survived, although some 18C houses can be seen in Upper Water St and Trevor Hill. St. Patrick's church, on the hill, is said to be the first built for the Protestant faith in Ireland, but it was seriously damaged in 1689. The porch retains the arms of the founder, Sir Nicholas Bagenal (1510?–90?), Marshal of Ireland. The **White Linen Hall** dates from 1783, while Francis Johnston may have designed the mansion of 1826 now accommodating the Bank of Ireland. The RC **Cathedral** (1826, Thomas Duff) has a fine if eclectic and much added to interior. **Newry Museum** (10.00–17.00, Tue, Thur & Fri, all year) in Bank Parade has a good section on the canal, local history and archaeology.

Around Newry

West on the A25, where the Dublin-Belfast line crosses the road, is the Egyptian Arch (Dargan, 1851), a convincing example of the Egyptian Revival style and worthy of the Temple of Isis at Philae on the Nile.

Five miles southwest of Newry rises Slieve Gullion (573m) with a passage-grave on its summit. It is surrounded by a natural ring-dyke, known as the **Ring of Gullion**. At **Killevy**, on its eastern slope, is an old church, two in fact (9C and 13C), with a huge lintel over the west door. The hills which form the Ring are covered by rough landscape and form part of the historic natural defences of Ulster.

A mile-and-a-half northwest is **Derrymore House** (NT: adm. by appointment), a late 18C thatched cottage orneé built for Isaac Corry, MP, and last Chancellor of the Irish Exchequer. The Act of Union is said to have been drafted here in 1800.

Some two miles east on the Hilltown road, is Crown Mound, a motte and bailey 180m round.

Armagh and Navan Fort

From Portadown the A3 passes southwest through a fruit-growing district. with **Kilmore**, on the right. What appears to be a Round Tower, built into the massive square tower of the church, is in fact a medieval staircase. Towards Armagh (11 miles) is the village of **Richhill**. There is an imposing Dutch-style manor (1664–90). The family of Francis Johnston, the architect, came from here.

Armagh

■ Tourist Information. Bank Building, 40 English St, ☎ 01861-527808.
■ Library. Market House, Market St, ☎ 01861-524072.

Armagh has long been the ecclesiastical capital of Ireland. It is the seat of both Protestant and Catholic archbishops and is rich in historical associations. Because of its importance, it has suffered more from fire and slaughter than most towns of its size. Nevertheless a number of 18C buildings have survived, while the names of some of its principal streets—Scotch St and English St—recall the fact that it lay roughly on the border between the English and Scottish 'plantations' of Ulster, the former towards Tyrone, the latter towards Down.

The name *Ard Macha* (Macha's height) commemorates a legendary queen (4C BC), but there is little doubt that St. Patrick built a church on a hill called *Druim-saileach* (ridge of sallow) within a short distance of the pagan sanctuary of Emania. The plan of the rath surrounding the site of the church is still clear from the layout of the streets. It became a centre of monastic scholarship and attracted the attentions of acquisitive Vikings in 841, and later of pillaging Anglo-Normans. The High King Brian Ború and his son were brought here for burial after the Battle of Clontarf (1014).

In 1566 the town was sacked by Shane O'Neill, who was subsequently excommunicated. St. Malachy (1096–1148), John Richardson the divine (1664–1747)—whose *Proposal for the conversion of the Popish Natives of Ireland* (Dublin 1711), advocated the ordination of Irish-speaking ministers—and the architect, Francis Johnston (1761–1829) were born here, as was the organist and composer Charles Wood (1866–1926). A native of the county was the Rev. Gilbert Tennent (1703–64), one of the founders of the 'Log College' at Neshaminy, which became Princeton University.

On the left of the approach from Belfast is the Mall, above which on College Hill is the **Royal School**, founded by James I in 1608, and enlarged since, accommodated in a building of 1774, by Thomas Cooley. Amongst its pupils was Viscount Castlereagh and the disreputable Frank Harris, author of confessional and salacious autobiographies and other works. *My Life and Loves* (1923) was banned in Britain as pornography. Opposite is the **Armagh Planitarium**

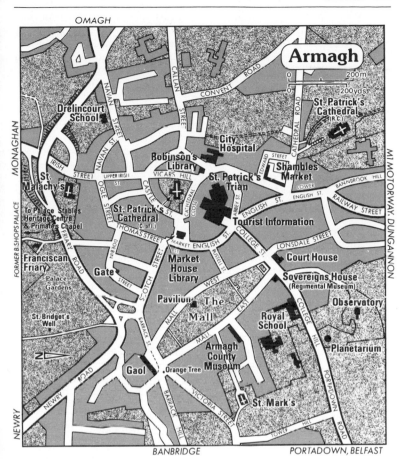

OMAGH

Armagh

0   200m
0   200yds

MONAGHAN

St. Patrick's Cathedral (R.C.)

Drelincourt School

NAVAN STREET

CALLAN STREET

CONVENT ROAD

CATHEDRAL ROAD

City Hospital

Robinson's Library

VICARS HILL

HOWARD STREET

Shambles Market

St. Patrick's Trian

BANNBROOK HILL

St. Malachy's

IRISH STREET

UPPER IRISH ST.

OGLE STREET

CASTLE ST.

CATHEDRAL CLOSE

ABBEY ST.

ENGLISH ST.

ENGLISH ST.

TOWER

RAILWAY STREET

M1 MOTORWAY, DUNGANNON

St. Patrick's Cathedral (C. of I.)

To Palace Stables Heritage Centre & Primates Chapel

FORMER B.SHOPS PALACE

FRIARY ROAD

THOMAS STREET

DOBBIN ST.

Tourist Information

COLLEGE ST.

LONSDALE STREET

Franciscan Friary

Palace Gardens

Gate

SCOTCH STREET

STREET

MARKET ENGLISH ST.

RUSSELL ST.

Market House Library

Court House

Sovereigns House (Regimental Museum)

St. Bridget's Well

BARRACK ST.

Pavilion

The Mall

MALL WEST

MALL EAST

Royal School

COLLEGE HILL

Observatory

Planetarium

PORTADOWN ROAD

Gaol

Orange Tree

Armagh County Museum

NEWRY ROAD

BARRACK STREET

VICTORIA STREET

St. Mark's

TOWER HILL

NEWRY

BANBRIDGE   PORTADOWN, BELFAST

(10.00–16.45 Mon–Fri; 13.15–16.45 Sat & Sun; £). The Observatory here (possibly by Francis Johnston) has been in continuous use since established by Archbishop Richard Robinson in 1791 and a Planetarium was opened in 1968. There is now a Hall of Astronomy (containing models of space-craft) and an Observatory open to the public.

Facing the north end of the Mall, a rectangular green, partly surrounded by Georgian houses, is the **Court House** (restored), an attractive work by Francis Johnston (1805–9).

County Museum

The County Museum (10.00–17.00 Mon–Fri; 10.00–13.00 & 14.00–17.00, Sat; £), on the east side of the Mall, illustrates the life and history of the town and county of Armagh. The Ionic building (1833) was once a school and opened in its present form in 1937. Among paintings are *Girls on a beach*, and a

Self-portrait, by G.W. Russell; and a naïve *View of Armagh* in 1810 by James Black (murdered in 1829). One section is devoted to folk craft (wood and metalwork, pottery and china, needlework; lace and linen manufacture), another to costumes (including uniforms of Armagh militia, yeomanry and volunteers, and of the Royal Irish Fusiliers). There are also rooms on the local ornithology and wild life, geology and a display of prehistoric artefacts found in the region, and general 'Armachiana'. The **Regimental Museum of the Fusiliers**, whose headquarters are in Armagh, stands at the north-east corner of the Mall.

The Boer War memorial is by Kathleen Shaw (1905), and from the south end of the Mall, overlooked by an imposing gaol, Scotch St leads up to the centre. No. 36, a Georgian town house built for Leonard Dobbin, has been restored. Its garden, in the course of excavation, may have been the site of St. Patrick's original church. From the Market House (1742; altered 1815), now a technical school, steep streets climb the cathedral hill (the ancient rath).

The Protestant cathedral

The cathedral, with a battlemented central tower, owes its present appearance mainly to Richard Robinson (1709–94), archbishop from 1765 and later Lord Rokeby of Armagh, and to Lord John Beresford (1773–1862), archbishop from 1822. It is a plain well-proportioned building in the Perpendicular Gothic style, extensively restored in 1834–37 by Lewis Cottingham. Beneath is a 12C crypt. The interior contains some good 18C–19C monuments, including that of Sir Thomas Molyneux (1661–1733, by Roubiliac); Archbishop Robinson (by Nollekens); and a recumbent statue of Dr Peter Drelincourt (1644–1722), Dean of Armagh from 1691 (by Rysbrack). There are also two fragments of an 11C market cross. The north transept contains 17C memorials to the Caulfeild family, Earls of Charlemont, sculptured fragments from earlier cathedrals and pre-Christian idols. Hanging in the north nave arcade is a French standard captured at Ballinamuck by the Armagh militia in 1798.

To the southwest, following the bank of the hill-fort of Ard Macha, is rebuilt Castle St (1730–40). To the northwest is the **Cathedral Library**, designed by Cooley, and endowed by Archbishop Robinson in 1771, with a Greek inscription above the entrance ('the healing of the mind'), and among the more important collections in Ireland.

In English St is **St. Patrick's Trian**, an interpretative centre which illustrates the history of Armagh from pre-Christian times to the present. There is also a child-centred section based on Swift's *Gulliver's Travels*. From here descend (right) past the Infirmary (1744; by George Ensor) and (left; at the bottom of the street) the Shambles (1827–29) to (right) Cathedral Rd.

Tanderagee Iron Age stone idol, St. Patrick's Cathedral

The twin-spired **Catholic cathedral**, also dedicated to St. Patrick, was begun by Thomas Duff in 1838 and completed by J.J. McCarthy in 1873. It stands at the head of a long flight of steps, on the upper terrace of which are the statues of the two archbishops under whom the cathedral was commenced and finished. The interior has been altered and 'improved' by successive architects as well as changes in liturgical direction, and presents a rather confusing clash of styles.

Southwest of the Protestant cathedral, in Navan St, are the buildings of Drelincourt's School (1740); while to the south, entered from Friary Rd, is the demesne of the (old) **Archbishops' Palace** (prior to 1767, to the design of Cooley), with a porticoed chapel of 1781, and a Classical interior. The **Palace Stables Heritage Centre** (10.00–17.30, Mon–Sat; 13.00–18.00, Sun, Apr–Sept; 10.00–17.00, Mon–Sat, 14.00–17.00, Sun, Oct–Mar; £) has been set up in the old stable block. Near the gate are the ruins of a Franciscan friary, founded in 1266, and destroyed 1565; and on an adjacent hill a huge obelisk, raised by Archbishop Robinson.

Navan Fort, or Emain Macha

An ancient coach road, leading due west from the cathedral hill, crosses the Callan by a charming old bridge, beyond which is St. Patrick's Well (a gnarled thorn bush is decked with votive offerings left by present-day pilgrims). **Navan Fort** (*Emain Macha*) rises 1.5 miles further on the right. This huge elliptical mound (view) occupies the site of Emania, the legendary palace of the Kings of Ulster for over 600 years. It was said to have been founded by Queen Macha, and was the headquarters of *Cu Chullain*, the heroic defender of Ulster in the *Táin Bó Cuailnge* and the Red Branch Knights under Conor MacNessa. In c 450 it was overrun by tribes from Connacht and the city and palace irreparably destroyed. It is the most significant pre-historic site in Northern Ireland, due to its complex and mysterious background as a centre of settlement and ritual.

In a building skilfully designed to blend into the landscape, the **Navan Visitor Centre** explains the history and archaeology of this important sequence of earthworks with a multi-media presentation.

From Armagh the A28 leads directly southeast to Newry via (6.5 miles) Markethill and **Gosford Castle**, the former seat of the Earl of Gosford. A later castellated pile in the Norman-Revival style was built by Thomas Hopper from 1819–39; it has been used to store public records in recent years, but its Forest Park is open to the public.

Alternative route from Armagh to Newry

A more interesting route is that via Tandragee, 11.5 miles due east from Armagh on the A51, passing Hamilton's Bawn (five miles), built in 1619 and destroyed in 1641, it was the subject of a poem by Swift

Thus spoke to my Lady, the Knight full of Care;
Let me have your Advice in a weighty Affair.
This Hamilton's *Bawn*, while it sticks on my Hand,
I lose by the House what I get by the Land;
But how to dispose of it to the best Bidder,
For a *Barrack* or *Malt-House*, we must now consider'
'The Grand Question debated' (Jonathan Swift, 1735)

There is a crannóg further east, at Marlacoo Lake. **Tandragee** (or Tanderagee), on the Cusher, a good trout stream in pleasant country, is dominated by its castle (c 1837), occupying the site of a fortress of the O'Hanlons, whose territory was confiscated under James I (it has been degraded to house a potato-crisp factory!). Count Redmond O'Hanlon (d. 1681), a descendant of the O'Hanlons, outlawed leader of a band of 'Tories', those dispossessed in the Cromwellian wars, and who levied tribute on the Ulster colonists from their stronghold on Slieve Gullion during the years 1671–81, was captured and shot, his head displayed on a spike at Downpatrick gaol, and is buried in the graveyard of **Ballynaback**, to the north of Scarva.

Follow the depression—once a boggy wilderness—that marks the boundary between Armagh and Co. Down. After two miles you by-pass (left) **Scarva**, the rendezvous of William III's armies in June 1690 before they marched to the Boyne. A gathering commemorates the event here annually (13 July) by the **Mock Fight**, where the battle is re-enacted by Orangemen (without casualties). In the demesne of **Scarva House** (c 1717; adm.) is a section of the **Dane's Cast**, the prehistoric earthen rampart that marked the ancient boundary of the kingdoms of Ulidia (North Ulster) and Oriel (Armagh and Lough). It remains distinct as far as Poyntz Pass and can be traced as far south as Jonesborough, beyond Newry. Cairn Cochy, a heap of stones 21m high, marks the site of a legendary battle in AD 332. To the east, at Lisnagade, is an extensive trivallate ring-fort.

Poyntz Pass (nine miles from Newry) takes its name from Sir Toby Poyntz, who in June 1646 defended the road into Down here against Hugh O'Neill, Earl of Tyrone. 'Tyrone's Ditches' in the demesne of Drumbanagher (right) still mark the Irish entrenchments.

Dundalk, Inniskeen, Cooley Peninsula, Carlingford

Before entering Dundalk on the N1 from Dublin and Drogheda you pass Dromiskin. Here the lower half of a Round Tower, which serves as a belfry, is all that remains of a monastery whose abbot was St. Ronan (d. 664). In the churchyard are the upper part of a sculptured cross and a ruined medieval church (13C–15C).

Dundalk

Dundalk (Tourist Information, Market Square, ☎ 042-35484, by-passed), the county town of Louth, is a prosperous manufacturing town, with breweries, printing-presses, and engineering works, and with a safe harbour at the head of its bay. The original dún (*Dún Dealgan*, Dealga's fort), was the motte of Castletown, a tumulus 2.5km west. This is the possible birthplace of the legendary hero Cuchulainn, who also died near here, defending this key position on the road to the north (see Clochafarmore, below, p437). The first name given to the present town was *Tráigh Baile* (Stradbally). Its subsequent history is one record of sieges. Edward Bruce, crowned King of Ireland in 1316, captured Dundalk the following year, but was also killed nearby in its defence in 1318. Later walled, it underwent six sieges between 1560 and 1650 (besieged by Hugh O'Neill, Earl of Tyrone in 1595, Phelim O'Neill in 1641 and the Cromwellian forces in 1648, among others), and its remaining fortifications were dismantled in the mid-18C. French weavers were brought over to start a cambric manufactory here in 1737, established by the Irish Linen Board.

The town was burned during the 'troubles' of 1922–23. In the town centre is **St. Patrick's church** (RC; c 1840), by Thomas J. Duff, in the style of King's College Chapel, Cambridge. In startling contrast is the **Doric Court House** (1813–18) to the north, by Edward Parke and John Bowden, its façade based on the Temple of Theseus, as published in James Stuart's *Antiquities of Athens* (1762).

To the east, off Castle Rd, is the 15C tower of a Franciscan friary (1240); the rest was destroyed in the 16C. In parallel Chapel Rd, nearer the centre, are the slight remains of a convent of Augustinian Crutched Friars. To the right of the main street leading north to the bridge is St. Nicholas (C. of I.), rebuilt in 1689 with the exception of its medieval tower, and altered early in the 19C by Francis Johnston. In well restored late 18C warehouses in Jocelyn St, is **Louth County Museum** (10.30–17.30, Mon–Sat, 14.00–18.00, Sun & BH, all year; £) which concentrates on the industrial history of the region. Adjoining the Dún, on which a folly was erected in 1780, is Bellow's Castle (1472–79), with a well-preserved keep with square angle turrets and crenellated parapets.

The interesting 13C fortress of **Castleroch** lies 6.5km northwest of Dundalk.

Louth and St. Mochta's House

An interesting brief detour may be made to Louth by following the R171 from Dundalk, bearing right off the direct road driving southwest, after 8km passing (right) Stephenstown House (1750). At **Clochafarmore**, (5.5km) you pass (left) a standing-stone associated with the death of Cuchulainn. He tied himself to the stone and allegedly kept the army of Queen Maeve at bay single-handed, until a raven alighting on his shoulder intimated to his enemies that he was dead (a scene commemorated in the GPO in O'Connell St, Dublin).

Louth, now a mere village, was once the chief place of the county. The religious house founded here by St. Patrick became one of the most famous in Ireland, producing (it is said) 100 bishops, but in the 9C it was pillaged by the Vikings. The present ruins are those of an abbey founded by Dermot O'Carroll, Lord of Oriel, in 1148. Near the abbey is **St. Mochta's House** (restored), a small oratory dedicated to the saint (d. 534) who was a companion of St. Patrick.

At **Inniskeen**, 7km north of Louth on the river Fane, is an imperfect Round Tower, all that remains of the monastery of St. Deagh (d. 560), the successor of Mochta. Patrick Kavanagh (1904–67), the most important poet writing in Ireland after the death of W.B. Yeats, was born here. The **Patrick Kavanagh Rural and Literary Resource Centre** (10.00–17.00 daily; annual literary weekend held in November), promotes understanding of his work. The surrounding area—the source of much of Kavanagh's poetry—is now being promoted as 'Kavanagh Country.'

From Dundalk, the R177 leads northwest, reaching the border at 9km, and continues as the A29. Three miles beyond, the left-hand turn leads to **Crossmaglen**, its large market square dominated by a British Army base, a frequent target of terrorist attacks. North of the base is the well-preserved prehistoric grave of Annaghmare.

The main road (B135) shortly skirts (right) the Dorsey, an extensive entrenched oval enclosure (120 hectares), probably contemporary with the Black Pig's Dyke, (see Ch.13), before entering Newtownhamilton. Veer northwest via Keady for Armagh (16 miles), also approached by a minor road (B31) forking right and driving direct through wooded country between Deadman's Hill (right) and Carrigatuke (366m).

5km beyond Dundalk the main road to Newry passes (left) the hill of **Faughart**, an ancient fort 11.5m high, where Edward Bruce was killed in 1318 in a battle against Sir Edward Bermingham.

You soon begin to ascend Ravensdale, the valley of the Flurry, gradually leaving behind the pastoral lowlands. In the next valley to the west is the Moyry Pass, where Hugh O'Neill barricaded the road (further west) into Ulster for five years (1595–1600). The square tower was built by Lord Mountjoy (1601). You shortly reach the border-post, with Slieve Gullion (573m) rising abruptly to the left, and after four miles enter Newry.

The Cooley Peninsula

Just north of Dundalk, turn right off the N1 onto the R173, for the Cooley Peninsula. The road runs along the northern side of Dundalk Bay, at Ballymascanlan passing near the **Proleek Dolmen**, 3.5m high, adjoining a passage-grave. After 17.5km the road turns north through **Grange**, with its quaint little church of 1762, passing to the west of **Greenore**, once the terminus of a ferry from Holyhead and since 1960 revived as a freight port.

Carlingford, charmingly situated on its lough, commands good views of the Mourne Mountains rising beyond its far shore, Slieve Foye (587m) being the highest. The town is said to have formerly possessed 32 'castles' in the days of the Pale, when every house on this border outpost was more-or-less fortified.

The first historic building seen as you enter is the **Abbey**, a Dominican house founded in 1305 by Richard de Burgh; the church has a square central tower and two west turrets. It is now **Holy Trinity Visitor Centre** 12.00–17.00, Mon–Fri, Easter–May; 11.00–17.00 daily, June–Aug; 12.00–17.00 weekends only, rest of year; £), dealing with the history of the town. Further on, to the right, is the parish church, also with a medieval tower; below it **The Mint**, a square tower with grotesque 15C Celtic-Revival carvings on its windows. Beyond this is the **Tholsel**, in part a rudely constructed town gate. In the main street is a square keep known as **Taaffe's Castle**. A short walk brings you to **King John's Castle**, built in 1210 by John de Courcy, a massive ruin occupying a horseshoe-shaped site overlooking the lough, and enclosing a courtyard with a loopholed gallery.

Omeath is a small resort opposite Warrenpoint. For Newry, cross the border just south of the viewpoint of Flagstaff and adjacent Fathom Wood (a bird sanctuary). The road skirts the **Newry Canal** and soon enters Newry.

20 · The Boyne Valley

The small territory covered in this chapter is exceptionally rich in historic sites, principally located in County Meath, but also in portions of the adjoining counties of Westmeath and Louth. The passage graves of the Boyne Valley Necropolis, **Dowth**, **Knowth** and **Newgrange** are the most impressive and significant antiquities of the Neolithic period in Europe, while to the east lies the extensive Iron Age cemetery of **Loughcrew**. As well as remains from prehistory, there are important sites and significant ruins from later periods; the **Hill of Tara**, (site of the palaces of the Celtic High Kings), early Christian monastic sites at **Kells** and **Monasterboice**; medieval and Anglo-Norman sites at **Drogheda**, **Trim**, and **Ardee** and medieval abbeys at **Bective** and **Mellifont**. **Slane Castle** is the most substantial 18C mansion in the region. Here also is the site of the **Battle of the Boyne** (1690), one of the last significant battles fought on Irish soil, in which the army of the Protestant William III (William of Orange) defeated that of his father-in-law, Catholic James II; significant for its relevance to the politics of contemporary Ireland.

Getting to the area
■ **Train**. Drogheda on Dublin-Belfast line.
■ **Air**. Dublin International Airport.

Listings
Ardee. **Red House**, Dundalk Rd, 19C former home of Chichester Parkinson-Fortesque, friend of Edward Lear, B&B, indoor heated pool (☎ 041-53523).
Castlebellingham. **Spenser House**, Kilsaran, patrician 18C house, racing stables, B&B (☎ 042-72254).

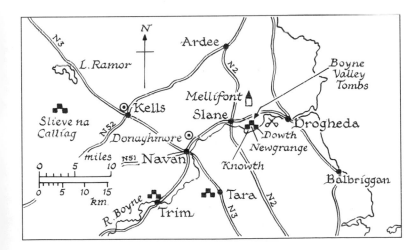

Drogheda. The Buttergate, Millmount Centre, attractive restaurant (☎ 041-34759); **Kieran Brothers**, 15 West St, shop-café (☎ 041-38728).
Duleek. Annesbrook, Classical country-house, B&B (☎ 041-23293).
Kells. Lennoxbrook, Carnaross, country-house B&B (☎ 046-45902); **Kells Hostel** (☎ 046-40100); O'Shaughnessy's, pub-food (☎ 046-41110).
Oldcastle. Loughcrew House and School of Gilding, country-house B&B, residential courses (☎ 049-41356).
Navan. Bermingham's, Ludlow St, traditional pub, good interiors (☎ 046-30055); **Hudson's**, Railway St, fine local restaurant (☎ 046-29231); **Swynnerton Lodge**, Black Castle, 19C fishing lodge on River Boyne, fishing rights, B&B (☎ 046-21371).
Newgrange. Newgrange Farm and Coffee Shop, on working farm (☎ 041-24119).
Slane. Conyngham Arms, gracious country town hotel (☎ 041-2415).
Trim. Bounty Pub, Bridge St, pub-grub (☎ 046-31640); **Knightsbrook House**, charming Gothick Folly, B&B (☎ 046-36740); **Wellington Court Hotel**, Summerhill Road, family hotel (☎ 046-31516).

Slane and the Boyne Valley Necropolis

From Dublin the N2 leads directly to Slane, passing some interesting wayside-crosses at Balrath, including a 16C cross 'beautified' in 1727. This cross carries two inscriptions, 'Orate-P-Aia Johanis Broin' (pray for the soul of John Broin) c !6C and 'Sr Andrew Aylmer of Mountaylmer Bart and his Lady Catherine Aylmer had this cross beautified AD 1727.' The **White Cross**, a far more elaborate monument, one of those erected in the neighbourhood during the late 16C by local benefactor, Dame Jennet Dowdall, is 2.5km to the east. On the east face is a Crucifixion, on the west face a Virgin and child in high relief, and the arms of the Bathe and Dowdall families. The crosses are important as the last flowering of the Irish high cross tradition.

The first stone church (*Damhliag*, stone church) in Ireland, at **Duleek** (turn east on the R150) is said to have been built by St. Patrick, and put in the charge of St. Cianan (Keenan). This was succeeded by a priory founded in 1182, of which the ruined church remains (adjacent to a gutted church), with tombs of the Bellew family and a cross of the Kells type. In the village is another cross (1601), erected by Dame Dowdall, and the castellated gateway of the demesne of the extinct earls of Thomond. Duleek House (c 1750, by Castle or his school). Drogheda lies 7.5km further northeast.

Descending to and crossing the Boyne, you enter **Slane**, a pleasant village with four matching Georgian houses facing each other diagonally in its centre. It was the birthplace of poet Francis Ledgwidge (1891–1917), killed at Ypres aged 26, in 1917. The **Francis Ledwidge Cottage Museum** (10.00–13.00 & 14.00–19.00 daily, Mar–Oct) contains memorabilia.

On a hill to the northwest (view) of Slane are the ruins of **Slane Friary** and College, rebuilt in 1512. Nothing remains of the earlier foundation although the church was used for worship until 1723. A large rath, 8m high stands on the west side of the hill. On the river bank near the parish church is the Hermitage of St. Erc, a Gothic ruin of various dates, dedicated to the first bishop of Slane, who mortified his flesh by standing all day up to his armpits in the Boyne. A five-storey flour-mill (1766) on the Boyne here, is well worth seeing; designed by David Jebb, engineer of the local canal works on the Boyne, it was described by Arthur Young as a 'handsome edifice, such as no mill I have seen in England can be compared with it'.

A short distance west is **Slane Castle**, its demesne set behind imposing gates (by Francis Johnston). It is a fine Gothick-Revival house incorporating an earlier castle built for William Burton Conyngham from 1785, largely by Wyatt and Johnston, with a round ballroom and library (the work of Thomas Hopper) with an ornate traceried ceiling. It was twice visited by George IV who had a penchant for Lady Conyngham (his portrait, by Lawrence, hangs here); the second visit was made in August 1821, after he became king. The castle was seriously damaged by fire in 1994; the demesne is a venue for outdoor pop-concerts.

The Boyne Valley Necropolis

'Boyne Valley Art', motifs from decorated kerbstone K67, Newgrange

The area between Slane and Drogheda (14km) contains perhaps the most impressive Neolithic passage-graves extant. The N51 (east) passes near the necropolis of **Brú** (pronounced 'Broo') **na Bóinne**, 'the palace of the Boyne' as it was known in early chronicles and legends, with the three great tumuli of Dowth, Knowth and Newgrange, visible on a ridge above the river Boyne. There are 26 such tumuli in the Boyne valley, approximately ten per cent of all those in Ireland. They can be reached by turning right 3km east of Slane.

■ **Note**. Newgrange and Knowth can only be visited from the starting point at the **Brú na Bóinne Visitor Centre** (09.30–18.00 daily; OPW; £), access by guided tour only.

The remarkable **Newgrange Tumulus**, unsurpassed among European passage-graves for size and decoration, rises to the southeast. The huge cairn of stones, 80m in diameter and 13.5m high, is surrounded by a circle of 12 of the estimated 38 monoliths originally there (Professor M.J. O'Kelly's 1962–76 excavations indicated that these post-date the tumulus). Within them is a ditch, and the base of the cairn itself is encircled by a kerb of 97 large stones carrying a dry-stone wall. Many of these stones are incised with complex and sophisticated spiral and other motives, now called 'Boyne Valley art', the original meaning of which is a subject of much debate, but it is more than likely that the designs are of astronomical significance. These motifs have been incised into the boulders by repeated tapping with smaller stone implements. There are some 700 inscribed stones distributed between the passage-graves of the Boyne; the largest known corpus of Neolithic art.

In front of the main entrance on the south side is the famous **Threshold Stone**, carved with the 'Triskel', a triple spirals motif which is unique to Newgrange, as well as concentric circles, diamonds, and other designs. Above the entrance is the 'roof box', an aperture in the roof of the passage, like a window, through which the sun's rays can penetrate. A passage 1m wide, almost 19m long, and

1.5–2.5m high, faced with huge slabs, some also incised, leads to the tomb itself. A lofty corbelled chamber, almost 6m high, it contains three recesses, richly decorated, each of which contain a hollowed stone basin, that in the east has a double depression. Only on 21 December, the mid-winter solstice, and some days before and after this date each year will the first rays of sunlight enter the passage through the roof-box and briefly illuminate the chamber. Radiocarbon-dating has confirmed that the tomb was constructed around 3100 BC, some centuries before the Egyptian pyramids, with which the Boyne valley tombs share the general principle of a large structure protecting a small interior burial chamber. It is believed that the tombs were built to hold the remains of the priest/kings of this Neolithic society of which little is known.

The improbable external restoration of the tumulus has been a source of considerable controversy and there is clearly a conflict between the architec-tonic tidiness of the reconstructed quartzite revetment (a retaining wall, held in place with concrete), and the rough megalithic nature of the original structure. The fact that the excavated remains contained large quantities of quartzite, which must have collapsed from above the kerb, does not of course prove the veracity of the current reconstruction, which has an unfortunate municipal look to it. It is interesting that the quartz had been originally quarried some 80km south, near Wicklow, and the sea-rolled pebbles, with which the revet-ment is peppered, had been gathered some 130km north in Co. Down.

In AD 861–62 the tomb was rifled of anything portable by the Vikings, who called it the cave of Acadh-Aldai.

The mound of **Knowth**,(Cnogba), dates from pre-3000 BC; earlier than Newgrange. Encircled by a kerb and 15 satellite tombs, it retains the largest collection of **passage grave art**, and is penetrated by two passage-graves of dissimilar construction (the eastern tomb is lit by the sun during the equinox), discovered during the excavations by Professor George Eogan in the 1970s–80s. The surface of the mound is honeycombed with souterrains or underground chambers mostly used for food storage, from the early-Christian period.

Rosnaree (the wood of the kings) lies to the west, on the far bank of the river. The legendary Iron Age King, Cormac of Tara was buried here at his own request, all efforts to carry his body across to Brú na Bóine being foiled by a sudden rising of the river which is comemmorated in a poem by Sir Samuel Ferguson

> Dead Cormac on his bier they laid:-
> "He reign'd a king for forty years,
> And shame it were", his captains said,
> "He lay not with his royal peers".
>
> And as the burial train came down
> With dirge and savage dolorous shows,
> Across their pathway, broad and brown
> The deep, full-hearted river rose.

Samuel Ferguson 'The Burial of King Cormac'

It was here on 12 July 1690 that the Williamites, who's magic was superior, crossed to turn the Jacobites' left flank (see Battle of the Boyne, p445).

From Newgrange, the lane zig-zags northeast to the great mound of **Dowth** (£), (*Dubhadh*) encircled by a stone kerb and pierced by two passage-graves, one of which, (difficult of access), is entered by a passage 8m long. Dowth Castle is a ruin, as is the medieval church, probably built from stones from a vanished outer ring of the tumulus.

To the east is **Dowth Hall** (c 1764) containing important late Rococco plasterwork in all the principal ground floor rooms, possibly by Robert West. The eccentric 6th Viscount Netterville who built it is said to have attended mass by sitting on top of the mound of Dowth and training his telescope on a distant chapel. John Boyle O'Reilly (1844–90), the poet and Fenian, was born at Dowth.

The lane continues northeast to cross the Mattock, 5km west of Drogheda, and the site of the Battle of the Boyne.

Slane to Navan

Running southwest from Slane to Navan, the N51 passes the formless ruins of Castle Dexter (3km); on the far bank of the Boyne rises the wooded demesne of Beau Parc House (1755), and on the river itself, just below a bridge on the left, is Stackallen Fall. Stackallen House (1710) is one of the few remaining early-classical country-houses in Ireland and its staircase is among the largest in the country. At **Dunmoe** is a 16C castle on the riverbank, burnt in 1799, while opposite stands the ruined church of Ardmulchan. Before entering Navan you reach **Donaghmore** (*Domhnach Mór*, the great church). A **Round Tower** (10C), 30m high, is remarkable in having a carving of the Crucifixion above the door, and no belfry windows, the latter as a result of 19C restoration. Little remains of the adjoining church (13C), said to occupy the site of the church of St. Cassanus, a disciple of St. Patrick. **Donaghmore Museum** (14.00–17.00, Mon–Sun, May–Oct; £), housed in a 19C workhouse is devoted to the history of the region.

After 2.5km you enter the busy but uninteresting town of **Navan** where the Blackwater and Boyne rivers meet, but its inhabitants 'have turned their backs upon the stream, scarce a glimpse of which can be obtained from any of its narrow streets'. Known in Irish as *An Uaimh*, the town has a long history, but its fortifications erected by Hugh de Lacy have vanished and its abbey was destroyed in the Cromwellian wars.

A wooden sculpture of the Crucified Christ by Edward Smyth (1792; his only recorded religious work) is preserved in the Catholic church (1836). West of the town is Navan Motte, an earthwork 16m high (not to be confused with Navan Fort, near Armagh). Some old mills remain by the riverbank. Lead and zinc deposits are being exploited in the vicinity, discovered in 1970.

In the church of **Johnstown**, to the east, is the medieval font from the old church of Kilcarn.

North of Slane

To the north of Slane on the N2, a right-hand turn (after 6km) leads 2.5km to **Old Mellifont Abbey** (10.00–17.00, May–June; 09.30–18.30, July–Sept; 10.00–17.00, Sept–Oct; OPW, £).

The first Cistercian house in Ireland, it was founded in 1142 by St. Malachy O'Morgair (*Mainistir Bhuithe*) on the site of a 7C convent and its ruins stand on the banks of the river Mattock, which here separates Co. Louth from Co. Meath. Of the church, consecrated in 1157, little more than the bases of columns and walls are left. The more interesting relics of the abbey dependencies are the massive gatehouse, the Chapter House (misnamed St. Bernard's Chapel), with its groined roof, foliated capitals, and 14C tracery (restored), and the two-storey **lavabo** (c 1200), an impressive octagonal building five sides of which still stand, each pierced by a round-headed doorway. It opens off the south cloister walk (exhibition at the **Visitor Centre**).

4km beyond this turning is the village of **Collon**, overlooked to the east by the Hill of Collon. **Oriel Temple** was built on the slope in the 1780s by John Foster, the last Speaker in the Irish House of Commons before the Union. Since 1938 it has been known as New Mellifont, and occupied by Cistercians. To the north west is Mt Oriel (244m).

After 6km a left-hand turn at Anaglog Cross leads to (1.5km) **Smarmore Castle** (14C and 19C), seat of the Taaffe family (see Ballymote). At **Woodtown**, some 5.5km further west, are the clear remains of the Pale boundary, an earthen rampart and fosse above the river Dee.

Ardee or the Ford of Ferdia

Ardee (*Baile Atha Fhirdhia*, the ford of Ferdia) takes its name from the long battle, in which Cuchulainn, the champion of Ulster, slew Ferdia, the legendary Connacht warrior. It was once an important outpost of the Pale, and a borough until 1800. A motte called Castleguard or Dawson's Mount defends the ford, but the more recent castle, restored in part, was founded c 1207 by the Anglo-Norman knight Roger de Pippard.

Two monastic foundations (Carmelite and Augustinian, or Trinitarian) are assigned to the knight and his descendant Ralph (late 13C). The remains of one of these are incorporated in the Protestant church, which contains the head of a 14C(?) cross, and a Gothic font found in Mansfieldstown grave-yard, near Castlebellingham (see below). The Catholic church (1829–60) is believed to occupy the site of the other. There is also a late-medieval fortified house in Market St called Hatch's Castle.

The N2 veers northwest from Ardee, and after 9km crosses the river Lagan into Co. Monaghan (Ulster) by the Aclint Bridge. An old fort and the Lagan Ford (replaced by a bridge 2.5km upstream) were the scene of negotiations for the truce of 1599 between Hugh O'Neill, Earl of Tyrone and leader of the Ulster Irish and Robert Devereux, Earl of Essex, governor-general of Ireland, commander of the armies of Elizabeth I. The truce was renewable on a six-weekly basis and described by his enemies in London as 'a dishonourable and dangerous treaty' which led to the latter's downfall.

The most important Gaelic musician and composer of the 18C, Turlough O'Carolan (1670–1738) was born just south of Nobber, about 20km southwest of Ardee. His harp compositions are still widely performed and his harp is displayed at Clonalis House, Co. Roscommon (Ch.2).

The memorials in the nearby Romanesque church of **Cruicetown** (west of R162) arc of interest. Kells (see below) is 13km from here. At 12km you pass (right) the spectacular ruin of **Killna Castle** (1780), the seat of the Chapman family, an illegitimate scion of which was T.E. Lawrence ('of Arabia'). **Ballinlough Castle** (5km beyond), has a round-towered crenellated range, added c 1730. It was enlarged in 1780, perhaps by Wyatt, and restored in 1939.

Delvin (5km) is a pleasant village on the Stoneyford river, with the remains of the 13C stronghold of the Nugent family (their ruined castle of Clonyn lies further to the west).

Slane to Drogheda; site of the Battle of the Boyne
The N51 from Slane approaches Drogheda (*Droicheah Atha*, bridge of the ford) (Tourist Information, ☎ 041-37070; mid-June-Sept) an ancient town, well situated some 5km from the mouth of the Boyne. It was a base of the Viking marauder Turgesius (Thorgestr) and later a bridgehead of the Anglo-Normans of the Pale. In 1395 four Irish princes made their submission to Richard II in the Magdalen monastery here. Of the numerous Parliaments held at Drogheda the most notable was that of 1494, which passed **Poynings Law**, enacting that no future law passed by the Irish Parliament would be held valid unless ratified by the English Privy Council. It was frequently the rendezvous of armies despatched by the Crown to quell the rebels of Ulster, and it suffered two memorable sieges in the 17C. In 1641, Sir Phelim O'Neill was beaten off by Sir Henry Tichborne and Lord Moore until relieved by the Earl of Ormond; and in 1649, when, after a stubborn defence by Sir Arthur Aston and 3000 men, it fell to Oliver Cromwell on 10 September. In the massacre that followed, some 2000 (Cromwell's own estimate) were put to the sword, and most of the rest transported to Barbados. In 1689 it was held for James II by Lord Iveagh, but surrendered the day after defeat at the Battle of the Boyne.

A new bridge partially by-passes the town to the west. South of the old bridge which crosses to the centre (Shop St) is Millmount (restored), the motte of the Anglo-Norman castle. There are slight remains of the town walls near it. The **Millmount Museum** (10.00–18.00, Tue–Sat; 14.30–18.00, Sun; £), incorporating the motte and a 19C military barracks, has a local history display. **The Tholsel**, at the north end of Shop St, is now a bank. A short distance to the east are the twin towers of **St. Lawrence's Gate** (13C), the only barbican remaining. In West St is St. Peter's church (RC), preserving the gruesome shrivelled head of Oliver Plunkett, in an elaborate reliquary (an arm-bone is in the North Cathedral, Cork). Plunkett (1628–81), Archbishop of Armagh, was hanged, drawn and quartered at Tyburn during the 'Popish Plot' persecutions, and canonised in 1975. The plot, fabricated by Titus Oates, notorious in his day as a perjurer, claimed that Charles II was to be murdered and England ruled by the Jesuits. Oliver Plunkett was among those imprisoned and executed in the hysteria which followed the revelations.

Further west, near the site of the West Gate, are the ruins of St. Mary d'Urso, consisting of the central tower of the church and one arch spanning narrow Abbey Lane; these ruins are those of an Augustinian friary of the time of Edward I.

In Fair St, parallel to and north of West St, is the Court House, while further east, at the corner of William St and Magdalene St, stands **St. Peter's** (C of I), rebuilt in 1740–53, with a later tower and spire by Francis Johnston (1787).

It contains a 14C font (on a modern base), some good plasterwork of Italian workmanship, and monuments, among them that of Chief Justice Singleton, by John Hickey. In the churchyard—on the wall—is the macabre tombstone of Edward Golding and his wife (early 16C) who are depicted as cadavers, and the graves of Oliver Goldsmith's uncle Isaac (d. 1769), and Bartholomew Vanhomrigh (d. 1703), father of Swift's 'Vanessa'. Further north is the 15C Magdalene Tower, all that remains of the Dominican abbey founded in 1224 by Archbishop Lucas de Netterville. South of Drogheda on the coast at Laytown, is **Sonairte, the National Ecology Centre** (10.00–17.00, Mon–Fri, 11.00–17.00, Sat, 12.00–17.30, Sun; Easter–Sept; £), a visitor and educational centre devoted to environmental and ecological issues, promoting the need for people to live in harmony with nature.

A short **detour** can be made to the northeast of Drogheda, descending the north bank of the estuary past (3km) **Beaulieu House**, a wide-eaved mansion in the Dutch style built in 1710–20 by Henry Tichborne and his son William. It occupies the site of the medieval castle of the Plunketts, which had been O'Neill's headquarters during the siege of Drogheda and was one of the first country homes in Ireland to be built without fortification. At Beaulieu Church, southwest of the House, note the 15C/16C macabre cadaver tomb-cover leaning against the church tower.

The Battle of the Boyne

From Drogheda the N51 ascends the northern bank of the Boyne, and in just over 1.5km reaches the remains of an obelisk near the mouth of the river Mattock that marked the site of the **Battle of the Boyne**. It was here, on 1 July (old style) 1690, (12 July by the modern calendar) that James II's hopes of regaining the English throne were shattered.

James's army was drawn upon the south bank at **Oldbridge**, beneath the steep slopes of Donore Hill. William of Orange (who was slightly wounded in a reconnaissance before the fight) detached part of his force to cross the ford of Rosnaree to the southwest, so turning the left flank of James's army, while the main body of William's forces, under General Schomberg, rushed the ford opposite Grove Island. Schomberg (see St. Patrick's, Dublin), who showed great courage, was killed in an Irish cavalry charge, but in the meantime another force had crossed the Boyne further east, cutting off any possible retreat towards Drogheda, and James's army was forced to retire in confusion over the hill to Duleek. About 10,000 Jacobites and 5,000 Williamites were killed in the conflict.

William's forces amounted to c 36,000, mostly Dutch, Germans, Danes, French Huguenots and Irish Protestants, while with James were about 25,000 French and Irish Catholics. James passed the night before the battle in the ruined church of Donore; King William's Glen, a little wooded ravine marks the spot where he was wounded. The Battle is one of the principal events commemorated during the 'Marching Season' in Northern Ireland, where political murals with the date '1690' are commonplace.

Also on the north bank is the demesne of Townley Hall (1794, by Francis Johnston; his only Classical house), with a remarkable rotunda and staircase.

A minor road following the bank of the Boyne leads shortly to Dowth Hill and Newgrange while Mellifont Abbey lies 3km northwest.

Drogheda to Dunleer and Castlebellingham

The R166 off the N1 from Drogheda leads to **Termonfeckin**. 3km beyond, is a 10C cross of the Kells type dedicated to St. Fechin (d. 665) and a 15C castle which, until 1613, was a residence of the archbishops of Armagh. Archbishop Oliver Plunkett lived at **Glass Pistol**. 3km further northeast near Clogher Head, commanding a distant view of the Mourne Mountains to the north, across Dundalk Bay.

Regain the N1 12.5km inland at **Dunleer** where the water-powered **White River Mill** (10.00–17.30, Mon–Fri, 14.00–18.00, Sun, May–Sept; £), is a working 19C cornmill. Nearby **Rokeby Hall** was built for Archbishop Robinson of Armagh by Thomas Cooley and Francis Johnston (c 1785).

The 18C castle at **Castlebellingham** (6.5km north of Dunleer on the N1, now an hotel) stands on the river Glynde. It replaces one burned in 1689 by the Jacobites whilst its owner, Colonel Thomas Bellingham, acted as a guide to William of Orange. In the churchyard lies Dr Thomas Guither, a 17C physician who is said to have introduced frogs into Ireland; James Napper Tandy (1740–1803), the erratic patriot, is also said to be buried here.

Monasterboice may be approached directly from Drogheda North on the N1 or south from Dunleer on the N1/M1 and turning west after (signposted) 7.5km.

Monasterboice

The ruins of Monasterboice (*Mainistir Bhuithe*) consists of two churches, a round tower and three crosses, two amongst the finest of their kind. These are the relics of a community founded by St. Buithe or Boethius. The larger and older of the churches is almost 14m long; the nave, entered by a rude square-headed door, was connected to the fallen chancel by a round arch, which has likewise collapsed. The smaller church (13C) is nearer the tower. The Round Tower, was probably built in the 9C; the entrance is 2m from the ground, and the small window above is the only one which is not square-headed. The burning of the tower in 1097 is the last recorded event in the history of the abbey.

> **The Crosses**. Of the three High Crosses (also known as Scripture crosses because they were used to explain scripture texts), the **West Cross**, 6.5m high, is made up of three stones—the shaft, the wheel-cross, and the capstone—perhaps a replacement—on which there are c 50 sculptured panels. They are so weather-worn that only one-quarter of the subjects have been identified; these represent scriptural scenes (of which the Crucifixion occupies the centre of its west face) or grotesque beasts. The monolithic **Muiredach's Cross**, nearest to the entrance, ascribed to Abbot Muiredach (d. 923), is over 5m high and much less worn. New Testament scenes, including the Crucifixion, appear on the east side, and scenes from the Old Testament, and Christ in Judgement, on the west face; the summit represents a gabled building with a tiled roof. The **North Cross** retains its original base and head; the original shaft and an ancient sundial are preserved in its enclosure.

Regaining the main road, with occasional views ahead of Slieve Gullion and the Carlingford hills, you pass (left at 5km) **Athclare Castle**, a good specimen of a fortified manor-house.

Northwest of Dublin

Leaving Dublin by the N3 beyond Black Bull, you reach (8km) **Dunshaughlin**, where the Protestant church retains an ancient lintel with a primitive carving of Christ crucified between two tormentors. The Court House is by Francis Johnston.

At **Lagore** (*Loch Gabhair*), c 1.5km east, in the bed of a former lake, was a crannóg that was a residence of local kings c 650–950 and for a time the seat of the *Ard Rí* (High King) after the fall of Tara. It was destroyed by the Viking, Olaf Guthfridson in 940, and excavated in 1934–36. The minor road leading northwest from Dunshaughlin approaches (4km) Killeen Castle (right) and, 2.5km beyond, **Dunsany Castle** (left), the ancient rival seats of the Fingall and Dunsany branches of the Plunkett family. Both were founded by Hugh de Lacy, and both were largely rebuilt in the 19C. The former, by Francis Johnston in 1802 and later by James Shiel, was gutted by fire in 1981; the latter, retaining its Norman core in the south-west corner, contains plasterwork by Michael Stapleton and a Gothick library attributed also to Shiel. It was long the home of the poet, Lord Dunsany (1878–1957) and contains some works of art and family relics. In the ruined church at **Killeen** (c 1465) is the tomb of its founder, Sir Christopher Plunkett; the old church at **Dunsany**, rebuilt by Nicholas Plunkett c 1450, contains a sculptured font and other Plunkett tombs.

Bective Abbey

Bective Abbey, on the left bank of the Boyne close to Bective Bridge (7.5km) is one of the more picturesque of the ruined abbeys of Meath. It was founded in 1147 for Cistercians by Murchad O'Melaghlin, King of Meath and soon rose to importance, its abbot being a lord of Parliament. Hugh de Lacy, procurator-general, who was accused of aspiring to the crown of Ireland and assassinated in 1186 was buried here. The abbey was rebuilt on a smaller scale in the 15C and after the suppression it was adapted as a mansion (c 1600). The buildings surround a central cloister, and a strong battlemented tower rises at the south-west angle. The dependencies on the east side have unusually thick walls, incorporating chimney-flues. To the northeast stand the ruins of Clady church (13C), near a bridge, perhaps coeval.

Tara may be approached by turning northeast from Bective along the south bank of the Boyne, and then right at the Bellinter crossroads. You pass (left) Assey Castle, and Bellinter House (18C; by Castle).

The Hill of Tara

9.5km beyond Dunshaughlin on the N3, a left-hand turn shortly ascends the **Hill of Tara** (10.00–17.00 daily, Oct–May; £), one of the more famous historic sites of Ireland (around which a thick mantle of romance has been woven). Little now remains apart from the hill on which there are a series of earthworks, together with a church.

In 1843, Daniel O'Connell, regarded as the father of Irish democracy, organised peaceful mass-meetings in order to generate popular support for repeal of the Union between Britain and Ireland (the movement proved unsuccessful) and chose this significant site for one of his 40-odd 'monster meetings' during his Repeal Campaign. It was attended by 100,000 or so.

Teamhair na Riogh, or Tara of the Kings, was originally the 'administrative capital' of the Kings of Meath (or North Leinster), and seat of the *Ard Rí* or High King (Iron Age; c1 BC–4 AD). Every third year a 'feis' or assembly was held, each province having their separate headquarters here. Under Cormac MacArt (227–66) the 'Teach Miodhchuarta' was erected for the triennial synods. It was his daughter Gráinne, betrothed to Fionn MacCumhail (Finn MacCoul), who eloped with Diarmuid O Duibhne (see p224). The romance of Diarmuid and Gráinne was one of the best-loved stories of the Fionn cycle of mythological tales, composed in Munster and Leinster in pre-Christian centuries.

The site was apparently of importance as early as the Bronze Age—The Mound of the Hostages in fact covers a passage-grave of c 1800 BC—and remained so until the interdict of St. Ruadhan in 563, when King Diarmuid MacFergus was cursed for offering judicial violence to a kinsman, but was not finally abandoned until 1022.

On the summit of the hill, with extensive views, is the *Ráth na Riogh*, the 'Kings' Rath' or royal enclosure, a slightly oval fortress (245m by 290m) with an earthern rampart and ditch. Within it are two mounds; on the east side, the *Forradh* or Royal Seat, and abutting it, in the centre of the enclosure, the *Teach Cormaic* or Cormac's House, near which (apart from the execrable statue of St. Patrick) is a pillar-stone marking the grave of insurgents killed at Tara in 1798. It is fancifully named the *Lia Fáil* (or 'stone of destiny'), as it is said to have formerly lain near the Mound of the Hostages (*Dumha na nGiall*, to the north of the enclosure), and was possibly the inauguration stone of the High Kings. According to tradition, Fergus Mór Mac Erc removed the *Lia Fáil* to Scotland when he conquered Argyle and Kintyre (c 6C) and it is the Stone of Scone, recently returned from Westminster Abbey to Scotland.

To the south are traces of the Rath Laoghaire (132m across), or Leary, King at the advent of St. Patrick in 432 and 1km beyond is the Fort of Maeve, another hill-fort. Passing the **Mound of the Hostages**, the most prominent monument at Tara, which is also the oldest (in fact it covers a passage-grave of c 1800 BC), you reach the **Rath of the Synods**, a trivallate earthwork (1C–3C AD) damaged at the turn of this century by those in quest of the Arc of the Covenant! In the adjoining churchyard (in the church of which is a medieval window) is a pillar-stone known as Adamnán's Cross, with a weathered figure supposed by some to represent Cernunnos, the horned god of the pagan Celts.

Further north are two parallel ridges, which mark the site of the great *Teach Miodhchuarta* (House of Mead-circling, of 'coasting'), assumed to be an assembly or banqueting hall, or even a ceremonial approach. To the northwest are three more circular earthworks, the nearest known as the *Rath Gráinne*; the others as the Sloping Trenches (*Claoin Fhearta*).

1.5km east of the main road, at **Skreen**, a well-sited hilltop village, is a ruined church of c 1341 with a later tower, and primitive cross. Earthworks here are supposed to mark the site of a stronghold to which Cormac MacArt retired. To the north are the slight ruins of Walterstown Castle, 3km beyond which (north-east) are remains of an ancient church and the fort of Danestown.

Continuing northwest on the main road, you pass near the ruined 13C church of **Cannistown** (left) and descend to cross the river Boyne at Kilcarn Bridge. **Athlumney Castle**, on the east bank, was a picturesque 16C manor, burned down, it is said, by Sir Lancelot Dowdall, a former owner, to avoid giving shelter to William of Orange. Adjoining it is a fine 17C house.

The Kells road climbs the western bank of the Blackwater, a lazy winding stream, the darkness of whose waters is attributed to a curse imposed on them by St. Patrick. After 2.5km you pass a turning (left) to (2.5km) **Ardbraccan House**. The main block was begun in 1776, with wings by Castle erected after 1734. The church (1777) has a medieval belfry. Bishop Pococke (1704–65), the historian, is buried here. The nearby limestone quarries provided stone for a number of Dublin's major buildings (Leinster House, Rotunda Hospital, etc.). Beyond, to the right of the main road, is **Liscartan Castle**, a fortress held in 1633 by Sir William Talbot, with two square towers; adjacent is a pretty little church. 15C **Rathaldron Castle**, on the opposite bank, is another square fortress.

After a further 3km, and also on the far bank, is **Donaghpatrick**, the 'Church of St. Patrick', near a large rath with four tiers of ramparts. Beyond it, in a bend of the river, is Teltown House, taking its name from the Hill of Tailte on the north bank, on the summit of which is the Rath Duhb, or Black Fort (view), built by King Tuathal, and later a burial-ground. The *Aonach Tailteann* (games in honour of the dead), were held here annually until 1168. An abortive attempt to revive them was made in Dublin in 1924. Here also took place the 'Teltown Marriages', an informal agreement to cohabit for a year, after which, if the couple disagreed, they might stand back to back in the centre of the rath, and walking north and south out of the fort, were considered free to wed again, a practice which is said to have survived until the turn of the 19C.

Kells

Kells, (*Ceanannas Mór*), a small market-town, once a famous centre of learning, still retains a number of interesting remains of its illustrious past. St. Columba, having received a grant of land from Diarmuid, son of Fergus Cerrbhol, founded a monastery here c 550. It flourished, producing in c 800 a magnificent decorated example of the Gospels, known as 'The Book of Kells', now on display in Trinity College Library, Dublin. A crosier made in the abbey is in the British Museum. The monks of Iona, expelled by the Vikings, took refuge here in 807, but between 920–1019 the abbey itself was plundered four times by the Vikings. The town was burned in 1170, and again by Edward Bruce in 1315, and the monastery was dissolved in 1551. Roger Mortimer, 4th Earl of March, was killed in a skirmish here in 1398; Robert Barker (1739–1806), the reputed inventor of the 'panorama', was born here.

Kells is the most important **High Cross** site in the country, with four magnificent and intensely decorated crosses. In the marketplace is the **Market Cross**, which has a frieze of horse and foot soldiers on the original base.

The top of its shaft and part of the wheel are broken, and apparently it was used as a gallows in 1798, after which it lay prone for a century.

From here you can ascend the street to the entrance of the churchyard. But first visit the building known as **St. Columba's House** (c 807) (the key is at a house on the right of the street here), a short distance further up the hill. This is a well-preserved example of the primitive corbel-constructed steeply-pitched stone-roofed church (compare Glendalough (Ch.1B, Cashel, Ch.5, and Killaloe, Ch.9). The lower storey is barrel-vaulted. The attic storey, known improbably as 'the scriptorium' is reached by a ladder; here it is possible to see the roof-construction at close quarters.

A Round Tower, pre-dating 1076 (without a cap) stands 30m high, in the churchyard. The entrance opening is round-headed; the windows above are square; the five (instead of the usual four) at the top are triangular-headed. At its foot is the largest of the **High Crosses**, over 3m high, with a Latin inscription (unusual in Ireland) 'Patricii et Columbae Crux' (the cross of Patrick and Columba). The other two crosses are known as The **Broken Cross** and The **Unfinished Cross**. Beside the church is an interesting unfinished example. Adjoining is the detached belfry, rebuilt in 1578, with a spire by Thomas Coolcy added in 1783. The Catholic parish church (1798) and the Court House are both by Francis Johnston. Little remains of the other old buildings of Kells except part of a tower of Walter de Lacy's ramparts.

2.5km east, on the far bank of the Blackwater, is the demesne of Headfort House (now a school), with an Adam interior of c 1771. The original design was probably by George Semple.

The Cavan road crosses the Blackwater at Clavens Bridge. 2.5km beyond at **Carnaross** (N3) you can turn left for the ruins of St. Kieran's Chapel and Well, on the south bank southeast of the bridge. The remains of four 'termon' or boundary crosses can be seen here; another stands in a ford on the river. Legend relates that St. Columba, envious of St. Kieran's crosses, determined to steal one under cover of darkness; but St. Kieran awoke when he was half-way across the river, and in the ensuing struggle he was forced to leave it where it has remained ever since.

The N3 later skirts (left) **Lough Ramor** before reaching the pleasantly-sited lakeside village of **Virginia** (19km from Kells), founded by James I at the colonisation of Ulster. Swift wrote the greater part of *Gulliver's Travels* in 1726 at the home of the Rev. Thomas Sheridan (1687–1738). Richard Brinsley Sheridan, his grandson, also spent much of his youth at Cuilcagh House, 4km to the northeast, south of the R178. North of this road lies **Killinkere**, the ancestral home of the American general, Philip Sheridan (1831–88). **Mullagh**, 9.5km southeast of Virginia, was the birthplace of the poet and novelist Henry Brooke (1703–83), who retired here in 1774 and was buried in an unmarked grave. He survived his wife and all but one of their twenty-two children. The sole survivor was Charlotte Brooke (1740–1793) whose *Reliques of Irish Poetry* (1789) is an early and important contribution to the revival of interest in Gaelic literature.

Oldcastle lies 11km southwest on the R195. **Slieve-na-Callighe** (Hill of the Witch; 277m) 5km southeast, is the highest of the three summits of the Loughcrew Hills. Some **32 chambered cairns** (Iron Age cemeteries) have been excavated here, the most perfect of which, on the hill-top, is notable for its supporting wall of stones. To the north is a stone seat known as the Hag's Chair. The executed archbishop of Armagh, Oliver Plunkett (1625–81) was born at Loughcrew, on the south side of the hill.

Trim to Laracor and Athboy

At **Newtown Trim** (1.5km east of Trim, on the R154) are the extensive remains of the **Cathedral of SS Peter and Paul**, founded by Simon Rochfort in 1206 for Canons Regular. The church, on the north bank, is a good example of the transition from the Norman to the Early English style, with graceful lancet windows. At the other end of the bridge are the ruins of a castle, with a large square keep, and a small chapel attached in the 13C to a priory of Crutched Friars. About 1.5km further on is the massive keep of Scurlogstown Castle (1080), with round towers at two of its corners. Bective Abbey lies further northeast to the right of the road to (14.5km) Navan.

Trim

Trim (*Ath Truim*, the ford of the elder-trees), the county town of Meath, is in a prime location on the Boyne, and retains several interesting historic buildings. The **Yellow Steeple**, (made of cream-coloured limestone) a ruined 13C tower that rises above the roofs of the town, was part of the Augustinian abbey of St. Mary, which is supposed to stand on the site of a convent founded by St. Patrick in 432. The Sheep Gate, nearby, and the fragmentary Water Gate, to the west near the river, are the only two surviving in the old town wall. The façade of the old gaol (c 1827) is by John Hargrave.

Trim Castle is the largest Anglo-Norman fortress in Ireland and has been dated by recent dendrocronological evidence (tree ring dating) to c 1172, with a second phase during the 1190s. The complex Greek-cross form of the 21m high keep which dominates the enclosure has no English or continental precedent and its military practicality is doubtful. The 20 angles of its external surface present numerous weak points to any potential attacker. The outer wall, guarded by ten D-shaped towers, is surrounded by a moat into which the Boyne could be admitted at will. The barbican is well preserved.

Here Richard de Burgh, Earl of Ulster, held court in Edward II's reign, and Richard II confined his cousins Humphrey of Gloucester and Henry of Lancaster (afterwards Henry IV) here because they were opposed to Richard's attempt as monarch to exercise greater control. It was the scene of several parliaments, and at one time housed a mint. Sir Charles Coote fell in its defence in 1642.

Talbot's Castle (modernised), near the Yellow Steeple, built in 1415 by Sir John Talbot, was bought by Esther Johnson ('Stella') in 1717 and sold by her the following year, at a profit, to Swift. The Dean likewise disposed of it, again at a profit, five months later; it was then converted into the diocesan school, where Arthur Wellesley (later the Duke of Wellington) received his early education, as did Sir William Rowan Hamilton, the astronomer. The Duke, who later (1790–95) represented Trim in Parliament, lived in Dublingate St, where he is commemorated by a pillar bearing his statue (repaired).

The tower of the **cathedral** (since 1955, of the Protestant diocese of Meath), with a Sheila-na-gig, dates from 1449. To the north, outside the old walls, are the scanty remains of a Dominican friary, founded by Geoffrey de Joinville,

Lord of Meath, in the 13C. In Mill St, the **Trim Visitor Centre** (10.00–18.00 daily, June–Sept; 10.00–18.00 Wed–Sun, Oct–May; £) has a multi-media exhibition on the history of the town.

South of Trim by the R158 is **Laracor**, a quiet little village of which Jonathan Swift was incumbent from 1699. Here are the paths where he used to stroll with 'Stella' (Esther Johnson) and Dr Raymond, the vicar of Trim; but the association is all that remains, for a modern church replaces that in which Swift used to preach to a congregation of a dozen (it retains the altar plate he used). The only authentic feature of the house where Stella lived from 1701 (with her friend Mrs Dingley) is the site.

The R154 continues northwest from Trim to (12km) **Athboy** (*Ath Buidhe*, the yellow ford) to the west of the Hill of Ward, the site of the Iron Age Palace of Tlachtga, formerly the scene of the festivities of Samhain, a Celtic festival held on the 1 November, marking the beginning of winter. During this period free passage was believed to take place between the natural and supernatural worlds.

Glossary

Ambulatory semicircular passage-way surrounding the apse at the east end of a church

Annagh marshy ground

Ard a high place

Atha a ford

Aras house

Aumbry wall-recess beside altar to hold sacred vessels

Baile a settlement or townland

Balla a wall

Ballagh marshy ground

Ballina an entrance, or ford

Bally a town; it has been estimated that there are no less than 5000 townlands in Ireland with names commencing with this prefix

Batter inward inclination of a wall face, usually external

Bawn (*Bo-dhaingan*, cattle enclosure) a fortified enclosure attached to a castle or tower-house

Beehive Hut small stone edifice, shaped like an old-fashioned beehive, and vaulted by corbelled construction; also *Clochan*

Ben a peak

Bivallate/Trivallate having two or three ramparts

Bog (*Bog*, soft) peat

Bullaun artificially hollowed stone, probably used as a mortar

Bun end of a road; foot of a hill; mouth of a stream

Cather, Caher, or **Cathair** a fort of dry stone construction, usually so-called when the structure is larger than a Cashel

Cairn a mound of stones heaped over a prehistoric tomb

Calp a dark limestone found principally in the Dublin region

Carrick or **Carrig** a stone walled enclosure encircling a church, monastery, or ring-fort

Cashel a Rath of which the bank is supported by a stonewall

Castle in Ireland, often merely a semi-fortified house, or manor-house; not necessarily fortified in the normal sense of the term.

Cathedral in Ireland, often a church of unpretentious dimensions

Chevaux-de-frise in Iron Age architecture, a defensive arrangement of stones projecting from the ground outside fortification

Chevet ambulatory with attached projecting chapels

Cill see **Kill**

Cist stone-lined burial pit in ground

Clachan a small group of dwellings or farm-buildings, but smaller than a hamlet

Clare a level; a plank bridge

Clochan a row of stepping-stones fording a river

Clogher a stony place

Clon a meadow

Commandery district under the control of one of the religious orders of knights, Hospitallers, Templars etc.

Corbel head sculpted head decorating a corbel projecting from a wall. It may support a floor, beams, or be the springing of an arch

Corrie a circular hollow at a valley head, often holding water

Crannog an island, often artificially built, in a lake or marsh, sometimes connected to the mainland by a submerged causeway; it was usually fortified by a palisade, and contained dwellings

Crocket carved projections, usually in the form of foliage, used as decoration on sloping surfaces (spires, canopies) in Gothic architecture

Currach or **Curragh** a small boat or coracle, formed of hides stretched over a lath framework, later of tarred canvas; a marsh or low plain

Cyclopean large scale, finely jointed and irregularly cut masonry

Dáil Eireann (pronounced Dau-il airan) the lower house of the Irish Parliament, the upper house being known as the Senate or Seanad. Both houses are referred to as the Oireachtas. Members of the Dáil (Teachta Dala) are known as TDs. The Prime Minister is the Taoiseach (pronounced Tee-shock)

Demesne enclosed park or garden surrounding a mansion; an estate

Derg or **Dearg** red

Derry an oak-grove

Diocletian Window large semi-circular window comprising three lights divided by two vertical mullions, the wider opening in the centre

Diamond in Ulster, the central square or market-place of a Plantation town. It can be any shape

Dolmen simple megalithic tomb formed of three or more upright stones covered by a cap-stone, and once enclosed by a mound, now known as portal tombs

Donag a large church

Dorter dormitory in medieval monastery

Drum or **Drom** a ridge or hillock

Drumlin a small hill, often oval in shape, formed by glacial action; a large part of Ulster is physically divided from the rest of the island by a belt of drumlins.

Dun or **Doon** fort

Ennis, **Inis**, or **Inch** an island

Esker an alluvial moraine or deposit of sand or gravel, usually left by an ice-sheet, and forming a sinuous ridge, sometimes used anciently as a track

Famine graves unmarked mass graves resembling earth barrows, of those who perished during the Great Famine of 1845–47

Fenian member of the Irish Republican Brotherhood, founded in 1858, to oppose British rule in Ireland

Fert grave, tumulus, mound

Fir Men (on lavatory entrances)

Fulacht Fiadh medieval outdoor cooking-place

Gaeltacht district in which the vernacular is still predominantly Irish

Gallan or **Gallaun** standing stone

Gallowglass mercenary soldier (*gall óglach*, foreign warrior), usually of Norse/Scots origin from Scotland and the Western Isles (13C–15C)

Garda; pl. **Gardaí** policeman (pronounced Gorda or Gordie)

Glen or **Glan** a valley or glen

Gothic European pointed-arched medieval architecture and its late 19C revival

Gothick Gothic revival of the late 18C–early 19C

Groin stone rib separating internal roof surfaces in Gothic architecture

Hiberno Romanesque Irish round-arched and decorated style of archi-tecture used prior to the Norman invasion and widely revived 1830–1930 during the Celtic Revival

IRA Irish Republican Army; from 1916–1921, the army of the Provisional Government of the Republic engaged in the War of Independence against Britain; currently the illegal guerrilla move-ment devoted to the unification of Ireland by force

Kelp type of seaweed, calcined for its properties as a fertiliser

Kill or **Cill** early monastic site, cell, or chapel

Knock or **Cnoc** a hill; there are some 2000 townlands in Ireland with this prefix

Lis earthen fort, or the green open space enclosed by a rath, on which livestock was penned

Liberty suburban area once beyond the jurisdiction of a mayor

Lough a loch or lake; sometimes an inlet of the sea

Loyalist (in Northern Ireland) working-class supporters of the Union with Britain

Machicolation in Medieval architecture, projecting wall parapet with floor openings through which molten lead, boiling water etc. could be poured on attackers

Mna Ladies (on lavatory entrances)

Mor big, great

Motte flat-topped mound, once fortified (by the Normans)

Moy a plan

Muck a pig

Mull a rounded height

Ogee in Gothic architecture, a moulding composed of a concave followed by a convex curve

Ogham c 4C–9C script formed of notches or lines representing twenty letters of the Latin alphabet, marked on either side or across the angle between adjacent surfaces of standing-stones, where they usually indicate a name (see p)

Orangemen from William of Orange (victor at the battle of the Boyne), members of the (Protestant) Orange Order, founded 1795, to oppose Catholic power

Orné ornamented rustic architecture of the late 18C-early 19C, usually associated with cottages of gate lodges

Oughter (uachtar) upper

Owen (less often *Avon)* a river

Passage-grave Neolithic tomb constructed as a stone-built passageway covered by a mound of earth and stones

Plantation referring to the settlement of the English or Scots in Munster after 1586 or Ulster after 1607

Poteen an illicitly distilled and highly potent colourless spirit usually made from potatoes, now from molasses

Rath circular rampart, often palisaded, surrounding ancient dwellings; see *Cashel*

Ros a promontory; also occasionally, a wood

Scellig or **Skellig** lofty crag or rock

Scots Baronial country-house style popular in late 19C, particularly in Ulster, with an emphasis on candle-snuffer turrets, crow-step gables and round corner towers

Sean old

Sheila-na-gig 'Sheila of the breasts' crudely carved medieval female figure in which the genitals are emphasised, displayed on the exterior of a building; possibly connected with a fertility cult, or as a defence against the evil-eye

Sinn Fein (pron. Shin Fane) 'Ourselves Alone'; an influential nationalist organisation (1903), founded to promote Home Rule; the present-day body is the (legal) political wing of the IRA

Slieve (*sliabh*) mountain

Souterrain underground chamber in a ringfort

Spandrels wall surface between adjoining arches, or between an arch and the surrounding wall

Strad a street

Strand the usual term in Ireland for a beach or shore

Teampull or **Temple** a church

Ten-pound Castle one built under the act of 1429, subsidising the erection of small forts in the Pale (see above) by the grant of the then substantial sum of £10

Termon boundary cross

Tholsel (Toll-stall) Town Hall or market house

Tobar, **Tober**, or **Tubber** a well, often believed to be holy

Toghers cross-country tracks made by timber or brushwood thrown down across boggy ground

Toome a tomb

Trabeate with a single stone lintel

Triforium in Gothic architecture, three-light vertical windows to a wall passage above nave arcade

Tull or **Tully** hillock

Turf peat or peat-fuel

Turas (Irish; a journey) route followed on Saint's day pilgrimage in early-Christian sites

Tyr or **Ter** territory

UDA Ulster Defence Association outlawed guerrilla movement devoted to maintaining British presence in Northern Ireland by force

Unionist individuals who regard their cultural identity as British and wish Northern Ireland to remain within the United Kingdom

UVF Ulster Volunteer Force, as UDA

Venetian Window with three openings, the central one taller, wider and round headed

Index

This is a comprehensive index to places described in the guide. It also includes geographical features such as loughs, rivers and mountains and important historical figures. Sub-indexes have been provided for Armagh, Belfast, Cork, Derry, Dublin, Galway and Limerick.